*Evatt: a man of tremendous intellectual power and vision.
Really a Titan—unappreciated by our sheep like community.*
KATHARINE SUSANNAH PRICHARD TO GUIDO BARACCHI, 1968.

Doc EVATT
PATRIOT, INTERNATIONALIST, FIGHTER AND SCHOLAR

KEN BUCKLEY
BARBARA DALE & WAYNE REYNOLDS

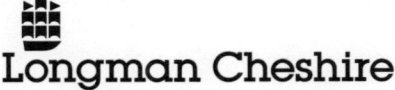
Longman Cheshire

Longman Cheshire Pty Limited
Longman House
Kings Gardens
95 Coventry Street
Melbourne 3205 Australia
Offices in Sydney, Brisbane, Adelaide, Perth and associated companies throughout the world.
Copyright © Longman Cheshire Pty Ltd 1994

All rights reserved. Except under the conditions described in the Copyright Act 1968 of Australia and subsequent amendments, no part of this publication may be reproduced, stored in a retrieval system or transmitted in any form or by any means, electronic, mechanical, photocopying, recording or otherwise, without the prior permission of the copyright owner.

Designed by Perdita Nance
Cover design by Rob Cowpe
Index by Russell Brooks
Set in 10.5/12.5 pt Sabon
Produced by Longman Cheshire Pty Ltd
Printed in Hong Kong

National Library of Australia
Cataloguing-in-Publication data
  Buckley, Ken.
     Doc Evatt.
  Includes index.
  ISBN 0 582 80719 0.
  ISBN 0 582 87498 X (pbk).
  1. Evatt, H.V. (Herbert Vere), 1894-1965. 2. United Nations—Officials and employees, Australian—Biography. 3. Cabinet officers—Australia—Biography. 4. Foreign ministers—Australia—Biography. 5. Judges—Australia—Biography. 6. Australia—Foreign relations—20th century. 7. Australia—History—20th century. I. Dale, Barbara, 1938- . II. Reynolds, Wayne. III. Title.
  994.04

The publisher's policy is to use paper manufactured from sustainable forests

Contents

Acknowledgments vii
Preface viii
Foreword x

PART I: LAW AND POLITICS: THE FIRST PHASE
1 The Formative Years 3
2 The Making of a Labor Lawyer 21
3 Balmain: Political Baptism of Fire 35
4 The Walsh–Johnson Deportation Cases 46
5 In State Parliament 51
6 Evatt versus Lang 65
7 Arbitration and the Depression 78

PART II: JUDGE AND SCHOLAR
8 Labor and the High Court 93
9 The Reserve Powers of the Crown 104
10 Historical, Literary and Artistic Circles 114
11 Writing Australian History 123

PART III: WAR, AND POST-WAR RECONSTRUCTION
12 From High Court to Parliament 139
13 War Crisis: Overseas Mission 1942 152
14 Civil Liberties in Wartime 168
15 Warplanes, Trade and Economic Plans 182
16 Postwar Reconstruction 195
17 Defence Powers and Individual Liberty 202
18 Attorney-General 1945–47: The High Court, and Industrial Relations 209

Part IV: International Affairs

19	Regional Security: the South Pacific	225
20	The Indonesian Revolution and Australian Security	245
21	Japan and US Policy in the North Pacific	264
22	The Empire as a Third Force?	283
23	The United Nations	302

Part V: Labor Government Problems

24	Banks, Judges, Doctors and ASIO	325
25	Democracy, the Coal Strike and the Defeat of Labor	340

Part VI: Leader of the Opposition:

26	The 1951 Referendum: Evatt's Finest Hour	355
27	Petrov, Politics and Security	369
28	The ALP Split	382
29	The Last Fight	396
30	Assessment	410

ACKNOWLEDGMENTS

This volume is a co-operative production. All three of the authors shared in the research on which the book is based and in the writing up of material.

As usual, thanks are owed to a large number of people and institutions. The staff of the Evatt Foundation are very helpful. On the administrative side, we are grateful for the work of Elsa Atkin, Marie Armstrong and Rowanne Couch. Without singling out other individuals, the authors extend particular thanks to those who were willing to be interviewed concerning their knowledge of H.V. Evatt. As usual, we also met with unflagging help from the staffs of the National Archives, the Mitchell Library and the National Library of Australia. We also made extensive use of the Evatt Collection of papers in the Library of Flinders University.

The research for this book was aided in part by a generous donation from the late Mr Neville Neich.

SYDNEY, 1994.

PREFACE

In 1968 the Evatt Foundation, then under the chairmanship of Cliff Dolan, former president of the ACTU, decided to commemorate the forthcoming centenary of Dr Herbert Vere Evatt by sponsoring the preparation of a comprehensive biography.

Dr Evatt, who was born in East Maitland in April 1894, has been the subject of several biographies, but the Foundation considered that a more substantial project was required in order to do justice to his contributions in a wide variety of fields—as politician, lawyer, judge, historian, legal scholar, civil libertarian, international statesman, and patron of literature and the visual arts.

The Foundation was also conscious that there was much documentary material about Dr Evatt's career which had not been utilised. Accordingly the project was undertaken on the assumption that it would take five years to explore this material as well as a wide range of other sources, including direct testimony from people who had been in personal contact with Dr Evatt. A considerable amount of research was carried out in archival sources overseas, especially in London and Washington DC. The Foundation decided to treat this as a major project, involving the necessary commitment of time and resources to make this research possible.

In January 1987, advertisements were placed calling for applications from would-be biographers, which elicited numerous applications. These were reduced to a short-list of six, and the final selection was made in November 1987.

Ken Buckley, the successful applicant, formerly Associate Professor of Economic History at The University of Sydney, has had a long and distinguished career as a labour historian. Barbara Dale, who was appointed as his research assistant in 1988, has had a long association with *Labour History*, the journal of the Australian Society for the Study of Labour History. In 1990, in recognition of her contribution to the project, she was designated as co-author.

In 1993, the Foundation also invited Dr Wayne Reynolds of the University of Newcastle to join the project as co-author. Dr Reynolds, whose contributions relate particularly to Dr Evatt's role in international affairs, gained his doctorate for a thesis concerned with Dr Evatt's work as Minister for External Affairs. Dr Reynolds is also the winner of one of the annual Evatt Essay prizes awarded by the Foundation.

The Foundation appointed a biography sub-committee to maintain liaison with the authors and to read drafts of the various chapters. The sub-committee comprised Emeritus Professor Sol Encel, vice-president of the Foundation; Professor James Hagan, Professor of History and Dean of the Faculty of Arts at the University of Wollongong; Suzanne Jamieson, of the Department of Industrial Relations at The University of Sydney; and Ted Wheelwright, formerly Associate Professor of Economics at the University of Sydney and also a vice-president of the Foundation. Although the members of the sub-committee made a number of comments and suggestions, the text of the book is the responsibility of the authors alone, and it is not an 'authorised' biography.

The biography sub-committee would also like to express its appreciation to the staff of the Evatt Foundation for the enormous amount of work and commitment involved in producing the text of the biography and in carrying out a wide variety of related tasks.

The Foundation acknowledges with thanks the interest and co-operation of the publishers, Longman Cheshire. It is noteworthy that Longman was responsible for publishing the biography of Dr Evatt's close colleague Ben Chifley, by the late L. F. Crisp, in 1961. Apart from Evatt's own biography of W. A. Holman, published in 1940, Crisp's book is one of the earliest scholarly studies of an Australian political figure, and it is entirely fitting that the same publisher should be involved in this case.

SOL ENCEL
ON BEHALF OF THE BIOGRAPHY SUB-COMMITTEE

FOREWORD

This is the fourth full-length biography of Evatt. Only one other Australian political figure, if my count is correct, has scored as many. Yet Evatt was never Prime Minister, and lost three successive elections as leader of the Opposition.

Why such interest in someone who failed so conspicuously to lead his party into office, especially when he is often remembered with a good deal less than affection? His biographers (and his surviving associates) all have unflattering stories to tell. Evatt was often a very difficult man to work with. He was suspicious of his colleagues and rude to his subordinates; he was arrogant; he was vindictive; he was an inveterate and sometimes clumsy intriguer. Even though (as his more enthusiastic biographers are quick to point out) these traits were often tempered by an impulsive generosity and familial affection, they hardly amount to a catalogue of virtues.

But they do amount to an interesting mix, especially when they are possessed by a man of such immense talent. Evatt had not one, but several careers, and in some of them he displayed real brilliance. As a barrister, he figured in cases of national importance, and won some striking victories on the basis of imaginative and original reasoning. As a judge, he propounded a doctrine that has the distinction of being accepted after his departure from the bench, and remaining a source of study for more than one generation of jurists. As a historian, he wrote a study of Governor Bligh that reshaped conventional interpretation, and a biography of W. A. Holman that demonstrated remarkable command over sources at a time when Australian labour history hardly existed.

These achievements alone would have qualified Evatt as a notable Australian, but moreover he was remarkable beyond his own country.

Evatt became one of those few Australians who won real fame in international politics. In 1948, he was elected as the third President of the General Assembly of the United Nations. In that role, he led the Assembly through years in which it intervened in dramatic incidents in Germany and Israel and captured the attention of the world's press and radio.

But it is not as one of Australia's few internationally famous political figures that Evatt has provoked four biographies. The first, Allan Dalziel's *Evatt the Enigma*, published only two years after Evatt's death in 1965, concentrated heavily upon Evatt's involvement in the great dramas of Australian politics in the 1950s: the High Court's rejection of the bill to ban the Communist Party, the referendum to empower the government to do so, the Petrov Affair, and the expulsion of the Industrial Groups from the Australian Labor Party. The biographies that have followed have presented Evatt against a broader background, but it is still the events of the early fifties that supply the most vivid of the conflicts in their narrative.

The conscription referenda apart, the events of the early 1950s produced the most passionate involvement of the Australian people in the politics of this century. The victory of the Allies in World War II produced great expectations in the labour movement for the remaking of a society that would prevent a recurrence of the Great Depression and the misery of the thirties. An overly ambitious Communist Party saw itself as a vanguard, and sought to use the Coalminers' Strike of 1949 to demonstrate the essential futility, even treachery, of labourism.

As Attorney-General in the Chifley Labor government, Evatt was one of the most aggressive architects of that strike's defeat. But its defeat did not save the government, and a Liberal–Country Party coalition led by Robert Gordon Menzies introduced legislation to ban the Communist Party. Evatt took a brief on behalf of the most notorious of the Communist-led unions, challenged the legislation in the High Court—and won.

Even at a distance of half a century, it is difficult to gauge the significance of that victory. In 1992, the Evatt Foundation held a conference which attempted that task, and published its proceedings in *Seeing Red*. Several papers trace Evatt's defiance of an Australian McCarthyism which sought to prevent the expression of critical opinion through fear of censure or reprisal. In Australia's Cold War, expression of any opinion which might have lent aid or comfort to the Communist Party was to be regarded as a threat to the safety of the realm, and therefore, potentially treacherous. Security Intelligence operatives ransacked the bookcases, opened the mail, and shadowed the movements of Communists and people they suspected of sympathising with them; they prejudiced their promotion, and secured their dismissal. We shall never know how this trend would have developed, because Evatt, more than any other man, stopped it. The victory in the High Court was a personal triumph; the victory of the 'No' vote in the referendum that followed resulted from a campaign which he led.

The price Evatt paid for his success was the hatred of many in the government and of some of its most powerful lay supporters. Their hatred was matched, in word and deed, by several inside Evatt's own party, who believed him either the dupe or the willing instrument of the Communists whose influence in the trade unions the Labor Party's Industrial Groups were attempting to destroy. His supporters saw him as a defender of the labour movement and of civil liberties against totalitarian suppression. Evatt became the leader of a Labor Party divided against itself. He ended that division, formally at least, at the Labor Party's Hobart Conference in 1955, where he denounced and expelled the Industrial Groupers as agents of a conspiracy organised by the Catholic Social Studies Movement to subvert the party.

Even before the Hobart Conference met, Evatt had come to believe himself the victim of another conspiracy. Amid some wild and well-photographed scenes at Darwin airport, Mr and Mrs Petrov, employees of the Russian Embassy, defected and sought asylum in Australia. The incident inevitably coloured the election campaign that soon followed, and resulted in another defeat for Labor. The triumphant Menzies government established a Royal Commission on Espionage. In the culminating political blunder of his parliamentary career, Evatt informed the Commission that he had contacted the Russian Foreign Minister to ask for his version of events. His enemies pointed to his misjudgment as evidence of madness; within a few years his friends began to ease him out of politics.

It is difficult for a historian to recreate the virulent animosity that Evatt provoked in those years. No other political figure has sustained such a remorseless campaign of abuse of such intensity over such a long period. Some of those who have reviewed his life have seen him in the fifties as undergoing a kind of martyrdom, as a tragic figure driven mad by the gods, powerless to use the great talents of which he was ultimately robbed entirely.

The last few years of Evatt's life were denouements to all of his various careers. But by that time he had affected the parliamentary Labor Party in ways that marked a distinctive break with its past. Evatt's predecessors as leader were typically men of working-class origin who had worked as tradesmen, joined trade unions and made their mark on them. Their union experience and reputation became the basis for their preselection, and later their promotion through the federal parliamentary Labor Party.

Evatt's background was quite different. His connection with the trade union movement was not as a member and official, but as a legal consultant and advocate. His preselection and his preferment within the party were not guaranteed by a trade union base, but depended largely on his repute as lawyer, judge, and man of intellect. In electing Evatt as leader, the parliamentary Labor Party recognised that it was possible for a champion of the rights of labour to arise from outside the ranks of the trade union movement. Specifically, it recognised that a Labor leader could be of middle-class background, and a man known for his learning. In doing that, the Labor Party made way for a change in its view of itself and of the movement it was pledged to serve.

For its first half century, labourism in Australia was essentially isolationist. The Labor Party would lead the forward march of the working class behind walls which kept them safe from the competition of foreign peoples (especially Asian peoples) or their cheap manufactures. Involvement in the war of 1914–18 did not change that belief; and when that part of the labour movement closest to the Communist Party attempted to commit the rest to support of the anti-Fascists in Spain in the late thirties, it failed. The Australian labour movement did not believe its country had a role to play in international politics.

No such reservation bound Dr Evatt. His international involvement in time of war he carried over into times of peace. He saw a role for Australia particularly but not only in the Pacific region as a broker between the pre-war colonial rulers and the nationalist parties and governments that the war had helped produce. As a small, rich, stable nation, Australia had the ability and perhaps the need to contribute to the peace of its region, and to that of the wider world. After Evatt, the labour movement has not returned to the isolation it had held up until World War II.

This biography, more than its predecessors, traces Evatt's role as someone who led Australia into a greater involvement with international politics. It draws on international sources much more extensively, and sets Evatt's public life against a detailed background of foreign relations in the forties and the fifties. But Evatt's battles of the fifties in Australia provide its greatest drama.

Although Evatt's arch rival Menzies is long dead, some of his other prominent opponents continue to lead public and politically active lives. As they recall their roles in those times in an increasingly mellow afternoon light, this book may help them make a judgement on what they did. For others, not at the time involved, it will above all provoke reflection on political and civil rights and what their protection may cost in personal, party and electoral terms.

PROFESSOR JIM HAGAN
PROFESSOR OF HISTORY—UNIVERSITY OF WOLLONGONG

PART I

LAW AND POLITICS: THE FIRST PHASE

CHAPTER 1

THE FORMATIVE YEARS

Hear the causes between your brethren and judge righteously between every man and his brother and the stranger that is with him. Ye shall not respect persons in judgment, but ye shall hear the small as well as the great...

DEUTERONOMY, CHAPTER I

When the young Herbert Vere (Bert) Evatt underlined that passage in the family Bible, he was affirming beliefs which he was to hold throughout his life, as a judge, a politician, and as President of the United Nations.[1]

Born on 30 April 1894 in East Maitland, New South Wales, he was the fifth of eight sons of John Ashmore Hamilton Evatt and Jane Sophia Evatt (née Gray). John Evatt had been born in India in 1851, where his father served in the British Army. The Evatts were an Anglo-Irish family which produced professional soldiers and Anglican clergy in about equal proportions, but John Evatt did not follow in their footsteps. Instead, after being educated in Dublin and Charterhouse school in England, he emigrated to Australia at the age of sixteen. There he gained employment as a providore for a steamship company operating between Sydney and Newcastle. After establishing himself as a man of some means, he married Jane Sophia (Jeanie) Gray in 1882 in the Anglican church at Morpeth. Jeanie, born in Sydney in 1863, was the eldest of a large family. Her father, John Thomas Gray, was Australian born, while her mother, Bridget, née Hall, had arrived from Ireland in 1857.

By the time Bert Evatt was born, his father was the licensee of the Bank Hotel in the main street of East Maitland. The family occupied living quarters at the rear of the hotel and employed a cook and a maid. Bert's early childhood was a happy one, with the companionship of his brothers, success at the local primary school, and the enthusiastic pursuit of cricket and football. In personality he was described as 'excitable, voluble, pugnacious, kind, tender-hearted, self-assertive, and accustomed to attention and praise'. He always wanted to have his own way in everything he did.[2]

His father, John, was a popular and gregarious member of the local community, generous to a fault; family lore has it that during the depression of the early 1890s he had often given money to those who had fallen on hard times. Bert's mother, Jeanie, was serious, strong willed and intelligent. She was profoundly religious and sang in the choir at the local Anglican church. Her sons were also encouraged to join the choir and to read the Bible. It was from his mother that young Bert acquired an early love of hymns and the Anglican order of service. In later years, he was fond of sitting down at the piano and singing hymns such as the 'Old Hundredth' and 'Jerusalem'. Another legacy of his mother's influence on Bert's early training was an abhorrence of smoking and a puritanical disdain for over-indulgence in alcohol. Bert the politician was also totally opposed to all forms of gambling.[3]

Family life in Maitland changed irrevocably with the sudden death from pneumonia of John Evatt, in October 1901. John left his widow, then aged thirty-eight, with six sons, ranging in age from eighteen years to the one-year-old baby Clive, two sons having died in infancy before Bert was born. For three years, Jeanie struggled to continue the management of the hotel in Maitland, but was eventually persuaded to move to Sydney. There she bought a two-storeyed house in Milson's Point, with a fine view of Sydney Harbour, a short distance from her parents' home in Kirribilli. Her married sisters lived in North Sydney and Mosman, and the extended family was able to provide comfort and support for Jeanie and her sons.[4] That support was important, for Jeanie had been used to domestic help in Maitland; now she had a large household to manage and six boisterous and growing sons to be clothed and fed. What she lacked in domestic skills she made up for in her high expectations of the boys' academic achievement, and they responded by trying very hard to please her. Bert in particular did not need prompting, and used to study until the early hours of the morning, a habit which he retained in later life.

Spiritual guidance was provided by the Revd W. Newby-Fraser of the local Anglican church of St John the Baptist at Milson's Point, where Jeanie played the organ every Sunday. The boys were encouraged to read their Bibles daily and to strive to live by Christian principles. An abiding concern for the less fortunate, and a belief in the worth of each individual, were a legacy of those early years. Bert Evatt, although in later years an irregular church-goer, retained a residual nostalgia for church music and was a generous benefactor to St Mark's Memorial Library in Canberra.[5]

Sydney in 1905 was a city of almost half-a-million people, its society still exhibiting vast disparities between wealth and poverty. It was a society where privileged families could reserve railway carriages for their exclusive use, hire a private tram for a picnic or close a public ice-skating rink for a private party.[6]

For those who were unskilled workers, casual day labour for the male breadwinner, interspersed with periods of unemployment, provided the bare necessities for a hazardous existence where illness or death could plunge the survivors into dire poverty. The area of North Sydney in which the Evatts settled contained a cross-section of working-class and middle-class families. The majority of the population was engaged in work relating to the maritime industry, with a smaller percentage employed in the supply of water, gas and sewerage, and in tanneries and glue factories. Although some wealthy and professional people occupied mansions on one-acre allotments, North Sydney proper was a strong working-class enclave, and the Labor Party had already established itself in the district.[7]

The ten-year-old Bert Evatt, as a promising student, was fortunate in gaining admission to the Fort Street Model School at Observatory Hill, where he spent the remainder of his school years between 1905 and 1911. In 1905, Fort Street School had not officially attained the status of a high school, although it prepared senior students for university matriculation and was a teacher-training institution. Consequently, tuition there was free, whereas Sydney High School charged fees. In 1905, education in New South Wales underwent significant reform, with the creation of post-primary schools for all children, the introduction of a new syllabus and the appointment of a new Director of Education, Peter Board. As a result, elements of the 'new education' movement, which Board had encountered on an overseas tour, were introduced into New South Wales schools.[8]

Since Fort Street had already attained a reputation for academic excellence, competition to enter the school was keen. Boys travelled from Penrith, Windsor and Campbelltown to attend, while some from the country boarded with relatives in the city. Those living in the local area of the Rocks and the city of Sydney were also entitled to enrol, so Bert Evatt was to encounter pupils from a wide cross-section of society at the school.

Alexander Kilgour, the headmaster of Fort Street during Bert Evatt's years at the school, was an outstanding administrator and a dedicated teacher who was to leave an indelible impression on his eager young pupil. Born in Edinburgh, he had emigrated to Australia as a boy with his parents and had himself been educated at Fort Street. He obtained his degrees at The University of Sydney as an evening student while teaching during the day, and was widely read and cultivated. Although a model of rectitude and a disciplinarian, Kilgour did not use the cane, relying instead on an 'air of quiet dignified authority that made any resort to corporal punishment inconceivable'. He had a reputation for driving his staff hard and 'had no tolerance for slackers and dullards'.[9] His students were encouraged to enter the professions, particularly law and medicine, while those who did not show potential towards those fields were referred to friends in the commercial world who could find them employment. Not only did Kilgour select good staff for Fort Street, but he ensured that the school library was well stocked. Departmental inspectors in their reports commented that the school 'compels admiration and challenges comparison with the best work of secondary schools in this State'.[10]

Many years later, Bert Evatt confided that the teachers at Fort Street had an important influence on his intellectual development, and certainly Kilgour in particular was a strong paternal figure to the growing boy. Their friendship lasted until Kilgour's death in 1944, with the benevolent retired headmaster usually sending a letter of congratulation on his former pupil's latest achievement.[11]

While at school, Evatt eagerly accepted positions of responsibility, being elected head prefect in 1911. He captained the cricket first XI, the rugby first XV and was also known as 'an enthusiastic supporter of the Australian game of football', being one of the members of a Fort Street team which visited Melbourne in 1910. The debating society provided a forum for the development of his talents as a speaker, while he was also successful as a prize essayist, winning the Chamber of Manufactures Prize for an essay on 'The Progress of Local Industries'.[12]

Dux of the school in 1911, Evatt was awarded the Bridges Prize 'for the boy who brings the greatest honour to the School during the year'. Among the books which he collected for prizes were Macaulay's *Critical and Historical Essays*; Hobhouse's *Liberalism* and Thomas Carlyle's *The French Revolution*. As Alexander Kilgour said in a speech in 1910, Fort Street boys were stimulated by 'the earnestness and ambition everywhere to be seen', and H. V. Evatt strove to exemplify the school's ethos. For Evatt it was true, as

Kilgour himself asserted, that 'the boy of poor parents had the same opportunity as the son of the rich man, and the best education that the State could afford was there for him'. The result was that manly, self-reliant, true-living boys were being turned out—boys with the power and the inclination to discipline themselves, with a high sense of duty, and who were to become valuable citizens of their country'.[13]

After his departure, Evatt retained close links with his old school, being President of the Old Boys' Union from 1922 to 1924, and establishing an essay prize in memory of his two brothers, Ray and Frank, who were killed in World War I.[14]

In the Senior Examination for 1911, Bert Evatt gained first-class honours in all except one of his subjects. He was runner-up to dux of the state. With such outstanding results, he won a bursary to The University of Sydney, which gave him free tuition and textbooks and an allowance of £20 per annum. St Andrew's College also awarded him the Horn Scholarship valued at £50 per annum, which provided free board and lodgings. The Horn Scholarship was awarded to assist 'deserving native students in logic, moral philosophy or divinity' and was held for three years.[15]

Thus, in 1912 Bert Evatt embarked on his years as an undergraduate at the University of Sydney, first in the Arts faculty, later in Law. The University enrolled about 2000 undergraduates at that time, and Arts was numerically a small faculty. All the lecture rooms were in the main building around the clock tower; the library consisted of one large room under the supervision of the librarian and poet, J. le Gay Brereton. Another Fortian, A. R. Chisholm, who went to the University four years earlier than Evatt, has left an interesting 'group portrait' of those years:

...the teachers gave me no vast fund of inspiration—though there were three or four exceptions. Some were masters of their subject, but poor exponents of it; a few were pedants rather than creative scholars; practically all were inaccessible...[16]

There were no tutorials in Arts subjects, and the few women students who attended lectures sat in the front rows, 'segregated by an unwritten law'. Photographs of the day show the formality of dress expected: male students always wore stiff collars and starched cuffs, tight trousers and rather long coats. A watch-chain was a desirable ornament. Boots were the fashion rather than shoes, which were considered effeminate, and all students had to wear academic gowns.

At the Presbyterian St Andrew's College, Evatt discovered not only the benefits of communal life, with its 'domestic supervision, systematic religious instruction and efficient tutorial assistance', but also 'intellectual competition, athletic sport, and Union, Club and Society activity, those qualities of influence, self-reliance, and leadership [which]...have not failed to find suitable and honourable expression'.[17] Yet, despite the camaraderie of dining hall and common room, debates committee and cricket field, and the *esprit de corps* which he extolled, there was a hint that Evatt's life-long battle against unwarranted privilege was about to begin. In December 1914, when editor of *St Andrew's College Magazine*, he argued against the abortive proposal for the formation of army companies based on GPS schools:

One would suppose a great public schools' education, however ill-digested, would at least have put us above the snobbishness of a certain grade of society, which is continually revealing its imperfections in the pitiful struggle to convince itself that it is not bourgeois at best; and which seems to expect the best campaigning material of the country to say that they will serve their King and Country on condition that they do not have to sleep in the same tent as some person who has not attended one of the great public schools.[18]

Evatt was to spend seven years in residence at St Andrew's College. In 1916, he became a college tutor in English and philosophy 'without any fee, provided he were permitted to live in College', which he continued to do until admitted to the Bar towards the end of 1918.[19]

Evatt formed two life-long friendships with contemporaries at St Andrew's, notably with Eric Dark and Vere Gordon Childe. Evatt first encountered Childe in the Philosophy I class in 1912, and they shared equal first place, with high distinctions, in the examinations at the end of that year. When Childe completed his Arts degree, he went to Oxford University on a postgraduate scholarship. On his return to Australia, he was appointed senior resident tutor at St Andrew's College from January 1918, while Evatt himself was there as a tutor in law. However, Childe's appointment was not to last: by May 1918 he had tendered his resignation, and the College Council resolved that it be accepted.[20]

The editor of the College magazine noted that Childe had 'won the respect and esteem of all the men' and hinted at the reason for his departure:

...Owing to the fact that in this as yet intolerant world, it is not possible at a time of crisis to hold social and political views contrary to those of the majority, it became desirable, in the interests of the College, that Mr. Childe leave us. He took the only proper course in the situation—that of voluntarily resigning—to the great regret of all those who knew him.[21]

Childe, by late 1917, had formed socialist and anti-war views, and may well have influenced Evatt's thinking. Yet Evatt himself, at least while he was an undergraduate, was circumspect in the expression of radical ideas, perhaps constrained by his mother's circumstances and his own reliance on scholarships and a college tutorship to support his university progress.

In that progress, he succeeded brilliantly. He graduated in 1915 with first-class honours in English, philosophy and mathematics, and the University Medal for philosophy. As an undergraduate in Arts, he won every available prize in his major subjects, as well as the Wentworth Prize for an undergraduate English essay (on 'the play within the play' in Elizabethan drama) and the Beauchamp Prize in 1915 for a long essay 'Liberalism in Australia'.[22]

Evatt was prominent not only in academic pursuits, but also in extra-curricular activities, where his zeal and desire for mastery were manifested in many spheres. In 1915, Evatt was elected President of the Undergraduates Association; he also served on the staff of *Hermes*, first as sub-editor, and then in 1916 as editor-in-chief. The Sydney University Union came into being in 1912–13, and Evatt was elected one of its first directors, in 1915–16 becoming the first undergraduate to be elected President of the Union.

In 1913, he had pressed for, and won, changes to the manner in which students in various faculties were represented on the executive of the Undergraduates Association, a body dominated until then by medical students. When Evatt retired as President of the Undergraduates Association, he was praised for the manner in which he 'had surmounted each difficulty with such regularity that he was looked upon by the committee as a leader and friend of very rare qualities'.[23]

These successes as an undergraduate demonstrated that Evatt was at least respected by his fellow-students, if not universally liked. He was never one to suffer from false modesty, and undoubtedly he inspired envy in some quarters. He sought approval from those in positions of authority within the University, partly to compensate for his lack of social status, but also because he genuinely respected and admired them for their intellectual eminence.

Evatt came to the notice of influential academics when he served on the Board of Directors of The University of Sydney Union with men such as Professor J. B. Peden. A testimonial that has survived from this period attested to his 'considerable capacity for management and executive ability' as President of the Union, and commented with some perspicacity that 'Mr. Evatt has shown when necessity arose that he possesses the courage of his opinions and when convinced that a certain line of action is the correct one has not hesitated to follow it although his actions may have operated to his personal disadvantage'.[24]

In University sport, while not an outstanding athlete, Evatt was an eager team player and an avid administrator—for example, honorary treasurer of the Sports Union, chairman for inter-faculty football and secretary of the University Cricket Club. In recognition of his services to sport, he was elected a life member of The University of Sydney Sports Union.

Meanwhile, his academic successes continued, with the award in 1917 of a Master of Arts in Philosophy for a thesis on 'Social and Political Tendencies in Australia'. Evatt had begun his law course after completion of the BA degree in 1915, and gained first place in both the Law I and Law II years. He completed the law degree by taking two sections and the final in one year, and graduated LL.B in April 1918 with first-class honours and the University Medal.

In 1916, Evatt became an Associate to the Chief Justice of New South Wales, Sir William Cullen, and this provided him with a small income while he was pursuing his legal studies. Not only did the position give him valuable experience, but it also made his name well known in the legal community. No doubt Evatt's prominence in student affairs and his membership of the Law Debating Society first brought him into contact with Sir William Cullen, who was also Chancellor of The University of Sydney, and Patron of The University of Sydney Union.[25]

Evatt's academic achievements and student activism are well documented, but it is more difficult to discern a coherent ideology emerging from the expression of social and political beliefs. The personal record is sparse, and much has to be inferred from his early published writings, and the intellectual environment of The University of Sydney at the time.

Initially, he was drawn to The University of Sydney Men's Christian Union, and in 1913 and 1914 he was treasurer of the organisation. In addition to its spiritual and missionary concerns, the Christian Union aimed to devote attention to the 'systematic study of social problems', and social study circles were introduced into the University for the first time in 1912. Evatt was also active on the committee which ran holiday camps for schoolboys in the University vacation 'to help the boys in strong Christian manliness'.[26]

Yet it was the teaching of Francis Anderson, Professor of Philosophy, which had a more important influence on Evatt's thought. Anderson had studied philosophy at Glasgow and had intended to enter the Presbyterian ministry. He arrived in Melbourne in 1886 to become an assistant in the Australian Church of the Revd Charles

Strong, whose liberal theology and concern for social questions seemed to offer more freedom of thought than the National Church of Scotland. However, after two years in Melbourne, Anderson came to Sydney to inaugurate, as Lecturer, the study of philosophy at The University of Sydney, and in 1890 he became first Challis Professor of Logic and Mental Philosophy there. His intellectual interests were wide ranging: in addition to logic, ethics and metaphysics, he taught psychology, economics and education before separate chairs were established in those disciplines, and retained an abiding interest in sociology. His lectures were clear and methodical, demonstrating 'keen critical power, graceful expression and moral emotion'. His philosophical position has been described as 'Christian Idealist', but 'tempered by the earlier traditional Scottish line of thought which emphasised the self and moral values'.[27]

More significantly, however, Francis Anderson was a disciple of T. H. Green, the philosopher of New Liberalism in England. Anderson's book on Green was published in Sydney in 1902, and in it he followed Green in asserting the primacy of the intellectual and spiritual over the material and mechanical causes of things. In rejecting Marx, Anderson insisted that will, intellect and morality were more important than material needs and desires; that the social order consisted of a community of ideals amongst individuals. The development of an ethical 'personality' was essential for the leaders of society, who, by their education and social policies, could reform the abuses of capitalism which destroyed the individual's personal development. As Tim Rowse states,

both [Green and Anderson] inherited the evangelistic belief in reforming 'social abuses' as a means to morally reconstructing individuals. This was to be the role of the modern state, with its expanded social concerns...The New Liberalism was...a practical, empirical maxim of state intervention to guide society's evolution towards more freedom for individuals.[28]

For Anderson, the State was 'society organised for the common good, for the protection of individuals, against groups, associations, unions of masters, or unions of men, who, without such common state action, would make freedom of individual development impossible'.[29]

However, Rowse does not perceive a later shift from Anderson's view of the State as benign. This may be seen in Anderson's notes for a lecture entitled 'The State and the Professions'. In it, he urged professional men to become involved in politics, because the moral integrity and independence of State officials could only be found in 'the existence of democratic forms of government, in free combination and discussion, and...in the existence of a great and free community outside direct government control'. Anderson, by 1920, feared 'a centralised omnipotent State, a monstrous organism from whose innumerable tentacles no man...could escape', and stressed the need to preserve democracy by maintaining the distinction between society and the State: otherwise, the 'interests of free scientific teaching, of free discussion and criticism and free combination, of moral as well as economic independence' would be threatened. Moreover, he wondered whether professional men had shown sufficient sympathy with 'the great social movement of our times, known as the labour movement'.[30]

An examination of the ideas expressed in Evatt's Beauchamp Prize-winning essay (1915), later published as *Liberalism in Australia*, reveals the extent to which the young Evatt was indebted to Anderson. Particularly in the concluding chapter on 'the New Liberalism', Evatt makes explicit its links with social progress:

The fundamental importance of liberty is seen to rest on the nature of 'the good' itself, and human progress is seen to be, in the main, social progress. The result is the idea that material wealth exists for the sake of the moral development of man, not man for the sake of material wealth; and Liberalism does its best to provide the external conditions for more efficient and fuller lives.[31]

The contractual theory of the State had been discredited, and freedom had changed from a negative to a positive concept.

However, in 1915 Evatt did not think that Socialism offered an alternative to the New Liberalism, and he criticised it for its 'mechanical interpretation of history, the over-emphasis on the economical factor, the supposition of a class war, the construction of Utopias'. Nevertheless, he conceded that in its association with the labour movement, Liberalism had 'undoubtedly been enriched', and it continued to be a 'living force'.

Sub-titled 'An Historical Sketch of Australian politics down to the year 1915', Evatt's essay on Liberalism traced its development from the governorships of Bligh and Macquarie, both of whom were subjected to the agitation of those free settlers who, although motivated by greed, were protesting against the caprice and arbitrariness of the system of government. Thus, the liberal movement was initiated by John Macarthur, and brought to fruition by W. C. Wentworth, John Dunmore Lang and William Bland. It is clear from the tone of this early chapter that Evatt had been well-schooled in the liberal historical tradition of trial by jury, opposition to press censorship and so on.

When his discussion moved to the 1850s, and the attainment of responsible government, Evatt was more critical of Wentworth as having lost touch with the more progressive elements in New South Wales, but praised him for opposing Lang's 'extreme' stand on independence from Britain. For Evatt, indiscriminate free selection, enacted by laissez-faire liberals in the 1860s, had merely led to an increasing monopoly of land, and its failure had reconciled Australian liberals to many forms of State interference, most notably the adoption of protectionist policies by the Commonwealth.

The rise of the Labor Party was credited with bringing about 'that stability of parties which has been so conspicuously absent in Australian politics'. Although Evatt emphasised that the development of State interference began before the advent of Labor as a political power, 'the various Labor parties contributed largely to the extensions of Government regulations and control, and thus reacted on Liberalism'. The success of the Labor parties in New South Wales, South Australia and Victoria from the 1890s was due to their 'practical list of proposals' and their emphasis on their 'fighting platform' at the expense of their ultimate objective. Both the caucus system and the Labor pledge came in for criticism from Evatt because they struck at the 'principles of the responsibility of Parliament to the people, and of the freedom of Parliamentary discussion'. Yet he acknowledged that, in the 1890s, the same system had given Labor a 'power and weight' beyond its numbers, so that its representatives could 'affect the fate of Governments and obtain concessions in return for support'. Evatt also agreed with those Liberals who opposed the principle of preference to unionists, while he predicted that Australian Labor parties, once they assumed the responsibilities of office, would become 'more and more dissatisfied with any Marxian scheme of reconstruction with its failure to recognise individuals and its quite frank materialism'.

In his consideration of the Australian Constitution, Evatt concluded that the challenge facing Australian Liberalism was to readjust the powers of States and Commonwealth; he was confident that the Commonwealth Parliament would receive additional powers 'by the will of the people'.[32] In that event, Liberalism would have to see to it that the newer and more national Constitution would be based on the principles of liberty and equality.

Evatt's essay on Liberalism received widespread praise within the University at the time, and in 1918 it was published in book form, having been prescribed as a Pass textbook in the University classes in sociology. George Arnold Wood, Professor of History, in his foreword acknowledged Evatt's success in overcoming the difficulties faced by those venturing as pioneers into the field of Australian history; moreover, Evatt had shown 'for the first time the meaning and the interest of a movement whose great importance will in future be more fully recognized'.[33]

Yet if Herbert Vere Evatt in 1915 adhered to the principles of New Liberalism, he was to move towards a more radical position. There were several reasons for this: the intellectual influence of V. Gordon Childe; Evatt's growing sympathy for the workers victimised after the 1917 general strike; and the emotional impact on him of the deaths of two brothers in the fighting on the Western Front.

Besides their move towards a radical political standpoint, Evatt and Childe had much in common. Both shared a distaste for the selfish pursuit of property and status; and Evatt would no doubt have been associated with Childe in the Public Questions Society at the University, which the latter helped to found. They both served on the Union's Reading Room and Archives Committee, as well as participating in Union debates. Childe joined the Labor Party in 1918.

Evatt himself was wary about expressing publicly ideas which might be viewed by the University authorities as dangerously radical. Nevertheless, there were signs that after 1916 he began to question the New Liberalism which he had previously professed. For instance, there is evidence that he sought publication of his views beyond the University. Writing in 1930, Henry E. Boote, editor of the *Australian Worker* during 1916–17, remembered Evatt 'as a young student calling upon me at *The Worker* office to ask my opinion of an essay on the capitalist system which he had written at the University'.[34]

Moreover, during the first eight months of 1917, a lively debate was carried on in the pages of *The Australian Worker*, inspired by an article of Professor G. A. Wood entitled 'Should We Have Imperial Federation?'. Wood answered the question in the affirmative, suggesting that Australian nationalism and the power of the worker to improve his standard of living could be secured within an imperial federation. Furthermore, such a federation was the best way to safeguard 'White Australia'. Responses to Wood were published on the letters page of *The Worker* over the ensuing months; and on 31 May 1917, an article appeared under the pseudonym 'Not at All'. For the cognoscenti at the University, the author would have been recognisable as H. V. Evatt, since he had earlier won an essay prize under the same pseudonym. The introduction to the article states that 'the following is the first of a series of three articles on Australian nationalism and Imperial Federation, and formed part of a thesis on the question by a student at Sydney University'.[35]

The reference was to Evatt's MA thesis, 'Social and Political Tendencies in Australia', which was awarded in April 1917. Unfortunately, all traces of it have vanished. There is no doubt, however, that Evatt was keen to take issue with Wood over his advocacy of imperial federation; in his opposition to it, Evatt aligned himself with C. H. Currey and W. J. Miles. No further articles by 'Not at All' appeared in the *Australian Worker* during 1917, perhaps because, from August 1917 onwards, the weekly columns were given over to the events of the general strike and, later on, to the arguments over the second conscription referendum.

In August 1915, when he was President of The University of Sydney Undergraduates Association, Evatt presented the National Belgian Relief Fund with £400 raised by students. Undoubtedly, he shared with his contemporaries a revulsion against German militarism and 'autocracy', and there is no evidence that he was opposed to Australia's involvement in the war, or to the recruitment of volunteers. Indeed, during 1915 he twice tried to enlist but was apparently rejected because of astigmatism. Commenting on the impact of recruitment of undergraduates at The University of Sydney, a writer in *Hermes* noted that 'the number of University men who have joined the expeditionary forces is now over 300, and every week fresh names are added; about 40% of these men were undergraduates attending lectures when the war started. Included in this number are three of the Directors of the Union for this year and six Directors of past years'.[36]

By May 1916, as the first referendum on conscription approached, Evatt, writing the editorial in *Hermes*, advocated the adoption of compulsory national service in Australia because it would

allow for proper organisation of our resources...it would resolve the doubts and difficulties of thousands of Australian youths and men who under our present system do not see their way clear to enlist...it would show that Australia is willing to sacrifice its all for an Empire which has given it absolute domestic freedom and virtual independence—it would prevent undue waste of effort...and it would be fairer to all.

At the same time, he agreed with the trade unions that there should be a 100 per cent tax on war profits. While conceding that 'conscription does mean a sacrifice of individual freedom for the sake of social freedom', he emphasised that the latter was to be placed first.[37]

A subsequent editorial in the August 1916 issue of *Hermes* reaffirmed support for conscription but deplored the tactics used by the 'military gentlemen...riding roughshod over the civilian population', as well as 'the paltry and despicable methods of the so-called Anti-Conscriptionists'. As President of the Union, Evatt appealed for letters and photographs of The University of Sydney graduates, students and staff on active service to be collected and placed in the University library, as a worthy record of their part 'in the great struggle to keep Australia free and inviolate'.

After the referendum, the editorial in the November 1916 issue of *Hermes*, written by H. V. Evatt and E. A. Woodward, commented on the part played in favour of the 'Yes' case by members of the University staff, and the difficulty in remaining neutral 'in the face of a great political and national crisis'. It was to be regretted that prominent graduates, especially members of the Bar, had realised too late their leadership responsibilities in guiding the people to a 'Yes' vote. The decisive majority for 'No' in New South Wales demonstrated the 'tremendous strength of national selfishness or local patriotism—that sentiment of Australia for the Australians'. The writers hoped that graduates and staff would never return to that 'contented quietism' which looks on at 'corrupt politicians playing the party game and passes by on the other side'.

By August 1917, *Hermes* was noting that nearly 1400 of the University's 'sons' had gone on active service. Among them was Frank Evatt, Bert's younger brother, who completed his first year of medicine by August 1916 under special regulations introduced by the University, and volunteered shortly after his eighteenth birthday. Ray Evatt, two years Bert's junior, had enlisted in January 1915, survived Gallipoli and served in France and Belgium as a lieutenant with the 20th Battalion, second Australian Division. From Belgium on 24 September 1916, Ray had written to his mother complaining that everyone in the AIF should be able to vote on the conscription question irrespective of age: 'I could, then, like 99% of the others, vote solid for 'NO' conscription...Show you what we think of this game'. By June 1917, Bert had become critical of W. M. Hughes and his break from the Labor Party; he intended to vote Labor because it had good policies and conscription was dead.[38]

Ray Evatt won the Military Cross for gallantry in action on 25 February 1917 on the Somme, but he was killed in action near Ypres on 20 September 1917. Writing more than twenty years later, in his book *Australian Labour Leader*, Evatt criticised Holman for failing to realise 'the tremendous strain and anxiety in every family from which a member was absent at the front. That burden...was almost too heavy to be borne'.[39]

After Ray's death, Bert made strenuous efforts to secure military permission for Frank's return to Australia on the grounds that he should continue his medical studies. Wounded in the battle in which his brother Ray had been killed, Frank Evatt was convalescing in England when Bert wrote to their uncle, Major-General Sir George Hamilton Evatt, retired Surgeon-General in the British Army, to intercede with military authorities. However, although the Director-

General of Medical Services recommended that Frank be allowed to return to Australia, General Headquarters in France refused permission. Returning to France in January 1918 as a gunner in the first field artillery brigade, Frank Evatt was involved in heavy fighting from March, when the German offensive began, right through the next six months until his death from wounds on 29 September 1918.[40]

Frank's death deeply affected Bert, who had had a special affinity with this younger brother, sharing with him a love of music and literature. It was Bert's painful duty to tell his mother of the death of another of her sons. Her grief and despair were so overwhelming that she was ill for many weeks.

A poem entitled 'November 12, 1918' by H. V. Evatt was published in *Hermes*, and expressed the deep anguish he felt on Armistice Day, when amidst the rejoicing he yearned

> *For those dear boys who never shall return,*
> *Our sweet young boys who bravely went along*
> *To meet with storm and pain and death, and yet,*
> *Faced all these terrors with a snatch of song,*
> *Oh! how I yearn for them and can't forget!*[41]

Nor did he forget. Their names were commemorated on plaques in St John's Church at Milson's Point, a memorial essay prize was established at Fort Street Boys' High School, and a bell in the War Memorial Carillon at The University of Sydney bears their names.[42]

Yet, even while he grieved for his two brothers, Bert had cause for personal joy; not only had he been admitted to the Bar, after obtaining his law degree with first-class honours and the University Medal, but he was in love with Mary Alice Sheffer (known to friends as 'Mas'). Bert had been introduced to her in May 1918 by his aunt, a neighbour of the Sheffers in Mosman, and he was instantly attracted to 'the beautiful, fair-haired girl'. She was nineteen and in her first term of Arts at The University of Sydney; he was twenty-four. In November 1918, Bert proposed, and knew at once, as he wrote later, that 'the greatest happiness in all the world (his love returned)—was his'. At the insistence of Mary Alice's father, a wealthy industrial chemist, they were engaged for two years, and during that time, as Mary Alice wrote, their 'confidence in one another grew fine and sure, so that our marriage was the true perfect mating of heart and soul and mind and body'.[43]

They were married on 27 November 1920 in the Congregational church, Mosman, and left for a honeymoon in Hawaii and California. On board ship to the United States, Bert was in his element as secretary of the passengers' entertainments committee which organised the games on the voyage. However, it was not merely a holiday:

he had been secretly commissioned by Prime Minister W. M. Hughes to report on the Japanese population in California, and he also carried a formal letter of introduction to the Governor of Hawaii. On Evatt's return, he wrote some newspaper articles about the racial problems caused by the influx of Japanese into those areas of the United States.

More important for the rest of his life was the earnest young man's good fortune in gaining a partner who was vivacious, strong-minded, independent and articulate. With her help and encouragement, Bert Evatt was able to expand his horizons beyond work and study, to acquire an interest in modern art and music, and to savour the fruits of his success.

Notes

1. Transcript of Interview with Mrs Mary Alice Evatt, 26 April 1973, Tape 1:2, Oral History Programme, National Library of Australia (NLA).
2. Family history provided by Justice Elizabeth Evatt; Interview with Mrs Jane Carter 16 May 1990; Kylie Tennant, *Evatt: Politics and Justice*, 3rd rev. edn, Sydney, 1981, pp. 3–8.
3. Mary Alice Evatt, Tape 1:2/7–8; Tape 2:2/43, NLA.
4. Interviews with Justice Elizabeth Evatt and Mrs Jane Carter, cited above.
5. A letter to Evatt dated 12 February 1960 from Bishop Burgmann, invited him to 'call at St. Mark's, which you helped to build, when you visit Canberra'. In his reply, Evatt promised not to forget to visit St Mark's 'on those occasions when I am in Canberra, as I regard the work of the Collegiate Library as one of the most important features of the intellectual life of our national capital'. Bishop Burgmann Papers, MS.1998, Box 7 file: Evatt, NLA.
6. Helen Rutledge, *My Grandfather's House: Recollections of an Australian Family*, Doubleday, Sydney, 1986, p. 96; pp. 107–8.
7. Anne O'Brien, *Poverty's Prison: The Poor in New South Wales 1880–1918*, Melbourne University Press (MUP), Melbourne, 1988, pp. 67–9; Shirley Fitzgerald, *Rising Damp: Sydney 1870–1890*, Oxford University Press (OUP), Melbourne, 1987, pp. 204–5; Andrew Moore, 'The Curse of the Kalahari: the North Sydney Bears and the Ghosts of 1921–22' in *Sporting Traditions*, vol. 5, no. 2, May 1989, pp. 157–8.
8. Jan Burnswoods and Jim Fletcher, *Sydney and the Bush: A Pictorial History of Education in New South Wales*, Dept of Education, Sydney, 1980, p. 139.
9. *Australian Dictionary of Biography* (*ADB*) article on Kilgour, vol. 9; A.R. Chisholm, *Men Were My Milestones*, MUP, Melbourne, 1958, p. 25.
10. C. Morris, *The School on the Hill: a Saga of Australian Life*, p. 64; L.E. Gent, *The Fort Street Centenary Book*, Sydney, 1949, pp. 42–3.
11. Interview with Sir Marcus Oliphant, Canberra, January 1991; Letters from Kilgour to Evatt, 22 December 1930, file: High Court: Congratulations on Appointment; and 6 August 1939, file: Evatt Publications: Correspondence—Rum Rebellion, Evatt Collection, Flinders University.
12. *Fortian*, December 1910 and May 1918, Fort Street Archives.

13 Quoted in Ronald S. Horan, *Fort Street: A History*, Sydney, 1989, p. 152.
14 *Fortian*, June 1924, Fort Street Archives; John Kerr, *Matters for Judgment*, 1978, pp. 37–8. Kerr won the prize in 1931, on the subject set by Evatt, 'Australia should be more enterprising in the Pacific'.
15 Manual for Public Examinations held by the University of Sydney, 1913, pp. 46–7, Sydney University Archives (SUA).
16 Chisholm, *Men Were My Milestones*, pp. 33–8.
17 Extract from an article by H.V. Evatt and R.A. Dart in the University Students' Handbook, published by the University Christian Union, 1917, and reprinted in the *St. Andrew's College Calendar*, 1918, p. 29, St Andrew's College Archives.
18 *St. Andrew's College Magazine*, no. 12, December 1914, pp. 2–3.
19 Minute Book, vol. 6, p. 28, 20 March 1916, St Andrew's College Council.
20 Ibid., 18 March 1918, 20 May 1918.
21 *St. Andrew's College Magazine*, no. 16, November 1918.
22 H.V. Evatt File, biography 779, Sydney University Archives (SUA).
23 Minutes of The University of Sydney Undergraduates Association, 13 July 1914; 19 April 1916, S.19 Box 1, SUA.
24 Testimonial written by O. Vonwiller, Acting Professor of Physics, University of Sydney, 9 November 1917, in private collection of Mrs Rosalind Carrodus.
25 *Fortian*, May 1918, Fort Street Archives; H.V. Evatt file, biography 779, SUA.
26 The University of Sydney Calendar, 1912, pp. 550–1; Calendar 1913, pp. 552–3; Calendar 1914, p. 564.
27 G.V. Portus, article on Francis Anderson in *Hermes*, November 1912, p.158; article on Francis Anderson in *ADB*, vol. 7.
28 Tim Rowse, *Australian Liberalism and National Character*, Kibble Books, Malmsbury, Vic, 1978, p. 39.
29 Francis Anderson, 'Liberalism and Socialism', Presidential Address to Section G of the Australasian Association for Advancement of Science, Proceedings, 1911, vol. XI, pp. 217–27.
30 Professor Francis Anderson Papers, Box 1, p. 27, SUA.
31 H.V. Evatt, *Liberalism in Australia*, Sydney, 1918, Introduction p. 2.
32 Quotations from this and preceding paragraphs are derived from H.V. Evatt, *Liberalism in Australia, passim*.
33 H.V. Evatt, *Liberalism in Australia*, Foreword, p. ii.
34 Boote to Evatt, 22 December 1930, File: High Court—Congratulations, Evatt Collection, Flinders University.
35 *The Australian Worker*, 18 January 1917, 31 May 1917.
36 *Hermes*, vol. 21, no. 1, May 1915, p. 8.
37 *Hermes*, vol. 22, no. 1, May 1916.
38 H.V. Evatt, *Australian Labour Leader: The Story of W.A. Holman and the Labour Movement*, Angus & Robertson, Sydney, 2nd edn, 1942.
39 Ray Evatt to Mrs. J.S. Evatt, 24 September 1916 from Belgium, 2DRL/0160, file 1, Australian War Memorial (AWM) Archives. Bert's increasingly critical

attitude towards Hughes and conscription is mentioned in a letter which Ray Evatt wrote to his mother Mrs. J.S. Evatt on 27 June 1917, 2DRL/0160, file 1, AWM Archives.

40 F.S. Evatt to H.V. Evatt, 3 December 1917, 2 DRL/0159, file 12/11/117, AWM Archives.

41 *Hermes*, vol. 24, no. 3, November 1918, p. 276.

42 D.R.V. Wood, *Bells of Remembrance: A History of the War Memorial Carillon, 1923–87*, Sydney 1991, p. 49. (Bell No. 28 was donated in 1928 by H.V. Evatt).

43 Wedding Book, in the possession of Mrs Rosalind Carrodus.

CHAPTER 2

THE MAKING OF A LABOR LAWYER

Every member in the ranks of Labor is part of a living movement marching towards an ideal and yet having a practical policy to submit to the people. The contest, therefore, is really one between the power of money on the one side, and practical and determined idealists on the other...The triumph of idealism is at hand.

H. V. EVATT

Before being a politician, H. V. Evatt was a lawyer. The legal profession which he joined was small in numbers and its members were comfortably situated. In New South Wales, there were about 170 practising barristers in 1919, together with over 1000 solicitors. About three-fifths of solicitors worked in Sydney, and the annual earnings of suburban solicitors were between £500 and £1000—at a time when average wages for male workers amounted to less than £250 per annum. Leaders at the Sydney Bar commanded incomes of up to £15 000 a year, while at the other end of the scale were barristers just starting in practice, with very limited incomes until they established themselves.

Evatt experienced no such difficulty. In his first year, he was briefed to appear as junior counsel in a big case concerning T. J. Ryan, Premier of Queensland. Ryan was the only Premier in Australia to oppose conscription in the referenda of 1916–17, in the course of which he was bitterly attacked by conservatives. Hitting back, Ryan sued a newspaper, the Melbourne *Argus*, for libel: the *Argus*, in an editorial, had accused the Ryan government of having entered into 'a paltry and contemptible conspiracy with Germans and other disloyalists'. Ryan chose H. D. Macrossan (a Queenslander) and H. V. Evatt to represent him at the High Court hearing in Sydney in 1919. It seems that Evatt was chosen as a result of Ryan (himself a barrister) having asked Richard Windeyer, KC, a leader of the Sydney Bar, to recommend a bright young barrister.[1]

There was no clear victory for either party in this case. Naturally, Macrossan was most prominent on Ryan's side, but Evatt was probably noted in the legal profession as a man of promise for the future. Furthermore, this was Evatt's introduction to the practical interpretation of the law of libel. As it happened, when Evatt commenced work at the Bar in March 1919 he read in chambers with A. R. J. Watt, KC, who specialised in libel cases.

Of course, in his early years at the Bar, Evatt served an apprenticeship at much lower court levels. As he wrote later, a young barrister had to become familiar with the everyday practice and the rough-and-tumble work of the profession:

...the practical application of the teachings of the law, particularly the law of procedure, evidence and pleading, must be mastered. The trade must, so to speak, be absorbed through the skin and become incorporated in the man himself...the tricks of the trade must be known, the devices must be used or avoided, and, above all, they are not to be thought about too subtly but are to become the almost unconscious stock-in-trade.[2]

Police court work provided good grounding for legal practice. One such case involving Evatt in his early days at the Bar was the defence of P. S. Brookfield, who represented Broken Hill metalminers in the New South Wales Parliament. Brookfield was a militant trade unionist and socialist, noted for uncompromising and fiery speeches. He strongly opposed conscription in the referenda of 1916–17, defended the Russian Revolution and advocated direct action rather than arbitration in industrial disputes. As a result, he attracted the attention of police and other authorities and was repeatedly fined for making statements to prejudice recruiting, using insulting language and so on. The particular incident which brought Evatt in to defend Brookfield related to a speech by the latter at a public meeting in the Sydney Domain one Sunday. Brookfield was charged with an offence on the ground that, in the hearing of one Constable McMurray, he used the following words:

One of my friends has just come round to tell me that there is the usual tribe of police pimps taking notes and, if so, I hope they take everything down. I have respect for the policeman in uniform, who comes boldly forward when he comes on the scene. We have to admire that policeman; but I have no time for the lying, perjuring pimps who come round here taking notes.

In court, Brookfield did not deny saying this, but he added that he had not been aware of Constable McMurray's presence in the Domain at the time. Evatt, for the defence, urged that Brookfield's words had not been levelled at McMurray in particular. As Evatt put it, although the words were 'harsh and severe, they were simply a criticism of certain methods, and of a certain class, as distinct from an individual'. It was a reasonable defence, but Evatt reckoned without his client's outspoken character. Under cross-examination by the prosecutor, Brookfield acknowledged that he had been convicted for similar offences in the past and he volunteered the information that one such occasion was in 1917, 'when McMurray couldn't write shorthand when the judge asked him to'. Thus Brookfield, in his eagerness to show up the 'police pimp', let out the fact that he knew McMurray by sight. The magistrate was therefore able to take the view that Brookfield's statement in the Domain had a personal application to Constable McMurray. Brookfield was fined £5, which probably did not worry him much, if at all. His defence counsel was left to reflect upon the desirability of clients being able to curb their tongues under hostile questioning.[3]

The fact that Evatt represented Labor parliamentarians in both these cases does not in itself mean that he sought them out. He may have simply accepted briefs as they were offered to him. Macrossan did this in acting as senior counsel for Ryan, despite the fact that Macrossan was a prominent politician on the non-Labor side. Nevertheless, the Ryan and Brookfield cases presented significant similarities, which probably attracted Evatt's sympathy. Both Ryan and Brookfield were subjected to severe court questioning concerning their activity in the anti-conscription movement and other challenges to the Commonwealth government. Questions of civil liberties, relating to censorship and police surveillance, were also raised. Had Evatt known that his own mail was tampered with, he would have been furious: he was not the sort of man to remain quiet under such an indignity. Yet ironically, the examination of Evatt's letters by an official censor provides us with important information as to Evatt's political views at the time.

The letters in question were from Evatt to his friend, V. G. Childe, who, after being virtually forced to resign from his tutorial position at St Andrew's College in the University of Sydney, went to Queensland and took a school teaching job. As a socialist and pacifist, Childe was under surveillance by the Department of Defence, his mail being censored. At least two of Evatt's letters to him were secretly read by an official censor who summarised their contents for Intelligence purposes. The originals of Evatt's letters, written at the end of 1918, did not survive, but the censor's reports on them were retained in Commonwealth archives.

Evatt, who was about to complete his term as associate to Sir William Cullen, wrote from the Chief Justice's Chambers at the Supreme Court, Sydney, and this may have stimulated the censor's interest—a potential subversive mixing freely with judges? Actually, however, the main purpose of Evatt's letters was to commiserate with his friend on uncertain employment prospects and to express the hope that Childe would soon be able to return to Sydney. There was also a reference to George Clarke, another young tutor at St Andrew's. As Evatt wrote: 'we both regard you [Childe] as our political father'. Here perhaps was scope for official speculation about a subversive cell at the College—if it be assumed that the discussion of unorthodox ideas could be dangerous. To conservatives, Childe and his friends were objects of suspicion, because they were radical intellectuals. Worse, they were incorruptible and not cowed by victimisation. In truth, they represented a threat to the established order primarily through their ability to promote ideas by disseminating them in print. There is no evidence of their involvement in organisations such as the Industrial Workers of the World (IWW) or militant trade unions. Childe himself became a member of the Labor Party before he went to Queensland in 1918, but he was 'not a revolutionary'.[4]

The most intriguing aspect of Evatt's letters is an indication that he was taken aback by the way in which his book, *Liberalism in Australia*, had been received when published earlier in 1918. The book was simply a reproduction of the university essay written by Evatt three years before, from which it appeared that the author was a latter-day liberal. Moreover, as Evatt informed Childe in a letter of 3 December 1918, the book had been adopted as a text by Meredith Atkinson, an academic who was closely associated with the Workers' Educational Association (WEA) of New South Wales. Evatt was unhappy about this development: Atkinson's strong pro-conscription stand had alienated him from radicals such as Childe, and the WEA formally dissociated itself from Atkinson's views. For his part, Evatt indicated to Childe his own embarrassment at being publicly identified with bourgeois ideas which he no longer espoused. Consequently, Evatt was thinking of writing a book renouncing bourgeois liberalism, and he suggested that Childe might collaborate with him in the project.

Nothing came of the idea, and it is difficult to imagine how Childe, whose brilliant study *How Labour Governs* was published a few years later, could possibly have shared in authorship of a work with someone like Evatt who was much less interested in developing concepts of political theory. Certainly, there was an area of general agreement—Evatt's comment on the recent English (Khaki) general election was that the result was 'terribly bloody'—and it is evident that Evatt had travelled a long way in his discussions with Childe. Even so, important differences remained.

Childe's own political development as a radical was predictable enough. For example, he was secretary of the Oxford University Socialist Society in 1917 before he returned to Australia and became involved in the anti-conscription struggle. Yet Evatt was initially on the other side in that conflict, though with some reservations, and it is astonishing that by 1919 he had swung round to a radical position. The censor commented that Evatt was 'quite prepared to follow Childe blindly', but this was a misjudgment. Both men were affected by the immediate post-war ferment of ideas and political activity, revolving around such events as the Russian Revolution and a series of major industrial conflicts in Australia. Socialism was on the labour agenda, and there were efforts to establish One Big Union to embrace all workers. Conservatives were fearful of these developments until a sharp economic slump in 1921–22 put a damper on them. By that time, Childe had gone to England, where he remained, becoming an archaeologist of international renown.

There is one other clue to Evatt's volte-face from his original support for conscription. Twenty years later, in a review of Ernest Scott's book, *Australia During the War*, Evatt noted that although 'the invasion of Belgian territory by German forces soon became the great war slogan' in Britain and Australia, it was now known that the British government had more important reasons for deciding to enter the war. In this context, Evatt referred to the writings of E. D. Morel and others in 'qualifying the dogmatic judgment of war time'.[5]

Although Evatt did not amplify the reference to Morel, it presumably related to Morel's book, *Truth and the War*, published by the National Labour Press in London in 1916. In this work Morel, a socialist and anti-imperialist, raised questions of international trade rivalries, militarism and the secret diplomacy of great powers in the decade before the outbreak of the war. In a documented fashion he argued that Germany was not wholly responsible for the war and that the war should be concluded by a just and lasting peace settlement in which peoples, not simply governments, must be given an adequate say.

These democratic ideas would have appealed to Evatt. Further, in his book review, he criticised Scott for virtually ignoring the great public services of such men as Tudor and Scullin, Mannix and

Blackburn, Storey and Boote, 'and other Labor leaders like Messrs. Lyons, Curtin, and Gardiner...The fact that the military service overseas of Australians continued upon a voluntary basis was mainly due to the efforts of these men, and it may be that, in a brave new world, history will not condemn but greatly praise'.

Whether Evatt had read Morel's book at the time of publication is not known. The work was assailed by conservative critics in Britain and it may be assumed that Australian authorities did their best to prevent importation of it. Yet Childe would undoubtedly have read and endorsed the book while he was in England in 1916–17. A link is evident in the fact that Morel strongly praised the work of a voluntary body, the Union of Democratic Control, and Childe on returning to Sydney in 1917 joined the Australian Union of Democratic Control as a means of opposing attacks on civil liberties. Thus it seems reasonable to suppose that Childe brought a copy of *Truth and the War* back to Australia with him, lending it to friends such as Evatt who were likely to be impressed by a reasoned critique of war propaganda and national hatreds.

After 1918, Evatt did not resile from his new-found conviction that the wartime attempt to introduce conscription for service overseas was wrong. Nor did he again write in the vein of Liberalism in Australia, although some reflection of that work may be seen in his biography of W. A. Holman. In the Sydney suburb of Mosman, where he then lived, Evatt joined the Australian Labor Party (ALP) in May 1920, three months after the local branch was established. Nevertheless, his radicalism was quickly modified in a practical direction about this time. The idea of collaborating with Childe in writing a book was not pursued. Instead, Evatt's continuing interest in politics found expression in two articles published in 1920–21.

The first concerned the social problem of a shortage of housing available for rent and the consequent rack-renting by unscrupulous landlords. The situation was exacerbated during the Great War. In 1915 a Labor government in New South Wales passed an Act providing for the establishment of Fair Rents Courts to determine rents on the application of tenants or landlords. In referring to the origins of the Act, Evatt noted that the government responsible for it was

still 'socialistic' in the way suggested by Metin in his phrase 'Socialisme sans doctrines'. Their theoretical objective, providing for the socialisation of all the means of production, distribution, and exchange, was still kept in the background, and prominence was given to the immediate fighting platform consisting of definite practical schemes, quorum magna pars the Fair Rents Act.[6]

Pointing out that in fact only one Fair Rents Court was established—in Sydney—Evatt examined the workings of that court in such detail as to suggest that he may have practised in it himself. He concluded that the Act had worked reasonably well in stabilising rents. Acknowledging that there was still a housing shortage in Sydney, he agreed that rent-control had probably deterred some investors from putting funds into housing, but he argued that this was no more than a subsidiary effect as there was also an acute housing shortage in places such as Melbourne, where there were no Fair Rents Courts operating.

This article was the product of extensive research and it was clearly written by a lawyer concerned with the functioning of the courts. The article was also of immediate political interest. In March 1920 a new Labor government, headed by John Storey, took office in New South Wales (after a period of Nationalist government), and Storey's Attorney-General, E. A. McTiernan, introduced to the Legislative Assembly an amending Bill aimed mainly at extending rent control to tenants of small shops and offices. This intention was frustrated by the Legislative Council, with the result that the question of fair rents was still an issue in New South Wales elections in 1925 and later.

The second article bearing Evatt's name was not attributed to him alone. It was written jointly with another barrister, T. R. Bavin, who was an older man, already well established in political life on the non-Labor side. Later, between 1922 and 1925, Bavin was Attorney-General in a Nationalist government; and later still he was Premier of New South Wales. Thus a literary association between him and Evatt looked rather odd, especially in the light of Evatt's earlier article: in parliamentary debate on McTiernan's Bill to amend the Fair Rents Act, Bavin spoke against it on the ground that it was likely to limit capital investment in housing. Yet the article written by Bavin and Evatt was on the subject of statutory price-fixing which, in terms of government intervention, could be regarded as being on a par with rent-fixing.

The co-authors got around this problem by adhering severely to a factual account of the development of price-fixing arrangements in the various Australian States and the Commonwealth during the Great War. These measures were designed to restrain sharp price rises, particularly for food, and to curb the activities of speculators. Public resentment of 'profiteers' led to legislative action by conservative as well as Labor governments. For example, a Nationalist government in New South Wales established a Necessary Commodities Commission in 1919, following earlier Labor moves to control prices. Bavin himself was associated politically with rural industries and was critical of the operations of middlemen in marketing. In 1920, he sat in the

New South Wales parliament as a Progressive, rather than Nationalist, leader—although the two groups were allied against Labor. In these terms, the collaboration between Bavin and Evatt in writing on the subject was not as surprising as it might appear.

Examination of the style of writing suggests that Evatt took the initiative and contributed most to the article. The conclusion concerning wartime price-fixing appears even-handed, yet Evatt's skill may be discerned in it:

On the whole, the consuming public had their interest safeguarded, and, what was perhaps even more important, they thought that they were being protected against undue profit-making. Further, the small trader was made secure against the danger of markets being cornered...the feeling of security was vitally important to Australia, and it took some years from the commencement of the war for the word 'profiteering' to acquire general acceptance and the privilege of being printed in newspapers and statute-books without inverted commas.[7]

Like the earlier publication on fair rents, this article, despite its uncontentious form of presentation, was of contemporary political significance. Written in 1920, though not published till the following year, it provided historical background for legislation. The Labor Party in New South Wales in 1920 campaigned on the need to improve the effectiveness of price regulation, and when the Storey government took office it passed a Profiteering Prevention Act, providing for the establishment of a court with power to fix maximum prices and rates of profit. Bavin opposed the Bill in the Legislative Assembly, arguing that it failed to define the concept of 'excessive profit'. Nevertheless, the legislation came into force—after the Legislative Council had limited its duration to a period of two years. In practice, the Profiteering Prevention Court had considerable difficulty in determining what was 'unreasonable profit' in particular cases, so that the Act proved a disappointment to its sponsors. Moreover, the economic depression of 1921–22 was accompanied by a general reduction in the price level, so that government regulation in this area ceased to be a contentious issue even before the scheduled demise of the court.

❖

An underlying factor in cordial relations between Bavin and Evatt was the professional camaraderie of members of the Bar. McTiernan, too, was on quite good personal terms with Bavin in the 1920s. However, this point should not be exaggerated. Law was a very conservative profession, concerned mainly with business matters and the protection of property. The small number of lawyers who were sympathetic towards the labour movement could expect to be regarded by their colleagues with some suspicion, unless they had proved themselves exceptionally able in professional matters. Evatt was in the latter category, yet Sir Richard Kirby recalls an incident during his own time as a law student in the 1920s, when Evatt and Bavin contested an election for the position of patron of the University Law Society. The group of students canvassing votes for Bavin did not bother to ask Kirby about his intentions. It was enough for them to know that he was a product of The King's School, Parramatta, a bastion of conservatism. Sure enough, Kirby voted for Bavin, who won the election comfortably.[8]

The field of industrial law was not a promising one for ambitious young lawyers. Workers' compensation litigation was in its infancy, particularly until a major legislative change in New South Wales in 1926. The amount of arbitration court work was increasing, but much of the advocacy here was handled by union officers rather than lawyers. Within the labour movement there was considerable hostility towards lawyers, concerning both their fees and their time-consuming practices. Such legal advice as trade unions required was dealt with by a handful of solicitors and barristers. There was little scope for professional specialisation and it is probable that those lawyers who were attracted to union work were motivated by sympathy for workers.

While trade union funds for the payment of lawyers were limited, there was another possible source of fees: briefs from government. In his early years at the Bar, Evatt received two briefs from the New South Wales government. It was a Labor government, but there is no suggestion of political connection in the allocation of these briefs. Indeed, there was no contact between Evatt and Attorney-General McTiernan before 1925. The first brief related to what became known as the *Engineers* case of 1920. This arose out of an application by the Amalgamated Society of Engineers (ASE) to the Commonwealth Arbitration Court for an award of better wages and conditions for ASE members. These members were located throughout Australia and there was certainly an interstate dispute between them and employers. However, the ASE application for a Commonwealth award included engineers in State-owned sawmilling establishments in Western Australia; and the High Court, in earlier cases, had ruled that employees of State enterprises (notably the railways) were not within the scope of federal arbitration power. Now, in 1920, the question of jurisdiction was re-opened when Judge Higgins referred the ASE application to the High Court for consideration of this point. The union was ably represented by a young Melbourne barrister, R. G. Menzies.[9]

The reference to the High Court caused several States to brief counsel to defend what were deemed to be State interests. Among those at the Bar table were Flannery, KC, and Evatt, appearing for New South Wales. They were unsuccessful. The court decided to overrule its earlier decisions, thus bringing workers in State instrumentalities within the jurisdiction of the Commonwealth Arbitration Court. It was a landmark in the process of extending Commonwealth powers, although it seems that the High Court (somewhat changed in composition from its original membership) needed no great persuasion to reach its decision in 1920.

Evatt, as junior counsel, played little part in the formal proceedings, although no doubt the experience of an important constitutional case was valuable to him. This was Evatt's first encounter with Menzies and there were paradoxical elements in the situation: Menzies represented a trade union and argued the case for central power; Evatt represented a government which stood for State rights.

Evatt's second government brief at this time was much more important in determining his career path. A Royal Commission, under Justice Edmunds, was appointed to enquire into the administration of the railway and tramway services of New South Wales. The Commission was assisted by Watt and Evatt, counsel for the government; and two other lawyers represented the Railway Commissioners. The background was a very serious industrial dispute some years earlier, in 1917. Beginning as a protest by engineering workers against working conditions in railway and tramway workshops in Sydney, the strike soon involved employees in a number of other industries. In effect, there was a general strike. The Nationalist government of the State claimed that the strike was aimed at disrupting the war effort, and a great deal of animosity was generated. The government was determined to win, bringing strikebreakers in to keep some railway services running; and after about six weeks the unions conceded defeat. The railwaymen went back to work on the basis of oral assurances that they would not be penalised for taking part in the strike, but the settlement also stated that the Railway Commissioners were to have discretion in filling all vacancies.

In fact, there was victimisation. Many railwaymen were not reinstated in their jobs, while others were demoted with reduced pay and loss of accumulated pension entitlements. At the same time, strikebreakers were retained in their jobs if they wished to stay and were given preferential treatment by the Railway Commissioners. Naturally, this situation created much bitterness in the labour movement in the following years, especially as a number of trade unions with members employed on the railways were deregistered by the New South Wales Industrial Arbitration Court, their places being taken by tame company unions which appealed mainly to those workers variously described as 'loyalist' or 'scab'. Incidentally, one lawyer who played a part in securing recognition of the bogus unions by the Industrial Arbitration Court was T. R. Bavin.

In 1920, there were still about 2000 railwaymen who had applied unsuccessfully for re-employment, and the new Storey government appointed the Edmunds Royal Commission to enquire into the situation. A number of unions were represented at the Commission's hearings, and they elected to present their cases through the counsel appearing for the government. Thus Watt and Evatt were kept busy. It may be remarked that one of the union witnesses was J. B. Chifley, a locomotive engine-driver who had been sacked at the end of the strike and was then, on appeal, re-employed at the lower grade of fireman. The Edmunds Commission provided the first occasion for a meeting of the future Prime Minister and his deputy leader.

The Commission began its hearings in October 1920 and continued intermittently for a year. While Watt took the lead for the government counsel, Evatt established his own particular area of interest in relation to the way in which appeals within the railway management system had been dealt with after the strike. As noted in the Report of the Commission:

A complaint was made by Mr Evatt and the Union Secretaries that although the awards governing some of the employees...laid down a certain method of investigating charges, such method was not followed by the special appeal boards.

In short, Evatt was concerned about denial of natural justice, notably through failure to supply an accused person with information as to the nature or particulars of the charge. Evidence from witnesses established this point to the satisfaction of Judge Edmunds, who decided that 'in the cases indicated in the schedule to this report the employees did not get a fair and reasonable enquiry, and that the refusal to regard them as eligible for re-employment was unjust'.[10]

For the rest, Edmunds' recommendations were very moderate. He considered that the former railway employees should be deemed ineligible for re-employment only if they came into one of the following categories: having taken a prominent part in the 1917 strike; committed sabotage or intimidation or used offensive language or behaviour; avowedly adopted militant unionism as a rule of conduct in railway service. On this basis, Edmunds recommended that the Railway Commissioners should revise all cases of men who had been deemed ineligible for re-employment and should review cases involving seniority or superannuation. However, it was too late for such measured words. Although the State Cabinet in June 1921 decided that the Attorney-General should contact Watt with a view to having the taking of evidence wound up within a fortnight, the Edmunds Commission report was not presented to the government until February 1922. This was only a month or so before a State election which Labor lost; and the new government took no action on the Edmunds report.[11]

Bert Evatt's passionate concern for civil liberties, for which he was later renowned, first came to the fore in the Edmunds enquiry. The affair was not a matter of a few days in court—the Commission sat for a total of 148 days—and according to Evatt's wife, Mary Alice, the transcript of evidence as presented was read every night in their home. Evatt's intensity of feeling about the victimisation of railwaymen came out in the State election campaign of 1922 when he spoke at meetings, especially in the constituency of Wollondilly, held by the Nationalist leader Sir George Fuller—who had been acting-Premier at the time of the strikes of 1917. A further indication of Evatt's involvement may be discerned with respect to V. G. Childe's book, *How Labour Governs*, which was published in London in 1923. In the preface, Childe wrote that he was deliberately limiting the scope of his study to the years up to 1920. As he had been private secretary to Premier John Storey for a period after that, before going to London, he could hardly write about the later period without breaching confidence. Nevertheless, Childe did incorporate in the book a detailed summary of the findings of the Edmunds Report of 1922. It may be assumed that Evatt sent a copy of the report posthaste to his friend.

One point was evident to Evatt from the fate of the Edmunds enquiry: the remedying of wrongs and injustice in such matters was not necessarily amenable to court proceedings. Rather, it depended upon governmental action and determination. Evatt was already a member of the Labor Party but this did not necessarily mean full commitment. In the light of Evatt's repeated public references to the Edmunds Commission in the next few years, it seems that his experience with the Commission was crucial in forming his resolve to throw in his lot with the labour movement. It was not only a matter of instinctive support for the underdog. For the first time in his life, Evatt had come into constant contact with unassuming yet principled workers like Ben Chifley. They were fundamentally decent people, who, in the case of skilled workers, were proud of their craftsmanship. Locomotive engine-drivers were regarded as being among the aristocrats of labour—not the sort of people to be slighted. Evatt liked and respected such people. He was also a practical idealist, confident of contributing to change for the better. In 1925, he was reported as saying:

every member in the ranks of Labor is part of a living movement marching towards an ideal and yet having a practical policy to submit to the people. The contest, therefore, is really one between the power of money on the one side, and practical and determined idealists on the other...The triumph of idealism is at hand.[12]

True, this was a politician's speech, made in the course of an election campaign which resulted in Evatt's election to the New South Wales Parliament. Evatt knew, if only from reading Childe's book, that there were corrupt practices in the labour movement and that in particular the Australian Workers' Union (AWU) was subject to a 'Tammany system of cliquism and favouritism'. Nevertheless, Evatt's idealism was genuine. He was never on the 'moneyed' side, although he was fortunate in being free from personal financial problems. The legal fees earned from the Edmunds Commission brief provided a comfortable cushion for a barrister recently launched into practice, and in the following years Evatt's reputation grew, both among lawyers and in the eyes of the general public.[13]

Andy Watt and Bert Evatt, working together as senior and junior counsel, were a highly successful team, particularly in defending a Sydney newspaper, *Smith's Weekly*, against writs for libel. *Smith's Weekly* in the 1920s was a lively, iconoclastic and aggressive paper which attracted many such writs from aggrieved persons. The paper's owner, Sir Joynton Smith, found that Watt and Evatt formed a winning combination—their standard method of defence was to attack—and he engaged them time after time. These cases were often sensational, attracting the press, and Evatt learned a lasting lesson about the value of publicity and good contacts with journalists.[14]

These particular court appearances were probably regarded by Evatt as being both good fun and a source of substantial fees. There were other kinds of case, as in July 1924 when Evatt appeared as junior counsel to Windeyer in defending a number of trade union officials, part of a maritime transport workers' group, who were charged with conspiring to pervert the course of justice. The matter related to providing a crew for a ship regarded as unseaworthy by workers. The men were acquitted in court, and this was increasingly the type of case in which Evatt was marrying his legal skills with his labour sympathies.

Evatt was also busy as a writer and academic in these early years. He regularly wrote law reports for the Melbourne *Argus*. In March 1922, The University of Sydney appointed him to a lectureship in legal interpretation, a position which he held for four years. Richard Kirby remembers him as an earnest lecturer who had an aura of intellectual superiority about him. He did not mix easily with other people and he had no fund of small talk. Law students respected his legal standing, but he was sometimes the butt of practical jokes—he was regarded as being beyond the pale socially, since he was a supporter of both Labor and rugby league football.[15]

NOTES

1. D.J. Murphy, *T.J. Ryan: A Political Biography*, University of Queensland Press (UQP), St. Lucia, 1975, pp. 339, 443–4. Windeyer had some experience of cases with a political background. In 1918 he appeared before the Street Royal Commission on behalf of twelve IWW men who had earlier been convicted on serious conspiracy charges. There was reason to believe that the prosecution evidence was tainted.
2. H.V. Evatt, *Australian Labour Leader: The Story of W.A. Holman and the Labour Movement*, p. 158.
3. Quoted from an undated press cutting in possession of Mrs R. Carrodus. Brookfield was killed—in an unrelated incident—in March 1921.
4. T.H. Irving, 'New Light on *How Labour Governs*: Re-discovered Political Writings by V. Gordon Childe', *Politics*, 23 (1), May 1988, p. 73. See also Irving's paper, 'The Origins of *How Labour Governs*', Annual Conference of Australasian Political Studies Association, August 1988. We are indebted to Terry Irving for drawing our attention to Evatt's censored letters in Australian Archives, MP95/1, file 167/57–76.
5. H.V. Evatt, 'Australia on the Home Front, 1914–1918', *Australian Quarterly*, IX (1), March 1937, pp. 68, 73.
6. H.V. Evatt, 'A "Fair Rent" Experiment in New South Wales', *Journal of Comparative Legislation and International Law*, 3rd series, II, 1929, p. 12. The article was relied upon heavily, for the period covered, by the New South Wales Royal Commission on the Landlord and Tenant Act in 1961.
7. T.R. Bavin and H.V. Evatt, 'Price-fixing in Australia during the War', *Journal of Comparative Legislation and International Law*, III, 1921, p. 212. Emphasis in the original.
8. Interview with Sir Richard Kirby, Sussex Inlet, 26 April 1990. Later on, he proved to be the exception to the rule about The King's School conservatism.
9. Menzies' role is considered by John Rickard, *H.B. Higgins: the Rebel as Judge*, Allen & Unwin, Sydney, 1984, pp. 277–80.
10. Report of Edmunds Commission, New South Wales *Parliamentary Papers*, 1922, 3, p. LVIII.
11. List of matters dealt with by Cabinet, 1921–22, State Archives, Attorney-General's Department, 9/5106.1.
12. *Labor Daily*, Sydney, 13 February 1925.
13. Vere Gordon Childe, *How Labour Governs*, MUP, Melbourne, 2nd edn, 1964, p. 174.
14. Joynton Smith, in *My Life Story*, Cornstalk, Sydney, 1927, described Watt and Evatt as '"Smith's" famous fighting counsel', pp. 267–8. See also the apt comments by Kylie Tennant, *Evatt: Politics and Justice*, pp. 4l–4.
15. Interview with Kirby; Blanche d'Alpuget, *Mediator: a Biography of Sir Richard Kirby*, MUP, Melbourne, 1977, pp. 14–15.

CHAPTER 3

BALMAIN: POLITICAL BAPTISM OF FIRE

Since 1919 the greater portion of the time (of the ALP) was taken up in fighting disruption, schism and communism.
H. V. EVATT, 1927

To understand the political position of a person like Bert Evatt, in the process of becoming active in the Australian Labor Party, it is helpful to have some knowledge of the party's structure and processes. The ALP operated at several levels. At bottom there were local branches—Labor Leagues, as they were still called in the 1920s—comprising workers and middle-class people plus some farmers and small capitalists. Branches elected delegates to the annual State conference of the party, which decided matters of policy and elected a State executive to exercise general control between conferences. Trade unions, which were an integral part of the ALP, had separate representation at State conferences, so that they influenced the composition of the State executive.

Unions were also influential in another respect. Party branches conducted ballots of their members to preselect candidates for parliamentary seats; and members of unions affiliated to the ALP were entitled to take part in preselection ballots in the areas where these members lived. Arrangements for this were ill-defined and it was possible for union officials to organise a bloc vote, sometimes employing forgery and other fraudulent means. The Australian Workers Union (AWU, the largest union) was adept at this sort of trick. Furthermore, this union, with a network of organisers in country districts, played a crucial role in persuading electors to vote for the ALP. Thus the AWU was prominent, occasionally dominant, at the levels of State conference and executive. Incidentally, the executive was responsible for overseeing the process of preselection for parliamentary elections.

The net result in New South Wales in the 1920s was that there were constant disruptive struggles for control over the party. There were divisions between trade unions and Labor members of parliament, the unionists being mainly interested in industrial matters such as wages and hours of work; between one set of union leaders (notably the AWU) and others; between Labor members of parliament and the State executive of the party; and between shifting factions within the Labor caucus. A further complication was federalism: the various State Labor parties had a large degree of autonomy in relation to the federal organs of the party and this was accentuated by the relative success of Labor in New South Wales in the 1920s. The federal Labor Party remained out of office until 1929, whereas in New South Wales—the largest State—the Labor Party held office from 1920 to 1922 and from 1925 to 1927.

Internal dissension and machine politics within Labor ranks were widely publicised by the press. To some extent, the disputes were over policy matters and ideology, particularly between moderates and socialists, and it could be argued that such debate was healthy in a democratic organisation. However, much of the in-fighting was personal in nature. There were vicious incidents, and sometimes ALP members were expelled from the party, allegedly for disloyalty but actually because the faction in control at the time seized an opportunity to get rid of some of its opponents. Evatt himself, in a speech to the Rozelle East branch of the party on 1 July 1927, decried factionalism, saying: 'Since 1919 the greater portion of the time [of the party] was taken up in fighting disruption, schism and communism'.[1]

Evatt knew about corruption and ballot-rigging in the labour movement. In the early 1920s there was strong suspicion that ballots for elected positions in the AWU in Sydney were rigged in favour of a union faction led by J. Bailey. In fact, he was using ballot boxes fitted with sliding panels so that when the voting ended—but before counting began—the papers in the locked boxes could be examined and those which did not support Bailey's ticket could be replaced by others more to his liking. The same AWU boxes were used at State ALP conferences until a day of reckoning came in 1923. As a number of the boxes were being carried into the conference hall, one box was dropped on the floor and its sliding panel fell out for all to see. The conference then set up a committee to investigate the incident, although 'the AWU officials were incensed that the Labor Party was accusing them of being crooks...AWU bosses didn't do things like that—not much!'. Nevertheless, the enquiry committee reported against Bailey and his friends, and, in the words of Clyde Cameron:

it became very obvious that the person who wrote the findings was none other than this up-and-coming lawyer, named Herbert Vere Evatt. The language of the committee's findings was not the sort of language you'd expect from ex-coalminer Willis or any other members of the Committee...[Evatt] was asked to advise them on the matter.[2]

If there was so much skulduggery going on, it might well be asked how it was that people like Evatt were attracted to the Labor Party. Broadly, the answer is that for those thoughtful people interested in politics and reform who had no ties to wealth or privilege, there was little alternative. This was obvious enough to most working men and women in New South Wales. For example, a Labor government in 1920 adopted the principle of a 44-hour working week and the Industrial Commission proceeded to implement this in State awards. Then, in 1922, a Nationalist government enacted a reversion to the 48-hour principle. Three years later, a new Labor government passed a Forty-Four Hours Week Act for workers under State awards. In other matters also, Nationalist administrations repeatedly undid the measures of their predecessors, so that reform was not assured.

Contrary to some perceptions, the decade of the 1920s in Australia was not a particularly prosperous one. Economic growth was slow and there was an average of eight per cent unemployment. Employers generally approved Nationalist moves to force cuts in wages, although some small business people were unhappy about certain aspects of conservative rule. Thus in the New South Wales election campaign of 1925, the Business Tenants' Association of New South Wales urged a vote for Labor against the Fuller government:

Cabinet is composed of double-dealers and venal shufflers. Its word is not worth a pinch of salt. It dishonoured a pact made with the BTA to relieve traders from the poisonous activities of the rack-renting property owner.[3]

The attraction of the Labor Party for Evatt was partly that it stood for the have-nots, against the representatives of wealth and privilege entrenched on the other side of the political fence. Beyond that, Evatt believed in progress, and Labor had a clear programme of reform. Internecine fights and backbiting in the Labor Party often left a sour taste in the mouth, yet the party was the only major one which gave ordinary people a real opportunity to take part in political life. Besides self-seekers, the party had many members who were idealistic and visionary—men and women who thought in terms of a better and more just society, not simply immediate tangible gains. Evatt appreciated the aspirations and hopes of these people and worked with them to achieve common goals. Of course, many Nationalist supporters also held ideals, but they were based on the values of an established conservative order. There were virtually no bitter struggles in that camp over policy or leadership, because a 'natural' leadership founded upon birth, property or status assumed control. Equality did not enter into calculations.

After joining the ALP in Mosman, Evatt was successively secretary and president of that branch. He extended his range of contacts when he became honorary legal adviser to the ALP, and in that capacity he played a part in condemning ballot-rigging, as related earlier in this chapter. Then, in October 1924, he was appointed as chairman of the ALP's Fighting Platform Committee, whose task was to draft a policy statement for use in the next State election. At the same time, Evatt decided to make a bid for a parliamentary seat himself.

There was no prospect of winning a seat for Labor where Evatt lived—Mosman, on Sydney's North Shore, was a relatively well-to-do area. Instead, Evatt focused his attention upon Balmain, an inner-city constituency which was much larger than the suburb of that name. Balmain was an industrial area whose working-class population included significant numbers of waterfront workers, engineers, tramwaymen (there was a big tramway depot in the constituency) and coalminers (the Balmain coal mine, extending under the harbour, was still functioning). Furthermore, Balmain had its own popular rugby league football club—and Evatt was honorary legal adviser to the New South Wales Rugby Football League.

As a first step towards becoming a Labor parliamentarian, Evatt had to win a preselection ballot. He prepared shrewdly for this contest by writing a series of seven articles about the victimisation of workers after the 1917 railway strike. These articles, published at weekly intervals in the *Labor Daily* in September–October 1924, damned the Nationalists and railway authorities. Evatt used much detailed evidence presented to the Edmunds Royal Commission but not published along with the report of that Commission. As the *Labor Daily* concluded in an editorial:

Never has there been a more withering exposure of dishonorable conduct than that so ably and convincingly set out in terms of studied moderation...by Dr. H.V. Evatt, M.A. LL.D. Labor's duty is clear, as he says. It is to declare that Labor will reinstate every victimised man, restore every lost right, and compensate those who were so foully wronged.[4]

The articles created a deep impression in the labour movement. They were reprinted in the *Australian Railways Union Gazette* and were strongly approved by *Common Cause*, the organ of the Miners' Federation. By the end of the year, the collected articles were on sale as a separate pamphlet. Nevertheless, some traditional Labor supporters were resentful of Evatt. One S. Sloane wrote to the *Labor Daily*, describing him as someone 'who has only just blown in to the movement, who knows next to nothing about it'. Attacking strongly, Sloane noted that Evatt put

'Dr' before his name, and 'LL.D' after it...I am compelled to ask if he is the Mr. Evatt who wrote a book on 'Liberalism' some time ago. If so, the labour movement should wake up to him, judging him by his own words in print, and which are strongly anti-Labor.

W. J. Walsh, of the Glebe ALP, responded by saying that Evatt's articles dealt with a matter which had been neglected by the ALP, and that Evatt's titles and degrees had been earned through work—they were not honorary. Tom Glynn, another supporter of Evatt, felt that he deserved credit for having overcome the biases of his class.[5]

Given the fact that intellectuals were generally regarded with suspicion in the Labor Party, Evatt's publicity material at this time was rather provocative in emphasising his educational attainments and university record. His own how-to-vote card in 1925 portrayed him in a barrister's wig and jabot, which may have caused some workers to shy away from him. On the other hand, his emphasis upon the need for free education at all levels probably attracted support from many working-class families in Balmain—in 1923, the Fuller government had re-introduced fees for high school pupils in New South Wales.

Evatt cleared the preselection hurdle easily. The electoral system at the time provided for multi-member constituencies. Balmain had five representatives in the State parliament and twenty-one people were nominated for preselection by local Labor Party members. At the ballot in November 1924, Evatt was second only to J. Quirk, who was one of the three sitting Labor MLAs for the constituency. Actually, in primary votes, Evatt topped the poll in every Party branch except Rozelle, where Quirk received an exceptionally high vote. Quirk's supporters had issued a how-to-vote ticket which listed candidates in order of preference, while omitting Evatt's name from the list. Nevertheless, Evatt was strongly supported by a number of trade unions, notably the Australian Railways Union, which included tramwaymen in its membership. Much more dubiously, there is an unsubstantiated story that the Orange Lodge in Balmain favoured

Evatt and that similarly the local Amalgamated Engineers' and Boilermakers' Unions were strongly Masonic. Religious sectarianism had declined since the State election of 1922, and Evatt himself was in no way a bigot, but he was regarded as a Protestant.

Mary Alice Evatt was ecstatic about the preselection result. She kept a personal diary or Commonplace Book, on the first page of which she wrote:

*This may be a Commonplace Book but pasted on the Opposite Page is the Man who has seen to it that the life of Mary Alice is **not** a Commonplace Life'.*[6]

On 4 November 1924, Mary Alice recorded that her husband had been preselected as a candidate for Balmain, adding:

I am delighted thereat and also full of yearning to plan an election campaign for March...I must think out plans for the house so that everything will run smoothly and I shall be able to take part freely in the political fight.

Mas then noted a question, evidently addressed to Bert: 'Do you definitely intend to go in for Federal politics later on?' 'Yes.'

The tone may have been rather breathless, but there was no mistaking the resolve. Mas was already actively involved in politics, and not just as an adjunct to her husband. She had ideas of her own and her papers show that she was engrossed in the works of the English socialist, William Morris. Partly, no doubt, this was because Morris's artistic interests appealed to her own endeavours in painting, but she was also attracted to Morris's romantic utopianism and his activities in the Socialist League in London in the 1880s. Mary Alice was particularly interested in questions of education and in 1924 she read a paper on the subject at a conference of the Women's Organising Committee of the ALP in Sydney. She advocated raising the age for compulsory education to sixteen, stressing that this and other educational reforms should apply to girls as well as boys. Indeed, she urged that 'a woman should be Minister for Education'. She spoke out sharply, as indicated by a draft of the speech in her papers:

When I think of our schools in this State the fact that strikes me most forcibly is that our children are being thrown into the industrial furnace at an age when they are but a sacrifice to the capitalistic system.[7]

A State election was scheduled for May 1925, and in the campaign leading up to it Mas proved herself an efficient and energetic organiser. She spoke at a special meeting for women electors in Balmain, arranged publicity for her husband in the local press, and, with a group of women, canvassed from door to door in the constituency. She enjoyed the experience, saying:

I remember canvassing the whole of Glebe...They were such a nice, jolly lot of people in Balmain, and all interested in sport. I think that was one reason my husband liked so many of them. Strangely enough a lot of them came from Maitland...Clive [Evatt] helped us in this election...I still remember coming down to Glebe one night very tired with my husband, and we heard a well-known voice in the distance saying 'Vote Number One for Dr Evatt'. Remember 'Better the devil you know than the devil you don't know'. We thought that was a very funny recommendation for voting. But Clive was a good campaigner of a totally different type to his brother...sometimes in those times people would perhaps get a little tough and they used to throw tomatoes or potatoes or eggs at him, and Clive would just pocket them, you see he was a good fielder from cricket...He'd say, 'Ha, the Sunday dinner, good. Now come on, a few more'. And then of course they'd start to roar with laughter and he'd have them all listening to him. And he was a very good speaker. I think he quite enjoyed campaigning; I did, too, because I'd never got to know so many people or so many different points of view...it was my first experience of coalminers, who...would always stick up for Labour, they'd always support each other, they would never give in. They were a wonderful lot of people.[8]

Evatt himself spoke at more than 150 meetings during the campaign, one such meeting being in company with E. G. Theodore, ex-Premier of Queensland. On that occasion, Evatt attacked Sir George Fuller's election policy speech. As Evatt pointed out:

Sir George endeavoured to discredit Labour candidates by identifying them with the revolutionary proposals of Russian Communism. He stated that Labour's candidates were 'Reds', 'Bolsheviks', and 'Communists', and that we were controlled from abroad. That is absolutely untrue. (Cheers). The Labour movement...has always stood, and will while I have anything to do with it, for the policy of Australia first. (Loud applause). No, it is not the Labour movement which is controlled from abroad.

Evatt went on to turn Fuller's criticism around by saying that in fact the Nationalist Party was beholden to big pastoral, shipping and financial interests controlled by London capital. Thus it was the Nationalist Party which was 'subject to some domination and control from other countries'.[9]

At another meeting, Evatt elaborated on the differences between Labor and Communism, as he saw them:

Communism and the Communist Party aim at a dictatorship of a class, such dictatorship to be reached by revolutionary means. The Labor movement, on the other hand, put forward definite and practical proposals such as restoration of the shorter working week...In short, whereas Russian Communism was revolutionary and unscientific, Labor was evolutionary and scientific. Labor aimed at adding some nobility, some beauty and some splendour to life, and this ideal could be achieved by legal and constitutional action.[10]

Evatt was fortunate in having a number of experienced Labor supporters working for him in Balmain. One of them, for example, was J. S. Rosevear, who became a federal Labor parliamentarian in the 1930s and 1940s (and was Speaker of the House of Representatives in the latter decade). These people were very familiar with the constituency, which had a strong sense of local identity. Equally versed in election procedures was another supporter of Evatt, E. C. Riley, who was a federal Labor parliamentarian in New South Wales from 1922 to 1934. Quite different in background was a group of university people. It so happened that in April 1925 an Oxford University debating team visited Sydney. Among the team's members was Malcolm MacDonald, son of a former British Labour Prime Minister, and some Labour supporters at University of Sydney arranged a reception for MacDonald junior. Evatt was in the chair for the occasion, which resulted in the formation of The University of Sydney Labour Society, 'to further the objects and ideas of the Australian Labour movement'. Evatt was elected President of the Society, and a leaflet was issued, supporting him in the Balmain election.[11]

Evatt made enemies as well as friends, and his political future was in some jeopardy through renewed criticism directed at his book, *Liberalism in Australia*. The matter was raised sharply at a meeting of the New South Wales Labor Council by a delegate, T. J. O'Sullivan, who drew attention to the fact that in the book Evatt had objected to both the principle of preference to trade unionists in employment and the ALP system of requiring party candidates to sign a pledge of support for party discipline: Labor representatives were required to vote along lines determined by the party platform and caucus. Beyond this, O'Sullivan took particular exception to a passage in the book which opposed State aid to church schools. Evatt had written: 'The only solution to the question of State aid is to refuse to recognise any denomination, for that is the only method of avoiding reactionary movements in the direction of church establishment'.[12]

On the last of these points, Evatt was on relatively safe ground, as ALP policy did not include State aid to denominational schools. Nevertheless, O'Sullivan questioned whether Evatt should have been preselected as a Labor candidate for Balmain. While this matter was being considered at several meetings of the Labor Council, the *Labor Daily* (official organ of the ALP) sprang to Evatt's defence against the 'spiteful attack' on him by the anti-Labor *Daily Guardian*. In the view of the *Labor Daily*, Evatt's original essay was 'Labor in spirit, tone and feeling, and...the subject of "Liberalism"...was selected by the University, and not by Dr Evatt'. Evatt himself, in a letter to the *Australian Worker*, described the criticism, based upon views expressed by him many years earlier, as 'frivolous'. He went on to say that

the essay as a whole is radical in outlook, and treats Labor as the radical party in Australian politics. I was always regarded at the University as Labor in sympathy...I have never in my life been a member of any political party except Labor.[13]

The outcome was that O'Sullivan withdrew his motion to set up a Labor Council committee to investigate Evatt's political past. O'Sullivan probably calculated that he would lose if he pushed the motion to a vote. A further point in connection with the attack upon Evatt is that O'Sullivan made a sarcastic reference to Evatt, 'fresh from his mansion in Mosman', seeking to win the support of the hard-working men and women of Balmain; but Bert and Mary Alice Evatt had already forestalled this type of sniping by moving their home to a house in Leichhardt, within the Balmain constituency. They were on the electoral roll in time to vote for Bert on 30 May 1925.

There was evidently some support for Evatt in the Labor Council (which had recommended that reinstatement of the railwaymen of 1917 should be part of ALP industrial policy); and there was also a strong feeling that the Council's name should not be used publicly in connection with the controversy until the Council had decided its own position. Whatever Evatt may have written years ago, he could not be faulted on his attitude towards current Labor policy, and he had already signed the party pledge. The episode attracted an unusual degree of press attention because Evatt was not cast in the traditional mould of Labor candidates.

Of course, other candidates also had their quota of campaign upsets. One which was not so much a problem as an occasion for mirth concerned J. Quirk, who was a postman in Rozelle for many years before being elected to represent Balmain in the New South Wales Parliament. His publicity leaflet for the election of 1925 referred to him as having received his education in the hard school of experience and as having 'foundered' the Letter Carriers' Association. Apparently his supporters took their candidate's name to heart when it came to spelling.

Labor won that State election, one notable example being the taking of four seats in Balmain instead of three as previously. The newcomer was H. V. Evatt, who topped the poll easily with 14 733 primary votes, which was more than the aggregate received by the five Nationalist candidates. The other three Labor candidates elected for Balmain received 13 434 primary votes between them, while two Communists trailed the field of fourteen candidates with a total of 239 votes. It was a great victory for Evatt and it boosted his ego. As noted by Bede Nairn, the principal historian of Labor in this period, Evatt still had 'a lot to learn about politics and Lang'. This was all too obvious when the new Labor parliamentary caucus met to elect members of Cabinet. There was a large field of candidates for ministerial positions from the ranks of the forty-three members of caucus, and Evatt was one of those nominated. It was a bad mistake: any old hand could have told him that caucus did not take kindly to a newcomer, however brilliant his reputation, who attempted to thrust his way to the front before proving himself in Parliament.[14]

Evatt was soundly defeated in the ballot. He received only eight votes, well below the number cast for the lowest successful candidate. In the process, he antagonised Edward McTiernan, who had been Attorney-General in the Labor government of 1920–22 and was subsequently Labor spokesman on matters of law. Having performed well in those positions, McTiernan could reasonably expect to be appointed Attorney-General again when Labor won the 1925 election. Evatt did not directly oppose him—the practice was for caucus to elect the requisite number of Cabinet positions, specific portfolios being then allocated by Premier Lang—but there were so few lawyers in caucus as to make it evident that Evatt was eyeing the attorney-generalship for himself. Undoubtedly he felt capable of doing the job. In the event, McTiernan secured thirty-four votes in the caucus ballot and was appointed Attorney-General by Lang. Almost certainly, Lang would have chosen McTiernan for the position even if Evatt too had been successful in the ballot. This was by no means the last time that Evatt needlessly offended people by indifference to their feelings.

With hindsight, it may be said that it was probably to Evatt's benefit that he did not become a minister in the Lang government. The exercise of power as a minister would have made him more bumptious; and he would have been bound by the principle of Cabinet solidarity. He would have restricted his attention largely to one area instead of ranging widely and speaking freely on many matters. In any event, he did not appear to be worried by his defeat in caucus as he prepared for the next session of Parliament, which opened in August. Before this, he formally severed his connection with the Mosman ALP by resigning from presidency of the branch there.

NOTES

1 Molesworth Papers, Mitchell Library, MSS.71, Box 6.
2 Interview with Clyde Cameron, Adelaide, 3 May 1988. Cameron derived this story from talks between himself and both Evatt and Bailey much later. He described Bailey as being 'as straight as a gun barrel; that is, physically'.
3 NSW State Archives, Attorney-General's Department, Special Bundle, Fair Rents Act, 5/7777.2.
4 *Labor Daily*, 21 October 1924.
5 Ibid., 30 September 1924, 1 and 4 October 1924.
6 File on Evatt, Mary Alice, Miscellaneous, Evatt Collection, Flinders University.
7 *Daily Telegraph*, 26 August 1924. The typed draft of the speech was edited by Bert Evatt, not for content but for conciseness of expression.
8 Transcript of interview with Mary Alice Evatt, April–May 1973, National Library of Australia, Canberra.
9 *Evening News*, 12 May 1925; *Labor Daily*, 15 May 1925.
10 *Labor Daily*, 23 May 1925.
11 Ibid., 22 April 1925.
12 *Daily Guardian* 17 and 18 April 1925. The passage on State aid appeared in *Liberalism in Australia*, p. 44. It may not be coincidental that R.J. Stuart-Robertson, a preselected Labor candidate in Balmain, who showed some resentment towards Evatt, was a Catholic. So was J. Quirk, another candidate.
13 *Labor Daily*, 18 April 1925; *Australian Worker*, 22 April 1925. Evatt, led by Watt, represented the *Labor Daily* in a court case at this time—which helps to explain that paper's support for, and its rival's antipathy towards, Evatt.
14 Bede Nairn, *The 'Big Fella': Jack Lang and the Australian Labor Party, 1891-1949*, MUP, Melbourne, 1986, p. 94.

CHAPTER 4

THE WALSH–JOHNSON DEPORTATION CASES

The complex and subtle reasoning of these two cases has ever since been of great importance in cases dealing with the Commonwealth's power to deal with alleged sedition by executive discretion.
GEOFFREY SAWER

In 1925, besides making his debut in Parliament, Evatt was engaged in a very important legal action concerning Commonwealth powers of deportation. This followed a case with some similar features in 1923 when the Commonwealth government moved to deport two Irishmen who had come to Australia—on British passports—to raise support for the Irish republican cause. The government set up a board to go into the matter but Watt and Evatt, representing the Irish envoys, challenged the jurisdiction of the board. The two barristers went to the High Court to argue that the particular section of the Immigration Act used in the case of the Irish envoys was invalid, that the envoys were not 'immigrants' in the sense of being people who came to settle in Australia, and that the board should be stopped from proceeding further. The court, while agreeing that the board had no power to do more than advise the Minister, upheld the Commonwealth's power to deport temporary visitors as well as those who came intending to stay. Thus the Irish envoys were actually deported by executive action. Watt and Evatt lost the case—but they became well acquainted with the law on immigration.

In 1925, the law was again tested, this time in relation to Australian trade unionists. The context was a series of industrial disputes in the maritime industry, where militant seamen sought to establish a form of job control despite the deregistration of their union by the federal Arbitration Court. The Bruce–Page government was infuriated. Consequently, in July 1925, the Immigration Act was amended in certain respects, notably by providing for the deportation of any person who was not born in Australia and had been convicted 'at any time' of a federal offence relating to trade or arbitration, if the relevant Minister was satisfied that the continued presence of that person in Australia would be 'injurious to the peace, order or good government' of the Commonwealth.

This amendment of the Immigration Act was clearly directed against certain leaders of the Seamen's Union, but it had much wider implications. A large proportion of all Australians were immigrants, and active trade unionists among them might easily be convicted of an offence in the course of a strike. Whatever might be said by arbitration tribunals, the trade union movement generally upheld the right of workers to strike. Accordingly, there were strong protests as the amending Bill passed through Parliament. The New South Wales Labor Council saw it as 'a dastardly attempt on the part of the Nationalist Government, acting in the interests of the Shipping Combine, to break down the organisation of the Seamen's Union'.[1]

Matters came to a head in August, when members of the British Seamen's Union went on strike, tying up ships in Australian ports. The Federated Seamen's Union of Australasia, whose President, Tom Walsh, was a Communist, gave financial support and encouragement to British sailors in the name of international solidarity. This was the last straw as far as the Commonwealth government was concerned: it reacted by initiating deportation proceedings against Walsh and another leader of the Seamen's Union, J. Johnson, who was assistant secretary of the Sydney branch. There was a furious response from the labour movement throughout Australia. In New South Wales, the Labor Council described the issue as 'one of the most important matters coming before the working class movement in the country since the days of conscription'; and the new Lang government refused to provide the Commonwealth with police assistance in connection with the matter. In other States also, there were expressions of support for Walsh and Johnson, including the collection of funds to pay for their legal representation.[2]

When the two seamen's leaders answered summonses to appear before a special deportation board in Sydney to show cause why they should not be deported, 'the old firm' of Watt and Evatt, instructed by R. Meagher & Co., appeared on their behalf. As in the earlier case of the Irish envoys, Watt challenged the jurisdiction of the board, on the ground that it was not a properly constituted court, but the board overruled his objections and, over a period of about two months, took evidence from witnesses. There was no dispute about two facts. First, that Walsh had been convicted on several occasions since 1919 for offences connected with industrial disputes. Second, Walsh had arrived in New South Wales as an Irish immigrant in 1893, and Johnson had arrived from Holland in 1910 and had become naturalised in 1913. The Commonwealth government, through its legal representative, E. Lamb, KC, was mainly concerned to produce evidence that the Federated Seamen's Union and its leaders had seriously disrupted Australian transport and interstate trade. Watt and Evatt responded so vigorously that it became a matter of common gossip as to 'whether the board was trying the affected persons or the affected persons were trying the board'[3]

At the conclusion of the hearing, the deportation board, in line with the recent amendment to the Immigration Act, recommended that Walsh and Johnson should be deported. Proceedings were then removed to the High Court, a forum for hard law and logic. Here Evatt took up most of the running on behalf of the two seamen. Presumably in recognition of Evatt's profound knowledge of constitutional law, Watt left it to his junior to develop a complex line of reasoning. Evatt examined the various constitutional powers, including that relating to trade and commerce, which were relied upon by the Commonwealth government, and argued that they were inapplicable to the Walsh–Johnson cases. Specifically, although the constitutional power with respect to immigration could be used to justify legislation concerning deportation, it was not relevant to a person who had ceased to be an immigrant by making his permanent home in Australia, as Walsh and Johnson had done. A majority of the High Court justices adopted this reasoning. As Chief Justice Knox put it in his judgment:

a person who has originally entered Australia as an immigrant may, in course of time, and by force of circumstances, cease to be an immigrant, and become a member of the Australian community. He may, so to speak, grow out of the conditions of being an immigrant and thus become exempt from the operation of the immigrant power.[4]

The court held that Walsh and Johnson were no longer immigrants and were therefore not within the scope of the Immigration Act. Further, all members of the court held that in any case a person who had come to Australia before the establishment of the Commonwealth in 1901 (as Walsh had) could not be treated by the Commonwealth as an immigrant. Walsh and Johnson were both freed immediately and were awarded legal costs against the government. As to the significance of this case, considered in conjunction with that of the Irish envoys, Geoffrey Sawer notes that 'the complex and subtle reasoning' employed 'has ever since been of great importance in cases dealing with the Commonwealth's power to deal with alleged sedition by executive discretion'. It may be added that while the reasoning was primarily Evatt's, tribute is due to Andy Watt for his extraordinary generosity in giving way to Evatt, enabling him to argue the constitutional aspects in full in the High Court. In this case, Evatt made his mark as a great lawyer.[5]

Evatt also received great acclaim in the labour movement. The case was extensively reported in the press throughout Australia and it gave Evatt an element of national stature for the first time. He also took part in the federal election campaign in November 1925, notably on behalf of J. B. Chifley, a candidate for a seat in New South Wales which included Bathurst.

Chifley, like the ALP as a whole, was defeated in that election. The Bruce–Page government gave strong emphasis to issues of law and order, such as the seamen's militancy and the 'Red' menace. When the election result became known—before the High Court proceedings in the Walsh–Johnson case opened—an editorial in the *Australian Worker* was very despondent:

Unless the deportation can be prevented by legal action, it will take place, for the simple reason...that the people, by their freely given votes, have exhibited an utter indifference to principles for which men of the same race staked their property and gave their lives long ago.[6]

This gloomy mood throws into relief the scale of Evatt's victory in the High Court. On 16 December 1925, the same newspaper happily greeted the court's decision: 'There is great joy in the camps of Labor.' At a more practical level, the executive of the New South Wales Labor Council a year later drew up a proposal to establish a Trade Union Defence Fund. This was in recognition of the fact that the Council had been caught short at the time of the Walsh–Johnson case and had found it necessary to appeal to the miners for financial assistance.

The Bruce–Page government amended the Commonwealth Crimes Act in 1926 so as to provide for the deportation of persons not born in Australia, who were involved in certain types of industrial dispute. This power remained on the statute book but was not in fact used to deport anyone: Evatt's success in the Walsh–Johnson case still served as a warning to those whose instinctive reaction to opposition was to ban or banish resisters.

NOTES

1 NSW Labor Council Minutes, 2 July 1925, Mitchell Library, A.3844, FM4/1132.
2 Ibid., 3 September 1925.
3 *Sydney Morning Herald*, 13 October 1925.
4 Judgment quoted in *Sydney Morning Herald*, 19 December 1925.
5 Geoffrey Sawer, *Australian Federal Politics and Law, 1901–1929*, MUP, Melbourne, 1956, p. 252.
6 *Australian Worker*, 25 November 1925.

CHAPTER 5

IN STATE PARLIAMENT

I look forward to the time when the principle of democracy which applies to the political side shall apply also to the industrial side, and when workers in industry shall have an opportunity of controlling it.
H. V. EVATT

When the newly elected Legislative Assembly of New South Wales got down to business in August 1925, it was soon evident that Evatt intended to play a full role in parliamentary proceedings. His Labor colleagues expected this of him. Indeed, for his maiden speech, he was given the responsibility of moving the address-in-reply proposing the adoption of the Governor's formal message foreshadowing the Lang government's programme for the parliamentary session.

Evatt's speech for the occasion was workmanlike. He referred confidently to a number of the legislative proposals, including the removal of any doubt about the eligibility of women for appointment to the Legislative Council. On this point, Evatt noted that 'certain lawyers are of opinion that the phrase "any person" does not mean what it says, that it does not include females'. His remark had a sting in it: 'perhaps the women who may be appointed as the result of this [proposed] amendment of the law will assist in closing [abolishing] the Legislative Council'.[1]

Evatt also referred particularly to two matters which had already been dealt with at an administrative level by the new government. Premier Lang had directed the Railway Commissioners to restore full rights of seniority to workers involved in the 1917 strike, while Tom

Mutch, the Minister for Education, abolished high school fees. On the latter point, Evatt said that until the previous government had reimposed such fees, it had been accepted policy in New South Wales that

children in the public schools should have an open road from the primary school right through to the University. I am proud to stand in this Parliament...and say that any opportunity I had in my life is due to the people of this State in connection with the public schools system.[2]

The *Sydney Morning Herald* on 13 August 1925 added a pen-portrait of Evatt to its report of his maiden speech. He was described as fluent:

He does not want for an easy flow of words. He has a clear, resonant voice, a boyish figure almost, he spoke with all the earnestness of youth, but, as was suggested by someone in the House, that very quality might be a weakness in Parliament, where a saving grace of humour is a great asset. Perhaps Dr Evatt will be seen to better advantage as he becomes used to the House.

Actually, it took Evatt some time to become used to the procedures of Parliament and the Labor caucus. Two weeks after his maiden speech, he was again on his feet, this time querying an announcement about the government's intention to change the parliamentary sitting hours. Traditionally, the Legislative Assembly began its business at 4 o'clock in the afternoon and continued till an undetermined hour, often late at night. This suited the convenience of members who retained business or professional interests. A barrister, for example, could move easily from a court when it closed (at 4 p.m. or earlier) to Parliament House. The Lang government, in line with traditional Labor opinion that members of Parliament should concentrate upon their parliamentary duties, changed the sitting hours so as to provide for opening at 10 a.m. and closing at 6 p.m.

In announcing this, the Attorney-General, McTiernan, said that the old system dated from a time when 'a small leisured class controlled the destinies of this House'; and it had permitted 'a few singularly privileged gentlemen in this Assembly to carry on their business or their profession'. Disarmingly, McTiernan added that he would be personally affected by the change: 'day sittings hurt me, but I believe in the greatest good for the greatest number'.

Evatt took exception to these remarks, which he regarded as 'very improper and uncalled for'. In his view, this was an attack directed primarily at barristers, 'an honourable class in the community'. As for the substance of the change in sitting hours, Evatt acknowledged that he was bound by a prior caucus decision, yet he made it clear that he considered the change to be an 'experiment' for the current session. Evatt gained no plaudits from his Labor colleagues for this outburst. They expected him to confine such views to meetings of caucus and they had no sympathy for the desire of barristers to be free to practise in courts whilst being members of Parliament. In terms of Labor principles, the caucus was right. Nevertheless, there was something to be said for exceptions from the principle, at least in Evatt's case. As it happened, proceedings in the Walsh–Johnson case, which were of great importance to the labour movement, began at precisely this time.[3]

Remarkably, Evatt was able to balance his commitment to the Walsh–Johnson case and his involvement in parliamentary proceedings in such a way that the one was very little hindrance to the other. Indeed, in the last four months of 1925, he was more deeply concerned in parliamentary business than were any of his colleagues, apart from those who had ministerial responsibilities. Besides contributing to parliamentary debate on five major Bills, Evatt was influential in the drafting of legislation. For example, he was a member of a small committee of caucus which dealt with the Forty-Four Hours Week Bill, one of the most important items in the Labor programme. Evatt then debated this Bill at length in the Legislative Assembly. Quoting with approval an earlier statement by Justice Higgins concerning the desirability of fewer hours of daily toil so as to give workers more leisure and 'opportunity for the things that make life worth living', Evatt tackled head-on the Opposition claim that a shorter working week meant less production. Rather, he argued, the result would be less absenteeism and reduced rates of sickness and accident.

Indeed, Evatt envisaged a time when it would be possible to have a standard working week even shorter than the proposal for forty-four hours in the Bill. He also believed that reductions should be effected by Parliament itself rather than by arbitration tribunals. He added an interesting response to an interjector's question as to whether he was prepared for the workers to control industry:

I look forward to the time when the principle of democracy which applies to the political side shall apply also to the industrial side, and when workers in industry shall have an opportunity of controlling it...they should have a direct interest in it. I have heard hon. members opposite call that sort of thing 'job control', but we look at the question from a different point of view altogether.[4]

Although the Opposition leader, Bavin, was strongly opposed to the Bill, he complimented Evatt upon his extensive research and 'the seriousness of the effort he has made to raise the discussion on this subject to a higher plane'. Such courtesy did not preclude sharp exchanges between the two men, as in debate on an Industrial Arbitration (Amendment) Bill in October 1925. This Bill was designed mainly to replace the New South Wales Court of Industrial Arbitration by an Industrial Commission and to introduce a tier of conciliation committees into the structure of arbitration. In addition, there was provision for preference in employment for trade unionists, and a schedule of unions to be recognised by the new Commission was attached to the Bill for this purpose. Bavin criticised this schedule for omitting the bogus unions formed at the time of the 1917 railway strike. Evatt spoke in favour of recognising only genuine unions, using evidence from the Edmunds Commission to devastating effect concerning the way in which the Railway Commissioners had abetted the setting up of bogus unions. The Legislative Council then objected to the concept of absolute preference and amended the Bill accordingly. Two years later, a new Nationalist government passed an Industrial Arbitration (Amendment) Act of its own devising.[5]

Careful preparation and analysis were hallmarks of Evatt's parliamentary speeches. They were punctuated by quotations from various authorities and references to comparable situations in other countries. This characteristic was seen at its best in connection with a Bill for the Abolition of Capital Punishment in September 1925. McTiernan presented the Bill in the Legislative Assembly and ran through the main points in its favour. Following him, Evatt spoke in the same vein, emphasising particularly the irrevocable nature of capital punishment, despite the possibility of errors of judgment. 'Error under such circumstances is so serious and reflects so much upon the reputation of the State itself that it should never be allowed to occur', said Evatt. The supporting argument was a tour de force—an erudite marshalling of evidence from the fields of philosophy, sociology and legal history. Evatt referred to the views of eminent criminologists, such as the Italian Lambroso, and he cited cases from Britain, France and Australia to show 'how dangerous it is to predicate of any man that he is beyond redemption...even a murderer of the worst possible description may in the end render some useful service to society either in gaol or out'.[6]

Although the speech was received with respectful attention by those members of parliament who were capable of grasping the argument, it counted for nought in the outcome. When the Bill reached the Legislative Council, it was nullified by an amendment providing for the retention of the death penalty for one particular kind of crime—murder. This amendment was initiated by the conservative leader of the Council, Professor John Peden, who was the respected former university law teacher of both Evatt and McTiernan. Evatt no doubt recalled wryly that in his own maiden speech a little earlier he had referred to Peden and Bavin as law reformers of some note. The hard reality was that when a Labor government was in office, numbers rather than humane consideration and understanding were paramount in the Council, whose members were appointed for life terms by the State Governor.

Whilst Evatt's speeches were relevant to the Bills under discussion, he did not confine himself to the terms of legislation. There was a refreshing originality about the way in which he looked beyond the immediate situation so as to envisage possible development of concepts and practices. He was also distinguished from most of his Labor colleagues by his readiness to acknowledge weaknesses in some measures put forward by the government—a tendency which probably did not endear him to Lang. These aspects of Evatt's approach were clearly in evidence in debate on a Bill to amend the Workers' Compensation Act in November 1925. Evatt regarded this Bill as being second only to the Forty-Four Hours Week legislation in order of importance on the government's programme. It was also a matter on which Evatt spoke with personal knowledge of the way the system worked and the concepts involved.

Some knowledge of the historical background is necessary here. In the nineteenth century, in the absence of State social security benefits, employees who were off work as a result of injuries were in danger of starving. The plight of their families was worse still if the breadwinner were killed. In English-speaking countries, the position in common law was that an employee injured at work was not entitled to compensation unless it could be proved that the injury was due to the employer's negligence. From the 1880s, the position of some injured workers was ameliorated by legislation in the form of Employers' Liability Acts, but there remained the basic problem of a worker's inability to recover compensation from an employer for loss of wages, irrespective of the cause of injury. This difficulty was the subject of Workmen's Compensation Acts.

In 1897, the first such Act in Britain embodied the 'no fault' principle: the employer's liability no longer depended upon his negligence or that of other employees. In cases where workers who were covered by the scheme were totally disabled through injury at work, the employer was liable to continue paying up to half the previous weekly wage. Australian States passed Acts modelled on the English legislation, New South Wales in 1910 being one of the last to do so. The funding for these schemes, as Evatt expressed it in 1925, represented 'a form of "farming-out" taxation by the State'. In other words, employers who felt it necessary to insure against risks of industrial injury did so by taking out policies with insurance companies. The costs of premiums on these policies were generally passed on by employers to their customers—in effect, a tax on the community. Injured workers benefited and so, to some extent, did shareholders in insurance companies. A big new field of operations was opened by these companies.

The New South Wales Workers' Compensation Act was amended in 1916 and 1920 but was clearly in need of further amendment by 1925 when J. M. Baddeley, Minister for Labour and Industry, introduced a new Bill. He explained it as providing for a range of enlarged benefits for injured workers, as well as increasing the number of workers covered by the scheme. The insurance of such workers by employers was made compulsory, as experience had shown that under a voluntary system some employers failed to take out insurance policies to cover their workers, who therefore suffered badly in the event of injury.

Evatt delivered a major speech on this Bill, supporting Baddeley's statements yet going well beyond them. The lawyer in Evatt was plain as he emphasised that the Bill was not concerned simply with the workers' compensation principle of paying benefits according to a scale set out in the legislation (notably, weekly payments of up to two-thirds of an injured worker's average wage, plus payments for dependants). The Bill also dealt with common law rights in cases where injury was due to negligence on the part of a fellow employee. Under the old doctrine of common employment, such an injured worker could not take action for damages against his employer. Although the doctrine was modified by employers' liability legislation, it still retained some effect until 1926. In Evatt's view, the 'most important clause' in the new Bill was one which 'abolishes the whole doctrine of common employment...It will give the employee the option in practically every case of determining whether he will proceed on his common law rights against the employer or whether he will proceed under this bill for compensation'.[7]

In support of the idea of compelling industrial employers to insure their workers against accident, Evatt said that there must be 'certainty that the compensation which is absolutely due...shall be paid'. The logical corollary was that the State 'should provide the machinery for the employer to insure, and that means a scheme of State insurance'. The concept was not new. For example, when Victoria passed its first Workers' Compensation Act in 1914, it included compulsion for employers to take out insurance policies. Furthermore, as it was likely that some employers would be unable to insure privately because they were poor risks in the eyes of insurance companies, a Victorian State Accident Insurance Office was set up. It was not designed to compete against insurance companies, which consequently accepted its existence.[8]

On the other hand, insurance companies in New South Wales were seriously worried by the possibility that the alternative example set by Queensland might be followed. In that State a radical Labor government in 1915 established a State Insurance Office which was given a monopoly of workers' compensation business. Labor argued that insurance was as much a public utility as were railways, which were State owned, and that insurance company premiums were too high, leading to excessive profits. The Queensland move proved a success, and in 1925 there was some expectation that the new Lang government in New South Wales would follow suit. In fact, the Labor election manifesto, published in *The Labor Daily* on 28 May 1925, promised specifically: 'Labor will create a State Insurance Office, and reduce insurance rates (as in Queensland)'.

Consequently, it was rather surprising that the Workers' Compensation Bill which was brought into the New South Wales Legislative Assembly in November 1925 made no provision for the establishment of a government insurance office. No doubt this reassured the insurance companies, and so their friends in Parliament did not object to the Bill in principle. Instead, Opposition criticism focused upon the likely cost of the various changes: it was said that big increases in insurance premiums would be required, which would be a burden on employers. Evatt, for his part, while defending the Bill vigorously, lifted the level of the debate with some percipient comments. He referred to the fact that government insurance offices had been set up in many States in North America, and the State insurance scheme in Queensland had resulted in a fall in insurance premiums. Without going so far as to advocate a government monopoly of workers' compensation business in New South Wales, Evatt said:

I presume the insurance companies which enter into this class of business will agree about the premiums, and that will in substance mean a monopoly on the part of private companies.

Thus, he observed, if the State itself were to enter the field, that would 'have the advantage of seeing that there is competition between the State, on the one hand, and the combination—if there is a combination—of insurance companies, on the other'.[9]

The Legislative Council was unusually forbearing in its treatment of the Bill, which passed into law and was due to come into effect in July 1926. Shortly before this date, the Accident Underwriters' Association of New South Wales issued a schedule of new premium rates which its members intended to charge under the Act. Incidentally, this action confirmed Evatt's suspicions about insurance companies operating as a combination fix charges. The rates laid down in the schedule were extraordinarily high but the companies assumed that the government would be forced to accept them for fear of collapse of the workers' compensation system. Actually, Lang responded to the challenge by establishing the Government Insurance Office (GIO) to conduct workers' compensation business in competition with insurance companies. The GIO expanded rapidly. Another important factor was that a number of relatively small Australian insurance companies decided to register with the new Workers' Compensation Commission to carry on business under the Act. In effect, there was a break-away from the Accident Underwriters' Association, which was dominated by giant English-based companies such as Sun Insurance and Prudential Assurance.

Lang initially decided, without consulting Cabinet or caucus, that the GIO would charge the same high rates of premium as those set by the big companies. Caucus took exception to this; and many of its members wanted the government to assume a monopoly of the business. Later in the year, under pressure from caucus, the premium rates charged by the GIO and by registered companies were reduced by one-third or more. The matter caused 'some little heartburning about the Premier', as Lang's deputy, P. F. Loughlin, said with deliberate understatement.[10] Evatt himself played no part in these developments, as he was overseas for six months in 1926. After his return to Sydney, he was critical of Lang, referring subsequently to lost opportunities:

The party decided in favour of a State monopoly of insurance. This would have resulted in lower premiums. The workers would also have had their claims viewed by a State Office with sympathy, not suspicion. In view of the direct mandate to Mr Lang, his inaction in this respect is extraordinary.[11]

The first Lang government, which was in office for about two years from June 1925, acquired a reputation as a government of reform, although it may be noted that the major legislative items of this nature were largely dealt with in Parliament in the first six months of office. Criticism of reform was particularly strong in the Legislative Council, where Labor proposals were frequently amended or negated. The need for Labor to do something about the power of the Legislative Council came up sharply at a caucus meeting in October 1925, one day after the Council had virtually killed the Bill to abolish capital punishment. An incensed caucus carried unanimously a motion, put by Evatt, in favour of abolishing the Council through the appointment of sufficient new members to swamp it.

Lang's reaction to this was cautious. Advised by McTiernan on constitutional aspects, Lang first sought the approval of Governor de Chair for the appointment of a large number of Labor nominees to the Legislative Council. The Governor was very reluctant to do so until finally, in December, he agreed to appoint twenty-five new members. Lang and the labour movement as a whole hailed this as a victory, and certainly the Labor strength in the Legislative Council was substantially increased. Nevertheless, Labor remained in a minority in the Upper House.

In the Legislative Assembly, Bavin as leader of the Opposition strongly criticised the appointment of the new members of the Council, arguing that the Governor had been misled by Lang and that if it were to become an established principle that a government could create as many new members of the Council as it needed to secure a majority for itself, then the existence of the Council would become absurd. The last point, while true, ignored the fact that previous conservative governments, while repeating the fairytale that appointments to the Upper House were non-political in nature, had always ensured a conservative majority there. Evatt, deputed by McTiernan to put the government's case in reply to Bavin, did so in style, citing relevant constitutional precedents. In the case under discussion, said Evatt:

The King's representative has acted on the advice of his responsible Ministers, as he is bound to do. It is no breach of the Constitution...The constitutional position not only in New South Wales, but in every other portion of the self-governing dominions of the Empire is this: Where there is a majority in the popular House for the Government of the day, every act whether it is a prerogative or a statutory power nominally exercisable by the Governor must, in accordance with the constitutional practice, be exercised on the advice of responsible Ministers, and on the advice of nobody else.[12]

In January 1926 the Lang government, with full encouragement from caucus, decided to abolish the Legislative Council. Radical reform of the Council was a long-standing item in the ALP platform and it was clear that the Governor was not willing to appoint any more Labor nominees to the Council. Lang himself saw a good opportunity to bolster his position in the Party by leading the public demand for abolition of the Council—a demand which was very popular throughout the labour movement. A Bill proposing to abolish the Council was introduced in the Council itself but was defeated. This was not surprising: not only were there too few Labor-appointed members to form a majority, but some were unwilling to follow the Party line by voting their positions and perquisites out of existence.

Lang then switched his attention back to the attitude of the Governor, who claimed that he had discretion to accept or reject government advice concerning appointment of more members of the Upper House. Without consulting either Cabinet or caucus, Lang decided to send his Attorney-General to London to try to persuade the Dominions Secretary, L. S. Amery, to inform Governor de Chair that he was bound to accept the advice of the New South Wales government on the matter. This was a curious manoeuvre by a Premier at the head of a Labor government which usually asserted its rights against imperial authorities in Whitehall. It was all the more odd in that Amery had already made clear his intention not to intervene between the Governor and the Cabinet in Sydney. Thus McTiernan's mission was doomed to failure. However, this was not material to Lang's aim of strengthening his position of dominance in the Labor Party by operating as a popular hero.[13]

McTiernan's visit to London took him away from Sydney for six months in 1926. Coincidentally, Evatt was also away during this period. Actually, knowledge of Evatt's impending departure became public before Lang announced his decision to send McTiernan to London, and there was some feeling among members of caucus that it would be opportune to ask Evatt to make representations to the Colonial Secretary while he was in London. Instead, Lang chose McTiernan for the job. It was a proper decision—after all, the Attorney-General was the government's principal legal officer and there was little need for his presence in Parliament, as that institution was in recess for practically the whole period of McTiernan's—and Evatt's—absence from Sydney. A further consideration for Lang was that McTiernan was one of his loyal supporters, whereas Evatt was apt to conceive and enunciate ideas of his own.

An illustration of this was a thoughtful article which Evatt contributed to the *Labor Daily* shortly before going abroad. He considered the situation which would arise if the ALP were successful in doing away with the Legislative Council. Evatt pointed out that there would then be no constitutional barrier to a move by a future Nationalist government to create a new Upper House, which would be so constituted (perhaps through a property franchise) as to have a permanent conservative majority, entrenched against the possibility of being swamped by new appointments. Consequently, 'the abolition of the present Legislative Council of itself would not necessarily mean the permanent advancement of the Labor movement in this State, unless accompanied by subsidiary constitutional changes'.[14] Evatt suggested that one such change might be implementation of that part of the ALP platform which called for 'Initiative, Referendum and

Recall' (of elected representatives). He was not dogmatic about this, being concerned mainly to argue the case for serious consideration of the problem. Apparently, no other Labor leaders had given serious thought to the matter—least of all Lang, who probably reckoned that the Legislative Council would not be abolished anyway.

❖

In making 'his first trip Home', as the *Labor Daily* described it, Evatt was accompanied by his wife, Mary Alice, who was farewelled by a number of prominent Labor women in Sydney. For Bert Evatt, the occasion for the visit to London was an appeal to the Privy Council in a case of alleged libel by *Smith's Weekly*. Evatt represented the newspaper in this matter, which was of no particular social significance. More important, a Congress to discuss world migration was held in London under the auspices of the International Federation of Trade Unions and the Labour and Socialist International. McNamara, the federal secretary of the ALP, knowing that Evatt expected to be in London at the time, invited him to represent Australian Labor at the Congress, along with W. H. Kitson, a delegate from Western Australia.

Evatt accepted the invitation, along with credentials from the Melbourne Trades Hall Council. He played a prominent part in the Congress, although its proceedings were dominated by representatives of labour organisations from various European countries. These particular delegates, while acknowledging a need to regulate the international movement of migrants so as to protect them, were primarily interested in emigration from Europe, where unemployment was a serious problem. Admittedly, relief of pressure on the labour market in the countries of emigration might result in increasing pressure, with a corresponding fall in standards of living, in the countries to which emigrants went. It was therefore agreed that economic conditions should be taken into account, in the interests of the international labour movement. In the view of most delegates, Australia offered the best prospects for emigrants, and a motion was submitted to the Congress to the effect that purely political reasons should not interfere with freedom of migration. Australia was not mentioned in this motion but there was little doubt that the White Australia policy was a target.

Certainly, Evatt had no doubt. He vigorously opposed the idea of absolute freedom of migration, saying that in the opinion of the ALP:

Australia could and should be developed as a white man's country. That policy was based largely on the economic fact that the introduction of coloured labour would lower and ultimately destroy the standard of living which had been built up in that country. There was also the practical impossibility today of assimilating Asiatic races without the deterioration of the races concerned...There was a great deal of unemployment in Australia, largely owing to unrestricted immigration. Australian labour was opposed to the present invasion of Southern Europeans, especially Italians, who received little for their work and retained anti-labour ideals, which were cultivated by Fascist organisations.[15]

In making these remarks at the Congress, Evatt was simply enunciating the racist views of Australian Labor and, indeed, of the great majority of Australians. In Melbourne the following day, in a comment upon Evatt's speech, Prime Minister Bruce wholeheartedly supported the White Australia policy. It was the manner, rather than the content, of Evatt's speech which was startling: for the first time, a large international gathering heard this outspoken Australian who was little concerned about offending the sensitivities of many workers' representatives in the audience. He was apparently unmoved by the reaction of a delegate of the All-India Trade Union Congress, who was reported as saying about white people:

By all means let them protect their own interests, but if the only means they could find of doing that was the segregation and exclusion of the coloured races, then it was good-bye to the solidarity of labour.[16]

Over the three days of the Congress, Evatt—supported by delegates from other British dominions, such as Canada—worked to have the motion favouring complete freedom of migration jettisoned. He succeeded in this endeavour because most delegates were concerned to achieve unanimity in Congress resolutions. For the rest, Evatt was happy with resolutions such as one which advocated the abolition of private migration agencies, while urging that government agencies should confine their activities to supplying information to prospective migrants. Further, immigrants should be encouraged to join the appropriate trade union in the host country.

This did not exhaust Evatt's active interest in international affairs during his stay in Europe. He went to Geneva to observe an International Labour Organisation conference and noted that the Australian government had failed to ratify a number of earlier conventions, such as on night baking, on the grounds that the Commonwealth Parliament lacked constitutional power to legislate on these matters.

On questions of war and peace, Evatt's views at this time were insular. On his return to Sydney, he advised against Australian ratification of the Locarno Pact, which related to Germany's western boundaries. He reckoned that it was only a matter of time before there was another war between France and Germany. 'It is difficult to see why Australia should insure the peace between these nations which have been at enmity for centuries', he concluded. In adopting this isolationist standpoint, Evatt was well in the mainstream of ALP attitudes on international affairs.[17]

During their stay in London, the sympathies of Bert Evatt and Mas were sharply engaged by their experience of the great general strike in May 1926. As strangers, they did not play a direct part in this stirring event in which coalminers and other workers fought unsuccessfully against wage cuts and other attacks upon their standards of living. However, the recollections of Ida ('Bill') Cantwell indicate clearly that the Evatts were on the side of the strikers. Bill Cantwell, whose taste in political reading ran to Marx and Engels rather than William Morris, was the wife of a journalist, and this Australian couple had become shipboard friends of the Evatts while travelling to London. There, the two couples exchanged social visits—in particular, Bill and Mas went to plays and art galleries together. Bill Cantwell recalled later that when the general strike broke out they attended meetings called to support the strikers and that Mas as a matter of principle used to walk five miles to Bill's flat rather than use one of the buses operated by strike-breakers. Evatt himself said later that he had seen some of the miners' homes, which were 'exceedingly bad'. When the Evatts left London later to return to Australia, they were seen off by the Cantwells; and characteristically Bert Evatt said, 'Don't let them anglicise you, Canty'.[18]

In retrospect, some curious intersections appear in relation to Evatt's presence in London during the general strike. In particular, two other Australians were there at the same time. One, known to Evatt, was McTiernan, although the two men seem to have had little or no contact in London. The second Australian was R. G. Casey, who was later an important political opponent of Evatt, especially on foreign policy. In 1926, Casey was a young External Affairs Liaison Officer in London, garnering information on the official organisation of strike-breaking activities. Almost certainly, Evatt knew nothing of Casey then.[19]

One very small cog in the strike-breaking machinery was a Cambridge University student named George Godfrey. Like many of his friends, he thought it good fun to help keep transport and other services running while workers were on strike. In Godfrey's case, he was enrolled as a special constable and was given a truncheon. When the strike was over, he was allowed to retain the truncheon as a memento and he took it with him when he emigrated to Australia later. In Sydney, Godfrey became a journalist, a trade union leader and an active member of the ALP. He happened to be president of the Mosman branch of the ALP in 1955, when Evatt's opponents in the party tried to get rid of Evatt by claiming that he had failed to renew his annual membership. It was Godfrey, by this time a strong supporter of Evatt, who saved him by ensuring a speedy renewal of membership through the Mosman branch. Godfrey died in 1989, still in possession of his truncheon, though it seems unlikely that he ever mentioned it to Evatt.[20]

Notes

1. *NSW Parliamentary Debates*, vol. 101, 12 August 1925, p. 69.
2. Ibid., p. 70.
3. Ibid, 27 August 1925, pp. 432–4, 437–40.
4. Ibid., vol. 102, 17 September 1925, p. 878. The Opposition reference to 'job control' was a dig at the policy of the Seamen's Union.
5. Ibid., p. 884.
6. Ibid., vol. 101, 3 September 1925, p. 570.
7. Ibid., vol. 103, 19 November 1925, pp. 2439–40. The justified expectation was that larger sums of compensation were obtainable through common law action than through statutory workers' compensation claims.
8. Ibid., vol. 103, p. 2435.
9. Ibid., vol. 103, pp. 2436–7.
10. Ibid., vol. 108, 22 November 1926, p. 1346.
11. *Truth*, 5 June 1927.
12. *NSW Parliamentary Debates*, vol. 105, 21 and 24 December 1925, pp. 3763, 3895.
13. Bede Nairn, *The 'Big Fella'*, pp. 114–15, shows from de Chair's unpublished memoirs that he had paranoid visions of Lang being a puppet of 'foreign elements' aiming to establish a Communist government in New South Wales at this time.
14. *Labor Daily*, 2 March 1926.
15. *The Times* (London), 24 June 1926.
16. Ibid., 25 June 1926.
17. *Sydney Morning Herald*, 6 September 1926.
18. *Labor Daily*, 6 September 1926; Interview with 'Bill' Cantwell, Sydney, 7 June 1988.
19. Andrew Moore, *The Secret Army and the Premier*, NSW University Press, Sydney, 1989, pp. 62–3.
20. George Godfrey Papers, held by his daughter, Mrs Jill Padman.

CHAPTER 6

EVATT VERSUS LANG

I am sorry to say of Mr Lang that he is a menace not merely to good Government, but to the workers themselves...The vanity of this man, never small, has grown to colossal and grotesque proportions.
H. V. EVATT, 1927

While Bert Evatt was in Europe in 1926, Lang was engaged in a battle for control of the Labor Party in New South Wales. At Party gatherings, Lang spoke about the legislative achievement on such matters as the 44-hour week, industrial arbitration and workers' compensation. He was acclaimed by local Labor Leagues and trade unions. Lang consolidated his position through short-term alliances with leaders of the New South Wales Labor Council. Yet his success in securing mass support in the labour movement was not matched by his position in the parliamentary Labor Party. A growing number of members of caucus, including some Cabinet ministers, resented Lang's authoritarian attitude and his disinclination to give credit to anyone but himself.

Discontent came into the open concurrently with the opening of a new session of parliament in September 1926, when Loughlin challenged Lang for the leadership of the Party. In the caucus ballot, Lang was saved by only one vote—cast in his favour by McTiernan on his way back to Sydney from his unsuccessful mission to London. McTiernan voted by radio telephone from the ship on which he was travelling. It is unlikely that Evatt, who had returned to Sydney only a few days earlier, played any part in organising the challenge to Lang, but according to Lang, Evatt was among those who voted against him. Certainly, Evatt took a keen interest in two elements of caucus disaffection: dissatisfaction with Lang's handling of the workers' compensation issue; and the spread of rumours that four unspecified members of the Labor caucus had been bribed by Nationalist opponents. On the latter point, the allegations were aired by the *Labor Daily*, and as Lang was a director of that newspaper there was some suspicion that he might be implicated in an attempt to create a diversion or to pay off old scores. At all events, the allegations impugned the integrity of members of parliament, especially Labor members; and caucus decided, despite some opposition from Lang, to move for the establishment of a parliamentary Select Committee to investigate the allegations. Evatt proposed this in the Legislative Assembly, and when the Committee was set up, Evatt was appointed as its Chairman.

Lang was among those called to give evidence to the Select Committee but, under questioning by Evatt and others, he was very evasive about the extent of his knowledge. In the outcome, the Committee reported judiciously that there was no reliable evidence to support the allegations. There was some criticism of the role of the *Labor Daily*, which struck back at the Labor members of the Select Committee, saying:

The comradeship between these sky-blue, skim-milk Laborites and their political foes...is evidently much stronger than their regard, either for the Labor Movement, or its mouthpiece, the Labor Daily.[1]

Evidently, Lang regarded Evatt with disfavour by this time, and there were other indications of antipathy between the two men. However, Lang was able to brush aside the Select Committee report, as its publication coincided with a special conference of the State ALP in November 1926. That conference overwhelmingly resolved to confirm Lang in the leadership of the parliamentary Labor Party 'for the period of the present Parliament'. In other words, for the time being, caucus was deprived of the power to choose its own leader.

Lang's triumph was not complete, as faction-fighting continued. Early in 1927, there was a top-level split as two State executives emerged, each claiming to control the Party in New South Wales. However, Lang was so decisively in control by May 1927 that, as Bede Nairn puts it, 'he could have defied his cabinet, his caucus, the Conroy [anti-Lang] executive and the Federal Labour [sic] Party authorities'. The federal executive in the following months backed away from confrontation with Lang.[2]

These events demoralised Labor MPs in New South Wales. At the legislative level, the last year of this Lang government saw the passing of a number of relatively minor Acts, although there was one which was of appreciable significance. This was a proposal to impose a tax of a half-penny per copy on newspapers. The proposal was introduced by Lang, as part of the annual Budget. Nominally, the measure was designed to increase State revenue but it was clearly aimed at metropolitan newspapers, which faced an increase of fifty per cent or more in cover-price. Questions of principle were also raised—by the *Australian Worker* among other publications—concerning taxes on knowledge. When the proposed tax was considered by caucus it was approved and was then adopted by parliament. Evatt was among those who voted for the Finance (Newspapers Taxation) Act, although he did not speak on it. Earlier, however, in the caucus discussion, Evatt had questioned the constitutional validity of the proposed tax.

The tax on newspapers came into force in January 1927, and several newspaper proprietors began proceedings in the High Court to challenge its legality. Evatt also appeared, on behalf of Smith's Newspapers Ltd, seeking an injunction on a subsidiary matter: whether newspapers should have to charge an increased price, in order to pay the tax, in the interim before the High Court decided the constitutional question. Evatt's point was left in abeyance, as it was agreed that the court would make an early decision on the main issue. Evatt was again present, as a junior barrister, when counsel for the main newspapers argued (against McTiernan, representing the Lang government) that the tax was an excise duty and was therefore not within the powers of the State of New South Wales. The High Court accepted this argument, ruling that the Act was invalid. Accordingly, the government dropped the tax.

Although Evatt was not overtly criticised by Labor colleagues concerning his role in the newspaper tax affair, resentment of his 'superior' attitude surfaced at the same time in connection with a Liquor (Amendment) Bill, a minor piece of legislation which nevertheless attracted attention from wowsers. Evatt voiced some doubts about the Bill. It was passed by the Legislative Assembly, but in the process Evatt was absent from a vote on a particular clause. The result was a report to caucus by the Labor Whip, Davidson, criticising Evatt and some others over their undisciplined attitude towards the Liquor Bill. Evatt defended himself in caucus. He was reported as saying that Davidson's attack was 'malicious, vindictive and untrue'.[3]

One exchange in this caucus discussion was reported in the following terms:

Dr Evatt: This memorandum bears internal evidence of not having been composed by Mr Davidson.
Mr Davidson: What evidence?
Dr Evatt: The fact that it is couched in coherent English, for one thing.[4]

This delightful story—accompanied by a reporter's comment: 'They do love one another!'—may be apocryphal, yet the words have a ring of truth. Indeed, Lang suspected that Evatt himself was in the habit of 'leaking' information to the press, while Evatt suggested that Lang instigated Davidson's report.

The spat was of little importance except as an indication of the way the wind was blowing. Much more significant were problems relating to the Family Endowment Act of 1927. The legislation was foreshadowed in the ALP election platform in 1925, in the form of a promise to provide for 'poor children not covered by the basic wage'. This formulation referred to the periodic determination of basic wages—or 'living wages', as they were termed in New South Wales—which were supposed to cover the needs of standard households consisting of adult male labourer, wife and children. A much smaller living wage applied to single women, but it was the male wage which was the focus of attention. Formally, calculations of the basic wage made no extra allowance for families with more than the standard number of children, and this became an important consideration when the question of child endowment came up.

The Lang government made no move in relation to child endowment until the end of 1926, when A. B. Piddington, the New South Wales Industrial Commissioner, made a pronouncement on the living wage—a pronouncement which was apparently designed to apply to a family of man, wife and one child. Piddington had been expected to declare an increased living wage, but instead he left the rate for adult males unchanged at 84 shillings per week, while indicating that this amount was linked to his belief that a child endowment scheme should be introduced as a supplement. This, in effect, forced the Lang government to decide upon the terms of its own policy. The crucial issue was whether a payment of 5 shillings per week for each child should be made as a simple addition without effect upon the declared living wage or, alternatively, the basic wage should be reduced, since it was theoretically based upon an assumed number of children in a household. Clearly, the second proposition was much more acceptable to employers.

Evatt went to the nub of the matter in legal terms. He pointed out to caucus that Piddington, under the Arbitration Act, had authority to fix a living wage but had no power to couple this with the question of child endowment. Thus, in Evatt's view, the Commissioner had exceeded his powers and the government should apply to him for a re-determination of the living wage in line with the Act. Cabinet decided not to do this, although trade unions were taking their cue from Evatt's comments. While the government remained undecided as to its course of action, union leaders were conscious of the fact that the living wage was lower than expected. The Labor Council on 16 December 1926 expressed its 'disgust' at Piddington's pronouncement and called upon the Parliamentary Labor Party to 'immediately bring into operation an effective basic wage'.[5]

Caucus set up a committee to consider child endowment; and Evatt, who was a member of this committee, continued to assert that it was necessary to separate the issue of the living or basic wage from that of child endowment. At a full caucus meeting in February 1927, Evatt and his supporters appeared to be in the majority in opposing a specific proposal from Cabinet. This proposal was that although 5 shillings per week endowment should be paid for every child in New South Wales, it would be subject to a family means test. More significantly, in cases where the children's parents worked under federal awards, smaller amounts of endowment were to be paid for the first two children in a family. The rationale for this proposed discrimination was that the federal basic wage was four or five shillings a week more than its State counterpart, and the federal basic wage purported to cover a larger family (with three children) than did the New South Wales living wage. Thus the Cabinet plan linked child endowment with the basic wage.

For this reason, caucus rejected the plan, preferring a scheme which did not differentiate between workers on federal awards and those on State awards. Subject to a fairly generous means test, 5 shillings per week was to be paid to the mother of *every* child, and this was the form in which the Family Endowment Bill was originally presented to the Legislative Assembly. It was passed by that body but was then amended and held up by the Legislative Council, where it was argued that the cost would be too high. To break the deadlock, Lang then arranged a conference between political managers in both Houses (primarily Lang and Peden), who discussed child endowment and the living wage. Out of this unusual, though prescribed, procedure came agreement on two points. First, the Industrial Arbitration Act was to be amended so as to require Piddington to make living wage determinations on the basis of the needs of a family consisting of a man and wife without children. Second, the payment of child endowment would be subject to a very severe means test: it was not to be paid so as to increase the weekly income of a family beyond the aggregate of the living wage and 5 shillings for each dependent child.

This deal between Lang and Peden, firmly establishing child endowment as a corollary of the living wage, was made without reference to the Labor caucus. A corresponding amendment to the Arbitration Act was rushed through the Legislative Assembly, and only Evatt was quick enough to register a protest. He asked: 'Is nothing to be said about these amendments?' Evatt pointed out that while the next declaration of a living wage would presumably be on the proposed new basis, there was no guarantee that the Family Endowment Bill would ever come into operation. The Legislative Council could not be trusted, and there might be an early election. Actually, Evatt's suspicions on this score were unfounded. The Legislative Council had gained more than it expected from Lang, and the Family Endowment Act duly came into effect. However, it became clear in the following year that only a relatively small proportion of children benefited. The calculation effectively excluded the children of skilled workers and many others who were paid margins above the living wage.[6]

In July 1927, Piddington declared a new male living wage of eighty-five shillings per week, which differed by only one shilling from the previous amount, despite the fact that in the interim the formal requirement to take account of the needs of children in families had been eliminated. The immediate effect was to defer for a year or two the potential threat to the living wage arising out of legislative change. Nevertheless, trade union leaders strongly believed that an appreciably larger living wage should have been in force in 1927. Lang parried such discontent by acclaiming the principle of child endowment, saying that half a loaf was better than no bread.

Lang headed off a revolt in caucus in May 1927 by suddenly tendering the resignation of his government and being re-appointed Premier by the Governor on the clear understanding that an election would be held as soon as possible. In effect, Lang got rid of the old Cabinet, including such able men as McTiernan, and appointed mostly compliant mediocrities in their place. The reconstructed Cabinet never had to face the Legislative Assembly: Parliament was prorogued, although fresh State elections were not held until five months later. In the meantime, there was much bitterness and confusion in the Labor Party. McTiernan described Lang as 'a dictator'. Not to be outdone, Evatt said that Lang was 'the biggest crook in the Labour movement'.[7]

This outburst was followed by a measured 14-point statement, published in a newspaper, *Truth*, in which Evatt analysed Lang's character and record. In relation to both the 44-hour week legislation and workers' compensation, said Evatt, Lang had deprived members of the party of credit for their work, yet there was 'no evidence that Mr Lang studied a line of either Bill. He never discussed them in party or in the House'. Similarly:

> Mr. Lang is not entitled to the credit for the attempt of the party to solve the problem of the Legislative Council. Mr McTiernan, as Attorney-General, and I...worked untiringly in this connection. No one knows this better than Mr Lang...Yet he has gone repeatedly to meetings and with 'I did this' and 'I did that' worked himself up into a fine frenzy...The plain truth is that the work and research put in by members of the party, on this great constitutional question, was subsequently bungled by the typical Lang touch—crude bluster and intimidation.[8]

In the same statement, Evatt ventilated several matters on which he had previously remained silent. One related to his deep concern for the railwaymen victimised in the 1917 strike. As noted in the previous chapter, Lang (as Minister for Railways) took administrative action in 1925 to restore rights of seniority to these workers. However, before this could be implemented, one of the 'loyalist' railway workers, on Bavin's advice, applied to court for an injunction; and a judge ruled on a technical point that the Railway Commissioners, in terms of the Act under which they operated, could not legally comply with the instruction from Lang. Evatt's criticism was that Lang had put at risk the proposed restoration of seniority to the former strikers by 'attempting to carry out the scheme without legislative sanction'. Furthermore, 'it was the wish and desire of the party to go much further in the way of compensation for the injuries done to the victimised men'.

Another point of criticism was that Lang had 'ignored the necessity of unemployment insurance', despite the fact that the platform for the 1925 election had referred to establishing such a scheme on the lines of existing legislation in Britain and Queensland. Evatt in caucus had raised the question of unemployment, but without success. A further matter, which obviously galled Evatt, was put by him in these terms:

> Mr. Lang in his more expansive moments has even claimed the credit for preventing the deportation of Walsh and Johnson...This is, perhaps the most impudent claim of all. Walsh and Johnson would have been deported but for the decision of the High Court of Australia. I have yet to learn that Mr Lang is a member of that tribunal.

Evatt concluded this scathing attack as follows:

> I say of Mr. Lang that he is a menace not merely to good Government, but to the workers themselves. His sincerity is tested by his readiness to

throw into the melting pot all the party's achievements, mainly in order to satisfy motives of personal revenge against his Cabinet Ministers...The vanity of this man, never small, has grown to colossal and grotesque proportions. He believes and acts as if he were not merely the whole Labor party, but the State itself.[9]

Evatt was not alone in the Labor Party in his criticism of Lang. The Balmain State Electoral Council of the party congratulated him on 'his fearless attitude in denouncing the undemocratic dictatorship exercised by Mr Lang'. Lang responded angrily; and the *Labor Daily* did its best to belittle Evatt, sneering that 'Evatt, instructed by Evatt, on behalf of Evatt, is some little whirlwind—for the defence'. McTiernan chose not to stand for re-election to Parliament.[10]

In August 1927, the ALP in New South Wales held preselection ballots to decide upon its candidates for the coming State election, in which there was to be a reversion to the old system of single-member constituencies. The Lang-dominated State executive of the Party had a strong influence over the preselection results, ensuring that Lang's opponents were defeated. In Balmain, Evatt faced several rival candidates, including a coalminer, H. Doran, who worked in the local Balmain pit. The result of this preselection contest was that although Evatt won more votes than any of the other candidates, he was defeated by Doran on allocation of preferences. There were allegations of fraud—one supporter of Evatt told of a kerosene tin with a hole in it being used as a ballot box—and a fresh ballot was held in Balmain two weeks later. The result was the same, despite complaints that many AWU members, who were expected to vote for Evatt, had been disfranchised through manipulation of election procedures by the ALP State executive. In the case of voting by Balmain miners, there was very loose supervision, causing Evatt to remark: 'If you had seen the voting at the pithead...you would have said, "Good God! Is this democracy?"' Lang gained the support of the Miners' Federation by promising that the government would take over the Balmain mine, which faced closure otherwise.[11]

The State executive endorsed Doran as the official Labor candidate for Balmain. Evatt announced that despite this he would stand for re-election to Parliament as a Labor representative, whereupon the executive promptly expelled him from the Party.

Evatt's action was based partly on his belief that he had been cheated by the executive, but he also claimed that Communists in Balmain had infiltrated the ALP and were using the miners as part of a plot to achieve power through the Labor Party, instead of putting forward avowed Communist candidates as in 1925. Doran was known as a man who had studied industrial history and Marxian economics at a Labour college. In effect, then, Evatt was using a diluted version of the standard assertion by Nationalists and the conservative press that the Labor Party under Lang was controlled by Communists. This propaganda played upon fear, ignoring the facts that the Communist Party had no prospect of organising a revolution and that from 1926 its members no longer had decisive influence even in the New South Wales Labor Council. Lang himself was consistently anti-Communist throughout his political career.[12]

Labor lost the State election held in October 1927, although the party secured forty-three per cent of the votes cast—or nearly forty-six per cent with the inclusion of two successful independent Labor candidates. Those two were Evatt and Mutch. Evatt polled 6722 votes in Balmain, against 5949 for Doran. In view of the traditional Labor solidarity behind an endorsed Party candidate, this was an outstanding achievement by Evatt, although it may be noted that no Nationalist candidate stood in the constituency. This may have resulted in some conservative voters preferring Evatt as the more moderate candidate, but it is just as likely that such people voted against Evatt, recognising him as a more formidable opponent of the Nationalists than Doran was likely to be. Probably a more important factor was that traditional Labor supporters felt freer to vote for Evatt in the absence of a Nationalist candidate: whatever the result, the Balmain seat would not go to the Nationalist Party.

Evatt had some useful friends in the labour movement, particularly among trade unionists. The New South Wales Labor Council, although it supported Lang, was impressed by Evatt's stand on the living wage and child endowment as well as his attitude towards immigration—a subject on which Evatt spoke and wrote after his visit to London. Henry Boote, editor of the *Australian Worker*, was also well disposed towards him.

Evatt continued to appear in court cases affecting workers. One offshoot of the celebrated Walsh–Johnson case raised an interesting question of women's rights in law. Following the High Court judgment which freed Walsh and Johnson, each man sued the Commonwealth government for £20 000 damages for unlawful imprisonment. Likewise their wives, Adela Walsh and Amy Johnson, each sued for £5000 damages for distress and illness occasioned by the imprisonment of their husbands. Indeed, Adela Walsh, at the time of her husband's arrest, was pregnant; and she subsequently lost the baby through premature birth. The federal Attorney-General's Department had no sympathy for her. It compiled a damaging dossier on Tom Walsh for possible use in court, and this contained a secret report by Major H. E. Jones of the Commonwealth Investigation Branch, saying: 'Adela Pankhurst is a clever and well educated woman...well able to supply the brains and subtlety to her evilly disposed and revolutionary husband [Walsh].'[13]

When the federal Crown Solicitor's Office in Melbourne asked Owen Dixon, KC, for a legal opinion on the Walsh–Johnson writs, he had no difficulty in concluding that as the two men had been unlawfully imprisoned they were entitled to bring actions against those responsible. However, the writs issued by the wives raised more complex issues. Their claims for damages were based on the argument of loss of consort. In English law, a man might claim redress for the loss of his wife's society (since the law had traditionally regarded the wife as his property), but it was by no means clear that a female spouse had a comparable entitlement. Dixon referred to a number of recent precedents in British courts before advising that, on balance, the Walsh and Johnson wives could not legally sustain the actions they had initiated. He was wrong, as it happened.

There was considerable delay in dealing with the substance of the writs as the Crown raised questions of law in the Supreme Court of New South Wales. There, H. V. Evatt appeared for the Walshes and Johnsons and successfully argued that since the Woman's Property Act came into force, the rights of a wife were equal to those of a husband in matters such as loss of consort. The court accepted this argument in March 1927, agreeing that the two women had good causes for action. Thus the issue of principle was won by Evatt. However, the sequel was an anti-climax. First, the writ issued by Tom Walsh was dealt with by a judge and jury. This time, H. V. Evatt was led by W. Holman, KC, in appearing for the plaintiff. Lamb, KC, acting for the defendant, called no evidence—he was evidently content to have the matter dealt with as expeditiously as possible.

The result was that the jury awarded Walsh damages of only £25. Three days later, a similar process resulted in an award of £20 to Johnson. The new Attorney-General, J. G. Latham, congratulated Lamb and his associates on this outcome. There followed an equally swift despatch of the cases brought by Amy Johnson and Adela Walsh. H. V. Evatt was again junior counsel, with a new leader, W. J. Curtis, KC. Mrs Johnson was awarded £60 damages, and when Curtis suggested to Lamb that Mrs Walsh would also accept £60, plus twenty guineas for medical expenses, Lamb agreed to settle on these terms and on the understanding that there would be no appeal in any of the four actions instituted by the Walshes and Johnsons. That concluded the affair. Of course, Walsh and Johnson were notorious as militant union leaders and it may well be that the juries involved felt that the arrest and imprisonment of the two men was more or less what they deserved. Their wives were tarred with the same brush.[14]

Bert Evatt enjoyed a good personal following in Balmain. He had a record of hard work in the constituency, and during the election campaign of 1927 there were reports of support for him from various groups, including engineers, waterside workers and labourers. On the eve of the election, he made a point of thanking women's committees in Rozelle and Balmain for their assistance. Mary Alice Evatt had a hand in organising these activities. Moreover, the only Party rule he had broken (admittedly an important one) was that which related to standing in an election against an endorsed ALP candidate. Certainly, Evatt had criticised the Party leader in very forthright terms, but Lang responded just as sharply—alleging, for example, that Evatt and other dissidents were being financed by the Nationalist Party in their election campaigns.

Although Evatt retained his seat in parliament, he did so at the cost of being divorced from the Labor Party. A number of his colleagues in the parliamentary Labor Party over the previous two years probably welcomed the break. He was a university man and a successful barrister, in a party where people with this kind of background were regarded with suspicion—and there was some justification, for in Labor experience, courts and lawyers were primarily used against workers, in the interests of property-owners. Abe Landa, a Sydney solicitor who began a long association with Evatt about this time, remarked that when Evatt was first elected to parliament in 1925, he was accepted on the Labor side for his ability, but 'nobody really put down the red carpet for him'. He was envied for his rapid rise; and 'if Bert had been a boilermaker he would have been perhaps better off'. Furthermore, Evatt was disliked for being rude, 'although he didn't mean to be. He would call me a "b…" one minute and the next minute he would be talking as though nothing had been said'.[15]

After the 1927 election, Evatt was cut off from the parliamentary Labor caucus. Admittedly, with a Nationalist government in office, there was not much scope for effective action on the Labor side, but there was some organised opposition. Evatt was excluded from it as an independent MLA. He proved to be remarkably subdued in this parliament. Evatt often abstained from voting, or absented himself, because he did not wish to be on record as voting against the Labor Party even if he disagreed with it. On one matter, Evatt had a particular reason for neither voting nor speaking: a move by the new

Premier, Bavin, to return to afternoon/evening sittings of the Legislative Assembly. The Labor Party unsuccessfully opposed this proposal but it may be assumed that Evatt welcomed greater freedom for himself to engage in court work.

To judge by his parliamentary speeches, only two major areas of politics attracted Evatt's sustained attention in the three years from October 1927. One was the living wage and child endowment; and the other was Commonwealth–State relations. On the latter issue, although mud-slinging between Commonwealth and State authorities was standard practice, Evatt was more serious in approach. Using federal roads legislation and immigration as examples, he argued that the Commonwealth was centralising power through its greater control over revenue. He said:

unless you have readjustment of these powers between the Commonwealth and the States, the States will gradually disappear, not through the will of the people, not through political action, but through economic pressure applied by offering grants...to the various States with a string attached to these grants in each case.

Yet Evatt was not a simple States-righter. He went on to say that he did not wish to be misunderstood:

I do not believe in this cry of States' rights at all. I believe in the Canadian system of giving unlimited power to the Commonwealth, but I believe that the proper way to do it is to submit it to the people for their judgment and not be pointing a pistol at the head of the States through the cruel and undemocratic principle of economic pressure.[16]

NOTES

1 *Labor Daily*, 13 November 1926. On the other hand, the *Australian Worker* (organ of the AWU) accepted the Committee's findings.
2 Bede Nairn, *The 'Big Fella'*, p. 149.
3 *Sydney Morning Herald*, 9 March 1927.
4 *The Bulletin* (Sydney), 24 March 1927, p. 44.
5 NSW Labor Council minutes, Mitchell Library, A3844, FM4/1132.
6 *NSW Parliamentary Debates*, vol. 111 (24 March 1927), p. 2531. Lang's account of this episode, in his autobiography, *I Remember*, pp. 223–4 (published in 1956) was characteristically misleading.
7 *Sydney Morning Herald*, 30 May, 4 June 1927.
8 *Truth*, 5 June 1927.
9 Ibid.
10 *Sydney Morning Herald*, 24 June 1927; *Labor Daily*, 25 June 1927.
11 *Australian Worker*, 31 August 1927. It was alleged that a number of the miners who voted did not live in Balmain.

12 John Hirst, in 'Communism and Australia's Historians', *Quadrant*, no. 265, April 1990, uses a quotation from Evatt at this time to argue that the Communist threat was very real and has been deliberately played down by left-wing historians. In making this political point, Hirst appears to be unaware of the specific situation in Balmain in 1927 which gave rise to Evatt's concern.
13 Australian Archives 467, Special File 12, Bundle 32.
14 Ibid.
15 Interview with Abram Landa, 5 June 1989.
16 *NSW Parliamentary Debates*, vol. 112, 15 November 1927, pp. 299–300. In debate on the Workers' Compensation Act in 1925, Evatt acknowledged a dilemma: a comprehensive Commonwealth scheme of national insurance would be better than providing workers' compensation on a limited State basis, but in practice it was the New South Wales Labor government which was willing to act.

CHAPTER 7

Arbitration and the Depression

If the Industrial Commission is altered in such a way that it will be unsympathetic towards the needs of the workers on the living wage, there may easily be...a substantial reduction in the living wage which will, of course, have its effect on various other wages and salaries.

H. V. EVATT

One of the first steps taken by the Bavin government in New South Wales in 1927 was to amend the Arbitration Act. As Evatt realised, this was aimed at diluting Piddington's power by providing for the appointment of two additional Industrial Commissioners to share his responsibilities, particularly in relation to living wage declarations.

The two barristers, M. E. Cantor and K. W. Street, who were appointed to the Commission were conservative in attitude. In 1928, they favoured an application by employers for a fresh enquiry into the living wage, on the ground that the 1927 declaration had been based on wrong principles. Cantor and Street considered that this declaration had not been based simply on the needs of a man and wife without children. Piddington dissented and was supported by Evatt, who appeared before the Industrial Commission to represent the AWU. Piddington realised that employers were aiming at a substantial reduction of about 11 shillings per week in the living wage, this being the estimated cost of maintaining one child.

Piddington was outvoted by his fellow judges on the question of whether to hold a fresh enquiry, and Evatt became heavily involved in representing the AWU at this public enquiry by the Industrial Commission. Indeed, Evatt was the only representative of trade unions at the enquiry. In effect, Piddington and Evatt strove to salvage something from the wreckage resulting from Lang's earlier opportunism. Piddington, as chief Industrial Commissioner, was most prominent in this, yet he acknowledged that Evatt provided much of the ammunition.

Evatt argued that the child endowment scheme should not be used as a basis for a reduction in the living wage. He also contended, as noted in the subsequent judgment of Justices Street and Cantor, that

one result of adopting the construction of the Act suggested by the employers...would be, as he [Evatt] put it, the almost complete destruction, for a period of one year, of the new scheme of child endowment.[1]

Evatt's submission on this matter related to an extraordinary anomaly in the Family Endowment Act. Besides stipulating reductions in child endowment payments in cases where family earnings were greater than the living wage, the Act provided that such earnings be calculated as an average of the amount received by the family in the preceding twelve months. Thus if there were any cuts in the official living wage, the effect in terms of consequential reductions in child endowment payments would be compounded by the twelve-month averaging process which purported to show that the worker was earning a higher living wage than was so in reality. Piddington described this as a 'crowning absurdity'.

Street and Cantor had no answer to Evatt on this point, except to say that the Industrial Commission had to work in terms of its own Act, not the Family Endowment Act. In October 1929, the Commission decided by a majority that 72 shillings and sixpence per week would constitute a proper living wage. This represented a reduction of 12 shillings and sixpence. However, a formal declaration of a new living wage was deferred to enable parliament to consider the results which might flow from it. The Bavin government, facing a State election within a year, decided that such a large reduction for poor people was politically untenable. Consequently, through a statutory amendment, the Industrial Commission was virtually instructed to declare a new living wage of 82 shillings and sixpence for a family supposedly consisting of man, wife and one child. At the same time, the Family Endowment Act was amended so as to eliminate payment for the first child in a family; and, to take some account of the anomaly emphasised by Evatt, the calculation of average earnings in relation to child endowment payment was to be on the basis of the previous quarter, not a whole year.

For the purpose of declaring the new living wage in December 1929, the Industrial Commission engaged in a public enquiry for only a few hours, as the result had already been ordained by the government. However, Evatt was again present to represent the AWU and he took the opportunity to raise questions about the female living wage. According to Piddington, Evatt argued that

in the case of the female wage the Court's hands are not trammelled, as they are in the case of the male wage, by the manacles of prescribed arithmetical calculations, but are free to establish a true judicial living wage...Dr Evatt also pressed upon our consideration the modern importance of women's work in industry, and the acceptance of the principle of 'equal pay for equal work' in the Treaty of Versailles.[2]

This was a very progressive viewpoint for the time, yet Evatt was not looking for a miracle. The Act required the female living wage to be fixed as a proportion of the male rate. The proportion proposed at this enquiry was fifty-four per cent and Evatt urged an increase to fifty-nine per cent, which would have given a female basic wage worker a few extra shillings per week. However, this plea was rejected on the ground that no time was available to receive evidence on the point. A new female living wage of 44 shillings and sixpence was declared.

One aspect of the child endowment scheme has been overlooked by historians. Federal arbitration awards, embodying the concept of a basic wage, applied to less than half—perhaps forty per cent—of all Australian wage workers. The others were covered by decisions made by State tribunals. Differences resulted. For example, at the beginning of 1930, the federal basic wage was well above the newly declared living wage for New South Wales. Part of the difference was made up, in effect, by the payment of child allowance, unique to New South Wales. The other side of the coin was that a high proportion of workers under federal awards in New South Wales were ineligible for child allowances because of their relatively high wages. However, there was a sharp change in position as the depression deepened. The federal basic wage fell rapidly as a result of automatic cost-of-living reductions associated with price-falls, in addition to which a ten per cent cut in real wages was imposed by the Commonwealth Arbitration Court in 1931.

There were no such court-imposed wage reductions in New South Wales, and a new Labor government there successfully resisted employers' moves to secure a formal reduction in the living wage, at least until 1932. Thus the State's living wage became appreciably higher than the Commonwealth basic wage and one consequence of this was that a substantially larger number of federal award workers in New South Wales were eligible for child endowment payments by the State. In addition, more families became eligible as a result of cuts in their income due to the spread of part-time working and, in many cases, covert cuts in wages to levels below award rates. These developments had not been foreseen, yet it is a fact that for a year or two when the depression was at its most severe, the child endowment scheme assumed something like the major importance originally envisaged for it and fought for by Evatt. However, from 1933 the federal basic wage and the New South Wales living wage were approximately equal.[3]

Evatt acquired considerable knowledge of arbitration processes through participation in various cases, particularly living wage enquiries between 1927 and 1930. Years later, he put this to use in an article which, despite its title, related to State as well as Commonwealth arbitration. In this article, Evatt differentiated between two kinds of arbitrator: those who worked towards industrial justice and improvements in living standards; and those who aimed 'merely at preventing a dislocation of industry' through strikes or lock-outs. In the first category he placed 'great arbitrators like Higgins, Piddington and Heydon'. Some other arbitration judges were named in the article without being categorised. Street and Cantor were not mentioned at all.[4]

Evatt also passed implicit judgement on some arbitration court judges in his book, *Australian Labour Leader: W. A. Holman*, published in 1940. On page 547, he referred to the substantial cut in the basic wage standard imposed by the federal Arbitration Court in 1931, which 'reduced that standard to a point considerably below Mr Justice Higgins's famous Harvester award of 1907'. In making this decision in 1931, the court, in Evatt's comment, 'was operating for once with amazing celerity'.

The Great Depression of the 1930s is traditionally dated from 1929, yet its initial effects were apparent in Australia well before then. The rate of economic growth slowed, stagnation set in and unemployment rose from 1927. Employers, supported by Nationalist governments, tried to cut costs (especially wages) by direct action and through arbitration courts. In 1928–29 there was a series of bitter industrial disputes, particularly affecting the waterfront, the timber industry and coalmining. The federal government moved to restrict the power of trade unions and to strengthen sanctions against strikes.

Evatt became involved indirectly in one dispute in 1928, when marine cooks went on strike. They were defeated, but before that point was reached the secretary of the New South Wales Labor Council, J. S. Garden, was reported to have made a certain reference to the use of scab labour on ships. Accidents, he remarked,

occur in the best of regulated families. The new [scab] cooks will not be very good sailors and will have to go to the railing occasionally. They may lose their balance. In which case the water is damp, the sea is deep, and dead men do not tell tales.[5]

For this, Garden was arrested and charged under the New South Wales Crimes Act with incitement to murder. In court, Garden was represented by H. V. Evatt and W. J. McKell. The defence contended that 'there was not the slightest evidence that there was ever a cook...[or] any particular section of the community...incited' by Garden's statement; and Evatt added that the statement was a jocular remark made in the course of a conversation between Garden and a journalist representing a newspaper known to be antagonistic towards the union movement. The jury acquitted Garden. However, he was immediately charged again, this time under the Commonwealth Crimes Act, with intimidation. The prosecution was based on the same words used by Garden, and Evatt argued that as his client had already been acquitted on similar charges he could not be tried again for the same alleged misdemeanours. The magistrate put this point aside for the time being and proceeded to hear evidence. The result was the same: Garden was acquitted because there was no evidence that he had tried to prevent anyone from taking employment in the shipping industry.[6]

An interesting sidelight on Evatt's role in this case was that while his client Garden, along with Lang, was strongly criticising the AWU (which had disaffiliated from the Labor Party in 1927) about certain matters, Evatt himself was at the same time also representing the AWU before the Industrial Commission. Antagonism between Garden and the AWU did not deter either of them from engaging Evatt's legal services, presumably because he was recognised as the best advocate on the labour side. Incidentally, Evatt seems to have drawn the line at representing employers in industrial matters—or perhaps he was not approached to do so. Representing employers on issues such as libel was a different matter. Evatt frequently did this.

Garden was before a court again in 1929, this time in connection with a strike by timber workers against a federal award which increased hours for timberyard employees from forty-four to forty-eight per week. Garden and a number of other union leaders were charged with intimidation, preventing timber workers from working, conspiracy and other offences. Evatt and other lawyers represented these accused unionists and secured their acquittal, but there was perhaps more public interest in a Supreme Court writ filed by Evatt, alleging contempt of court in several articles and editorials published in the *Sydney Morning Herald*. Evatt argued that this material was unfair and injurious to his clients, being clearly designed to imply that they were guilty of the conspiracy charges which were pending. The argument was upheld: the newspaper proprietor was fined £200 for contempt of court.

Shortly after this, in November 1929, Evatt—in lawyers' jargon—'took silk'. The press reported that the new KC intended to devote his time to a legal career and he was not expected to stand for re-election to Parliament. It may be added that Evatt's legal practice was broad, not restricted to the jurisdictions mentioned so far. He was engaged in several cases which resulted in greater benefit for employees under the Workers' Compensation Act, although in 1929 the Bavin government amended the Act with a view to restricting its application.

Another move by Bavin to reverse the policy of the previous government was directed against the railway strikers of 1917, and this vindictive action remained in force until 1931. The repeated seesaw of policies, varying according to whichever party was in office, probably left Evatt frustrated and disillusioned with politics and it is significant that he made no parliamentary speeches at all in the session which extended from September 1929 to June 1930. Perhaps it would be more accurate to describe his attitude as being a compound of frustration with Nationalist reaction and some disenchantment with Labor politics as practised by a party dominated by Lang, for Evatt did not lose interest in the workers' struggle to defend living standards at this time. Bert and Mary Alice Evatt were personally involved in providing aid for the poor in Balmain. The Evatts, with their adopted son Peter, were living in Balmain itself, having moved there from Leichhardt after the reversion from multi-member to single-member constituencies.

As an industrial suburb, Balmain was badly affected as unemployment mounted in the depression. Mas later recalled the grinding poverty of the time and the local efforts to alleviate its effects. With others she organised a committee of women, which collected clothing materials and borrowed sewing machines for needy women to work on in rooms obtained rent free in the Balmain town hall. As Mas explained:

they're very independent, people in Balmain, they didn't want charity, but what can you do if you've got nothing to put on your baby, or if you haven't even got the money to get to the hospital? Do you know they used to hang on to their wedding rings until time to go to the hospital…where they'd have the babies, and so they'd have…just a small amount of money to be able to get there. This struck me as really terrible. And the women organised to try and help everyone who was in that position, and this made them very much more friendly to each other, you know.[7]

———❖———

One political consequence of the onset of depression was a clear victory for Labor in federal elections in October 1929. McTiernan was one of the ALP candidates elected. Evatt showed no inclination to make a similar move to the Commonwealth Parliament, although he had friends in the federal party, one of them being Theodore, deputy-leader of the ALP. Indeed, Theodore, according to one report, had been present at a meeting in Balmain in 1927 when Evatt launched a strong attack upon Lang; and Theodore had his own reasons for disliking Lang.

The new federal government, with J. H. Scullin as Prime Minister and Theodore as Treasurer, faced enormous difficulties. In the first place, there had been no simultaneous election for the Senate, which therefore remained dominated by a strong Nationalist majority. It was to be expected that before long the Senate would thwart important Labor legislative proposals—and this in circumstances of a rapid deterioration in the economy. A bold Labor administration might have circumvented this at an early stage by forcing a double dissolution of parliament, with the aim of securing a Labor majority in both Houses. However, such a move was not seriously contemplated—Scullin proved to be among the weakest of all Australian Prime Ministers.

Even without adequate legislative control, the federal government could influence events by executive action. There was power to appoint trustworthy people to certain positions, although the Scullin government was loth to expose itself to conservative criticism on the score of bias. This was equally true of appointments to certain judicial bodies. Two such bodies, with influence over wages and conditions of work, were the Commonwealth Arbitration Court and, at one remove, the High Court. Previous Nationalist governments, recognising the realities of power, had no hesitation in appointing such men as E. A. Drake-Brockman as judges in the Arbitration Court, despite his background as a Nationalist politician and a former President of the Australian Employers' Federation. In contrast, the Scullin government made no move to change the composition of the Arbitration Court. The position in relation to the High Court was different. The prestige and independence of a High Court seat, together with infrequency of retirement from it, meant that normally a government had relatively little opportunity to affect the complexion of the court by appointing to it someone of the same political persuasion as the government. Nevertheless, from the time of Griffith and Barton there were numerous examples of politician–lawyers being appointed to the High Court bench.

When the Scullin government took office, the position on the High Court was unusual in that there were only six judges instead of the standard complement of seven—Justice Powers had resigned in July 1929. Chief Justice Knox followed him in March 1930, so that there appeared to be two vacancies on the court although the government was not obliged to fill either of them. Already there was press speculation about the possibility of Evatt and McTiernan being appointed to the High Court. *Smith's Weekly*, in remarking upon this, described Evatt as a man of brilliant intellect. In inimitable style, the paper sketched Evatt's career to date, mentioning his introduction of professional league football into Sydney University:

> To the priggish section in the University, this was the crime of an Outsider. But, since Bert Evatt was an intellectual giant among the students of his year...he defeated the snobs with a Napoleonic completeness of victory.[8]

Then, the columnist continued, Evatt entered Parliament 'and was asked to adjust himself to Jack Lang. The ordeal found him out. Genuine intellect and Jack Lang cannot move parallel'. However, Scullin and his Attorney-General, Brennan, scotched the rumours early in 1930 by stating that the government did not intend to make any additional appointments to the High Court. The decision was justified on the grounds of economy: it was said that the volume of the court's work did not warrant more judges.

At the same time, the federal government was losing a crucial industrial battle. Ever since March 1929, the coalminers of northern New South Wales had been locked out of work by their employers, who demanded a heavy cut in wages. Nationalist administrations which were eager enough to act against workers on strike refused to prosecute colliery proprietors responsible for a lock-out. The new Scullin government was expected to act decisively to end the long dispute and to relieve the desperate miners. Instead, the government fumbled the issue. There was still no prosecution of mine-owners. The most hopeful move was to refer the dispute to the Commonwealth Arbitration Court, where Judge Beeby followed the usual practice by making an interim award ordering the re-opening of the mines at pre-stoppage rates of pay. This suited the miners but not their employers, who took the matter to the High Court on the ground that the dispute was not an interstate one and that therefore the federal Arbitration Court had no jurisdiction over it.

Evatt, KC, appeared before the High Court as a representative of the Commonwealth government in this matter. His case was that the dispute was genuinely interstate in character, as demonstrated by the fact that there had been a short sympathy-strike by miners at Wonthaggi in Victoria. Evatt failed to convince a majority of the High Court, which took the view that the portrayal of the dispute as interstate in character was artificially manufactured for the occasion. This was probably true but it was an arid judgment which disregarded the industrial realities of the situation. Evatt had the consolation of being supported by Justice Isaacs' dissenting judgment. In Isaacs' view, the coalminers and the proprietors had been brought into the Arbitration Court to settle 'a serious national industrial quarrel that has caused…widespread injury in the community; and…[now] they are summarily ejected from that tribunal, with the conflict still active and its consequences unaverted'.[9]

Isaacs notwithstanding, the majority judgment spelled defeat for the miners, who returned to work on reduced rates of pay in May–June 1930. One general consequence was that the federal government lost a great deal of support among its Labor adherents, who were sympathetic towards the miners. Conversely, the Labor Party in New South Wales grew in strength as Lang voiced potent demands—for example, advocating the commandeering of the mines in order to re-open them. A further factor in improving Labor cohesion at the State level was a repair of the rift in relations between the ALP and the AWU which had existed since 1927. In October 1930, Labor in New South Wales won a big electoral victory. Lang was back as Premier. Evatt was out: as expected, he did not nominate for re-election to State parliament.

Meanwhile, the federal government floundered. One of its few legislative achievements was to amend the Conciliation and Arbitration Act. Among the provisions of the Bill introduced for this purpose was the repeal of a section of the Act, introduced in 1928, which required the court to take account of economic effects in making an award. This change, justified on the ground that, in principle, a government should bear full responsibility for public policy, was of vital interest to trade unions at the time, as rapid deterioration in economic conditions provided scope for argument by employers that wages should be reduced by arbitration tribunals.

Nevertheless, there were some unexpected consequences of the legislative changes. G. J. Dethridge, Chief Judge in the Commonwealth Arbitration Court, soon made it clear that he intended to continue to take economic circumstances into account when dealing with specific industries: it had been implicitly necessary to do so before 1928, so the formal requirement embodied in the Act in 1928 made no difference to the situation—and its repeal in 1930 could likewise be ignored. The AWU was shocked by Dethridge's statement, for at the time he had before him an application from the Graziers' Association of New South Wales for a severe reduction in shearers' wages. The general secretary of the AWU walked out of the Arbitration Court hearing—an unprecedented move for a union which was known as the staunchest supporter of the principles of arbitration in the labour movement. The union was reported as saying: 'Surely the Government will not permit its policy to be over-ridden by a Court appointed by its discredited enemies'.[10]

H. V. Evatt was brought into the dispute in August 1930, when the Graziers' Association took action in the High Court against the *Labor Daily* for allegedly inciting shearers to go on strike against an award. Indeed, there were some strikes after Dethridge awarded reductions of about twenty per cent in the pastoral industry. Evatt defended the newspaper company largely on technical grounds, that it was not a party to the award in question. The court in effect rejected his argument but noted that the newspaper article had not been repeated nor was it likely to be: an injunction would be granted by the court if similar material were published again. It may be added that if a penalty had been applied under the Arbitration Act it would have been a fine of only £100. The Graziers' Association was primarily aiming to intimidate with an eye to the future.[11]

While Arbitration Court judges, enjoying tenure of office for life, were thumbing their noses at one section of the amended Act of 1930, the High Court proceeded to nullify other sections which provided for the appointment of conciliation committees. What became known as the *ARU* case arose from applications to the Arbitration Court by Railway Commissioners of several States for the setting aside of certain awards so as to provide for a reduction of wages. The Australian Railways Union then procured the appointment of conciliation committees in terms of the Act—a move which may well have been designed to delay proceedings. In fact, there was little delay, as the Arbitration Court itself intervened and ordered the setting aside of the awards in October 1930. The ARU responded with an appeal to the High Court to rule that when conciliation committees were appointed, the Arbitration Court was left with no jurisdiction in the matter. Maurice Blackburn appeared for the ARU, while Evatt intervened on behalf of the Commonwealth government, in effect supporting the union.[12]

The High Court, instead of considering directly the question raised by the ARU, ruled that the sections of the 1930 Act which related to conciliation committees (consisting primarily of government-nominated representatives of parties to a dispute, with power to make decisions by majority) were void: the scheme amounted neither to conciliation (that is, settlement by agreement) nor arbitration (since the process did not involve hearing the actual parties to a dispute). Thus, this part of the Act was held to be outside the government's constitutional powers relating to conciliation and arbitration. The ruling effectively by-passed a separate question raised outside the High Court by E. A. McTiernan, MP, who wrote to Senator J. Daly, the acting Attorney-General, to query the power of the Arbitration Court to set aside an award. The court had done this in the railways case on the ground that it could take a financial emergency into account. Daly, in reply to McTiernan, acknowledged that the Arbitration Court did indeed have power to set aside an award, but this power was intended largely as a punitive measure 'in the case of grave misconduct by the parties...it was never intended that the power to set aside awards should have been exercised by the Court on the ground that a state of emergency had arisen'.[13]

Naturally enough, trade unionists regarded the High Court judgment in the *ARU* case as a lawyers' quibble designed to undermine legislation enacted by a Labor government. In reaction, powerful union leaders felt more strongly than ever that it was wrong for there to be no High Court judges who were sympathetic towards the labour movement. Although the decisive move to appoint Evatt and McTiernan to the High Court bench originated in the federal parliamentary Labor caucus, there was undoubtedly union pressure behind the scenes. That Evatt was a great constitutional lawyer was, in the eyes of people in the labour movement, much less important than the fact that he and McTiernan had demonstrated not only sympathy with Labor but an ability to put that sympathy to service in the interests of workers in arbitration proceedings.

An interesting illustration of the intensity of union feeling on this subject comes from a letter of 27 January 1931 written by the general secretary of the ARU to both the Prime Minister and Attorney-General Brennan. By this time, not only had Evatt and McTiernan been appointed to the High Court but Chief Justice Isaacs was retiring from it in order to take up the position of Governor-General. The ARU letter expressed 'considerable concern' at the government's announcement that it did not intend to fill the vacancy created by the retirement of Isaacs. It continued:

In these days when Arbitration Courts are setting themselves above legislative functions or, at least, are endeavouring to become law-makers rather than interpreters of Parliamentary legislation, it is considered that no further risk should be taken as was unfortunately taken prior to the appointment of Justices Evatt and McTiernan. The action of the Government in not making earlier appointments has caused the workers of Australia millions of pounds [loss].[14]

Despite this, Scullin did not fill the new High Court vacancy. He was determined to have no repetition of the furore which had broken out over the appointments of Evatt and McTiernan.

NOTES

1 *NSW Industrial Arbitration Reports*, vol. 28, part 1 (1929), pp. 379–80, 426.
2 Ibid., pp. 530–1.
3 Fran Jelley's helpful article on 'Child Endowment', in *Jack Lang*, Heather Radi and Peter Spearitt (eds), Hale & Iremonger, Sydney 1977, does not refer to developments from 1928 onward.
4 H. V. Evatt, 'History of Federal Arbitration', *Australian Quarterly*, vol. ix (September 1937), p. 21.
5 *Sydney Morning Herald*, 13 June 1928.
6 Ibid., 23 June, 18, 21 and 25 September 1928. Actually, the Commonwealth intended to launch its own prosecution the day after Garden's statement became public knowledge, but a State policeman got in first.
7 Transcript of interview with Mary Alice Evatt, NLA.
8 *Smith's Weekly*, 11 January 1930
9 Quoted by Robin Gollan, *The Coalminers of New South Wales*, MUP, Melbourne, 1963, p. 191.
10 *Argus*, 11 June 1930.
11 44 *Commonwealth Lar Reports* (CLR), 1930–31,1–10.
12 44 CLR, 1930–31, 319 ff.
13 Daly to McTiernan, 5 December 1930, Australian Archives 432, 30/2301.
14 Australian Archives A432, 31/205. The calculation of loss related to delays due to a Full Bench not being available to deal with a certain case.

PART II

JUDGE AND SCHOLAR

CHAPTER 8

LABOUR AND THE HIGH COURT

The non-Labor parties do not have to make deliberately 'political' appointments to the Bench; they only have to choose from a small group of men whose professional eminence singles them out for judicial preferment, and those chosen will nearly all be as a matter of course supporters of non-Labor parties or apolitical men.
GEOFFREY SAWER

In August 1930, Scullin, Brennan and another federal Minister left Australia to attend an Imperial Conference in London. They did not arrive back in Australia until January 1931, and in the meantime the economic situation had deteriorated markedly. A growing number of Labor MPs, especially those from New South Wales, felt that the federal government was drifting and defeatist; and one expression of discontent was a decision by caucus in December 1930 that the two vacant positions on the High Court should be filled. This was about a week after the High Court judgment in the *ARU* case. Cabinet then proceeded to appoint Evatt and McTiernan to the positions. Scullin, when he learned what was afoot, cabled a protest from the ship in which he and Brennan were returning to Australia. While not objecting to Evatt and McTiernan personally, Scullin and Brennan took the view that it would be wrong for Cabinet to accept political direction concerning appointments to the High Court and it would expose the ALP to criticism. Scullin's prime concern was to preserve public respectability and he urged that the decision be deferred until he and Brennan were able to take part in the discussion and to express their strongly held views. It was too late—Scullin's cable, it was said, was not received until after Cabinet decided upon the appointments. Evatt's elevation dated from 19 December 1930 and McTiernan's from 20 December.[1]

Of course, the two appointments were political in the sense that they were made by the government of the day. The same was true of all High Court judges, and with one exception (Rich, in 1913) each owed his position to a conservative government. They were men of legal eminence and of no apparent or conscious bias, who could be relied upon to make sound decisions in cases where important political or property interests were at stake. As Geoffrey Sawer puts it:

The non-Labor parties do not have to make deliberately 'political' appointments to the Bench; they only have to choose from a small group of men whose professional eminence singles them out for judicial preferment, and those chosen will nearly all be as a matter of course supporters of non-Labor parties or apolitical men with middle-of-the-road or conservative temperaments, certainly not likely to be enthusiastic supporters of ALP policies.[2]

A government which wished to appoint a barrister who was both eminent and inclined towards Labor had far fewer options available to it—the total number of Labor sympathisers among lawyers was small. In 1930 this made the federal government vulnerable to charges of political bias in appointing Evatt and McTiernan. Yet there is much to be said for the view that appointments to the highest court in the land should not be the prerogative solely of conservative, not to say elderly, lawyers whose contacts with ordinary people are extremely narrow: inevitably, judges are influenced by their own social, economic and political values. The intensity of the conservative attack upon Evatt and McTiernan was probably due in part to the likelihood that they would remain on the High Court bench for many years. Evatt was only thirty-six years old at the time.

There was general approval of the appointments in Labor circles. Even Lang considered them beneficial. As he remarked later: 'We had much more time for Evatt as a lawyer than as a politician'. Conservatives, however, were critical. The *Sydney Morning Herald*, for example, editorialised about political appointments: 'politics should have nothing to do with judicial office'. Criticism was also voiced by members of the Bar in New South Wales and Victoria. The Victorian Bar issued a public statement concerning the circumstances surrounding the High Court appointments, saying:

If judicial appointments are to be discussed and regarded as political rewards or opportunities for political service to be dispensed by political parties, the judicial office will inevitably be degraded, and the fair, honest, and efficient administration of the law will be threatened.

On the other hand, R. G. Menzies, KC, wrote a personal letter of congratulation to Evatt—while simultaneously deploring McTiernan's lack of outstanding qualifications. The brilliance of Evatt's legal career was generally acknowledged, yet it was said that others had been passed over who had equal ability, together with stability and maturity of years.[3]

Neither Evatt nor McTiernan responded in public to the criticism of their appointments. The latter was undoubtedly hurt by it, but Evatt had a thicker skin. He had no doubts about his own ability and he was aware of the part played by political considerations in such matters. Later he wrote about an occasion when it was being mooted that C. G. Wade, a lawyer and former Premier of New South Wales, might be appointed as Chief Justice of the State. Evatt commented that 'Wade was a conservative, a qualification which can transform a plodding blockhead into a great jurist'. Furthermore, accusations of political bias in judicial appointments came from the left as well as the right in 1931. Thus a Labor man in Sydney, who had supported the appointment of Evatt and McTiernan to the High Court, attacked what he termed 'inspired propaganda' in the press to the effect that Sir Owen Dixon should be Chief Justice of the High Court. In the view of this critical commentator, 'Sir Owen Dixon has been for years the legal mouthpiece of capitalism and the Employers' Federation in Melbourne, in all legal industrial proceedings, as Victorian union leaders can testify'.[4]

On appointment, Evatt had to withdraw from two cases in which he had been briefed. One was the Mungana affair, a civil court matter in which E. G. Theodore was seeking to clear his name of allegations of corruption. The other case in which Evatt was involved was more important, concerning a constitutional issue of much interest to him. In the previous year the Bavin government in New South Wales secured an amendment to the State's constitution so as to require that the Legislative Council could not be abolished without a prior referendum on the subject. Moreover, this legislative amendment itself could not be repealed without a referendum. Soon after the Lang government was voted into office in 1930, it introduced Bills to repeal Bavin's amendment and to abolish the Legislative Council. The Bills were passed, but no referendum was held and, inevitably, Nationalist opponents resorted first to the Supreme Court (where Evatt appeared for the Lang government) and then to the High Court.

When the High Court considered the case in 1931, Evatt took no part because of his earlier involvement as counsel. The Court's judgment, that the parliament of New South Wales had power to make its constitution more rigid in the manner adopted in 1929, went against the new Lang government. However, the judgment was not unanimous: it resulted from a majority of three to two, the dissentients being Duffy (Chief Justice) and McTiernan. It was an interesting division, as there is little doubt that if Evatt had sat in the case he would have come down on the same side as McTiernan. On the other hand, it must be said that the majority judgment was upheld by the Privy Council in 1932.

One other High Court case might be regarded as a hangover from the political past of both Evatt and McTiernan. Known as the *Garnishee* case, this was a matter of major constitutional significance. It arose out of a Financial Agreement entered into by the Commonwealth and the States in 1928, which was embodied in an amendment of the federal Constitution the following year. Under this Agreement, the Commonwealth assumed responsibility for the public debts of the various States, while the latter in effect agreed to pay the Commonwealth the interest due upon these public debts. The Agreement was put to the test in the depression in 1931–32, when the Lang government decided not to pay interest on those New South Wales government bonds which were held by persons overseas, mainly in Britain. In 1932, a new federal government headed by Lyons—following the fall of the Scullin government—moved to implement the Financial Agreement by passing a drastic Financial Agreements Enforcement Act authorising the Commonwealth to garnishee—that is, seize—New South Wales government revenues so as to pay the debts owed and thus avoid international default by Australia. There was then a struggle between the Lyons and Lang governments for control over New South Wales public revenues, and the constitutional validity of the Financial Agreements Enforcement Act was challenged in the High Court.

By a majority of four to two, the High Court upheld the validity of the legislation. The majority consisted of Rich, Starke, Dixon and McTiernan, while Duffy and Evatt were in the minority. Both sides had reasoned and persuasive arguments to support their judgments, and it is in such circumstances that the political inclinations or idiosyncrasies of individual judges may be important—they may exercise their biases without appearing to do so. In this particular case, the decision of McTiernan was crucial in the balance. In effect, it meant support for a conservative Commonwealth government against a Labor State government, and this came as a surprise to people who had known McTiernan as a Labor adherent before his appointment to the High Court. As against this, it could be said that McTiernan had consistently advocated greater powers for the central government, and the States had adopted the Financial Agreement of 1928 of their own volition. In McTiernan's view, the Agreement was worthless unless there was some way of enforcing its provisions. It is also possible that McTiernan saw in the case a good opportunity to separate himself from both the Lang Labor Party and H. V. Evatt: McTiernan was demonstrating publicly his independence as a judge.[5]

Different considerations applied to the two dissentient judges in the *Garnishee* case. Duffy was widely known as a supporter of the rights of States as against the Commonwealth. Evatt's judgment was more complex, being based on a technical argument that a State's revenue could not be expended except in terms of an Act of its Parliament, and in the current case the Parliament of New South Wales had passed no relevant Act. Further, Evatt argued, the federal Act was discriminatory in providing for the enforcement of the Agreements by the Commonwealth, but not by the States against the Commonwealth. Beneath the legal subtleties lay an issue of material substance, not simply one of constitutional interpretation. Years later, Evatt referred to the *Garnishee* case (without mentioning his own part in it) and described the Financial Agreements Enforcement Act as a piece of legislation which 'business and financial controllers considered necessary to meet an emergency'. Conversely, the Act could be regarded as being against the interests of workers, at least in New South Wales, where they had hitherto suffered less severe wage reductions than at the federal arbitration level.[6]

Evatt's judgment in the *Garnishee* case may be best interpreted as a matter of keeping faith, not so much with the Lang Labor Party (which was badly split) as with the ordinary people in the labour movement. Evatt was concerned to continue, as far as possible, to shield workers from the worst effects of the depression. He sought to do so in the *Garnishee* case, not directly (there was no mention of wages at the hearing) but through a plausible legal argument.

When Lang still defied the Commonwealth government after the High Court decision, the Governor of New South Wales, Sir Philip Game, dismissed him from office. This was followed by an election in New South Wales in 1932, which resulted in defeat for the Labor Party. Remarkably, Lang did not institute a court challenge to Game's action in dismissing him. Consequently, the question of whether the Governor acted within his constitutional powers in summarily sacking a Premier who commanded a majority in Parliament was left undecided. However, in 1936, Evatt, in the course of a scholarly survey of the reserve powers of the Crown, studied the Lang–Game episode. On balance, Evatt seriously doubted whether the Governor's action could be justified constitutionally: his proper course, if he believed that ministers were breaking the law, would have been to wait at least until a court decided upon the alleged illegality. In New South Wales, wrote Evatt, 'legal proceedings could have been instituted before the ordinary Courts of law, and...appropriate declarations obtained and injunctions issued'. Had Evatt known in 1936 that advice to just this effect was drafted in the Dominions Office in London at the time of the crisis in 1932—but never sent to Game—he would have felt his opinion vindicated.[7]

As is clear from the *Garnishee* case, there were significant divergences of opinion between Evatt and McTiernan on the High Court. McTiernan was jealous of the higher public esteem generally accorded to Evatt. Nevertheless, the reserve or tension in relations between Evatt and McTiernan did not detract from the fact that they had much in common. Their experience of the labour movement gave them extensive understanding of workers and their problems, whereas other judges had little or no contact with the poor. Evatt and McTiernan retained a degree of sympathy for underdogs and the organisations which represented them. Such empathy was badly needed in the depression of the 1930s and it became particularly noticeable in cases involving workers' compensation and trade unions. It was not simply a matter of making sympathetic judgments in cases where the law could be construed in such a way as to permit such action. It was also relevant that Evatt and McTiernan knew a great deal about industrial and labour law. The High Court benefited from this, and within a year of the appointments of Evatt and McTiernan to the Court, it was clear that they were making a difference.

One example of this arose out of the Commonwealth Arbitration Court's cut of ten per cent in award wage rates in 1931. The Australian Insurance Staffs' Federation appealed to the High Court for exemption from the decision, on the ground that its award could not be legally varied so as to prescribe minimum wages lower than those set out in the employers' previous log of claims. As it happened, the current insurance award was an agreement made by consent of both parties in 1927, with the result that the employers' ambit claim at that time had not been for absurdly low wage rates as it would have been had the case gone through the standard arbitration procedure for disputes. Justices Rich, Dixon, Evatt and McTiernan upheld the Insurance Federation's argument, while Duffy and Starke preferred the argument put forward by R. Menzies, KC, for the Atlas Assurance Co. and other insurance companies. The case itself was not of major importance yet it is apparent from a reading of the separate judgments that the four judges who comprised the majority had a much more comprehensive grasp of precedents in this area than had the two dissenting judges. In particular, Evatt and McTiernan were very familiar with practice concerning the concept of ambit claims in arbitration cases.[8]

Much more sharp and intense than the relationship between Evatt and McTiernan were the feelings of hostility exhibited by Starke towards both of them. Starke simply believed that the other two men should not have been appointed to the court and were not worthy of his notice.

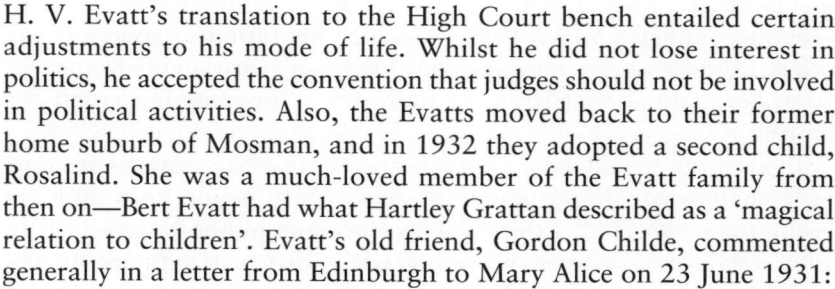

H. V. Evatt's translation to the High Court bench entailed certain adjustments to his mode of life. Whilst he did not lose interest in politics, he accepted the convention that judges should not be involved in political activities. Also, the Evatts moved back to their former home suburb of Mosman, and in 1932 they adopted a second child, Rosalind. She was a much-loved member of the Evatt family from then on—Bert Evatt had what Hartley Grattan described as a 'magical relation to children'. Evatt's old friend, Gordon Childe, commented generally in a letter from Edinburgh to Mary Alice on 23 June 1931:

I'm glad to have your new address, by the way I assumed you'd leave Balmain when electoral necessities ended...Bert will find the High Court very heavy for a while, I know Alec did at first before he got into the way of untying marriage knots and hanging murderers...I and everyone are thoroughly sick of Macdonald & Co [British Labour government]. But there is no alternative less bad, the CP [Communist Party] being quite hopeless here. I've become a political agnostic.[9]

Removal from Balmain did not mean cutting all former ties. According to the *Sunday Sun* of 1 November 1931, Evatt was contributing £40 per month to the Balmain Distress Relief Committee. He was also giving the committee two guineas per fortnight for a competition among unemployed youths in the district, as well as ten guineas for a special Christmas competition. Such generosity, usually with a specific focus, was characteristic of Evatt. For instance, in the 1920s he instituted an annual essay prize at his old school, Fort Street. In 1931, this prize was won by a working-class lad from Balmain named John Kerr, who was in his final year. He wished to go on to the university to study law but could not afford to do so. He went to see Evatt to explain his problem. Impressed by Kerr's ability and initiative, Evatt then gave him a scholarship of £50 per year to enable him to go to university. This was a foundation stone in the career of a student who later became Governor-General of Australia—and, in 1975, an object of rage and derision in the labour movement.

Evatt did not publicise his acts of generosity. Thus the prime source of information about his scholarship for Kerr was Sir John himself many years later. The sum of £50 was not small change: it was equal to Evatt's own annual salary as a university lecturer in the early 1920s. Of course, it might be said that he could afford to give freely by 1930, when his legal practice was very extensive.[10]

Evatt sustained a substantial drop in income when he was appointed to the High Court bench on a salary of £3000 per annum. It was customary in such cases for colleagues and journalists to remark upon the difference in income, while overlooking security (tenure for life for High Court judges), prestige and power. All such factors were weighed by those concerned before they accepted offers of appointment. Evatt and McTiernan had no hesitation in accepting the offers. Abe Landa, in recalling that Evatt was then a very successful barrister, added that 'Bert Evatt never talked money much for himself'.[11]

Evatt's relative lack of concern about personal finances may be viewed alongside an intriguing incident, which would have reflected badly upon the High Court if it had become public knowledge. In June 1931, as a means of coping with the great depression, the Premiers' Plan was adopted, with the support of conservatives. Under the plan, Commonwealth and State governments agreed to make substantial reductions in public expenditure (including salaries and pensions), as well as reducing interest rates and increasing taxes. Wages and prices were falling and there was much talk of a need for equality of sacrifice. The following month, Scullin in a private letter suggested that the High Court judges might make a personal contribution to the financial emergency through a voluntary reduction in their salaries. Some, if not all, of the judges were outraged by this idea. Chief Justice Duffy met Scullin to discuss the matter and then, on 10 August 1931, a reply to the Prime Minister's letter was drafted. This reply noted that the judges' salaries had not been increased since the establishment of the High Court, and stated firmly:

The Constitution provides (Sec. 72) that the remuneration of the Justices shall not be diminished during their continuance in office...we are unwilling to do anything that affects or weakens, directly or indirectly, this provision of the Constitution. The primary purpose of the prohibition against diminution was, as has been said, not to benefit the Judges, but, like the clause in respect of tenure, to attract good and competent men to the Bench and to promote that independence of action and judgment which is essential to the administration of justice...

And any gift or contribution to the revenue of the Commonwealth which would in effect be a deduction from the judicial salary would, in spirit if not in letter, be obnoxious to that provision. The Chief Justice, at his interview with you, pointed out that the Justices of this Court cannot be treated as ordinary officers in the Public Service. They make a considerable pecuniary sacrifice in accepting and holding office, and that certainly was the case with us...[12]

So much for the spirit of equality of sacrifice. No trade union could have been tougher in protecting the interests of its members. At the same time, there was recognition that it would be diplomatic to offer a token concession:

In the circumstances, what we propose to do is this. At present, an allowance of four guineas per day is paid to each Justice during his absence on official duties from the State in which he resides. We shall not, on and from 1st September next, claim or accept any portion of this allowance. But it must be understood that each Justice is at liberty to withdraw from this arrangement whenever he decides to do so.

It was further acknowledged in the letter that the value of this proposal was lessened by the fact that it had already been decided, as an economy measure, to rearrange the sittings of the full court so as to confine them to Sydney and Melbourne, eliminating visits to the other State capital cities. Scullin was much too respectful to tell the judges, in blunt Australian argot, what they could do with their mealy-mouthed proposal. Nor did he expose them to public charges of self-seeking or hypocrisy. No information about the judges' attitude was made public by the government.

Unfortunately, it is not known how many of the High Court judges subscribed to the letter quoted above. McTiernan's recollection, half a century later, was that he, Rich and Dixon decided to consent to a voluntary reduction in salaries, but that Duffy, Starke and Evatt declined. However, McTiernan's memory was hazy on this matter. He stated on another occasion that Rich was mean and had a grievance about travelling expenses dating from World War I—which suggests that he would not have been happy to make a concession in 1931. Further, McTiernan was inclined to be malicious in remarks about Evatt.[13]

The final outcome is not clear. The *Australian Law Journal* in September 1931 reported briefly that reductions of judges' salaries had been arranged in most States and that the High Court judges had 'fallen in with the scheme for the national economy, some by consenting to a reduction of salary, and others by waiving their travelling allowance'. In fact there was no reduction in the salary level of £3000 per annum, although it appears that the travel allowance in some cases was not drawn for a period of two years. Indeed, Prime Minister Lyons wrote to Evatt in 1932 thanking him for stating that in the year to June 1933 he did not intend to make any claim for travelling allowances other than the actual costs of transport. As Evatt was usually firm in upholding the dignity of any institution with which he was associated, he may well have signed the letter in question in 1931. On the other hand he was not personally worried about his income and he was generous in donating part of it to people suffering in the depression. As far as is known, the same could not be said of any of his brothers on the High Court bench.[14]

While a High Court Judge in the 1930s, Evatt made a number of remarkable contributions to legal history. Some of these, in so far as they are dealt with in his published books, are referred to in following chapters. However, full consideration of his judicial work would require a much larger biography than can be conveniently encompassed in a single volume. Consequently, this material is being published separately in a monograph, *H. V. Evatt and the High Court*.[15]

Suffice is to say here that, as a member of the court, Evatt played a significant role in opposing censorship, the official proscription of radical political literature and attempts to repress suspect political organisations. He also stood out against the distortion of immigration rules in order to keep out certain foreigners deemed politically undesirable by government. And he objected to professional bodies of lawyers and doctors exercising discrimination against Jewish refugees in Australia. Furthermore, Evatt strongly asserted workers' rights to strike in industrial disputes. In all such cases, Evatt's judgments were informed by liberal and humane considerations. McTiernan very often took the same standpoint in cases concerning workers, whereas other members of the High Court did their work with little apparent concern for the people involved. Following the law was their duty—the problem with this formulation was that judges also create law, and most lawyers worth their salt can produce plausible arguments to support submissions.

Notes

1 According to Warren Denning, *Caucus Crisis: The Rise and Fall of the Scullin Government*, Cumberland Argus, Parramatta, 1937, p. 73, Senator Daly as acting Attorney-General was the 'prime mover' in the High Court appointments. A resentful Scullin reconstructed Cabinet soon after, and Daly was dropped from it.

2 Geoffrey Sawer, *Australian Federalism in the Courts*, MUP, Melbourne, 1967, p. 64.
3 J.T. Lang, *The Great Bust*, McNamara reprint, Katoomba, 1980, p. 316; *Sydney Morning Herald*, 19 and 23 December 1930; Menzies' letter in Evatt Collection, File on High Court: Congratulations on Appointment (Flinders University).
4 H.V. Evatt, *Australian Labour Leader*, pp. 247, 420; letter from T. Mack, *Labor Daily*, 13 January 1931. Dixon was appointed to the High Court in 1929.
5 Brian Galligan, *Politics of the High Court*, UQP, St. Lucia, 1987, p. 109; Geoffrey Sawer, *Australian Federalism in the Courts*, p. 67.
6 H.V. Evatt, *Australian Labour Leader*, p. 555.
7 H.V. Evatt, *The King and his Dominion Governors*, Cass, London, 1936, pp. 173–4. For the Dominions Office draft advice, see John Manning Ward, 'The Dismissal', ch. 10, Heather Radi and Peter Spearritt (eds), *Jack Lang*.
8 45 CLR, 1931, 409.
9 Evatt Collection, Flinders University, File on Childe.
10 John Kerr, *Matters for Judgment: An Autobiography*, Macmillan, Melbourne, 1978, ch. 3.
11 Interview with A. Landa, 7 June 1989.
12 Draft typed letter, unsigned, found among miscellaneous papers of E.A. McTiernan. Actually, the real value of salaries rose substantially during the depression, as prices fell.
13 For example, McTiernan alleged privately that in 1925, when Evatt was under attack by Catholics in the labour movement over his book, *Liberalism in Australia*, Evatt and his wife bought up all remaining copies of the book. There is no corroboration of this story from any other source.
14 Lyons to Evatt, 12 September 1932, Evatt Collection, Flinders University, File: High Court correspondence 1930–40. It may be added that Evatt was a minor beneficiary in the will of R.D. Meagher, prominent solicitor and politician, who died in 1931.
15 Ken Buckley, 'H.V. Evatt and the High Court', publication anticipated for late 1994.

CHAPTER 9

THE RESERVE POWERS OF THE CROWN

The moral of the precedents is the need for definition, regulation and enforcement of the Crown's reserve powers, for very damaging inferences are apt to be drawn from the fact that, in each of the two cases...it was the official Labour Party and its supporters which were seriously disadvantaged, both by the exercise of, and by the prevention of the exercise of, a reserve power.
H. V. EVATT

Until World War II, most Australians saw themselves, in Alfred Deakin's words, as 'independent Australian Britons', proud of their British cultural and political heritage. In the 1930s, however, there was a resurgence of the 1890s debate about Australian cultural identity and the extent to which Australian nationalism could be accommodated within a wider imperial framework. Tensions were created when Australian interests did not coincide with British interests.

Evatt's legal and historical writings of the 1930s should be viewed in the context of that debate. They complement the concerns and values already demonstrated in his earlier career in State politics and on the High Court, and they provide an insight into his thinking about the relationship between British law and Australian development, and about the emergence of the labour movement.

As C. Hartley Grattan said, Evatt displayed 'consistent solicitude for the interests of the small man as against the big man, for the rebel as against the authoritarian, for social justice as against institutionalised machinery for supporting the status quo'.¹ For him, the law in Australian society had to operate for the benefit of all its members if a truly democratic system were to survive; democracy was endangered when the processes of the law were vulnerable to manipulation by vested interests. In times of social crisis, the law could be used as a weapon; the threat to democracy could come from groups within Australia, or it could come from the Crown's representative. Yet at no time did Evatt advocate a dissolution of all ties with the Empire—rather he foresaw a gradual devolution of power to the Dominions, which would continue to be linked within a British Commonwealth.

Evatt's thesis, 'The Royal Prerogative', for which he was awarded a doctorate of laws in 1924, showed remarkable prescience for its time. In it he argued that Australia could achieve independence within the British Empire without alteration to the Constitution, by virtue of 'the flexible application of common law principles concerned with the prerogatives of the Crown, and the operation of constitutional conventions relating to responsible government'.²

Evatt's concern about Australian autonomy had no doubt been fuelled by the experience of World War I and the Peace Conference of 1919. When Britain declared war on 4 August 1914, it was assumed that Australia, as one of the Dominions, was automatically at war, since the Australian Constitution gave Britain control over external affairs and defence. A small advance towards international recognition was made when the allies gave the Dominions separate representation at the Peace Conference. However, although the peace treaty was signed for Australia by an Australian Minister, it was also signed by the British delegate for the empire as a whole. The Dominions became separate members of the League of Nations, could be chosen as members of the League Council, and in the case of Australia, could be given a mandate.

In the light of these events, Evatt claimed in 1924 that 'the Dominions have assumed the status of full nationhood', and that 'the Prerogative should be still invoked in order to *maintain and consolidate such status* and so *retain our constitutional salvation*' (his italics).

Evatt assumed that the supremacy of imperial legislation over Australian law would continue 'forever', but hoped that 'the Courts, interpreting that common law, will find in the Prerogative of the King an instrument which can and should assimilate legal to political facts.' Actually, it was not until 1986 that the *Australia Act* brought to an end that supremacy of British law over the Australian Commonwealth, States and Territories to which Evatt referred. Only then was the full independence of the Australian political and legal system established. Nevertheless, as early as 1924, Evatt was asserting that 'the Prerogatives of the Crown so far as the Commonwealth of Australia is concerned can only be exercised in respect to...foreign affairs on *the advice and responsibility of the Commonwealth Executive*' (Evatt's italics).[3]

The Balfour Declaration, approved by the Imperial Conference of 1926, confirmed that the United Kingdom and the Dominions were 'autonomous communities in the British Empire, equal in status', and that the Governor-General was not a representative or agent of the British government. The Imperial Conference went further: among other things, it recommended that when appointing Governors-General, the King should act on the advice of responsible ministers in the Dominions. The principles of the Declaration and the Conference of 1930 were subsequently incorporated into the Statute of Westminster (1931), but Sections 2 to 6 were not to extend to Australia, New Zealand or Newfoundland unless they were adopted by the parliament of the Dominion concerned. No law of the British parliament was to extend to any of the Dominions as part of its law other than at the request and with the consent of that Dominion. While he was on the High Court, Evatt relied on the development of Dominion status in construing the external affairs power—in *R. v. Burgess ex parte Henry*.[4]

It was not until 1942, when Evatt was Attorney-General and Minister for External Affairs in the Curtin government, that Australia officially ratified the Statute of Westminster, as from 3 September 1939. Throughout the 1930s, conservative Australian governments had conducted foreign affairs as though Britain had never enacted the Statute. This was not only due to their reluctance to abandon a 'colonial' outlook, but also because of a lack of unanimity amongst the States. In 1939, Menzies assumed that when the King, on the advice of his United Kingdom ministers, declared war, Australia was automatically at war. However, with a Labor government in office in December 1941, there was a separate Australian declaration of war against Japan. A special power was issued by the King acting under Section 2 of the Constitution, granting the Governor-General power to declare war. Evatt, as Attorney-General, refrained from expressing any opinion as to whether this specific authorisation was necessary.

In the early 1930s, some constitutional lawyers argued that because the States of Australia were not represented at the imperial conference which led to the Balfour Declaration, the principles expounded there did not apply to State governors. According to Leslie Zines an academic legal authority, after the adoption of the Statute of Westminster, *both in respect of matters of legal form (such as advice to the Queen) and imperial law there were marked disparities between the status of the Commonwealth and the States. The Commonwealth was not bound by the Colonial Laws Validity Act; the States were. The Commonwealth was freed from any restraints on its power to make extra-territorial laws; this provision did not apply to the States. The Commonwealth Government could give advice direct to the Queen; the States had to proceed through a British minister.*[5]

There is no doubt that the dismissal of the Lang government by Governor Game in New South Wales in May 1932 gave impetus to Evatt's study of the reserve powers of Governors and Governors-General, *The King and his Dominion Governors* (1936). In it, he built on the work of his unpublished doctoral thesis on the Royal Prerogative, but extended the scope of his analysis to take into account important political and constitutional developments which had occurred since the thesis was written. As Evatt explained to Nettie Palmer in 1937:

The book was written partly with the object that the intelligent reader would make the point that the conventions are not defined because they always work against the Left party.[6]

In the preface, Evatt stated that his analysis was based on two postulates: the permanence of the Crown, and the continued existence of a system of parliamentary democracy. He was convinced that 'constant research' into 'all the present-day implications and tendencies' of that system was essential, otherwise 'it may change, or be changed, without popular approval given with full knowledge, into something very different'. With this in mind, he had chosen 'important modern instances where the exercise of the reserve power [of the Governor] has given rise to dispute'. Later in the text, he referred to

vagueness and uncertainty of the rules governing the exercise of the reserve powers of dismissal, dissolution, and veto by the Crown in England or its representative in the Dominions...today the position is befogged by conflicting authority, and by inconsistent or ambiguous precedent.[7]

For Evatt, the Balfour declaration and the Statute of Westminster did not address the problem of the reserve powers, and he concluded that their extent should be defined, preferably in statute form. He acknowledged that on some future occasion the exercise of the reserve powers might be 'the only possible method of giving to the electorate an opportunity of preventing some permanent and far-reaching constitutional change'. Nor did he think it desirable that the office of Governor-General should become a 'mere reflection' of an existing Dominion administration, because there was no predicting 'to what lengths certain persons may not be prepared to go in the exercise of legislative power'.[8]

The desirability of a definition of the reserve powers was given added impetus by the comments of contemporary observers. One of the targets of Evatt's criticism in *The King and his Dominion Governors* was the Scottish constitutional lawyer and historian, Professor A. Berriedale Keith, whose later writings were 'freely interspersed with condemnatory references of an extreme, almost violent character to those who entertained opposing views'. Keith's works were often quoted as authority by participants in constitutional disputes—in some instances the professor himself cabled his observations across the world, giving a 'spot diagnosis' which consisted of a mixture of political facts and political comment. Moreover, the Australian press quoted Keith approvingly, especially when he criticised the actions of Labor governments: he had been 'lyrical' in his praise for Game in 1932 when Game dismissed Lang's ministry, and had condemned the appointment of Sir Isaac Isaacs as Governor-General. For Evatt, questions of constitutional practice were 'not, or should not be, party questions'.[9]

After analysing the opinions of other British constitutional textwriters such as Todd, Bagehot and Laski, on the exercise of the reserve powers of the Crown, Evatt concluded that those interested could cite a precedent or constitutional convention 'to find support for or against almost any proposition'. Hence the need for definition.[10]

The major part of the book, however, is devoted to a detailed and exhaustive analysis of disputes between Governors and Ministers, in Australia, the United Kingdom and other Dominions. The purpose was to demonstrate the extent of a Governor's discretionary authority in a particular situation, and the nature of the reserve powers of the Crown, with special emphasis on the power to grant or refuse dissolutions of parliament and to dismiss ministries.

The tone is lofty and dispassionate, in keeping with Evatt's stature as a High Court judge. There is none of the drama, the personal and political conflicts which were an essential element of the story. While Evatt provided some historical background to each of the episodes described, the reader is given very little sense of the political or social contexts within which the Governors and ministries were operating. Nevertheless, his main purpose was to draw attention to the lack of a definite and consistent set of rules which Governors could follow in times of crisis, and this he did in a clear and comprehensible style, accessible to both lay and professional readers.

According to Evatt, it was the emergence of Labor parties throughout the English-speaking world which signalled the need for a shift away from the old reliance on a code of political morality to which liberals and conservatives adhered, whereby 'conventional understandings' had characterised British and Dominion constitutions. The members of the labour movement

were no longer satisfied with a mere reference to rules and understandings which were nowhere defined except so far as definition might be found in the essays of Bagehot or the daring but inaccurate generalizations of Dicey.

In the Dominions, the new parties

cannot see the 'rules' written down in any authoritative way, and they come to suspect the rules the more if they are brought into operation against their desires...If parliamentary government is to endure, it is essential that the terrain of this constitutional no man's land should be finally explored.

There were several contentious episodes in recent Australian history which Evatt had in mind when he made these comments. Not only did they reveal inconsistencies in the policies pursued by Governors, but they also pointed to a tendency for a Governor to act in a manner harmful to the political interests of the Labor Party, either on his own initiative or on the advice of the Dominions Office.

In November 1916, Sir Gerald Strickland, the Governor of New South Wales, had been recalled by the British government after refusing Holman, the Premier who had broken from the Labor Party over the conscription issue, an extension of one year to the life of the existing parliament. The Governor had refused Holman's request on the grounds that the Assembly had not declared confidence in the new ministry, and because Holman had originally been commissioned to form a government as leader of the Labor Party, a majority of which had declared no confidence in him. However, Holman had appealed to the Colonial Office, and Strickland was recalled. At the general election in March 1917, Holman was successful in returning to office with the support of some Labor defectors and the newly formed 'National Party'. In this instance, Evatt agreed with Keith, that 'on the constitutional rules hitherto observed in Australia, the Governor was fully entitled to act as he did'.

According to Evatt, the imperial authorities had intervened on the side of Holman and his ministers, although everything indicated that they would have been defeated if an election had been held immediately. Such imperial intervention was 'uncontrolled by governing rule or practice'.

Another constitutional crisis occurred in New South Wales in 1926, as recounted in Chapter 5 above. Attorney-General McTiernan, on his mission to England in 1926, pointed out to Amery, Secretary of State for the Colonies, that Governor de Chair's claim to have complete discretionary authority in appointing members of the Legislative Council under Clause VI of his instructions was not warranted by instructions issued to Governors-General. Amery, however, insisted that the Clause could only be changed if all Australian States unanimously approved, and given the political differences between the States at that time, this was, according to Evatt, an unrealistic requirement, 'tantamount to refusal of the request'. Moreover, Amery made clear to McTiernan that he did not believe that the British government should intervene in the internal affairs of New South Wales by issuing specific instructions to the Governor on how he should act. As Evatt commented, 'nowhere is there any ruling [by Amery] as to whether and to what extent the Governor possesses a discretion to refuse to act upon the advice of his Ministers'.

In spite of having been in the Legislative Assembly as a Labor member at the time of this crisis, though not in the ministry, Evatt treated this subject quite dispassionately, carefully separating legal from political considerations. Governor de Chair's partisanship is more clearly identified in the article on him in volume 8 of the *Australian Dictionary of Biography*, but Evatt refrained from openly criticising him in his book.

The uncertainty regarding a Governor's discretion remained unchanged when, in May 1932, Lang's second ministry, only half way through its term, and with a majority in the Legislative Assembly, was dismissed by Governor Sir Phillip Game. The Assembly was dissolved 'because of a supposedly illegal act on the part of Ministers, although redress...was obtainable in the Courts of law'. Game had acted on his own initiative, since, nominally at least, imperial intervention 'had become out of order...by such rulings as...the imperial conference declarations'. Evatt summed up:

The moral of the precedents is the need for definition, regulation and enforcement of the Crown's reserve powers, for very damaging inferences are apt to be drawn from the fact that, in each of the two cases...it was the official Labour Party and its supporters which were seriously disadvantaged, both by the exercise of, and by the prevention of the exercise of, a reserve power.

Governor Game's dismissal of Lang in 1932 was given detailed examination by Evatt in chapter XIX of *The King and his Dominion*

Governors. He warned that Lang's dismissal had set a very important constitutional precedent which illustrated the 'confusion and anarchy' resulting from the absence of binding rules for the exercise of the reserve power. In Evatt's view, 'too much was left to the Governor's decision upon what are really questions of fact and opinion'. Instead, there should be recourse to 'the organs exercising the judicial power, or to a specially constituted tribunal'.

Evatt admitted that there were practical difficulties in defining the reserve power, but he asserted that constitutional practice could be defined and controlled by legislation to be passed by the parliament having the relevant jurisdiction. Such an enactment could declare 'the rules which were to govern the appointment and dismissal of Ministers of the Crown, the dissolution of Parliament, and the special position of the Premier in the Ministry'. There was, according to Evatt, no difficulty in giving binding force to legislation of this character. All that was necessary to make it valid and effective would be to specify 'the remedies obtainable against the Governor and Ministers if the constitutional rules laid down were broken'.

In conclusion, Evatt warned that it would be wrong to assume that a Governor-General would always be 'a mere tool' in the hands of the dominant party. A Governor-General 'could not safely exercise his reserve powers unless he had good reason to suppose that the electorate would vindicate his action'. However,

...the absence of definition may prevent an over-careful Governor-General from acting when he should, just as it may enable an imprudent or over-zealous Governor-General to act where no reasonable ground for intervention exists. In each case an error may be fatal to the best interests of the people, which are committed in the last resort to the care of the Governor-General or Governor.

Although Evatt's original doctoral thesis was not published in full until 1987, the typescript was frequently consulted in The University of Sydney Library by students of constitutional law. In 1938, R. H. Long Innes—a Supreme Court judge in Sydney and a friend of Evatt—made a passing reference to the thesis in a letter to Evatt, who was then in London. The context was that Innes had recently given judgment in a court case involving Crown copyright in statutes and, as he told Evatt, it seemed unlikely that there would be an appeal to the Privy Council against the judgment. Innes commented:

I am rather sorry; it isn't often I feel sure that my conclusions are correct, but in this case—based as they so largely were upon the as yet unpublished work of Mr. Justice Evatt 'Some Aspects of the Royal Prerogative'—I feel unusually confident.[11]

As for *The King and his Dominion Governors,* Evatt undoubtedly intended the book to become a standard reference for scholars and constitutional lawyers and although its material was poorly organised in Geoffrey Sawer's opinion, it was influential in this way. For example, John Barry informed Evatt that in a political crisis in Victoria in 1943 the State Governor had consulted Evatt's book 'assiduously'.[12] On the other hand, McTiernan—a practical-minded judge—criticised Evatt's opinion that the reserve powers of the Crown should be defined by legislation. McTiernan's private comment was terse:

That's all rubbish...[Evatt] wanted to codify it and have a law case about it. If the Governor declined, go and have a case about it. Does that finish up in the Privy Council?[13]

Evatt's hopes for definition of the reserve powers of the Crown remained unrealised. Zelman Cowen, in his Introduction to the second edition of *The King and his Dominion Governors* in 1967, acknowledged that there might be difficulty in reducing the reserve powers to certainty by legislation, although, in Cowen's view, Evatt's 'general thesis remains persuasive'. Ironically, another Governor-General, Sir John Kerr, having carefully read the same book, decided in 1975 to exercise the reserve powers by dismissing the Whitlam government. Sir John defended his action by reference to the existing reality of the reserve powers and the fact that Evatt's recommendation that the powers be codified had not been implemented. Nevertheless, it may be surmised that if Evatt had been still alive he would have regarded Kerr as an illustration of what Evatt referred to as 'an imprudent or over-zealous Governor-General' taking advantage of the absence of definition of reserve powers.[14]

NOTES

1. C. Hartley Grattan, 'Evatt of Australia', in H.V. Evatt Papers, MS.1309, Mitchell Library.
2. L. Zines, Commentary, in H.V. Evatt, *The Royal Prerogative*, Law Book Company, Sydney, 1987, C.1–2.
3. Evatt, *The Royal Prerogative*, pp. 84, 159.
4. H.V. Evatt, *The King and his Dominion Governors: a Study of the Reserve Powers of the Crown in Great Britain and the Dominions*, 2nd edn, Cheshire, Melbourne, 1967, pp. 192 ff; 55 *CLR*, 1936, 608.
5. Zines, Commentary in *The Royal Prerogative*, C8.
6. H.V. Evatt to Nettie Palmer, 1937, Vance and Nettie Palmer Papers, MS.1174/1/5278 folder 71, NLA.
7. H.V. Evatt, *The King and his Dominion Governors*, p. 268.

8 Ibid., p. 198.
9 Ibid., pp. 3–7.
10 Ibid., p. 268. Except where otherwise indicated, succeeding quotations in this chapter are also derived from Evatt's *King and his Dominion Governors*.
11 Letter in Evatt Collection, Flinders University. *File*: Overseas Trip, 1938.
12 Barry to Evatt, 27 September 1943, Barry Papers, NLA, MS 2505/10/63–4.
13 K. Buckley, 'Edward McTiernan and the High Court' (unpublished MS held by Law Foundation of NSW). Nowadays the Judicial Committee of the Privy Council is no longer a problem in this respect.
14 H.V. Evatt, *The King and his Dominion Governors*, Introduction by Z. Cowen; John Kerr, *Matters for Judgment*, Macmillan, Melbourne, 1987, ch. 4.

CHAPTER 10

HISTORICAL, LITERARY AND ARTISTIC CIRCLES

Unless trades unionists throughout the world are always ready to sacrifice their personal interests, their safety, or even their lives for the amelioration of the lot of the poor, their elaborate organization may perish overnight either in a holocaust of terror and force or in the slower process of legal repression.

H. V. EVATT

Evatt's next published book, *Injustice within the Law*, ventured beyond purely legal studies and into the realm of social and political history. He examined the story of the Tolpuddle Martyrs, the six Dorchester labourers who in 1834 were sentenced to seven years transportation to Australia for administering unlawful oaths to those joining their fledgling Agricultural Workers' Union.

The centenary of their conviction in 1934 had seen the publication by the British Trades Union Congress General Council of *The Book of the Martyrs of Tolpuddle*, but this was the product of many authors, and lacked unity of treatment. The case had been neglected by legal historians and had been given scant attention in relevant Law Reports, whereas in Evatt's opinion, it was 'of great importance from the point of view of legal history and the general principles of the administration of criminal law'.[1]

Evatt proceeded to show that the Home Secretary in the Whig Government of the day (Lord Melbourne) and the magistrates, who were local landowners, conspired to prosecute the six labourers in order to make an example of them to others who may have been considering joining trade unions. Possibly Evatt had in mind recent Australian political history when he commented that 'a vindictive administration of the law for political ends has not yet been held to be an "unlawful" conspiracy'.[2]

The published correspondence between Lord Melbourne and the local landowner and magistrate, James Frampton, was examined by Evatt to prove that their real object was the destruction of trade unionism, at a time when membership of Owen's Grand National Consolidated Union (GNCU) had increased to over half-a-million, striking fear into the hearts of both Whigs and Tories. The initiative came from Frampton, who wrote to Melbourne about the local situation in Dorset where, as a result of drastically reduced wages, the Agricultural Workers' Union had been formed by the Loveless brothers in October 1833 on the advice of two delegates from the GNCU. Frampton offered to arrange for 'trusty persons' to infiltrate the organisation and identify those involved. He sought Melbourne's help about how to proceed, and after obtaining legal advice from the Home Office Melbourne suggested that the leaders could be prosecuted for administering secret oaths, provided sufficient evidence could be obtained from informers.

By March 1834, Frampton had obtained the necessary evidence, and contrary to the impartiality required of magistrates, acted as both prosecutor and preliminary judge at the same time, his object being to crush the union. Melbourne selected the charge to be preferred and stressed the advantage of a speedy trial. Conveniently, the foreman of the Grand Jury which decided whether the accused would be committed for trial was Ponsonby, Melbourne's brother-in-law; the judge who presided at their trial, Sir John Williams, was Baron of the Exchequer. The petty jurors, who were all farmers, had been carefully vetted in order to exclude tradesmen and Methodists, a section of the community to which the accused belonged. For Evatt, this was a misuse of the jury system because 'a jury consisting of the labourers' real peers, not of their bitter opponents, would certainly have acquitted them'. However, the evidence against the prisoners 'was sufficient, if true, to support the verdict and finding of the jury'.

Although trade unions had been legal since the repeal of the Combination Acts in 1824 and 1825, the Tolpuddle labourers had been indicted under a section of the Unlawful Oaths Act of 1797 and a subsequent Act of 1799 outlawing societies which required members to take an oath. This allowed the judge scope to sentence them to seven years transportation. As Evatt said, 'the clear object of the prosecutors was that [trade unions] should not operate at all, despite the repeal of the Combination Acts'. However, he agreed with legal opinions that the decision was 'still regarded as a good authority on the true interpretation of the Unlawful Oaths Act of 1797'.

The conduct of the trial by Judge Williams was not criticised by Evatt, given the evidence presented, but the punishment of seven years transportation was described as 'severe' and 'cruelly unjust'. The judge, in his summing up, had stated that the legal punishment was imposed as 'an example and warning', for the security of the country and the maintenance of law and order.

Writing to Melbourne after sentence had been passed, Frampton assured him that 'the conviction and prompt execution of the sentence of transportation has given the greatest satisfaction *to all the Higher classes...*' (Evatt's italics), and urged the government to resist appeals for clemency, as the sentence would have a great impact on all labourers. Melbourne and the local magistrates deserved condemnation, according to Evatt, 'for combining to abuse the proceedings of the Courts for the attainment of an illegitimate end, that is, the suppression of trade unions, however lawfully they might be conducted'.

The clergy of the established Church of England did not escape Evatt's criticism. They were, with one exception, hostile to the labourers' cause, having taken up petitions designed to prevent the spread of unionism throughout the county. George Loveless regarded himself as having been victimised, partly because he was a Methodist; he characterised the vicar of Tolpuddle as 'that hireling parson'.

Evatt did not dwell in much detail on the experiences of the six convicted labourers in the Australian colonies, but he did absolve the colonial governors, Bourke and Arthur, from charges of victimisation, placing responsibility for the suffering on the authorities in England. In 1836, King William IV, despite his hostility to trade unionism, was persuaded by the more moderate Lord John Russell to grant free pardons to the labourers, and they all eventually returned to England.

In his discussion of the consequences of the case, Evatt agrees with J. L. and B. Hammond, who claimed that Melbourne was successful in breaking the spirit of the starving men in the villages: wages in Dorset remained the lowest in England for two generations, and trade unionism was suppressed throughout the agricultural districts. By August 1834, Owen's Grand National Consolidated Union was rapidly losing members and broke into factions.

There were lessons to be drawn from the case, which Evatt had no hesitation in spelling out. Firstly, lawyers should be interested because the case represented 'the very coronation of injustice', yet there was no technical breach of the law. Secondly, it was the public and parliamentary agitation of a determined minority which led to the pardons, even though they were not granted until unionism had been suppressed. Nevertheless, 'the extreme punishment was thereby mitigated'. Finally, the case illustrated the fact that oppression and cruelty do not always fail, for

unless trades unionists throughout the world are always ready to sacrifice their personal interests, their safety, or even their lives for the amelioration of the lot of the poor, their elaborate organization may perish overnight either in a holocaust of terror and force or in the slower process of legal repression.

It is noteworthy that Bishop E. H. Burgmann, Anglican Bishop of Canberra and Goulburn, and a friend of Evatt's, agreed to write a Foreword to the book, in which he remarked that 'neither churches nor courts rise much above the prevailing opinion of the time'. Burgmann was well aware that the law could 'fairly easily be twisted into an instrument of injustice'. As Warden of St John's College, Morpeth, he had called for a fair trial for the thirty men charged after the Tighe's Hill eviction riot of June 1932. In a speech to a meeting at Newcastle Town Hall on 8 November 1932, he criticised the decision to conduct the trial in a rural location and not in the industrial area where the riots took place, contending that the accused should be tried before a jury of their peers and in their own neighbourhood. Clive Evatt acted for the defence.

In a subsequent letter, Bert Evatt praised Burgmann's speech for dealing with

a very difficult and little understood question, involving grave principles. I did not think there was anyone in Australia who sufficiently cared, or appreciated, the importance of the matter...It is a great shame on Church leaders who ought, at least, to be disinterested, that your courage is equally to be admired.[3]

Although Evatt's letter to Burgmann conveyed a sense of cultural isolation, he was able to share his concerns about Australia's future with a circle of friends and acquaintances from the art and literary worlds.

The depression, Australia's declining birth rate, a sense of instability exacerbated by Lang's dismissal in New South Wales, and an awareness of a growing threat from Japan, all combined to inspire a burst of cultural nationalism and an obsession with the 'spirit' of Australia. At the federal government level, repressive censorship of literature, both for political and moral purposes, had placed at least 5000 books on the banned list, including such classics as Huxley's Brave New World, Hemingway's *Farewell to Arms* and Defoe's *Moll Flanders*.[4]

During 1934 and 1935, two issues united intellectuals, academics, artists and clerics into an activist and nationalist group—the Kisch case, involving restrictions on immigration, and censorship. William Macmahon Ball, then lecturer in political science at The University of Melbourne, founded the Book Censorship Abolition League in 1934, and Brian Fitzpatrick, a radical intellectual and historian, was one of its leading members. Australian nationalists such as writers Vance and Nettie Palmer joined the League, as did Katharine Susannah Prichard. However, its membership was not confined to those of left-wing sympathies—a number of prominent liberals and conservatives such as Eggleston, Bland and Scott also joined.[5]

The Lyons government's attempt to bar Czech-born Egon Kisch from entering Australia in 1934 to attend a peace congress in Melbourne again brought together the same activists. The case forced local writers to face the issue of intellectual freedom, and the Fellowship of Australian Writers formed a 'Cultural Defence Committee', headed by P. R. Stephensen and Frank Clune.[6]

A Kisch Defence Committee was established, and its members included writers Katharine Susannah Prichard, Vance Palmer and Jean Devanny, artist Max Meldrum, and academics Professor Walter Murdoch and Macmahon Ball. The Revd Albert Rivett addressed a meeting of 20 000 in the Sydney Domain, and Bishop Burgmann sent a message of sympathy to the Committee. Detained on board the ship *Strathaird*, Kisch was told by visitors that the barrister A. B. Piddington 'has got the authorities in a corner, and Mr. Justice Evatt himself says that the statements of the alleged information from England are ridiculous'.[7]

This last reference was to Evatt's hearing of the case in the High Court, and there is no evidence to suggest that he was in direct contact with members of the Kisch Defence Committee at the time. However, Evatt's stand in the case gave him a certain cachet amongst intellectuals, and by 1937 he was corresponding regularly with Nettie and Vance Palmer and Brian Fitzpatrick, and had been introduced to the American journalist and historian C. Hartley Grattan by the novelist Miles Franklin. Grattan later remembered that his attention had been 'insistently called in London to Evatt as an Australian worthy of scrutiny by Harold Laski whom I had frequently encountered on various occasions in New York'. Moreover, the fact that Grattan had met Laski and the Webbs 'raised [Grattan's] stock with Evatt'.[8]

In 1937 and 1938, Grattan was resident in Australia on a Carnegie Fellowship; on an earlier visit in 1927, he had met Nettie Palmer, who wrote a Foreword to his short critique entitled *Australian Literature* (1929). Even though she thought him wrong in some details, Palmer praised Grattan for his remarkable understanding of Australian literature, which helped to ease the isolation of Australian writers. As Geoffrey Serle has stated, he was the first and most perceptive outsider to pay any attention to Australian literature. Moreover, Laurie Hergenhan has remarked that Grattan expressed 'a sense of the specificity of national cultures arising out of his sense of America's colonial and post-colonial experience and out of his broader conception of culture'.[9]

Grattan shared with Miles Franklin an admiration of Furphy's *Such is Life* as a 'superb book' to be valued for its 'insistence on the worth and unique importance of the common man...one of the fundamental Australian characteristics'. That this view of Furphy was shared by Bert Evatt is obvious from a letter written to him by Miles Franklin, expressing her delight that 'one of our own authors, and such a truly Australian one', had been quoted in one of Evatt's High Court judgments: 'It is because you are high among the literati as well as high among the jurists that you have applied the passages, native and imported, with such effect'.[10]

Evatt's friendship with Hartley Grattan was a productive and intellectually sustaining one, and lasted until a few years before Evatt's death. Indeed, it was a measure of Evatt's respect for Grattan's understanding of Australia that he was asked to write a Foreword to *Rum Rebellion*. Later, Grattan's study of Evatt's book on Holman, *Australian Labour Leader*, originally intended as an introduction, was printed as a separate article in *Australian Quarterly*. On Evatt's advice, Brian Fitzpatrick's manuscript of *British Imperialism in Australia* (1939) was sent to Grattan for his comments, and Fitzpatrick agreed to incorporate Grattan's suggestions into his book. It is not surprising that Fitzpatrick referred to an 'Evatt–Grattan–Fitzpatrick solidarity'.[11]

More important, perhaps, than Grattan's influence in Australian literary circles was his role as a publicist for Australia in the United States. In 1940, he spent ten weeks in Australia and New Zealand as part of a fact-finding mission for the Institute of Current World Affairs to assess the impact of war on the two countries. After the American entry into the war in December 1941, he prepared news from Australia for the American News and Information Bureau in New York, and wrote for *Asia* and *Harpers* on Australian subjects. For his part, Evatt sought advice from Grattan about the establishment of the Australian Embassy in Washington in 1942.[12]

On subsequent visits to New York, Evatt always found time for a visit to Grattan and his family, no matter how busy he was. In 1947, Grattan edited the book *Australia*, as part of the United Nations series. The chapters, by various contributors, revealed the scope of Grattan's interests and the extent of his acquaintance with specialists in the fields studied. Among those who contributed were Brian Fitzpatrick, S. J. Butlin, Lloyd Ross, Vance and Nettie Palmer, Bernard Smith and E. H. Burgmann. Grattan himself contributed a chapter on the social structure of Australia.

❖

In the early 1930s Mary Alice Evatt took art lessons at George Bell's School in Melbourne with Russell Drysdale and Peter Purves Smith. She also met Cynthia Reed, the owner of a modern design and furniture shop who, with her brother and sister-in-law, John and Sunday Reed, was a patron of aspiring young Australian artists. It was through Cynthia that Bert and Mary Alice were introduced to the young painter Sam Atyeo and his fellow-student Moya Dyring, both of whose experimental paintings drew on pictorial ideas derived from Cézanne and Picasso. They were to remain life-long friends of the Evatts, Sam later introducing Bert to Picasso in Paris in 1946.[13]

In Sydney, Mary Alice also took lessons at the George Street School of Grace Crowley and Rah Fizelle. Since she was a frequent visitor to Melbourne, travelling with Bert when he attended High Court sittings there, Mary Alice provided a vital link between the two art schools at a time when communication and travel by artists between the two cities was quite limited.

During a sojourn in Paris, in 1938, Mary Alice studied painting at a studio atelier in Montparnasse while Bert indulged his passion for art by haunting the Louvre and other galleries. In a letter to Vance Palmer, he remarked that 'my preference for the Moderns and the Primitives (is) entirely confirmed. Before Raphael the sureness of handling of fundamental colour was always evident and the rejection of irrelevant detail was merciless...The Moderns from Manet Van Gogh Cezanne Gaugin Toulouse Lautrec to Modigliani and Picasso have in substance restored to painting the clear beauty of the Primitives, using the spirit of the old genre'.[14]

In 1939, Bert Evatt opened the first exhibition of the Contemporary Art Society, held at the National Gallery of Victoria. It provoked controversy in the art world, coming after the founding of the conservative Australian Academy of Art in 1937, which was sponsored by R. G. Menzies. In his speech opening the exhibition, Evatt attacked the Academy for its 'unwarranted assumption of pontifical authority' and accused it of preventing progress, encouraging ossification, and discouraging genius.[15] As Geoffrey Dutton has remarked:

It was Evatt, not Menzies, who had the future of Australian art on his side. The artists showing at the Contemporary Art Society's Exhibition included Russell Drysdale, Sali Herman, Peter Purves Smith, Albert Tucker, James Gleeson, Noel Counihan, V.G. O'Connor, David Strachan and Sidney Nolan.[16]

The Evatts consistently bought paintings and drawings from struggling young artists such as Drysdale and Nolan, often giving them away to friends and relatives, to local councils and to art galleries.

In the second half of 1939, Sir Keith Murdoch, the managing director of the Melbourne *Herald*, brought to Melbourne an exhibition of French and British Modern Art. It was later taken to Sydney by the *Daily Telegraph*, where Margaret Preston and Bert Evatt were guide lecturers. It was from this exhibition that the Evatts purchased a painting by Modigliani, a portrait of the artist, Morgan Russell, as well as works by Soutine, Leger and Vlaminck.[17]

NOTES

1. H.V. Evatt, *Injustice within the Law*, Law Book Co, Sydney, 1937, pp. 2–3.
2. Ibid., pp. 42–3. Except where otherwise indicated, all quotations in this chapter are from Evatt's book.
3. E.H. Burgmann, Foreword to *Injustice within the Law*, p. viii; H.V. Evatt to Burgmann, 17 August 1933 and pamphlet entitled 'Justice', Bishop Burgmann Papers, MS.1998, Box 7—Eviction Case, NLA; E.H. Burgmann to Evatt, 19 August 1933, Evatt Collection, Flinders University.
4. Craig Munro, Introduction to P.R. Stephensen, *The Foundations of Culture in Australia*, Allen & Unwin, Sydney, 1986, pp. viii–ix.
5. Leonie Foster, *High Hopes: The Men and Motives of the Australian Round Table*, MUP, Melbourne ,1986, pp. 66–7.
6. Craig Munro, Introduction to P.R. Stephensen, op.cit., p.xiii.
7. E.E. Kisch, *Australian Landfall*, Macmillan, Melbourne, 1969, pp. 34, 68, 86.
8. C. Hartley Grattan Papers, Box 30, File 4; and Manuscript Notebook on Dr H.V. Evatt, page 40, Box 30, File 2, Harry Ransom Humanities Research Center (HRHRC), University of Texas at Austin.
9. Geoffrey Serle, *From Deserts the Prophets Come: The Creative Spirit in Australia 1788–1972*, Heinemann, Melbourne 1973, p. 238; L. Hergenhan, 'Recovering American Connections', *Overland*, 121, 1990, p. 73. See also Hergenhan's essay, 'The C. Hartley Grattan Manuscript Collection: A Critical Introduction', in Dave Oliphant (ed.), *Perspectives on Australia*, HRHRC, the University of Texas at Austin.
10. Miles Franklin to Evatt, 24 August 1940, Evatt Collection, Flinders University, file: High Court Resignation, 1940.
11. C. Hartley Grattan, 'Australian Labour Leader', in *Australian Quarterly*, vol. XII, no. 3, September 1940; Brian Fitzpatrick to Grattan, 28 September 1938, Box 37, file 2, C. Hartley Grattan Papers, HRHRC, University of Texas at Austin.
12. D.B. Bryson, 'C. Hartley Grattan: an American Intellectual and Reformer 1925–45—An Evaluation', BA Hons. thesis, Flinders University 1974.

13 Geoffrey Dutton, *The Innovators*, Macmillan, Melbourne, 1986, pp. 67-8; Richard Haese, *Rebels and Precursors: the Revolutionary Years in Australian Art*, Allen Lane, Melbourne 1988, pp. 20–1; Ken Buckley, Interview with Sam Atyeo, Vence, France, 20 Sept. 1988.
14 Evatt to Vance Palmer, 6 August 1938, Palmer Papers, MS. 1174, 1/5414, NLA.
15 Note by Frank Hinder in Cantwell Papers, MS.1919, ML.
16 G.Dutton, *The Innovators,* p.68.
17 Dutton, op.cit., pp. 57, 67; Interview with 'Bill' Cantwell, 7 June 1988.

CHAPTER 11

WRITING AUSTRALIAN HISTORY

Political Labour's struggle towards socialism is dependent upon Mill's hypothesis that mankind shall 'continue to improve'. At times the condition seems to be impossible of achievement...But victory may be at hand if only courageous leadership and loyal devotion both remain.
H.V. EVATT

The year 1938, which marked 150 years of European settlement, inspired the reappraisal of Australian history by two historians who were writing outside the academic establishment—Herbert Vere Evatt and Brian Fitzpatrick. Both were to adopt a radical revisionist perspective, Evatt in his *Rum Rebellion*, and Fitzpatrick in his *British Imperialism and Australia 1783–1833*. The two corresponded during the course of writing, Fitzpatrick sending Evatt a typescript copy of his book and Evatt offering an Introduction to it. Fitzpatrick agreed that 'the implications are ill understood, of the originating circumstances of Australian society, and I think my own interpretation will be strengthened—I believe you will be in accord with it—by your stressing your view in an introduction'. Moreover, he intended 'to take advantage of your permission, and use some of your facts and arguments in my *British Empire* thing. I agree that it would be a mistake to omit the important constitutional illustrations of the Imperial modes of exploiting Australia'.[1]

The story of the overthrow of Governor Bligh on 26 January 1808 undoubtedly attracted Evatt for a number of reasons. He had already examined the royal prerogative of colonial and State Governors in his doctoral thesis and in *The King and his Dominion Governors*, and as an undergraduate had written *Liberalism in Australia*. Bligh, moreover, had not been treated kindly by historians, and Evatt's sense of fair play and his concern for those wronged by powerful vested interests led him naturally to the defence of Bligh.

In Evatt's *Rum Rebellion*, Bligh was depicted as a high-minded and firm Governor acting in the broader public interest in his attempts to carry out faithfully his instructions from the English government by encouraging the small farmers. Yet he was 'the victim of a corrupt system, which, through combination, forestalling, monopoly and licentiousness, aggregated the wealth of the colony in the hands of a few unscrupulous men'.

According to historical tradition, 'Bligh was the tyrant, and Macarthur the hero who ended the tyranny'. What was required, according to Evatt, was a close examination of official historical records and a questioning of dogmatic statements and prior assumptions. These official records for New South Wales had been selected and edited in 1901, those for Australia in 1916, and in *Rum Rebellion* Evatt subjected them to the scrutiny of a critical legal mind, trained to detect inconsistencies and contradictions in evidence and the absence of incontestable facts.[2]

In 1931, George Mackaness, Evatt's former English teacher at Fort Street and an amateur historian, had published a two-volume life of Bligh. Although the work was comprehensive and overwhelming in its detail, Mackaness did not attempt to judge the legal disputes which, for Evatt, characterised the rebellion.

Other historians, such as Arthur Jose, had simply repeated the generally accepted version that it was Bligh's 'overbearing conduct' which had caused not only the mutiny against him on the *Bounty* but also the rebellion against him as Governor of New South Wales in 1808. According to Evatt, Bligh's opponents had skilfully disseminated propaganda against him both before and after the rebellion, and the correspondence they sent back to England was given credence by the influential political patrons of his opponents. W. C. Wentworth, who published *A Statistical, Historical and Political Account of New South Wales* in 1819, had repeated 'false and malicious rumours' that Bligh had been engaged with the merchant, Robert Campbell, in commercial speculations. Wentworth, however, was by no means an impartial commentator on the rebellion, his father d'Arcy having been dismissed by Bligh as an assistant surgeon to the New South Wales Corps for having illegally used convict labour on his property. Wentworth's 'tremendous invective', allied with his allegations against Bligh, influenced educated opinion in the early part of the nineteenth century, and were accepted as substantially correct. John Dunmore Lang, in his *History of New South Wales*, published in 1852, won praise from Evatt because he tried to redress the balance by attributing the causes of the rebellion to the misconduct of the military and trading groups, but he did not have access to the contemporary documents which Evatt had available to him.

The editor of *Historical Records of New South Wales*, published in 1901, F. M. Bladen (a barrister), is the subject of criticism by Evatt throughout his own book, not only for perpetuating the 'original legend' about the rebellion, but for being unwilling to 'handle it fearlessly'. He was 'never as generous to Bligh as he was generous to Macarthur and the officers of the Corps'.

Having established that previous writings on Bligh were flawed in some way, Evatt proceeded to give historians a lesson in historical method: the historian who is not trained in the science of legal investigation 'labours under a considerable handicap in reaching sound conclusions...for he is sometimes ready to accept documents at their face value, and to regard them as possessing equal significance. Often, he treats the letters of a person, subsequently made available to the public, as providing evidence as much in favour of the writers as against them'. Evatt clearly defined the techniques which he would bring to bear in his investigation into the overthrow of Bligh: the 'importance of credibility, of general character and of habit and system is increasingly recognised by the Courts'.[3]

The legal proceedings of the Johnston court martial held in England in 1811 provided key evidence for Evatt about Bligh's overthrow, because Macarthur, Johnston and Bligh were all present as witnesses subject to skilful cross-examination. Moreover, Evatt justified his focus on the proceedings of several cases which came before the Criminal Court of New South Wales prior to Bligh's overthrow by claiming that, because there was no legislature, no municipal government or independent press, the courts were 'the true forum of the little colony' where individual or public grievances could be expressed. The conflict between Bligh, who exercised a 'legal dictatorship' in favour of the farmers and poor settlers on the one hand, and Macarthur and the officers of the New South Wales Corps, characterised as 'wealthy traffickers and monopolists' on the other, thus 'necessarily assumed the form of legal contests'.

In the early chapters of the book, Evatt built up a very convincing case against John Macarthur, much as a barrister in court attacks the credibility of a witness for the prosecution. He described the way in which Macarthur and the officers of the New South Wales Corps undermined the authority of Governors Hunter and King, who preceded Bligh, and how the attacks on the three Governors were 'causally related'. In the case of King, Macarthur tried to get the officers of the New South Wales Corps to boycott the Governor. He in turn was determined to force Macarthur to leave the colony. King's lengthy despatch denouncing Macarthur to the Colonial Secretary, and accusing him of extortion and rapacity, went missing in transit to London, and Evatt concluded that either Macarthur or a close associate arranged for the document to be stolen or destroyed. As a result, Macarthur was able to state his case to authorities in London first, before King's side of the story could be heard.

Moreover, during his visit to England, Macarthur succeeded in gaining the patronage of Lord Camden, Secretary of State for the Colonies, who was impressed by Macarthur's plans for a wool industry. On his return to New South Wales in 1805, Macarthur carried a letter from Camden directing King to make a grant to him of 5000 acres of pasture. By this time, Governor King knew he was to be recalled, because of his constant differences with the military officers. According to Evatt, King regarded himself as 'utterly humiliated and defeated by Macarthur's double triumph'.

Having established the power of Macarthur within the colony, Evatt introduced the reader to Governor Bligh. Not only had Bligh been treated unkindly by historians but he had suffered condemnation from Hollywood in the 1930s film of the *Bounty* mutiny. Yet most of the evidence for Bligh's so-called 'tyranny' came from partisan sources. Bligh had acted with inflexible resolve to carry out orders, and his few disciplinary measures were not harsh when judged by contemporary standards.

Having examined Bligh's log book from the *Bounty*, Evatt admitted to 'a deep sense of respect and admiration, even of affection, for the man responsible for it', who loathed laziness and inefficiency, although his 'brusque and occasionally rude manner must have hindered his advancement'. Evatt acknowledged that such personality traits contributed to Bligh's downfall: 'the tragedy is that such faults of manner are as much calculated to cause disaster to true greatness as more serious blemishes of character'. Ironically, Evatt might well have been describing himself in this thumbnail sketch.

Evatt stressed the degree of public support for Bligh, the petitions received from the small landholders calling for free trade and the administration of justice by free settlers; his definite reform programme in the areas of police, the magistracy, public works, education and the prohibition of the rum traffic. It was Bligh's determination to proceed against those engaged in a sordid exercise in alcohol trafficking that brought about his overthrow. In order to explain how such a situation had arisen, Evatt analysed five leading court cases which preceded Bligh's overthrow. By this means he sought to demonstrate the tactics used by Macarthur to rally political and military support.

Recently, Evatt has been criticised for focusing too narrowly on these legal cases instead of canvassing the broader political and economic issues involved. Actually, Evatt dismissed the arguments of the economic historian, Edward Shann, who in 1930 had praised the New South Wales Corps officers and their associates for 'nobly fighting for trade and exchange freedom against quasi-socialism or communism'. Rather, Evatt asserted, it would be more accurate to regard Macarthur as 'the representative of the rising capitalist group...and the forces of combination and monopoly'. Moreover, in three of the cases which Evatt examined, he indicated that the motives of the accused were mainly financial.

Bligh was deposed shortly before Macarthur was due to stand trial for his defiance of the Governor. Evatt's reply to the question of whether Macarthur was guilty of sedition was that on two out of three counts, Macarthur would probably have been convicted by a jury acting honestly and reasonably if the trial had proceeded in January 1808. On the evidence, he intended 'to stir up disaffection against the Governor'.

According to Evatt, Macarthur and Lieutenant-Colonel Johnston, the commander of the New South Wales Corps, conspired to manufacture a false document, which called on Johnston to overthrow Bligh: most of the signatures on it appeared later, after the coup. Evatt, for his account of what happened in New South Wales from the time of Bligh's arrest to the time of his departure for England years later, relied on the transcripts from the court martial of Colonel Johnston, a source which none of his predecessors had used before. As a result, Evatt concluded that Johnston's evidence was 'false in important respects', although the full facts never became known to the court martial.

Macarthur himself avoided punishment by leaving the colony for England in 1809—Evatt claimed that 'it is almost certain that he received legal advice that if he returned to NSW he would do so with a noose around his neck'. Both Macarthur and Johnston had a powerful patron in the Duke of Northumberland. Johnston was found guilty of mutiny by a general court martial in England in 1811, and was sentenced to be cashiered. Undoubtedly, said Evatt, the mitigation of his punishment was due to the opinion that Johnston had acted as the mere instrument of Macarthur who was beyond the reach of the court, as he was not subject to military law. Nevertheless, Macarthur remained in self-imposed exile in England for eight years.

The authors of the first major study of the subject since Evatt have acknowledged that *Rum Rebellion* made an 'enduring contribution' to the debate on the rebellion and its causes.[4] Some historians, however, have criticised Evatt for his partiality towards Bligh and his hostility towards Macarthur; for his harsh condemnation of the character of the New South Wales Corps; and for his failure to recognise that the extent of economic and social change in New South Wales by 1806 had rendered Bligh's vision of a static, agrarian society, rather than a pastoral economy, unworkable.[5]

Evatt ignored evidence that Bligh had started his own private farm in the Hawkesbury district with land granted to him by Governor King, and that he maintained it with provisions from the government stores and convict labour—although that was an activity for which Evatt condemned the officers of the New South Wales Corps. Bligh, moreover, had an interest in supporting Andrew Thompson, his farm manager, against Macarthur in a court case, but Evatt failed to mention the association.

Nevertheless, for Evatt and for Brian Fitzpatrick, the officer-traders deserved condemnation because, by controlling the price of spirits, the colony's unofficial currency, and using the labour of convicts fed and clothed from government stores, they had established a monopoly which benefited them rather than the economy as a whole.[6]

Evatt took the high moral ground by criticising the New South Wales Corps for its excesses and by exaggerating the extent of the criminal element among its members, but recent historical research indicates that the officers and men of the Corps were no worse than those of other British regiments on overseas duty at the time, and that the local convict component and ex-military prison recruits made up 'only' 20 per cent of the total. Moreover, apart from the ringleaders, most of the officers who took part in Bligh's overthrow in 1808 were not those who had been associated with the officer-trading monopoly which had reached its peak in 1798. Nevertheless, by focusing on the ringleaders such as Johnston, Evatt identified those who by long service and established networks were clearly the most influential.[7]

The strong defence of Bligh's character and actions which Evatt mounted in *Rum Rebellion* precluded him from making a balanced assessment. There is no doubt that Bligh's personality, displayed in his self-righteousness, rigidity and authoritarian manner played an important part in isolating him from potentially powerful supporters in the colony, such as the wealthy emancipist traders. However, Evatt deserves praise for his awareness of the political role of the courts. As David Neal, a lawyer-historian says, Australian historiography has not reflected Evatt's insight about the importance of the rule of law in the colony's politics: in the absence of representative institutions, the courts served 'as a de facto parliament', providing a 'public forum both for opposition to the governor's policy, and for the governor to have his authority underlined...Law became the means of expressing and contesting the differing conceptions of social and economic relations in the colony'. Indeed, it was only when it appeared that Bligh had legally cornered Macarthur that Bligh was deposed.[8]

In his Introduction to Brian Fitzpatrick's *British Imperialism and Australia, 1783–1833*, published in 1939, the year after *Rum Rebellion*, Evatt acknowledged the importance of economic interpretation of Australia's early history. The penal settlement of Australia was not a closed economic system but was always subject to the control of the English government of the day, which 'sought to protect what it considered to be the economic interests of the governing classes of England'.[9]

Moreover, of fundamental importance was the appropriation of the Crown lands of the colony:

The partial adoption of the Wakefield scheme discouraged the poorer settler, shattered the labourer's hopes of land ownership, and deliberately manufactured a proletariat for the purpose of supporting and extending capitalist technique. This led to vital social and political changes...[10]

Those 'vital social and political changes' led on to the emergence of the Labor Party, and it was this subject which was to command Evatt's attention in his next book, published in 1940, *Australian Labour Leader: The Story of W. A. Holman and the Labour Movement*.

While still writing the book on Holman, Evatt took sabbatical leave from the High Court, and in April 1938 he sailed to England with his wife Mary Alice. The trip was not merely an overseas working holiday, nor was its main purpose to extend the judge's contacts with the legal fraternity. There was also a political dimension, judging from some letters of introduction which Evatt carried with him. A letter from W. Forgan Smith, Labor Premier of Queensland, to Clement Attlee, Leader of the British Labour Party, mentioned that Evatt was 'desirous of meeting prominent members of the Labour Party'. Another letter was from the Labor Premier of Tasmania, A. G. Ogilvie, to Sir Walter Citrine, secretary of the British Trades Union Congress, stating that Evatt would be 'making a study of conditions abroad'.[11] At a lunch at Cambridge University later, he was entertained by Stafford Cripps and also met Nehru and Ernest Bevin.[12]

Before leaving Australia, Evatt had been appointed a representative of the Australian Board of Control at the Imperial Cricket Conference. Not only did this allow him to contribute to the administration of a game of which he was a devotee, but it also gave him an opportunity to make useful social and political contacts for the future.

In October 1938, Evatt spent a week at the Harvard Law School, giving a lecture on labour relations and methods of arbitration, and conducting discussions with faculty members. Dean Erwin Griswold, then a junior member of staff at Harvard, recalls that he was 'very much impressed by him at the time...he seemed to have a flexibility and a breadth of outlook which was not always found in British judges, including some Australian'.[13]

Felix Frankfurter, a friend and confidant of President Franklin D. Roosevelt, was a Professor of Law at Harvard at the time, and he arranged for Evatt to meet the President. There is no record of the conversation, but in the Evatt collection at Flinders University there is a letter from Roosevelt thanking Evatt for the copy of *Rum Rebellion* which had been forwarded to him. The President noted that 'it was a pleasant reminder of our conversation last October. This work is clearly a noteworthy contribution to Australian history, and I assure you that it will be a valuable addition to my library'.[14]

Felix Frankfurter, who was appointed to the United States Supreme Court in 1939, was one of the most important informal diplomatic contacts in Washington for many foreign diplomats, by virtue of his close ties with Roosevelt. Evatt was to renew the acquaintance in February 1942, when Australia needed American help.

———❖———

W. A. Holman died in 1934, without having published his memoirs, and Evatt, in his biography of the man, made extensive use of Holman's unpublished reminiscences which ran to several hundred pages, as well as other private papers such as those of W. M. Hughes and D. R. Hall, who were both still alive at the time. Another major source was the *Australian Worker* and, in his Preface, Evatt acknowledged his debt to its editor, H. E. Boote.

Substantial research was required for Evatt's *Australian Labour Leader,* a book of 574 pages, which surveyed the political landscape of New South Wales from 1891 to 1934 and Holman's place in it. No doubt Evatt was able to gain easy access to research material by virtue of his position as President of the Board of Trustees of the Public and Mitchell Libraries, but he also relied heavily on the assistance of barristers Keith and John Brennan and of his associate Percy Burgess, whom he thanked in the Preface.

Evatt arranged the material into a chronological narrative, beginning with the arrival in Australia in 1888 of the seventeen-year-old William Holman. In a letter to Vance Palmer, who had written a critique of the manuscript, Evatt justified the technique he had adopted:

My theory of writing was this: to collect the facts, select them and reject them on the basis of relevance and to separate my conclusions and opinions from the narrative ...Therefore, if your opinion does not correspond entirely to my own, that is the type of result at which I was specifically aiming. I have undoubtedly allowed personal knowledge and sympathy to find a place in my judgment...Brian Fitzpatrick said something like this unconsciously when he wrote that 'it looked as though two different people combined to write the book'. The procedure I adopted meant exactly that...[15]

In his efforts to achieve objectivity, Evatt assiduously excluded his own name from the narrative, even where he was personally involved, for example, in the Walsh–Johnson cases of 1925–26.

The first half of the book was devoted to Holman's early years in the labour movement, through the 1890s and up to the election in New South Wales of the Labor government of J. S. T. McGowen, in which Holman was Attorney-General. The amount of space taken up by this early period indicates the importance Evatt attached to Holman's role as a grass-roots organiser in the movement, his perseverance in spite of setbacks and his skill in appealing to a broad cross-section of society. As the Labor Party sought to gain office in its own right, socialist doctrines were thrust into the background, and greater emphasis was placed on liberal, radical or reformist proposals which appealed to a wider audience, 'including Irish Catholic and Australian Nationalist groups'.[16]

Moreover, Evatt obviously identified to some extent with Holman who achieved fame without money or influence, and who possessed 'great courage, a first-class brain, an endless capacity for hard work, a fine physical appearance, a magnificent speaking voice, and, above all, a compassionate heart'.[17]

The focus of the book was very clearly on the role of individuals in the history of the labour movement:

What was achieved by Australian Labour was achieved by men of courage, imagination and integrity. Similarly, where there was failure, it was caused or contributed to by the weakness and errors of individuals.[18]

In Evatt's view, Holman's greatest achievement as Premier was his creation of State enterprises such as the State brickworks, metal quarries, and the Monier pipe and reinforced concrete works to compete with private monopolies which had been overcharging the public and the government. Praise for Holman's talents as a parliamentary tactician, outwitting the conservatives in the Legislative Assembly, was tempered by criticism of his failure to press home

Labor's advantage: in the early years, when he had public support, he should have secured the appointment by the Governor of additional members to the Legislative Council for Labor's policies to be implemented. Evatt blamed Holman's inaction on the refusal of the Labor Party to condone the nomination to the Council of his friend and supporter, the raffish entrepreneur H. D. McIntosh, sports promoter and newspaper proprietor. McIntosh's influence on Holman was merely hinted at by Evatt, probably because McIntosh was still alive when the book was published. For instance, he financed Holman's trip to England in 1913, and this appeared to place Holman under an obligation to him.

According to Evatt, Holman was a socialist by intellectual conviction, but he was hindered by institutional barriers. Labor's programme had to be implemented 'within the forms and framework of a capitalist society', where legal and constitutional barriers impeded to some extent. As Evatt put it: in Australian Labour's history, too little of socialist doctrine was quite as dangerous as too much. For leaders like Holman, a choice was difficult. Political victory would be prejudiced if the cry of 'Red' or 'Socialist' or 'Extremists' could be used to frighten the middle-class voter; on the other hand, the workers might lose faith in political Labour if opportunism and expediency replaced firm adherence to important socialist objectives.[19]

Once Holman began to enjoy the luxuries of public office, he lost touch with the common people and neglected the rank-and-file in the Party. He was impatient of restraint from the decisions of Labor conferences, and occasionally ignored them: 'he tended to regard his personal opinions on tactics (as well as on policy) as basic tenets of the whole labour organization'.[20]

Holman had very little personal experience with trade unions and had a hostility towards their use of the strike as a weapon. The great strike of August 1917 occurred while he was in England and after he had left the Labor Party, but he could not be exonerated from some blame for the harsh reprisals against railwaymen condoned by his deputy, Fuller. The trial and imprisonment of the IWW twelve was an over-reaction to a perceived threat in wartime, but was further evidence of the illiberal and anti-labour tendencies of both the federal and state governments. Evatt allowed this to pass without condemning Holman.

On the constitutional issue of Commonwealth versus State powers, Holman set himself at odds with the federal Labor Party. When Hughes sought to increase the powers of the Commonwealth against monopolies by referendum in 1911, and again in 1913, Holman voiced his opposition. He feared that the more progressive legislation and better wages and conditions in New South Wales would be jeopardised by forcing conformity with lower standards in other States. His influence on the rejection of the proposals was considerable.

Evatt devoted almost one quarter of the book to the war years 1914–18, and the issue of conscription and the split in the Labor Party. However, he tried not to apportion blame, showing that there was intransigence on both sides.

It is perhaps understandable that Evatt left the reader to judge, given that in 1940 many of the participants in the anti-conscription struggle were still active in federal politics, and indeed were in powerful positions in the ALP—Curtin and Calwell for instance. However, he did not make a coherent and thorough analysis of the conscription issue 1916–17, nor did he successfully explain why, by his own estimate, Labor's two greatest leaders, Hughes and Holman, could not reconcile their ambitions and ideals with the conformity required by the Labor Party machine. Evatt blamed the war for causing a 'catastrophic cessation' of the progressive legislation Labor had introduced. At the outbreak of war, Holman, an avowed Francophile, diverted his energies into patriotic activities, establishing a network of recruiting agencies.

Evatt found it 'amazing' that Holman's break from the Labor Party should have been final, 'for opposition to compulsory military service had never been an essential feature of Socialist or Labour policy in Australia'. What he did not sufficiently emphasise, however, was that many of those who had earlier supported compulsory military service did so on the assumption that it would only be given full effect if Australia itself was directly threatened. Conscription for overseas service was a different matter, and Evatt did not make the distinction emphatically enough. As Vance Palmer told him, those who opposed conscription questioned the rightness of fighting an enemy in France, but 'obviously Hughes and Holman, both recent arrivals, wouldn't feel this as instinctively as the bulk of the working class who had known no other country'. Evatt's reticence may perhaps be explained by Australia's reliance in 1939–40 on the recruitment of volunteers for overseas service.[21]

In examining the decision of Hughes and Holman to leave the Labor Party, Evatt modified his criticism of them by asserting that they were misled by others about the success of the recruitment drives in 1916–17. He implied that conscription was unnecessary anyway, and that it was tragic that other options could not have been explored.

Holman's transition to Nationalist Premier was described quite dispassionately by Evatt, including the fact that he immediately proceeded to obtain twenty-three nominations to the Legislative Council from the Governor. That his skills as a parliamentary tactician were thenceforth used to organise the employers and their political representatives was noted without comment. Rather, the focus was on Holman's declining prestige, with revelations of maladministration and scandals involving corruption in the awarding of government contracts. While, as Evatt remarked, Holman did not personally gain, he showed errors of judgement.

In the concluding chapters, Holman's career as a barrister after his defeat in the State election of 1920, and his membership of federal parliament as a Nationalist backbencher 1931–34, are discussed within the context of State and federal politics in the 1920s. Evatt skilfully charted the rise of the Country Party and the resulting shift to the right by the Nationalists, which left Hughes and Holman isolated and powerless.

Evatt's biography of Holman was flawed in some respects. It was praised by book-reviewers but was not enthusiastically greeted by everyone in the labour movement. Brian Fitzpatrick, though unwilling to offend Evatt, evidently felt that the author dealt too tenderly with Holman—who, in Labor terminology, was a 'rat' who deserted the Party. Evatt's sweeping assertions that Holman changed 'the entire outlook' of the citizens of New South Wales on political problems and that he was 'the first Australian statesman to inaugurate a planned economy for the social and material advancement of a whole State' were open to question.[22]

Nevertheless, the book was a remarkable achievement. In effect, it was contemporary history, written by someone who had lived through much of the period under consideration. Furthermore, for a person who had been actively involved in politics to produce a scholarly study of the subject was a very difficult task. Yet Evatt did so, in a manner unmatched by writer-participants in the half-century since then. It is no detraction from the accomplishment to remark that in writing the book, Evatt had personal reasons for preoccupation with the difficulties faced by leaders of the Labor Party. He had in mind the possibility of once more entering the political area himself.

Despite Holman's ultimate failure, Evatt ended his book on an optimistic note. In what may be seen as a political manifesto, he wrote:

Political Labour's struggle towards socialism is dependent upon Mill's hypothesis that mankind shall 'continue to improve'. At times the condition seems to be impossible of achievement...But victory may be at hand if only courageous leadership and loyal devotion both remain.[23]

In 1979, another Labor leader, Neville Wran (Premier of New South Wales) contributed a significant Foreword to an abridged edition of *Australian Labour Leader*. While paying tribute to Evatt's

writing—'the book retains its original freshness, grace and style'—
Wran made particular reference to Evatt's account of the Labor Party
split in 1916 and compared it with the later split of 1955, in which
Evatt played a major part. Although 'the spirit of disinterestedness
was absent' among protagonists on both occasions, the split of 1955
was not inevitable in Wran's view: 'splits which involve no fundamental issue of principle, but merely reflect an excess of factionalism,
can never be condoned or justified'.[24]

Thus, Wran implicitly criticised Evatt's role. Yet it should be noted
that Wran has always been a pragmatist, never more than marginally
interested in what Evatt referred to as 'Labour's struggle towards
socialism'. In this context, Wran begged the question. For Evatt and
his supporters, the issue at stake in the struggle against the Industrial
Groupers in the Party in 1955, as shown later in this volume, was
indeed one of principle, going to the heart of Labor's hopes and
aspirations.

NOTES

1 Brian Fitzpatrick to H.V. Evatt, 10 July 1937, Evatt Collection, Flinders University, file: Fitzpatrick, Brian; Fitzpatrick to Evatt, 1 April 1939, Evatt Collection, Flinders University, File: Publications—*The King and his Dominion Governors*—Letters of Thanks (b).
2 H.V. Evatt, *Rum Rebellion: A Study of the Overthrow of Governor Bligh by John Macarthur and the New South Wales Corps*, Angus & Robertson, Sydney 1938, pp. 352,1.
3 Ibid., pp. 6–9 ,13–14. Except where otherwise indicated, subsequent quotations in this chapter are from Evatt, *Rum Rebellion*.
4 Ross Fitzgerald and Mark Hearn, *Bligh, Macarthur and the Rum Rebellion*, Kangaroo Press, Sydney, 1988, p. 18.
5 W.G. McMinn, 'Explaining a Rebellion: an Historiographical Enquiry', *Teaching History*, vol. 4 pt. 1, May 1970, 36–8.
6 Fitzgerald and Hearn, op.cit, pp. 17, 70–1; A.G.L. Shaw, article on Bligh in *ADB*, vol. 1; B. Fitzpatrick, *British Imperialism and Australia, 1783–1833*, 2nd edn, Sydney University Press, Sydney, 1971, p. 95.
7 T.G. Parsons, 'Courts Martial, the Savoy Military Prison and the NSW Corps', *Journal of the Royal Australian Historical Society*, 63, March 1978, 4; P. Statham, 'A New Look at the NSW Corps, 1790–1810', *Australian Economic History Review*, XXX, March 1990, 54.
8 David Neal, *The Rule of Law in a Penal Colony: Law and Power in Early New South Wales*, CUP, Cambridge, 1991, pp. 21–4.
9 Evatt, Introduction to Fitzpatrick, op.cit., pp. 7–8.
10 Ibid., p. 9.

11 W. Forgan Smith to C. Attlee, 11 April 1938, Evatt Collection, Flinders University—File: Overseas Trip 1938. A.G. Ogilvie to Sir Walter Citrine, 19 April 1938, Evatt Collection, Flinders University.
12 Kylie Tennant, *Evatt*, p. 102.
13 Dean Erwin Griswold to Justice Michael Kirby, 9 August 1990, in Justice Kirby's private collection.
14 Franklin D. Roosevelt to Evatt, 4 August 1939, Evatt Collection, Flinders University, File: Evatt Publications—*Rum Rebellion* Correspondence.
15 Evatt to Vance Palmer, 2 February 1940, Vance and Nettie Palmer Papers, MS.1174/1/5694, NLA.
16 H.V. Evatt, *Australian Labour Leader: The Story of W.A. Holman and the Labour Movement*, Angus & Robertson, Sydney, 2nd edn, 1942, Introduction, p. 2.
17 Evatt, *Australian Labour Leader*, p. 571.
18 Ibid., p. 4.
19 Ibid., pp. 569–70.
20 Ibid., p. 573.
21 Ibid., p. 571; Vance Palmer to Evatt, 13 December 1939, Evatt Collection, Flinders University, File: Evatt—Publications—*Australian Labour Leader*.
22 Evatt, *Australian Labour Leader*, p.570.
23 Ibid; p. 574.
24 H.V. Evatt, *William Holman*, Angus & Robertson, Sydney, abridged edition 1979, Foreword by Neville Wran.

PART III

WAR, AND POST-WAR RECONSTRUCTION

CHAPTER 12

FROM HIGH COURT TO PARLIAMENT

It's little use talking about Chamberlain and his gang—they are really sympathetic with Fascism because their one fear is insecurity through Socialism. Money first and to hell with their own country. Even Palmerston's jingoism was better than this black treachery.

H. V. EVATT

Moving now to the period of World War II, there was no significant Australian objection to joining Britain in war against Germany in September 1939. Nevertheless, there were still deep divisions in the community. Among conservatives, the United Australia Party belied its name: its leader, Menzies, was out of favour with an important section of the Melbourne financial/industrial establishment which organised the funding of the UAP; and there was serious friction between the UAP and its natural ally, the Country Party. Menzies himself, in the 'phoney war' period, maintained his pre-war desire for appeasement of Germany. Privately he hoped for a soft peace with Germany but he did not say this publicly for fear of opposition from the Australian press and some members of his own Cabinet.

On the labour side, there were bitter memories of the 1930s depression, and many workers anticipated making gains against employers in the improved employment position due to the war. Within Labor ranks, there was still strong dissension between factions, particularly in New South Wales. This was a sequel to the situation in 1931, when a group of federal Labor MPs from New South Wales—including J. Beasley, thereafter known as 'stabber Jack'—turned against the Scullin government. A special conference of the ALP retaliated by expelling the New South Wales State executive from the party. Despite this, Lang Labor supporters, defying federal authority, remained in control of the State party (and the associated group of federal Labor MPs) for some years. Gradually, however, the authoritarian Lang political machine declined in strength—the ALP remained out of government in New South Wales for nearly a decade from 1932 and in 1937 it was challenged by the formation of a faction known as Heffron (Industrial) Labor. This group secured considerable support from trade unions and enjoyed some success in State by-elections. Thus Clive Evatt won the seat of Hurstville in Sydney in March 1939.

Although H. V. Evatt kept aloof from party politics in the 1930s, he knew about these developments from his brother and other sources. The general picture of Labor faction-fighting was a depressing one, but Evatt was certainly interested in the proceedings of an ALP unity conference held in Sydney in August 1939. This was shortly before the outbreak of war, although it was clear that war was approaching. At the conference, the Heffron group (led by Hughes and Evans) was in a majority, and Lang's supporters were defeated in elections to the State executive. Then the ALP parliamentary caucus elected W. J. McKell as its leader in New South Wales. This ousting of Lang marked a decisive turning point in his position in the party, although he remained influential in a spoiling role.

While the unity conference was still in session, Bert Evatt wrote to Vance Palmer in Melbourne. The letter contained an intriguing statement: 'As to politics, they have formally asked me to stand: but I am rather disinclined as I think I could never stand up to the racket of it all'. 'They' were not identified, and there is no indication from other sources of a possible entry by Evatt into politics at the State level. It seems very unlikely that he would have been attracted to such an idea, and nothing came of it. If Evatt were to return to political life, it would be through federal parliament, as became clear in his subsequent private talks with friends and acquaintances.[1]

The friends ranged from Claude McKay, formerly editor of *Smith's Weekly*, to E. H. Burgmann, Anglican Bishop of Goulburn, but Evatt's closest political confidant at this time was probably H. E. Boote, a dedicated socialist. Boote was highly respected in the labour movement as a man of strong principles—manifest in the anti-conscription campaign in World War I—and he was still influential as editor of the *Australian Worker*. He was a trustee of the Public Library of New South Wales and a member of the Mitchell Library committee, whilst Evatt was President of the Public Library from 1937; and the two men often had a cup of tea or coffee together after meetings. Boote kept a personal diary, in which he recorded, for example, that on 13 February 1940 Evatt 'expressed very radical views—for a High Court Judge—on both local and world situations'. Boote did not exaggerate. A year earlier, Evatt wrote to Vance Palmer about the struggle against Fascism in the Spanish Civil War, adding:

It's little use talking about Chamberlain and his gang—they are really sympathetic with Fascism because their one fear is insecurity through Socialism. Money first and to hell with their own country. Even Palmerston's jingoism was better than this black treachery.[2]

These were strong views, which would have been unacceptable to many Labor leaders, let alone High Court judges. The letter also shows that Evatt's intense interest in foreign affairs antedates World War II and his appointment as Australia's External Affairs Minister. Incidentally, the determined anti-Fascist stand of Communists as part of united fronts in Australia and other countries probably disposed Evatt to regard them with friendly feelings in the years leading up to 1939. The sympathy was not entirely dissipated when Australian Communists, in line with their comrades elsewhere, abruptly reversed their attitude towards the war against Germany. Communist parties, after initially supporting the war effort, decided in the light of the German–Soviet non-aggression pact that the war was really imperialist in character and therefore could not be supported by workers.

Evatt had no sympathy with this view, which gave priority to Soviet interests over those of Australia. Nevertheless, he knew that there were grounds for thinking that Stalin entered into the non-aggression pact with Hitler as an expression of *realpolitik*, after Britain and France had procrastinated in negotiations with the Soviet Union to reach an anti-Fascist agreement earlier in 1939. The point was put to Evatt at some length in a letter sent to him in September 1939 by an Australian living in Britain. This friend, a journalist, also expressed an opinion that many big businessmen and politicians in Britain had 'always been prepared to make a deal with the Nazis...I fail to see what is to deter them again from reaching a compromise with Hitler'.[3]

There were parallels in Australia at this time. Menzies, who continued to regard Germany as a bulwark against the Soviet Union, wrote to S. M. Bruce, Australian High Commissioner in London, about the desirability of 'a new alignment of nations in which not only Great Britain and France, but Germany and Italy, combined to resist Bolshevism'. Evatt was unaware that Menzies was writing in these terms, but the judge was still suspicious about the British government's intentions concerning Russia. When the Russians attacked Finland, Evatt wrote to C.R. Attlee, leader of the British Labour Party, querying the policy of the party. Attlee replied that Labour in Britain was 'very much alive to the war against Fascism being switched over to a war against Russia', but that the party felt obliged to condemn aggression by Russia or any other power.[4]

The federal electoral prospects of the ALP received a fillip early in 1940. When Menzies appointed R. G. Casey as Australian Minister at Washington, Casey had to resign from his parliamentary seat of Corio, which was won decisively for Labor by J. J. Dedman in the ensuing by-election. Boote noted in his diary on 3 March 1940:

Evatt rang to talk about Labor win at Corio, and its probable effect on the political situation. He is still contemplating leaving the Bench and breaking into politics again. Would rather be in the hurly-burly of the House of Reps. than in the austere atmosphere of the High Court.

Through such men as G. Buckland (an AWU official who was also a member of the federal executive of the ALP), Boote sounded out the prospects for a return to political life by Evatt. Others involved included McKell, who was said to be in constant touch with Evatt about his mooted re-entry into politics. The path was far from smooth. For one thing, Evatt was not a member of the ALP—indeed, he had been expelled from it many years earlier—yet Party rules required candidates for pre-selection to have three years membership immediately prior to nomination. The only exception to this rule was an invitation from the executive of the party to contest a seat—and there were some Labor leaders who had doubts about Evatt's political standpoint. Boote recorded that A. S. McAlpine, Vice-President of the New South Wales Labor Council, had told him that

...it was being said about the Trades Hall and in inner Labor circles, that Evatt was going to leave the High Court Bench to lead an attack on those now in control of the ALP and infuse a more militant spirit into the party. Evatt himself has never said anything like that to me, though he has strongly criticised the present party leaders.[5]

Boote's assessment of Evatt's position was balanced. The judge was very critical of Lang and his supporters, yet he told Boote that 'if Lang broke away at the Easter Conference and formed another party, and ran candidates, it would make a difference in his [Evatt's] intentions, as he wouldn't care to find himself involved in a faction fight. He thinks the Beasley group very corrupt'. Lang did in fact form a breakaway Australian Labor Party (Non-Communist) in New South Wales in April 1940.[6]

Another serious problem which arose at the Easter conference of the State ALP concerned a resolution which denounced conservative attempts to switch the war's direction towards action against the Soviet Union. This became known as the 'Hands Off Russia' resolution, reflecting the strength of the left-wing Hughes–Evans group, which was said to be under Communist influence. There was a substantial amount of truth in this allegation, although Boote and Evatt—neither of them Communist—both reckoned the resolution to be worthy of support. John Curtin, federal leader of the ALP, thought differently. He considered the resolution to be costly to the party in terms of public opinion, and the federal executive ordered the New South Wales State executive to expunge the 'Hands off Russia' resolution from the minutes of the Easter conference.

Boote commented in his diary on 12 April 1940 that the federal executive order was a 'cowardly surrender to the capitalist press and politicians, in my opinion, and to the anti-Red and Catholic Action reactionaries in our own ranks'. Shortly after, Boote recorded that Evatt was 'entirely on my side as regards the big questions of the day, including international policy...The Judge is still ready to quit the Bench and enter politics...He would be a great acquisition to the Federal Party'. It is interesting to note in this connection Katharine Susannah Prichard's recollection that Evatt told her, before he left the High Court, that he was going to enter the political arena because he hoped 'to help the ALP to implement its platform'. She understood him to mean a socialist policy going much beyond winning the war.[7]

The German invasion of France and other European countries in May 1940 marked transition to a much more deadly phase of the war. One result was the replacement of Chamberlain by Churchill as British Prime Minister, which in effect put paid to Menzies' lingering hopes for a soft peace with Germany. At the same time, the Menzies government felt free to use the war situation to impose certain restrictions in Australia. First, the publication of a number of left-wing papers was banned; and then, in June 1940, the Communist Party and several other small groups were declared unlawful under National Security (Subversive Associations) regulations. There was some justification for these actions, in the light of the one-eyed Communist attitude towards the 'imperialist' war—the Soviet annexation of the Baltic states and other territories could equally be regarded as imperialist by non-Communists. On the other hand, Menzies was not loth to avenge the defeats suffered by conservative governments in the 1930s in their attempts to suppress allegedly subversive organisations.

The State executive of the ALP in New South Wales remained recalcitrant in dealings with the federal executive of the party concerning both the 'Hands off Russia' episode and Curtin's acceptance of a government amendment of the National Security Act which authorised industrial and military conscription in Australia. Then, in August 1940, the federal executive suspended the State executive and replaced it with a new one loyal to Curtin. Boote commented on this struggle:

Had lunch with Mr Justice Evatt…He is strongly on the side of the State Executive [the Hughes–Evans group] against the Federal body. His intention to re-enter politics was temporarily abandoned, he said, because of the split in the Labor Party. He wouldn't take part in a faction fight.[8]

Evatt's hesitation on this score helps to explain why, after the federal executive on 26 August decided unanimously to invite him to contest the seat of Barton on behalf of the ALP in the forthcoming election, he delayed for three days before accepting the offer and resigning from the High Court. Actually, Labor leaders were not offering Evatt very much. The Barton seat, in the southern suburbs of Sydney, had been held by a UAP politician for the past nine years, and although there was a general belief that Evatt could win it, not one Labor MP or candidate for a safer seat was willing to withdraw in his favour. Nevertheless, Evatt decided that if he were to change the whole course of his life it was now or never. His self-esteem was also boosted by publication and favourable reviews of his book, *Australian Labour Leader*, that year.

Evatt was not the only High Court judge who felt that a greater contribution to the war effort could be made by transferring to some other sphere of work. Earlier in August 1940, Chief Justice Latham—who had a sympathetic appreciation of Japanese interests, as against Chinese—was appointed Australian Minister to Japan; and in 1942 Justice Dixon accepted a similar diplomatic post in the United States of America. In both these cases, the judges were given official leave of absence from the Court and they returned to it in due course. Evatt, however, had to burn his boats behind him: it was unlikely that Menzies would offer him a diplomatic position, and it was necessary for Evatt to resign from the Court in order to stand for parliamentary election. His immediate reward was to receive congratulations from many people for his 'courage' and 'sacrifice'. Among the letters was one from a young barrister, Richard Kirby, who wrote that the resignation conveyed a delightful realisation:

Life still offers scope for magnificent actions and if talk at the Bar means anything your action has inspired the profession—tories included—when one thought inspiration was dead for ever.

It makes one realise that the legal profession and the race for the bench is not and should not be the be-all and end-all of one's aims.[9]

One of Evatt's first public statements in his election campaign was to the effect that party politics—and 'still less intra-party divisions'—should not be allowed to frustrate the war effort or stand in the way of attempts to improve social and economic conditions. However, Evatt recognised no contradiction between this and his own public attacks upon Menzies and the pre-war appeasement policy. In Evatt's words: 'Every bomb that now falls on London comes as a shattering proof that Mr Chamberlain was wrong and that Mr Menzies and his predecessors were wrong.' Menzies responded: 'I thoroughly agreed with what Chamberlain did at Munich and I still agree with what he did.'[10]

It is pertinent at this point to refer to a significant aspect of Menzies' early career, in contrast to Evatt's. Menzies, of course, was well known as a lawyer and a conservative politician. Less obvious were his links with big business. There was an instructive episode in 1935 on the occasion of a visit by Prime Minister Lyons and Menzies to London. In a dinner-speech there, Menzies was reported as saying that as the London-based banks which operated in Australia had become the object of political controversy, they 'could not go on saying indefinitely that they took no part in political controversy'. This encouragement to banks to come out more openly on the conservative political side may be regarded as a prelude to the great struggle over bank nationalisation more than a decade later, in which Evatt and Menzies fought on opposite sides.[11]

On his visit to London in 1935, Menzies may also have impressed big English insurance companies which did business in Australia and had connections with banks. Certainly, at the end of the year Menzies was appointed as a Melbourne director of the London-based Commercial Union Assurance Co. Ltd. This was in line with the practice of the English companies to appoint subsidiary boards of directors to advise on local affairs. No doubt Menzies' legal advice was useful. Indeed, he had expertise in the area, having been engaged some years earlier to give a legal opinion as to whether a move to establish a government insurance office in South Australia could be blocked in court. He advised that such obstructive action was likely to succeed. As far as is known, Evatt never became a director of any business, although he often gave free legal advice to his Labor parliamentary colleagues on personal problems from the 1940s onwards.

Evatt campaigned in style for the federal election held in September 1940. It is said that he spent £1500 from his own pocket to make up for receiving little financial assistance from the party's federal campaign committee. In the Barton constituency, enthusiastic supporters (who included Jessie Street, a prominent feminist) distributed an impressive brochure, entitled *Every Man the Maker of His Own Career*, which extolled Evatt's achievements from school days onwards. Indeed, the title was a translation of the Fort Street school motto. At a national level, he received extensive publicity from press and radio—it was not uncommon for a politician to become a judge, but a reversal of the process was unprecedented. In the event, Evatt as the official Labor candidate won the Barton seat easily, receiving 35 425 votes against 21 845 for the retiring MP. Two rival candidates, for Non-Communist Labor and State Labor, polled negligible votes. More generally, Evatt's prestige contributed to ALP gains in the election. However, the successes were more or less confined to New South Wales and were not sufficient to win government for Labor: the Menzies government remained in office, though dependent upon support from two independent MPs.

Winning a seat in the House of Representatives was only the first step for Evatt. He was determined not to be merely a backbencher. The aim was to play an important role in government, and as it was not feasible to form a Labor government after the election, Evatt was attracted to the idea of an all-party national government. This was a proposition floated by Menzies (who envisaged himself leading it) and rejected by Curtin and other Labor leaders. Evatt was so impatient after the election that he antagonised his own colleagues. Boote noted:

He has given the press an 11-point policy for a National Government! Points are taken from the policy put forward by the Labor Party for a Labor Government. Has Evatt so soon forgotten that Labor is strongly opposed to joining a Capitalist Ministry...I could sense that he is eager to be a Minister and that his eagerness governed his line of reasoning.[12]

After considerable discussion, in the course of which Evatt called for a national government to be led by a Prime Minister other than Menzies, the idea of an all-party government was shelved. Instead, Menzies agreed to the formation of an Advisory War Council, which would include some Labor representatives among its members. Evatt was dissatisfied with this outcome, according to Boote:

He's disappointed and disgusted with the Labor Party. They were afraid to press for power, he said. Curtin was woefully timid, and was merely going to endorse everything the Government did...They're all good pals together, apparently.[13]

Evatt's criticism of Curtin, though shared by some other federal Labor MPs in 1940–41, was rather unfair. Curtin, like Boote, feared that any Labor decision to join the Menzies Cabinet would precipitate a big split in the ALP. Despite his criticism, Evatt liked Curtin. As for Curtin's view of Evatt, this may be gauged from a story recounted by

Hartley Grattan, who met Curtin late in 1940. Referring to Evatt, Grattan told Curtin: 'If you can discipline and direct his ambition he will serve you well'. As Grattan recalled this incident: 'I shall never forget the look of amused appreciation that came into Curtin's face!' The plain fact is that nobody ever found it easy to discipline Bert Evatt, who by this time was becoming familiar in Labor circles as 'the Doc'. The term recognised his intellectual attainments, although it is probable that few people realised that Evatt, unlike medical practitioners, was entitled to use the appellation.[14]

Many traditional Labor supporters distrusted Evatt because of what they saw as his 'silvertail' legal background and his restless ambition. He had barely entered federal parliament before coming close to repeating the same mistake as in the New South Wales caucus in 1925. On that earlier occasion he had aimed at appointment as Attorney-General. This time, in 1940, he nominated for the position of deputy-leader of the ALP, a position held by F. M. Forde. However, Boote, knowing that many members of federal caucus were irritated by Evatt's presumptuousness, persuaded him to withdraw the nomination. He had to be content with being elected to the ALP's federal parliamentary executive (alongside J. B. Chifley, newly re-elected to parliament).

Another example of the unproductive nature of Evatt's relations with some important figures in the labour movement concerns C. Fallon, who was both federal president of the ALP and Queensland branch secretary of the AWU in 1941. Boote noted that at one point during the AWU national convention in Sydney that year, Fallon was called away to the phone. When he returned, he told Boote, 'It was that fellow Evatt! He plagues me with telephone calls'. Clyde Cameron attended that union convention as a delegate for the first time, and he recalls that before Curtin was called to speak, Fallon went round the delegates, saying that Curtin had 'lost his confidence, he's about to chuck it in, and I want you all to give him a standing ovation; and don't stop clapping until he sits down'. This was done, says Cameron, with the result that Curtin developed more and more confidence as he spoke. On the other hand, just before it was Evatt's turn to talk to the convention, Fallon told the delegates 'not to be moved by any feeling that we ought to give him a clap. So we didn't'.[15]

Moreover, Fallon launched into an attack on the concept of a coalition government, which Evatt was known to favour. As a result of this treatment—psychological warfare as practised in the labour movement—Evatt made a rambling and dispirited speech. Cameron (who had been impressed by Evatt's resignation from the High Court) remembers that Evatt was 'really shattered'. 'He liked to be told how good he was. If you told him he was good, he would know you were genuine. But if you told him he wasn't quite an "Einstein", he'd know that you were crook; that you were out to do him some damage. Nothing in between'.

Early in 1941, the ALP improved its political standing considerably. Unity within the party in New South Wales was basically restored through victory in a State election. McKell became Premier, and dissident groups such as the Hughes–Evans faction lost much public support. Further, the group of former Lang supporters led by Beasley in federal parliament re-joined the mainstream Labor group there; and one indirect consequence of this was that Evatt became a member of the Advisory War Council. In that capacity, Evatt had access to a considerable amount of confidential information, which showed disturbing delays in putting Australia effectively on a war footing. The war was going badly for the Allies. German forces in Greece defeated the British there, with the result that Australian soldiers were hastily evacuated, first from mainland Greece and then from Crete. There were considerable Australian losses.

In this situation, Evatt and Beasley, working closely together on the Advisory War Council, developed a critical role, which included giving the public more information about the seriousness of the state of affairs. Thus they declared in May 1941 that there was confusion and incompetence in the production of war munitions in Australia. There was a sharp official reaction to this disclosure when the Australian Associated Press sought to relay the Evatt–Beasley comments to the Canadian press. The Chief Censor in Melbourne held the cable back and was supported in this action by Casey, the Australian Minister in Washington. However, the government in Canberra decided to let the cable go so as to avoid any accusation of interference with the right of Evatt and Beasley to criticise. The incident was the subject of a Department of Defence Co-ordination file (Australian Archives A5954/1, 327/8). A little later, the Department (re-named Defence) established a file misleadingly headed 'Personal Correspondence—Dr Evatt'. This file, maintained for a number of years, consisted mainly of press-cuttings which showed Evatt in an unfavourable light. In effect, it was an Intelligence dossier, probably inspired by F. Shedden, permanent head of the Defence Department.[16]

———❖———

Prime Minister Menzies spent several months in Britain before returning to Australia in May 1941. There was growing apprehension, not only about the situation in Europe but over Japanese intentions, with Evatt urging the Advisory War Council that 'no further A.I.F. troops should be sent abroad, as every trained and equipped man in Australia was an additional protection against Japanese intervention'. Evatt greeted Menzies' return to Sydney with a confidential letter, expressing frustration and dismay over inadequacies in war preparations. It was a remarkably conciliatory letter which went so far as to tell Menzies that 'no-one at the present time questions your right to the leadership of the nation'. Evatt went on to offer his own full co-operation, not for a national government (which no longer seemed practicable) but for any move which Menzies might initiate to give supreme executive power to the War Council or a smaller body. This would enable Evatt and others to play a full part in the war effort. He concluded: 'My own purpose is to serve this country in the most suitable capacity for the period of this war, and then to give up political life as a career'.[17]

There is no reason to doubt Evatt's sincerity in this approach, but nothing came of it—Menzies reckoned that Evatt was trying to make political capital out of Australian problems in the Middle East. The result was that Evatt concentrated his efforts upon working for the downfall of the Menzies government. In July 1941, Menzies was warned by a friend, businessman Herbert Brookes: 'Dr Evatt has been staying in Melbourne lately and has had interviews with several prominent men generally supposed to be on *our* side politically'. Besides trying to undermine Menzies among conservatives, Evatt— along with Beasley and others in the ALP—was pressing Curtin to take decisive action against the government. There were problems of timing in this connection and Evatt felt that Curtin 'was too much influenced by Jim Scullin, whose moderation amounted to a calamity when he was Prime Minister'.[18]

Menzies, under constant criticism for weak leadership, resigned as Prime Minister, being replaced by A. W. Fadden of the Country Party in August. Six weeks later, Fadden's government fell as the two independent federal MPs who held the balance of power changed sides. They believed that the Labor Party could provide a more stable government. One of the independents, A. Coles, was disgusted with the failure of Menzies and the UAP; while Evatt had for some time cultivated the friendship of the other independent, A. Wilson, who held a Victorian rural seat. Thus a Labor government, with Curtin as Prime Minister, took office in October 1941. In the allocation of portfolios, Evatt became Attorney-General and Minister for External Affairs. He now had an opportunity to live up to Boote's earlier prediction of his political future:

[Evatt] is perfectly sincere...At present he's swayed too much by personal ambition and the flattery handed out to him by the capitalist press...but this phase will pass and he'll be a distinguished member of the party and a big Australian.[19]

Curtin's biographer, Lloyd Ross, had a less favourable view of Evatt and his relations with Curtin in the year or so before the party gained office:

Sometimes Evatt was really being disloyal to Curtin, sometimes he was carrying a bit further the ideas that Curtin had accepted, but always there was this very mixed personality [Evatt] that everybody admits quite freely was a very difficult personality to judge or to test.[20]

Ross acknowledged that Evatt, from the time that Curtin allocated to him the two portfolios, 'gave his leader all the loyalty he was capable of'. This praise was carefully qualified yet it is clear that Curtin as Prime Minister owed much to Evatt's ability and hard work. As Ross McMullin puts it, 'Curtin was soon raving about Evatt's ability to dictate word-perfect legislative clauses and cable messages on complicated issues'.[21] Both leaders were able to inspire others—in Evatt's case, less by oratory than by plain speaking, mixed with a dash of idealism. Evatt's relationship with associates was often poor in quality, yet he had some understanding of human nature. For example, in the letter which he wrote to Menzies in May 1941 he referred to the importance of high morale:

If I may say so with respect it is most unwise to suggest an era of great poverty after the present war. Man lives by hope as well as by fear.

NOTES

1 Evatt to V. Palmer, 27 August 1939, Palmer Papers MS 1174/1/5585, NLA.
2 Boote Diary, vol. 1, Boote Papers MS 2070, NLA; Evatt to Palmer, 16 January 1939, Palmer Papers MS 1174/1/5487. In contrast, Menzies in 1938 expressed full support for Chamberlain's policy of appeasing Hitler in relation to Czechoslovakia.
3 Frank McIlraith to Evatt, 21 September 1939, Evatt Collection, Flinders University. McIlraith was the London representative of *Smith's Weekly*.
4 Menzies to Bruce, 22 February 1940, quoted in David Day, *The Great Betrayal*, Angus & Robertson, Sydney, 1988, p. 42; C.R. Attlee to Justice Evett [sic], 26 January 1940, Evatt Collection, Flinders University.
5 Boote Diary, 10 April 1940.
6 Ibid., 12 March 1940.
7 Ibid., 27 April 1940; K.S. Prichard to F.E. Chamberlain, 21 February 1968, Ric Throssell Papers, MS 6201, Box 17, NLA.
8 Boote Diary, 8 August 1940.
9 R.C. Kirby to Evatt, 30 August 1940, Evatt Collection. File: High Court Resignation 1940. Another letter in this file, from a Presbyterian clergyman in Sydney, envisaged Evatt becoming Prime Minister of Australia in the not far distant future.

10 *Sydney Morning Herald*, 30 August 1940; *Sun*, 12 September 1940.
11 *Australian Insurance and Banking Record*, vol. 59, 1935, pp. 625, 1134. This has been overlooked by Menzies' biographers.
12 Boote Diary, 23 and 29 September 1940.
13 Ibid., 30 October 1940. The phrase 'good pals' embraced Menzies, Curtin and Forde.
14 Hartley Grattan Papers, University of Texas at Austin. Labor had sour memories of 'national' governments in World War I (under Hughes) and the 1930s (Lyons).
15 Boote Diary, 14 February 1941; interview with Clyde Cameron, 3 May 1988. Evatt was notorious for his use of the phone.
16 Australian Archives, A5954/1, 61/7. The gossipy nature of this file is indicated by an unsourced 'Political Portrait', apparently compiled in 1943: 'Dr Evatt has a mercurial and Celtic temperament, without unfortunately for himself, the usual Celtic charm of manner...he has never been popular with orthodox Bar circles'.
17 Advisory War Council Minute, 8 May 1941, quoted by Paul Hasluck, *The Government and the People, 1939–1941*, Australian War Memorial, Canberra, 1952, p. 357; Evatt to Menzies, 24 May 1941, Evatt Collection, File: War—ALP Government, Formation of, 1941.
18 Rohan Rivett, *Australian Citizen: Herbert Brookes, 1867–1963*, MUP, Melbourne, 1965, p. 196; Boote Diary, 18 August 1941. Sir Gilbert Dyett, federal President of the Returned Soldiers' League, was one of Evatt's Melbourne contacts, a connection which seems to have been established by John Wren, a wealthy businessman and Labor 'wire-puller'. See James Griffin, 'The Evatt–Wren Letters', *Eureka Street* vol. 2, September 1992, pp. 26–7.
19 Boote Diary, 8 October 1940.
20 Lloyd Ross Tapes, Transcript TRC236, LR2:2/37, NLA.
21 Lloyd Ross, *John Curtin: A Biography,* Macmillan, Melbourne, 1977, p. 224; Ross McMullin, *The Light on the Hill: the Australian Labor Party 1891–1991,* OUP, Melbourne, 1991, p. 213.

CHAPTER 13

WAR CRISIS: OVERSEAS MISSION 1942

Tell Mr Roosevelt and the Cabinet members to look out for their shirts. Evatt is going to tell, not ask.
N. JOHNSON, US MINISTER TO AUSTRALIA

The scope of World War II was greatly enlarged by two dramatic developments in 1941. In June, there came the German invasion of the Soviet Union. In December, the Japanese attacked the US fleet at Pearl Harbor. Thus three major powers joined in the war, making it truly global in extent.

Immediately after becoming External Affairs Minister, Evatt angled for Russian support in the event of Japanese forces moving southwards in Asia, as was feared. The Australian government was prepared to reciprocate in this connection, and the Soviet government was indeed appreciative of Australian declarations of war in December 1941 against countries (Finland, Hungary and Rumania), which were fighting with Germany against the Soviet Union. However, Evatt's broader objective was not gained. For one thing, when it came to the point, the Russians had no desire to be engaged in another war front in Asia whilst fighting for their lives in Europe. Besides this, the British government was not prepared to support an Australian move which might entail withdrawal of some Russian troops from the struggle against Germany. The interests of Britain and Australia diverged on this point.[1]

When the attack on Pearl Harbor impelled the United States of America into war (against Germany as well as Japan), Australians felt relief at having such a powerful new ally in the Pacific, especially as it soon became apparent that Britain, its attention concentrated on the war in the Middle East, felt unable to send substantial additional forces to the region it termed the Far East. In Australia, early feelings of relief gave way to very grave concern as Japanese forces advanced rapidly through southern Asia. Curtin's response was to turn uncompromisingly to the United States. Over Christmas 1941, he issued a public statement, the kernel of which was a forthright phrase: 'Australia looks to America, free of any pangs as to our traditional links or kinship with the United Kingdom.'[2] Not surprisingly, the statement angered Churchill. At the same time, Evatt instructed Casey in Washington to 'insist that in every conference between representatives of Associated powers...[Australia] must have the opportunity of separate representation even though it may appear unpracticable at first sight.' The era of British representation of Australian interests overseas was passing.[3]

In January 1942, the Australian War Cabinet was informed that the British government was considering withdrawal of troops from Singapore. Cabinet decided to make strong representations against this to Churchill through a cable from Curtin. Actually, in the absence of Curtin in Western Australia, Evatt amended one paragraph to make it read that evacuation of Singapore would be regarded as 'an inexcusable betrayal'. Churchill took immediate exception to this, but it must be said that the terse wording of the cable was due not so much to difference of viewpoint between Evatt and Curtin as to Evatt's strengthening of drafts prepared for Curtin by Shedden of the Defence Department.[4]

As it happened, Singapore fell to Japanese forces in February, and thousands of Australians were among the troops taken prisoner of war. In Australia, the debacle led to considerable public criticism of British leadership. Evatt, in the hope of securing support in Britain for his views, sent a confidential cable to Stafford Cripps, an influential Labour MP. Among other things, the cable criticised a recent speech by Churchill in which, said Evatt:

He [Churchill] went out of his way to praise Menzies solely in order to make political play against our Prime Minister. Incidentally Menzies privately described Churchill as suffering from a dictatorship complex which approaches megalomania.[5]

Evatt went on to inform Cripps that although the Australian government would have preferred to have a Pacific War Council established in Washington, Churchill had set it up in London. This, in Evatt's opinion, was designed 'to prevent the countries so closely concerned in the Pacific theatre as Australia and China from meeting in common council to decide upon common policy against Japan'.

Relations between the British and Australian governments deteriorated further concerning the deployment of Australian troops who had been fighting in the Middle East. Churchill had earlier approved the transfer of two of these Australian divisions to the Netherlands East Indies, as a support for the British bastion at Singapore. The 7th Australian Division was actually en route through Indian waters when Singapore fell, and this was followed by the bombing of Darwin by Japanese planes. Curtin, greatly alarmed by the Japanese advance, asked Churchill to re-direct the 7th Division convoy to Australia rather than to Java. However, Churchill decided that there was a greater need to divert the ships to Rangoon, so as to oppose Japanese troops advancing in Burma. The Australian government, 'owing to a misunderstanding' in London, was not informed of this until after the convoy had changed course.[6]

Curtin protested, insisting that the 7th Division be brought to Australia at once. Churchill asked the Australian government to reconsider its position and he secured President Roosevelt's support on the matter, but Curtin refused to budge. The Australian troops returned to defend their homeland. An interesting aspect of the episode was that Earle Page, the former leader of the Country Party, who had been appointed by the Fadden government as Australian Special Representative in the UK, sided with Churchill rather than the Australian government which he was supposed to represent. Evatt noted this in a cable to an Australian representative in the United States, saying that Page 'had instructions as to our view, but failed to carry them out'. Curtin, too, was critical of Page, who was in any case quite ineffective in his post in London. Sir Edward Cadogan, permanent head of the British Foreign Office, cuttingly recorded in his diary at this time that Earle Page had engaged in an argument at a War Cabinet meeting, but 'E.P. can never state a point (I don't know whether he ever grasps it)'.[7]

Following the Japanese victory at Singapore, and their occupation of Rabaul in New Guinea, UK troops were virtually out of the Pacific. Some American forces arrived in Australia early in 1942, but they were primarily concerned with the direction of the US war effort in the region as a whole. The defence of Australia itself was largely dependent upon rapid mobilisation of Australia's own resources of manpower and materials. Such mobilisation as had occurred before 1942 was only partial, and remedying this took time. The immediate aim was to secure supplies of arms from overseas for use if a Japanese invasion materialised. As an indication of the urgency of the position, Evatt cabled to Stirling, an External Affairs officer in London:

the flow of munitions here [Australia] is only a trickle. For instance the bulk of United States production of Tommy guns and ammunition for warships (twenty-five thousand guns) is going to the United Kingdom.[8]

In this desperate situation, the Curtin government asked Evatt to go on a mission to America and Britain. His reputation in official circles went before him. Nelson Johnson, US Minister to Australia, warned Washington: 'Tell Mr Roosevelt and the Cabinet members to look out for their shirts. Evatt is going to tell, not ask'. R. Cross, British High Commissioner in Canberra, had a definite bias against both Labor and Australians, regarding the latter as 'inferior people'. Cross cabled to his superiors in London concerning Evatt's projected visit, referring to the Australian Minister's 'nationalistic or possibly secessionist tendencies', and adding, 'I think it of special importance that Mr Churchill should, if possible, see a good deal of Evatt who has been inclined to disparage him'.[9]

On his long trip overseas, Evatt went first to Washington. He was accompanied by A. Smith (Secretary of the Commonwealth Department of Supply and Development) and W. S. Robinson, a businessman described as 'Adviser (Raw Materials)'. Also in the group was Mary Alice Evatt. This was at the suggestion of Curtin, who knew that Evatt had a pathological fear of flying and needed the emotional support which his wife provided. Robinson was a remarkable man, perhaps the most distinguished entrepreneur in Australian history. In the inter-war period, he was a key figure in the network of metal-mining and manufacturing companies known as the Collins House Group in Melbourne. This group—the core of which was the Zinc Corporation, with Robinson as its managing director—had international ramifications, and Robinson spent much of his time travelling between Australia, the USA, Britain and other countries.

In the course of his work, Robinson had established friendly relations with many influential politicians as well as businessmen, one of them being Winston Churchill. In 1935 it had seemed to Robinson that a European war was inevitable, so he began moves to create the Commonwealth Aircraft Corporation in Australia. Further, in the following few years he used his contacts to collect a mass of confidential information on the German aircraft industry, which he passed on to Churchill and his associates. When war broke out,

Robinson was occupied with dovetailing Britain's demands for base metals with the sources of supply in Australia and elsewhere. He also acted as adviser to the Menzies government, though apparently to little effect.[10]

The very close relationship which developed between Robinson and Evatt was extraordinary. On the surface, the big businessman and the Labor politician had little or nothing in common, apart from a strong Australian nationalist spirit. However, it was sufficient for each to recognise in the other a determination (and ability) to contribute greatly to winning the war. On this basis, supplemented by tact on Robinson's part, the two men established a genuine friendship which long outlasted the war. Robinson was by no means unmindful of his private business interests while accompanying Evatt on trips overseas, and these missions gave Robinson high priority—and an Australian diplomatic passport—for scarce transport in wartime conditions. Yet Robinson gave far more than he got. He used his connections to introduce Evatt to many friends who were in a position to influence events and policy.

Apart from this, Evatt in March 1942 used the good offices of Casey, who was well established in Washington, to meet American leaders such as President Roosevelt and his assistant, H. Hopkins, Justice Frankfurter and General Marshall. Evatt's prime concern was to stress Australia's urgent need for more war supplies, particularly aircraft. Years later, in talking to Australian Minister Eggleston, Harry Hopkins reminisced about Evatt's visit:

Hopkins said that Evatt came over very well briefed...and had several interviews with the President. He was not to be denied his assistance and secured rather vaguely worded promises from Roosevelt to the effect that he would give Australia aeroplanes.[11]

In fact, Evatt secured little by way of increased war supplies from his visit to the United States. This was partly because the Americans were more concerned with allocating resources for direct use by American forces under the command of General MacArthur, using Australia as a base. More significantly, Roosevelt and his colleagues knew about disagreements between the British and Australian governments, and the Americans adopted the British position as that of the much more important ally. American supplies for allies were largely committed to Britain and the Soviet Union; and Britain had strong procurement agencies in Washington. Evatt's entreaties went largely unheeded. Indeed, as Robinson noted, there were occasions when apparently firm arrangements for the supply of war material to Australia were not adhered to:

The snag appeared to be in U.S. General 'Benny' Myers' department—there the promised planes were always diverted to others. At last the trouble became unendurable and Dr Evatt was 'forced to remonstrate' (as anyone knowing Bert will recognise, this is one of the world's greatest understatements) to the U.S. top brass. The demoting of Benny Myers followed.[12]

Evatt registered one diplomatic success in Washington. Roosevelt agreed to establish a Pacific War Council there, consisting of representatives of several countries. The Council met for the first time on 1 April 1942, with Roosevelt in the chair and Evatt there to represent Australia. The initiative was clearly Australian—two months earlier, Curtin had cabled Lord Cranborne, British Minister for Dominion Affairs, expressing a desire for a Pacific War Council to be established in Washington 'as a council of action for the higher direction of the war in the Pacific'. As it happened, although the similar Council established in London (which did not include the Americans) was left to die a natural death after the setting up of the Pacific War Council in Washington, the latter body did not live up to Australian hopes that it would have executive and policy functions. The Americans were no more interested than were the British in giving small countries an effective role in policy formulation. The Pacific War Council remained advisory and consultative, and thus proved a disappointment to Evatt.[13]

Evatt's departure from America, after spending six weeks there, was welcome to some members of the Australian Legation staff in Washington. They resented Evatt's personal efforts in the field of diplomacy and his abrasive style. Alan Watt, the first secretary, wrote confidentially to J. D. L. Hood in the External Affairs Department in Canberra:

While Mr Casey and the Minister were both here, there was complete confusion. I had two masters, no discretion, and legation work suffered. After Mr Casey left things eased somewhat...I have seen...all senior Australians in Washington (including myself) trodden on, discarded, not used.[14]

Oblivious or indifferent to such hurt feelings, Evatt flew out of the USA to Britain. W. S. Robinson, who accompanied him—Mas remained behind, suffering from tonsillitis—recalled the discomfort of the sixteen-hour flight in his memoirs:

no heating, a five inch plank to sit on...and an oxygen mask which had to be lifted off the face every five minutes to prevent its freezing to the skin...we struggled out of the bowels of the plane looking like nothing on earth. 'Bert' was most anxious to be photographed but I declined.

While not missing an opportunity for publicity, Evatt, according to an American, on arrival in London simply told journalists: 'I have come to report, observe, and consult.' He was impatient to get on with the task in which he had so far been unsuccessful: to obtain large war supplies for Australia and to ensure for his country an adequate share in the direction of the overall war effort. Moreover, Evatt was under pressure from Curtin to produce results, and both men were spurred on by the threat of Japanese attack. As Evatt communicated to Bruce: 'I believe very short period ahead of us will determine whether our country will be overrun.'[15]

Prior to arrival in Britain, Evatt cabled to Bruce the text of a letter of introduction from W. M. Hughes to Churchill. Hughes (who had replaced Menzies as leader of the UAP) wrote that Evatt had an 'intense admiration' for Churchill and had 'great influence in Australia'. There was in fact an affinity of attitude between Evatt and Hughes in certain respects. Makin noted that at one meeting of the Advisory War Council, Hughes had said that 'if ever you wanted to get anywhere with British public men it was necessary to "crack them hard"'. Whether Hughes' commendation of Evatt was valued by British politicians may be doubted. Certainly, W. S. Robinson carried far more weight. As a trusted friend, he had easy access, not only to Churchill but also to some of the Prime Minister's close advisers, notably Brendan Bracken, British Minister of Information, and Oliver Lyttelton, Minister of Production (who had big business interests in non-ferrous metals). Robinson also had a talk in May 1942 with another old acquaintance, J. M. Keynes, concerning economic matters likely to affect Australia in the post-war period.[16]

Apart from Robinson's efforts as a go-between, Churchill himself recognised the desirability of improving Anglo-Australian relations. In Australia, there had been considerable public criticism of the British position on the war in the Pacific. Some historians have suggested that Evatt was 'duchessed' by Churchill at this time. It is true that, at Churchill's invitation, Evatt and Robinson spent weekends with him at the Prime Minister's country house, Chequers; and Evatt was honoured by being admitted to membership of the Privy Council. Evatt was also well received when he spoke at meetings, including an address to a conference of the Labour Party in London. Yet he was in no way deflected from the purpose of his mission. Wherever he spoke, whether in public or at meetings of the British War Cabinet, he emphasised the threat that Japan posed to Australia and the consequent need to strengthen the forces available for defence of Australia.

S. M. Bruce, noting a conversation with Evatt soon after his arrival in London, wrote that on strategic problems Evatt was 'not too sound and has not got in his mind the whole picture, but is too inclined to think in terms of Australia only'. This note reveals much about Bruce's understanding of his own job: no British or US diplomatic representative overseas would have referred to his own country's interests in such qualified terms. At the same time, Bruce's comment went to the heart of conflict in relations between Britain and Australia. The British government considered it unlikely that the Japanese would launch a full-scale invasion of Australia—although the assessment was based more on hope than knowledge of Japanese intentions. If Australia were to be 'heavily invaded', said Churchill, Britain would come to Australia's assistance. How such assistance would be realistically provided was not specified, and there was a nasty implication that it would need to be deferred until the war in Europe was over. This strategic view was unacceptable to the Curtin government, which wanted weapons and munitions immediately to avert any Japanese invasion. The British government would itself have adopted a similar viewpoint if the positions had been reversed. Indeed, when German forces swept through France in 1940, the predominant concern of the British government was to evacuate its own troops through Dunkirk for the defence of Britain, not to throw more forces into the defence of France.[17]

For a full understanding of Evatt's mission to the United States and Britain in 1942, it is necessary to consider what was generally termed the 'Beat Hitler First' policy. Of course, this did not become relevant in practical terms until Japan entered the war, but there were secret Anglo-American defence staff discussions on the subject early in 1941. The British and American staff planners agreed upon a 'Beat Hitler First' strategy, although there was no formal endorsement of this by the respective governments. The Menzies government was aware of these talks but it seems unlikely that Labor Opposition leaders were informed.

In December 1941, after the attack on Pearl Harbor, Churchill flew to the United States and at a conference code-named Arcadia he and Roosevelt and their advisers decided upon a strategy of top priority for the war in Europe. The Combined Chiefs of Staff of the two countries based their operations on a secret document, named WW1, which embodied the agreement in firm and precise form. Australia was not informed of its existence or its terms, although Eggleston, Australian Minister to China in Chungking, had shrewd suspicions. He wrote to Earle Page in London: 'It is all nonsense to say that Britain and America cannot spare anything [for Australia]. The whole question is one of priorities, reserves and risk.'[18]

Unknown to Evatt, the WW1 agreement stultified his efforts in Washington to secure supplies for Australia. He was still ignorant of the agreement after arrival in London, saying at a press conference that Allied strategy did 'not contemplate concentration on one enemy' and there was 'great danger to the common cause in talking along the line, "Let us beat Hitler first"'. At his first meeting with the British War Cabinet on 4 May 1942, Evatt suggested that a reassessment of the general strategic situation might provide 'good grounds for strengthening the forces available for the defence of Australia'. Churchill responded appreciatively, without disclosing the existence of WW1.[19]

That same day Evatt, in order to examine the procedures for dealing with Australian requests for war material, attended a meeting of the London Munitions Assignment Board (LMAB). He refused to be diverted by discussion on whether Australian requests should be submitted to the London Board or the similar Board in Washington. Colonel E. Jacob, of the War Cabinet Secretariat, foresaw problems following this meeting. He told the Minister of Production in a memo that according to Bruce, 'Evatt says he is not interested in the machinery [of allocation]. All he wants is the stuff'.[20]

Evatt then arranged for a meeting between himself and the Chiefs of Staff, so that he could obtain a picture of the general strategy which served as a basis for the allocation of munitions by the LMAB, and at the same time he could emphasise the inadequacy of allocations to Australia. Preparatory to this meeting, held on 12 May, briefing papers drawn up for the Chiefs indicated that Evatt should be told that 'our basic strategic policy is not only firm and unchanged but is agreed with the United States'. A crucial element in the agreed strategy was encapsulated in the statement: 'Defeat of Germany whilst holding Japan. Only after Germany's defeat can United Nations assemble superior force against Japan'. The briefing papers also included a document, LMAB 42/17, for the information of the Chiefs of Staff.[21]

For the purpose of allocation of munitions to various theatres of war, LMAB 42/17 listed those theatres in order of importance as decided earlier by the Combined Chiefs of Staff in Washington. The Middle East was first on the list and Australia was fifth—after India–Ceylon and Hawaii. Attached tables showed the supplies projected by the Chiefs of Staff for allocation to each theatre of war in 1942. The number of airplanes for Australia was not impressive. It was not intended to communicate this information to Evatt at his meeting with the Chiefs of Staff but as an Air Ministry official commented later, 'Dr Evatt unfortunately saw them' (the tables). It would have been quite in character for Evatt simply to have seized a copy from the conference table—and his legal expertise in quickly absorbing the essence of a brief enabled him to grasp the significance of the papers.[22]

Next day, the Chiefs of Staff felt obliged to supply Evatt with a copy of WW1, the secret written agreement between Britain and the United States to 'Beat Hitler First'. Evatt derived some comfort from an incidental statement that the security of Australia and New Zealand must be maintained, but this was small consolation. He had to face the fact that there was no possibility of changing the basic strategy. Evatt was left with two options: he could attack Churchill for not consulting or informing Australia about WW1, in the hope that the British Prime Minister would be shamed into making concessions; or he could attempt to win Churchill over by more subtle tactics. After considerable thought, Evatt decided upon the latter course. This emerges from a cable which Evatt, after accompanying Churchill on a speech-making tour of Yorkshire, sent to Curtin on 17 May. Evatt told Curtin that, while making some progress in bringing Churchill to a realisation of the grave war threat to Australia, he (Evatt) was 'under the necessity of being persistent without being importunate'. Moreover, said Evatt: 'The fact is that when Churchill visited Roosevelt the strategy agreed on was primarily to concentrate on the defeat of Hitler'.[23]

At the same time, W. S. Robinson cabled Curtin, saying:

Evatt has experienced many difficulties most of which have been disposed of by his tact and patience...Evatt has established himself in the confidence of Churchill Cripps and the other important Ministers and in my opinion has made sure of their support for Australia.

Robinson's reference to Evatt's 'tact and patience' may have raised some eyebrows in Canberra, although he probably had in mind a BBC radio broadcast in which Evatt praised Churchill and appealed to the spirit of kinship between Britain and Australia. Remarkably, this broadcast elicited a telegram of warm congratulations to Evatt from Warwick Fairfax, proprietor of the *Sydney Morning Herald*. Very many Australians had been worried by the deterioration in relations between the two countries. Actually, Robinson was not yet sure that Evatt could be restrained from exercising his natural aggressive instinct. Robinson wrote a fine personal letter to his friend, Bert Evatt:

You have achieved much in this country. You have had a splendid reception...You have stated and pressed the case of Australia with 'great firmness'. Admittedly sometimes the depth of your feelings has put rough edges on your approaches...

With diffidence, I now submit a word of advice. I know you will regard it as sincere...I feel very strongly that the moment has arrived *when in your discussions and dealings with all men of importance...you should adopt an attitude which could not but be regarded as warmly appreciative of all that has been done in the past for Australia—all that has been promised and you hope Britain can do today...The judge and jury are on your side—don't please risk irritating much less criticising them.*²⁴

Robinson's advice was heeded. Evatt made a special plea to Churchill for fighter aircraft, and Churchill responded generously. At a British War Cabinet meeting, held on 21 May 1942 in the presence of Evatt, it was decided to send three Spitfire squadrons to Australia as a special contribution in the emergency. In proposing this, Churchill acknowledged that there were seven squadrons of planes in Britain manned by Australians, and two of these were to be included in the new contingent for Australia. The Chiefs of Staff objected: they considered that it would be preferable to make available Kittyhawk aircraft (less powerful than Spitfires) from the United States. However, Churchill brushed this aside. Evatt made a contribution to the discussion, saying that the arrival in Australia of three squadrons of Spitfires, including one manned by United Kingdom pilots, 'would have a tremendous effect' on Australian morale. Spitfires had great significance in the public mind because of their vital role in the Battle of Britain in 1940. Incidentally, Robinson was jubilant about Evatt's much more favourable opinion of Churchill. Robinson told Brendan Bracken: 'He [Evatt] came, saw and Churchill conquered'.²⁵

The Spitfires were to be additional to any planes already scheduled for despatch to Australia in 1942, and this was not the only gain made by Evatt. He secured agreement for acceleration of transport to Australia of other munitions, notably anti-aircraft guns. On Evatt's behalf, Robinson negotiated details of this with Lyttelton and Jacob. Evatt sealed his success by obtaining from General Ismay, Churchill's Chief of Staff, a written record of the decisions made by Cabinet. Then, on 28 May 1942, Evatt sent a long cable to Curtin, including the full text of WW1 and claiming success for his mission overseas. Subsequently, a number of commentators on the mission have damned Evatt with faint praise. For example, David Day described the achievement as 'illusory' and referred to the Spitfires as a 'rather minuscule force of forty-eight secondhand aircraft'. If these planes were indeed obsolescent, the anxiety of the British Chief of Air Staff to retain them becomes inexplicable. Further, New Zealand and South African representatives in London felt that the Cabinet decision was important enough to warrant their protesting at the speedy manner in which it was made.²⁶

In fact, the Chiefs of Staff in mid-1942 persuaded Churchill to delay the despatch of the Spitfires to Australia, on the grounds that they were urgently needed in the Middle East. Churchill apologised to Evatt for the delay and the squadrons did not arrive in Australia until late in 1942. Nevertheless, the warm personal relationship between Evatt and Churchill is exemplified in the wording of a cable from the latter: 'How are the Evatt Spitfire Squadrons getting on?' They were in good shape, as it turned out. Stationed at Darwin, the Spitfires proved to have the measure of the Japanese Zero aircraft; Curtin happily informed Churchill that the Spitfire pilots, in their first encounter with the Japanese, 'shot down six out of 15 enemy planes which raided Darwin...we had no losses'. It was a striking achievement for 'superseded' aircraft.[27]

Of course, it may be argued that the delay in arrival of the Spitfires detracted substantially from Evatt's initial success in securing Churchill's promise to send them. It has also been alleged that Evatt's prime concern at the conclusion of his visit to Britain was to make exaggerated claims so as to maximise political advantage for himself and the Curtin government. Undoubtedly, Evatt sought good publicity, but criticism of this misses the point of his achievement.

It was Evatt who persistently drew Churchill's attention to Australia's plight, and this brought results mainly as a consequence of Evatt's unearthing of WW1. It is very unlikely that any other Australian envoy, more polite and less suspicious than Evatt, could have ferreted out that document. Also, in view of claims (notably by Carl Bridge) that the information in the document was available to the Australian Cabinet before Evatt's visit to Britain, it may be noted that much later he queried Sir Frederick Shedden on the point. This apparently occurred in 1957, when Evatt may have been thinking of writing his memoirs; and Shedden, still Secretary of the Defence Department, was reputed to have the best collection of war records in Canberra. Shedden—no friend of Evatt—replied that 'the first advice received by the Australian government' that the US and UK governments had agreed upon a 'Beat Hitler First' policy was in Evatt's cablegram of 28 May 1942 to Curtin. Shedden overlooked Evatt's earlier cable of 17 May, but the difference of date is immaterial.[28]

As for the delay in sending the Spitfires to Australia, Curtin expressed 'surprise and concern' to the British government but he accepted the decision without protest. This was understandable, as the war situation in the Pacific had changed for the better. In May 1942, US naval forces engaged a Japanese fleet in battle in the Coral Sea. The outcome was not a definite victory for the Americans but it thwarted Japanese plans for a seaborne invasion of Port Moresby, dangerously close to the Australian continent. Then, a month later, a Japanese naval force was defeated by the Americans at the battle of Midway Island. This proved decisive in halting the Japanese advance towards Australia. Curtin continued to speak about the possibility of a Japanese invasion, but for most Australians the extremely acute pressure was relieved: the war was yet to be won but it was reasonable to hope or trust that it would be won outside metropolitan Australia.

One major factor in the strengthening of morale was publicity about Evatt's success in London, and he received a heartfelt welcome on return to Australia. Typical, though rather unexpected, was a congratulatory letter to Evatt from Justice McTiernan, who had not been favourably disposed towards Evatt on the High Court in the previous decade. Now McTiernan wrote to express his appreciation: 'You fought a very plucky battle to make others see the situation in the Pacific as we see it'. There were some who disagreed and remained silent. The extraordinary venom of Menzies' attitude is worth recording. In April 1942, the US Consul-General in Melbourne, Dickover, reported to Washington on a conversation between himself and R. G. Menzies, in which the latter referred to the Labor government as 'scum—positive scum'. In Menzies' view, Curtin was 'reasonably safe', but Ward and Evatt were 'positively menaces to Australia'. Menzies was so fanciful as to claim that Evatt had gone on his trip to Washington 'to get himself and his wife in a safe spot'. In making his remark, Menzies may have been unaware of Evatt's dread fear of flying but this does not excuse the scurrilous attack: he knew or should have known that his words would be relayed to the US government.[29]

Although Evatt's time on this first official visit overseas was very largely occupied with problems relating to Australian defence rather than foreign policy, he was involved in certain other matters. Thus he played a part in negotiations with the British Chancellor of the Exchequer, which resulted in an increase of fifteen per cent in the price paid by the British government for Australian wool. There was also some personal correspondence from well-wishers in London. One intriguing letter was from Doris Colles (once Doris Nolan), who wrote:

My dear Bert,
Somehow I feel I must write to you. I think it is over twenty-five years ago you and Paddy (Nolan) were talking of your ambitions—you were to be Prime Minister of Australia and he, Attorney-General. Do you remember? And now here you are almost if not quite where you said you would be.[30]

On his way back to Australia in June 1942, Evatt spent a week in the United States, renewing contacts with American and other leaders and continuing to press for more war supplies for Australia. He missed no opportunity, as indicated by a message sent to Churchill:

'All here are rejoicing at the result of the Midway battle...I beg you to consider whether it may not be possible to strike the enemy harder in the Pacific now that he is groggy'. Evatt also made public statements in America. One woman, Margaret Macpherson, was particularly impressed. She wrote to him, saying:

Half the Australians in New York are becoming languid little English gentlemen who don't in the least convey to American beholders the true virility and vitality of the country they so unworthily represent. That is one reason why we were so glad you came; you looked like an Australian, you spoke up like an Australian.[31]

It was an interesting comment. Perhaps the writer had in mind Australian bureaucrats like Alan Watt, a stickler for proper procedures, whose feathers had been ruffled by Evatt.

NOTES

1 Wayne Reynolds, 'H.V. Evatt: The Imperial Connection and the Quest for Australian Security, 1941-1945', Ph.D thesis, University of Newcastle (Australia), 1985, ch. 1.

2 Curtin's statement appears to have been counter-productive as far as the Americans were concerned. According to Casey, Roosevelt privately expressed 'the greatest distaste' for it. W.J. Hudson, *Casey*, Melbourne, OUP, 1986, p. 134.

3 W.J. Hudson and H.J.W. Stokes (eds), *Documents on Australian Foreign Policy* (DAFP), vol. v, Canberra, AGPS, 1982, Document 196, Evatt to Casey, 16 December 1941.

4 D.M. Horner, *High Command: Australia and Allied Strategy, 1939–1945*, Australian War Memorial, Canberra, 1982, pp. 150–4.

5 *DAFP*, vol. v, Document 335, Evatt to Cripps, 16 February 1942. Presumably it was this kind of remark that led J.D.B. Miller to say, in reviewing this publication (*Historical Studies*, April 1985, p. 457) that Evatt 'emerges as a simple-minded Left Book Club subscriber of the 1930s in his approach to foreign affairs'. This glosses over the fact that Left Book Club readers were much better prepared than their conservative critics to recognise and oppose the threat from fascism.

6 British War Cabinet Conclusions, Confidential Annex, 23 February 1942. PRO: CAB 65/29, W.M. (42).

7 Ibid; *DAFP*, vol.v, Document 359, Evatt to J. McMillan, 22 February 1942; David Dilks (ed.), *The Diaries of Sir Edward Cadogan 1938–1945*, Cassell, London, 1971, p. 429.

8 *DAFP*, vol. v, Document 387, Evatt to Stirling, 4 March 1942. This cable was to be passed on to Stafford Cripps.

9 N. Johnson, quoted in Christopher Thorne, *Allies of a Kind: The United States, Britain and the War against Japan, 1941–45*, Hamish Hamilton, London, 1978, p. 256; Cross to Dominions Office, 27 March 1942. PRO: PREM 4, 50/6.

10 Geoffrey Blainey (ed.), *If I Remember Rightly: The Memoirs of W.S. Robinson, 1876–1963*, Cheshire, Melbourne, 1967, pp. 177–81. See also Peter Richardson, 'The Origins and Development of the Collins House Group, 1915–1951', *Australian Economic History Review*, 27, 1, March 1987.
11 Eggleston Papers MS 423/10/820, NLA.
12 Robinson's *Memoirs*, p.188.
13 *DAFP*, vol. v, Document 289, Curtin to Cranborne, 21 January 1942.
14 Watt Papers, MS 3788, Folder 1, NLA, Watt to Hood, 16 April 1942. Casey had been appointed by Churchill as British Minister of State in the Middle East. Evatt, who was suspicious of Casey, was not sorry to see him go, yet the Evatts gave valuable assistance in the care of his children, who remained in Washington after Casey left. Casey was very appreciative.
15 J. Steel, *Men Behind the War*, Sheridan, New York, 1942, p. 379; *DAFP*, vol. v, Document 443, Evatt to Bruce, 26 March 1942.
16 Makin Diary, 20 Jan.1942, Norman Makin Papers, MS 7325, NLA; *DAFP*, vol. v, Document 438, Evatt to Bruce, 23 March 1942.
17 *DAFP*, vol. v, Document 481, Note by Bruce, 3 May 1942.
18 Ibid., Document 395, Eggleston to Page, 7 March 1942. Actually, Earle Page was present at a British Cabinet Defence Committee (Operations) meeting in January 1942, at which Churchill referred to the 'Germany first' strategy, but Page apparently failed to realise its significance.
19 Quoted in David Day, *The Great Betrayal*, p. 318.
20 PRO: CAB 109/43, LMAB 42/16.
21 PRO: CAB 109/40, J.P. (42) 491.
22 Quoted in Wayne Reynolds' thesis, p. 160. This is an excellent piece of work, and Reynolds deserves credit as the first researcher to locate the LMAB records in the PRO. David Day's account in *The Great Betrayal*, ch. 14, is inaccurate in some respects because he was unaware of the LMAB papers.
23 *DAFP*, vol. v, Document 490, Evatt to Curtin, 17 May 1942.
24 Robinson to Curtin, 17 May 1942; Fairfax to Evatt, 19 May; 'Robbie' to 'Bert', 18 May. Evatt Collection, Flinders University. File: Evatt—Overseas Trip 1942.
25 War Cabinet Conclusions, 21 May 1942. PRO: CAB 65/30, W.M. (42) 65; Note from Robinson to Bracken, 26 May 1942. PRO: PREM 4, 50/6/, Evatt's visit to UK, 1942.
26 David Day, *The Great Betrayal*, pp. 334–5. In his article in *Historical Studies*, vol. 22, October 1987, Day referred to the Spitfires as 'superseded'.
27 Churchill to Evatt, 17 December 1942, Curtin to Churchill, 3 March 1943. PRO: PREM 3, 150/7. The arrival of the Spitfires in Australia was not made public until March 1943.
28 Carl Bridge (ed.), *From Munich to Vietnam*, MUP, Melbourne, 1991, ch. 2; Australian Archives A5954/1, 61/7. Shedden's letter to Evatt was undated and absurdly marked 'Secret'. By an odd coincidence, Bruce in London on 30 May 1942 noted being told by Evatt that 'the great majority' of cables which Bruce received from Australia were drafted by Shedden and that 'although they might come over the Prime Minister's signature he probably had not given

them any consideration', *DAFP*, vol. v, Document 508. Curtin was Acting External Affairs Minister during Evatt's absence overseas.

29 McTiernan to Evatt, 16 July 1942, Evatt Collection, Flinders University, File: Evatt—Overseas Trip 1942; Memo of conversation between Dickover and Menzies, 24 April 1942, US National Archives, Washington, Lot Files, RG59, Lot 54D224 Box 4.

30 Colles to Evatt, 6 May 1942, Evatt Collection. Evatt and Nolan were university students together, before 'Paddy' joined the army in World War I and was killed in action. Also in 1942, J. Steel, in *Men Behind the War*, wrote that many Australians looked upon Evatt 'as a future leader of the Labor Party and Prime Minister'.

31 Macpherson (Mrs W.T. Albert) to Evatt, 13 July 1942, Evatt Collection.

CHAPTER 14

CIVIL LIBERTIES IN WARTIME

The aim and sole justification of all restrictions upon individual liberty is to prevent injury to the war effort...[but] there cannot be any absolute right of public trial in these cases of restriction of liberty.
H. V. EVATT, COMMONWEALTH ATTORNEY-GENERAL

The excitement of Evatt's mission overseas in 1942 tends to obscure the fact that he also held the ministerial portfolio of Attorney-General, traditionally regarded as more important than External Affairs. The Attorney-General's Department, through its responsibility in drafting legislation and regulations, and its oversight of court prosecutions, was pivotal in the area of civil liberties. Parallel with the war against external enemies, a struggle was waged internally in relation to democratic freedoms. There was general agreement among Australians that it was necessary to act against spies, saboteurs and the like, and that certain restrictions upon traditional rights were justified in wartime. Accordingly, a system of official censorship was instituted early in the war, aimed at preventing the enemy from obtaining information about such matters as the movement of Allied troops and ships. However, in the view of liberal-minded people, such restrictions should be kept to the minimum necessary for the purpose.

The war was said to be a struggle between dictatorship and democracy, and many who took that proposition seriously felt that there was little point in winning the war if freedom of speech and other civil liberties were eroded in the process. Once lost, such freedoms might be very difficult to recover after the war. These considerations were foremost in the minds of a small, yet determined, number of Australians, represented particularly by the Australian Council for Civil Liberties (ACCL). Prominent in this organisation was Maurice Blackburn, its president from 1940, described by an historian as 'a civil libertarian in the classic mould, more influenced by Mill than Marx'.[1]

Most important in the ACCL was its indefatigable secretary, Brian Fitzpatrick, who argued that the rule of law had given way to the rule of war. Fitzpatrick, who had had some contact with H. V. Evatt, had trade-union and left-wing political associations. In 1940–41 he led the ACCL in sharp criticism of government restrictions, recognising them as being primarily directed against elements on the left in politics. Two aspects of the problem were particularly worrying. One was the sweeping nature of the regulations promulgated under the National Security Act. For example, Regulation 42, in force from September 1939, provided that:

A person shall not—
(a) endeavour, whether orally or otherwise, to influence public opinion (whether in Australia or elsewhere) in a manner likely to be prejudicial to the defence of the Commonwealth or with the efficient prosecution of the war; or
(b) do any act, or have any article in his possession, with a view to making or facilitating the making of any such endeavour.

Secondly, power to enforce the regulations was delegated to a very wide range of people: Commonwealth and State officials, police, Army officers, and so on. Most of these authorities had little interest in civil liberties. Their natural bent was for restriction and they were inclined to act upon suspicion. Moreover, it became clear that many magistrates and judges were affected by patriotic fervour. This was particularly so in relation to people classified as enemy aliens, who were subject to various restrictions, including internment. Many anti-fascist refugees were lumped into this category simply because of their foreign birth, being placed in the same camps as supporters of the German or Italian governments. At the end of 1940, interned aliens were given the right to submit objections to an Aliens Tribunal, which could recommend their release; but these tribunals were not required to conform to standard court requirements of due process and were often unsatisfactory in operation.

Even in ordinary courts, justice could be rough. An illustration of arbitrary action comes from a case in Western Australia, where a raid on an elderly man, J. W. Coleman, resulted in the discovery of two copies of a Kalgoorlie Communist newspaper in his possession. Coleman was prosecuted for propagating unlawful doctrines—as advocated by a body which had been banned. Actually, these two issues of the paper contained references to Coleman's son-in-law, a German-born miner resident in Australia who had been interned. This particular reason for possessing the newspapers did not save Coleman: a magistrate found him guilty and sentenced him to four months hard labour. On appeal, the sentence was reduced to one month. The ACCL had raised the £50 necessary for the appeal, and Evatt donated £5 for the purpose. This was indicated in a letter from Blackburn to Fitzpatrick, saying: 'This is Evatt's fiver. It can be used for the WA case but he doesn't want any publicity'.[2]

Similarly, Evatt's cautious support for the ACCL was shown earlier in a letter from him to Fitzpatrick, who had invited Evatt to become a vice-president of the ACCL. Evatt (newly elected to the Commonwealth Parliament) responded:

I shall help Blackburn to the best of my ability but I prefer not to accept any office in the organisation—I do not think that the value of any help from me will be lessened thereby.[3]

Evatt's reluctance about formally associating himself with the ACCL was probably due to the fact that the organisation, by taking up cases involving Communists—at a time when the CP was unlawful—could be regarded as unpatriotic. It was a point which had caused some of the ACCL's original adherents to distance themselves from it. However, when issues of principle were at stake, Evatt was not inhibited from engaging in public debate, irrespective of whether he was supporting a Communist by doing so. A good example was the case of H. Ratliff and M. Thomas. These two men were active Communists, well-known as such in Sydney. They were arrested in November 1940 by Military Police Intelligence, a body alluded to later by a solicitor, J. B. Sweeney, in addressing a public meeting:

If you read the same encyclopedia as I do occasionally, you will find that there are three sorts of intelligence; firstly, they say there is animal intelligence, secondly, human intelligence and, thirdly, military intelligence...even below that you would have to put Military Police Intelligence.[4]

Following their arrest Ratliff and Thomas were charged with possession of some unlawful (Communist) pamphlets, together with a typewriter and a duplicating machine. Actually, the latter was not surprising, since Ratliff was by occupation a printer. However, the Deputy Crown Solicitor advised that the material could be used 'to establish a state of mind from which it may be inferred that the possession...was..."with a view to influence public opinion in a manner likely to be prejudicial to the efficient prosecution of the war"'. A magistrate, satisfied with this argument, imposed sentences totalling six months imprisonment with hard labour on each man. Though unrepresented in court, they had pleaded 'not guilty' and defended themselves defiantly, being proud of their political standpoint. Further, when the magistrate ordered them to enter into bonds to observe National Security regulations for the duration of the war, they refused to do so.[5]

There were some scattered protests against the sentences, and it was pointed out that Thomas was New Zealand born, while Ratliff was Australian. Indeed, Ratliff had fought at Gallipoli and in France for three years in World War I. These protests were to no avail: Ratliff and Thomas remained in gaol until they finished serving their sentences in May 1941. Six weeks later they were re-arrested and interned without trial, on the orders of the Minister for the Army, Percy Spender. Shortly after, Germany attacked the Soviet Union; and Ratliff and Thomas accordingly decided that the war was no longer imperialist in content. They were now willing to engage in an undertaking to support 'a maximum war effort to secure victory over Nazism and Fascism'. Further, to bring their plight to public attention, the two men went on hunger strike at the same time as they lodged objections against their internment.

This situation provoked many protests, particularly from trade unions. Evatt joined in, arguing publicly that Ratliff and Thomas had been interned without being charged with any offence and that they were being punished twice for the same offence. When a National Security Advisory Committee (otherwise described as a tribunal) met in July 1941 to consider the objections lodged by Ratliff and Thomas, it was faced with a difficult task. The two men, in a weakened condition, were brought into the court on stretchers; and there were threats of industrial action in their support. This time, they had the benefit of legal representation by J. B. Sweeney, who was very critical of the absence of legal rights customarily available to an accused person. Sweeney also noted that the chairman of the Advisory Committee was a retired Supreme Court judge named Pike. Before retirement, Pike was engaged almost solely in Land and Valuation Court work, which might be considered inadequate as a qualification for dealing with appeals by interned persons. However, when he volunteered his services to the Menzies government in 1940, the offer was favourably received; perhaps the knowledge that he was a member of the establishment Union Club in Sydney was sufficient guarantee of his rightness of judgment.[6]

The Advisory Committee did what it saw as its duty. Refusing to be influenced by evidence of industrial unrest over the internment of

Ratliff and Thomas, the Committee doubted whether the two men were sincere in their change of opinion about the war and their proffered undertakings. Accordingly, the Committee recommended that the two internees should not be released; and the government accepted this recommendation. More protest action followed, including a stoppage of work by about 100 000 workers in New South Wales. Evatt stated that the decision to continue internment was 'as unwise as it is unjust...a policy of repression.'[7]

A few months later, Evatt became Attorney-General and arranged for the release of Ratliff and Thomas on their signing suitable undertakings. Apparently, there was no cause for official concern about them thereafter. Quite apart from questions of justice, it could well have been argued that continuation of their internment ran counter to the professed aim of efficient prosecution of the war, as angry workers resorted to strike action entailing loss of production. Fitzpatrick at this time reported to officers of the ACCL concerning a long talk which he had with Evatt, including discussion of the Ratliff–Thomas case and two pending prosecutions of a comparable nature in Melbourne. Evatt promised to enquire into these cases. Further, Fitzpatrick wrote:

The Attorney-General discussed with me the general bearing of the N.S.W. Regulations touching civil liberties, and informed me that he had no intention of permitting proceedings of the kind of which we [ACCL] have had to complain on numerous occasions during the last 18 months ...Dr Evatt said that he considered a power to intern was necessary. I agreed but pointed out that as the Regulation 26 stood anyone could be interned arbitrarily. I made tentative suggestions for the insertion of safeguards into Regulation 26 and Dr Evatt appeared to accept the principle.[8]

Evidently, a strong rapport was subsequently established between Evatt and Fitzpatrick, although there were some differences of viewpoint. In the memo just quoted, Fitzpatrick noted that he had raised the question of the official ban on the CPA and other organisations but Evatt had indicated that its removal presented some difficulties in view of the composition of the federal Labor caucus. This was a reference to the influence of anti-Communist Catholics in the ALP, especially in Victoria. In fact, it was not till the end of 1942 that legality was restored to the CPA, although the Communists staunchly supported the war from mid-1941. Indeed, they used their influence among workers to head off strikes which might disrupt war production. Even so, when Evatt announced the lifting of the ban on the CPA, he was careful to make it clear that 'the decision evidences no sympathy by the government with any Communist views or doctrine'.[9]

In parenthesis, it may be said that it is doubtful whether the banning of the CPA was very effective. A rare indication of the flavour of those days comes from Eddie Maher, a young Communist worker at the time:

When the Party became illegal, I used to sell illegal Tribunes. Being a cricketer, a sportsman, well-known in Paddington...I would start at the Royal Hotel and finish at Bondi, and I would be blind drunk by the end—but I sold the Tribune and had none left. I would go with the Progress at the front and the Tribs at the back to avoid arrest. And the blokes in the pub would say, 'Ah, give us the illegal one, Eddie!'
We [also] raised money for gaoled comrades.[10]

Up to 1942, Evatt's involvement in issues of civil liberty was decidedly in line with his previous liberal record on the subject. Then the picture was blurred by official action against the Australia First Movement (AFM). This body, founded in 1941 by P. R. Stephensen, was projected as the nucleus of a new political party to be established once the war was over. Stephensen, an intellectual and writer of some distinction, was known mainly for his extreme nationalist views on Australian culture and politics. Through his monthly magazine, *The Publicist*, Stephensen churned out what an opponent, Cyril Pearl, described as 'a stale mixture of rabid anti-British nationalism, Nazi-inspired, and anti-semitism and windy Fascist pseudo-philosophy'. Stephensen and his associates were also believed to be pro-Japanese and this was certainly true of one prominent AFM member, Adela Walsh, who had moved far to the right in politics since the Walsh–Johnson case in 1925–26.[11]

The AFM was a motley collection of hopelessly incompetent cranks, comprising less than 100 members in Sydney. The insignificance of the organisation became apparent towards the end of 1941 when it held a number of public meetings. Attendance was poor and a number of those present (Communists, wharfies, servicemen) were hostile. Several brawls broke out. Evatt was aware of AFM activities, as the organisation was under surveillance by several security bodies, including the Commonwealth Investigation Branch attached to the Attorney-General's Department. Actually, the CIB did not favour very drastic action against the AFM. On the other hand, the Military Police Intelligence Section of the New South Wales police force (in co-operation with a group of army officers) considered that the AFM should be declared unlawful by Commonwealth authorities.[12]

Evatt did not act upon this recommendation. Instead, when it became known that the AFM was planning to hold another public meeting on 5 March 1942, the Attorney-General signed an order under National Service Regulations, prohibiting the meeting. The order was despatched to MacKay, the New South Wales Commissioner of Police. However, MacKay returned Evatt's order to Canberra, saying that it had been unnecessary to use or disclose it: the meeting was cancelled by Stephensen himself, after MacKay told him that the meeting would be banned by exercise of traditional police powers, as likely to cause a disturbance of public order. Evatt may have felt relieved to have the matter dealt with in this way. He appears to have thought highly of MacKay—who, a few days later, was appointed as the first Director-General of a new body, the Commonwealth Security Service, which was mainly concerned with the surveillance of aliens. The Service was to be under the administration of the Minister for the Army during Evatt's absence abroad.[13]

Stephensen came under criticism from all sides. For example, the State Labor Party called for the public trial of leaders of the AFM. In the New South Wales parliament, a Labor MP, Abram Landa, attacked Stephensen for his virulent anti-semitism. Evatt himself, like a great many other Australians, regarded the AFM as contemptible. He would also have been incensed if he had known that Stephensen planned to distort the manner in which Evatt had arranged for Australia's declaration of war against Japan (through the King, yet separately from Britain): in Stephensen's view, it could be inferred that a 'separate peace' between Australia and Japan would be in order. This would mesh with Stephensen's argument that Australia should not be in the war, which should be left for other countries to fight out. The argument is typical of Stephensen's remoteness from reality.

Even so, Evatt was not privy to the official decision to intern members of the AFM. He left Australia on his overseas mission on 9 March. That night, four people were arrested in Western Australia. Information about these arrests was then telegraphed, in sensationally worded form, to military intelligence headquarters in Sydney, with the result that Stephensen and fifteen other people associated with the AFM there were arrested on 10 March 1942. They were interned on the orders of Forde, Minister for the Army.

The four people in Perth were charged with conspiring to assist within Australia 'a public enemy, to wit, the armed forces of Japan'. It was alleged that these people planned to co-operate with the Japanese in the event of their invading Western Australia. The evidence for the allegation was very largely dependent upon the word of a police informer working for Detective-Sergeant Richards of the Special (political) Bureau of the State police. There was strong suspicion of a frame-up. As Hasluck moderately expresses it, there was 'ground for considerable speculation whether there ever was any substantial threat to security in the alleged conspiracy'. Nevertheless, two of the men were convicted in a Perth court in June and were given substantial prison sentences.[14]

The internment of the sixteen people in Sydney was based upon an Intelligence claim that there was an integral connection between them and the small Perth group. In practice, this amounted to no more than a similarity of views; and apparently the Perth group had heard vaguely about the AFM organisation in Sydney. There was no AFM branch in Western Australia and as Justice Clyne noted in his subsequent enquiry, the Sydney members of the AFM 'were completely unaware of the conspiracy alleged against the persons arrested in Western Australia'.[15]

Clearly, whatever may be thought about the episode in Perth, the operation against the AFM in Sydney was a gross blunder. Intelligence officers jumped the gun and bamboozled Forde into signing internment orders. Evatt was overseas and in his absence the Attorney-General's Department was not in charge of the matter. Actually, the Crown Solicitor, H. F. Whitlam, examined Stephensen's speeches and other papers and on 16 April 1942 told Sir George Knowles, the Solicitor-General, that there was nothing to indicate any contravention by Stephensen of any National Security Act Regulation or any other Commonwealth law. In other words, no matter how objectionable Stephensen and his associates might appear, they could not be charged with influencing public opinion in a manner likely to be prejudicial to the war effort. However, this did not protect them from internment.

In Parliament, Blackburn urged that the internees should be given a fair trial, but little notice was taken of this. He was highly regarded as a man of principle, but his influence among Labor MPs had declined after his expulsion from the Party by its Victorian Executive in 1941 for continued association with the Australia–Soviet Friendship League. In the eyes of most Australians, more important than questions of civil liberties were perceptions of Stephensen as a would-be traitor at a time of serious national peril. In addition, as far as the Curtin government was concerned, the Deputy Prime Minister—under the influence of security advisers—had bungled badly, but should be supported. In the ALP, solidarity was an important consideration.

❖

During his absence abroad in 1942, Evatt was so engrossed in external affairs that he had very little time to spare for domestic developments in Australia. There was one exception, involving Evatt's expertise as a lawyer. This was a question of constitutional validity of uniform taxation. The exigencies of war entailed a need for higher rates of Commonwealth income tax, which was complicated by the fact that the States also imposed income tax—and at rates varying between themselves as well as in relation to the Commonwealth. As a matter of equity and administrative convenience, in May 1942 the Treasurer, J. B. Chifley, introduced several taxation Bills, designed to make the Commonwealth the sole authority to tax incomes, and to ensure that tax rates would be uniform throughout Australia. This was of great significance in the long run, as it meant a permanent change in relationships between the Commonwealth and the States.

Inevitably, several States appealed to the High Court to declare the legislation invalid as a derogation of State sovereignty. Among these objectors were States which had Labor governments in office: their petty parochial interests overbore the fact that traditional ALP policy was to centralise power in the federal government. With a struggle in the High Court likely, Evatt sent a cable from Washington on 24 April 1942 to inform Knowles that

the best constitutional method by which uniform taxation can be secured and yet survive the test of a challenge in the Courts is by fixing the Commonwealth rate at such a level as will secure a sufficient overall taxation after allowing as a deduction from each taxpayer the actual taxes paid or payable to the States. This has its difficulties because, although it will secure uniformity, it still allows the States to tax unevenly.[16]

In the event, Chifley framed the legislation in such a way as to give the Commonwealth priority in payment of income tax without formally depriving the States of their power to tax. Exercise of such power by the States was made difficult by the transfer of tax officials and equipment from them to the Commonwealth. States which refrained from imposing income tax for themselves were to be reimbursed by the Commonwealth for their lost revenues. It was a subtle move, declared 'plausible' by Evatt. The legislation was challenged in the High Court by four States, but in July 1942 the Court upheld its validity. Chifley and Evatt correctly gauged the influence of the war on the judges' assessment of national interests.

This appears to have been the only matter of domestic Australian politics which attracted Evatt's attention while he was overseas. There is no indication that he was informed in any detail about the Australia First Movement internments and the part played in them by security organisations. If he had been aware of the facts, it is just conceivable that on one of his visits to Chequers, Evatt might have asked Churchill about British experience in such matters. As it happened, MI5 in 1941 stubbornly objected to the release of many aliens who had been hastily interned but were now regarded as safe by appeal tribunals. On one occasion, Churchill, generally a supporter of MI5, wrote in exasperation:

I have heard from various quarters that the witch-finding activities of MI5 are becoming an actual impediment to the more important work of the department. I am carefully considering certain changes, not only in MI5 but in the Intelligence and Secret Service control.[17]

If Evatt had known about this, he might have been less susceptible to special pleading by security authorities when he returned to Australia and inherited the AFM debacle from Forde. The Attorney-General moved fairly quickly to repair some of the damage due to Forde's naivety. Between August and October 1942, most of the sixteen people arrested in Sydney were released from internment, though they were still subject to certain restrictions, such as their freedom to move wherever they pleased. This action was taken in some cases following Advisory Committee recommendations, which Evatt adopted. In other cases, Evatt took the initiative himself, after consulting security officers. By the end of the year, only three AFM people—including Stephensen—remained in detention camps.

On 10 September 1942, Evatt made a comprehensive parliamentary statement on security matters. He referred to certain improvements in internment procedures, mainly aimed at shortening delays in the hearing of objections by tribunals—although the Security Service, subject to the Minister's oversight, was still to have the last word on decisions concerning the release of internees. Evatt also enunciated certain principles, admirable in themselves though carefully hedged with exceptions. He said: 'The aim and sole justification of all restrictions upon individual liberty is to prevent injury to the war effort of the country...full internment being reserved for cases where the possibility of injury to the nation is undeniable'. However, 'there cannot be any absolute right of public trial in these cases of restriction of liberty. In most cases it would not be possible to prove that the accused person had committed a specific offence.' The last two of these quoted sentences were in contradiction to what Evatt had said about a right to trial in the Ratliff–Thomas case earlier. They also represented a rationale for rejecting Stephensen's requests that he be put on trial so that he could defend himself. Habeas corpus no longer applied in wartime.

With specific reference to the AFM, Evatt made no acknowledgment of any official error. He endorsed the actions taken by Forde and Military Intelligence in relation to these 'enemies of Australia'. Indeed, while admitting that two of the four people put on trial in Western Australia were acquitted by a jury, Evatt justified continued internment of these two by referring to a hostile remark by a judge. Evatt concluded his statement by quoting damaging extracts from the correspondence of some unnamed people associated with the AFM in Sydney. These extracts, which appeared to support Forde's earlier parliamentary reference to the AFM internees as traitorous fifth-columnists, could not be tested in court in the absence of trials.

All in all, Evatt's statement was a deplorable attempt to cover up the blunders of Forde and Intelligence agents. As Craig Munro puts it: 'Evatt's political principles had proved as flexible as anyone else's'. The Attorney-General's statement was accepted at the time, when few people knew the facts, but the matter came back to haunt him in later years. Although Evatt was not responsible for the original decision to intern the AFM leaders, his continued attempt to vindicate that decision sullied his reputation as a civil libertarian. It would have been far better to have ignored the AFM. It had no influence nor did it have any communication with enemy forces or agents. Thus it represented no real threat to Australia. Even if the decision to arrest AFM leaders be accepted as a natural response to wartime fears, the injury due to that decision could have been reasonably contained once it was recognised in official quarters that a mistake had been made. Early release of the internees, coupled with an expression of regret—preferably by Forde—would have settled the matter in 1942. Instead, a cover-up was adopted as a means of salvaging Forde's reputation—not to mention the hides of some over-zealous, if not bent, security agents.[18]

Much more congenial to Evatt's cast of mind at this time was the Statute of Westminster Adoption Bill, which he introduced into the Commonwealth parliament in October 1942. The statute had been passed by the United Kingdom parliament in 1931. With the concurrence of the self-governing Dominions, the Statute of Westminster spelled out the right of each dominion to make its own laws and foreign policy and to give its own advice directly to the King. However, to preserve the appearance of equality, crucial sections of the Statute of Westminster were not to come into effect in relation to any particular Dominion until that dominion adopted the Statute by Act of its own legislature. In the 1930s, Canada and South Africa adopted the Statute, but Australia and New Zealand did not.

Actually, in 1937 Menzies as Commonwealth Attorney-General brought into parliament a Bill to adopt the Statute of Westminster but parliament was dissolved before it came to a vote. Evatt, to smooth the passage of his own Bill, gave this technical point as the reason for failure to pass the Bill in 1937, yet it seems that Menzies and other conservatives had been at best lukewarm: they felt that the reality of Australian independence was enough in itself and that formal adoption of the Statute would derogate from their stance as empire loyalists. In consequence, certain pieces of Commonwealth legislation could still be deemed invalid. In particular, the (British) Colonial Laws Validity Act of 1865—under which any colonial law which was repugnant to an imperial law might be declared void—remained in force.

The restrictive effect of the Act of 1865 was felt mainly in connection with shipping, as the British Merchant Shipping Act of 1894 was considered to have overriding force in relation to legislation such as the Australian Navigation Act. In speaking to his Bill in 1942, Evatt emphasised that the situation had acquired urgency because of the war. It was legally necessary to send certain Bills passed by parliament to the King for assent. Although it would not be in accord with constitutional practice for the King to refuse assent, the reservation of Bills for this purpose necessarily entailed delay. This had always been the case, but now the delay could apply even to certain National Security Regulations. Evatt particularly cited an amendment to the Navigation Act passed by parliament in June 1942, for which royal assent had not yet been proclaimed—four months later.[19]

Evatt's Bill was passed without difficulty, though not without disquiet on the part of some conservatives who felt that he was motivated by anti-British prejudice in bringing the matter up at this time. Evatt strenuously denied this, pointing out that the statute to be adopted was actually an Act of the British parliament. Moreover, he had stated his intention to deal with the matter a year earlier, soon after the Curtin government took office. More urgent matters had intervened, yet to Evatt the Statute of Westminster Adoption Act was a necessary step towards full independence for Australia, in law as well as practice. It may be noted, however, that the Australian legislation and the Statute of Westminster itself did not affect the powers of the British parliament with respect to individual States in Australia.[20]

Clarification of the powers of the Commonwealth in relation to Britain was one constitutional problem. The other side of the coin was the question of the powers of the Commonwealth as against those of the States. Evatt gave an early indication that this question had not been overlooked: on the same day that he spoke on the Statute of Westminster Adoption Bill, he gave parliamentary notice of a Constitution Alteration (War Aims and Reconstruction) Bill. With a view to dealing with expected post-war problems such as unemployment, the government proposed that the Australian constitution be amended so as to give the Commonwealth greater powers. Although the proposal was deferred for a year or two, it is interesting to note that in introducing the matter in October 1942, Evatt indicated an essential interaction between foreign and domestic policies. In doing so, he was applying and extending views formed during his years on the High Court. Now, in parliament, he said:

This country, like all the other United Nations, has pledged itself to the task of achieving the broad objectives embodied in the Atlantic Charter and in the historic declaration of the four essential human freedoms ...These declarations...are solemn pledges of our dedication as a nation to the great ends of economic security, social justice and individual freedom...the Australian nation, which pledged as a nation, must be endowed as a nation with legislative powers to carry out the pledges within Australia and its territories.[21]

NOTES

1. Robin Gollan, *Revolutionaries and Reformists: Communism and the Australian Labour Movement 1920–1950*, Allen & Unwin, Sydney, 1975, p. 97.
2. Blackburn to Fitzpatrick, 2 June 1941, Fitzpatrick Papers, MS 4965, 1/7290, NLA.
3. Evatt to Fitzpatrick, 8 November 1940, Fitzpatrick Papers, MS 4965, 1/619, NLA.
4. Ibid. Commonwealth Investigation Branch, verbatim report of speech by Sweeney, 6 August 1941, at meeting under auspices of Manly branch of the State Labor Party, Australian Archives A467, item SF 42/4. In 1973, J.B. Sweeney, QC, was appointed as a judge of the Australian Industrial Court.
5. AA: A467, SF 42/4, Bundle 90, Item 4, A–G File on Proposed Prosecution of Thomas and Ratliff. Incidentally, most commentators, including P. Hasluck, incorrectly reported the latter's name as 'Ratcliff'.
6. For Sweeney's criticisms, refer to footnote 4 above. Information about Pike and his offer of service is in AA: A472, W211.
7. *Sydney Morning Herald*, 24 July 1941.
8. Memo, Fitzpatrick to members of the Emergency (War) Committee of ACCL, 22 October 1941, Fitzpatrick Paper, MS 4965, 1/14341, NLA. Regulation 26 related to Restriction and Detention Orders.
9. Quoted in R. Gollan, *Revolutionaries and Reformists*, p. 129.
10. Interview with Eddie Maher, Sydney, 4 October 1989. *Progress* was the organ of the State Labor Party.
11. Pearl, quoted in Bruce Muirden, *The Puzzled Patriots*, MUP, Melbourne, 1968, p. 52.
12. Paul Hasluck, *The Government and the People 1942–1945*, Australian War Memorial, Canberra, 1970, pp. 722–6.
13. MacKay to Knowles, 7 March 1942. AA: A467, SF 43, Bundle 97, Australia First Movement.

14 Paul Hasluck, *The Government and the People 1942–1945*, p. 731.
15 Clyne Enquiry Report, p. 8. AA: A467, SF 43, Bundle 97, item 17.
16 AA: A4764/2, ES15.
17 Minute from Churchill, 25 January 1941, quoted in Neil Stammers, *Civil Liberties in Britain during the Second World War*, Croom Helm, London, 1983, pp. 55–6.
18 Craig Munro, *Wild Man of Letters: The Story of P.R. Stephensen*, MUP, Melbourne, 1984, p. 236.
19 The second-reading speech is in H.V. Evatt, *Foreign Policy of Australia: Speeches*, Angus & Robertson, Sydney, 1945, pp. 78–95.
20 S. Encel, *Cabinet Government in Australia*, MUP, Melbourne, 1962, pp. 46–8.
21 *Commonwealth Parliamentary Debates*, vol. 172, p. 1339.

CHAPTER 15

WARPLANES, TRADE AND ECONOMIC PLANS

I am making preparations for the forthcoming visit of Dr Evatt which, if the last occasion is any guide, is likely to be troublesome.
BRIGADIER JACOB, OFFICER ON CHURCHILL'S STAFF, 1943

At the Casablanca conference between Roosevelt and Churchill in January 1943, the basic war strategy—'Beat Hitler First'—remained unchanged. However, it was decided that a major offensive in western Europe was not feasible until 1944, and this meant that some Allied resources could be used for other purposes in the interim. The British favoured an attack in the Mediterranean. The Americans were not opposed to this but some of their leaders—General Macarthur in Australia, for example—felt that a greater proportion of resources should be committed to the Pacific war. In short, while preserving the basic strategy, a change of emphasis was conceivable.

Curtin, when he heard about the Casablanca conference, informed Churchill and Roosevelt that the Australian air force needed more warplanes, not simply for the defence of Australia but also for holding operations in the Pacific, which called for limited offensives against Japanese forces. By this time, bitter fighting by Australian troops along the Kokoda Trail had pushed the Japanese back in Papua, but they still held Rabaul and other centres in New Guinea. Beyond that, though still not distant from Australia, American forces were heavily engaged in the Solomon Islands. The Australian government was particularly concerned by delays in the supply of planes from the United States. In 1942, it was provisionally planned to expand the size of the RAAF to seventy-three squadrons by April 1943, but this figure had to be scaled down to about forty-five squadrons. Crews to fly more planes were available in Australia, but the machines were not. Understandably, the Americans gave priority to equipping their own squadrons based in Australia rather than the RAAF.

Curtin, in the absence of satisfactory responses to his cables, announced in February 1943 that Evatt was to go on another mission to the United States and Britain, mainly in an attempt to secure substantially more aircraft for the RAAF. Actually, Evatt did not leave Australia till six weeks later, so that his hosts had adequate advance notice. Brigadier Jacob, a military bureaucrat on Churchill's staff, told a colleague in the Air Ministry:

I am making preparations for the forthcoming visit of Dr Evatt which, if the last occasion is any guide, is likely to be troublesome.[1]

This irritated remark illustrates Evatt's reputation as a difficult man to deal with. He tended to be overbearing in manner, brusque to the point of being rude, and inclined to be suspicious and obsessive, sometimes bordering on a state of paranoia. He was also determined, forceful and effective; and it was these attributes which really worried people like Jacob and Portal, the British Chief of Air Staff. Before Evatt set off on his second overseas mission, the Joint Planning Staff of the British War Cabinet was busy assembling material to counter the arguments which Evatt was expected to present. Telegrams on the subject were exchanged frequently between Whitehall and senior British liaison officers in Washington.

If Evatt had known about these machinations, he might well have exploded and accused the air planners of double-dealing: whose side where they on? An honest answer, if forthcoming, would have been that these people had virtually no concern for Australia, so long as its importunate Prime Minister and Minister for External Affairs could be fobbed off. The big show was the war in Europe. In their own eyes, the bureaucrats were unquestionably right. Thus the Air Ministry policy of using hundreds of bombers in nightly poundings of German cities was pursued regardless of suggestions—though not from Australia—that the strategy was of doubtful effect in winning the war. In any case, Australia must wait.

❖

Evatt left Australia on his overseas mission in April 1943, bound initially for Washington. As in the previous year, he was accompanied by his wife, Mary Alice, and W. S. Robinson, but there were newcomers in the party this time, notably H. C. Coombs, Director of the Department of Post-War Reconstruction, and J. W. Burton, Evatt's private secretary. In pressing his case for more aircraft, Evatt adopted his usual practice of talking to the media and engaging in discussions with everyone, from President Roosevelt downwards, who might have an impact on decisions. Yet very little progress was made. Evatt's contacts were sympathetic while promising nothing. There were institutional barriers. The Munitions Assignment Board in Washington, like its counterpart in London, allocated war supplies according to general directives from the Combined US–UK Chiefs of Staff Committee. This meant priority for the aim of beating Germany first, and the Americans took their cue from the British in resisting claims from Australia. There were no Australian representatives on these boards.

A breakthrough came in May, when Churchill arrived in Washington to discuss future Allied strategy with Roosevelt. Australia was not invited to this Trident conference and it was a mere coincidence that it took place at a time when Evatt was present in Washington. Nevertheless, Evatt was able to have a long talk with Churchill and this, along with Churchill's realisation that many Americans wanted more stress on the war in the Pacific, probably influenced the outcome of the Trident conference. While maintaining the strategy of absolute priority for the war in Europe, the conference agreed to give more emphasis than previously to the war against Japan. Churchill referred to this at a meeting of the Pacific War Council in Washington, at which Evatt and Roosevelt were present. At the same time, Churchill expressed support for expansion of the RAAF; and Roosevelt agreed to supply more aircraft to Australia.[2]

In June 1943, Roosevelt committed the US government to supplying Australia, under lend-lease arrangements, with 'approximately 475 planes prior to the end of 1944. This is in addition to any previous commitments'. This number of planes was intended to complete the Australian seventy-three-squadron programme. Evatt happily cabled this information to Curtin and claimed full success for his mission. Yet Evatt reckoned without the ability of powerful military authorities to twist or frustrate the wishes of politicians. Of the planes promised, only 132 were made available to Australia from American production in 1943 and most of these were of superseded types. D. M. Horner disparages Evatt concerning his mission in 1943, saying that his success in the United States was illusory and that his 'main concern appears to have been to increase his own prestige'.[3]

This dismissive comment is in contrast to the general seriousness of Horner's worth as a military historian. Certainly, Evatt, as a politician, was aware that a general election was due in Australia later in the year and that the results of his mission could affect Labor's prospects in the election. Yet to emphasise this and Evatt's aggressiveness is to discount his efforts, while glossing over a critical question: could anyone else, representing a minor power, have achieved as much against such formidable obstacles? Evatt, a notoriously hard worker, told Curtin that he had 'never worked so hard or so untiringly on anything in my life'. As for the impression created by Evatt in the United States, he undoubtedly alienated some important people. Despite this, Sir John Dill, Chief of the United Kingdom Joint Staff Mission in Washington, informed Churchill that General George Marshall, US Army Chief of Staff, in a conversation with Dill 'expressed surprise that Arnold and King were able to produce as much as they have for Evatt'. Admittedly, Arnold and King acted rather reluctantly and at Roosevelt's urging—and the planes allocated by these officers were being phased out of production.[4]

Another aspect of Evatt's work, barely mentioned by historians, relates to his speeches, through which he presented Australia's viewpoint while overseas. He thus influenced public opinion, which in turn had to be taken into account by politicians in those countries. The extent of this activity is indicated by a personal letter from John Burton in Washington to Paul Hasluck in Canberra. The letter also illustrates a growth of close trust between Burton and Evatt:

I am enclosing a speech by Minister...We have turned out about 40 speeches—I have another 6 to do this weekend before going to Canada. As a matter of fact they are becoming less difficult. I find the Minister rarely has much idea of the line he wants to follow, and he will accept a draft quite easily. I have not had so many ideas put over for a long time!

The boss has behaved quite well, and everyone is commenting that he is much less difficult this time than last. I believe I have been able to help towards this end quite a bit and wonder how he managed last time, because the Legation staff are all hopeless.[5]

Horner's slighting remarks about Evatt relate primarily to the American section of the visit overseas. In June 1943, Evatt moved on to London, where he played upon what he regarded as his special relationship with Churchill. Specifically, Evatt suggested that, as a gesture comparable to the agreement about Spitfires the previous year, Britain should despatch some more squadrons of planes to Australia. Churchill, despite objections from his Chief of Air Staff, approved the idea and decided to send two RAF Spitfire squadrons. On balance, it seems little enough return for the fact that there were seventeen Australian squadrons serving with the Royal Air Force at the time, comprising 10 500 aircrew.

Actually, Churchill delayed formal notification of the decision on the two additional Spitfire squadrons until after the general election in Australia. He did not intend to give the ALP an electoral boost, and he was wrongly advised by the British High Commissioner in Canberra that the ALP was likely to lose the election. The Spitfires arrived in Australia in December 1943. In the meantime Evatt, back in Australia, arranged for the Commonwealth government to make a gift of a live platypus to Churchill. The External Affairs Department solemnly presented a memorandum of costs to the Commonwealth Treasury, including £96 for what was described as a 'platypussary' (a tank and burrows incorporated in one unit) and £44 for 'food for voyage; cost of digging worms and grubs'. The unfortunate creature, one of the shyest of all animals, died during the voyage, whereupon Churchill offered to have the animal stuffed by the Royal College of Surgeons.

Leaving aside such absurdities, it may be noted that Evatt was more concerned to establish cordial relations with Britain than with the United States. This was in contrast to the abiding impression left in the public mind by Curtin's statement in December 1941 about Australia looking to America for support. The statement was obviously true in terms of American supplies and armed forces in the Pacific. In certain other respects, the inferences commonly drawn from the statement were of doubtful validity. In Evatt's overseas missions in 1942–43, he took full account of the immense importance of US productive capacity: the United States was the prime country from which Australia could hope to obtain substantial numbers of aircraft. Nevertheless, in general diplomatic terms, Evatt applied himself more to cultivating good relations with Britain—although, of course, this policy was linked to Australian-American relations through the dominant figure of Churchill. For his part, Churchill saw good reasons, in terms of the future of the British Commonwealth, for keeping Australia favourably disposed. Wayne Reynolds sums up:

Central to Evatt's perception of the Empire in this period was his view that the United States was not only casual in its recognition of Australian strategic priorities, but was emerging as a future threat to Australian national interest. The one defence seemed to lie in the assertion of the Imperial connection.[6]

Elucidation of this point requires reference to economic relations between Australia and the United States, particularly in the broader context of British imperial trade. Australia had its own protective tariff system, and was also part of the sterling bloc of countries. British goods received preferential treatment in the Australian market and in return there were substantial preferences for some Australian exports in Britain and other parts of the empire. This was notably the case following the Ottawa trade agreements of 1932. In the American view, this system of trade preferences discriminated against the rest of the world. The United States wanted an extension of world trade, unhampered by tariff barriers, for the same reason as Britain itself had followed a policy of free trade in the nineteenth century: free trade was to the advantage of the dominant economic power—and after World War I, that meant the United States, not Britain.

The financing of the Allied effort in World War II provided US negotiators with a powerful lever to bring about a fundamental post-war improvement in the American foreign economic position. This flowed from the very strong position of the United States as a creditor nation. In 1941 (before direct American involvement in the war), the Lend-Lease Act provided for the supply of war materials to Britain on terms which bypassed the shortage of dollars by not requiring payment while the war lasted. This arrangement was extended in February 1942 by a Mutual Aid Agreement between the United States and the United Kingdom. The Agreement established the principle of reciprocal aid to the United States where appropriate, this being known as Reverse Lend-Lease. More significant in the long-term was Article VII of the Agreement, which bound the signatory governments to agree upon measures to expand post-war domestic and international economies, including 'the elimination of all forms of discriminatory treatment in international commerce, and...the reduction of tariffs and other trade barriers'. These future agreements were not spelled out.

In practice the provisions relating to Lend-Lease and reciprocal aid applied to Australia and other Dominions as well as Britain. However, Australia was not formally covered, and it was decided to remedy this simply by an exchange of Notes between the Australian and US governments. It is useful in this connection to distinguish the question of Article VII of the Mutual Aid Agreement from matters of Lend-Lease and Reverse Lend-Lease. Article VII worried some Australian Cabinet ministers, as indicated to the Australian Legation in Washington on 21 May 1942. The cable expressed the Commonwealth Government's 'tentative views' on the United States' proposals that Australia should give up some of its preferential position in empire markets in return for an improved position for some Australian exports in the American market. In a world of expanding trade,

a substantial agreement on these lines might well be made in the long-term interests of Australia. But unless positive action is taken to promote world trade, we should be left with the loss of an assured market for exports, while the benefit we would receive in the American market appears very uncertain. At the close of the war our position would be very precarious.[7]

This concerned the long term. More immediately, Evatt was affected, partly because his Department was involved in the foreign economic policy aspect and partly because at the relevant time in 1942 he was the only Commonwealth Minister in a position to engage personally in negotiations with counterparts in other governments. In Washington in June 1942, Evatt had intensive discussions with Dean Acheson, US Assistant Secretary of State, concerning the form of the proposed exchange of Notes on Lend-Lease and reciprocal aid between their respective governments. The two men reached tentative agreement, Evatt being primarily concerned to ensure that Reverse Lend-Lease from Australia should not be regarded as open-ended in nature. The point of this was the likelihood that reciprocal aid from Australia—mainly in foodstuffs and raw materials—would represent a substantial proportion of the value of Lend-Lease goods received from the United States. In fact, by the end of the war the proportion was seventy per cent or more, which was much greater than the comparable figure for reciprocal aid provided by Britain to the United States.

Evatt was satisfied with his discussions with Acheson; but the latter's superior, Cordell Hull, then ignored the tentative agreement and produced a draft exchange of Notes which expressed Australia's commitment to reciprocal aid in the widest possible terms. After some hesitation, the Commonwealth government accepted Hull's draft, subject to it being made clear that Australia's reciprocal aid was to be limited for the time being to US armed forces in Australia and its territories. The Notes, formally exchanged in September 1942, also stated that Australia accepted 'the principles' of the United States–United Kingdom Mutual Aid Agreement, yet Evatt refused an American request that Australia commit itself in writing to the terms of Article VII. 'Principles' did not necessarily embrace all of the terms.[8]

Then, in February 1943, the Australian government announced that it was granting the United States the status of most favoured nation under the Australian tariff. It is not entirely clear why this did not apply in the 1930s, although it appears to have been connected with Australia's trade diversion policy. It may have been reckoned that American exporters were doing well enough without special favours, for the United States regularly had a very favourable balance of trade with Australia, largely because the Americans kept out Australian wool to protect their own producers. Nevertheless, an American trade official in 1942 suggested to Evatt that Australia should give most favoured nation treatment to imports from the

United States. The matter was evidently not regarded as very important or urgent and the Australian decision in 1943 was probably aimed at conciliating the State Department as a prelude to Evatt's mission overseas. Cordell Hull responded with a message of appreciation to Evatt but it is doubtful whether this represented any softening of US attitudes on trade matters. The decision did not affect Australia's preferential Empire tariff.[9]

American trade officials became tougher in dealings with Australia. One US representative who had spent six months in Australia reported in Washington his dissatisfaction with Lend-Lease relations. He said that the United States was being looked upon as 'Uncle Santa Claus', and that Australians 'in their Lend-Lease requisitions for machinery always have one eye on postwar industrialisation and ...their requests might well be screened more carefully'. This kind of observation had an effect. Towards the end of 1943, the Australian government was notified of a decision by the United States to restrict the scope of Lend-Lease aid, this being associated with a request for Australia to extend its Reverse Lend-Lease.[10]

Economic considerations had already assumed greater significance than previously, and Evatt on his mission overseas in 1943 was fortunate in being advised by H. C. Coombs. Coombs was a young economist who reported from Washington to the Treasury in Canberra, but Chifley gave him a fairly free hand. Evatt was satisfied with the arrangement so long as Coombs consulted him on important aspects. Coombs provided vital expertise, not only in relation to Lend-Lease matters but also by representing Australia at international conferences in the United States concerning the form of a future monetary stabilisation fund and the need for an organisation to deal with food and agriculture. The US representatives emphasised the Article VII commitment to eliminate tariffs and other trade barriers, while Coombs expressed the Australian viewpoint that the commitment must be considered in the context of post-war expansion of employment and rising living standards. Evatt, too, in addressing the Hot Springs conference on food and agriculture, emphasised the importance of full employment. A little later, when Coombs moved on to London with Evatt, the Australian economist had useful talks on post-war commercial policy with Keynes and representatives of British dominion countries. Britain shared Australian misgivings about American trade policy.[11]

The Australian emphasis upon full employment—a matter of little concern to US representatives—came from the development of ALP policies for the post-war world. Not only was full employment socially desirable: it also required extension of Australian manufacturing with its heavy demands for labour. Already there had been a dramatic increase in secondary industries to meet war needs, and Australian tariff barriers seemed necessary to maintain this position after the end of the war. Consequently Evatt and his colleagues were suspicious of US trade objectives as reflected in Article VII. Moreover, Evatt was fearful that any public talk about possible tariff reductions might adversely affect Labor Party prospects in the approaching federal election. Actually, there was little public discussion about the matter before the end of the war.

Coombs' personal impressions of Evatt in 1943 are interesting as presenting aspects rather different from those generally portrayed by people who worked with him. Certainly, Coombs found him difficult and suspicious. Yet Evatt 'never resented disagreement, entering into argument in forthright and vigorous style and expecting the like in return'. Moreover, Evatt was 'capable of warm and friendly response'. Late at night, he often dropped in to see Coombs and Burton to talk about books, people and social issues:

In this mood he was an exhilarating companion. He was always reading six books at a time and his photographic memory enabled him to quote readily and aptly from a vast repertoire of literature.

As for Coombs' own special area of knowledge, his comment upon Evatt was acute: 'While not greatly interested in economic matters, he mastered a brief about them with the speed of a top flight barrister.'[12]

Another adviser who contributed to Evatt's informal education was W. S. Robinson, who enjoyed access to inside information as well as to influential people. Thus he was able to bring two important points to Evatt's attention concerning Reverse Lend-Lease. First, Robinson noted that the concerned attitude of Morgenthau, US Treasury Secretary, on this subject was probably influenced by the large external credits being built up by Canada, India and South Africa, whereas the position of Australia was quite the reverse. Second, Australian producers of lead and zinc concentrates sold their products mainly to the British and Australian governments at controlled prices. The US producers, on the other hand, sold at much higher prices to the US government. In consequence,

When Australia is debited with the value of goods and services from the US under Lend Lease, the US prices are based on the inflated values ruling in that country. In all except a few items, when Australia provides goods and services under Reverse Lend Lease, the costs are based on Australia's controlled and low level prices.[13]

Robinson's long-term interest lay in the establishment of an integrated aluminium industry in Australia. Before the war, there was only a small fabricating plant, which meant that Australia was very heavily dependent upon imports for its aluminium requirements. Robinson kept Evatt informed about the growing importance of aluminium as a new light alloy, not only in the manufacture of warplanes but also in extension of the use of aluminium to many other industries, particularly post-war civil aviation. As the industrialist dramatically expressed the point in a long memorandum supplied to Evatt in mid-1943: 'We are passing from the era of coal and iron to that of electricity and aluminium.' In Robinson's view, Australia needed to establish a large-scale aluminium manufacturing plant of its own: other countries could not be relied upon in this connection, as US, Canadian and British aluminium producers would discourage such competition from Australia.[14]

There were problems about giving concrete shape to Robinson's vision, as he recognised. One difficulty was that nothing was then known about the existence of vast deposits of bauxite, the raw material, in Australia. Robinson countered this with a belief, based on his extensive mining experience, that bauxite would be discovered soon; and the development of cheap hydro-electric power to smelt ores in Australia would help in establishing a viable industry. Even so, there were doubts about production costs for such a project, and Robinson argued that Commonwealth government subsidies and guarantees of a market were necessary. More remarkably, despite his predilection for private enterprise, he was prepared to agree to public ownership of an aluminium industry.

As it happened, Robinson's views meshed very well with Labor government plans to develop new manufacturing industries in Australia. Perhaps Robinson shrewdly adapted his project to such plans—after all, there was a long Australian history of public enterprise in the economy. Precisely what happened in this particular case is not clear. Evidently, Evatt played a key role, having listened attentively to Robinson's urgings. Curtin also thought highly of Robinson. In October 1943, Beasley, as Minister for Supply and Shipping, announced in federal parliament that the government intended to establish an independent Australian aluminium industry. Three months later, Evatt (standing in for Beasley while the latter was ill) informed Cabinet that the Tasmanian (Labor) government was prepared to share with the Commonwealth the costs of establishing a smelter in Tasmania, where hydro-electricity would be developed for the purpose. Actually, the new Bell Bay plant did not begin operations till years later, but the necessary legislation was passed in 1944.[15]

In August 1943, there was a general election in Australia, centred on the question of whether it was Labor or the Opposition which would be the better choice as a party to lead the war effort. In the campaign, Curtin's stature as a national leader and a man of sincerity and modesty was very impressive. In terms of drive and administrative efficiency, he was ably supported by three ministerial colleagues in particular: Chifley, Evatt and Beasley. Curtin naturally emphasised the good points of his government's war record—in which Evatt's two overseas missions figured significantly—while looking forward to a peaceful future and the development of Labor's post-war plans. The Opposition, on the other hand, was negative and disunited—Menzies was at odds with Fadden—and its record of war leadership was mediocre at best. In the private opinion of Frederic Eggleston, a thoughtful Liberal supporter, 'we lost the [1943] elections fundamentally because the Opposition leaders had no political philosophy which met the problems everyone in the world is thinking about'.[16]

Eggleston's remark may be considered alongside Judith Brett's historical commentary upon Menzies' customary emphasis on Australia's 'forgotten people'. By this, Menzies meant the lower middle classes, exemplifying the conventional virtues of family and home life and being identified neither with big business nor trade unions. No doubt Brett is correct in saying that reiteration of this theme played a significant part in Menzies' political success from the late 1940s onwards, yet the refrain was first enunciated by him in a radio talk in May 1942. Its effect in 1943 was nil: voters were concerned with matters of more substance and urgency. Indeed, Curtin himself referred to the 'forgotten men' in an election campaign speech then; but he was talking specifically about Labor's intention not to forget the armed forces, the great bulk of them 'drawn from the ranks of the workers'.[17]

Evatt's own election speeches were along much the same lines as those of Curtin, although the Attorney-General outlined in more detail Labor's post-war objectives, particularly in relation to full employment and the consequent need for national planning. Evatt followed Curtin in declaring that Labor would not socialise any industry in wartime. In rebutting Opposition claims that Labor would embark on such a programme, Evatt depicted the ALP as aiming to protect 'not only the industrial worker but the smaller trader, the man on the land, the professional classes, the ordinary housewife'. He added that he saw 'no difficulty in reconciling our full national development with a maximum of individual enterprise'. Also incorporated in Evatt's speechmaking was reference to the need for a post-war aviation industry in Australia, though this point was seemingly not attributed to W. S. Robinson (who may well have wished to stay out of public notice in this context). Further, it may be assumed that Evatt reminded select audiences of an initiative in which he took personal pride: the establishment at the beginning of 1943 of a Legal Service Bureau. This was designed to give free legal advice to servicemen and women and their dependants concerning special benefits such as relief from pressing obligations on rent and hire-purchase. The Bureau had offices in all capital cities. It may be added that when Evatt returned to Australia that year he brought with him a big bundle of letters from Australian servicemen in Britain to their relatives.[18]

The result of the general election was a landslide victory for the ALP. The party won forty-nine of the seats in the House of Representatives, against twenty-three for the UAP and Country parties, while the two Independents retained their seats. There was a swing to Labor in all States, and contrary to expectations the Party won a majority in the Senate. Thus for the first time since 1916, the ALP secured a majority in both Houses of Parliament. Evatt, in his seat of Barton, was returned overwhelmingly with 50 000 first preference votes from an electoral roll of about 80 000. He remained in charge of the same two portfolios in the new Curtin government.

Notes

1 Jacob to Crawford, 8 April 1943. PRO: CAB 109/41. Dr Evatt—1943. It is quite clear that British authorities were willing to concede to Australia no more than could be squeezed out of them.
2 An additional reason for Churchill's favourable disposition towards Australia at this time was that Evatt offered representation by the Australian government of Polish interests in the Soviet Union. Churchill was happy to accept the offer (David Day, *Reluctant Nation: Australia and the Defeat of Japan 1942-45*, OUP, Melbourne, 1992, p. 116).
3 D.M. Horner, *High Command*, pp. 259–62.
4 Evatt to Curtin, 12 June 1943, *DAFP*, vol. vi, Document 222; Dill to Churchill, 12 June 1943. PRO: PREM 3/150/8. General Arnold commanded US Army Air Forces, while Admiral King was US Chief of Naval Operations.
5 Burton to Hasluck, 3 May 1943, Hasluck Papers, AA: M1942/36.
6 Wayne Reynolds, 'The Imperial Connection', p. 193.
7 *DAFP*, vol. v, Document 493. Emphasis in the original.
8 S.J. Butlin and C.B. Schedvin, *War Economy 1942–1945*, Canberra, Australian War Memorial, 1977, pp. 135–6; Roger Bell, 'Australian-American Relations and Reciprocal Wartime Economic Assistance, 1941–6', *Australian Economic History Review*, XVI, 1 (March 1976). See also the heated debate between Bell and Schedvin in *AEHR*, March 1978.
9 Watt to Evatt, 4 March 1943. AA: A3300/2,255.
10 Memorandum, 9 June 1943, US State Department, RG59, Lot 54D 224—Australia—Political Affairs 1943.
11 H.C. Coombs, *Trial Balance*, Sun Books, Melbourne, 1983, ch. 1.

12 Ibid., pp. 39, 45–6.
13 Robinson to Evatt, 17 August 1943, W.S. Robinson Collection, File 70, Box 6, Melbourne University Archives. Robinson gave precise prices to support his argument.
14 Memo to Evatt, undated, W.S. Robinson Collection, File 70, Box 6, Melbourne University Archives; Day, *Reluctant Nation*, pp. 114–15.
15 Janette Ryan, 'The Development of the Australian Aluminium Industry 1944–1965', B.Ec. Honours thesis, Economic History Department, University of Sydney, 1981, pp. 1, 5–9.
16 Warren G. Osmond, *Frederic Eggleston: An Intellectual in Australian Politics*, Allen & Unwin, Sydney, 1985, p. 205.
17 Judith Brett, 'Menzies' Forgotten People', *Meanjin*, vol. 43 (2), June 1984, pp. 253–65; Lloyd Ross, *John Curtin: A Biography*, p. 328.
18 *Sydney Morning Herald*, 5 August 1943; *Daily Telegraph*, 18 August 1943.

CHAPTER 16

POST-WAR RECONSTRUCTION

Unless the High Court can be persuaded to take a very different and much broader view of the constitution than it has taken in the past...the difficulties of transition [from war to peace]...will be immensely exacerbated.

J. V. BARRY

Between 1943 and 1945, policies for post-war reconstruction of Australian society were developed in a coherent form, in large measure by a group of dedicated young public servants in the Department of Post-War Reconstruction established in December 1942. Its ministerial head was Chifley, although he seems to have given relatively little attention to the progress of reconstruction plans in 1943. This is understandable: war demands had priority with the Treasurer and it was generally agreed that implementation of reconstruction must await the termination of hostilities. Nevertheless, members of the Curtin government were much concerned about post-war prospects. As part of the labour movement, they entertained a vision of creating in Australia a society affording a better life for the people. In particular, they were determined to prevent reversion to the circumstances of the depression of the 1930s. These Labor views provided a broad framework for articulation of reconstruction plans.

Evatt appears to have been foremost in pressing for action in this respect and he had some early experience: in 1941, he was appointed as honorary research director of the Reconstruction Division of the Department of Labour and National Service under the Menzies government. Later, as Attorney-General, Evatt's particular concern was to ensure that the federal government was given greater powers to deal with a post-war situation which was expected to include problems of dislocation of industry and the need to provide jobs for demobilised troops. During the war the government had adequate powers to deal with such matters by regulations issued under the National Defence Act, but nobody could foretell how long the resort to constitutional defence powers would be permitted once the war was over. Consequently, in October 1942, Evatt brought into parliament a Bill to amend the constitution. The Bill was rather vague and general in its terms and this defect was seized upon by political opponents, including some State Labor leaders.

In view of this, the government did not proceed with the Bill or the original intention to hold a referendum on it. Instead, a Constitutional Convention of Commonwealth and State parliamentary representatives (Premiers and Opposition leaders) was held. Evatt, supported by W. M. Hughes, presented to the Convention an amended version of the Bill, and after further alteration it was agreed unanimously that the final draft should be submitted to State parliaments with a request that they agree to transfer certain powers to the Commonwealth for a period of five years after the end of the war. Such transfer would obviate the need for a referendum, which might be regarded as inappropriate or divisive in wartime conditions.

It is a remarkable testimony to Evatt's energy and forcefulness that one month before the Convention was held, he called together at very short notice about twenty public servants, academics and lawyers. They included Sir George Knowles, permanent head of the Attorney-General's Department, W. R. Hodgson (Evatt's counterpart in External Affairs), Kenneth Bailey (Professor of Public Law at the University of Melbourne), Paul Hasluck and John Burton. Evatt was the only government minister at the meeting and he told the others present that the purpose was to arrange for a book to be written. After discussion, an editorial committee was set up, which allocated responsibility for writing various sections of the book within a matter of weeks. Extraordinarily, a 188-page book entitled *Post-War Reconstruction. A Case for Greater Commonwealth Powers*, in the name of H. V. Evatt as author, was ready for distribution to the Constitutional Convention when it met. In Bailey's recollection, the initial draft of the book was primarily the work of Burton, although Evatt personally approved it. Evatt also proposed some safeguards of civil liberties, but he did not proceed with these at the Convention.[1]

The draft Bill agreed to by the Convention—including the Premiers, though some were reluctant—specified fourteen matters on which the States were to be asked to transfer their powers to the Commonwealth. These points included employment and unemployment, the organised marketing of commodities, profiteering and price controls, the production and distribution of goods, and laws relating to Aborigines. In the event, the hopes of persuading State legislatures to agree to referral of these powers were dashed in 1943. Two States, New South Wales and Queensland, passed the Bill as drafted; Victoria passed it, with the proviso that it would be acted upon only if all the other States passed the Bill; South Australia and Western Australia passed Bills with fewer powers than those agreed upon by the Constitutional Convention; and in Tasmania, the Legislative Council shelved the Bill, effectively rejecting it.

In stating this outcome in federal parliament in October 1943, Curtin said that the government now intended to deal with the matter by referendum. In effect, a year had been lost in a vain attempt to secure the agreement of the States, and it could be said that it would have been preferable to go straight to a referendum at the end of 1942, when there would have been less organised opposition. On the other hand, the Curtin government did not then have a majority in the Senate. After the general election in 1943, this problem was overcome, and in the following year Evatt introduced in parliament a Constitution Alteration (Post-War Reconstruction and Democratic Rights) Bill.

The Bill laid the necessary groundwork for a referendum seeking the approval of the people to amend the constitution by giving the Commonwealth government power to legislate with respect to the fourteen points adopted by the Constitutional Convention. Additionally, the Bill included certain safeguards, notably constitutional guarantees of freedom of speech and of religion. Thus one clause proposed: 'Neither the Commonwealth nor a State may make any law for abridging the freedom of speech and of expression'. This was modelled largely on the US Constitution's Bill of Rights and, in speaking on the clause, Evatt showed that he was fully conversant with the leading US Supreme Court cases on the subject, particularly the judgments delivered by such great liberals as Brandeis and Holmes.

Brian Fitzpatrick, while supporting the referendum proposals, thought that Evatt's introduction of clauses guaranteeing political rights might well be 'just a sweetener'. Yet Evatt's action was consistent with his record. Indeed, two years earlier, a friend, J. V. Barry, wrote to Evatt, referring to the fact that Bert Evatt had publicly advocated some constitutional guarantee of civil liberties. After seeking further information on this, Barry went on to say that he himself had been pondering fruitlessly upon *what seems to me to be the inevitable chaos that will arise when the cessation of hostilities deprives the Commonwealth of the unifying power it now exercises under the necessities of war. Unless the High Court can be persuaded to take a very different and much broader view of the constitution than it has taken in the past, it looks inevitable that the difficulties of transition, appallingly great though they are in themselves, will be immensely exacerbated.*[2]

A substantial 'sweetener' in the Constitution Alteration Bill passed by parliament in March 1944 was that its provisions, comprising the fourteen points and the civil liberty guarantees, were specifically stated as only temporary in character. They were to be limited to a period of five years following the end of the war. Evatt envisaged that before the expiration of that period of transition from war to peace, there would be a comprehensive reconsideration of the constitutional situation. Meantime, in piloting the Bill through parliament, he went to great pains to explain the need for it, clause by clause. The government also published a booklet by Evatt, *Notes on the Fourteen Powers and the Three Safeguards*. However, this was not widely distributed—it does not appear to have been available in bookshops. Certainly, in the referendum campaign, the Opposition case was presented much more effectively in the media, particularly the Murdoch press. Menzies and others argued that existing Commonwealth powers were quite adequate, and additional powers would enable Labor to pursue a policy of socialisation and control. It was an argument calculated to appeal to voters who were weary of wartime regulations.

There was, in fact, some pressure within the ALP for adoption of thorough-going socialist policies, but there was very little reflection of this among Labor parliamentarians. Planning was one thing; socialism quite another, whatever the rhetoric for the benefit of the faithful. Even in relation to planning for the future, many of Evatt's Labor colleagues appeared lukewarm, if not indifferent, towards the importance of winning the referendum in August 1944. Evatt himself worked tirelessly to secure a 'Yes' vote; and when he was campaigning in Tasmania, Mary Alice made a contribution by speaking to women over the radio in Hobart. Nevertheless, the outcome was a decisive vote in favour of 'No'. A majority in only two States voted 'Yes'; even in New South Wales and Queensland, where State parliaments had passed the earlier Powers Bill, 'No' voters predominated.[3]

An important factor in the result was the traditional reluctance of Australians to approve proposals for changes in the constitution. There was also a major tactical blunder in presenting voters with a long list of proposed powers on an all-or-nothing basis, instead of splitting the package into smaller parcels, one or more of which might well have been approved in the referendum. It seems that Chifley and Evatt were mainly responsible for the decision to present all points in the form of one Yes/No question: according to Geoffrey Bolton, this was against Curtin's better judgement. Yet it was reasonable, in the light of the earlier bipartisan Constitutional Convention, to believe that the comprehensive proposal for the fourteen points would be acceptable, thus in one stroke clearing the way for Labor's post-war aims.[4]

The setback in the referendum did not deflect Labor from planning for a better future for Australians. Coombs and Chifley concentrated particularly on the objective of full employment and with it the need to keep inflation under control. Evatt, in full agreement with the objective, made a substantial contribution towards achieving it through his External Affairs portfolio. At one international conference after another, Australian representatives argued that high levels of employment were essential in all major countries, not only for the benefit of their own people but because of their effect on the rest of the world. Policies of full employment in Australia were considered heavily dependent upon growth in international trade and increases in standards of living. Thus in a parliamentary statement by Evatt on 8 September 1944, he praised another Minister, Beasley, for his persuasive advocacy at a recent conference of the ILO in Philadelphia. Beasley had urged the conference to recommend that governments consider entering into an international agreement on domestic policies of employment and unemployment. Evatt commented:

Fortunately there is already a large measure of appreciation by all the nations of the British Commonwealth of the importance of making domestic policies concerning employment a subject for international negotiation and international agreement.[5]

Evatt's aim in this context was not simply to influence other countries towards an Australian viewpoint. He also sought to involve Australia in international treaties or conventions, with obligations which could be regarded as binding in international law. Thus, in terms of the doctrine developed by Evatt in 1936 in the High Court case of Goya Henry (*R. v Burgess*), the Commonwealth would gain power to legislate on the given subject without any specific constitutional amendment. Such use of the Commonwealth's external affairs power was already available before 1944, but it acquired greater significance after the failure of the 1944 referendum. For example, if the subject of an international agreement was full employment, it could be assumed that the Commonwealth was competent to legislate so as to give effect to its own international commitment.

This avenue to greater powers for the Commonwealth was limited in scope, and undoubtedly Labor's defeat in the referendum constituted a substantial barrier to plans for post-war reconstruction. Nevertheless, early progress was still feasible in some areas, particularly social services. Already, in 1942, Commonwealth provision had been made for widows' pensions; and in the following few years some other gaps in a comprehensive system of benefits were filled, mainly on the initiative of Chifley. Labor maintained a decisive majority in federal parliament, and the High Court did not act to withdraw the expansive interpretation of the Commonwealth's defence power until a reasonable period elapsed following the end of the war. Furthermore, the ALP did not give up the fight to secure greater powers for the Commonwealth after 1944.

Yet the referendum of 1944 should be recognised as a watershed: it marked a crucial moment in the movement for social and democratic renovation between 1944 and 1949 in Australia, accompanying the international defeat of Fascism. It was not a matter of progress becoming impossible. Rather, the Labor defeat in the referendum meant that reform would be protracted and piecemeal—and in the process, momentum was lost, enthusiasm was dissipated and opponents recovered. What Chifley referred to as Labor's 'beacon, the light on the hill', came close to being doused at the end of the 1940s. Many important decisions were dependent upon approval by the High Court and lengthy negotiations with the States. Evatt illustrated the latter point in a paper which he read to the Australian Institute of Political Science in January 1944:

For example the elaborate Wheat Industry Assistance plan of 1938 depended on agreement between the Commonwealth and the States. But the plan had taken three full years to work out. On the contrary, under the war-time powers of the National Security Act, the Commonwealth War-time Wheat Industry Stabilisation Scheme was brought into being in a matter of months.[6]

NOTES

1 Paul Hasluck, *Diplomatic Witness*, MUP, Melbourne, 1980, pp. 61–2; Kenneth Bailey, transcript TRC 121/20, 1: 2/24, Oral History Programme, NLA. Hasluck was not impressed by the quality of Evatt's book, but Isaacs, formerly Governor-General and High Court judge, considered that the book was 'very comprehensive and informative' (Isaacs Papers, MS 2755/2/102, NLA).

2 Fitzpatrick quoted by Don Watson, *Brian Fitzpatrick: A Radical Life*, Hale & Iremonger, Sydney, 1979, p. 161; Barry to Evatt, 19 November 1941, Barry Papers, MS 2505/1/208, NLA. Barry was a prominent Melbourne barrister and civil libertarian.
3 *Mercury* (Hobart), 27 July 1944. Similarly in the general election campaign of 1943, on one occasion when Bert was ill, Mary Alice deputised for him by reading his speech over the radio from their home in Sydney. She received considerable acclaim for this.
4 Geoffrey Bolton, *The Oxford History of Australia*, vol. 5, 1942–1988, OUP, Melbourne, 1990, p. 29. The information about Curtin's viewpoint is uncertain.
5 H.V. Evatt, *Foreign Policy of Australia: Speeches*, p. 218. Hasluck in *The Government and the People 1942–1945*, pp. 466–7, doubts whether Beasley was as successful on this occasion as Evatt suggested in parliament.
6 D.A.S. Campbell (ed.), *Post-War Reconstruction in Australia*, Australasian Publishing, Sydney, 1944, p. 245.

CHAPTER 17

DEFENCE POWERS AND INDIVIDUAL LIBERTY

Evatt's instincts were, I think, radical...his instinct was always to support the underdog, even if the underdog happened to be a communist.
K. H. BAILEY, COMMONWEALTH SOLICITOR-GENERAL

The Australia First Movement was again on Evatt's agenda early in 1944, when he announced the appointment of a federal bankruptcy judge, T. S. Clyne, to review the AFM cases. Actually, by that time only Stephensen, out of the sixteen AFM people arrested in Sydney, was still in internment, but Menzies and others were questioning whether the internments had been justified. Evatt, in announcing the Clyne enquiry, made clear his own intention to vindicate the Curtin government's record in the matter.

Justice Clyne's enquiry lasted for more than a year, and his report amounted to a whitewash of the government's actions. The detention of those arrested in Sydney was held to be justified, 'as it was in fact recommended by the Army authorities'. At the same time, Clyne thought it 'proper to add' that the Army authorities were not justified in recommending the detention of eight of the sixteen; and he recommended compensatory payments for them, ranging from £350 to £700. Apart from this, the main item of interest in Clyne's investigation concerned the security situation in Western Australia. Under cross-examination it became apparent that one F. J. Thomas had operated as an undercover police spy, first in 1941 in relation to the activities of Communists, and then a year later with reference to a small right-wing group regarded with suspicion by Military Police Intelligence. The evidence presented to Clyne indicated strongly that Thomas was probably an agent-provocateur and a person of dubious character who had also been illicitly engaged in the sale of sly grog.[1]

Thomas, whose secret reports were largely responsible for the four arrests in Perth which were the basis for action against the AFM in Sydney, was the agent of detective-sergeant G. R. Richards of the Western Australia police force. Richards—nicknamed the 'Black Snake', according to historian Stuart Macintyre—was chief investigation officer of the Security Service in Western Australia at the time of the Clyne enquiry. He came to public attention again later, when he was the chief ASIO officer in the Petrov case.[2]

The Clyne enquiry was a bonanza for lawyers, one of whom was J. W. Shand, KC, who appeared for the Department of the Army and Security Services. On 8 May 1945, Shand made an unexpected submission to the enquiry: 'it is not suggested that there is any reason at present why the detention of P. R. Stephensen should be continued.' However, no official action was taken until August, when Stephensen was released from internment on the authority of an order which purported to be signed by Evatt. Actually, according to John Burton, Evatt had agonised over the matter for a long time without being able to make up his mind; and meanwhile Burton, in accompanying Evatt on journeys, was required to carry a locked case containing papers for Stephensen's release which awaited Evatt's signature. Again according to Burton in an interview much later, he decided to make up Evatt's mind for him by forging the Minister's signature on the document revoking Stephensen's detention order. This was an extraordinarily bold and risky action for a public servant to take, and Burton's position would have been untenable if there had been a furore over Stephensen's release. As it happened, there was no public outcry and Evatt said nothing. The Clyne report was tabled in parliament in September 1945, and shortly afterwards Forde, as Minister for the Army, stated that the government would adopt Clyne's recommendations concerning compensatory payments. Evatt was overseas at this time.[3]

As Attorney-General, Evatt had responsibilities for the treatment of aliens, although the Army was in charge of internment camps. Actually, the interned AFM people were not aliens; but in relation to other groups of internees and refugees Evatt went some way towards redeeming his claim to be an upholder of civil liberties. It was a very complex area of jurisdiction, involving security and political and religious interests, as well as civil liberties. As an early step, Evatt in

1942 appointed an Aliens Classification Committee, consisting of Arthur Calwell as chairman, J. V. Barry, and three other persons. Their task was to classify aliens 'according to their degree of reliability from the point of view of security' and to make recommendations as to the restrictions which might be imposed upon them.[4]

One problem was the extremely insensitive treatment of Jewish refugees (many of them from Germany, Austria and Italy) by Australian authorities. Jewish organisations in Victoria gained support from the Australian Council for Civil Liberties; and Fitzpatrick, in making representations to Evatt, found him a sympathetic listener. Evatt was opposed to the raucous anti-semitism from the right in Australian politics, including the AFM group before its members were interned.

There was another ethnic pressure group in Melbourne. The Italian community had its own problems. Some of its members had been opponents of Mussolini from the 1920s, while a more numerous group had supported his regime. In both categories there were naturalised British subjects, which did not prevent internment of many of them. In 1943, an anti-fascist group in Melbourne formed the Free Italy Movement and secured Evatt's official permission to work amongst Italians in aid of the Allied war effort. The Free Italy Movement also sought the release of all anti-fascists from internment camps. Although Calwell was apparently not directly associated with the Italian Movement, he sought liberalisation of official policy towards the internment of Italians who had become naturalised citizens of Australia.[5]

There was a stronger Italian organisation on the right, supported by the Catholic Church in Victoria. Indeed, Archbishop Mannix is reported to have declared at a rally in September 1943: 'Mussolini is the greatest man living today'. Calwell by this time was hostile to the Free Italy Movement, and the Victorian branch of the ALP was strongly influenced by Catholics. In November, Curtin—on the recommendation of Mannix—authorised the appointment of G. Vaccari to act as a liaison between the Commonwealth government and the Italian community on certain matters, including detention under National Security Regulations. This was done with the approval of the Security Service, despite the fact that Vaccari had been an outspoken supporter of Italian fascism in Australia in the 1930s. By March 1944, Evatt was aware of Vaccari's dubious background and in reply to a parliamentary question the Attorney-General stated that Vaccari had not been appointed to represent the Italian community: he had been authorised on humanitarian grounds to make representations to Commonwealth departments concerned with the welfare of persons of Italian origin. Evatt said nothing to indicate that he himself had been given a lesson in the intricacies of Church and Labor politics in Victoria.[6]

In 1943–44, Fitzpatrick on behalf of the ACCL made frequent representations to Evatt about refugees and other persons, often in relation to government regulations framed by Ministers. For example, there was National Service Regulation 51A, gazetted by J. J. Dedman, the Minister for War Organisation of Industry. Under this regulation, any seaman not born in Australia could be imprisoned merely on the recommendation of an Allied naval officer or the agent of a shipping company. Dozens of merchant navy men were held in Australian prisons as a result, sometimes for no more than being drunk. Evatt, after receiving persistent complaints, agreed to have the regulation amended.[7]

On the whole, Fitzpatrick was satisfied by the Attorney-General's response on civil liberty matters, yet Evatt would not go beyond certain limits. This was firmly indicated in a case involving a British subject who had worked in Japan before the war and was regarded by the Security Service as pro-Japanese. Accordingly, he was confined, under a Restriction Order, to residence in a country town in Victoria or New South Wales. In 1945 he wished to move to Queensland to take a job there and the ACCL supported his case. Evatt responded with a stiffly-worded telegram:

Matter is primarily one for decision of Director of Security who is of opinion that it would be detrimental to security interests...Your suggestion regarding publicity and Parliamentary action is quite unwarrantable. I am as much in favour of the protection of civil liberty as you are but I shall not jeopardise defence security contrary to the unanimous view of those who are fully aware of the facts.[8]

By the end of 1943 it was clear that Germany and Japan, while still menacing, had lost the initiative in the war. One reflection of this was the Commonwealth government's decision to stabilise the RAAF in Australia at a strength of about fifty squadrons, as against Evatt's target number of seventy-three during his mission overseas earlier that year. Similarly in relation to the general Australian war effort in the Pacific region, there was to be a significant readjustment. In short, although fighting capacity was sustained at a high level, there was seen to be no need to continue diverting extra resources to it. There was an acute shortage of manpower in civilian industry and it was considered desirable to concentrate more upon production of food and clothing for use by Allied forces. Accordingly, from 1944, there were releases of men from the Australian armed forces, particularly for employment in primary industries.

In these changing circumstances, Evatt established an independent War Regulations Advisory Committee, including Barry and another leading member of the ACCL, to recommend as to which wartime regulations should be repealed or modified. Incidentally, Evatt had kept a critical eye on various National Service Regulations, as indicated in December 1942 when he persuaded Cabinet to redraft a proposal by Dedman designed to prohibit the employment of domestic servants as a means of conserving manpower (actually, the servants were women). According to Hasluck, Evatt intervened on that occasion because he was 'the member of Cabinet most sensitive to the reactions of the middle-class vote and most eager to placate it'.[9]

Another reason for government action was a sharp increase in the number of appeals to the High Court, challenging the scope of the Commonwealth's defence powers. Professor Bailey, as a consultant to the Attorney-General's Department from 1943, found himself increasingly involved in advising on such matters. The challenges came from States, objecting to Commonwealth encroachment on their own powers, and from employers resenting regulations, concerning prices for example. One case that Bailey recalled later was a challenge by the Victorian Chamber of Manufactures to regulations seeking to improve lighting standards in factories and to economise on the use of power. This challenge was successful in the High Court, on the ground that the regulations did not have a sufficiently real connection with the war effort. Another successful challenge in 1943 was directed against regulations to control admissions to universities, where some students—for example, in medicine—were exempted from military service until they graduated. Bailey felt that the High Court was wrong in deciding that the university faculty quota system did not have a real connection with the war. He also felt that Justice Starke's judgment in the matter indicated a belief that the government sought to seize control of the education process under cover of war needs, which was not so.

Although these were relatively minor cases, they were a portent for the future. Indeed, early in 1943 a barrister who had been appearing before the High Court reported to Evatt 'some very interesting conversations with some of the Members of the Bench'. He warned Evatt:

I gathered from more or less direct statements some of the judges do not think much of Socialism and their decisions might be affected by the fact that they consider your Government is trying to attain Socialism under the guise of National Security.[10]

Bailey became Commonwealth Solicitor-General in 1946 and had easy access to Evatt. Thus, Bailey's impressions of the Attorney-General carry some weight. Evatt not only showed lack of consideration in his dealings with many people—partly due to the pressure under which he worked—but he also extended this to Knowles, the permanent head of the Department. According to Bailey, Evatt was frequently offensive and rude to Knowles, deliberately humiliating him in the presence of others. Evatt 'used to ring up Knowles at all times of the night or morning...half past one in the morning... sometimes making some quite trivial enquiry'. Somewhat at odds with this recollection was Hasluck's remark, from the External Affairs perspective, that 'Evatt could neither ignore Knowles nor disregard his professional standing...to anything like the extent to which he ignored Hodgson and reduced his effective status'.[11]

On matters of more substance, Bailey said:

Evatt's instincts were, I think, radical. This is...a contentious proposition. Some people say at heart he was really a liberal rather than a radical...my own impression was strongly that his dominating direction was radical. More radical than Chifley in a way, less radical in some ways. He was not, I think, as doctrinally wedded to the party platform as Chifley was, but his instinct was always to support the underdog, even if the underdog happened to be a communist, I don't think that he minded that in the least. Chifley might have been a bit more careful about that than Evatt.[12]

NOTES

1 Transcript of Clyne Enquiry, p. 1818. AA: A467, SF 43,Bundle 96, item 1.
2 Stuart Macintyre, *Militant: The Life and Times of Paddy Troy*, Allen & Unwin, Sydney, 1984, pp. 60–1.
3 Clyne Transcript, p. 2266. According to Evatt's private secretary, the Attorney-General was 'never happy with the whole business of the Australia First Movement' (Allan Dalziel, *Evatt the Enigma*, Lansdowne, Melbourne, 1967, p. 27).
4 Copy of letter Evatt to Calwell, 15 September 1942, Barry Papers, MS 2505/ 12/29, NLA.
5 G. Cresciani, 'Italian Anti-Fascism in Australia 1922–1945', in E.L. Wheelwright and Ken Buckley (eds), *Essays in the Political Economy of Australian Capitalism*, vol. 3, ANZ Books, Sydney, 1978, pp. 86–101.
6 Evatt to Vaccari, 26 November 1943, *DAFP*, vol. vi, Document 336; *Commonwealth Parliamentary Debates* (*CPD*) vol. 178, p. 1832. Evatt in February 1944 arranged for discontinuance of Vaccari's authority to make representations in relation to the Italian community.
7 Evatt to Fitzpatrick, 31 August 1944, Fitzpatrick Papers, MS 4965, 1/7839, NLA.
8 Attorney-General to Fitzpatrick, ACCL, 25 February 1945, Fitzpatrick Papers, MS 4965, 1/6697. No further information is available on this matter.

9 Paul Hasluck, *The Government and the People, 1942–1945*, p. 353. Hasluck also notes (pp. 544–5) that the Advisory Committee set up by Evatt in June 1944 was quite effective.
10 Quoted in Brian Galligan, *Politics of the High Court*, pp. 144–5.
11 Kenneth Bailey, transcript TRC 121/20,2: 2/8, NLA; Paul Hasluck, *Diplomatic Witness*, p. 35.
12 Kenneth Bailey transcript, 2:2/7. The interview with Bailey was recorded in mid-1971.

CHAPTER 18

ATTORNEY-GENERAL, 1945–47: THE HIGH COURT, AND INDUSTRIAL RELATIONS

[Evatt] said that we would be accused of packing the bench if we increased the court to nine judges.

A. A. CALWELL

The war in Europe ended in May 1945. On 5 July, Curtin died, being succeeded briefly by Forde as Prime Minister. At the time, Evatt was on a ship returning to Australia from the San Francisco conference which drew up a charter for the United Nations Organization. There was some irony in the fact that recently Evatt had privately urged that Forde be recalled from that conference to act as Prime Minister during Curtin's illness. Evatt was not motivated by worry about the situation in Australia—it was not known that Curtin was dying, and Chifley proved to be a very competent acting Prime Minister in the absence of both Curtin and Forde. Evatt's prime concern was to remove Forde from San Francisco where Forde asserted his seniority as Australian representative, despite being out of his depth intellectually and an embarrassment and hindrance to Evatt's negotiating capabilities.[1]

As it happened, Forde arrived back in Australia just before the death of Curtin and was duly sworn in as Prime Minister. A week later, the ALP federal caucus voted for Chifley as Party leader and Prime Minister, with Forde as his deputy. Evatt, not yet back in Australia, did not contest the election; and if he had done so, it is unlikely that he would have been successful against Chifley. Evatt's ambitions now lay on the wider international stage of public affairs—which is not to say that he would have foregone an opportunity to become Prime Minister had it been within his grasp. It would be fair to say that Evatt's contribution as an international statesman was not only of great value to his own country and to others but was almost certainly more important than anything he might have been able to achieve as Prime Minister of Australia.

In 1945, particularly after the surrender of Japan in August, the most urgent task facing the Commonwealth government was to facilitate transition from a wartime economy to one attuned to the needs of civilian production. Jobs were required for hundreds of thousands of demobilised servicemen and women, munition workers and others. Many wartime economic controls remained in force to guide the process, and the transition was remarkably smooth over the next few years. Instead of the heavy unemployment which had been feared, there was an expansion of the economy, accompanied by shortages of labour. Australia was not unique in this respect.

The Chifley government, besides its involvement in daily affairs, had a reform programme to implement. To some extent this was done through joint arrangements with State governments, such as for the great Snowy River construction scheme for irrigation and the generation of hydro-electric power. There was also co-operation between the Commonwealth and New South Wales governments to establish a Joint Coal Board to supervise a troublesome industry. During the war itself Evatt, like Curtin, was incensed by shortages of coal due to repeated strikes, although Evatt stated: 'In my opinion, the industry as a whole—and this applies to both sides—is blameworthy'.[2]

Labor's plans extended beyond such measures to embrace major changes in social services and the restructuring of certain industries. There were two early moves in this direction. First, a Pharmaceutical Benefits Act was passed in 1944, designed simply as a relatively inexpensive instalment of a comprehensive health scheme. The Act provided free medicine: the government undertook reimbursement of the costs of certain medicines prescribed by doctors and dispensed by chemists. To keep costs down, proven drugs were to be listed in a comprehensive formulary, and only those prescriptions which conformed with this were to be free. This limitation gave doctors an opportunity to air their objections to 'socialised medicine'—irrespective of, indeed contrary to, the interests of poor patients.

Second, there was the Australian National Airlines Act of 1945, which established a government corporation, Trans-Australia Airlines (TAA), to conduct interstate air services, and which also set up an Airlines Commission to control civil aviation generally. The Commission had power to take over (subject to compensation) privately owned interstate airline companies, and it was evidently intended to do so. This legislation met fierce opposition from private interests and their supporters in federal parliament. In moving the Bill, Drakeford, the Minister for Civil Aviation, pointed out that private airlines were coming together to form a monopoly and that the Commonwealth already had much capital invested in ground facilities such as aerodromes. He also emphasised that, in constitutional terms, the Commonwealth undoubtedly had power over interstate air transport. Government spokesmen had some difficulty in parrying Menzies' reminder that, in the election campaign of 1943, Curtin had said Labor would not socialise any industry in wartime. However, Chifley, in replying to the parliamentary debate in July, said:

The proper monopoly, if there is to be one, is a government monopoly. That is our purpose...This Bill is largely a post-war project, because the organisation that it provides for cannot be created for some time. The people will have the opportunity next year to give their judgment.[3]

It is difficult to determine Evatt's precise position in relation to this legislation. He was certainly committed to it as a senior member of the government, and undoubtedly he would have advised on legal aspects at Cabinet meetings, if he had been present. Actually, Evatt was overseas for considerable periods of time. Not only was he away at the San Francisco conference in the early part of 1945, he also spent the latter months of the year in Europe and the United States for conferences concerning peace terms (chiefly with Italy) and in connection with the Allied occupation of Japan. He did not participate in the parliamentary debate on the Australian National Airlines Bill. Indeed, he became so engrossed in negotiations overseas that the Australian War Cabinet thought it necessary to send him a cable

requesting that the Government be kept informed of his activities in connection with his discussions with United Kingdom Ministers and the Council of Foreign Ministers. He is also...to be informed that the Government does not wish to be involved in controversial matters relating to Europe which do not affect Australia's vital interests.

Evidently, some of Evatt's colleagues felt that his interpretation of External Affairs responsibilities was too far-reaching.[4]

In November 1945, the High Court upheld a challenge to the constitutional validity of the Pharmaceutical Benefits Act, primarily on the ground that the provision of medical and pharmaceutical services was not specifically referred to as a Commonwealth power in the constitution. In fact, only old age and invalid pensions were expressly enumerated, so that this court decision laid open to challenge other current social services such as child endowment and unemployment and sickness benefits. Shortly afterwards, the High Court gave a decision on a challenge to the Australian National Airlines Act. The court upheld the provisions under which a government interstate airline was established, yet denied the government a right to drive private airlines out of business, on the ground that this would infringe freedom of trade and commerce under Section 92 of the constitution. Garfield Barwick, in appearing for the private operator, Australian National Airlines, cleverly emphasised individual freedom: he argued that his clients were under attack through the legislation because they were private. This approach was acceptable to all the judges sitting in the case.

These two court decisions—coincidentally announced while the federal Attorney-General was overseas—were serious setbacks to Labor's reform programme. They threatened the basis for radical change and focused attention upon the High Court's function and attitudes. In personnel, the court had not changed since Evatt was a member of it, except that his resignation in 1940 was promptly followed by the appointment of Dudley Williams, generally reckoned to be a lawyer's lawyer—a man of conservative instincts, though without party political affiliations. Before the end of the war, Latham and Dixon returned to the bench from their temporary government positions. It soon became apparent that with the exception of McTiernan—who was the sole dissentient in the *Pharmaceutical Benefits* case—the six High Court judges were unsympathetic to Labor's aims.

There were several possible ways of changing this situation to Labor's advantage. There was a hope that some aged judges would retire. At the time of the *Pharmaceutical Benefits* case in 1945, Rich was eighty-two years old and Starke, seventy-four. Evatt had this in mind when he sent a confidential note to Chief Justice Latham, informing him that the Prime Minister and the Attorney-General had agreed to recommend to Cabinet increases in High Court judges' salaries to £4000 per annum. Evatt added with rather ponderous humour:

As this will mean a pension of £2,000 p.a., I think, in the interest of the court, that 2 resignations should follow!! However, that is for others to decide...[5]

Evatt's hope was forlorn. There was no compulsory retirement age; and both Starke and Rich were determined to sit it out on the bench until Labor lost office, thus forestalling appointment of more forward-looking replacements.

Another option for the Chifley government was to increase the number of High Court judges. This might be done in order to pack the court in the government's favour, as Roosevelt had proposed in relation to the US Supreme Court in the 1930s. Even before the critical High Court decisions in 1945, Calwell (supported by Ward) persuaded Cabinet that the total number of judges should be raised to nine. The decision was taken in Evatt's absence overseas, and on his return he intervened strongly to secure agreement to only one additional judgeship, not three. According to Calwell's recollection of the Cabinet meeting in January 1946, Evatt

said that we would be accused of packing the bench if we increased the court to nine judges...I said that if our proposal could be described as one of packing the bench, then the successful plot that put Evatt and McTiernan on the bench...was certainly an instance of packing.[6]

In this case, Calwell may be said to represent a standard, if crude, Labor view of politics and the High Court, whereas Evatt was concerned about legal proprieties, especially in relation to a court of which he had been a member. Beyond this, the Labor government would undoubtedly have lost much public credit if it had introduced legislation to enlarge the High Court as Calwell wished. Evatt's preferred alternative, of one additional appointment, could easily be justified. The High Court had had seven judges from 1912, a number reduced to six from 1933 as an economy measure. Restoration to the original size in 1946 was no great change. Indeed, it was unlikely to alter the balance of opinion on the court, a matter on which Calwell's proposal had real merit if Labor were to implement its programme.

As it was, Evatt bungled the business of appointing one additional member of the High Court. Some names were suggested—J. V. Barry, for example—of lawyers who were well-qualified professionally while being sensitive to Labor aspirations. Yet Evatt recommended W. F. Webb for the appointment. Webb was Chief Justice of Queensland, and in 1946 was the Australian judge on the International War Crimes Tribunal in Tokyo. Apparently, Evatt was impressed by his work in that capacity, and other senior members of Cabinet, such as Forde, may have supported Webb because of Queensland connections. Calwell reckoned that Evatt, in favouring Webb, was courting the Catholic vote: Archbishop Duhig of Brisbane canvassed for Webb. In the upshot, Webb was appointed to the High Court, although lawyers generally did not regard him as eminently suited to the position. Geoffrey Sawer remarks that if Webb had any pro-Labor sympathies, they 'never showed in his judgments'. He did not actually take up his duties on the court until 1948.[7]

Perhaps Evatt was sanguine—unduly so, as it turned out—about overcoming High Court conservatism through another referendum on Commonwealth powers. In March 1946, with the support of Chifley, Evatt secured the approval of federal caucus for three separate referenda questions to be voted on at the same time as the general election scheduled for that year. These questions took up and extended some of the proposals which had been rejected in the referendum held two years earlier. As embodied in legislation providing for the referendum of 1946, power was sought for the federal government on three matters: provision of specified social services, including medical and pharmaceutical benefits; laws with respect to terms and conditions of employment in industry; and laws relating to the organised marketing of primary products, free from the restrictions of Section 92 of the constitution.

In considering the Bills for this purpose, the Opposition did not express complete disagreement. For example, most of the existing social services were regarded as acceptable. However, Evatt, in piloting the legislation through parliament, accepted a suggestion from Menzies that as the question on employment included a qualifying phrase, 'but not so as to authorize any form of industrial conscription', a similar qualification should be attached to the social services question. The suggestion seemed unobjectionable, but as interpreted later in the High Court with relevance to medical services it was of critical importance.

In voting on the referendum in September 1946, the proposal concerning social services was carried, which meant that Labor was free to proceed with another Pharmaceutical Benefits Act to replace the one ruled invalid by the High Court. The other two proposals were narrowly defeated. Actually, they both received overall majorities of votes, but there were majorities in only three, not the requisite four, of the six States. The result in the case of organised marketing was not as restrictive as it seemed, for a major section of the Country Party supported such marketing in principle.

As for the general election held at the same time, it was fairly straightforward. In 1945–46, Evatt himself was frequently criticised in the press for being away from Australia so much, and Menzies attacked Evatt's foreign policies as being destructive of the unity of the British Commonwealth, but this criticism appears to have had little or no effect. Evatt responded sharply with ridicule:

The Menzies theory is that Australia should be a complete cypher in international affairs. Under the anti-Labor regime in this country, the only discernible foreign policy was appeasement of Hitler and Japanese Fascists, which resulted in active encouragement to our enemies to prepare for war.[8]

Facing a reinvigorated Liberal Party, the ALP in 1946 lost a handful of parliamentary seats yet retained a comfortable majority. However, one of the Labor representatives defeated was Forde in Queensland, and this necessitated an election for a new deputy leader of the Party. Federal caucus on 31 October 1946 elected Evatt to the position in an exhaustive ballot. The other candidates included Ward, Dedman and Calwell; and Evatt was evidently unsure of his prospects in the ballot, as indicated by a letter from him to John Wren earlier that month. Evatt asked Wren to use his influence with certain members of caucus 'but *only* if you can move with absolute certainty: in such a situation I really need a friend like you...I have worked flat out to help the party as they all know'.[9]

This letter, the existence of which became known only very recently, calls for frank comment. Of course, there is nothing novel in a politician seeking votes to advance himself. Yet in this particular case Evatt, a highly respectable Labor leader, was covertly soliciting a favour from a man with a sleazy reputation. In his earlier years, Wren operated as an illicit bookmaker, associating with ex-criminals. He then became wealthy via horseracing and other businesses, in Melbourne and Brisbane. Through generous donations to select causes, he gained influence in Labor circles and the Catholic Church. He anticipated benefits in return for his money—in the case of the Church, a cynic would say that Wren aimed to buy his way into heaven through his close association with Archbishop Mannix. Incidentally, Dalziel, Evatt's personal secretary, mentions that Evatt, when he was in Melbourne, frequently visited that eminently political prelate.[10]

Unsavoury though Evatt's connection with the manipulative Wren appears, two comments are in order. First, it is unfortunately true that ambitious men, particularly in politics, are not necessarily repelled by the dubious character of some people who can help them, and are not reluctant in seeking their help. Evatt was by no means the only Labor politician who secured assistance from Wren; Arthur Calwell admired Wren.[11]

Second, there is the fact that, whereas influence in the Liberal Party was wielded behind the scenes by wealthy businessmen and companies, in the ALP a comparable role was played by the trade unions. Individual Labor politicians could usually rely upon support from the trade unions of which they were members, and each union had a network of alliances with other unions. Thus, blocs of votes could be organised for inner-party purposes. Furthermore, it was important for

Labor politicians to keep in touch with trade union opinion. For example, when Ben Chifley visited Sydney he usually had a chat with Reg Downing about Trades Council developments. Downing, besides being a Minister in the New South Wales Labor government from 1941, had a strong background as a trade union officer and organiser.[12]

Evatt, on the other hand, had no such traditional base and had to cast around for support as occasion arose. In the circumstances, it is rather surprising that he won the ballot for deputy leadership. Whether Wren gave him any assistance in this is unknown and seems rather unlikely in the light of an incident earlier in 1946, also covered in the Evatt–Wren letters. This concerned an entirely different matter. At United Nations meetings in the United States, Evatt was heavily involved in a long debate about Spain, which had been refused admission to the United Nations because of Franco's association with the regimes of Hitler and Mussolini. The question then arose as to whether the Franco regime constituted a threat to peace necessitating action by the Security Council. The Soviet Union wanted dramatic action against Spain; Britain and the United States were reluctant to have any action taken; and Australia through Evatt adopted an intermediate stance which was nevertheless clearly anti-Franco. In Australia, press reports gave a garbled account of this situation, and Stan Keon, a Labor member of the Victorian parliament, publicly attacked Evatt's stand as 'pro-communist'. Two archbishops—probably Mannix and Duhig—came to the same conclusion, according to Wren, and it was at their behest that Wren contacted Evatt to protest.

Evatt's cabled reply on 10 June 1946, as shown in the Evatt–Wren correspondence, was a stout defence of his position. He pointed out that he was 'actually opposed to the extreme course recommended by the Soviet' and that the 'principles upon which Franco's rule is based are fundamentally opposed to the tenets of Catholicism'. Evatt concluded by saying: 'I must adhere to the principles advocated by me on behalf of Australia and I trust you will give a fair and just interpretation to all my actions'. Thus to his credit, Evatt refused to yield to the private remonstrance. Presumably the contents of his cable were passed on to the two archbishops, though it may be doubted whether they were convinced by the argument in the enveloping anti-communism of the time. Wren himself no doubt worked on the basis of exchange of favours.

As Attorney-General, Evatt had particular responsibilities in the area of industrial relations. As noted above, in 1946 he was in charge of legislation providing for a referendum, and one of the three questions voted upon related to greater power for the Commonwealth with respect to the terms and conditions of employment in industry. In effect, the intention was to circumvent the section of the federal constitution which confined the Commonwealth to providing machinery for conciliation and arbitration in interstate industrial disputes. The proposal was that the Commonwealth would also have the right to intervene directly in such matters. For example, it could have taken action similar to that of the New South Wales Labor government in 1947. That government, under pressure from unions exasperated by delays in the Commonwealth Arbitration Court over a claim for a reduction in working hours, passed a Forty Hours Week Act for employees under State awards, which had the effect of forcing the hand of the federal Arbitration Court.

Following the failure of the referendum on industrial employment in 1946, the possibility of federal legislation on hours of work did not arise. In any case, it is unlikely that the Chifley government would have wished to take such action in 1947. It is necessary to look at issues of industrial relations in the context of the government's economic policy. Chifley, on becoming Prime Minister, retained the Treasury portfolio, and throughout he was a very cautious, parsimonious Treasurer. Moreover, his government—whatever its plans for certain industries—did not entertain ideas of establishing a socialist regime. Provisions to regulate or control private investment expenditure were weak, which meant that ultimately a policy of full employment was dependent upon the co-operation of capital. This—the classic dilemma of a social democratic government in a capitalist society—had serious consequences for the labour movement. To keep inflation in check, it was deemed necessary to control wage increases. In this connection, it was not a matter of Chifley and his economic advisers baulking at improvements in living conditions. Rather, they sought to moderate the extent and pace of such improvements, and this suited employers.

Most Australian workers instinctively had a different perspective. At the end of World War II, in a situation of shortage of labour, they saw opportunities to gain better wages and conditions. Employers were on the defensive. Yet paradoxically, it was the Chifley government which held wages down, insisting upon protracted arbitration proceedings. As Tom Sheridan, historian of industrial relations, argues,

if market forces had been unimpeded, both private and public employers would have conceded improvements in wages, hours, leave and the rest more rapidly than they did. It was the ALP which, headed by the federal government, diverted much of its energies to blocking and diverting the spontaneous forward surge by the workforce.[13]

Although Chifley and his associates used their influence in the labour movement to considerable effect in this respect, there were many serious industrial strikes. Communists led the way in direct action and were followed by many militant ALP members in trade unions. Moderate union leaders, fearing loss of their own positions of authority, established Industrial Groups within particular trade unions. The Groupers, as they came to be termed, aimed at countering the Communist threat by gaining a seal of approval for themselves from the Labor Party, which was regarded by workers as their party in a way that the CPA was not. However, the Groupers then became targets for covert infiltration or takeover by the Movement, a fervently anti-Communist Catholic body established by B. A. Santamaria in 1941. As a further complication, there was a developing Cold War. As in other capitalist countries, so in Australia, right-wing political organisations played upon fear of Communism. Their efforts included attempts to associate the ALP with the CPA in the public mind, and the ALP leaders moved to the right in order to counter this.

Some of the results were evident in industrial relations and civil liberties. Evatt's own position is not entirely clear. Chifley was undoubtedly the dominant figure in determining the federal government's domestic policy and in general it can be said that Evatt was content to follow the Prime Minister's lead in this area, just as Chifley allowed Evatt to make the running in most aspects of international affairs. Occasionally there was a convergence of national and international affairs, as in 1947 when Evatt piloted the Approved Defence Projects Protection Bill through parliament. In doing so, he was fortified by a resolution passed by the federal executive of the ALP, congratulating Chifley and Evatt upon their firm stand 'against the proposed black ban on the rocket range project'. The Bill stemmed from an agreement under which the Commonwealth government provided the British government with a range in South Australia for testing missile guidance systems—whereupon Communists and others tried to organise a trade union boycott of the construction project. In an official pamphlet, Evatt quoted a leading Communist as saying, 'The rocket plan is part of the Attlee–Bevin and Chifley–Evatt policy of turning Australia into an imperialist base'. In reality, this was a case where Evatt's role as External Affairs Minister conflicted with his traditional stance on issues of civil liberty, and Australia's foreign policy interests took precedence.[14]

The Bill was said to be aimed at preventing sabotage of approved defence projects—in the first instance, the testing of long-range weapons. Officially, there was no connection with atomic warheads, although there was some press speculation on this point. The Bill provided penalties of fine or imprisonment for any person who, without reasonable cause or excuse, obstructed such a project by boycott or threat of boycott. This was extended to any person who, by speech or writing, advocated or encouraged the prevention or obstruction of a project. Evatt denied that this was an undue interference with freedom of speech. He also claimed that the fundamental trade union right to strike was not affected. This, he said, was because a strike was 'an action by workers to improve their industrial conditions', whereas a boycott or black ban of the kind contemplated in the Bill was 'a misuse of industrial power, not for the purpose of improving the conditions of workers but for a political or international purpose contrary to the defence policy of the Government and the Parliament'.[15]

This was a very dubious distinction, and in the parliamentary debate the Opposition pointed out that the government had not tried to apply it to recent union boycotts of shipping vessels carrying Dutch goods destined for Indonesia. Doris Blackburn, a left-wing Independent MP who had been elected after the death of her husband, attacked the Bill from another direction. She described it as 'a coercive measure of the worst kind undertaken in a time of peace', and asked: 'at what point does [freedom of] speech become incitement to sabotage?'. She also pointed out that official ALP policy included as an objective: 'To amend the Crimes Act by repealing the sections relating to political or industrial offences'.[16]

Opposition to the rocket range at Woomera was not confined to Communists. Other opponents included pacifists and people concerned about the welfare of Aborigines in central Australia. Communists picked up this point, and Evatt was probably stung by a comment in a pamphlet:

Rights of small nations is what Dr Evatt says he fights for. The utter hypocrisy of his plea is exposed by the treatment of the Australian aborigine...in the interests of a Big Power rocket range and armament race.[17]

The Australian Council for Civil Liberties was also concerned about the Bill, and Fitzpatrick requested Evatt to redraft it in order to restrict its application. Evatt was willing to consider this but he was due to depart on a visit to Japan, and the Bill passed quickly through parliament, the Opposition being generally in favour of it. Blackburn claimed that the government had fallen for an Opposition stunt based on the Communist bogy; and Evatt provided some support for this view by his insistence that the prime justification for the Bill was the adherence by Australian Communists to Soviet interests.[18]

A month or so earlier, Fitzpatrick wrote to Evatt about press reports that the Minister intended to repeal obnoxious sections of the Crimes Act dating from the inter-war period of conservative government. Fitzpatrick expressed the hope that such repeal would follow the lines of criticism of the Act articulated by Evatt himself in the High Court in 1932 in the case of *Hush v. Devanny*. Evatt replied that the Act was indeed under extensive review. However, no amending Bill came to light. Doris Blackburn, as a vice-president of the ACCL, was probably aware of this correspondence.[19]

As for the Woomera rocket range, it seems that the CPA dropped any plans to impose a black ban on its construction, so that no criminal charges were laid under the Approved Defence Projects Protection Act. Indeed, the Act was never invoked. Nevertheless, it remained in force for potential use in relation to other defence projects to be proclaimed later. Notably, there was the Menzies government's approval of British atomic weapon tests in Australia in the 1950s. The approval registered both the subordination of Australian interests to the interests of other countries and a callous disregard for the welfare of Aborigines.

A further tentative shift to the right by the Chifley government in 1947 may be discerned in important amendments to the Commonwealth Conciliation and Arbitration Act. Actually, the prime purpose of these changes was simply to increase the number and power of conciliation commissioners. In this way, it was hoped, procedures would become more informal, even though questions of the basic wage, female minimum wages, and standard hours of work were reserved for consideration by judges of the Arbitration Court. The amending Bill, with its emphasis upon conciliation, to a large extent re-asserted the proposals of the Scullin government in 1930. At the same time, the Chifley government rejected employers' proposals advocating legislative restoration of pre-1930 penal clauses concerning strikes and lock-outs. On the other hand, the government did not adopt proposals by the Australian Council of Trade Unions (ACTU) aimed at eliminating sanctions against unions. As Evatt remarked in speaking to the Bill, it remained open to the court to insert prohibitions on strikes or work bans in awards, as had been done—though rarely—in some cases in the 1930s.[20]

Further, existing provisions relating to the deregistration of organisations, secret ballots under court orders, and the cancellation or suspension of awards were retained in the Act as sanctions. This degree of caution on the part of the Chifley government may be related to a major metal trades dispute in Victoria at the time, which the Opposition used as a means of attacking the government, despite the fact that Chifley did not support the striking unions.

Another legislative amendment affecting industrial relations in 1947 reflected more credit upon Evatt, from a trade union point of view. The Stevedoring Industry Bill brought in by Evatt in effect did away with the Transport Workers' Act of 1928 which, by requiring the licensing of waterside workers, was known to them as the 'dog collar' Act. The new Act provided for a Commission to regulate work on the wharves. Richard Kirby, a barrister who had been a member of the Evatt Brains Trust in the 1930s, was appointed chairman of this commission, Chifley being as much concerned as Evatt to persuade him to take the job. Stevedoring, like coal-mining, was an industry in which relations between workers and employers were hostile and Communist influence was strong.

NOTES

1 S.M. Bruce assessed Forde as 'a very well meaning and quite amiable person with an unrivalled capacity to mouth platitudes' (Bruce to McDougall, 20 April 1945, *DAFP*, vol. viii, Document 74). Nevertheless, Forde was well regarded by his colleagues in Canberra.
2 Melbourne *Herald*, 11 November 1942.
3 *CPD*, vol. 183, pp. 4770–1. In fact, the Act was not proclaimed until the day after the surrender of Japan.
4 War Cabinet Minute, 19 September 1945, *DAFP*, vol. viii, Document 251.
5 Evatt to Latham, undated (probably 1946–47), Latham Papers, 1009/62/812, NLA. The Salaries (Statutory Offices) Adjustment Act of 1947 provided for increases in judges' salaries. At the time, a High Court judge, on retirement after not less than fifteen years service, was entitled to a non-contributory pension equal to fifty per cent of salary. Evatt himself had been ineligible when he resigned in 1940 after a shorter period of service.
6 A.A. Calwell, *Be Just and Fear Not*, Lloyd O'Neil, Victoria, 1972, p. 197.
7 Geoffrey Sawer, *Australian Federal Politics and Law 1929-1949*, p. 182.
8 *Daily Telegraph*, 15 February 1946.
9 Quoted in James Griffin, 'The Evatt–Wren Letters', *Eureka Street*, vol. 2, September 1992, p. 28. Underlining in the original.
10 Allan Dalziel, *Evatt The Enigma*, p. 58.
11 *ADB*, vol. 12, pp. 580–3.
12 Interview with R.R. Downing, Sydney, 22 October 1992.
13 Tom Sheridan, *Division of Labour: Industrial Relations in the Chifley Years 1945–1949*, OUP, Melbourne, 1989, p. 318.
14 H.V. Evatt, *Hands Off the Nation's Defences*, Canberra, July 1947.
15 *CPD*, vol. 191, 3 June 1947, p. 3248.
16 Ibid., pp. 3660–1.
17 Alf Watt, *Rocket Range Threatens Australia*, South Australian State Committee, ACP, Adelaide, n.d., p. 11.

18 Fitzpatrick to Evatt, 11 June 1947, Evatt to Fitzpatrick, 30 June 1947, Fitzpatrick Papers MS 4965, 1/8647 and 1/8653, NLA.
19 Fitzpatrick to Evatt, 24 May 1947, Evatt to Fitzpatrick (telegram), 23 June 1947, Evatt Collection, Flinders University.
20 Jim Hagan, *The History of the ACTU*, Longman Cheshire, Melbourne, 1981, pp. 189–90.

PART IV

INTERNATIONAL AFFAIRS

CHAPTER 19

REGIONAL SECURITY: THE SOUTH PACIFIC

It is obvious that there will have to be zones of security in areas like South-east Asia and the South and South–west Pacific. Of crucial importance to Australia's own security will be such islands as Timor, New Guinea, the Solomons, the New Hebrides, Fiji, and New Caledonia.

H. V. EVATT, 1943

By way of an introduction to consideration of Evatt's role in international affairs, it may be said that one of the greatest difficulties in modern diplomacy has been the attempt to develop a regional scheme for the Asia–Pacific area. Australia's geographical location has forced it into a unique role as a Western nation when such schemes have been attempted—invariably in times of crisis. Deakin's proposal for a Pacific Pact was an attempt to fashion a security system in the wake of the withdrawal of British power and the dramatic expansion of Japan. Lyons' proposal in 1937 was similarly a reaction to British weakness in the Far East, American isolationism and the aggression of Japan in China. On the eve of World War II, Menzies could only lament the tendency of the British to minimise the problems of the distant East, which to Australia was 'the Near North'.

The problem was to persist during the war. The Allies had no effective plans for dealing with Japanese aggression and their hastily constructed regional command arrangements were quickly swept away. The American defence scheme for Australia seemed to be a residual afterthought of an ally preoccupied with 'beating Hitler first'. As the Allies prepared for the peace they continued their neglect of the Pacific region. The problem was that many of their decisions had major implications for the Pacific region. The American demands to end colonialism; the talk of recognising China as a major regional power; the attempt to take island bases by the United States Navy and by American airlines; and the ultimate attempt to model a regional scheme to contain Communism and restore Japanese power—all suggested to Evatt that there would be no comprehensive regional settlement unless he initiated action to that end.

Evatt left office in 1949 calling in vain for a regional settlement that he had foreshadowed when becoming Minister for External Affairs in 1941. Despite the fact that a number of historians have seen Evatt as simply wanting American protection, his view of the region was far more comprehensive than that. To Evatt, regionalism was an essential factor in the United Nations and the post-war Commonwealth. It was central in defence planning and diplomacy. It was of vital concern to civil aviation and immigration. It dominated his thinking with respect to the peace treaties. It was a consistent strand that ran through all of his policies in office.

For all that, his policy evolved. Australia was a small power without membership on the higher councils that directed the war and planned for the peace. Evatt had to react to events as they occurred. Initially the trauma of war conditioned his view of the region. Of immediate concern were the strategically placed islands that controlled the approaches to the continent—Timor to the north-west and New Guinea to the north. His attempts to secure these islands were central to his diplomacy and to his regionalism thereafter. Evatt's regional plan announced so dramatically in the 1944 Australia–New Zealand Agreement was a response to American plans to change colonial arrangements and to acquire bases. His post-war appeals for a comprehensive regional settlement need to be read against American economic plans designed to secure dominance in civil aviation and later to restore Japanese power. In the process, Evatt welded together an elaborate regional synthesis that was designed to protect Australian strategic and economic interests. In the event it was to prove unattainable while he was in office—it still remains so.

Evatt's first survey of the Pacific region, after assuming office in October 1941, was forced by the imminent prospect of war in the area. European colonial powers had responsibility for much of the region and yet there were no regional defence plans in place. May 1940 had changed all that. The French had effectively lost Indochina

Bert carries bat (circa 1905)
Copyright Flinders University

Evatt the young Doctor

***Bert and Mary Alice Evatt:** young lovers*
Copyright Flinders University

Counsel for the Defence
L to R: Watt, Evatt and Meagher in the Walsh–Johnston Deportation case
Copyright Flinders University

New South Wales State Election, 1925
From the *Labor Daily* newspaper

Family and friends in New South Wales in World War II
L to R: Premier McKell, Senator Ashley, Mary Alice Evatt, Peter Evatt, Penelope Evatt, H. V. Evatt, Clive Evatt, Elizabeth (later Justice) Evatt, unknown and Billy Hughes
Copyright Flinders University

Evatt and Churchill
Copyright Flinders University

Going my way? H. V. Evatt and General MacArthur
Copyright Flinders University

Dr Evatt when Minister for External Affairs with Mr Chifley, Prime Minister
Copyright John Fairfax and Sons Ltd

Bert and Mary Alice Evatt—riding ships of uncertain State
Copyright Flinders University

Evatt wields the gavel at the United Nations, 1947

H. V. Evatt, C. R. Attlee and others, 1948?

when it was occupied by Japan in mid-1941, an act which led to crippling American sanctions, which in turn threatened to escalate into war. The Americans, however, had not indicated to the Australians or to the British what precisely they would do in this eventuality. British help, on the other hand, was unlikely. The Singapore base stood as a great symbol but Britain's commitment to the Far East would depend on the war in Europe. In late 1941, however, German troops were approaching Moscow and Rommel threatened the Middle East.

Evatt was made aware of the extent of Australia's peril on 7 November when, at a meeting of the Advisory War Council, he asked the visiting British Minister at Singapore, Duff Cooper, for the 'real plans' for the defence of the Far East. Evatt greeted the response—that Britain would abandon the Mediterranean if necessary to save Singapore—in silence, but others present saw that to be 'a very remote possibility'.[1]

Evatt obviously shared this view, and given Australia's strategic isolation at that juncture his objective was to avert war with Japan, even if that meant appeasement. Consequently, he was prepared to support US Secretary of State, Cordell Hull's, last-ditch bilateral discussions between the Japanese and the Americans in the weeks before Pearl Harbor. When the talks looked like breaking down, however—prompting the Australian legation in Washington to warn Evatt that 'an explosion might come at any time and at short notice'— he took his first step in calling for a regional conference to deal with security. It was, argued Evatt, 'time to talk frankly' to the Japanese and avoid the 'pinpricking policies' pursued by the Americans and British. What Evatt had in mind was an agreement which would allow the relaxation of the US embargo if the Japanese would withdraw from Indochina—an initiative which would leave Japan free to prosecute its war in China. Evatt explained his position to the House of Representatives on 27 November:

the occasion of the imposition of economic restrictions upon Japan was that nation's military advance into Indo-China...I do not see why it should be impossible for Japan to retrace her steps and make it possible to ease the present economic restriction.

Once war had been averted by this, Evatt foreshadowed a regional security conference, but when he listed those countries that should be guaranteed against aggression in any regional arrangement he specified the Netherlands East Indies, Thailand and the Far East Province of Russia. China was not included—Evatt conceding only that he hoped that Britain 'would not look on with equanimity' if Japanese attacks there were to be 'redoubled' in intensity. These were dangerous times and as Evatt explained his position to Australian legations on 29 November, 'China does not want to be treated as a pawn in this game...neither does Australia'.²

Ultimately the talks broke down and, as war engulfed the Pacific, Evatt, having seen the failure of Allied diplomacy in the Far East, now witnessed the failure of military strategy as well. He was not to realise, until his 1942 mission to Britain, that the basis of that strategy was 'Beat Hitler First', but from the beginning he sought to have Australia sit in common council with the main Allies in the Pacific theatre. The chickens had come home to roost for the British who had in 1921 replaced their traditional alliance with the Japanese with the pious hope that the threat of the Singapore base would deter aggression. Beyond that they had a Pacific strategy based on the expectation of American intervention. But what were American plans? This problem, raised in acute form in the weeks after Pearl Harbor, forced Evatt to initiate planning for the region. From the first, as he later reflected, Australia's 'emphasis is on Pacific security'.

Before Pearl Harbor there was no adequate co-operation between our countries in relation to the military situation in the Pacific. This was despite the great danger that Japan, known to be an active supporter of the two other Axis powers, would enter the war. Pearl Harbor forced the Pacific nations to unite. The first tentative and hastily improvised organization known as ABDA was created. In it American, British, Dutch and Australians were included in a defensive military set-up. Soon, however, it had to be liquidated as the greater part of the territories directly affected were occupied by the enemy, as one bastion after another fell.³

Britain's regional defence organisation—ABDA—was overstretched. They were hard pressed to defend India, let alone Australia. When this became tragically obvious in early 1942, Australian defence planners were forced into a strategic analysis of the region for the first time. Herein, Evatt's first sortie into what was to become a feature of his term as Minister of External Affairs, was over the identity of an 'Anzac Area'. The objective was to focus Allied planning on the security of Australia as a main base rather than to leave it where it had always been—beyond the operational focus of the Allies. This area was designed to cover Australia as well as New Zealand and islands in an arc from New Guinea to Fiji. Australia was to be the main base from which to launch the counter-offensive. Britain was to be encouraged to anchor Far Eastern defence there rather than concentrate on India. In early January, Evatt accordingly pressed the British to extend ABDA to include the defence of the Australian mainland. He also impressed upon Casey, at the Australian Legation in Washington, the need to ensure that American reinforcements be sent in adequate numbers and not positioned only in order to secure the American Pacific base chain in Samoa, Fiji and New Caledonia.[4]

Evatt wanted Allied planning to secure Australia as a central base in the Pacific. In reality the Allies had no such plan. The British and the Americans would stand on the defensive in the Pacific and their theatres of operations were to be divided. The main British base would be India—although they promised to 'cover' the Indian Ocean approaches to the Australian west coast—and the main American base was Hawaii. The fate of the Anzac Area and the strategy it presupposed was sealed by the decision of the Combined American and British Chiefs of Staff in January to truncate the 'Anzac Area' by detaching Australia into the 'Southwest Pacific Area' and placing New Zealand and the islands in the 'South Pacific Area'.[5]

Much writing concerning Evatt's mission to the United States in 1942 has concentrated on his attempts to secure a voice for Australia in the planning of the Pacific campaign through the Pacific War Council. A major objective of the mission was also to get the Americans to accept the Anzac Area. Evatt questioned their ability to ensure joint planning and co-ordination given these command arrangements, especially as the Army under General MacArthur had responsibility for Australia and the Navy under Admiral King would have responsibility for New Zealand.

At the beginning of the 1942 mission, Evatt was inclined to hope that the Pacific War Council would sort out the problems of regional co-ordination and the attendant problems of Army–Navy rivalry, but he was soon disillusioned. By April he was already aware that Australian regional planning was in tatters—for now. The Pacific War Council itself was irrelevant. Roosevelt had only consented to it to 'make everybody happy', but he never intended it to have power. It became a talkfest without access to the Anglo-American committees that made the detailed decisions on the conduct of the war. Evatt summed up the problem to Curtin:

any attempt to introduce detailed consideration of equipment problems is inadmissible, because it causes complete confusion, with China, United Kingdom, Australia, New Zealand and the Netherlands East Indies all taking up somewhat different attitudes.[6]

Evatt understood in 1942 the harsh reality that Australian views on strategic planning in the region were of no account. The only influence that Australia could bring to bear was by supporting General MacArthur, as Commander of the South-West Pacific Area, in his requests for resources to the Combined Chiefs of Staff in

Washington. That in turn was to prove difficult as he was to learn in London in 1942 of the 'Beat Hitler First' Policy. Pearl Harbor had not altered the neglect of the Pacific.⁷

❖

The command arrangements for the Pacific were an outcome of the immediate strategic situation after the initial Japanese assault in 1941–42, and they had to be accepted. Within a year, however, Evatt was again forced to enter the vexed question of defining Australian regional security—this time over the issue of colonies. He became aware after the American victory at Midway in June 1942 that the Roosevelt administration was planning major changes to future colonial organisation. At first, press releases by US officials, such as that by Sumner Welles in July 1942, indicated that the Pacific War would usher in 'the death of imperialism'. In October, *Life* magazine published an 'Open Letter...to the People of England' stressing that while Americans might disagree among themselves about war aims, 'One thing we are sure we are not fighting for is to hold the British Empire together'. In December, on the anniversary of Pearl Harbor, at the Eighth Conference of the Institute of Pacific Relations at Mont Tremblant in Canada, alarmed Australian officials reported to Evatt that there had been a sustained attack on British colonialism by American delegates.⁸

The Americans also took concrete steps to end European colonialism. In August 1942 Hull called for a joint Allied statement on the future administration of colonies and held out the possibility that a few 'principal' or 'parent' states, like the United States, Britain and China, might take the lead here. By March 1943 Roosevelt himself made his views known to the Allies represented on the Pacific War Council in Washington. He informed them that in considering the disposal of Japanese-mandated islands, China must play a central part. He went further, however, and insisted that China should resume control of Hong Kong and that the French colonial empire should be put under United Nations trusteeship. These ideas surfaced dramatically at the Cairo Conference in December 1943 when Roosevelt sought to replace French trusteeship over Indochina by Chinese tuusteeship, and further indicated that certain territories seized by Japan after 1931 would be restored to China after the war.

Evatt was not new to the colonial question. In 1935 he produced a study—'The British Dominions as Mandatories'—in which he developed the argument that mandatory powers were responsible to world opinion as 'trustees' for colonial subjects.⁹ But he did not enter the developing debate over colonies after 1942 simply to apply his 'liberal-socialist' views to the question; he reacted to developments in the United States and Britain. Evatt was caught unaware by the Hull proposals for a joint declaration and was inclined at first, as he explained to the Australian Parliament on 3 September 1942, to dismiss any need to go beyond the Atlantic Charter—which had embodied the general war aims of freedom from oppression, but had not specifically addressed the question of colonial peoples. Significantly, he added that in the case of the Pacific 'the first principle which must be applied is that of security'. Privately, however, he objected to any 'approach arising mainly from a desire to meet current criticism in the United States'.[10]

That was exactly what the British were proposing to do. They were in a difficult position, because they could not lightly dismiss the policies of so powerful an ally, but the British were not going to allow themselves, as the Colonial Secretary Lord Cranborne said in response to the Hull declaration, to surrender their empire and be 'manoeuvred by the Chinese and Americans'. Positive steps, however, had to be taken. The British government was prepared to agree to a joint declaration by 'Principal States' as Hull wanted, and they agreed that there should be some accountability about colonies to such states. In December the British Cabinet accordingly accepted regional commissions along the lines of that established in the Caribbean in March. In the Far East this would allow at least a measure of 'consultation' with the other 'parent states', with the possible inclusion of India. On 13 July 1943 these ideas were conveyed to the House of Commons in an address by the new Colonial Secretary, Oliver Stanley, when he endorsed the possibility of establishing regional commissions.[11]

Evatt was determined to take a lead in formulating any proposals for the region. He rejected the idea that any proposed declaration on colonies could be 'definitive' in the 'South West Asian Region'. His concern was security. He told the British in January 1943 that 'he had in mind the relinquishment of parts of the Netherlands East Indies' and that 'the course of the war in this theatre has demonstrated that control or supervision over neighbouring territories will be vital to the future security of Australia'. He did not delimit a specific region at this stage but sent a cable from the Australian government to the British on 5 February 1943 that declared that

the Commonwealth Government wish it to be clearly understood...that it regards Australian specific strategic and economic interests as extending to South East Asia, the South West Pacific and the Pacific areas.[12]

After Stanley's announcement concerning the establishment of regional commissions Evatt followed the lead of the South African Prime Minister, Smuts—who had reacted by declaring that South Africa would establish a commission covering southern and central

Africa—and proposed his own. In a major review of international affairs delivered in the House of Representatives on 14 October 1943 he drew the line:

In one of his speeches, Mr. Churchill indicated that he favoured the establishment within the framework of a world organization of a system of subordinate regional councils. Such reference to zones brings me to another vital part of our foreign relationships. While Australia's interest in the future of Europe is undoubted, it is obvious that our predominant interest must lie in the Pacific regions. Australia has a leading part to play in those regions.

He then listed those 'island neighbours' in which Australia had 'a particular interest' as a 'result of the war'. The Solomons 'should maintain sufficient bases'; New Caledonia should have 'an important place in the future security of the South-West Pacific'; Timor 'in enemy hands is a constant threat to Australia'; and 'I envisage New Guinea, both Australian and Dutch, as an integral part of the Pacific zone'.[13]

Evatt was more direct with the Americans. After the speech Evatt met with John Minter, the First Secretary of the US Legation who graphically described the Australian's 'defence line'. Evatt

turned in his chair and with a pencil drew a line across a map of the South Pacific which was on his wall. The line started at Timor, extended through Dutch and Australian New Guinea and on through New Britain and New Ireland, then down through the Solomons, the New Hebrides, New Caledonia, and New Zealand. He then drew another line starting at the Philippines, running through the Carolinas, Marianas and Marshalls, to meet a perpendicular line running from the Aleutians through the Hawaiian group and down to American Samoa. He said, 'This I think should be Australia's and this should be yours. All of yours, except Samoa, is above the equator. Ours is all south of the Equator and constitutes a natural line of defence'.[14]

The next development for Evatt was shattering. In November 1943 China discussed the question of the disposal of Pacific islands at the Cairo Conference as a member of the 'Big Four'. China's entry on to the scene threatened all—the White Australia policy, regional security and Australia's objective to be recognised as the leading Pacific power. No less than Hughes at Versailles, Evatt wanted to preserve the White Australia policy. In January 1942 he had argued that the approval for Eurasian and Chinese women and children to come to Australia as refugees should be regarded as a wartime relaxation only. During British negotiations with China over the abrogation of extraterritoriality, he steadfastly refused to enter any agreement which might infringe the White Australia policy, despite assurances from the

Australian Ambassador in China, Eggleston, that the immigration laws were not threatened in any way. During his 1943 mission abroad, Evatt defended Australia and New Zealand as 'strong and progressive peoples whose civilisation is based on a long European background' and called upon the people of Britain, as he told one audience in Leeds, to build a white post-war Australia of twenty-five million people. On his return to Australia, Evatt developed a theme that he carried into the United Nations, often occasioned by bitter debates with Chinese delegates over the 'domestic jurisdiction' of immigration:

the basis of all our population increase is the principle of White Australia, which is fully recognised by the United Nations as absolutely necessary.[15]

Evatt had been receiving disturbing reports in 1942 that the Americans looked upon China as 'the light of Asia and a very great democracy', leading him to caution Bruce in London before the Mont Tremblant Conference that 'care' should be taken 'that Chinese imperialism...does not replace older imperialisms'. He saw danger, therefore, in Roosevelt's remarks at the Pacific War Council in May 1942 that the French should not have their Pacific possessions returned after the war. In 1943 China was the likely candidate to fill the vacuum in Indochina. At the Moscow Conference in October, China was invited to sign the Four Power Declaration, confirming its status as a major power, a development that led to Evatt's rejection of China's Big Power status. The declaration, in his opinion, would 'lose much of its positive value if China is included'.[16]

It was the 'concessions made to China' at Cairo that caused Evatt, as he explained to the British High Commissioner in Australia, Ronald Cross, to proceed with the calling of a regional conference. He gave Cross a list of the nations that should attend such a conference, and the Chinese were not included—leading them to appeal to the United States with a view to overturning the proposed conference. That hardly surprised Evatt who defended his initiative by claiming that in the south-west Pacific Australia would provide 'a European counter-weight to American or Chinese policy'.[17]

Evatt returned to the proposal that he had raised in the crisis of 1941. There should be an international conference to oversee the peace settlement in the Pacific, a move that would arrest unilateral action by the United States. The first step in this was the convening of a conference between Australia and New Zealand in Canberra in January 1944. The idea of the conference, and of the signing of a formal treaty with New Zealand, was Evatt's alone. It gave him the opportunity to provide a dramatic indication of some of the key parameters underlying Australian attitudes—the notion of an Anzac region which straddled the Allied strategic division of the Pacific of 1942; the refusal to accept the monopoly of the Big Four in determining policy; and a reminder that the Agreement supported 'the accepted principle that every government has the right to control immigration and emigration in regard to all territories within its jurisdiction'.

To give effect to these principles Evatt adopted Smuts' idea and proposed a 'South Seas Regional Commission' (SSRC) which would be based on 'Melanesian and Polynesian races'—leading the British High Commissioner, Cross, to observe that the SSRC 'would constitute an instrument which will aid in imposing a bar to infiltration by Chinese migrants into the South West and South Pacific'. Evatt himself did not pretend otherwise. He emphasised in Parliament later the need to differentiate between the immediate 'area of influence' of the commission which was concerned with 'the welfare of the native peoples of Melanesia and Polynesian areas', and the rest of the Asian region.[18]

Apart from the fact that the Australia–New Zealand Agreement represented a repudiation of American plans for the future of the region, it also demonstrated the extent to which the American alliance of December 1941 was enforced. Evatt was realistic when he drew the line on the chart for Minter's notice indicating America's major concern with the North Pacific. That had been the case in the past and indeed was to be reflected in the command arrangements at the end of the Pacific War with the return of the Australian area of operations to the British, under Mountbatten in the South East Asia Command. That, for Evatt, was a welcome arrangement. Regional planning throughout 1943–44 within the Australian government was based not on an impending American alliance, but a restoration of Commonwealth defence.[19]

That was a main objective of the January 1944 conference. The Canberra Agreement also demonstrated that, if nothing else, the war had taught him the importance of air power. These two factors—the links to the Commonwealth and the importance of air power—provide a thread that runs from the Agreement down to the so-called Manus controversy two years later. They also combined to force Evatt to modify even further his attempts to define an area of strategic responsibility for the Pacific dominions.

❖

Evatt attracted strong American criticism when he announced to the world on 21 January, as he signed the Australia–New Zealand Agreement, that

Absurd claims have sometimes been advanced in connection with wartime construction of naval, military and air installations. Both

Governments accept the undoubted principle of international practice that such construction does not in itself afford any basis whatsoever for territorial claims after hostilities have been concluded.

Pointedly the American legation related this specifically to the implications for their plans to extend civil air links throughout the Pacific:

*The civil aviation portion of the agreement is most significant. It contemplates international air trunk routes operated by an international air transport authority owning all the necessary aircraft and ancillary equipment. It also contemplates the prior specification of the international trunk routes by international agreement subject to this that both Governments assert the right of each country to regulate all air transport services within its own national jurisdiction and its neighbouring territories and also the right to use Australian and New Zealand personnel and resources not only on the national services but also to a fair degree on and in relation to the international air trunk routes. **If such an international agreement cannot be obtained to control international air trunk routes, both Governments will support a system of air trunk routes controlled and operated exclusively by Governments of the British Commonwealth of Nations under Government ownership.*** [20]

A major question underlying Evatt's thinking was the security of Australia from long-range bombing, a factor that required the possession of bases in an arc from Timor to the Admiralties.[21] An associated question was the extent to which air power would allow Britain to restore its fortunes. Its naval power had long been in decline, but air power promised a new beginning. Roosevelt himself had indicated to the Pacific War Council as early as 17 February 1943 that there would have to be 'redistribution of sovereignty' in the Pacific since 'the influence of air power will require new strategic studies to preserve peace'. In March he went further and advised the New Zealand government that he was aware of Australian and New Zealand interests in post-war civil aviation but the United States was interested in organising routes through the Pacific from South America and Mexico. 'The problem' was that many islands en route were French.[22]

In June 1943 Roosevelt inquired about the Navy's conclusions as to the relative strategic importance of the Pacific islands. He was interested in two particular groups—French Polynesia and the Marquesas—which seemed to control the strategic routes in the South Pacific. He suggested that air transport experts visit the islands to assess their suitability as air bases. In the event Rear Admiral Richard E. Byrd led a mission in September which included representatives of Northeast Airlines, Transcontinental and Western Air, United Airlines, Pan American Airways, American Airlines, and the American

Export Airlines. Byrd's objective was to locate 'exactly what air routes, islands, strategic areas, etc., are essential for the combined purposes of commerce and political and military strategy'. As Louis observes, 'On the eve of the Cairo Conferences, the President now had the precise military information he required. Though Roosevelt might talk about trusteeship territories in a slapdash fashion with Churchill and Chiang Kai-shek, he knew precisely what issues were at stake for American security'.[23]

So did Evatt. During 1943 Forsyth, the architect of much of Evatt's planning in the Department of External Affairs on Trusteeship, was set to work to study the operation of the United States air ferry service in the Pacific and to assess its links to projects designed around the needs of post-war civil aviation, particularly in British and French possessions. Evatt noted the importance of Forsyth's enquiries in a letter to Watt on 30 July 1943 when he argued that the question of post-war civil aviation was 'coming to a head'. He went on to point out that the head of the Australian legation in New Caledonia, Ballard, had been given the job of initiating 'a special enquiry in New Caledonia and the New Hebrides' regarding American planning in aviation and the resumption of civil administration. In requesting that Watt, at the Washington Legation, also study the matter of 'what post-war plans are being laid' by the United States in the Pacific, he noted that 'there seems to be a lack of United Kingdom interest on the one hand and rather too lively an American interest on the other. The fate of these islands has obvious importance in any security system and in post-war trans-Pacific aviation'.[24]

Historians have ignored Evatt's attempts to enlist French help in an effort to thwart nascent American planning for the region at this juncture. The French were a buffer to both Chinese influence and American economic penetration. Roosevelt coveted French bases in the Pacific and elsewhere for use by American airline companies after the war. He detested de Gaulle and refused to recognise the Free French Committee of National Liberation. At the same time as the Australia–New Zealand conference, the French Committee of National Liberation had sponsored the Brazzaville conference which adopted resolutions enshrining principles of trusteeship for the French colonial empire. This marked the beginning of a major campaign waged by de Gaulle in 1944 to get American recognition of the Committee and of the legitimacy of Free French colonial aspirations.

At the Canberra Conference, Evatt proposed that any South Seas Commission to discuss colonial problems should invite the participation of the French Committee of National Liberation. This invitation was extended, he said, 'because we owe a peculiar debt to Fighting France, especially in relation to the early defence measures against

Japan both in the New Hebrides and in New Caledonia'. Furthermore, he went on, Australia 'is publicly pledged to do its utmost to maintain the sovereignty of France in its present South Pacific possessions'. The statement was mockery of the record. The Australians themselves had initiated the seizure of New Caledonia from the Vichy Government, and they had regarded the New Hebrides Anglo-French condominium as a disaster from its inception in 1907. The invitation in 1944 was in fact an important intervention into Great Power diplomacy. Evatt knew of American plans to take responsibility for French Pacific bases and of Chinese ambitions in Indochina.[25]

His initiative prompted American anger and therefore British embarrassment. So determined was Roosevelt over French colonies that Churchill himself, while eager to restore the French to their empire, preferred to 'let this sleeping dog lie'. Only after the 'Overlord' landings in June 1944, with the Free French once again on the continent, did he conclude that Britain 'could now safely recognise' de Gaulle's committee as the provisional government of France. Yet Evatt sought to secure British recognition in January 1944 for the Committee of National Liberation as the French provisional government and to openly pledge to support its claim to their Pacific possessions. Writing directly to Evatt, Churchill thundered that 'I will never consent to quarrel with the President of the United States on account of the antics of General de Gaulle'.[26]

Despite differences with the British over de Gaulle, Evatt saw the Commonwealth connection to be vital. Following news of the Byrd mission, Evatt worked to strengthen British interest in the Pacific. He informed them that the American air bases constructed in the Pacific 'have the appearance of permanent rather than merely wartime' measures. To counter this, and foreshadowing Curtin's appeals nearly a year later at the Commonwealth Conference, he stressed the need that 'the present and future operations in the South West Pacific make it most desirable that the British flag should be kept flying prominently'. Significantly, he argued that heavy bombers such as Lancasters should participate in the Pacific offensive 'not only from the military point of view but from the broadest Empire policy'.[27]

He didn't get the bombers but he got a sympathetic response. The British were keen to restore the system of imperial communications which had been set up in the 1930s. The Empire Air Mail Scheme in 1935 had been a joint British-Australian venture and therefore had ensured Qantas control of the Singapore –Sydney leg of the route. The American airline, Pan Am, had been kept out of the Australian market. In September 1943 the British Air Ministry, having already resisted American calls for a post-war system of 'freedom of the air', therefore rejected any attempts to transfer sovereignty of the Pacific islands to the Americans. British planners could not at that stage of the war challenge American predominance in the production of transport aircraft, but they could exploit their ownership of airfields around the world as a basis for developing civil aviation.[28]

On 1 October news broke of the Truman Committee's report to the United States Congress which indicated that bases built with Lend-Lease Aid should be controlled by the Americans. Ominously, members of the committee believed that 'Britain everywhere was outsmarting America, whose interests were not being pursued with the same vigour as Britain's'. As one of the Senators summed up the problem, 'America has invested hundreds of millions of dollars in Britain, Africa, Australia and India, yet there is not a single spot in these countries where our planes can land after the war'.[29]

Evatt's rejoinder was made in Parliament on 14 October. He emphasised the need for Australia to have a 'zone of security', but added that there was also a need for Australia to discharge responsibility in 'what I have called the extended defence zone'. In 'such a zone it is plain that Australia must be armed with the necessary air resources both civil as well as military'. He also associated Australia with the British position in their talks on post-war aviation with the United States—that in the event of a failure of international co-operation in the development of post-war civil aviation, then 'common understanding' would be reached within the Commonwealth. That position was enshrined in the Australia–New Zealand Agreement.[30]

The Americans, not surprisingly, objected strongly to the Australia–New Zealand Agreement. Roosevelt complained to Eggleston that 'he did not like the Anzac Pact', while Hull told Curtin, who was on his way to the Commonwealth conference in April 1944, that 'we were almost flabbergasted at certain provisions' of the Agreement. Evatt was the focus of their concern. He had behaved 'outrageously'. He had attempted to prejudice a more orderly attempt to deal with regional security in the context of a more general security system.[31]

That, at least, was the public assessment. Privately the Americans realised that the agreement marked a turning point in their relations with the Commonwealth. Minister Johnson provided a sober assessment when he pointed out that Australia had come to occupy 'a position of very real importance to the Empire...Australia and New Zealand emerged as close supporters of Empire interests in the Pacific area'. Johnson saw Evatt as asserting an interest in the Pacific islands because the British had been unable to do so by virtue of the 1916 treaty with Japan which had guaranteed Japanese possessions in the Pacific in return for their participation in World War I. When reflecting on the civil aviation policy, Johnson lamented to Hull that 'all fit into an Empire domestic scheme of economy that is closed to the outside world'.³²

Nor did the British see it differently. The US State Department noted that the agreement was 'heartedly' supported by the British press while Churchill, in Eden's words, 'said that he was rather glad that the incident had occurred...It was most important to do nothing to antagonise Evatt, who was now "on our side"'.³³

In January 1944 Evatt had at last identified his 'region'. The inner arc of islands anchored on Timor and New Guinea, a factor underlying his complicated assessment of the Indonesian revolution later, and Manus Island in the Admiralty group. Manus was vital to the defence of the Australian east coast, but it was also a secure link in a chain of Commonwealth bases. His refusal to countenance the transfer of the base to the Americans is explicable in the context of his attempts to associate Australian regional planning with that of the Commonwealth. Evatt turned his back on the Americans as far as immediate planning was concerned, and looked forward to a reinvigorated Commonwealth as the best guarantee of Australian national and regional security.³⁴

The retention of Manus Island was based on the assumption that in any future war the role of the United States would be uncertain. The role of the British Commonwealth, on the other hand, was fundamental. Indeed, as we will see, a number of elements combined to ensure that the Australian government at the end of the war turned back to Britain as opposed to accepting the inevitability of an alliance based in the first instance on the United States. Until the mid-1950s, planning for global war was based on the primacy of imperial defence. Regional planning was based on the principles laid down at the Australia–New Zealand Agreement—the British role was paramount while the Americans were seen as having a role north of the Equator and would work out their relationship with British Commonwealth defence chiefs at a later date.

The Manus dispute itself arose out of an American claim to strategic trusteeship of a number of island bases in the Pacific in October 1945. Manus was not the main objective—in fact the Americans dismissed it as being of slight importance. Nor did the Australians react immediately by noting its importance. The simple fact was that the Americans were laying claim to a string of air bases that would extend their control of trans-Pacific communications while denying any reciprocal rights to the British Commonwealth.³⁵

Australian planning for post-war civil aviation was from the first based on ensuring access to a share of international routes via agreement with the British. Any such agreement, however, conflicted with American plans for a deregulated market—or a so-called 'open skies' policy. Civil aviation was a very obvious case of an area where the Commonwealth gained strength from operating as a unit.[36]

Evatt knew it. His primary objective after the American claim was to enlist the support of the Commonwealth at the April 1946 Prime Ministers' Conference in London, which he attended with Chifley.[37] Chifley himself explained to the conference the overall position of the Australian government by emphasising the principles of the new Commonwealth defence policy. In the Pacific, Australia would lead in the devising of 'an agreed' common defence scheme, 'in the first instance between the Governments of the United Kingdom, Australia and New Zealand, and thereafter with the United States Government'. 'It was', he emphasised, 'against this background that the Australian Government viewed the United States' request for military bases in the Pacific'.

Evatt laid out for the conference the more detailed thinking of Australian defence planners. The American claim to 'exclusive rights' at Canton, Christmas and Funafuti Islands

was based on the ground that these islands were important stepping-stones in the direct line of communication between the United States and Australasia. But that was the very ground on which the Australian government could not agree that exclusive rights should be conceded to the United States; for these islands were vital links in Australasian communications to the United States.

Evatt was supported by Prime Minister Nash of New Zealand who gave the conference the details of the proposed empire trans-Pacific routes, especially signalling the importance of the locations mentioned by Evatt. Not surprisingly Evatt received the unequivocal assurance of Attlee that the bases would only be granted as part of a common defence scheme for the Pacific area.[38]

Evatt's subsequent talks with the Americans in June and July were conducted on the principle that the Americans would have to concede 'reciprocity' in the use of bases. At no stage did he relent on the question of the overall question of bases —but agreement on Manus was related, for the Americans, to this far more important issue. And for that reason agreement was not possible. Significantly their decision in April 1947 to drop their request for the base came after the conclusion of Anglo-American talks where the United States at last conceded the reality of a trans-Pacific Commonwealth system of aviation—and one subject to regulation. The Pacific Air Agreement of December 1946 provided landing rights in Honolulu and San Francisco for Britain while Pan American Airways had at last secured landing rights at Sydney, thereby ending a dispute that had dogged relations between the two sides over air transport since the Depression. More importantly, the American 'open skies' policy would have to wait till a much later period.[39]

Manus was indeed vital in the Australian arc of islands in its own right and would have to be accessible to British forces at the outset of any conflict, especially now that the Australians had responsibility for regional planning on behalf of the Commonwealth. But its viability as a base entirely presupposed the existence of imperial sea and air communications in the Pacific.[40]

Evatt finally summed up his position in a report to the House of Representatives on 11 November 1946:

Manus Island is only one of the places that are involved in a proper regional plan for the reciprocal use of bases. Also involved is the use of other bases, including British possessions such as Fiji, possessions held jointly such as at Canton, and New Zealand possessions.[41]

Five years earlier Evatt had anxiously witnessed the collapse of the Imperial position in the Far East. Now, after the war, he placed his faith in the restoration of the Commonwealth as the basis for regional planning. But the war had raised the prospect of invasion from the northern islands, and this memory remained firmly in place as Evatt shaped Australian policy to take account of nationalist revolution in Asia.

Notes

1 AA: A2682, Min. 560. The same day the British government advised the Australians by cable 'that no independent action by ourselves will deter Japan because we are so fully occupied elsewhere', A2679, Item 135/1941, Cable M350, Secretary of State for Dominion Affairs (SSDA) to Australian government, 7 November 1941.

2 *CPD* vol. 169, pp. 972–3. The cables dealing with the November–December crisis in the Far East are in AA: A3390/99, no item number, 'Japan–America'. Evatt followed the broad outline of Hull's 'Modus Vivendi' proposal in attempting to secure this trade-off, but unlike Hull wanted a major regional conference to address the underlying causes of the conflict in China.

3 H. Evatt, 'The Future of the Pacific', *Pacific Historical Review*, vol. 14, no. 2, June 1945, p. 147.

4 The documents on the Anzac Area are in AA: A2673, Min. 1776 and A2670, Item 118/1942 and Supplements 1 and 2. Evatt's cables on the subject are in A3300/219. See also M. Matloff and E. Snell, *Strategic Planning for Coalition Warfare, 1941–1942*, US Government Printer, Washington, 1952, pp. 156–8.

5 Public Record Office (PRO) CAB 66/22, WP (42) 94; AA: A2679, Item 14/1942, Cable 44, Casey to Evatt, 8 January 1942.
6 AA: A3300/233, Cable ES 17, Evatt to Curtin, 23 April 1942.
7 W. Reynolds, 'H.V. Evatt: The Imperial Connection and the Quest for Australian Security, 1941–1945', Ph.D thesis, Newcastle University, New South Wales, 1985, ch. 2.
8 Reynolds, 'Evatt and the Imperial Connection', chs 4–5.
9 Mandates were held on the assumption that social and economic conditions were maintained and that the ultimate objective was to grant independence to colonial subjects. In reality, a wide discretion was granted to the strategic and economic needs of colonial powers, especially with respect to 'C class' mandates, the type applied to New Guinea after Hughes' efforts at Versailles.
10 N. Harper and D. Sissons, *Australia and the United Nations*, Manhattan Publishing Company, New York, 1959, pp. 48–9; *CPD*, vol. 172, p. 82; AA: A989, Item 43/735/321; unnumbered cable, Evatt to Bruce, 3 September 1942.
11 W. Louis, *Imperialism at Bay 1941–1945: The United States and the Decolonization of the British Empire*, Clarendon Press, Oxford, 1977, p. 2. The problem with the British position was that their general views on the 'region' did not accord with that of the Australians. To London the 'Far East' had always been a region in itself. In December 1941, for example, they had developed regional planning through the 'Council of the Far East'. Churchill envisaged a Supreme World Council after the war presiding over three regional councils—the Pacific, Europe and America; but in January 1943 Eden spoke of a 'South Asian Council' that would include China and the United States. PRO: CAB 66/262, WP (43) 31; CAB 66/73, WP (43)233; W. Churchill, *The Second World War*, vol. 4, Cassell, London, 1951, pp. 717–18.
12 Evatt's cables are in PRO: DO 35/1895; AA: A2937, no item number, 'Post-War Colonial Policy'; A989, Item 43/735/321.
13 H.V. Evatt, *Foreign Policy of Australia*, Angus & Robertson, Sydney, 1945, pp. 141–6. The detailed work on colonial policy during 1943 was done by W.D. Forsyth. See AA: A989, Item 43/735/3,1021.
14 J. Reed, 'American Diplomatic Relations with Australia During the Second World War', Ph.D thesis, University of Southern California at Los Angeles, 1969, p. 259.
15 Reynolds, 'Evatt and the Imperial Connection', ch. 4; E. Andrews, *Australia and China: The Ambiguous Relationship*, MUP, Melbourne, 1985, ch. 4.
16 Evatt drafted this cable which was sent as No.244, Curtin to SSDA on 16 September, 1943, *DAFP*, pp. 511–13.
17 PRO: CAB 99/30, BCM (45) 2nd meeting.
18 PRO: CAB 66/48, WP (44) 169; *CPD*, vol. 177, p. 74.
19 AA: A5954/1, Item 294/1; Minute by Defence Committee, 28 and 31 December 1943, No. 288/1943 —'Future of Southwest Pacific Region—Conference Between Australia and New Zealand Ministers, January 1944'. The attached report specified Australia's desire to obtain Manus Island and Timor as the anchor points in the strategic arc designed to defend the

northern approaches, but realised the need for British help in the wider region, especially in naval and air defence.
20 United States National Archives (USNA) RG 59, Lot Files, 54D224, Box 5, 'Australia–New Zealand Agreement'—Statement by Evatt. Original emphasis.
21 AA: A5954/1, Item 294/1, Defence Committee Minutes, 28 and 31 December 1943. The Defence Chiefs' assessment was that Australia would need protection against long-range bombing from bases within 1000 miles of Australia's industrial centres. Timor would protect Darwin, and the Admiralties, the east coast. Beyond that, given Australia's limited resources, there would be an 'imperial obligation'to 'ensure that air transport routes are strategically disposed for defence'.
22 Roosevelt Papers, Box 168, Folder 2, Pacific War Council Minutes 17 February 1943. Kay, *New Zealand External Relations*, vol. 1, p. 42.
23 Louis, *Imperialism at Bay*, p. 273.
24 AA: M1942/1, Item 36, Letter, Evatt to Watt, 30 July 1943. In October 1944 the American State Department reported Evatt as concerned with the United States 'gobbling-up air bases and territory'.

USNA RG59, Lot Files, 54D224, Box 5. Even the US Congress acknowledged that the Australia–New Zealand Agreement was an attempt by the British empire 'to secure post-war civil aviation and shipping advantages in the Pacific', Reed, 'American Diplomatic Relations with Australia', p. 317.
25 Evatt pursued this line of reasoning for a long time thereafter. On 29 November 1944, the State Department's Division of British Commonwealth Affairs produced a Memorandum—'Further Views of Dr. H.V. Evatt on Pacific Questions'—in which it was noted that Evatt 'regarded the retention of New Caledonia by France as necessary and characterized the British and American policy towards China as...not in accordance with the realities of China's current position'. USNA RG 59, Lot Files, 54D224, Box 5, 'Australia–New Zealand Agreement'.
26 The Evatt–Churchill exchanges are in PRO: DO 35/1540. Thorne is the one historian to comment on Evatt's attitude towards the French at this juncture. He is baffled by the fact that the only 'blunt speaking' regarding the French far-eastern empire in 1944 came from Canberra, 'surprisingly so in view of the greater desire of Australia...to see reforms made in the field of colonial administration'. He also finds surprising Evatt's support at San Francisco in 1945 for the restoration of the French to their Indochinese colonies. He does not consider that Evatt had the same motives as India, which supported the French 'for security, anti-Chinese and pro-imperialist reasons'. C. Thorne, *Allies of a Kind: The United States, Britain and the War Against Japan, 1941-1945*, OUP, Oxford, 1978, p. 469.
27 Evatt's cables are in AA: A989, Item 43/735/321; PRO: CAB 66/47, WP (44) 108; PREM 3/150/8.
28 The Australian government was kept informed of British concerns during 1943. Already in April, Bruce was able to advise that the British wanted to work in concert with the Australians in operating air services in the event that an international agreement proved to be unworkable. AA A5954/1, Item 345/1.

29 AA A5954/1, Item 345/1. The Americans were taking action. At the end of August, the Australian Minister in Washington, Sir Owen Dixon, handed Hull a note complaining of 'very greatly increased difficulties' in securing transport by air for Australian civilians with the US Air Transport Command. Cordell Hull Papers, Library of Congress, 'Airplane priorities to and from Australia', 30 August 1943.

30 H.V. Evatt, *Foreign Policy of Australia*, p. 150.

31 Eggleston Papers, ANL, MS 423/10/838; Kay, *New Zealand External Relations.*, vol. 1, p. 276. Hull sent a memorandum to Roosevelt on 31 May describing Evatt as 'behaving outrageously' and that he was offended by the references that Evatt had made, in an explanatory note about the Agreement, to Roosevelt's comments on Pacific bases—especially to New Caledonia. Truman Library, PSF 23, Diplomatic Correspondence—Australia 1942–44.

32 Reed, 'American Diplomatic Relations with Australia', pp. 315–20.

33 PRO: CAB 66/47, WP(44)108. Press reactions are in AA: A989, Item 43/735/324 and A816, Item 11/301/511.

34 Scholarly comment on the post-war period has focused on the attempts of the Australian government to secure a regional alliance with the United States. In this context Evatt has been seen as not only failing to secure this but as damaging Australia's bilateral relationship with the Americans in the process. The Department of External Affairs has been seen as harbouring idealistic visions for the future, focused on the United Nations, while Defence is seen as the locus of attempts to revive the Commonwealth connection. See, for example, G. Pemberton, *All the Way: Australia's Road to Vietnam*, Allen & Unwin, Sydney, p. 5.

35 USNA RG59, Lot Files, 54D224, Box 5; Reed, 'American Diplomatic Relations with Australia', p. 317.

36 AA: A5954/1, Item 1818/3. The Australian Defence Committee on 4 April concluded that there was 'a necessity for an overall empire plan, of which a base in the Admiralties would form a part'. It then went on to note that many of the bases that the Americans were claiming 'are of little strategic importance to us' but 'the islands are geographically well placed on the trans-Pacific air routes...facilities have been developed by the Americans on Christmas, Funafuti and Penrhyn Islands'.

37 The British Chiefs of Staff Appreciation of the American request for bases had been sent to Australia before the conference. It emphasised the importance of United States defence assistance but added the important qualification that 'the Ministry of Civil Aviation is anxious that we should retain our right to civil aviation facilities'. On 23 January the British government made it clear that discussions would proceed with the Americans after the Commonwealth had established 'which bases were to be used for civil [aviation]'. AA: A5954/1, Item 1801/2.

38 AA: A5954/1, Item 1818/2, PMM (46) 3rd meeting, 24 April 1946. The briefing papers from the defence planners are in A5954/1, Item 1818/3.

39 L.G. Churchward, *Australia and America, 1788–1972: An Alternative History*, APCOL, Sydney, 1979, pp. 161–2.

40 The details of Evatt's talks are in AA: A5954/1, Item 1818/2.

41 *Current Notes*, 17, 11, November 1946, p. 717.

CHAPTER 20

THE INDONESIAN REVOLUTION AND AUSTRALIAN SECURITY

In 1949, the Dutch recognised Indonesian independence 'in return for the safeguarding of Dutch investments. The Dutch also retained...the ethnically distinct territory of western New Guinea, West Irian...this suited the Australians'.
GEOFFREY BOLTON

On 8 June 1950 Evatt, then leader of the Opposition, strongly associated himself with the policy of the Menzies government in rejecting Indonesia's claim to West New Guinea. He declared that the problem could not be solved without the full agreement of the Netherlands and further that

the interest of Australia in such a settlement is not indirect, but very direct. The interest should and can be adequately safeguarded. The sovereignty of the Netherlands in Western New Guinea is undoubted and if the Netherlands Government wishes to retain that sovereignty, the situation cannot be altered except by acts of aggression by Indonesia.

Furthermore, argued Evatt, not only did 'ethnic considerations' preclude the attachment of West New Guinea to Indonesia since it was 'part and parcel of the South Pacific', but any change of status of West New Guinea might threaten the security of Australia.[1]

The West New Guinea incident reveals that Evatt, although he has been seen as the 'midwife of Indonesian independence' by the former Indonesian Foreign Minister, Dr. Subandrio, approached this issue from a very different perspective.[2] Evatt had clear visions of the region—this had been enshrined in the Australia–New Zealand Agreement. Indonesian nationalism on the other hand was a much more complex and uncertain issue. Well before there was agreement on the nature of an Indonesian state, and on the area that such a state would cover in the vast archipelago to Australia's north, Evatt had formulated his own ideas about the future of the region. These were very much wedded to his wartime experiences and the desire to ensure that in future the security of Australia would be safeguarded.

The Netherlands East Indies (NEI) straddled Australian communications to the British base at Singapore in the inter-war period. Australia was therefore anxious to secure the lines of communication to the focus of imperial defence in the Far East, and thus to influence the defence preparations of the NEI. In developing diplomatic contact the overriding concern was security. The Lyons and Menzies governments had already taken steps to establish Australian legations in the Asian region so as to give them assessments that did not rely on the prior analysis of the British.[3] Evatt picked up the threads in this regard with respect to the NEI; he adopted the advice of the Australian representative in London, Stanley Bruce, and requested the Dutch to allow the appointment of a senior Australian diplomat to Batavia, capital of the NEI, rather than through London, the seat of the Dutch Government in exile. He also called upon Portugal, the colonial power responsible for part of the island of Timor 'one of the main points of entrance into the Commonwealth' to enter into a defence arrangement with Australia.[4]

Evatt therefore saw the need for a defence arrangement to cover approaches to Australia, but there were major obstacles. The Dutch were willing to co-operate but they lacked the forces. In the case of Portuguese Timor, European considerations were to have a major impact on regional defence preparations. The experience shaped Evatt's policies for the rest of his time in politics. With the likelihood of Japanese occupation of the island, thereby threatening Darwin, an Australian–Dutch force was despatched to Dili. The Portuguese government, anxious to preserve their enclave at Macau, immediately protested to their ancient allies the British. The British government was presented with a major clash of priorities—to the Australians, Timor was the one area where they would 'declare war on the Japanese irrespective of the attitude of the United States', but the

Portuguese occupied a strategic position on the Iberian peninsula and in the Azores. The European theatre had priority. The Foreign Office therefore expressed its 'regret' for the Australian action while the British Chiefs of Staff refused to lend support for the 'military necessity' for the operation. The Australian government was accordingly reminded of the danger to Gibraltar and of the 'consequences to the *general strategy* of the war'.[5]

Faced with this there seemed little that the Australians could do. Britain, after all, had overall responsibility for the defence of the south-east Asian region. Curtin accused the British of 'double dealing' but agreed nevertheless to the withdrawal of the forces, and Evatt lamely advised the Australian Chiefs of Staff to keep the position of Timor 'constantly under the notice of [the British Commander of the Far East] General Wavell'. But his inclination was to assume little from that quarter. He fired off a cable to David Ross, an Australian with consular rank in the British Foreign Service serving in Portuguese Timor, that he was not 'in Dili as a servant of the [British] Foreign Office, but as an Australian Commonwealth officer'. Despite the fact that Ross had been accredited in October 1941, only on Christmas Eve did Evatt raise the need of such direct access to the Australian government. All that Ross could do was confirm Evatt's worst fears—the Portuguese defences were in an appalling state.[6]

In the short term Evatt could only explain the shambles by stressing to Parliament that

When Portugal protested violently, we were prepared to retrace our steps, in order to avoid embarrassment between London and Lisbon. An agreement with the Portuguese Government was made for the withdrawal of Australian and Dutch occupying forces, providing that the Portuguese forces were sent to carry out the defence of the colony against Japanese invasion.[7]

After the rapid fall of the NEI and Portuguese Timor, however, Evatt laid the groundwork for securing for Australia the strategic approaches to the Australian continent. It was obviously impossible to claim an active role in the defence of the entire Indonesian archipelago, but there were parts of it, especially in Timor and Dutch New Guinea, which were of central importance to Australian security. He thus sought outright annexation of Timor, but for the rest of the Indonesian archipelago he was prepared to accept the restoration of Dutch authority, subject to a defence agreement that would recognise Australian interests.

At first Evatt sounded out the British and the Americans. He told the British High Commissioner in Canberra, Ronald Cross, that he had in mind the relinquishment of sovereignty of 'parts' of the NEI and, in discussions at the US State Department, he raised the general question of the 'selective' use of Dutch bases. During Evatt's visit to Britain in 1943 he again pressed the need for any settlement to take account of Australian security, but as part of this, 'Australia should have Timor'![8]

As in 1942, Evatt's initiative foundered on the rock of global strategy. The Americans were threatening to abolish the colonial order altogether, a prospect which concerned the Australians, and the British viewed Evatt's blatant demand from the perspective of the war in Europe. The British needed bases in the Azores. It says something of their concern over Evatt's feelings on this matter that they did not tell him while he was in London in 1943 that they were then holding talks with the Salazar government with a view to accepting Portuguese sovereignty after the war over its colonies. Only after he returned to Australia in August did Evatt learn of the British assurances to Portugal.[9]

Any thought of annexation was out of the question. Evatt did not give up on the possibility of direct control of Timor, but for the immediate future he had to try different tactics. He now sought to ensure Australian security by claiming an interest in the joint control or supervision of colonies as part of any future regional settlement.[10] Cordell Hull had foreshadowed trusteeship proposals in 1942 and had also indicated that regional arrangements for colonies would have to take account of the wishes of so-called 'parent states', such as the United States. Using this, Evatt argued that in the Pacific any reorganisation of colonies would have to take account of security as 'the first principle which must be applied'. It was in this context that Evatt announced Australia's desire to collaborate with the Dutch, involving the use of their bases.

This policy was to be fought out later in the context of Evatt's proposals on trusteeship in the United Nations, but his focus was always on the immediate security implications for Australia—and others knew it.[11] The Dutch reacted to the first declarations about Australian 'partnership' in the post-war control of the Netherlands East Indies by handing the Australian Government an aide-mémoire on 14 May, rejecting co-operation at that level. When Evatt invited the Dutch to attend the Canberra conference 1944—the one that produced the Australia–New Zealand Agreement with its call for a regional settlement—the Dutch refused.[12]

Evatt did not, however, conduct his campaign on colonies solely at the abstract level of diplomacy as some historians have concluded.[13] Far from using trusteeship as a means of removing European imperialism for ideological or 'idealistic' reasons, he attempted to secure a defence agreement from the Dutch and the Portuguese bilaterally. In November 1943 Evatt instructed Bruce to propose to the Netherlands government-in-exile that it accord Australia a long lease over Dutch Timor and Dutch New Guinea, stressing that they had been left defenceless in 1941–42. In November the Dutch, fearing Australian designs and wanting themselves to prepare for the liberation of their eastern territories, advised the Australians that they would be sending Dr. H. J. van Mook there as Lieutenant-Governor of the NEI. Evatt, to discourage 'complacency by the Dutch about an imminent reoccupation of the NEI', unsuccessfully attempted to stop the appointment. After this, while the Australians prepared to mop up Japanese forces in the NEI without Dutch forces, Evatt continued his efforts to secure informal and confidential discussions on defence with the Dutch—in vain.[14]

Evatt wanted to extract concessions from the Dutch and it set him on a course of meddling with their colonial policy until 1949. The Portuguese, however, were not to return at all. Fully aware of the storm brewing over trusteeship, he publicly attacked their colonial administration and threatened to put 'the facts and record of their weakness and evasion in handling their responsibilities in Timor... before the peace conference' after the war. In late 1943 Evatt stressed that Australia, not Portugal, had taken 'all practical steps' to defend the island, leading Portuguese President Salazar to denounce plans to have the Australian flag 'fly over Timor'. In 1944 Evatt answered calls by the Opposition to secure Timor for defence reasons by suggesting, ambiguously, that Australia was 'bound' to 'favour' the restoration of Portuguese sovereignty by virtue of the strategic position of the Azores. That of course would change at the end of the war.[15]

With the sudden cessation of hostilities in August 1945, Evatt immediately proposed that the Portuguese extend to Australia a 100-year lease over Portuguese Timor. Furthermore, he unilaterally announced that Australia alone would take the surrender of Japanese forces there. Thereafter he used the argument that the investigation of war crimes would require the presence of Australian forces on the island for some time. In the meantime he demanded that the British make no provisions to transport Portuguese forces to the Far East until there was a 'long term agreement' with Australia over the island's future.[16]

All this hardly reflected Evatt's trust in any future system of international security. Quite the opposite. Like Hughes after World War I, Evatt pursued single mindedly the interests of Australian security. Australia needed New Guinea and Timor as part of its future defence planning. Evatt kept that objective in clear focus as he claimed the right of Australia to intervene in the affairs of the Indonesian archipelago as a 'principal power' after 1945.

Formulating policy in respect to the South-East Asian region after the surrender of Japan was an enormous task. Ravaged by war, the region was now plunged into nationalist revolt with the prospect that Communism would also become a significant problem. Trading relationships had been shaped around the links between the colonies and the metropolitan powers—nowhere was there an integrated national economy. Accordingly there were no plans for the region when Japan was suddenly knocked out of the war. The Americans were preoccupied with Europe and did not formulate their first analysis of Indonesia until June 1947. There was no proposal for an American 'Marshall Plan for the Far East', and even then only in draft form, until February 1949. The Soviets delayed their own planning for the region until the Polish conference of September 1947 while the British did not put in place a detailed regional defence scheme—ANZAM—until 1949.[17]

This context is important in explaining Evatt's position in late 1945. Firstly the prevailing turmoil in the region reinforced his concerns about security. Secondly there was no consensus about the region—let alone the final boundaries of any future nation states. Finally, it was clear that while the major powers had insisted on having a dominant position in the determination of the international security system, they lacked policies with respect to the future of the Asia–Pacific region. For all its bravado, the declarations of the 1944 Australia–New Zealand Agreement stood alone as a guide to future planning in the region.

Events thereafter moved quickly. The independent Republic of Indonesia was proclaimed by Hatta and Sukarno on 17 August 1945, and immediately declared by the Dutch to be illegal. The British, now responsible for the Indonesian region since its incorporation that same month into Mountbatten's overstretched South-East Asia Command (SEAC), only had a small Special Operations Executive group inside Indonesia and they reported that the 'Nationalists were confused in their aims and badly organised'. Nor did they enjoy support among the peasantry, the SOE team concluded. Evatt therefore had no basis for accepting the credentials of the Republicans. But he was, on the other hand, aware that Mountbatten himself was anxious to restore Dutch control as quickly as possible. The SEAC commander recoiled from the enormity of administering an archipelago of some two million square kilometres and 128 million people, especially with the outbreak of fighting between Dutch and Republican forces. He therefore looked to bilateral talks between the Dutch and the Republicans to arrive at a settlement.[18]

That, of course, conflicted with Evatt's general position, stated so often since the Australia–New Zealand Agreement in January 1944, that Australia should be involved in any talks aimed at a regional settlement in the Pacific. Evatt had a clear view of what he wanted in the region and that presupposed the restoration of the Dutch to their colony. Beyond that he lacked an understanding of the motives and the strength of the nationalists. Indeed he had his own advice on the details of the Indonesian situation only when William Macmahon Ball was attached to SEAC as Australia's political representative in October 1945. Significantly, Macmahon Ball fully understood the basis on which he was to assess the situation. He confirmed this to Evatt immediately after reaching Batavia by cabling that 'Australia must take an active part in diplomatic negotiations (between the Nationalists and the Dutch) and do everything to prevent developments which ultimately may threaten her security'. Pointedly, Macmahon Ball was inclined to discount the strength of the nationalists and even reported that the 'eclipse' of Hatta and Sukarno would be 'permanent'. In any future government the Indonesians, he added, would lack 'technical and administrative competence' and would therefore need European assistance.[19]

Within this framework, Evatt wanted Australian involvement on the basis that it was a 'security power' in the region. It is clear from his first reactions to Macmahon Ball's cables that he did not question the right of the Dutch to return or to intervene 'in the internal affairs of the Netherlands Indies'. 'Our interest', Evatt told Chifley on 23 November, 'lies in security'. In this connection, he went on, 'the sovereignty of the Netherlands is a fact internationally recognised'. But he was determined that 'the question of sovereignty and self government cannot be allowed to impede these [Allied] forces in the fulfilment of their legitimate, urgent and paramount task of executing the Japanese surrender terms', the basis of course for Australian primacy.

Unfortunately it was not that simple. Demonstrating Australian credentials as a security power, as in the overall question of the armistice with Japan, also provided difficulties for Evatt in Indonesia. He put the case to Chifley on 23 November. It was clear that the British wanted an 'early solution without further commitment of forces', he said, yet the situation was 'rapidly deteriorating' with the failure of talks and the outbreak of fighting between the Indonesians and the Dutch. The only option as Evatt saw it, given this, and the fact that 'the United States wants to keep out', was that 'Australia is now the only power likely to act'. That of course meant extending the period of time for Australian troops in the NEI to police the surrender of Japanese forces and to give effect to the armistice conditions. This tested directly his assertion that Australia had rights in the region as a 'principal' or as a 'security power'.[20]

The problem was that it was also difficult in this situation to demonstrate that Australia was such a power. Even in early 1944, Evatt's proposals to establish bases in the region had been attacked not onlyby the British as 'grandiose', but also by the Commander of the Australian army, General Thomas Blamey, as 'beyond the capacity of Australia'. Now, in the midst of crisis over Australia's security screen, Evatt had the ground cut from beneath him when Chifley told him on 26 November, that while agreeing fully

with you regarding the Australian security interests in [the] settlement before the situation further deteriorates...I am sure Cabinet would not agree to commitment of force which your proposal implies. It will be difficult to accept even [the] proposal to leave Australian troops at Borneo, nor do I think [an Australian] offer of mediation is...practical.[21]

Answers at that juncture did not readily present themselves. The waterside unions were boycotting Dutch ships, Chifley seemed to be sympathetic to their pro-Republican position, yet in a major appreciation of Australia's strategical position in February 1946 the Defence Committee re-emphasised the view that Australia had a major security interest in the NEI. Indeed the latter report also cast doubts on basing planning for the region on the United Nations by drawing attention to its 'fragile structure', and advised that there was a 'pressing need to ensure Empire security'.[22] In that case the British attempts to restore Dutch sovereignty, albeit with concessions to the Republic regarding internal self-government, would have to be acknowledged.

Evatt was locked into this position when in February and March, following talks with the Dutch,he argued that Australia recognised the rights of the Netherlands in the South-West Pacific. Australia had, he said, 'vital interest in the preservation of the wartime friendship with the Dutch in relation to the Netherlands East Indies'. Evatt had shifted his position, however, on the Portuguese. He still stressed that Timor was of 'great importance' to Australia. Following exactly the Appreciation of the Defence Chiefs, he argued that 'In enemy hands during the war this possession was a danger continually threatening the safety of Darwin'. But in a much more conciliatory gesture, reflecting his failure to enlist Allied support for Australian 'security power' pretensions in Timor, Evatt spoke approvingly of the Portuguese President, Salazar, and welcomed the negotiation of bilateral agreements with Portugal covering defence and aviation. It was hardly surprising that at this stage Evatt opposed the attempt by the Ukraine to refer the problems in Indonesia to the United Nations. He wanted to secure defence co-operation bilaterally and he resisted any attempt to impugn SEAC's activities in the NEI. Earlier, in November 1945, he had argued that the dispute in Indonesia was not a matter of 'domestic jurisdiction' for the Dutch and the Republicans only. At that juncture it was his intention to involve Australia in a regional security arrangement, especially one that would secure base rights. He envisaged no broader international action. Despite Evatt's well-known commitment to UN fact-finding activities elsewhere, here he opposed the idea—much to the delight of the British and the Dutch.[23]

His support for the British and Dutch did not stop there. As Attorney-General, Evatt also moved to break the deadlock over the ban on Dutch shipping. On 26 February 1946 he promoted a compulsory conference of unions under the auspices of the Commonwealth Conciliation Commission during which 'some quiet threats' were made that if the ban was not lifted the Stevedoring Commission would be dissolved. This important body controlled all waterfront labour and allowed for the representation of the Waterside Workers' Federation. The threat was seen by them, rightly, as an 'attempt to force us into supporting the Dutch against the Indonesians' and it carried 'the obvious Evatt touch'.[24]

There was more to Evatt's position than that. He was then laying the groundwork for the Australian case to be put at a Commonwealth Conference in April and the Peace Conference in Paris in August. Following the line of the Defence Committee Appreciation he recognised the fundamental importance of securing Commonwealth support for a plan of regional security. While this was much broader than simply Indonesia, it enabled Australia, as Evatt said to the British, to claim use of bases in such places as Koepang in Dutch Timor before any settlement was concluded in Indonesia with the Republicans. In similar vein, at Paris, Evatt welcomed the participation of the Dutch in the South Seas Regional Commission by virtue of their control of the western portion of New Guinea. His aim, therefore, was still to assert the primary interest of Australia to be involved in Republican–Dutch negotiations and to persist with attempts to enlist British support for the detachment of those parts of the archipelago that were of importance to Australian security.

The problem was that the British were not prepared to exert pressure on the Dutch, an important European ally, or to become involved in an area well beyond British strategic reach—especially one as messy as this. In October at Cheribon, Java, Anglo–Dutch–Republican talks cleared the way at last for Britain's withdrawal—if nothing else. Despite Evatt's consistent efforts to secure Australian participation at these talks as a 'principal party', he was unsuccessful. All that he could secure —and that by virtue of the Commonwealth connection—was the admission of an Australian 'advisor' to the British delegation. Characteristically, Evatt made great play of this in public, claiming that 'Australia's representatives are sitting side by side with the representatives of Great Britain in attempting to settle the dispute'. But it was an attempt to disguise yet another failure. The previous year he saw the claim as a security power reduced to nought. Now the claim to use the British connection was flawed as SEAC handed over full control to the Dutch on 30 November. In the meantime the Australian base rights were as far away as ever and the internal situation in Indonesia after Cheribon rapidly deteriorated.[25]

While Evatt was without the advantage of SEAC control in Indonesia, he did not modify his policies. He may have been less sanguine about the prospects for securing bases in early 1947 in the NEI other than in Dutch New Guinea, as Renouf suggests, but that—and Timor—had always been the main objective. He took encouragement from the fact that there were as yet no defined borders for the area. In December 1946 the Dutch had excluded West New Guinea from their newly created state of 'East Indonesia'. This fitted in with Evatt's thinking concerning the South Seas Regional Commission which was initiated at the January 1947 Canberra conference. The area to be covered by the commission included West New Guinea, which was geographically and strategically separate from the rest of Indonesia. He also hoped that a similar commission would be established for South-East Asia, an area in Evatt's estimation of 'greater political maturity', and therefore readier for independence—unlike the areas of strategic importance to Australia.[26]

If Evatt expected smooth sailing after the final signing of the Cheribon agreement at Linggadjati in Java on 25 March he was soon to be disappointed. Open warfare broke out as the Dutch started their 'police actions' in June. Initially Evatt wanted to stitch up a regional trade and security agreement with the Dutch immediately after Cheribon, even holding out the prospect of a favourable settlement of their £7.5 million war debt to Australia in return for a base in Timor. 'Security concerns', as Margaret George argues, were 'paramount', but the Dutch dismissed the 'imperialistic' attempt to trade debt for bases. Evatt also used the continuing boycotts against Dutch shipping in an attempt to secure a joint Dutch–Republican appeal to the Australian government to mediate in the restoration of trade with Indonesia.

The fact that Evatt's thinking was wedded to the issue of security was also evidenced by his initiation of attempts to have the Governor of Portuguese Timor visit Australia. This, contrary to the wishes of the Portuguese—who saw the visit as purely ceremonial—was seen by Evatt as an opportunity to initiate detailed defence planning for Timor. Evatt announced to the Parliament on 6 June 1947, after his report on Australia's 'mediation' on trade with the NEI, that the visit would facilitate preparations 'on the basis of a war-time understanding' with the Portuguese in respect of commerce, air communications and defence.[27]

It is clear that at that point Evatt still had very limited security objectives in mind. With the Dutch threatening police action, in June he appealed to the British and the Americans to intervene in Indonesia, and in that context he argued that Australia would also offer its 'good offices' to the disputing parties. The problem for Evatt was that he had no support for his policy. The Netherlands and the Portuguese did not want to compromise their control of the colonies. The Dutch not only rejected his offer of Australia's 'good offices', but also complained that his involvement had been a 'source of annoyance'. Nor would the British intervene. Despite Evatt's attack on the 'lessening of British interest' in South-East Asia they were not going to jeopardise relations with a key European ally. The Americans, without plans for the South-East Asian region, put their faith in the hope that the talks between the Dutch and the Indonesian Republicans would yield a 'moderate solution'.[28]

Evatt now turned to the UN, but this path was forced on him. In the face of the reluctance of the English and the Americans to push the Dutch to make concessions, India took steps to internationalise the dispute by referring it to the Security Council on 29 July 1947. Historians have ignored the reasons for Evatt's attempts to pre-empt India's intervention into the Indonesian problem. In taking this action India emerged as a major regional player, and one that was a member of the Commonwealth. The Indian government readily admitted that a main motivation in taking a lead on Indonesia was as part of a 'bid for political leadership in Asia'.[29] India—not Evatt—provided the impetus to involve the UN, a step he found 'slightly embarrassing'. But once this step was taken, Evatt kept with the Indians in the UN—at least until action at that level threatened his real objectives.[30]

The Americans themselves forestalled major UN involvement by offering 'good offices' to the Dutch on 31 July, a respite that allowed Evatt to revert to his traditional position of attempting to assert Australian primacy and to mediate in the dispute. On 5 August, therefore, he instructed the Australian Ambassador in Washington, Norman Makin, to suggest that Australia 'act jointly with the United States in a capacity of mediator and arbitrator'. Ironically, while the Americans dismissed this as 'largely motivated by Mr. Evatt's desire to play a leading world role and to take the limelight wherever possible', it was the Indonesians themselves who accepted Australia in this role on 10 August.[31]

Australia thereafter developed the reputation of being a Republican partisan, but Evatt had broader objectives. From his point of view, support for the Republic did not compromise his quest for bases since it was only one of a number of states inside the United States of Indonesia (USI). As far as the determination of regional security was concerned he still fell back on the argument, as he said in a press release on 3 February 1948, that there should be 'greater participation by those countries which actually participated in war and made a substantial contribution to victory'. That would involve not the Indonesians but, as he wrote in the *New York Times* on 4 April, the Dutch who 'should retain overall political guidance' over the USI. In the Parliament four days later he ignored Indonesia in a major statement on international affairs but stressed that a key principle of Australian foreign policy was 'To strengthen Pacific defence by appropriate regional arrangements'.[32]

In fact he was still without any real knowledge of the Republican leaders, a point which he only began to address in 1948 when he sent Macmahon Ball on a mission to assess their capabilities. Evatt wanted to end the bloodshed, and saw the Dutch police actions as largely responsible for it, but the Dutch were also the key to winning concessions on the bases. His insistence on an arbitral role for the United Nations Good Offices Committee (GOC) was intended to force an end to the fighting which was delaying a settlement and obstructing the defence needs of Australia.[33]

The Republic was energetically supported by members of the Department of External Affairs, especially by its secretary, Burton, and Critchley on the GOC. Evatt himself, however, was prepared to play down support for the Republic when this threatened relations with the Dutch. In August 1947 for example, he acceded to a Dutch request to oppose any attempt to have the Republic admitted at a meeting of the United Nations Commission for Asia and the Far East (ECAFE)—a move that would have signalled its international status. In September he even attempted personally to influence the Dutch by visiting Holland, but a major motive here was also to enlist their support for his impending nomination for the Presidency of the United Nations General Assembly. For all that he got nowhere. The Dutch shunned him while the GOC could do little other than adopt the pose of anxious spectator as the position deteriorated in late 1948 with a Communist revolt in September and the announcement by the Dutch of a second 'police action' on 19 December.

Evatt's reaction to the second police action and his subsequent decision to raise the question of Indonesia in the General Assembly has been seen by many commentators as the beginning of a more internationalist policy. His critics saw him as influenced by his election as President of the General Assembly, where his 'personal ambitions...predisposed him to adopt a United Nations rather than perhaps an Australian attitude to the complex political problem in Indonesia'.[34]

Evatt certainly used the opportunity in December to force the police action to a vote in the Security Council. He also wanted a much stronger stand than that proposed by the United States which refused to blame the Dutch and called on further reporting by the GOC to assess responsibility. Having failed in the Security Council, Evatt moved to place the Indonesian question on the agenda of the General Assembly in March 1949, much to the annoyance of the Americans and the British. Evatt in turn, recalled Dean Rusk, raised 'strong objection' to any deferral of debate in the Assembly. The British meanwhile were told by Burton, who had already attacked the Americans for their failure to use economic sanctions against the Dutch, that failure of the Batavia talks would cause Australia to raise a 'hullabaloo' in the General Assembly.[35]

Evatt seemed to be setting out in other radical directions as well. In January 1949 he reported that Australian attendance at a conference at New Delhi, called by Nehru, was 'of crucial significance' since 'Australia wanted to live in closest harmony with its newly-emerging neighbours in South East Asia'. To many, Australia's attendance as the only Western nation at this conference signalled a major attempt to eject the Dutch, and was an implied threat to the White Australia policy. He also seemed to have reversed course on smoothing relations with the Dutch, as he accused them, without substantiation, of organising 'a continuous employment of propaganda and press agencies to interfere with the Government of Australia in the performance of its supreme executive functions'.[36]

Evatt, however, had not altered his objectives: circumstances had changed and he knew well enough that small powers ignored broader changes at their peril. It was apparent that appeals to the Americans and to the British were futile. The Americans were not prepared to countenance UN interference with an important NATO ally, although in 1949 they came to see Indonesia as an important part of their Asian strategy. Not only was it a major source for raw materials needed for the rehabilitation of Japan, but an Indonesian nation would be, in the view of the State Department a 'southern anchor' to the American island defence chain north to Japan.[37]

The diplomatic situation within the region was also changing. The New Delhi conference was only part of a more sustained attempt by the Indian government to capture the initiative on the question of Indonesia. Australia's decision to put the issue on the General Assembly agenda kept it in step with India, which took the same action. But Nehru took it further. In April the Australians were outmanoeuvered when the Indian government proposed that stronger action should be taken in the event that the Batavia talks failed to arrive at a satisfactory solution. They proposed to the governments that had attended the January Delhi conference that individual governments impose economic sanctions and disallow Dutch rights of transit.

Evatt, however, did not want to go that far. While he publicly expressed his policy in the House of Representatives on 21 June as being in step with India in advocating conciliation with the approval of the General Assembly, he was more concerned about securing a security agreement for South-East Asia. This was to be negotiated between the Australians, British, French and Dutch, as he had always wanted, after the conclusion of an acceptable agreement between the Republic and the Dutch. Unlike Burton and Critchley, who conducted the detailed issues concerning the fate of the Republic itself, Evatt wanted to expedite a broader regional settlement.

The need for haste became apparent in July. Not only were American plans for the region causing concern, but the Republican delegation forced Evatt into the open by claiming West New Guinea as part of the USI. As Kylie Tennant observed, Evatt, if he had been in office in 1962 when the Liberal government acquiesced in proposals to hand over West New Guinea, would 'have moved heaven and earth to prevent a land frontier between Australia and an Asian Power'.[38]

He tried. On July 28 the Department of External Affairs advised the Dutch of the position taken consistently by Evatt since the Anzac Pact of 1944, that West New Guinea was not Asian—it was geographically, ethnologically and politically a part of New Guinea. Furthermore New Guinea had been included in the Australian-declared Pacific security zone in 1944. Discussions were held between Dutch and Australian External Affairs officers in August and September 1949, during which it was agreed that West New Guinea would be excluded from the transfer of sovereignty to the USI. Evatt did not spell this out specifically when he presented his report on Indonesia in the House of Representatives on 7 October. Nor did he clarify the precise arrangements that he had in mind for the island, but he revealed his views on the Republic's claims by dismissing it as merely one of a number of 'other Indonesian governments'.

Behind the scenes he was at that time arguing through the South Pacific Commission against Indonesia having any role in any UN trusteeship. Not surprisingly the Dutch understood from this that Australia wanted such a role in the administration of West New Guinea under UN trusteeship and offered it accordingly on 18

October. Evatt, however, was vague in his reply, declining to agree immediately while welcoming the general proposition that it be placed under trusteeship. His actions confound scholars at this point. George argues that Evatt did not press the Australian case because of the impending Federal elections. Renouf finds his attitude to be a riddle. The most plausible explanation is that he did not have to say more—the Dutch themselves were working to detach West New Guinea from the USI and were to achieve success at the Round Table Conference in November. Beyond that he would be inviting a Republican and Indian backlash. Nehru had exposed the limits of Evatt's support only six months earlier. For the moment, as he confided to the British on the eve of the elections, Australia favoured a trusteeship 'within a couple of months of the Netherlands transfer of sovereignty to the USI', an arrangement that would sidestep Republican claims.[39]

The same thinking was evident in relation to Timor. In 1948 and 1949, following the visit of the Governor of Portuguese Timor to Australia, Australia succeeded in getting the grant of agricultural and mining concessions on the island. Evatt also had some success in getting the Portuguese to look upon Australia, as they explained at their Washington legation, 'as the representative of Western Civilization in the South, but as maintaining a bridge with the peoples of India and Southern Asia'. Evatt was also keen to have the Portuguese Governor visit New Guinea, an indication that he wanted the colony associated with that strategically vital area.[40]

There is no direct evidence that Evatt proposed the unification of the two halves of the island in the way anticipated for New Guinea. But it seems clear that this was his objective throughout. In 1945 Eggleston had discussed Timor with the Americans and relayed Australia's opposition to split trusteeships, citing the problems over the New Hebrides condominium. In February 1948 Evatt was informed by the Australian Consul in Dili of 'a rumour of the impending transfer of Dutch Timor to Portugal', but apparently no action was subsequently taken. Evatt's policy was more subtle—to cement ties through gradual penetration of the island, especially with respect to civil aviation as the forerunner of air defence ties. As the Joint Planning Committee concluded in August 1947, 'firm defence arrangements' would be 'inappropriate at this stage'.[41]

Evatt, in late 1949, had not shifted his thinking. UN trusteeship would deliver the bases. He knew only too well that when Australia negotiated a trusteeship agreement for New Guinea in 1946, it did so in defiance of majority opinion on the General Assembly and successfully insisted on total control of the territory. He remained wedded to the system of security based on the inner ring of islands to the north. The Republic was in occupation of another part of the archipelago and others like Burton and Critchley could be exercised by its fate, as long as that did not clash with the vital defence interests of Australia in the region.

By 1949 things were not as easy as they had been in 1944, when a fellow Asian dominion did not challenge Evatt's attempted regional hegemony. Of greater significance the Americans after 1947 had formulated proposals for the region, and they gave a renewed urgency to the question of regional security. Gone was Roosevelt's misplaced trust in China as a great power in Asia. Now his successor, Truman, wanted the region to be remodelled in the interests of the nation that had just been defeated, and one that Australia had feared above all others—Japan.

NOTES

1 A. Vandenbosch and M. Vandenbosch, *Australia Faces Southeast Asia: The Emergence of a Foreign Policy*, University of Kentucky Press, Lexington, 1967, p. 43. This was, of course, the position taken at the 1944 Canberra conference.
2 Margaret George, *Australia and the Indonesian Revolution*, MUP, Melbourne, 1980, p. 4.
3 For the work of the Menzies government in securing closer ties to the NEI see AA: A2670, Item 335/1941; A2973, 'Netherlands East Indies'. On Timor see A2679, Item 50/1941; A2973, Item 114/45; PRO: CAB 65/19,103 (41) 5; *CPD*, vol. 169, p. 259.
4 AA: A3300, Item 174; *CPD*, vol. 169, p. 972. Neither initiative was successful. The Dutch refused direct diplomatic access to their colony while the Portuguese were not prepared to risk the Japanese seizure of their far more important possession at Macao.
5 PRO: CAB 79/19, COS (42) 2nd. meeting; FO: 371/31728, Cable 23, SSDA to Australian government, 8 January 1942. For a general discussion on this see Peter Hastings, 'The Timor Problem 2', *Australian Outlook*, vol. 29, no.3, December 1975.
6 AA The Evatt—British/Ross cables are in A2679, Item 125/1941; PRO: FO 371/31727.
7 *CPD*, 17, pp. 56–7. The Portuguese troops were still en route from Lorenco Marques when the Japanese captured Timor. Lionel Wigmore, *Australia in the War of 1939–1945: The Japanese Thrust*, Australian War Memorial, Canberra, 1957, p. 475, n. 2.
8 J. Reed, 'American Diplomatic Relations with Australia during the Second World War', Ph.D thesis, University of Southern California, August 1969, pp. 243–4; PRO: CAB 65/34, 85 (43) 1. The basis for the Timor claim lay in the anxieties of the government which pressed MacArthur throughout 1942 to invade the island. Evatt himself was sent a large number of cables after February 1942 reminding him of the importance of Timor. The Australian Chiefs of Staff were accordingly asked to provide an appreciation on the strategic significance of Timor and they concluded in December 1942 that

while it was a key base for launching an invasion against Australia's north this was not then likely, given Japanese problems after Midway. AA A5954/1, item 564/2—3; MP 1587/1/0.

9 PRO: CAB 65/23, WM (41) 77th Conclusions; DO 35/1598, Cable 1022, SSDA to Australian Government, 25 August 1943.

10 Evatt argued that the United States should understand that 'the course of the war in this theatre has demonstrated that control or supervision over neighbouring territories will be vital to the future security of Australia'. AA: A3300/262, Cable 308, Evatt to Dixon, 31 March 1943.

11 At the San Francisco Conference and the Commonwealth Conference which preceded it in 1945 Evatt directed his remarks in the debate on trusteeship to Indonesia and questioned the motives 'of some at least of the returning powers'. The Indian delegation leader, Sir R. Mudaliar, saw Evatt as 'debating the case for the landlords', while the British saw him as 'steadfastly' viewing the trusteeship issue 'through the wrong end of a telescope focused on Timor'. PRO: CAB 99/30, BCM (45) 12th meeting; DO 35/1865, Letter, Cochram (British Delegation to the San Francisco Conference) to Stephenson (Foreign Office), 2 June 1945.

12 M. George, *Australia and the Indonesian Revolution*, p. 17; W. Reynolds, 'H.V. Evatt: The Imperial Connection and the quest for Australian Security, 1941–1945', Ph.D thesis, University of Newcastle, 1985, p. 259. At least the Dutch were invited; Evatt did not extend an invitation to the Portuguese.

13 N. Harper and Sissons, *Australia and the United Nations*, pp. 48–9; P. Hasluck, *Diplomatic Witness: Australian Foreign Affairs 1941–1947*, MUP, Melbourne, pp. 211–12.

14 M. George, *Australia and the Indonesian Revolution*, p. 19.

15 *DAFP* 6, pp. 280–2, Cable SL 4, Evatt to Bruce, 20 February; *DAFP* 6, pp. 560–1, Cable 119A, Bruce to Curtin, 21 October 1943; CPD, 179, p. 236. The reference to Australia being 'bound' followed Britain's assurances to restore the colonies to Portugal. Reynolds, 'Evatt and the Imperial Connection', p. 270.

16 The cables Evatt exchanged, mainly with Bruce in London during August, are in AA: A2937, Item 114/45.

17 M. Schaller, *The American Occupation of Japan: The Origins of the Cold War in Asia*, OUP, Oxford, 1985, ch. 8; R. Ovendale, *The English-Speaking Alliance: Britain, the United States, the Dominions and the Cold War 1945–51*, Allen & Unwin, London, ch. 6.

18 P. Dennis, *Troubled Days of Peace: Mountbatten and South East Asia Command, 1945-46*, Manchester University Press, Manchester 1987, p. 83; R. McMahon, 'Anglo-American Diplomacy and the Reoccupation of the Netherlands East Indies', *Diplomatic History*, vol. 2, no.1, Winter 1978, pp. 6–7.

19 Macmahon Ball's cables to Evatt are in the 'External Affairs File—Indonesia', Evatt Collection, Flinders University. See also Alan Rix, *Intermittent Diplomat: The Japan and Batavia Diaries of W. Macmahon Ball*, MUP, Melbourne, 1988, pp. 237–65.

20 At that stage the Australians were responsible for Borneo, Sulawesi and most of the eastern islands. Their troops were on the spot and, unlike the British in

Java, had experienced no difficulty in restoring Dutch civil administration. This, and possibly the desire to have Australia assume greater responsibilty in the region on behalf of the Commonwealth, lay behind Mountbatten's desire to have Britain and Australia 'impose' a settlement in the event of the failure of Dutch–Republican talks. Dennis, *Mountbatten*, pp. 130, 155.

21 The Evatt–Chifley cables are in the 'External Affairs—Indonesia' file, Evatt Collection, Flinders University; C. Thorne, *Allies of a Kind: The United States, Britain, and the War Against Japan, 1941–1945*, OUP, Oxford, 1978, p. 259; D. Day, *Reluctant Nation: Australia and the Allied Defeat of Japan 1942–45*, OUP, Oxford, 1992, pp. 184–5.

22 AA: A5954/1, Item 1662/4.

23 *Current Notes*,vol. 17, no. 3, March 1946, pp. 148–9; A. Renouf, *Let Justice Be Done: The Foreign Policy of Dr. H.V. Evatt*, UQP, St. Lucia, p. 169.

24 R. Lockwood, *Black Armada*, Australasian Book Society, Sydney, 1975, p. 192.

25 AA: A5954/1, Item 1662/1, '1946 Conference: Defence Brief'; A2700, vol. 28, Submission 11 'Prime Ministers' Conference in London, 1946'; George, *Australia and the Indonesian Revolution*, ch. 4.

26 Renouf, *Let Justice Be Done*, p. 173; George, *Australia and the Indonesian Revolution*, pp. 67, 70.

27 George, *Australia and the Indonesian Revolution*, p. 74. *Current Notes*, vol. 18, no. 6, June 1947, p. 403. At this stage Australia had included Timor in its regional plan developed in the context of Commonwealth defence. The British had agreed to include Timor inside the Australian naval station following the communication to the Admiralty of 'very strong views about the importance of Timor to Australian security'. Defence Committee Minutes in AA: A2031, Item182/1946; A1838/2, Item 378/7/1/2; A5799/1, Item 1945/1947.

28 Foreign Relations of the United States (*FRUS*), 1947–, vol. 6,'The Far East', pp. 924, 976.

29 The independence of India was seen to have major implications for Australian security. Evatt attempted to impress upon Nehru the benefits of 'Dominion status' for the Republic and to involve India formally in Commonwealth Defence planning. AA: A1838/1, Item 87/1/3/2B; A1838/2, Item 169/10/11/2 Part 2 and Item 169/12 Part 1; A5954, Item 1687/15. He also reminded them, in a display of wishful thinking regarding the Commonwealth, that after years of 'bitterness' Britain and Eire now came to realise that, because of the war, 'the two countries came to realise their need of each other'. *Current Notes*, 19, 7, July 1948, p. 430.

30 American cables on the attitude of the Indian Government from early July are in *FRUS*, 1947, vol. 6, 'The Far East', p. 992.

31 *FRUS*, vol. 7: 1947– 'The Far East', pp. 1014-15. Makin made no attempt to disguise Evatt's role in offering Australia as a mediator. When pressed for the reasons why Australia had waited five days after the American offer, he replied 'that Evatt was somewhere at sea and perhaps it had been difficult to communicate with him'.

32 *Current Notes*, vol. 19, no. 2, February 1948, p. 91; George, *Australia and the Indonesian Revolution*, pp. 101, 103–4. The Department of External

Affairs in April ventured the 'hard-headed point' that the interests of Australia's security might be better served by the Dutch 'giving way to local nationalist movements as they coalesced, while remaining in full control in outlying and more backward areas *indefinitely*'.

33 G. Greenwood, *Approaches to Asia: Australian Postwar Policies and Attitudes*, McGraw-Hill, Sydney, 1974, p. 287; *FRUS*, vol. 6, 1948– 'The Far East and Australasia', p. 2. In a shallow review of Australian relations with the United States in August 1948 the State Department dismissed Evatt's attempts to mediate as reflecting an Australian 'domestic tradition of arbitration'. The authors of the review entirely ignored the security issues from Australia's perspective and focused rather on Evatt's personal motives in pursuing policies throughout this period.

34 Harper, *A Great and Powerful Friend*, p. 219. See also Ann Curthoys and John Merritt, *Australia's First Cold War: Vol. 1. Society, Communism and Culture*, Allen & Unwin, Sydney, pp. 105–6.

35 USNA, Lot Files 54D224, Box 5, 'Australia—Letters to and from Embassy'; RG 84, Box 70, 'US Mission to UN'; Harry S. Truman Library, Dean Rusk Papers, 'Indonesia', 12 April 1949. The Americans reported the Dutch to be 'floored' by Evatt's action. The US mission to the UN called in their British counterparts on 1 April only to learn that Evatt had not informed them either of the General Assembly proposal and declared that 'His people were very angry at Evatt'.

36 Evatt Collection, Flinders University, External Affairs Files,'New Delhi Conference on Indonesia',20 January 1949. The Evatt—Teppema exchanges are in AA: A4311/1 Item 4/3. The Australians also impressed upon the United States that they were closely in step with Nehru. *FRUS*, vol. 7, 1949: 'The Far East and Australasia, Part 1', p. 404.

37 USNA, Lot Files 54D224, Box 5: 'Australia—Letters to and from Embassy'. Burton in particular attacked the US preoccupation with the Western Union and the Soviets as causing poor impressions in Asia over Indonesia. Schaller, *The American Occupation of Japan*, p. 156.

38 Kylie Tennant, *Evatt: Politics and Justice*, p. 201.

39 George, *Australia and the Indonesian Revolution*, p. 148; Renouf, *Let Justice Be Done*, p. 186. Any doubts about what Evatt's policies might have been had the Chifley government been returned, were dispelled by his strident attacks on anything that suggested the transfer of West New Guinea to the Indonesians in the 1950s. See P. Edwards, *Crises and Commitments: The Politics and Diplomacy of Australia's Involvement in Southeast Asian Conflicts 1948–1965*, Allen & Unwin, Sydney, 1992, pp. 200–1.

40 AA: A5799/1, Item 87/1949, 'Relations with Portuguese Timor'.

41 USNA, Lot Files, 54D224, Box 5; AA: A1838/1, Item 756 Part 1, 'Portuguese Timor'; A5799/1, Item 87/1949, 'Relations with Portuguese Timor'. The Menzies government continued the policy with detailed planning into the arc of islands covering Timor and Dutch New Guinea. See A5799/1, Item 100/1950, 'Strategic Significance of Dutch New Guinea'; A1838/1, Item 756/1, Part 2, 'Portuguese Timor, 1954'.

CHAPTER 21

JAPAN AND US POLICY IN THE NORTH PACIFIC

American policy towards Japan was based on 'vested interests who wanted to build up Japan as bulwark against Communism'.
H. V. EVATT

War with Japan was a watershed in Australian history. Australia had federated in the shadow of an emerging imperial Japan. After 1901, Japanese expansion into continental Asia was never far from the thinking of defence planners and diplomats in Australia. The diplomacy of the Lyons and Menzies governments was very largely driven by attempts to keep abreast of events unfolding in 'the near north', as Menzies called it, after the Japanese invasion of Manchuria in 1931. The near run of 1942, and the confirmation—provided by the 'Beat Hitler First' strategy—that Australia could not rely on traditional allies in Asia—resulted in an active diplomacy under Evatt. Like his predecessors, Evatt kept Japan clearly in view in the process of developing policy. Central to his efforts was a desire to play a major role in the Japanese Peace Settlement and to effect a comprehensive settlement for the region. Both eluded him during his term in office, as they have eluded his successors.

Evatt wanted the total disarming of Japan and a revolutionary restructuring of its social and economic structure so that it would never again threaten the region. Its feudal institutions would be replaced by those of the West. A democratic constitution would be promulgated with protection of civil liberties. Trade unions would protect Labor and at the same time lead to higher levels of consumption. The Emperor would be put on trial and his household never again be allowed to become a rallying point for those advocating imperial expansion.

In developing his policy, however, Evatt clearly understood that the war had reaffirmed that Australia was, at the end of the day, a small nation. The Pacific War had been won by the Americans, and they were determined to dominate developments after the armistice. This was driven home on 26 July 1945 when the terms for a Japanese capitulation were announced at Potsdam by the major powers. The Australian government first learned of the announcement in the press. Evatt condemned this but could hardly have been surprised by it. The 'Beat Hitler First' policy; the ineffectual Pacific War Council; the Cairo Conference; the final prospect at San Francisco of a general peace settlement brokered by the Big Four...all had prepared Evatt for the possibility that Australia's policies regarding the Pacific peace settlement would be ignored by the major powers. Evatt therefore made it immediately clear after the announcement that Australia's policies were based on two propositions—that Australia had a right as a 'party principal' to participate in the formulation of the peace treaty, and that treaty should deal with Japan harshly.

The period from the Potsdam Declaration to the emergence of a consistent American policy towards Japan in 1947 was one in which Evatt sought to secure the right of the Australians to share in a general Pacific peace conference which, he hoped, would also establish a system of regional security. Well before the Potsdam Declaration, however, he had prepared the groundwork in anticipation that he would have to press hard to secure Australia's role. He initiated the Australia–New Zealand Agreement (the Anzac Pact) in January 1944, frustrated by the domination of the war effort by the Big Three, to make the point that Australia expected to be fully consulted about the Pacific peace settlement. In order to impress upon the Big Three Australia's credentials, Evatt constantly drew attention to its war effort, particularly in the Pacific. The problem with this argument was that he had to wage a relentless battle against those in Cabinet, especially Chifley and Dedman, who were anxious to release manpower from the services in order to bolster the production of foodstuffs for the increasing number of Allied forces in the Pacific theatre. Similarly Evatt strongly defended the Australian Military Forces from charges that the Americans had relegated their role to that of 'mopping up' the Japanese in rear areas—leading the US minister in

Canberra to conclude that this emphasis on the maximum use of Anzac forces in the Pacific 'would give Australia the right to insist upon having its voice heard and considered in the making of any plans by the US for the future of the Pacific'.[1]

The Americans had other ideas. Despite Evatt's attempt to influence the course of events with the Anzac Pact in 1944, the US State Department by March 1944 had sketched the outline of a virtually exclusive occupation of Japan with only token Allied forces. In similar vein the US Navy, with the support of the Army, raised objections to the setting up of any Allied body for the Pacific which would interfere with occupation plans. These directions were clear to the British by May 1945 but since they were unable to challenge US dominance in the Pacific they were content to secure no more than a few minor amendments to the draft ultimatum to Japan after Potsdam. Anticipating the inevitable response from the dominions, Sir Alexander Cadogan at the Foreign Office lamely noted that Britain had no choice other than to accept that the Americans would not fully consult the other Allies and that this should be pointed out to the Dominions.[2]

The first test of Evatt's proposition that Australia should have 'Party Principal' rights in Japan came with the refusal of the United States to extend an invitation to Australia to sign the instrument of surrender in Tokyo Bay in September 1945. It was only after his strenuous efforts, supported by an embarrassed US mission in Canberra, and by MacArthur, that Australia was conceded the right by the United States government to sign the instrument 'as an independent nation'. Far from recognising Australia's status as a 'principal' or as a 'major belligerent', the invitation was also extended to other nations, lesser powers in the Pacific theatre in Evatt's view, such as the Netherlands, Canada and France.[3]

The fiasco over the signing of the Instrument of Surrender was part of a more significant problem. The only body overseeing the peace treaties was the Council of Foreign Ministers, and this was composed only of the major powers—including China, a nation whose inclusion in the Pacific settlement was feared by a White Australia. Evatt therefore took his case to the Council, which met in London in September, to counter the 'deplorable tendency' to treat Australia as a 'subordinate'. The Australian government, he argued, should be afforded full opportunity to participate in the occupation of Japan, 'not as a subsidiary but as a Principal Pacific Power'.

The problem was that this demand raised the sensitive issue, among members of the British Government as well as members of the Australian armed services, of Australia's role as a member of the Commonwealth. Quite apart from the diplomatic considerations, there were logistical reasons for arguing that any Australian participation in the occupation of Japan would be as a member of a combined Commonwealth force.[4]

This left Chifley unmoved—he insisted on separate participation. Evatt, however, wanted Australian participation on any basis—if not as a principal, then the Commonwealth was a useful alternative. But if Australia was to accept this arrangement, then Evatt was determined that it should be given command of the Commonwealth Occupation Force. At first glance this was surprising. After the Potsdam Declaration, Evatt's outbursts about the dominance of the Big Powers did not spare the British. Evatt had, in the words of the British High Commissioner in Canberra, fanned a press campaign to 'white heat' over Britain's failure to support Evatt's call that Emperor Hirohito be tried as a war criminal. Furthermore Evatt had accused the British Foreign Secretary of not supporting Australia's wishes to be represented at the armistice negotiations—leading to a stiff denial and a formal protest. Despite this, and the personal disdain for Evatt shared by a number of the British, there was common ground. Evatt wanted a greater share for Australia in the Pacific peace settlement and the occupation of Japan. At the same time, the British recognised that in the Pacific they were very much a minor player compared to the United States; British interests were in Western Europe, the Middle East and the Indian Ocean. Evatt's acceptance of the offer to lead the Commonwealth in Japan, firstly in relation to the Occupation Force and later the control machinery, coincided with the interests of the British government.[5]

Dealing with the Americans was a difficult business and it was only through the Commonwealth that Evatt could ensure that Australia had access to the councils representing the major powers. Consequently when the Allied Council for Japan was finally convened in April 1946 the Australian representative, W. Macmahon Ball, took his seat as the representative of the Commonwealth. In fact this 'swing' to the Commonwealth represented a more general trend in Australian defence, economic and foreign policy, and Evatt clearly regarded developments in Japan as quite consistent with it, especially since the 'Commonwealth' now offered leadership to Australia as its main power in the Pacific. It was the first step in a regional arrangement that was to last until Australia's decision to fight in Vietnam.

Commonwealth leadership, however, was not the sole basis of Evatt's claims for Australian representation in the Pacific settlement. Evatt had ingeniously raised the question of Emperor Hirohito's role as a war criminal in the face of strident opposition from the United States, which was determined to use the Emperor's prestige as a means of ensuring support for the Occupation. This issue, however, furnished Evatt with an early argument for advocating a basis for Australian participation in both the peace settlement and, more importantly, in leading the reoccupation of islands such as Timor, which Australia required for the construction of a system of regional security. It was also to prove the forerunner of his later insistence at the UN investigative committees of inquiry with wide-ranging powers. Australia was going to insist on the thorough investigation of war crimes, and the day after the Potsdam Declaration he released the investigations which had been done on behalf of the Australian government by Sir William Webb, the Australian War Crimes Commissioner. Whatever Evatt's personal feelings about the treatment of Australian POWs by the Japanese, he was determined, in the immediate aftermath of Potsdam, to tie the crimes of the Emperor to the need to impose a hard peace so that Japan might not again become an 'economic aggressor'. Booker has accused Evatt as having 'little genuine concern for the principles of law' over his determination to put Hirihito on trial. Webb himself, however, concluded that the question ultimately had to be decided at the highest 'political' level. More to the point his efforts did not go unrewarded. Sir William Webb was chosen President of the International Military Tribunal for the Far East. It may well have been a factor in Evatt obtaining, in October 1945, American approval of Australian membership of the Far Eastern Advisory Commission (later the Far Eastern Commission—FEC) in Washington where he assumed the seat himself.[6]

By the beginning of 1946 Evatt had secured an apparently formidable basis to ensure that Australian interests could be represented in the machinery that would supervise the armistice in Japan and address the broader issues of Pacific security. It had been no mean feat to arrange to sit in common council with the major powers. The problem now was to influence the peace settlement itself. Unfortunately, gaining access to the control machinery in Japan was not sufficient. The Americans had no intention of allowing the other Big Powers to influence American occupation policy. The real question then became for Evatt the nature of United States policies and the extent that these were compatible with those of Australia.

For the first two years of the Occupation MacArthur, as Supreme Commander of the Allied Power (SCAP), dominated. He ignored the Allied Councils that were responsible for broad Occupation policy, and took discretionary measures on the pretext that it was 'administrative action'. This rankled with the Australians, who found Mac-

Arthur erratic. Some of his measures, especially the restoration of Japanese whaling, were seen as threatening, and indeed pointed to the need for international guidelines. Yet he operated without clear policies. As late as November 1946 Evatt took comfort in the fact that while MacArthur 'as Supreme Commander must have tremendous power...the general policy is not yet fixed'.[7] Ultimately, when the Americans did formulate policy, MacArthur was far from being the problem.

Evatt's views were clear from the outset. He put his case to the FEC when it first addressed the broad policy issues in October 1945. He wanted stringent economic restrictions as well as specific measures to eliminate the armaments industry. At this stage he had some reason to be optimistic. Planners in Washington also insisted upon strict controls on Japanese heavy industry and directed that the giant industrial monopolies—the zaibatsus—be broken up and that Japanese society be remodelled on liberal, democratic lines. Indeed at the end of 1945 American government missions to Japan drew attention to the fact that Japan enjoyed a higher standard of living than many of her victims. Consequently reparations would not only be a punishment but also a means of ensuring that the disparities between Japan and its neighbours would be eliminated.

The extent to which security drove Evatt concerning the Japanese peace settlement in the early stages was demonstrated over Japanese whaling, which also served as an illustration of Evatt's diplomacy. He was absolutely determined to defend his position on this critical issue. Yet he was pragmatic, using every device that he could.

In August 1946 MacArthur authorised a fleet of Japanese whalers to operate in the Antarctic in the 1946–47 season to relieve the protein shortage within Japan. The action was justified as administrative and as coming within the scope of a directive on fishing and whaling given to him on 13 November 1945, before the Allied Council had come into existence and before the FEC had developed policy on the issue.[8]

To Evatt the action constituted a move to rehabilitate Japanese shipping, and as such was a matter of major policy. He therefore challenged on the FEC the validity of the SCAP directive. Australia had never agreed, in Evatt's view, to Japanese whaling in Antarctic waters, and he emphasised that Australia 'has great territorial interests' there. The US State Department conceded something to Evatt by emphasising the 'purely temporary character of the projected expedition' but they rejected the attempt to elevate the status of the control machinery—SCAP had the power to authorise it as a matter of administrative action under the directive issued to him as Supreme Commander in November 1945. Ultimately Evatt had no choice but to accept the American action as a *fait accompli*. He therefore had to take the Americans at their word on the FEC—this was a mission designed to relieve an immediate shortage of food.[9]

Evatt was content to let the matter rest there as far as MacArthur was concerned. He could hardly challenge the right of SCAP to take such action in terms of his directive. But he could work within it. He had, after all, been used to doing just that during the war when Washington used the directive to MacArthur as Commander of the South-West Pacific area to deflect Australian arguments about the inadequacy of supplies to that theatre. Evatt therefore accepted that administrative action was necessary to feed the Japanese, and issuing orders to procure fish was obviously covered by this. The expedition should go ahead, but Evatt now sought to have it 'controlled and operated exclusively by Allied personnel'. He supported a joint venture by Britain, Australia, New Zealand and Norway—but not by the United States. He also attempted to limit the actual area in which the Japanese could fish as a question of major policy. Any future extension would have to be authorised by the FEC!

In addition Evatt extended the fight to other arenas. He enlisted British help with the argument that Australia had a 'direct interest in the proper control and development of the whaling industry'. He found ready support among other whaling nations such as Norway, which were not keen to see the return of their pre-war competitor. They in turn proceeded in the course of 1947 to draw American attention to the very poor past record of the Japanese in killing young whales, thereby threatening the world supply.[10]

In the end, despite the argument concerning FEC authorisation, and the pressure of the world whaling industry, SCAP sought authorisation from Washington on 4 May 1947 for a second whaling mission to the Antarctic. Evatt's response was dramatic and unambiguous. On 6 June he released a comprehensive statement on international affairs in the House of Representatives in which he stressed that the time had arrived for an international solution for the peace settlement with Japan.

It is increasingly desirable that an early peace settlement with Japan should be negotiated. We have been increasingly perturbed to notice a tendency towards the piecemeal disposal of matters that should be dealt with as a whole in a peace treaty with Japan.

In the address he also sought to pre-empt any future appeal to food shortages as a justification for whaling by stressing that the United Nations should take 'concerted action' for economic reconstruction through the Food and Agriculture Organisation (FAO) and the Economic Commission for Asia and the Far East (ECAFE) both of which included Australian representatives. He also wanted to head off the possibility that whaling might become the basis for the revival of Japanese shipping. Despite Australian information to the contrary, he cited the 'waste' of the Japanese on the first whaling expedition and he cautioned that the disposal of the Japanese fleet must be the subject of peace settlement. In this context he foreshadowed Australia's bid for lighter vessels suitable for the Australian coastal and inter-island trade.[11]

What is significant about this speech is that Evatt revealed the futility of working through the Allied control machinery. As he was to do repeatedly in his diplomacy, when Evatt was rebuffed at one level he did not hesitate to work at another. He foreshadowed action by UN agencies; spoke of Commonwealth diplomatic action to concert policy on the settlement; and announced that Australia was taking unilateral action to forestall the threat to its interests in Antarctica. In April, he declared, Australia had despatched a scientific mission, thereby commencing the work of laying Australian claims to primacy in the area—a step that was to become a fundamental foreign policy objective thereafter for both major parties.

The heart of the problem, as Evatt said bluntly, was that 'The presence of Japanese ships in Antarctic waters was a threat to Australian security'. As a result the Americans came under strong pressure from Australian diplomats in late June—Macmahon Ball recalling 'all sorts of telegrams arriving from Canberra about whaling'. The campaign culminated with Evatt's press statements on 23 and 27 June which warned that the re-establishment of the Japanese industry in Antarctic waters 'in effect means the creation of naval potential'.[12]

The whaling issue came at a critical juncture in the post-war occupation of Japan. To the Australians the decision to allow Japanese whaling foreshadowed a move to take major decisions that would determine the future of Japan and the region in advance of a peace settlement, and along lines that were too 'soft'. There were other signs as well. In May the Australian government presented an aide mémoire to the Americans protesting against the participation of Japanese officials in international conferences such as the rice study group in India—leading the United States the next month to present a policy paper to the FEC suggesting that the way be cleared for Japanese to travel abroad. The aide mémoire also drew attention to 'Japanese penetration' of phosphate mining on Angaur, in their former Palau Group mandate and now UN Trust Territory. Once again, however, the Americans rebuffed these criticisms on the basis of the administrative authority accorded SCAP in his directive.[13]

These decisions were taken by SCAP and seem not to have followed any American overall plan for Japan, and certainly not the region.

Clearly the Americans had been concerned to dominate the Occupation, but they did not indicate a clear direction in their thinking about the role of Japan until 1947. The Cold War, along with the increasing burden of maintaining the Occupation, caused them to consider the need for a 'soft' peace settlement. Even more threatening to Australia was the thinking from Washington that sought to link an industrially revived Japan which would take the leading role in South–East Asia with a similar strategy in Western Europe based on the regional dominance of Germany.[14]

---❖---

It became apparent to the Australians during 1947 and 1948 that despite their efforts to secure an early settlement the United States wanted postponement so as to allow a revival of the Japanese economy. In order to build Japan as a 'bastion against Communism', production would have to be boosted; trade with South-East Asia (as opposed to China which was increasingly seen as likely to be 'lost' to the West) expanded; the purges against the Japanese right wing be switched to a move against organised labour; and the restrictions of the earlier Occupation be removed. All of this was to be done unilaterally—any pretence of consultation with the Allies in the FEC was dismissed.

This change of policy goes some way to explaining Evatt's trip to Japan in July 1947 where he succeeded in restoring relations with MacArthur—even at the expense of the sacrifice of the Australian representative on the Allied Council for Japan, William Macmahon Ball. There is no doubt that Macmahon Ball had vigorously followed Evatt's policy in Japan and was justifiably concerned that he did not receive Evatt's backing against MacArthur. Evatt's public support for MacArthur gave Macmahon Ball little option but to resign. In private he was snubbed. Evatt was notorious for his poor treatment of subordinates. Evatt's apparent volte face, however, in not supporting Macmahon Ball, needs to be considered against the reasons that lay behind the mission.

Macmahon Ball was dispensable—MacArthur was not. The change of American policy towards Japan in 1947 was coupled with a concerted drive from Washington to lessen MacArthur's power, especially since he was now determined to effect a radical transformation of the Japanese economy by breaking up the giant corporations—the zaibatsus. The General was also opposed to any changes to Occupation policy and argued instead for an early peace settlement—policies apparently motivated by his own desire to be seen as a great 'trust-buster' and social reformer, but also designed to lay the groundwork for an attempt to become President of the United States. Whatever MacArthur's shortcomings had been, he was now advocating policies similar to Evatt's.

Evatt was certainly aware of this. MacArthur readily confided in the British Representative in Japan, Sir Alvary Gascoigne, in early March 1947 that he favoured an early peace treaty and that Marshall and his aides in Washington 'paid heed' only to 'Wall Street whose main holdings were in Europe'. The General dismissed the efforts of senior US Defence and State Department officials—the 'tycoons' such as 'Draper, Harriman and Forrestal'—who saw the deconcentration of Japanese industry 'as a threat to their business interests'.[15]

This line of argument was taken up by Evatt later when he told the British High Commissioner in Canberra, E. J. Williams, that American policy towards Japan was based on 'vested [financial] interests who wanted to build up Japan as bulwark against Communism'. In reporting this, Williams went on to say that 'he [Evatt] developed the fantastic idea that there should be a social democratic bloc of the three Commonwealth Labour Governments between the United States and the USSR'.[16]

MacArthur also supported an early peace settlement. He told MacMahon Ball on 6 March 1947 that he welcomed Evatt's position on this and that he also shared his view that the occupation should move under United Nations control to tackle a new and more difficult phase—the economic reconstruction of the country. Furthermore he thought that Australia should 'take a principal part in the Pacific settlement [and] he was sorry you [Evatt] had not come to Japan'.[17] In April, however, Evatt was further advised by Macmahon Ball that MacArthur was faced by the prospect of political control going back to 'reactionary groups'. This was soon followed by dramatic news that indicated the overall thrust of American policy and the extent to which Washington was seeking to undermine MacArthur. On 8 May 1947 Undersecretary of State, Dean Acheson, attacked MacArthur's policies in a public address in Cleveland , Mississippi, and foreshadowed that United States foreign economic policy would restore 'the greatest workshops of Europe and Asia—Germany and Japan'.[18]

It made little sense to attack MacArthur given these developments. Far from undermining Macmahon Ball by supporting MacArthur, thereby losing 'the chance to become involved in a constructive Japan policy', as Rix contends, Evatt's policy at this juncture was precisely that—to become involved in a Japan policy before the Americans proceeded with the reconstruction of Japan on their own terms.[19]

Evatt was not duchessed by MacArthur during the visit to Japan— the basis for a successful mission had been laid in March when Evatt learned of MacArthur's position. While Evatt's instructions were seen by Macmahon Ball as 'vague' after March, they were specific on the point of not causing 'unnecessary antagonism with MacArthur'. The focus of the mission was on ensuring relations with MacArthur, with one news source indeed suggesting that Evatt had come 'in order to identify himself with General MacArthur'. Macmahon Ball himself was astonished, as he later reported, that while in Japan Evatt paid little attention to the previous disarmament of the country, but rather directed his concerns to the next phase of control—'which might be necessary for perhaps ten years'. Consequently, Evatt spent his time in discussions in Japan presenting his views on the peace settlement and attempting to secure American assurances that Australia would be represented as a 'party principal' in any negotiations. This did not mean that during the visit the battle over whaling ceased—it had been taken up in the FEC where it was, despite Allied support, being lost. But beyond that Evatt, like Macmahon Ball himself, looked to the coming Canberra Conference of the Commonwealth in August where the substantive issues would be discussed. The mission to Japan was part of Evatt's diplomacy. The FEC was another part, and the scientific mission to Antarctica yet another.[20]

Evatt's mission to Japan has to be placed in context. Evatt tried to arrest the drift of events in Japan by a series of initiatives from the beginning of 1947. Firstly he called for an early peace settlement, with Australia attending as a 'Party Principal', and then sought to exploit the apparent desire of MacArthur for this and for Evatt's Japan policy; secondly he wanted to secure Commonwealth support for a 'hard' peace; thirdly he wanted a regional pact in the Pacific to police the new order.

On his return to Australia he assured the Parliament that the vital work lay in the future:

My consultations with General MacArthur showed a broad agreement on the steps to be taken in preparing the treaty, on the principles that should be contained in it, on the type of supervisory machinery that should be established under it and on many of the other important matters with which the settlement must deal.[21]

Evatt now wanted to arrest the piecemeal decisions over Japan and at a more general level to impede American attempts to secure Pacific bases in advance of a general settlement. In that sense he had attempted to use MacArthur. The settlement would put Japanese obligations, as Rosecrance argues, 'on a contractual basis'. But to secure this Evatt also sought to exploit Australia's role as the leading

Commonwealth nation in the Pacific. By proposing, in March, a Commonwealth conference to consider the peace settlement, Evatt not only attempted to exploit the general concerns about the possibility of a 'soft peace', but he also put the British on notice that he would oppose a peace brokered by either the FEC or by a bilateral arrangement between the British and the Americans. As one New Zealand official then reported

Dr. Evatt said he feared that the Americans might settle things without full consultation with the active belligerents, mainly because of their desire to exclude the Russians. He said he would send a cable to the United Kingdom Government to the effect that the Japanese settlement should not be discussed at (the FEC)...I had gathered from officials earlier that Australia took the view that they could not afford not to be present in the preparatory work of the treaty, and that Dr. Evatt would get representation 'by hook or by crook'.[22]

Using the Commonwealth had its drawbacks. Since the days of the Imperial Federationists at the turn of the century the Canadians had always spoken against developing a fixed Commonwealth policy. And, as then, the Canadians inevitably charged that any such meeting 'should not be expected to lead to [the] formulation of a single Commonwealth policy to which all members of the Commonwealth would be committed in the later stages of the Japanese settlement'.[23]

The British, however, were fully supportive of Evatt's initiative even if they were careful to publicly disclaim that it was their aim to produce an 'agreed' Commonwealth position on the Japanese Peace Treaty. To them the American vision of Japan as a major regional force in the containment of Communism threatened Britain's position in South-East Asia where Malayan rubber and tin went a long way to redressing the trans-Atlantic trade deficit. Like the Australians, the British feared that in rebuilding Japan, the United States would enhance the Japanese position in South-East Asia to compensate for their loss of markets in Manchuria and Korea. The British therefore shared Evatt's view that strict industrial controls and extensive reparations would lessen Japanese economic dominance in South-East Asia.[24]

Evatt, as usual, prepared thoroughly for the conference, which met in Canberra in August, straight after his return from Japan. Part of that preparation was the publication of his statements on the Japanese Peace Settlement which coincided with the conference.[25] He had also been seeking since June the views of the Defence Committee on the strategic aspects of the settlement with Japan and had been conducting an active correspondence with the British and New Zealand governments on the main subjects to be dealt with at the conference.[26]

Evatt was, as a result, furnished with a comprehensive plan that largely reflected their views and one that envisaged a 'hard' peace settlement, international control of Japan and a blueprint for regional development as a whole.

Far from tolerating the integration of Japan into the regional economy, Evatt sought economic restriction within Japan and a multilateral regional solution. Specifically, Evatt argued that Japan should not be treated like Germany after World War I, where that country was allowed once again to 'menace' the security of the world. To ensure this he repeated the Defence Committee's call for major controls on shipping—'limited to a maximum sufficient for [the] satisfactory conduct between Japan's main islands' with provision for limited overseas trade under strict Allied supervision—and argued that the surplus merchant marine should be distributed to the key Pacific War belligerents. As far as pearling was concerned, he embarrassed even his solid supporters from New Zealand with the demand that this, 'if approved at all', should not extend below 10 degrees North. His most significant emphasis, given the American desire to develop Japan as a leading regional industrial power, was the insistence that Japan would not be allowed to acquire raw materials, such as 'the tin and rubber which she snatched at in the Indies and Malaya', on 'her own terms and whenever she wishes'. Evatt here envisaged on-going 'supervision' of Japan's imports and stocks of vital raw materials as essential for 'the safety of Australia'.[27]

Evatt's intention at the Canberra Conference was to mount a comprehensive challenge to American policy, with the prospect of a Commonwealth bloc.[28] He informed the US State Department, for example, that 'all Commonwealth governments were approaching the settlement along parallel lines'—hardly a position acceptable to the Canadians who were at pains to point this out. But he also used the opportunity to stress in the United Nations that the latter should take a much more active role in international economic planning. He criticised past 'piece-meal' approaches and reminded members 'That all nations have a stake in international economic cooperation'. Read against his concern that Japanese trade in acquiring raw materials be carefully supervised, Evatt's appeal at the UN that regional commissions should be accorded 'substantial authority' also served to reinforce Australia's security:

Australia as a member of the Economic Commission for Asia and the Far East will participate earnestly in its work. Our economic ties with countries in this area have developed substantially during and since the war. Our mutual trade has increased four fold compared with before the war...and we are making exchanges of products in short supply, and of information and industrial techniques.

Apart from all this Evatt pressed the New Zealand and British governments for 'vigorous and prompt action to substantiate the Australian claim to 2 500 000 square miles of Antarctica' ![29]

Evatt left little to chance. He sought to influence events in Japan at the end of 1947 by exercising every diplomatic lever Australia possessed and cited variously the credentials of belligerent status, regional security, United Nations authority and Commonwealth leadership in the Pacific. It was, however, to be of no avail as the United States moved to effect a settlement on its own terms.

This became dramatically apparent during 1948 following an orchestrated campaign by George Kennan in the State Department and General William Draper, under-secretary of the Army, to strengthen Japan. Kennan visited Japan in early 1948 and received wide publicity with headlines, inspired by Draper, such as 'Drastic Change in Policy of US Envisaged—Kennan Visits seen as Move to Build up Japan as Anti-Red Bulwark'. At the same time Draper published a report on Japanese industry by the private consultant Clifford Strike which concluded that reparations would cripple the Japanese economy. Finally, Draper himself led a mission to Japan in March 1948 which drew together the threads of the new policy. In April he concluded that Japan needed access to cheap raw materials and markets in Asia and that the deconcentration program should be terminated. SCAP would have to radically change course. By the middle of 1948, however, MacArthur, by then thoroughly undermined by the advocates of the new policy, submitted, moving forcefully to the right, starting a systematic purge of the 'radicals'.

Evatt had moved to associate himself with MacArthur in July 1947 in an attempt to resist just this course of events. Now the General lamely confided to Kennan, one of his harshest critics, that 'He had been able to make some impression on Evatt when he was here but he had no doubt that he would begin to backslide when he had been back in Australia for some time'.[30]

In fact Evatt had praised the work of MacArthur. He knew the source of Australia's concerns. He had followed the campaign in the American press against 'deconcentration' of Japanese industry—the breaking up of the zaibatsus. This had been inspired by Draper's leaks of information to United Press and the International News Service. In a major statement on International Affairs on 8 April 1948 Evatt declared that

It is clear that the United States thinks it would be useless at present to continue with the plan for the holding of a peace conference in relation to Japan. What is the reason? First of all, it is quite correct that the Soviet Union would claim [the right to use the veto]…But of course there have been changes too, in the attitude towards the Soviet Union in the last few months. There have been visitors like Mr. Kennan. There is what is called the Strike Report and the Draper Report, and a great deal of newspaper discussion with regard to Japan, to the effect that it would not be wise to pursue the policy laid down in the Potsdam declaration in regard to the industrial capacity of Japan and that it would be wise to review it.

Evatt then roundly condemned this approach. 'I say that it will be an evil day for Australia if Japan is given the capacity to rearm...The Australian people will never agree to the re-building of Japan to a stage where it might be a threat to our security'. He was not prepared to let 'power politics' and the 'fears and suspicions' of the Cold War impede the settlement—it could, he concluded, be effected 'in a few days' since it should, referring to the Potsdam Agreement and the FEC's 'advices'...'be essentially a matter of working out the agreements already made'.[31]

The Americans were seeking to take precisely the opposite action and it was becoming increasingly clear to Evatt that any prospect of an early settlement was unlikely. To counter this he stepped up the campaign against the American changes throughout 1948 through more traditional channels. In the FEC the Australians vainly fought American pressure to relax travel restrictions on Japanese representatives and to authorise the creation of a Japanese Maritime Coastal Patrol. In late April the Americans exercised a veto over a New Zealand attempt to delay the expansion of the Japanese merchant marine foreshadowed in the Diet's Maritime Safety Authorities Bill. This led Patrick Shaw, the Australian official appointed to represent the Commonwealth on the Allied Council for Japan, in a manner reminiscent of the Macmahon Ball period, to charge that SCAP had acted beyond his authority. Immediately after this the Australian embassy in Washington presented an aide mémoire arguing that the FEC should as a matter of principle adopt a policy on Japanese whaling in Antarctica.[32]

Despite all this the Americans were unmoved. In June the Americans informed the Australians that they were authorising a third whaling expedition. Further they used the opportunity to dismiss a wide array of Australian concerns. Arguing from the premise that 'the United States Government is in a unique position in the matter of the revival of Japanese trade' the Americans in an aide mémoire dismissed the FEC's attempts to restrict Japanese travel; the Australian views on the Maritime Safety Authorities Bill; the attempts to restrict the area of Japanese fishing; and the building up of Japan's industrial capacity. Finally, concluded the Americans tartly, they hoped that the Australians could 'move forward' with the United States in solving the many problems in the reconstruction of Japan.[33]

Evatt continued his calls for 'an early settlement' and for 'care not to give Japan a war potential' for the rest of his time in office and on to the Opposition benches. The attitude of the Americans in 1947 and 1948, however, marked the effective end of his hopes of securing an early treaty. He indicated his bitterness in a discussion with the British High Commissioner in Canberra, E. J. Williams, on 15 April 1948. 'Evatt', reported Williams, 'was now veering away from his earlier attitude of closer cooperation with the United States' because of their policies on Japan.[34]

The Americans too knew that their rough handling of the Australians had caused a revision in Evatt's thinking. In a review of relations with Australia conducted by the State Department in August 1948 it was concluded that Evatt had now abandoned his previous position of adopting a 'parallel role' with the United States and had adopted a 'more neutral role'. Significantly they did not put this down to his desire to exercise his influence in the United Nations but rather conceded that 'Special attention should...be paid to the basis of Australian policy regarding Japan and the origin of their suspicion of our intentions'.[35]

The impasse over Japan forced Evatt to look to policies that challenged American plans for the region. In a speech that could have been scripted for a later de Gaulle, Evatt declared in June 1949 that

It is a fundamental mistake to have our policies in relation to Germany and Japan determined merely as a by-product of our relationship with Russia...The problems of France in relation to Germany are analogous to those of Australia, New Zealand and the Philippines in relation to Japan. You re-arm Japan and remove all the restrictions to which it agreed in the Armistice and so develop its war potential, and you are quite satisfied that in any future struggle in the Far East Japan will do the bidding of the western democracies. That is a fallacy.[36]

Like de Gaulle, Evatt had his own ideas on the future of the region in which he lived. Australian wartime experiences, followed by US policy in the occupation, led Evatt to fear that an unreconstructed Japan could yet again threaten the region. Before 1941 Australia looked to Britain to protect it against Japan. Now Evatt was to continue that policy.

Japan was a central concern of Evatt's policies as Minister of External Affairs. He was adamant that Australia, as a wartime belligerent and as a regional power that could again be threatened by a rearmed Japan, would be involved in any regional settlement. His policy was absolutely clear from the end of the war. Japan would be disarmed and reformed. Under no circumstances would Evatt tolerate any act that would give Japan a war potential. Initially, he was concerned by isolated instances such as the authorisation of Japanese whaling in Antarctica and the mining of phosphate on Angau. By 1947, however, it was no longer the erratic policies of MacArthur that concerned him but the development of firm American policy to rearm and industrialise Japan as a bastion against Communism. American Cold War priorities ignored Australian insecurity about the Pacific.

NOTES

1. AA: A2670, 55/1944; Roger Bell, *Unequal Allies: Australian–American Relations and the Pacific War*, MUP, Melbourne 1977, p. 176.
2. Michael Schaller, *The American Occupation of Japan: The Origins of the Cold War in Asia*, OUP, Oxford, 1985, pp. 6–7; Christopher Thorne, *Allies of a Kind: The United States, Britain, and the War Against Japan, 1941–1945*, OUP, 1978, p. 656.
3. D.M. Horner, *High Command: Australia and Allied Strategy, 1939–1945*, Allen & Unwin, Canberra, 1982, p. 420.
4. Alan Renouf, *Let Justice be Done: The Foreign Policy of Dr. H.V. Evatt*, UQP, St Lucia, 1983, p. 197; Horner, *High Command*, p. 420.
5. PRO: DO 35/180; CAB 122/493, COS (45) 172; CAB 81/46, PHP (45) 29.
6. W. Reynolds, Ph.D thesis 'H.V.Evatt: The Imperial Connection and the Quest for Australian Security, 1941–1945', University of Newcastle, 1985, pp. 335–9; M. Booker, *The Last Domino: Aspects of Australia's Foreign Relations*, Collins, Sydney, 1976, p. 71.
7. Norman Harper, *A Great and Powerful Friend: A Study of Australian American Relations Between 1900 and 1975*, UQP, St Lucia, 1987, p. 160; *Japanese Peace Settlement: Statements by the Minister of External Affairs*, Australian Government Publishing Service (AGPS), Canberra, 1947, p. 63.
8. The Australians initially discounted the argument that the expedition was warranted because of the food shortage in Japan—A. Rix, *Intermittent Diplomat: The Japan and Batavia Diaries of W. Macmahon Ball*, MUP, Melbourne, 1988, pp. 101–2. They responded on 13 January 1947 by submitting a draft revision of the fisheries policy proposing the limitation of Japanese fishing with authorisation only through the FEC. This led to strong exchanges between the Australians, who perceived a threat to their security, and the Americans, who dismissed this along with the 'proposed appropriation by the FEC of administrative responsibility in fishing and whaling'. Cable, US Political Adviser in Japan to Secretary of State,13 January 1947, *Foreign Relations of the United States*, vol. 6 , 'The Far East', Washington, 1972, p. 164, FRUS.
9. R. Rosecrance, *Australian Diplomacy and Japan,1945–1951*, MUP, Melbourne, 1962, p. 38.
10. Aide-mémoire, British Embassy, Washington, to the Secretary of State, 30 April, 1947, *Foreign Relations of the United States*, vol. 6, 'The Far East', p. 207. It is more likely that their real concern, however, as they added here, was to ensure their own supply and further to secure the allocation to Britain of Japanese factory ships as reparations, FRUS.

11 *Current Notes*, vol. 18, no. 6, June–July 1947, pp. 378–405. Evatt claimed that the Japanese had discarded oil-bearing bones and that they did not 'regard the International Whaling Regulations seriously'. This charge was not defensible. The expedition had been given a relatively clean bill of health by the Australian observer aboad and SCAP modified Japanese whaling vessels so that they could extract oil after they had returned. *FRUS*, 1947, vol. 6, 'The Far East', p. 223.

12 *FRUS*, vol. 6, *The Far East*, 1947, pp. 230–47; Rix *Intermittent Diplomat*, p. 216; *Current Notes*, vol. 18, no. 6, p. 409.

13 *FRUS*, vol. 6, 'The Far East', Memorandum of Conversation by Chief of the Division of North East Asian Affairs, 29 May 1947; T. Reese, *Australia, New Zealand, and the United States: A Survey of International Relations 1941–1968*, OUP, London, 1969, p. 93.

14 M. Schaller, 'MacArthur's Japan: The View From Washington', *Diplomatic History*, vol. 10, no. 1, Winter 1986, p. 10.

15 Schaller,*The American Occupation of Japan*, p. 127.

16 Ibid., ch. 4; PRO: FO 371/70202A Cable, E.J.Williams to Sir Eric Machtig, 15 April 1948.

17 Rix, *Intermittent Diplomat*, pp. 185–8. Given these remarks, along with the public attacks in the United States from January 1947 (see Schaller, *The American Occupation of Japan*, pp. 91–5) to the effect that MacArthur had gone too far in attempts to remodel the Japanese economy, it is hardly surprising that Evatt was not prepared to attack the General openly, despite his earlier actions and attitudes.

18 Ibid.; R. Kay, *Documents on New Zealand External Relations: vol. 3: The Anzus Pact and the Treaty of Peace with Japan*, Wellington, p. 15; Schaller, *The American Occupation of Japan*, p. 97.

19 Rix, 'Macmahon Ball and the Allied Council', p. 26.

20 Rix, *Intermittent Diplomat*, n. 28, p. 285, pp. 278–9; *FRUS*, vol. 6, 1947, 'The Far East', pp. 473–4.

21 Rosecrance, *Australian Diplomacy*, pp. 85–6.

22 Ibid. p. 73; Kay, *Documents on New Zealand External Relations*, p. 10.

23 Kay, *Documents on New Zealand External Relations*, pp. 26, 31, 36. It is clear from the documents marshalled by Kay that New Zealand fully supported Evatt's attempts to secure Commonwealth support before the Americans modified their policies. Evatt stuck literally to the proposition that Australia represented the Commonwealth in the Pacific and dismissed the Canadians as having 'relatively remote interests compared with Australia'. As late as September 1949 he reprimanded Bevin for discussing Japan with the Americans without first consulting the Australian government—Letter, PRO: PREM 8/966 Attlee to Chifley, 28 September 1949.

24 FO 371/63766–84; Schaller, *The American Occupation of Japan*, pp. 100–1.

25 *Japanese Peace Settlement: Statements by the Australian Minister for External Affairs, the Right Honourable H.V. Evatt, MP*, Department of External Affairs, Canberra, August, 1947.

26 He duly received a blueprint for a hard peace. The Defence Committee indeed advised that it was 'in our interests that Allied control of Japan should

continue indefinitely'! The report was particularly hostile to the loosening of control on Japanese fishing, whaling and sealing and sought to restrict the size of the merchant marine by limiting all vessels to 5000 gross tons. 'Strategic Aspects of the Peace Settlement with Japan', Report by the Defence Committee, 24 June 1947, AA: A816/1, 19/304/481—Attachment 1.

27 Kay, *Documents on New Zealand External Relations*, pp. 58–209. The New Zealanders agreed with Evatt's view that 'security must be the overriding consideration despite the American intention to restore Japan to its position as workshop of the East...as a bastion against Russia', AA: A4144, item 640.

28 In this context Evatt made great play with the role of the new dominions in the region—especially India—which served to strengthen the focus on the Commonwealth Conference as against the American focus on the FEC. Kay, *Documents on New Zealand External Relations*, p. 51.

29 Cable 328/47, Australian Ambassador to the Acting Secretary of State, 2 September 1947, *FRUS*, vol. 6, 'The Far East' 1947, p. 516 (the British government assured the Secretary of State orally on 9 October that there was no agreed policy formulated at Canberra, ibid, p. 534); *Current Notes*, vol. 18, no. 9, October 1947, pp. 625–6. Evatt even sought, and emphasised, a review of world economic conditions at 'each session' of the Economic and Social Council; USNA, Lot Files 54 D224, R59, Box 4 'Australia Policy File'—'Pressure to Secure Title to Australian Antarctic'.

30 *FRUS*, 1948, vol. 6, 'The Far East', Conversation between MacArthur and Kennan, 5 March 1948.

31 *Current Notes*, vol. 19, no. 5, May 1948, pp. 265–7.

32 Kay, *Documents on New Zealand External Relations*, p. 256.

33 *FRUS*, vol. 6, 'The Far East and Australasia', 1948, pp. 737–827.

34 PRO: FO 371/70202A, Unnumbered Cable, E.J.Williams to Sir Eric Machtig, 15 April 1948. On 28 May the Foreign Office added that 'the Anzac Powers are in a fog over the whole matter and had a pathological fear over...Japan', Memorandum of Conversation by Marshall Green, 28 May 1948, *FRUS*, vol. 6, 1948, 'The Far East and Australasia'.

35 *FRUS*, vol. 6, 1948, 'The Far East and Australasia', Policy Statement of the Department of State—'United States Relations with Australia', 18 August 1948, p. 3.

36 Rosecrance, *Australian Diplomacy and Japan*, p. 149.

CHAPTER 22

THE EMPIRE AS A THIRD FORCE?

My view is that if one speaks of 'powers', the British Commonwealth can be the third group of powers. Its contribution to victory was of the same order as that of the Soviet Union and the United States of America.

H. V. EVATT

Australia during the Pacific War was exposed to an unprecedented influence from outside the Commonwealth as Washington took on the major responsibility for defeating Japan. Yet it has been increasingly acknowledged by historians that the swing to the United States was not intended to be at the expense of Imperial ties and in any case did not long endure. By the middle war years there was a decided turn back to the British connection. Historians have concentrated on the two major declarations by Curtin as evidence of this—his December 1941 'without any pangs' speech and his May 1944 'Fourth Empire' speech.

Evatt has largely been ignored in all of this. His biographers have concentrated on those things that made Evatt exceptional. They draw attention to his commitment to 'principle' in the conduct of foreign affairs, and argue that he was legally well qualified to ply his craft on the world stage. Much of Evatt's work, however, was developed in close co-operation with others. Australia was a small power with limited influence. Policy often was made as a reaction to much larger forces. Evatt was well aware of Australia's strategic and economic situation and the potential benefits of maintaining the Imperial connection. This provided a major thread that linked his seemingly inexhaustible and diffuse array of policies to 1949.

The 'swing' to Washington in 1941–42 was forced by the circumstances of war and did not long endure. The Americans were seen as erratic in policy, and dismissive of their small ally's concerns. Their views on the post-war settlement held dangers in the region for Australia. They were also seen as a threat to the Australian economy. Apart from Australia's dependence on British imperial trade it was a cardinal point of policy to use tariffs generally to promote industrialisation.[1]

The Australian government had realised in 1942 that its attitude to the loss of preference in British markets would depend on the extent to which the United States would limit its income from exports and move to home consumption. The question of tariffs would also depend on the US attitude to the establishment of an international trade system. Failure to reach accord on either issue would result in an Australian commitment to 'Empire economic solidarity'.

Evatt quickly realised that there was little reason for optimism. The United States was wedded to international free trade and prepared for 'competition with all comers'. The Americans therefore looked to maximising the role of private companies and keeping the role of international regulation to a minimum. Evatt became aware of this during his overseas mission in 1943. The American proposals for a 'Stabilisation' Fund took up much of the time of the Evatt delegation. For Evatt, the plan envisaged too much international control and too little credit funding for any future World Bank. The American Treasury wanted a fund of $5 billion and little scope for exchange rate depreciation for nations suffering trade deficits. The British, on the other hand, wanted a fund of some $26 billion and a large measure of freedom to make exchange rate adjustments. Evatt accordingly welcomed the British position and argued that in the event that the Fund was not given adequate reserves, or that it did not take measures to avoid 'persistent credit balances'—an obvious reference to the United States—then Australia should have the right to withdraw.

This was the position consistently followed thereafter by Evatt. In May 1944 Evatt and Chifley persuaded a reluctant Cabinet to authorise Australia's attendance at the Bretton Woods Conference, which was to formulate proposals for an International Monetary Fund and a Bank of Reconstruction and Development. In so doing, Australia refused to give any commitments to exchange rate stability without international agreement on full employment.[2] It was, as Bell has argued persuasively, *a convenient rationalisation for Australia's determination to use import restrictions, high tariffs and the Ottawa agreements to ensure full domestic employment and promote an increasingly diversified economy.*[3]

Civil aviation, and the attendant question of bases, furnished an early illustration of the importance of the Commonwealth connection. The Americans would not assist in the building of an Australian aircraft industry but the British would.[4] With the news that the Americans were attempting to undermine Britain's markets in Latin America, and the associated revelation that Roosevelt wanted to employ Latin America as a base for American civil air penetration into the Pacific, the Commonwealth link became an essential defence. By 1943 civil aviation policy, along with trade policy as a whole was predicated on post-war co-operation with the Commonwealth. Not only did this have implications for regional defence strategy, it also went to the heart of Australia's post-war plans for industry.[5]

The Americans had not only failed to give comfort in international trade talks on the employment question but less than one week after the surrender of Japan the Truman Administration suddenly announced the termination of Lend-Lease, threatening the trading position of Britain and many nations in the sterling bloc. The move was strongly condemned by the British and Australian governments. Furthermore, the Americans refused any bilateral trade agreement with the Australians, which Evatt had hoped for in January 1945, and went on to offer instead a bilateral air transport agreement in an attempt to break up the Commonwealth bloc and to force the question on the bases.

They were to be disappointed. The Commonwealth position on aviation was reaffirmed at the Prime Ministers' Conference in 1946—resulting in the public debate over Manus—and empire preferences emerged unscathed. Evatt defended Australia's position by reminding the Americans that the 'sterling bloc is a perfectly normal association in which, as a practical convenience, Australia would deal with foreign countries'. The Ottawa system was in any event, he went on, the reaction of the empire to the United States Smoot–Hawley tariff of 1930. In this connection, he said,

If we are to find expanding markets for our farm products, and a reasonable share for them for our new industries, we can expect to buy more from others. If not, we must buttress our defences and build as we can at home.[6]

Evatt had the latter in mind. The Chifley government up to 1949 followed a policy described aptly by one historian as 'protecting the sterling area'.[7] Evatt himself came to regard the Commonwealth as a 'Third Force' between the United States and the Soviet Union. That policy was, as we have seen, largely a reaction to American attempts after 1947 to build Japan as a regional bastion against Communism, but it was also of immense significance economically.

In Europe the Marshall Plan proposed to treat Britain as a European power rather than as the leader of the Commonwealth. For Evatt the Commonwealth fulfilled two essential needs. At the strategic level it promised to secure trading and diplomatic benefits, as well as access to military planning and technology. At the regional level it provided a defence scheme that augmented, and indeed came to replace, that which had been foreshadowed at the Canberra Conference in 1944. As he explained in a BBC broadcast on 10 May 1946

*we are reaching a stage in British Commonwealth relations at which there is a division of functions on a **regional** basis for certain purposes. It has become possible for a Dominion to act not only for itself but also for the United Kingdom and other Dominions as well. Another recent development suggests the integration of British Commonwealth activities concerned with specific functions. Three examples of this functional integration are to be found in British Commonwealth agreements concerning first, tele-communications, second, civil aviation, and third, the disposal of wool surpluses.*[8]

The view that the Commonwealth could emerge as one of the Big Three has been attributed to Curtin, with his appeals at the 1944 Prime Ministers' Conference for a more united policy in a 'Fourth Empire'. Evatt anticipated this position well beforehand when he spoke of the necessity for improving the machinery for Commonwealth co-operation on 14 October 1943. Events thereafter emphasised the advantages of the Commonwealth to Australia in the region. The Australia–New Zealand Agreement added force because of its appeal to the importance of the empire in regional defence and air power in 1944. The following year it was as a representative of the Commonwealth that Evatt secured Australian representation in the control machinery to supervise the peace settlement in Japan.

The major revelation as to the benefits of the Commonwealth, however, came after the dropping of the atomic bomb. Chifley regarded it as being of 'considerable importance' to ensure Australian participation in the development of atomic power, and he agreed in 1944 to the Australians conducting a secret search for uranium in the Mount Painter area in South Australia for the British. But he had greater ambitions. He wanted the industry developed in Australia and in consequence he wanted to sound out Mark Oliphant. Oliphant was one of the Commonwealth's leading nuclear physicists and had worked in the Manhattan Project to develop the bomb. It fell to Evatt, during his visit to London to address the Council of Foreign Ministers, to contact Oliphant to explore the possibilities and to entice him to return to Australia to take charge of the new field.

Evatt met Oliphant in September 1945, and learned of Britain's post-war plans to develop atomic energy for military and industrial purposes. He was also told of the existence of the so-called Gen 75 Committee which had been set up under the chairmanship of Sir John Anderson in August 1945. The Committee was to make recommendations on broad policy concerning atomic energy. The problem, as Oliphant informed Evatt, was that the United Kingdom was bound by agreement with the United States and Canada not to release information to the dominions. Beyond that, Evatt was advised that the United States was anxious that any large-scale production should be confined to the North American continent.

Evatt saw immediately the possibilities for Australia. He advised an eager Chifley that the Commonwealth itself should develop atomic energy, arguing that

It would be difficult, for technical reasons, to carry out the whole of the development and production programme in the United Kingdom, but with the co-operation of the Dominions the project could be carried out on an adequate scale within the Empire.

He emphasised the importance of atomic energy to Australia because of its military and industrial possibilities, especially in view of the shortage of coal and oil supplies. If Australia were to participate in the development of atomic energy, as Canada was then doing, he insisted that the British would have to release technical information so that the Australian government could develop its own atomic project. He did not then indicate that Australia would host the primary research and development—that would be done, in the light of Oliphant's advice, in Britain. In the short term, however, Australia could send skilled scientists to help.[9]

The month after this cable was sent, Britain agreed to the establishment at Woomera of a site to test missiles, a scheme that promised to transfer to Australia much valuable research and development. Evatt again grasped the implications of this for Australia. He wrote to Chifley on 13 November that the British Isles were vulnerable to rocket-delivered atomic weapons and that 'British policy would have to take this into account'. For the future he dismissed American attempts at atomic monopoly, arguing that 'it would be extraordinarily difficult to suppress research into atomic energy'. Such research, he concluded, had 'a constructive side' since atomic energy 'might gradually free mankind from industrial occupations which are now extremely burdensome'.[10]

The first step for Evatt was to gain Australian representation on the Gen 75 Committee, but in proposing this he revealed the inconsistency in Britain's position. Co-operation with the United States was essential, yet this very co-operation restricted the extent to which the 1946 Commonwealth defence policy could be realised. Evatt's embracing of the latter reflected the extent to which the Australian Government realised that only through the Commonwealth connection was it likely to realise gains in atomic power, rocketry and air power.

Evatt was buoyed by his trip to Britain. He explained enthusiastically in the House of Representatives on 13 March 1946 that Commonwealth 'co-operation has reached the highest peak in history'.[11] This was confirmed at the Prime Ministers' Conference in May when the Australian delegation raised the question of Australia's role in any future system of Commonwealth defence. As Oliphant had forecast, Britain was far from conceding that she was not a world power. Rather, the lesson of the war was that a greater degree of imperial unity was necessary if the British Commonwealth was to be a major power. Commonwealth planning would involve, as we have seen, an adequate chain of air bases, but it would also involve the development of resources 'in different parts of the Empire for the manufacture of munitions'. Australia would be in a position of regional leadership since, as the Conference was told, 'Economy of force requires that the initial responsibility for securing Empire interests should be borne, so far as is practicable, by the nation nearest to, or most immediately affected by any particular area'.[12]

Evatt drew the implications of this for the development of atomic power. He summed the position up at the 1946 Prime Ministers' Conference by emphasising that American supremacy in atomic armament and the industrial application of nuclear energy would

accentuate the disparity between the industrial power of the United States and other nations with smaller natural resources, such as Australia, in spite of the fact that the fundamental discoveries of atomic energy were made in Europe.[13]

The policy received bipartisan support thereafter. Evatt's concerns were shared by Menzies who asked in the House of Representatives on 8 November 1946 how it was that the United States came to have a monopoly of weapons when three countries produced the bomb in the first place. Evatt revealed his hand and stated optimistically that the Americans 'will have that monopoly for only a limited period, of course, because scientists of other countries will be busy on atomic research'.[14]

Evatt's early recommendations, following the thinking of Oliphant, reflected the general policies designed to position Australia so as to allow participation in the new field. Separate missions sent from Britain to Australia advanced planning on joint aircraft production; munitions development; and the formation of a joint intelligence bureau. In June 1946 Australia participated in the Commonwealth Defence Science Conference and fellowships were offered to Australian scientists to study at the Harwell reactor in Britain. The Bureau of Mineral Resources was established in 1946 to co-ordinate the search for uranium and the Australian National University was established, with central billing going to the School of Nuclear Physics under Oliphant.[15]

Evatt was in a excellent position to assist the work of Oliphant at the ANU. Oliphant had made it clear that his needs would be enormous. He had convinced Evatt and Chifley that the impact of the atomic bomb would be profound and that his School of Nuclear Physics would cost £500 000—out of just over £800 000 allocated for the whole of the ANU. Oliphant also needed special steel for the construction of a cyclotron, the accelerator or 'atom smasher' that led to speculation that it would be used for the construction of the atomic bomb. Cabinet, sitting 'ga ga' as his biographers recall during Oliphant's unprecedented presentation of his proposals, readily granted him the money; BHP was pressed to make special arrangements for the steel; and Evatt directed the Australian scientific missions to secure—through reparations negotiations—cyclotrons in Japan, where he knew that there were at least three, and Germany. Oliphant for his part kept Evatt well briefed. In debates later on the UN Atomic Energy Commission he gave Evatt detailed calculations on bomb yields, leading 'horrified' US officials to accuse him of 'revealing secret information without authority'![16]

It was in 1947, however, that Evatt's hopes of developing the nuclear industry in co-operation with the British seemed realisable. He was still attempting to secure United Nations control of atomic energy, but as he announced in the Parliament on 6 March 1947, Australia aimed to strengthen British Commonwealth security arrangements. The Commonwealth remained the cornerstone in the absence of a system of collective security. The extent that this was so was indicated when Evatt associated himself with Menzies' remarks regarding the 'more complete integration of the British Empire'.[17]

What lay behind these remarks was the breakdown in co-operation between the Americans and the British in the development of the bomb. The Americans had passed the McMahon Act following the disclosure by the Soviet defector Gouzenko of high-level infiltration of the British atomic program. There is every reason to suppose, as Evatt did, that their action was based on opposition to the construction of atomic piles outside North America. The Act forbade the exchange of information with other nations with respect to the use of atomic energy for industrial purposes and constituted a step in United States attempts to dominate the West's armament production.[18]

The British government reacted in a fashion that was to have enormous implications for Australia. Firstly it decided to develop its own bomb. Secondly it decided to have some atomic plants built outside Britain so as to avoid strategic vulnerability. Canada was ruled out because it sided with the United States in disagreements and, being a dollar country, especially in the midst of the sterling crisis in 1947, would be a serious drain on reserves.

By November 1947, in view of the inability of the British to build water-cooled reactors and in keeping with the strategical dispersion of defence resources throughout the Commonwealth, the Australians decided to proceed with the construction of an atomic pile. The pile was to be an integral part of the British programme and was seen to be the basis of a future nuclear industry which would provide power as well as plutonium for the manufacture of atomic bombs. It was to be accorded the maximum degree of security.[19]

There were other compelling reasons for security. The Anglo-Australian Joint Project was at last concluded on 1 April 1947, formally giving the go ahead for the Woomera Rocket Range. The programme was assuming major proportions by the end of 1947 with some sixty-nine of Australia's best physicists, engineers and mathematicians ear-marked for training in Britain. The range itself was then absorbing £6 million a year—by 1952 it chewed up over £50 million and the joint project constituted nearly ninety per cent of the entire Defence research and development budget.[20]

Clearly the dream of a nuclear Australia was not Evatt's alone, but he was very much to the fore in the early attempts to lay the foundation of the industry. What is not clear is the extent that Evatt's involvement was driven by a desire to allow Australia to have access to nuclear weapons. Burton recalls that Evatt was heavily involved in defence matters and it seems likely that this extended to the question of the atomic bomb.[21] Of interest here is the relationship between Evatt and Colonel Alfred Conlon, the Director of Research and Civil Affairs. Conlon kept closely abreast of post-hostilities planning in Britain and Australia—so much so that Evatt warned him 'to keep out of foreign affairs or he'd break his wrist'. Nevertheless Conlon shared Evatt's views on defence and foreign affairs. He agreed, for example, with Evatt's use of the Commonwealth to secure Australian representation internationally and on the acquisition of islands to the north. Like Evatt, Conlon played a role in moving Oliphant to the ANU. The establishment of universities was essential to the nuclear programme in Britain and the research had obvious military significance. Sir Mark Oliphant recalls that Conlon 'was very much to the fore' in establishing the ANU and got on very well with him personally. Despite this, as Sir Mark now recalls, 'his name has been virtually expunged from the record'. Given the enormous resources devoted to the School of Nuclear Physics, the interest of the military in the ANU was understandable.[22]

Evatt's role in initiating the Approved Defence Projects Protection Act in 1947 also suggests that he was heavily involved in attempts to get Australia into the atomic club. Historians such as Crisp have argued that Evatt's concern in drafting the legislation was the Communist threat to Woomera. The British ballistic missiles to be tested at Woomera were naturally designed to carry nuclear warheads. Evatt himself published a pamphlet in 1947 titled *Hands off the Nation's Defences* in which he put the case for Australian participation in the development of weapons of mass destruction:

The Government recognizes that some people are genuinely concerned that Australia, in agreement with Britain, should be building a range for testing and guiding powerful weapons of mass destruction. But the present position in relation to international proposals for abandoning the use of weapons of mass destruction is by no means satisfactory... [Australia] has declared its willingness to abandon all weapons of mass destruction once an international system is established whereby the preparation and use of those weapons can be prevented anywhere and everywhere in the world.

In beefing up Australian security Evatt also wanted to demonstrate the suitability of Australia as a site for an atomic pile.[23] Tennant was on the mark over twenty years ago when she wrote that Evatt in 1947

was evolving a scheme whereby atomic power would be developed in the central deserts of Australia at Woomera...Evatt was a hard man to unwind from a cherished opinion. He persisted that so far Australia had not found oil. Atomic power could transform the country; Britain was ready to join the venture.[24]

The development of atomic energy involved, as Evatt had known from the first, the highest security. This legislative basis therefore was the Defence Projects Protection Act, which imposed penalties of up to twelve months gaol or a £5000 fine or both for hindering 'by speech or writing' the carrying out of any approved defence project. In similar vein the reaction of the Chifley government to anything that smacked of a threat to power supplies in 1949 may be read against this policy.

The attempt to demonstrate the reliability of Australian security, however, did not work. In July the following year the Americans, either to block Australian nuclear ambitions or from genuine fears as to the security position in Australia, formally advised the Australian Military Mission in Washington that Australia would receive no more classified information from the United States.[25] This move not only placed further restrictions on the British in their sharing of information with the Australians, but meant that the recently established system of training Australian personnel in British defence establishments was in jeopardy. Central in the American assessment of the problem in Australia was Evatt himself. He was 'suspicious of [American] intentions' but pointedly the Americans concluded that 'the degree of our support from Australia frequently will be influenced by the intimacy of our relations with the United Kingdom'.[26]

With the failure of the United Nations to secure control over atomic weapons, and concerns over the directions of many American policies, the appeal of the Commonwealth remained for the Australians. Britain at least offered some access to advanced technology and remained the focus of Australian trade. That had been evident to Evatt as early as the 1944 Anzac Agreement, and subsequent events seemed to confirm that position. By 1948 Evatt held grave fears concerning American resistance to the Anglo-Australian Joint Project at Woomera, upon which Australian defence strategy rested. Furthermore the Americans then looked to the development of Japan as a so-called bastion against Communism. Both policies, to the United States, pointed to Britain's role in Europe. Evatt's answer was to embrace the view that the Commonwealth could act as a 'Third Force' between the United States and the Soviet Union. He announced in Parliament on 8 April

> *My view is that if one speaks of 'powers', the British Commonwealth can be the third group of powers. Its contribution to victory was of the same order as that of the Soviet Union and the United States of America.*[27]

In June Evatt repeated Curtin's wartime call for the establishment of a Commonwealth Secretariat, while in July he defended the right of South Africa, despite the election there of the Malan government which was committed to apartheid, to remain in the Commonwealth.

Significantly, he argued that the exclusion of South Africa was 'inimical to the security of the Commonwealth', a factor of some importance given its stocks of uranium and its strategic location in Commonwealth communications. In this connection Evatt laid heavy emphasis on the 'functional activities' of the Commonwealth. He instanced the importance of joint defence machinery, aviation, supply, telecommunications among other things and in a pointed reference to Canada, stressed that Australia has 'been able to co-operate more closely and frequently with Britain than other dominions'.[28]

Evatt's appeals to the Commonwealth as a 'Third Force' were also the basis in 1948 for a number of international initiatives. He went to some lengths to bring India into a system of Commonwealth defence, even though the Indian government had withdrawn its contingent from the Commonwealth Occupation Force in Japan. He also tried to persuade the Indians, unsuccessfully, to hold ministerial meetings at least twice a year.[29]

The same concern with preserving the membership of the Commonwealth was evident in Evatt's reaction to British attempts to treat Ireland as a 'foreign country'. In September 1948 Evatt learned of Ireland's intention to repeal the External Relations Act. Since 1936 this Act had provided for Ireland's 'external association' with the Commonwealth. It was a weak bond but when Evatt heard of the impending action by Britain he became 'extremely indignant'. The fact that he had no previous involvement in Irish affairs and would gain no electoral advantage suggests that he was concerned about the implications of Ireland's move towards total divorce from the Commonwealth. Evatt's idea of Commonwealth could accommodate Indian republicanism, and again in the case of Ireland, as John O'Brien concludes, he 'was less concerned with structures than with the essentials of the Commonwealth'. When the British reacted to the Irish initiative by declaring the citizens of Eire to be 'ordinary aliens', Evatt responded with a unique if clumsy compromise. Commonwealth citizens, he argued, should be entitled to the rights and privileges of citizens of Ireland. 'It was a fact that an Australian would never think of himself as a foreigner in Eire any more than an Irishman would think of himself as a foreigner in Australia'. As a result he succeeded in getting the British to accept a formula which allowed for reciprocal citizenship between the British Commonwealth and the Irish Republic. Quite apart from the constitutional question Evatt was concerned about the possibility that Britain would take retaliatory economic action against Ireland. He threatened to dissociate Australia from any action against Ireland and argued for the continuation of current trade arrangements.[30] The Irish decision to proceed, however, had the consequences that Evatt feared. The

Republic was not represented formally at future Commonwealth Prime Ministers' Conferences or meetings to deal with the stability of the sterling area.[31]

Significantly, Evatt's intervention in the Irish affair came while he was attending the Prime Ministers' Conference in October 1948, where he made a solid attempt to strengthen the sterling area. With an international trade agreement as far away as ever, Australia's economic future in 1948 was bound up in the fortunes of the sterling area. At the conference Evatt reported that Australia had done all that it could to support sterling. He noted that Australia had restricted dollar imports from $263 million in 1947–48 to only $190 million in the current year. This gave grounds for optimistism about the economic future of the Commonwealth. On the other hand he questioned the prospects of a multilateral system in the near future. The 'United Kingdom', he pleaded, 'had little to fear from a policy of buying boldly from the sterling area'. This was because

The Australian Government had always looked upon the United Kingdom as their most important market...Within the sterling area the United Kingdom's income from exports was determined by the amount of her purchases, and she could afford to buy to the limit of the capacity of the sterling area countries to supply. If, for instance, Australia's income were increased by greater exports to the United Kingdom, Australia's power to purchase abroad was so much the greater; and, as Australia bought most of her requirements from the United Kingdom, the trade of both countries would then balance at a higher level...Such a policy would only be dangerous if Australia bought largely from dollar countries, but this could be checked by her strict control over dollar imports.

To secure the sterling area, and the interests of the Commonwealth as a whole, Evatt argued throughout the conference that 'machinery' should be devised to avoid the wartime practice of not consulting the dominions. In short, he was advocating that the Commonwealth become what he described in the following year as a 'self-sufficiency group'.[32]

As Lee has shown, the continuing dollar shortage experienced by the sterling bloc forced Britain itself to consider the possibility of abandoning multilateralism in mid-1949. The extreme position was to divide the Western world into two currency blocs: a sterling bloc and a dollar bloc. The Attlee Cabinet rejected this option as inconsistent with Britain's strategic need for close relations with the United States and Canada. Some 'constructive compromise' would have to be sought.

Evatt, on the other hand, had no doubts. The plight of the sterling bloc, as he argued in June 1949 at a preparatory meeting for the

Commonwealth Finance Ministers' Conference called to debate the dollar crisis, was largely the fault of American policy. They had imposed restrictions on the sale of strategic materials to the Eastern bloc and had taken measures to build up Japan and Germany in competition with Britain. Evatt wanted to free up East–West trade and to threaten the Americans with 'a non-dollar autarky'.[33]

———❖———

At the 1948 Commonwealth Conference Evatt readily accepted the views of the British chiefs that the ultimate security of Australia was attainable only in the context of an overall plan of Commonwealth defence. That was obvious in the case of air power and the development of modern weapons, but it had profound implications for Australian defence planning in the Pacific region.

Since 1944 Evatt had anticipated a regional scheme of Commonwealth defence but he could get no indication of specific British planning. He summarised his position in November that year, arguing that

Australia was always on the horns of a dilemma: they were bound to the Empire by ties of blood, and by economic ties, but that more and more they were coming to the realisation that their political future as a people was cast in the Pacific. London...was mostly concerned with India,... Canada was preoccupied with its relations with the United States... Australia felt very much alone.[34]

The problem was that Evatt could not get recognition for Australian defence interests in the region without the Commonwealth link. This was made dramatically clear by his attempts to intervene in Indonesian affairs after the demise of SEAC. Whatever Australia's role on the GOC Evatt had no basis for his 'arc of islands', including Timor and Dutch New Guinea. In 1947 that area indeed threatened, due to American planning to contain Communism in Asia, to be integrated with a reindustrialised Japan. Evatt, therefore, looked to the Commonwealth in the region to act as he hoped it would act generally—to strengthen Australia's hand against the Americans.

At an international level this took the form of appeals in Commonwealth forums for a general treaty in the Pacific which would deal also with the Japanese settlement. His use of the 1948 Prime Ministers' Conference was typical when he said that

Japan must not be allowed to establish a dangerous war potential. The United States were inclined to proceed on the assumption that they could alone determine the future of Japan. This was an assumption the Commonwealth nations could not accept.[35]

Evatt also wanted urgent British Commonwealth defence planning in the region. At the 1948 conference he was emphatic that joint planning could commence immediately between Australian and British Services, despite the hesitations of the Australian Joint Services Staff in London.[36] Such planning, which formed the basis of the British Commonwealth's ANZAM regional defence scheme in 1949, operated on the assumption that Australia would secure the lines of communication to Malaya. In time of war that meant of course the occupation of the 'arc of islands' as fundamental to such planning.

There was another compelling reason for Evatt's assertion of the importance of Commonwealth regional planning by 1948. India had gained independence the previous year. Evatt was certainly aware of the importance of India in the defence of the Commonwealth. British Defence planners had briefed the 1946 Prime Ministers' Conference, which Evatt attended, and concluded that it was of 'the utmost importance to retain India as a main support area'.

In hindsight it would be easy to see the loss of India as critical to the British defence position East of Suez, yet the implications of India's independence in 1947 on Britain's position in the Far East, as Coral Bell concludes, were ignored by British planners for another twenty years. Certainly Evatt sought to plug India into Commonwealth defence planning. He also helped to steer republican India into the Commonwealth and to gain the valuable friendship of Nehru by plying his legal skills on India's constitutional problems.[37]

India provided a cornerstone of any future regional scheme within the Commonwealth and Nehru's policies had the potential to be of great benefit. At the 1948 conference Evatt 'strongly supported Nehru' in emphasising the need for economic improvement within the area. Foreshadowing the later Colombo Plan he regarded 'positive action' by the Commonwealth as the best defence against Communism in the region. Here was an alternative thesis to American containment policy. Nor should Asia become a Japanese quarry:

Dr. Evatt expressed agreement with Pandit Nehru's statement of the need for industrial development in India and the other less developed countries of the Commonwealth. This was a matter in which Australia desired to assist. In particular she recognised the need for capital goods in South Africa, India, Pakistan, South-East Asia and Ceylon.[38]

He kept in step with the Indians over the question of Indonesian independence and in 1949, following the outbreak of revolt in Burma and the threat of that country to leave the Commonwealth, spoke of 'India and Australia taking a lead in restoring peace in Southeast Asia'. His aim, as he explained in a cable to the Australian embassy in Washington on 18 May 1949, was to develop a regional pact within the Commonwealth and 'thereafter' with the United States and other nations with possessions in the area.[39]

That led Evatt to accept Britain's general regional priorities in the Malayan Emergency which broke out in 1948. Defence planners in Australia had already resolved the vexed question of how to anchor Australia's defences to the north-west by looking once again to the base at Singapore. Manus Island, as Evatt repeated in Parliament, was the 'Scapa Flow of the Pacific',[40] and as such covered the north-eastern approaches. But there was no comparable position, in the absence of bases in Timor and Dutch New Guinea, off the north-west coast. Nor was there as yet a comprehensive plan for Commonwealth defence in the region. There was, however, a recognition that the retention of Singapore as a base 'was essential for the continuance of British influence in South East Asia'.[41]

The Communist threat to Malaya thus portended disaster for Australia and the Commonwealth. With its valuable tin and rubber, it was the second largest earner of dollars in the sterling area. Further, as Evatt feared in 1947, it was also a potential market for a resurgent Japan. Finally it was also an anchor for a future system of Commonwealth defence in the region.

Evatt's concern to preserve British rule was heightened by his fear of Chinese expansion and he thus became an early convert to the cause of suppressing the Communist insurrection in Malaya. He learned of the British assessment that the insurrection was Chinese and Communist when he stopped at Singapore en route to Europe on 23 July 1948. Evatt accepted that the insurrection 'was a minority attempt to sabotage, not only the present British rule here, but the true independence movement, which is of course Malay'. He also felt that Australia should agree to sending arms to the colony, notwithstanding threatened action by the Seamen's Union to implement bans.[42]

Evatt reacted in a similar fashion in June the following year when the British position in Hong Kong was threatened by the new Communist Chinese state. Britain was willing to recognise the regime and to continue commercial relations, but it was also prepared to reinforce the garrison in order to avoid damage to British prestige in the Far East. Evatt was in Britain on a visit when this crisis occurred. When the British approached him to enlist his help he agreed readily that Hong Kong should be defended and even anticipated that Australia would send air and naval reinforcements. He also gave an undertaking that following his return to Australia he would personally explain the British view in Cabinet.

Evatt added the acceptance by the Peoples' Republic of China of the territorial integrity of Hong Kong as a condition for Australia's recognition of the Communist Chinese government in October, a position often assumed to have been adopted solely because of the potential of domestic electoral backlash.[43]

This was yet another instance of Evatt adopting the same diplomatic posture towards the Chinese as that followed by the British. Like Britain, he rejected the notion that the Soviet Union dictated policy to Peking and warned against action by the West that would lead to the severing of contacts with China. Significantly he called for commercial contacts to be maintained with the Chinese through Hong Kong.[44]

In 1949 Evatt accepted that Australia was a small power whose fate was tied to the Commonwealth. While he was hardly passive in accepting this he did not question the fundamentals of that relationship. The British market helped to pay the bills. In the event of global war he recognised the need to co-ordinate with the Commonwealth. Equally he supported the Commonwealth in its defence of regional interests. Whereas the Americans presented hostile policies, or at best indifferent ones, the British connection seemed to be comprehensive. Past loyalties had been given a new impetus by the advent of atomic energy and air power. Planning in the context of the Commonwealth promised very real benefits in the future—if only the opposition of the Americans could be overcome or the British could be enticed to rely more on the Commonwealth itself. The Commonwealth also offered a means of maintaining dialogue with the new nation states of the region—especially the key ally of the past, India. In the process Evatt viewed the region in a fundamentally different way from that of the Americans. Containing Communism and restoring Japan in the process ignored the possibilities of a more 'positive approach' to regional security. Regional peace must rest on comprehensive plans. Past association with the Commonwealth offered the best safeguards if this could not be achieved, but Evatt also looked to the future. In the event that a new system of collective security through the United Nations might meet the objectives of Australian policies, then Evatt seemed to be well suited to the task of attempting to mould the organisation to that end.

NOTES

1. Roger Bell, *Unequal Allies: Australian–American Relations and the Pacific War*, MUP, 1977, ch. 5. Despite the Pacific War, the Roosevelt administration in 1942 was suspicious of Australia's use of Lend-Lease Aid. Australia as a base 'vital to the defence of the United States', was eligible for military assistance, but not, according to the Americans, for goods that would be used for competitive economic purposes. A similar suspicion lay behind the master agreement of Lend-Lease which was signed in February 1942 by the British. Article VII of that agreement was designed to eliminate 'all forms of discriminatory treatment in international commerce', including the Ottawa

preferences of the British empire. With two-thirds of Australian commerce with the empire, Australia was heavily influenced by this clause.

2 *DAFP 6*, pp. 384–5, Cable 117, Evatt to External Affairs, 26 May 1943; *CPD*, vol. 177, p. 577 and vol. 180, p. 2118. 'Bretton Woods', *Economic Record*, 20, December 1944, pp. 149–50.

3 DAFP, pp. 202–4; R.N. Gardner, Sterling–Dollar Diplomacy in Current Perspective: The Origins and Prospects of our International Economic Order, Columbia University Press, New York, 1980, chs. 5–8; Bell, Unequal Allies, pp. 111–12. It was a central part of Evatt's missions abroad to press the case of full employment. See, for example, AA: A989, Item 44/735/150, Part 2; Evatt Collection, Flinders University, '1943 Mission'.

4 The objective of the Australian Air Board was complete independence from overseas supply in the construction of heavy bombers. The British Ministry of Aircraft Production promised every assistance in creating the capacity to produce Lancaster bombers. The bombers would also be converted and used as the first civilian carriers. Butlin and Schedvin, *War Economy 1942–45*, pp. 410–19.

5 AA: A5954/1, Item 606/2, 'Postwar Trade', 1943. The file contains British cables to Australia outlining fears that the Americans were deliberately trying to force them out of Latin American markets. Roosevelt's views on the aviation links to Latin America are in A989, Item 735/838, 'Transport—Civil Aviation—Pacific Island Bases'. Commonwealth countries, with the exception of Canada, provided a united front against the Americans in conferences with the Americans on civil aviation from 1943 to 1947. In October 1943 a Cabinet committee chaired by Lord Beaverbrook recommended that in the post-war period there should be an all-British air route connecting Britain and the dominions. The dominions were to service their sections of the route. In 1945 BOAC and Qantas began services on the 'Kangaroo route'. J. Stroud, *Annals of British and Commonwealth Air Transport, 1919–1960*, Putnam, London, 1962.

6 H.V. Evatt, *Australia in World Affairs*, Angus & Robertson, Sydney, 1946, p. 91.

7 D. Lee, 'Protecting the Sterling Area: The Chifley Government's Response to Multilateralism 1945–9', *Australian Journal of Political Science*, vol. 25, no. 2, 1990.

8 Evatt, *Australia in World Affairs*, p. 189. Original emphasis.

9 Evatt Collection, Flinders University, Cable EC 29, Evatt to Chifley, 26 September 1945; M. Gowing, *Independence and Deterrence: Britain and Atomic Energy 1945–1952*, vol. 1, Macmillan, London, 1974, pp. 24, 147; A. Cawte, *Atomic Australia 1944–1990*, University of New South Wales Press, 1992, p. 10. The Defence Committee gave Evatt a briefing paper in February 1946 that embraced these views and laid down the principle that was to dominate official thinking for the next fifteen years: 'Superior scientific development can, if secrecy be preserved, redress the balance between a weak nation and a strong one and this is of profound significance to Australia'. AA: A5954/1, Item 1662/4, 'Appreciation of the Strategic Position of Australia', February 1946.

10 Evatt Collection, Flinders University, Cable 1022, Evatt to Chifley, 13 November 1945.

11 H.V. Evatt, *Australia in World Affairs*, pp. 181, 123.

12 AA: A5954/1, Item 1662/4; A5799/1, Item 46/1 'Cooperation in Empire Defence'.
13 AA: A2700, vol. 28, Agendum Number 1197, 'Atomic Energy', 5 June 1946.
14 *Current Notes*, 17, 11, November 1946, p. 712.
15 AA: A5954/1, Item 1662/1, 'British Commonwealth Conference, 1946—Defence and Security'; P. Morton, *Fire Across the Desert: Woomera and the Anglo–Australian Joint Project 1946–1980*, AGPS, Canberra, pp. 11–29; Cawte, *Atomic Australia*, pp. 13–14.
16 S. Cockburn, and D. Ellyard, *Oliphant: The Life and Times of Sir Mark Oliphant*, Axiom Books, 1981, pp. 144–51, 194.
17 *Current Notes*, vol. 18, no. 3, March 1947, p. 185.
18 F. Cain, 'An Aspect of Post-War Australian Relations with the United Kingdom and the United States: Missiles, Spies and Disharmony', *Historical Studies*, vol. 23, no. 92, April 1989, p. 202.
19 AA: A5954/1, Item 1385/3, 'Proposed Construction of an Atomic Pile in Australia'; Gowing, *Independence and Deterrence*, chs 5–6.
20 P. Morton, *Fire Across the Desert: Woomera and the Anglo–Australian Joint Project, 1946–1980*, AGPS, Canberra, 1989, pp. 37–8; AA: A4926, vol. 5, Agendum Number 111, 'United Kingdom—Australia Joint Project', Howard Beale, 12 April 1956.
21 Interview with John Burton recorded by Tom Sheridan. Copy held by the Evatt Foundation.
22 D. Horner, *High Command: Australia and Allied Strategy 1939–1945*, Allen & Unwin, Sydney, 1982, pp. 322, 397, 420. Interview with Oliphant, 20 January 1991.
23 L.F. Crisp, *Ben Chifley: A Political Biography*, Angus & Robertson, Sydney, 1961, p. 359.
24 K. Tennant, *Evatt: Politics and Justice*, Angus & Robertson, Sydney, 1970, p. 201.
25 F. Cain, 'Missiles and Mistrust: US Intelligence Responses to British and Australian Missile Research', *Intelligence and National Security*, vol. 3, no. 4, October 1988.
26 *FRUS*, vol. 6, 1948, 'The Far East and Australasia', p. 8. In 1949 the Secretary of Defence, Shedden, noted that Australian co-operation with Britain in the development of atomic energy rankled with the Americans. One of the reasons that the British did not locate their pile in Canada was the fact that all the uranium supplies were taken by the Americans. AA: A5954/1, Item 1687/15, 'Some General Impressions From a Visit Abroad, 1949'.
27 *Current Notes*, vol. 19, no. 5, May 1948, p. 263.
28 Ibid., no. 8, August 1948, p. 544; PRO: FO 371/70202 A, unnumbered cable, E.J. Williams to Sir Eric Machtig, 15 April 1948.
29 AA: A816/32, Item 14/301/348, 'Planning for Cooperation in British Commonwealth Defence, 2/1948'; A816/30, Item 14/301/351, 'Prime Ministers' Conference, London, October 1948'.
30 J. O'Brien, 'Ireland's Departure From the British Commonwealth', *The Round Table*, vol. 306, 1988, pp. 179–94; N. Quirke, 'Dr. H.V. Evatt's Role

in Ireland's Declaration of a Republic and Break from the British Crown and Commonwealth 1948–49', Evatt Foundation Essay, 1988, p. 1.
31 N. Mansergh, *Survey of British Commonwealth Affairs: Problems of Wartime Cooperation and Post-War Change, 1939–1952*, OUP, London, 1958, p. 298.
32 AA: A816/1, Item 11/302/13, 'PMM (48)', Meetings 2–13. Lee, 'Protecting the Sterling Area', p. 190.
33 Not surprisingly the CIA in 1949 assessed the Chifley government as 'suspicious of what it regards as American economic imperialism'. A key factor in Australia's refusal to accept dollar loans or to sign a bilateral trade treaty at this juncture was attributed to the acceptance of imperial preferences and 'a sympathetic bond with the Labor Government in the United Kingdom'. USNA RG 59, Lot Files 54D224, Box 3: 'Australian Economy—General'.
34 R. Kay, *Documents on New Zealand External Relations: Vol.1. The Australia–New Zealand Agreement 1944*, Government Printer, Wellington 1972, p. 280.
35 AA: A816/1, Item 11/302/13, PMM (48): Meeting of Prime Ministers 1948, 3rd meeting, 12 October 1948.
36 AA: A816/52, Item 14/301/353,'Strategic Planning in Relation to Co-operation in British Commonwealth Defence'; A816/30, Item 14/301/351, 'Prime Ministers Conference, London, October 1948'.
37 C. Bell, *Dependent Ally: A Study in Australian Foreign Policy*, OUP, Oxford, 1988, ch. 5. AA: A2700, vol. 28, Agendum Number 11, 2 July 1946. Tennant, Evatt, p. 239. Evatt's policies regarding India were scripted by the Australian Defence Committee. See A5954/1, Item 1662/4, 'Appreciation of the Strategical Position of Australia, February 1946'.
38 AA A816/1, Item 11/302/13, PMM (48): Meeting of Prime Ministers, 1948, 5th Meeting, 13 October 1948. Nehru welcomed Evatt's stress on Commonwealth action, adding that 'though many Indians might envy the material prosperity of the United States, few would welcome the consequences of applying to India the principles of American capitalism'.
39 AA: A1838/1, Item 378/3/1.
40 'Scapa Flow' refers to the major fleet base in Scotland protecting Britain.
41 AA: A2031, Defence Committee Minute 279/1947, 'Strategic Importance of Singapore', 12 August 1947; A5799, Item 47/109; *Current Notes*, vol. 20, no.2, February 1949, p. 266. The *Age* on 7 July 1948 noted that Malaya was 'Britain's centre in this part of the world…If communism were to win in Malaya the iron curtain may reach down to Timor'. P. Edwards, *Crisis and Commitments: The Politics and Diplomacy of Australia's Involvement in Southeast Asian Conflicts 1948-1965*, Allen & Unwin, Sydney, 1992, p. 38.
42 Edwards, *Crisis and Commitments*, ch. 3.
43 C. Waters, 'Anglo-Australian Diplomacy 1945–1949: Labour Governments in Conflict', Ph.D thesis, ADFA, 1990, pp. 257–64. Evatt Collection, Flinders University, 'Australian Attitude Towards Recognition', 25 October 1949.
44 USNA 800 Series (Internal Affairs of States—Australia), Box 6166.

CHAPTER 23

THE UNITED NATIONS

The Honourable Member...said that I must speak as an Australian. I have never spoken in any other way. Australia's contribution to international affairs has been made, to a large extent, through the United Nations.
EVATT IN PARLIAMENTARY DEBATE, 1949

Evatt achieved international fame for his work on the United Nations. He was an unceasing defender of the organisation during his entire period in parliament and had been active in a vast number of its activities. He was indeed one of its architects.

The UN was established at the San Francisco Conference, which was held between 25 April and 26 June 1945. The conference was intended to ratify the draft plan of the future world organisation prepared by the Big Four at Dumbarton Oaks. The centrepiece of their proposals was the veto—unanimity of action by the Big Powers was felt to be essential by them in order to overcome the deficiencies of the old League. That view was too narrow for Evatt. He attacked the veto on behalf of the 'small powers' and mustered twenty votes from the fifty countries present, despite the solid opposition of the Big Powers. Failing to overcome it by direct assault he chipped away at it by broadening the scope of the organisation and strengthening the role of the General Assembly and the Economic and Social Council. In the process Evatt was careful to present Australia's credentials as a 'security power' which should be given a seat on the Security Council as a 'non-permanent' member.

Evatt also earned a reputation at San Francisco as an indefatigable worker, labouring around the clock and participating in some twenty committees. He submitted thirty-eight amendments, twenty of which were wholly or partly incorporated into the Charter. His stamp was put on the final clauses of the Charter dealing with Trusteeship, regional organisation, the economic and social objectives of the UN, Domestic Jurisdiction and on a number of procedural questions. Evatt had crashed on to the world scene and was hailed in the press as the conference 'hero'.[1]

Evatt's achievements there helped to cement his credentials as an international statesman thereafter. He carried the fight against the Big Powers to the Paris Peace Conference in 1946 and represented Australia on a number of UN subcommittees and on the Security Council. In 1948 he was rewarded with the Presidency of the General Assembly.

Evatt earned the reputation of being one who would not hesitate to use the UN to conciliate conflict between the rivals in the Cold War. To the consternation of the Americans and the British, he seemed not to take sides. Evatt wanted the UN in Iran, for example, to conduct a thorough investigation which would include the 'reasons behind the Soviet refusal to withdraw troops'. The issue was not, in Evatt's view, just a dispute between the Soviets and Iran, as Britain and the United States had seen it. Similarly, during the Berlin blockade, imposed by the Soviet Union after the Western Allies announced the economic integration of their occupation zones into the state of West Germany, Evatt appealed for reconciliation. In Korea he did not go along with the American attempt to sponsor elections only in their zone of occupation in the south of the country. On no occasion, he argued, had the UN been given evidence to suggest that the Korean dispute could not be resolved nationally. To Evatt it was a question of due process. If the facts had been collected and assessed, then 'The Council should govern its actions and decisions accordingly'. If it did not, then of course it was up to the Assembly.[2]

In these cases Evatt pointed out the wisdom of his position taken since the San Francisco Conference—that in the event that the Big Powers fell out and resorted to the use of the veto in the Security Council, the General Assembly must ensure that the issues could be openly investigated and debated. Providing that this procedure was not abused, Evatt assumed that the merits of each case could be assessed and the organisation could then take the appropriate action. More than that, as he argued in the Iran case, 'a party to a dispute must refrain from voting', a move that the lawyer hoped might short-circuit the veto.[3]

Evatt also outflanked the Big Powers in the UN by stressing that international peace was not simply secured by security measures, it also needed 'positive' measures. The initial wartime successes of Japan in Asia, and the reverses suffered by some colonial powers in war and then in the restoration of their regimes, dictated a need for change. Organisations such as the United Nation Relief and Rehabilitation Administration (UNRRA) and the Food and Agriculture Organisation (FAO), in Evatt's view, had to be adequately supported by the world community to tackle the root causes of war—social and economic insecurity.[4]

Evatt's activism spread to Australian diplomats involved in UN work—and they gained similar reputations, especially among the Americans. In Korea, Australian delegates on the United Nations Temporary Commission on Korea (UNTCOK) were seen by the State Department as 'difficult and uncooperative'; in Greece, Glasheen on the United Nations Special Committee on the Balkans (UNSCOB) was the 'enfant terrible' and Australian delegates were generally 'obstructionist'; in Indonesia, the Australian members of the Good Offices Committee (GOC) were proving 'embarrassing'; on the UN Atomic Energy Commission the 'various spokesmen for Australia, except Hasluck, have always been troublesome'; the head of External Affairs, John Burton, was—like the Australian representative in Japan, Macmahon Ball—said to be sympathetic to the Communists. And Evatt was 'the most frightful man in the world'.[5]

At home Evatt's activism in the UN earned him the enmity of the Opposition, which saw it as against the interests of Australia as a Western Ally. He was also seen as following contradictory policies, especially with respect to UN involvement in matters of 'Domestic Jurisdiction', an article in the UN Charter for which Evatt had been largely responsible. But the most damning charge was that he had ignored Australian national interests. The following exchange took place when Evatt reported to parliament on 21 June 1949 on his work in the General Assembly.

Evatt: *I claim this for the General Assembly of the United Nations, in respect of which I am mainly speaking tonight.*
Beale: *Why not speak as an Australian ?*
Mr. Deputy Speaker: *Order! The Honourable Member must remain silent.*
Evatt: *I would not care if the Honourable Member did not remain silent. He said that I must speak as an Australian. I have never spoken in any other way. Australia's contribution to international affairs has been made, to a large extent, through the United Nations.*[6]

Evatt's friend Hartley Grattan assessed him as 'an Australian nationalist'. In this sense Evatt strengthened Australian diplomatic machinery, improved the selection of staff through the cadetship system and extended extra-Commonwealth ties, especially in the region. His nationalism, however, also took account of the opportunities afforded by the Commonwealth and the UN. Evatt did not see any contradiction here. Nor was he naive—despite his active role on the UN he was aware of its limitations from the beginning. The Dumbarton Oaks draft for a future international organisation in 1945 had stated as principle what Evatt had discerned in the wartime conferences between Roosevelt, Stalin, Churchill and later Chiang Kai-shek—that the peace settlement and the UN machinery would be dominated by the Big Powers. Having failed to eliminate their veto at San Francisco he warned of acute 'pessimism' in world affairs and counselled against the 'risks of a big power peace'.[7]

Evatt saw much in the UN that would benefit Australia, but he did not allow it to conflict with national interests. He continued his emphasis on the need for the organisation to take measures to secure 'Full Employment', as he had stressed in other multilateral forums. He saw the FAO as valuable since Australia was a 'country with over 150 000 workers dependent on the export of agricultural products'. He was successful in having Australia host the first UNRRA conference, held at Lapstone in the Blue Mountains, and in pressing for the regionalisation of that body—a step designed to ensure that it did not adopt a 'Europe first' priority. It also provided an opportunity to demonstrate Australian regional leadership—Evatt was conscious of Chinese UNRRA ambitions at Lapstone.

His amendments in the UN on trusteeship gave adequate protection to Australian strategic interests in New Guinea. Yet the emphasis on reporting to a Trusteeship Council opened up opportunities for Australia to influence the colonial policies of those powers,like Portugal, France and the Netherlands, which held possessions of interest to Australia. This involved questions of colonial welfare, but he never lost sight of the ultimate possibilities concerning defence cooperation.[8]

Evatt's amendments concerning domestic jurisdiction were designed to protect Australia's control of its immigration and economic policies, including the right to apply them to its territories. He called for UN action on civil aviation, telecommunications and commodities trade, but he was hardly surprised that, as he told the General Assembly in September 1947, 'it was an extraordinary fact' that it had not yet made a 'review' of the current world economic situation.[9]

Evatt certainly gained a reputation as champion of the small powers in the UN but his claim was for Australian pre-eminence. Following the lead of Canada, he argued that Australia was entitled to representation on the Security Council as a 'Middle' or 'Security'

Power. In the Pacific region in particular, it was a 'Principal Power'—as Hull had called them—with major welfare and security responsibilities. A constant claim he made, overlooked by historians, was that Australia should also be entitled to participate in the peace settlement by virtue of its war record. The suggestion that Evatt was inconsistent over the question of domestic jurisdiction overlooks the fact that Evatt made a distinction between those nations that had fought the Axis and those that had not. The former had fought global Fascism and Evatt was determined that the UN and the peace settlements would rid the world of that evil.[10]

Evatt wanted to give the UN an active role in ensuring that former Fascist states were purged of this ideology before they could be admitted for membership. He summed up the general position the day after the dropping of the atom bomb on Hiroshima.

It is most undesirable that the United States Government take unilateral action. The procedure that we favour is for political agreement followed by military and other specific arrangements.[11]

His overriding consideration was Japan. He had insisted that it 'was part and parcel' of the Axis in 1941 and was determined that the peace settlement would ensure sweeping changes in its social and economic organisation. He had been opposed to the possibility that the settlement might not be made with respect to all the Axis powers and according to these principles. His justifiable fear was the development of 'piecemeal arrangements' by the Great Powers. The Cold War kept the settlement outside the UN and at the same time led to the very forces, in Evatt's view, that the UN should check.[12]

Evatt had called for extensive purges as early as September 1945, when he insisted that Italy should be governed by a 'genuinely democratic regime capable of eliminating Fascist remnants'. After that, as Dunk summed up the Australian policy, 'it should be a matter for the Italian people themselves as to whether they look to the West or to the East'.[13]

The following year the question of Spain was raised in the UN by Poland. When the British delegate, Cadogan, argued that action against Spain should be resisted because the policies of the Franco government were essentially matters of 'Domestic Jurisdiction', Hodgson, acting on Evatt's instructions, argued in the General Assembly that 'a fascist government could threaten international peace and security by virtue of its domestic policies and its relations with reactionary groups in other states'. When the UN committee returned a verdict that Spain 'might' in future constitute a threat to peace, Evatt insisted, against solid American and British opposition, that the Security Council should act 'speedily and effectively', and not tie the question up in the International Court for 'months and years'. In the upshot Britain recognised the Spanish government and the Americans sent Marshall Aid to the Franco regime, a move Evatt condemned as the 'worst blunder since the war'.[14]

Moves to 'contain Communism' in 1947 left the war on Fascism unfinished. Evatt was acutely conscious of the developing problem in Japan, but he also dismissed the 'so-called epurazione' or purge of Italian Fascists as 'wholly unsuccessful'. He appealed to the Assembly to 'act urgently' to effect a settlement in Germany where it was still the case that 'Nobody knows what production will in future be permitted or what trade and political structure will be permitted'. To ensure that the process was carried forward, Evatt introduced an amendment into the UN specifying that no new member could be admitted which had been at war with any of the United Nations since September 1939, unless recommended by the Security Council.[15]

South Africa had been admitted. When South Africa came under attack in the UN for seeking to annex South West Africa, its former mandate, and then for the treatment of the non-whites enshrined in the apartheid programme in 1948, Evatt sprang to its defence.

South Africa was one of the few nations that from the beginning stood firm against aggression. So let those who are so ready to pass judgement upon others take all this into account...I pay tribute to Mr. Lawrence and General Smuts for the magnificent war job of the Union of South Africa. I do not like their being pilloried here. Nor do I like to enter upon a comparison of the conditions in South Africa so far as freedom and practice of democracy.[16]

Despite the Cold War Evatt's fight against Fascism remained undiminished in 1948. With the relaxation of controls in Germany and Japan, and the criticism in the Australian Parliament that the Government was not actively taking steps against Communism, Evatt saw the need to demonstrate that the UN should not be 'bogged down' by the Cold War. He reminded Parliament that Fascism had its origins in repression against Communists and then Jews, and that 'We are against totalitarianism under whatever name it may be paraded'. Chifley himself cabled Attlee that Australia was not convinced about the desirability of forming a Western Alliance against the Soviet Union, 'particularly where undemocratic Governments like Greece and Spain are included'. In these cases Chifley argued that 'considerations of strategy' should not be allowed to dictate policy.[17]

On the surface Greece was an illustration of Evatt's concern that the UN impartially conciliate a dispute between opposing sides in the

Cold War. But there was more to it than that. He was aware that UN action there would prove to be an important precedent for action in the Pacific. The crisis in Greece also tested his position on Fascism and domestic jurisdiction. Greece, unlike the Axis powers, was not an enemy in World War II. Its territorial claims against Albania in Northern Epirus, which had precipitated conflict initially with its northern Communist neighbours, were based on the state of war that had existed between Italy and Greece since 1940—Albania then being an Italian possession. Greece had referred the issue to the Security Council which organised an enquiry, but one which focused on the 'aggression' from the north. The internal reasons for the civil war then raging in Greece were ignored.[18]

The matter was referred to the General Assembly by the United States after deadlock in the Security Council. On 1 October 1947 the Assembly established the UN Special Committee on the Balkans (UNSCOB), but the terms of the Committee were restrictive. It was to 'observe compliance' with the recommendations of the Assembly (which of course had blamed the problem on northern aggression) not investigate anew the ground covered by the original Security Council Investigating Commission. To the Americans, it was important that UNSCOB operate in the context of their overall strategy to 'save Greece'. As the US Embassy in Athens later saw it

UNSCOB must continue to operate in Greece with the active support and interest of the non-Communist members of the UN. It should not again be necessary to prove the Greek case...UNSCOB should cast aside impartiality and come to Greece with positive instructions to save her. The non-Communist world must realise that Greece is on our side.[19]

Evatt, however, was aware of the nature of the Greek government and the extent to which problems within that country were based on internal oppression. Atyeo, who had represented Australia on the Security Council commission, told him on 12 March 1947 that the Greek government was 'very far to the right' and that 'no solution is possible until it becomes a whole lot more democratic'. The 'problem', he reported, was that by the terms of the American reference to the General Assembly, UNSCOB was confined to action consistent with UN protection 'of the political independence and the territorial integrity of Greece'.[20]

Ashenden has argued that Evatt tended to go along with the American position. Evatt 'presided', he charges, over the UN's rapid decline into 'a cold war cockpit'. Through the UN he 'helped to legitimate and justify American imperialism and the Greek regime it sponsored'.[21] This is misleading: in fact Evatt did not go along with the American plans for Greece. The 'obstructionist attitudes', as the Americans saw it, of the Australian delegates on UNSCOB in 1948 reflected the views of Evatt. The Australian delegates stressed 'conciliation', as opposed to merely cataloguing border incidents, but went on to argue that there should be fresh Greek elections. These elections should be accompanied, in the view of the Australians, by reforms to labor laws, the withdrawal of foreign armed forces, participation of Leftist elements in the government and internationally supervised aid. This was entirely in line with Evatt's rejection of the Greek election results of March 1947. He announced in the House of Representatives on 6 June 1947 that there should be 'unfettered new Greek elections' to be accompanied by an amnesty for all political prisoners—then numbering some 25 000.[22]

The American State Department dismissed these views out of hand. It stood by the election results and argued that there was no legal requirement for the Greek government to initiate the reforms proposed. The suggestion that internationally supervised aid should replace bilateral US aid, which was then critical for the survival of the oppressive Greek government, was seen as 'impractical'. Evatt was reminded that the imperative concern of the Americans was the 'effective functioning of observer groups'. Thereafter the Australian delegates on UNSCOB were isolated—their entreaties to concentrate on mediation were ignored. Hodgson and Glasheen could do little other than question the UNSCOB findings on the basis that its observers had no access to three of the four countries concerned and could only take evidence from witnesses produced by Greece. [23]

UNSCOB, as a fact-finding instrument of the Assembly, seemed to be an example of just the sort of machinery that Evatt envisaged so that the UN could perform its role. Yet he dismissed it as a failure. It had not attempted mediation and had not made contact with the northern states. He therefore resolved to sidestep it and to use his position as President of the General Assembly to head a small neutral conciliation committee. To the Greeks and the Americans he 'effectively paralysed between December 1948 and June 1949' the work of UNSCOB.[24]

Evatt secured Assembly backing for his initiative in November 1948 and the discussions were conducted at Lake Success in the United States. This gave him considerable latitude compared to the restrictions encountered on UNSCOB. It is clear that he saw the border issue as of relatively minor importance, in line with Atyeo's advice, and that he expected settlement now that 'the three uncles'— the United States, Britain and the Soviet Union—were not involved. He avoided the external issues such as the Cominform, assistance to the guerillas from the northern states, and the previous conclusions of UNSCOB. On the other hand he stressed that 'the internal situation' within Greece was the source of the conflict—it had prevented firm commitments as to the border question.

In April 1949 he further revealed his concerns about the domestic situation when he appealed to the Greek government to refrain from the execution of trade unionists. He was careful to present this as a 'personal' appeal, but coming from the President of the UN General Assembly, and from one who had received international press for his defence of Church leaders in the Eastern bloc, the Greeks saw it as interference and denounced the move accordingly to the UN. Nevertheless, Evatt's appeal is credited with saving the life of Ambatielos, leader of the Seamen's Union, and others.

In the same month Evatt received word from the Greek guerillas that they would co-operate in the holding of new elections. While there is no evidence that Evatt replied to this request, he did, on 12 May, put to the Greek government the possibility that they might offer elections and an amnesty. At that juncture, however, he received a dramatic reminder of the limitations of action through the UN. On 14 May the US Secretary of State declared publicly that 'the basic issue in the Greek situation is the violation of Greece's northern frontier...internal questions such as amnesty and elections are for the Greek Government'.[25]

Evatt was criticised at the time by Atyeo for not carrying the fight to the General Assembly and making an announcement on UNSCOB in his 18 May address. He was particularly anxious that Evatt comment on the situation within Greece. In fact Evatt, as he had done in Japan when he had reached the limits of diplomacy with MacArthur, transferred the fight elsewhere. It wasn't that he 'embraced the Western Bloc', thereby emasculating the UN, as Ashenden contends. The Americans would not budge on domestic jurisdiction. Evatt did what he could on UNSCOB and attempted personal conciliation when UNSCOB failed to produce the desired results. In the process he went well beyond the brief to refrain from suggesting changes within Greece—with predictable results.

Evatt turned away from the UN when further action was futile and put the problem to the Council of Foreign Ministers on 25 May 1949. To the consternation of the British, he linked the question of the Civil War, as a Greek domestic matter, to the intervention of the northern neighbours. The whole question of Greece, 'both internal and external', argued Evatt to an incredulous Bevin, 'can now be treated as one'.[26]

This had been Evatt's position from the beginning. As the Australian representatives on the Balkan Commission reported to him in November 1947

*A Statesmanlike politico-economic solution of the Greek problem might have been possible. The one proviso was that the relations of Greece with the northern neighbours should have been treated as a Balkan problem in itself, not as a strategic conflict between the Great Powers.*²⁷

Evatt had approached the crisis in Greece mindful of the precedents that it would set in the Pacific and with an awareness of the limits of UN action. In Palestine, Evatt regarded the role of the United Nations as 'a striking example' of the organisation's potential to intervene in complex disputes and to effect solutions without the involvement of the Great Powers. In fact the whole matter had been placed before the United Nations because of its complexity. As he said when reviewing the issue in 1949

*When the United Kingdom brought the question of the future government of Palestine before the United Nations in April 1947 many people were afraid to touch it. They thought it was insoluble. Palestine was bitterly disputed by the Jews and the Arabs; it had special associations for the three great worldwide religious groups—Christians, Jews and Moslems; it was of great strategic importance to several of the Great Powers and to other nations too. Yet the Palestine problem did not break the United Nations: the United Nations broke the Palestine problem.*²⁸

In contrast to Greece, Evatt here pleaded due process. He related the 'steps' that had been adopted, from 'investigating the facts'; getting 'concrete proposals before the committees'; reconciling opposing views; and to finally passing resolutions through the Assembly. Thereafter it was a matter of adhering to these resolutions until the proclamation of the State of Israel in 1948, a measure that earned Evatt the acclamation of a grateful people.

There is no doubt that Evatt played a critical role in the United Nations deliberations over Palestine. In May 1947 the Australian delegation successfully moved, in the General Assembly, the resolution to establish a committee of enquiry to investigate the issue. The United Nations Committee on Palestine (UNSCOP), unlike UNSCOB, would be made up exclusively of smaller 'neutral' powers—including Australia. In September, when UNSCOP unsurprisingly failed to produce a unanimous report, Evatt exercised decisive control over the next stage of the Assembly's deliberations. While the Arab delegates claimed that Evatt manipulated the debate, a charge that persists with some historians to this day, Evatt deftly organised a debate that had to take account of the fact that the groups were absolutely irreconcilable. The Jews wanted a homeland and the Arabs threatened war if it was granted.²⁹

Evatt himself chaired the Ad Hoc Committee that the Assembly had appointed to develop recommendations on Palestine. Here the Arab Higher Committee and the Jewish Agency were free to openly express their views 'without restriction'. To ensure the development of specific proposals, however, Evatt appointed three subcommittees to consider alternatives. Committee 1 dealt with the Majority Report of UNSCOP which had favoured partition, while Committee 2 dealt with the Minority Report which favoured a unitary state. Evatt himself headed a third committee that would attempt to reconcile opposing views, a measure that in any case followed seventeen meetings of the Ad Hoc Committee that made it clear that there was no common ground. Behind the scenes he spoke to the Arab and Jewish delegations separately. By 28 October he confided to Atyeo that he 'now' realised that their positions were too far apart and that partition was the only way out. Despite this he continued to attempt to get the Arabs and the Jews together via meetings of go-betweens—George Marshall, the US Secretary of State, for the Jews, and Prince Faisal of Saudi Arabia for the Arabs.[30]

The General Assembly voted for partition on 9 November 1947, but when fighting broke out following this, the Americans and the British had second thoughts. The Americans now proposed trusteeship, which they put before the General Assembly in March 1948. In the Security Council they were reluctant to take enforcement action following Israel's declaration of independence on 15 May, citing the 'uncertain' status of the new state. In September the Americans supported a plan by the United Nations Special Mediator on Palestine, Count Folke Bernadotte, to reduce the territory of Israel by over half—a recommendation that cost him his life.

To Evatt this change of policy was an attempt to reverse a binding decision of the General Assembly. 'The authority and credit of the United Nations is now committed' he declared. He argued, successfully, that the United Nations was obliged to take enforcement action 'irrespective of the status of Israel' since a threat to peace had occurred. He attacked the attempt to reduce the new state saying that 'there was nothing sacrosanct about the Bernadotte Plan'. He also sought to have Israel admitted to the United Nations—a move that would overcome concerns about its 'status' and which would allow the fledgling state to arm itself. Only on the question of the internationalisation of Jerusalem did Evatt disappoint the Israelis when they demanded sovereign control of the city. Here again Evatt pleaded that the UN was committed by the terms of the November 1947 Assembly resolution.[31]

Palestine was seen by Evatt as the most successful UN operation during his time there, but his stand throughout reveals that he was aware of the implications of the issue for developments at home and in the Pacific. He was also consistent in his handling of the issue with the need to develop policy in the context of the Commonwealth.

The failure to secure a peace treaty with Japan weighed on Evatt in 1948. On 2 May the Americans were given an insight into Australia's priorities when Evatt, explaining his concerns that the trusteeship plan would 'bypass' the United Nations, appealed to Truman.

It is quite clear that the Palestinian problem, though caused independently, is nevertheless now related to the central problem of tension between the great powers. Failure to reach settlement in Palestine, as in the Japanese treaty, is merely a by-product of the major problem...the time has come for you, the President of the United States...to make a bold move to find the solution of Palestine, Japan, Germany, and the other situations which could be a cause of war.[32]

The issue also reflected his concern that it should not provide any dangerous precedents for the White Australia policy. As the Australian delegation to the United Nations saw it during the Assembly debate on the UNSCOP report:

In fact from Australia's point of view there would be a narrow line between the United Nations attempting to impose upon Palestinian Arabs an obligation to admit further Jewish immigrants and the United Nations attempting to open the doors of Australia to Asiatic immigration on the pretext that failure to do so might endanger the peace and that Australian immigration policy was contrary to the principles of the Charter in so far as it involved racial discrimination.[33]

The conclusion reached from this was that the only way to admit further Jewish immigration would be by partition.

There is some evidence, however, that Evatt had decided on this course well beforehand. Renouf reports that Evatt told near associates in September 1945 that the Jews should have a permanent home. There is, however, no evidence that this was due to lobbying of Evatt on the question by Zionists, although they specifically targeted him as early as 1942 and kept close contact thereafter.[34]

It is unlikely that this lobbying in itself was decisive. Zionists lobbied hard over the internationalisation of Jerusalem in 1949—to no avail. The Catholic lobby was stronger, and Evatt was not unaware of their influence in the ALP! Nor was he unaware of the influence of the Latin American vote in the UN which swung behind him on this issue. It is hazardous to go further and identify personal influences—especially where Evatt is concerned. The strong influences of his friends, Max Freilich and Felix Frankfurter, were at the very least neutralised by Cardinal Gilroy and Eris O'Brien.[35]

In fact Evatt intervened in the issue only when the British made it clear that the mandate was becoming an acute embarrassment to them. Initially Evatt saw the problem in Palestine from the Commonwealth perspective. As Clyde Cameron today remembers it, 'He had to overcome the double-dealing of the British in World War 1 when the Arabs were deceived on the one hand, and the Jews on the other'. Evatt, in March 1946, indicated that the British could not simply abrogate the Balfour Declaration of 1917 which had promised the Jews a homeland. But he was also aware that the Peel Report of 1937, that had seen the solution to be partition, had foundered on the rock of Arab opposition. This in turn had led the British government in 1939 to restrict Jewish immigration to Israel. To complicate matters even further, the question of Jewish immigration had strained British relations with the United States after the war. The State Department could sympathise with the British strategic needs which dictated a policy sympathetic to the Arabs, but Truman was susceptible to the powerful Jewish lobby, and this led him to advocate increased immigration. That, and the sheer cost of maintaining the mandate, led the British to hand the whole problem to the UN.[36]

Before then Evatt kept in step with the British. During the peace negotiations over the Italian colonies he had expressed the need for the Commonwealth to maintain bases throughout the Mediterranean. When Zionists lobbied him they were always careful to play down the strategic argument. Freda Kirchwey, the prominent pro-Zionist editor in the United States, implored Evatt to 'take up' the cause of Israel—'the one energetic democratic element in the whole of the feudal Middle East'—but she was careful to add that 'I am not overlooking oil and strategic interests attaching to this area'. It was a wise addition since these were included as major points of consideration in ensuring Australian support for Britain during the Assembly debate over the UNSCOP reports. During the UNSCOP investigation itself, the Australian members roundly condemned other delegates when they sought to protest against the hanging of three convicted Irgun terrorists. Evatt also agreed readily to comply with a British request to seek Australian government authority for an intake of European Jews into Australia, thereby relieving the British of embarrassment over Palestine.[37]

The Opposition in Australia made much of the withdrawal of Britain from Palestine as a sign of Evatt's faith in the UN at the expense of Commonwealth defence. The reality was, as he tried to explain to Parliament in April 1948, the

United Nations did not take it up on its own initiative. The British Government had made up its mind to withdraw its troops from Palestine...I am speaking of the stage reached when the United Kingdom almost in desperation brought the matter to the UN.[38]

Thirty thousand British troops could not keep the peace. On the contrary—the situation was getting worse. Even Smuts had seen the wisdom of partition. And throughout Evatt received regular reports from the Australian Embassy in Washington that Zionists there were lobbying the President to use dollar diplomacy in order to influence events in Palestine. Evatt, therefore, determined that partition should occur as quickly as possible, despite the recognition that the bloodshed would continue. That would be a matter for the Jews themselves (who would be armed under the partition plan) and for the Security Council. As Bell has concluded, Evatt's 'largest impact', as President of the General Assembly, as far as British policy-makers were concerned, 'was not on Cold War issues, but on the partition of Palestine'.[39]

Evatt's policies in the UN were developed with the knowledge that Cold War could easily become world war, and one that would involve the use of nuclear weapons. He feared proliferation and was concerned for the protection of Australia, either through the links to the Commonwealth or through international control of atomic power. Australia took steps to enter the new field outside the UN. As noted in the previous chapter, however, in formulating policy in the UN Evatt could do little other than react to developments. Australia after all, as he knew from Oliphant, was not in the atomic club.

The problem here was that the UN was to have a very limited role. The Americans, British and Canadians, as Evatt cabled Chifley on 14 November 1945, 'passed the buck' to the United Nations Organisation on atomic collaboration, but this was to be confined to the 'peaceful' use of nuclear energy—it did not extend to nuclear weapons. In fact the Americans had also at this point made up their minds to restrict the transfer of data about the bomb to the British and Canadians as well as others.

Evatt immediately seized on the possibilities of UN action. He advised Chifley of an argument that was to become central to his position on the UN:

Under the Charter [the UN] can make recommendations regarding armaments. As the Charter also contains the principle that 'facilities' are to [be] provided against an aggressor...I am of the opinion that facilities include new inventions and explosives [such] as the atomic bomb.[40]

The key, of course, was the Security Council, membership of which carried the additional benefit of membership of the UN Atomic Energy Commission (UNAEC). On 13 November 1945 Evatt became aware, from a speech by the influential Republican Senator Stassen, of the possibilities of Security Council control of the atomic bomb. Stassen envisaged ultimate possession by the Security Council of a stock 'of about twenty five' atom bombs. Evatt found the prospect horrifying. He told Stassen that the fate of Australia would be threatened by such an arrangement, emphasising that 'the only countries which would feel the effects of the devastation would be countries which are not members of the Security Council'. He went on to develop an argument that was to become of increasing importance as the Cold War developed. He strongly put to Stassen the proposition that 'the problem of the destructive use of atomic energy cannot be separated from the general problem of international relationships'. He did not leave it at that. He wanted Australia to be seen as having the qualifications to join the club. It was after all, an important supplier of raw materials. 'Thorium', he said, 'was found in quantity in only three countries, Brazil, Australia and British India'.

Evatt therefore moved heaven and earth to secure access to the Security Council and the UNAEC. In the event he secured Australian representation for two years as one of the non-permanent members of the Security Council and became the first chairman of the UNAEC! He wanted access to any UN committee that was involved in international security. When he became aware, on the UNAEC, of British fears that nuclear disarmament without reductions in conventional arms would disadvantage them in both Europe and in Asia, he took up this debate as Chairman of the UN Commission for Conventional Armaments. He even attempted, without success, to have Australia represented on the UN's Big Power Military Staff Committee.[41]

Evatt's time on the UNAEC was overshadowed by American determination to monopolise nuclear information. His fears that this would become a major problem were confirmed in May 1946 when the United States presented the UN with a report prepared by the Chairman of the Tennessee Valley Authority, David Lilienthal, followed in June by one presented by the head of the US Delegation on the UNAEC, Bernard Baruch. Lilienthal called for the UN to control all raw materials and development of 'peaceful' atomic power. The United States, the report went on, would only dismantle its stockpile of bombs after the establishment of a UN system of controls. Baruch developed the latter theme and sought to have the UN put in place strict and 'enforceable' sanctions against those nations that violated such UN controls. He envisaged no veto—a step designed to thwart any opposition to UN enforcement action.

In public Evatt welcomed the reports, particularly the elimination of the veto and the possibility of Security Council enforcement action. He was, however, under no illusions as to the purposes behind the plans. The Lilienthal Report, he advised the Department of External Affairs on 30 May 1946, was designed 'to protect the United States from atom bomb attack. It preserves her supremacy in atomic armament and scientific application for a considerable period'.[42]

Evatt saw the key to safeguarding Australian interests as dependent on the Lilienthal timetable which, he argued, would have to be 'equitable'. It was 'essential', he insisted, that the sequence of events identified by Lilienthal 'should occupy the minimum time'. To that end he attempted to use his friendship with Baruch, and his position as Chairman of the UNAEC, to move as quickly as possible. Furthermore he wanted a 'treaty' to secure the confidence of the Soviets and countries such as Australia which would have to surrender their control over raw materials—the admission ticket to the nuclear club.[43]

To the Americans, Evatt, in 'wanting to settle the problem of atomic energy control during his chairmanship' of the AEC, was simply making a 'grandstand play' before Australia left the Security Council and the AEC in November 1947. But Evatt knew that if the UN was to have such authority over the process outlined by Lilienthal, then the UNAEC should be 'independent' of the Security Council, where of course the Soviets would exercise the veto. On the other hand, the concern of the UNAEC with security issues and the need to address the question of sanctions meant that it could not operate as an organ of the Assembly. With these considerations in mind, Evatt wanted the Americans to consider expanding the AEC so that, as the Australian representative Plimsoll requested informally, 'the retiring members could continue...and thus their experience and knowledge would not be lost'. Not surprisingly, the Americans 'gave him no encouragement on this idea'.[44]

Evatt did not leave it at that. He continued to be 'troublesome' in the UN. When the Americans announced the closure of Trust Territory at Eniwetok Atoll in December 1947 to prepare for atom tests the following year, Hood, on Evatt's instructions, 'complicated things' by demanding a report under the terms of the Trusteeship Agreement of the UN. Never comfortable with the American notion of 'Strategic Trusts' before a general settlement could be effected in the Pacific, the question of nuclear testing was no more acceptable to Evatt than American attempts to use the islands for civil aviation or Japanese phosphate mining.[45]

In 1948, with the deepening Cold War and Australia off the UNAEC, Evatt returned to action in the General Assembly. He had already announced in the Australian Parliament in April that Soviet fears over the failure of the Americans to destroy their nuclear stockpile were 'understandable'. But when the Allied nuclear club attempted to dismiss further debates in the UN in October on Soviet plans for disarmament, Evatt introduced, according to the Americans, a 'dangerous amendment'. This was designed to allow the debate to continue in the Assembly, but more to the point it presented the Americans as resistant to international action at a time of acute international tension. In public he denounced the failure to consider alternatives to the Soviet disarmament proposals and argued that the UNAEC should be instructed to continue meetings and conclude the 'treaty'. In private he scolded the Americans for 'deliberately' keeping Australia off the sub-committee that was responsible for considering draft resolutions that would be submitted to the Assembly.[46] This should, however, be kept in perspective. Evatt was aware that the UN had limitations. In the absence of UN action Evatt knew that the Anglo-Australian Joint Project would ultimately ensure Australia's entry into the nuclear club.

That was Evatt's general position towards the UN. It had no jurisdiction over the all-important peace settlements and the Big Powers were determined to keep vital issues outside its control. Moreover, Evatt himself wanted to confine its role. He brought to it definite ideas on economic policy, trusteeship, regionalism, domestic jurisdiction and law. These policies had been largely the outcome of the war and Evatt's assessment of Australia's place in the post-war order. In this sense Evatt made a distinctive contribution. Labor leaders in the past had distrusted schemes for world government. Hughes placed no faith in the League as a guarantor of Australian regional security and Curtin looked to a reinvigorated Empire. Evatt shared their ideals but he saw the potential benefits of the UN. He used it as a tool and he wielded it in Australian national interests.

NOTES

1 H.V. Evatt, Australia *in World Affairs*, Angus & Robertson, Sydney, 1946, pp. 130–1. N. Harper and D. Sissons, *Australia and the United Nations*, Manhattan Publishing Company, New York, 1959.

2 R. O'Neill, Australia and the Korean War, 1950–53: Vol.1: Strategy and Diplomacy, AGPS, Canberra, 1981, p. 8.

3 AA: A1838/T189, Item 854/10/2.

4 Current Notes, vol. 18, no. 9, October 1947; H.V. Evatt, Foreign Policy of Australia, Angus & Robertson, Sydney, 1945, p. 198; Evatt Collection, 'UN Cables'.

5 USNA RG 59 Box 2095; RG 84 Boxes 75 and 178. G. St. J. Barclay, *Friends in High Places: Australian–American diplomatic relations since 1945*, OUP, Oxford, 1985, ch. 1.

6 *Current Notes*, vol. 20, no. 6, June 1949, p. 757.
7 F. Poyas, 'A Hazardous Occupation: Dr. H.V. Evatt's 23 Year Friendship with C. Hartley Grattan', Conference Paper, Bond University, 1990; Evatt, *Australia in World Affairs* and 'Risks of a Big Power Peace', *Foreign Affairs*, January 1946.
8 *Current Notes*, vol. 15, no. 10, October 1944, p. 291 and vol. 16, no. 2, February 1945, p. 31; N. Pyke, 'Australia's UNRRA Contribution', *Australian Outlook*, vol. 3, no. 2, March 1949; Evatt Collection, Flinders University, 'UN -Trusteeship'.
9 *Current Notes*, vol. 15, no. 8, September 1944, p. 220; AA: A3300, Item 529.
10 Harper and Sissons, Australia and the United Nations, p. 164; C. Bell, Dependent Ally: A Study in Australian Foreign Policy, OUP, Oxford, p. 38.
11 AA: A1066, Item H45/1014/2, Cable 217, Commonwealth Government to Addison, 7 August 1945.
12 When the Americans delayed the peace settlement in 1947 with the development of the Cold War in Europe, Evatt moved to secure terms in Japan before it too became a bastion against Communism. On 18 September 1947 he told the General Assembly that the 'Peace Settlement of the Pacific need not await the settlement in Europe'. AA: A3300, Item 529. Evatt also refused to entertain the separate settlement of Korea and Siam without that of Japan. USNA RG 84, Box 84, 'Korea'. In March 1948 he complained that the settlement of Trieste was taken outside the UN, causing Australia to fear 'a sudden decision by the Great Powers to write the Japanese Peace Treaty'. USNA RG Box 68, 'Mission to UN Files', Memorandum of Conversation with Evatt, 31 March 1948.
13 Evatt Collection, 'External Affairs—Europe', no date; AA: A1066, Item H45/1013/1/9, Cable 292, Dunk to Evatt, 11 September 1945.
14 The cables dealing with Spain are in AA: A1066, Item 45/28/7; A3196, 1946, 0.6997/98; USNA RG 84, Box 90, 'Spain 1945—1949'.
15 Evatt Collection, 'External Affairs—Europe', no date; AA A3300, Item 529, Address by Evatt to Assembly, 18 September 1947; USNA RG 84, Box 68, 'Security Council'.
16 AA A1068, Item PI 47/5/3/1, 'Speech by Evatt in Committee 4—Trusteeship', 8 October 1947. In Commonwealth forums Evatt defended the Malan Government, dismissing calls to expel South Africa from the Commonwealth as 'sheer defeatism inimical to the security and wellbeing of the Commonwealth'. USNA, 800 Series, Box 6166, 'Internal Affairs of States—Australia', Cable 1673, US Embassy, London to Secretary of State, 30 July 1948.
17 *CPD*, vol. 196, p. 622; PRO: FO 371/70189, Item W918, unnumbered Cable, Chifley to Attlee, 22 January 1948.
18 Greece had been descending into a state of civil war since 1944. Successive British—backed governments embarked on a policy of gaoling and terror that spawned resistance, largely concentrated in the mountainous north of the country in 1946. Despite claims of the Greek government that this 'northern' resistance was organised by the neighbouring Communist states of Yugoslavia, Albania and Bulgaria, the British themselves did not accept that without qualification. In August 1946 a parliamentary delegation acknow-

ledged that many had fled north to escape the terror of the extreme right. The Security Council investigation in Greece had taken place between January and June 1947—the period in which the United States moved to implement the Marshall Plan and to announce the Truman Doctrine. Not surprisingly the American-dominated Commission was anxious to focus on the activities of Greece's northern neighbours and to avoid any 'inordinate interest in Greek internal affairs'. USNA, RG 84, Box 68, US Security Council Files—'Appraisal of the UN Secretariat Attached to the Balkan Commission', 21 July 1947. J. and G. Kolko, *The Limits of Power: The World and United States Foreign Policy, 1945–1954*, Harper & Row, New York, 1972, chs 8, 12.

19 USNA, RG 59, 501—'Files on UN—Greece', US Consulate General, Istanbul to State Department, 3 April 1948 and Despatch 803, 2 August 1948.

20 Evatt Collection, 'UN Balkan Commission', Letter, Atyeo to Evatt, 13 March 1947. Atyeo also complained of the 'active bias' of the Secretariat and the fact that there was very little evidence specifically related to frontier incidents. USNA RG 84, Box 178, 'US Mission to UN—UNSCOB'.

21 D. Ashenden, 'Evatt and the Origins of the Cold War: Australia and the US with the UN in Greece, 1946–49', *Journal of Australian Studies*, no. 7, November 1980, p. 95. See also A. Renouf, *Let Justice be Done: The Foreign Policy of Dr. H.V. Evatt*, UQP, St. Lucia, 1983, p. 243.

22 *Current Notes*, vol. 18, no. 6, June 1947, p. 382. Ashenden makes the case for Evatt's central role in shaping policy in Greece, despite Burton's claim that he (Burton) had 'considerable influence'. See Ashenden, 'Evatt and the Origins of the Cold War', p. 85, no. 37. On the problems of the election, including manipulation of electoral lists and intimidation of the Left see Kolko, *Limits of Power*, pp. 223–4.

23 The American reports on UNSCOB are in USNA RG 59, Boxes 2095–7. The Australian files are in AA: A1838/T189, Item 852/20/1, Parts 1-6.

24 USNA RG 84, Box 80, 'Greece: the Evatt Conciliation Discussions', Report by Harry Howard.

25 USNA RG 84, Box 80, 'The Evatt Conciliation Discussions'.

26 PRO: FO 371, Items 78458 and 78475.

27 Evatt Collection, Flinders University, 'Overall Assessment of the Facts Ascertained', November 1947.

28 AA: A3318, Item L49/1/3/3 Part 1, 'Peace—How can it be Achieved', Speech by Evatt to the United Nations Associates, 7 April 1949.

29 C. Bell, *Dependent Ally: A Study in Australian Foreign Policy*, p. 39. Bell accuses Evatt of 'manipulating the rules of procedure'. Adelman has recently written that the structure of the committees was seen by the Americans and the British as militating against conciliation. H. Adelman, 'Australia and the Birth of Israel: Midwife or Abortionist', *Australian Journal of Politics and History*, vol. 38, no. 3, 1992, p. 356.

30 USNA RG 84, 'US Mission to UN Files', Box 57, Memorandum of Conversation with Atyeo, 27 October 1947 and Box 86 , Memorandum of Conversation with Evatt, 28 October 1947.

31 AA: A1838, Item 852/20/2, 'Palestine'; USNA RG 84 Box 87, 'US Mission to UN Files—Palestine'; H.V. Evatt, *The Task of Nations*, New York, 1949.

32 Truman Library, Naval Aide Files, Box 21, Letter, Evatt to Truman, 2 May 1948.
33 Adelman, 'Birth of Israel', p. 365.
34 Renouf, *Let Justice Be Done*, p. 247. On Zionist lobbying of Evatt, designed to counter especially the anti-Zionist Isaac Isaacs, see M. Freilich, *Zion in Our Time: Memoirs of an Australian Zionist*, Morgan Publications, Sydney, 1967; R. Gouttman 'First principles: H.V. Evatt and the Jewish Homeland', in W.D. Rubinstein, *Jews in the Sixth Continent*, Allen & Unwin, Sydney, 1987.
35 Especially in an election year. See A. Dalziel, *Evatt the Enigma*, Lansdowne Press, Melbourne, 1967, p. 60; R. Gouttman, 'Jerusalem from the Antipodes: A Political View, 1947–1967', *The Australian Journal of Jewish Studies*, vol. 6, no. 2, 1992; B. Murphy, *The Brandeis/Frankfurter Connection: The Secret Political Activities of Two Supreme Court Justices*, OUP, New York, 1982. The American State Department at the time concluded that Evatt's stand on Jerusalem was due to 'many Catholic voters in Australia'. USNA RG 84, Box 36, 'US Mission to UN Files', Partition of Palestine, 19 November 1949.
36 Interview with Cameron, 4 May 1988; Gouttman, 'First principles', p. 270; S. Rutland, *Edge of the Diaspora: Two Centuries of Jewish Settlement in Australia*, Collins, Sydney, 1988, p. 307.
37 Evatt Collection, 'External Affairs File', Letter, Freda Kirchwey to Evatt, 15 July 1947; PRO: DO 35/1833, Item WR 207/7/45, Note by Ben Cockram, 23 June 1946; USNA RG 84, Box 60, 'Delegates Brief: Second Session of the General Assembly, 1948'.
38 *CPD*, vol. 197, p. 742.
39 AA: A1067/1, Item 46/2/3/11, 'US—Relations with UK'; A1068, Item 47/34/1/2, 'US Relations with UK'; PRO: FO 371/70189, Item W918, Strategic Arrangements after the Partition, 12 August 1947; Bell, *Dependent Ally*, p. 39.
40 Evatt Collection, 'Overseas Trip—1945', Cable E32, Evatt to Chifley, 15 November 1945.
41 AA M1943/1, Hasluck Correspondence and Subject Files, Letter, Hasluck to External Affairs, 19 January 1946. Evatt also followed the work of other associated bodies working generally in the industrial and nuclear area such as the Inter-Allied Reparations Committee and its Committee of Industrial, Technical and Scientific Patent Rights. A1067, Item ER46/19/1/2.
42 AA: A1838/T184, Item 720/1, Part 1, Cable UN 171, Evatt to External Affairs, 30 May 1946; A2700, vol. 28, Agendum Number 1197, 'Atomic Energy', 5 June 1946.
43 AA: A1838/T184, Item 720/1, Part 1, Cable UN 189, Evatt to Chifley, 12 June 1946 and Cable 848, Evatt to Department of External Affairs, 25 June 1946; Truman Papers, Naval Aide Files, Box 20—DOS Briefings—AEC. The Cabinet position at this time was that Australia's 'defence interests' were safeguarded by the control of materials. A2700, vol. 25, Agendum 1126, 'Control of Uranium Bearing Ores'.
44 USNA RG 84, Box 68, 'Mission to UN Files—Atomic Energy', Conversation with Plimsoll, 18 November 1947; Box 75, 'Attitude of Various Delegations

in the UNAEC Negotiations'; P. Hasluck, *Diplomatic Witness: Australian Foreign Affairs, 1941–1947*, MUP, Melbourne, 1980, p. 279.

45 USNA RG 59, Department of State: 501. BC—'Atomic Energy'. Hood could hardly have been surprised with US insistence that they would test weapons 'pending the establishment of a fully effective system for the control of atomic energy'.

46 *FRUS*, 1948, vol. 1, General: The United Nations: Part 1, pp. 457, 480.

PART V

LABOR GOVERNMENT PROBLEMS

CHAPTER 24

BANKS, JUDGES, DOCTORS AND ASIO

To place a ban on the Communist party means that it would be necessary to pass a law providing that people must not approve of Communist ideas or objectives, and that it shall be a criminal offence.
H. V. EVATT, 1948

In the era of television, historical myths may be created virtually overnight. In 1988, ABC TV presented a series entitled *The True Believers*, which portrayed the ALP in the period from 1945 to 1955. The material was interesting, dramatic and powerful in impact: a great many viewers received images and impressions which will probably remain with them for the rest of their lives. Understandably, the main character—at least up to the time of his death—was Prime Minister Chifley. He appears as a very likeable person, modest and unassuming, firm and reliable, leading the Party and the nation in important achievements at a difficult period. In essentials, this picture is realistic and *The True Believers* largely reinforced the prominent position held by Chifley in the Labor pantheon.

The portrayal of Evatt was quite different in character. It seems to have come mainly from a federal Labor MP on the right who was hostile to Evatt and who regularly recounted malicious anecdotes. The result in *The True Believers* is that Evatt is depicted as a rather frenetic person of little significance with an overweening ambition for the Prime Ministership—which he failed to achieve. There is no suggestion of powerful intellect or attractive qualities. Even in presenting a case for nationalisation of banking to the High Court, Evatt is shown as a rather ridiculous figure. Granted that he was a very difficult person to comprehend, this one-dimensional portrayal was a travesty of the truth. Yet of such stuff are myths made.

A clear example of ignorance and prejudiced treatment of Evatt in *The True Believers* concerns bank nationalisation, with reference to which there is a strong insinuation that Evatt was the prime mover in policy, as well as the person mainly responsible for its failure. Actually, it was Chifley, not Evatt, who pushed for greater public control over banks, culminating in an attempt to nationalise them. It is useful to consider the background here, for two reasons. First, the Labor defeat over bank nationalisation—taken in conjunction with adverse High Court judgments on pharmaceutical benefits and national airlines—was crucially important to the Chifley government. Second, the matter throws light on the relationship between Chifley and Evatt.

Banking was a subject on which Chifley was very well informed. As a member of a federal Royal Commission on Banking in the late 1930s, he became convinced of the need for firmer regulation of the operations of the private trading banks by a central bank responsible to the federal government. Indeed, in a minority report, Chifley recommended nationalisation of banks. This accorded very well with the long-standing hostility of Labor towards monopolistic bank power over credit and interest rates—a hostility deepened by the way in which the private trading banks and the Commonwealth Bank together frustrated the policies of the Scullin government in the Great Depression.

As Commonwealth Treasurer in World War II, Chifley was responsible for imposing upon the trading banks a structure of control in the national interest. These regulations were derived from the constitutional defence power and, as the war came to an end, it was necessary to decide what should replace them by way of more permanent legislation. The outcome, in 1945, was the passing of the Commonwealth Bank Act and the Banking Act. Between them, these Acts placed greater emphasis on the Commonwealth Bank's competitive role; they made the bank, under a single Governor, responsible to the government; and they increased the bank's regulatory powers over the private trading banks, notably through the 'special accounts' system, whereby the central bank could compulsorily 'call up' varying proportions of trading bank deposits so as to influence the amount of credit available in the community.

Some Labor MPs, such as Dedman and Calwell, would have preferred to legislate directly for bank nationalisation in 1945, but most were willing to defer to the views of Curtin and Chifley. The latter, in particular, while not abandoning the idea of nationalisation, felt that controls of the kind proposed would be adequate to ensure that banking operations were appropriate to the aims of full employment and stable economic growth. As for Evatt's standpoint, Dedman's impression was that 'the Doc never had much of an idea of economics' and in relation to bank nationalisation 'would have been more concerned what the electors might think of it rather than [whether] it was good legislation from the point of view of the country generally'.[1]

Although the private trading banks were generally critical of the legislation passed in 1945—it threatened their unfettered profit-making capacity—they concentrated particularly upon a provision which required public bodies, including local government authorities, to do all their banking business with the Commonwealth Bank or State banks. Actually, this provision was not brought into effect until 1947. When that happened, the Melbourne City Council challenged the Banking Act in the High Court. It was no coincidence that Melbourne contained the head offices of five of the nine major trading banks. Two States (South Australia and Western Australia) intervened in the case in support of the Melbourne City Council, while Victoria (then under a Labor government) did so in support of the Commonwealth.

The decision of the High Court in August 1947 came as a surprise to the Chifley government, as the government was relying upon a straightforward interpretation of the Constitution, which gave power to the federal parliament with respect to 'banking, other than State banking'. Indeed, a majority of High Court judges agreed that the section of the Banking Act which directed public bodies not to give their banking business to the private banks was a law with respect to banking. Nevertheless, the court judged that this section of the Act was constitutionally invalid because it discriminated against the States or violated one of their essential functions. On the latter argument, put forward by Rich and Starke, it may be remarked that whilst the States certainly needed access to adequate banking facilities this did not mean that some of those facilities must be available from private banks. More reasonable was the view propounded by Latham and Dixon to the effect that State immunity from discrimination was implicit in the nature of the federal system and operated to restrict Commonwealth legislative powers. Williams subscribed to both adverse opinions. McTiernan alone dissented from the other judges.

The High Court decision left untouched the major part of the Banking Act, making no comment on it. Thus it could be reckoned that the federal government still held adequate control over the banking system and that it would be best to accept the Court's judgment without more ado. This appears to have been Evatt's inclination. However, Chifley took the view that the private banks, having savoured a partial victory, would challenge other aspects of banking legislation when a suitable opportunity arose. The banks had deliberately refrained from expressing their acceptance of the 'special accounts' system. As Evatt wrote later, Chifley aimed essentially at full control over banking, yet because

under the constitution as interpreted by the Court, the indirect method was of doubtful validity, he was prepared to stake all on the direct method. It would be as wrong to say he did this out of doctrinaire pedantry, as that he was opposed, as doctrinaires are, to socialisation.[2]

Consequently, Chifley's abrupt response to the High Court decision was to promote a Banking Bill which provided for nationalisation of the private trading banks, subject to just terms of compensation for their property. The move was approved by Chifley's colleagues and by the ALP as a whole, since it had been part of the ALP official platform since 1920. Chifley, in his second-reading speech on the Bill on 15 October 1947, stated that the Attorney-General, before going overseas a month earlier (prior to which, Evatt had been back in Australia for only three weeks), had given 'close attention to the legal and constitutional aspects...and laid down the main lines on which the preparation of the measure has proceeded'.[3]

The Bill represented a threat to the interests of a key section of the Australian capitalist class, whose adherents launched a massive attack upon the legislation well before it passed through parliament. Widespread public meetings were organised, propaganda was disseminated and bank staffs were encouraged to speak out in support of their employers. White-collar workers were deeply concerned, and the Federal Council of the Australian Bank Officials' Association decided to oppose bank nationalisation on the ground that members would be subject to industrial conscription—despite the fact that the legislation gave protection to continuance of employment for bank staffs. The banks also appealed for support to people who held bank accounts. Sometimes the results were not as anticipated: when Evatt's daughter, Rosalind, received one such circular from the E.S.&A. Bank at a later stage in the campaign, she promptly passed it on to her father as an illustration of bank tactics. Yet on the whole the bank campaign was very successful. The first fruits were evident in November 1947, when the Cain Labor government of Victoria was decisively defeated in an election.

While all this was going on, Chifley failed to provide leadership for Labor supporters. He wanted the Labor response to the bank's campaign to be restrained in tone, but in practice the response was belated and slow moving, lacking inspiration. Given the party numbers in parliament, there was no doubt about the Bill being passed, yet it was clear that when that eventuated the banks would initiate a challenge in the High Court. Indeed, the government facilitated this. At a meeting of the Labor caucus on 26 November, the acting Attorney-General, McKenna, announced that it had been agreed by both sides that as soon as the Bill received royal assent there would be an application to the High Court in the hope of obtaining a reasonably quick decision on the case. It was expected that whichever side lost in the High Court would appeal to the Privy Council, and McKenna thought that the matter could be finalised by both courts within a period of nine months. In fact, it took much longer.

At the same caucus meeting, Chifley proposed the deferment by the ALP of 'all meetings in the capital cities in reference to the Bill'. Labor regarded the subject as *sub judice*—a foolish attitude to adopt, as it meant vacating the political arena in favour of a decision to be made by a small number of judges. No doubt those eminent lawyers would formally frame their judgments in terms of the constitutional powers of the Commonwealth but in reality they were dealing with an issue of public versus private interest, on which they were inevitably influenced by their own prejudices. It might be said that the High Court, in making its decision, would be unaffected by any current political campaigns, but this would be to assume that the judges were not human beings. As it was, before the court began its hearings on the bank nationalisation case, public opinion polls showed a strong trend in favour of the private banks—and the ALP was doing virtually nothing to counter this.[4]

The banks and their allies in politics and the press were certainly not inhibited in their preparations to fight on, no matter what the court's judgment might be. What began as a vigorous defence of private banks became a broad campaign leading up to the next federal election—a campaign which merged with fear of Communism. Two weeks after the Labor caucus meeting referred to above, R. G. Casey, federal president of the Liberal Party, wrote to about a hundred representatives of large companies and businesses, soliciting confidential donations to a political fund designed to raise £100 000 to combat socialism. As Casey put it:

Labour has openly declared its intention of the complete socialisation of our country. Although labour is 'officially' opposed to Communism, there is little doubt that the eventual aims of the Australian Labour Party and of the Australian Communist Party are indistinguishable...

A new phase in Australian politics is developing—socialism versus free enterprise. The Banking Legislation is the opening shot in the campaign—but it will not end with the Banking Legislation.[5]

❖

Evatt, loyal to his Party's decision to proceed with bank nationalisation, personally led the presentation of the Commonwealth government's case to the High Court. He began in a startling fashion by asking two of the judges to disqualify themselves from hearing the case on the ground that they held interests in private banks which were plaintiffs in the action. Evatt's information was that Judge Williams was a joint shareholder in two banks, the beneficial interest being enjoyed by his sister, while Judge Starke's wife also held shares in two of the banks. Bailey, as Commonwealth Solicitor-General, had earlier tried to soften what could be construed as a personal attack by telling Starke that both Chifley and Evatt were confident that his wife's shareholdings would not influence Starke's judgment but that other people might suspect bias on his part. Starke was not impressed, and he and Williams declared that they had 'no pecuniary interest' in the shares of private banks. Chief Justice Latham then rejected Evatt's submission on the point.

If Evatt had been successful in this opening gambit, he would have been acclaimed for bold tactics. Failure meant that in retrospect his judgement was regarded as faulty: he had needlessly antagonised two or more members of the Bench which was to hear the case. Evatt was not in a position to say publicly that he did not expect Starke and Williams to favour the Commonwealth viewpoint regardless of what was said in court. Furthermore, Evatt was probably far from optimistic about the outcome where other members of the court were concerned. Perhaps for this reason, Evatt argued the Commonwealth's case at inordinate length, taking up seventeen of the thirty-nine days of the hearing in March–April 1948.

Rather surprisingly, Latham seems not to have been alienated by Evatt's imputation of possible bias on the part of Starke and Williams. That conclusion may be drawn from the warm tone of a letter written by Latham to Evatt a little later, while the High Court judgment on bank nationalisation was still reserved. Admittedly, the letter had no reference to the court case and it was addressed to Evatt in his capacity as Minister for External Affairs. Latham, as a former Australian Minister to Tokyo, retained a keen interest in overseas regional affairs and it was natural enough for him to congratulate the government upon its announced intention to improve contacts between Australia and South-East Asia, particularly by providing fellowships to Asian students for study in Australia. Nevertheless, it seems rather odd that Latham chose to do so in a friendly letter to Evatt at this juncture.[6]

It was at this time, too, that the Chifley government suffered a setback in yet another referendum on constitutional powers, strongly advocated by Senator McKenna. On this occasion the question was the government's attempt to gain power to control prices and rents—in effect, to continue wartime practices, the authority for which had expired the previous year. The proposal was rejected by voters in May 1948, although most State governments operated similar controls until some years later.

The High Court gave judgment in the bank nationalisation case in August 1948. Garfield Barwick, KC, in leading the case for the banks, had argued that the Act should be deemed invalid on five alternative grounds. The outcome was complicated by the fact that the six judges delivered five separate judgments. No doubt this personal indulgence, resulting in later uncertainty as to precise collective reasons, was the product of much cogitation. Rich and Williams jointly adopted virtually all the grounds put forward by Barwick, while Starke was not far behind in his support for private enterprise. Dixon, too, though more cautiously, upheld the same free-market doctrine. Taking these four judges together, there was a clear majority of opinion that the Act, by prohibiting private banking, infringed Section 92 of the Constitution and was therefore invalid.[7]

Evatt's main argument had been that whilst Section 92 related to freedom of interstate 'trade, commerce, and intercourse', this did not include banking. Furthermore, the Act did not prohibit banking: it merely selected the persons or agencies which should be permitted to engage in it. Both Latham and McTiernan accepted Evatt's argument in relation to Section 92. They therefore dissented from the majority of the Court on this crucial issue. In thus upholding the Act, Latham and McTiernan considered that some of its provisions infringed upon the concept of 'just terms' of compensation for the banks, but this was a matter which could easily have been remedied by subsequent legislation. However, this would not have altered the Court's majority ruling on interpretation of Section 92, so the government decided to appeal to the Privy Council. It was probably an unwise decision: precedents suggested that it was unlikely that the Privy Council would overrule the Australian High Court.

Evatt apparently thought otherwise. When the Privy Council hearing began in London in March 1949, he was present (together with other counsel, including English lawyers) to put the Commonwealth's case. He did so at tiresome length which probably bored the judges. Evatt's confidence in his own powers of advocacy told against him, especially as he was at the same time very heavily engaged in work in New York at the United Nations. He would have been wise to allocate to other lawyers the presentation of the Commonwealth case to the Privy Council, but he was influenced by knowledge that his Labor colleagues regarded him (a former member of the High Court) as the best man for the job. Evatt shared that belief and he was indeed an authority on constitutional law. Nevertheless, his other commitments were extremely burdensome.

Political opponents were aware of the distractions and gave the impression that on one occasion Evatt asked the Privy Council to adjourn its hearing of the banking case because of clashes with Evatt's work timetable. Besides this, H. Holt, a Liberal MP, criticised Evatt for holding two major ministerial portfolios:

Our present Minister for External Affairs is to be found very rarely in Australia, and then only for short periods. He has no leisure in which to deal with tremendously important matters connected with the Attorney-General's Department.[8]

Actually, the case presented by Evatt to the Privy Council, though laboured in form—it traversed all the precedents concerning Section 92—reads well. He argued that Section 92 'does not embody any conception of freedom of trade...or freedom to trade in the sense that freedom of competition is to be unrestricted'. In Evatt's view, the substantial guarantee provided by Section 92 was that 'legislative or executive restrictions in respect of the passage of goods or persons across the State boundaries shall not be adopted either by the Commonwealth or the State'. Consequently, 'the "freedom of trade" which is denied, for instance, by a law creating a State monopoly has no connection with the specific freedom of passage or movement across the State frontiers'. As a further illustration: 'The Post Office monopoly does not impede freedom of correspondence, but merely, as it were, canalizes its course'.[9]

Evatt's argument was of little avail against the private banks' case presented to the Privy Council by Barwick, who skilfully adapted his style to the occasion. In July 1949, the Council dismissed the Commonwealth government's appeal concerning bank nationalisation. The reasons for thus upholding the Australian High Court's majority interpretation of Section 92 were not published until three months later, shortly before an Australian general election. In retrospect, it is apparent that the Privy Council's attempt to justify its decision by framing a general formulation of Section 92 'bristled with vagaries and contradictions...The rhetoric and forms of legalism ...barely cloaked a basic preference for liberal individualism'. Nevertheless, the effect in political terms was decisive: bank nationalisation was killed. Indeed, nationalisation as a general policy appeared to be dead for the foreseeable future.[10]

Evatt, whilst acknowledging defeat for the present, tried to salvage something from the ruins. In a letter to the Attorney-General of New South Wales, he analysed the Privy Council's reasons for judgment and concluded that the intervention in the case by the Labor governments of New South Wales and Queensland in support of the Commonwealth had been vindicated. This was because some passages in the Council's stated reasons indicated a disposition to agree with Evatt's views rather than those of Dixon and other judges, concerning interpretation of Section 92 in relation to State regulation of transport and organised marketing. There was some justification for Evatt's legal analysis on this point but he was inclined to overlook contradictory indications of Privy Council reasoning. The political reality of the next decade and later was that Dixon's interpretation of Section 92 was dominant: judge-made doctrine—not based on any explicit expression in the Constitution—ruled.[11]

Ironically, a differently constituted High Court, in the *Crayfish Case* in 1988, swung back towards Evatt's interpretation of Section 92. It now appears that the Constitution would not be held to debar bank nationalisation. However, this *volte-face* came much too late for Evatt—and for a Labor Party which has turned decisively away from nationalised ownership of any industry.[12]

Provision of social services was another important area where conservative forces were able to enlist the aid of the High Court to block reform. In relation to the constitutional validity of legislation on medical and pharmaceutical benefits, the Court had two bites of the cherry. The second occasion arose after the referendum in 1946 which gave the Commonwealth specific power to legislate on the subject. As a result of the referendum, the Chifley government anticipated no constitutional difficulty over the Pharmaceutical Benefits Act which McKenna, Minister for Social Services, piloted through parliament in 1947. The Act was substantially the same as that which had been invalidated by the High Court in 1945, before the referendum.

The government reckoned without the intransigence of medical practitioners, who were fiercely independent and highly respected in the community. Their union—the Australian division of the British Medical Association (BMA)—was both grasping and outspoken in the interests of its members, besides being involved in a similar political struggle against introduction of a national health scheme in its home territory, Britain. In Australia, the Chifley government's scheme was that medicines and appliances were to be provided at public expense, paid for on presentation of doctors' prescriptions as dispensed by chemists. To simplify administration of the scheme, Commonwealth prescription forms were provided.

When the scheme came into effect in mid-1948 it was boycotted by the BMA and its members, who regarded it as the forerunner of nationalised medicine. As this refusal to co-operate threatened to nullify the scheme, the government responded with further legislation, stipulating that those doctors who wished to prescribe medicines on which benefits were payable must do so on standard Commonwealth forms. As all the routine drugs were included in the official formulary, this effectively meant that doctors, on penalty of £50 for non-compliance, were compelled to participate in the scheme—and all patients were given the right to reject formulary prescriptions and free benefits. The fact that this was in the interests of the great majority of patients was lost sight of in the hullabaloo of protest from the BMA.

When the validity of the Act was challenged in the High Court by the BMA, Evatt as Attorney-General of the Commonwealth argued with reference to the crucial Section 7A of the Act:

All that section 7A does is to forbid medical practitioners to write prescriptions for pharmaceutical benefits otherwise than on forms provided by the Commonwealth. It does not compel medical practitioners to write any prescriptions...merely makes certain that in the case of the medical practitioner determining that the patient needs a prescribed benefit—one of the drugs on the formulary—he shall not refuse to take the step which will give the patient that very drug prescribed by him as being necessary to the patient's health.[13]

Despite this, four High Court judges, headed by Latham, decided that the Act was invalid, on the ground that Section 7A was a 'form of civil conscription' which was forbidden by the new section of the constitution adopted as a result of the referendum in 1946. Dixon and McTiernan dissented from this opinion. Dixon said that 'the expression "civil conscription" cannot be equivalent simply to compulsion'. McTiernan took the argument further by noting the wartime context:

The word 'conscription' standing by itself generally means military conscription...To compel a civilian in time of war to darken the windows of his house is not to conscript him...The Pharmaceutical Benefits Act...does not attach any medical practitioner to the service of the Commonwealth.[14]

As against this, Latham argued that the government's scheme was the thin end of the wedge. He said that if Section 7A were held to be valid, there would be nothing to stop the addition of other requirements, so that 'the whole practice of a doctor could be completely controlled'. This phrase indicates a readiness to clutch at straws to bolster a conservative ideology. There was also an atmosphere of solidarity with the most reactionary of all professions, medicine. A general election was only a few months ahead when the Court in October 1949 delivered its judgment on the second Pharmaceutical Benefits Act.

❖

Up to 1949, the High Court was not directly concerned with attacks upon the Chifley government which related to Communism and the Cold War. Outside the Court the Liberal–Country parties increasingly concentrated upon this subject as a means of discrediting the Labor Party. Notably, there was an Opposition motion of censure of the government in April 1948 for having allegedly failed to take action against Communism in Australia. Fadden, the Country Party leader, urged that the CPA should be banned. Evatt vigorously rejected this view:

What would be involved in the banning of the Communist party? To place a ban on the Communist party means that it would be necessary to pass a law providing that people must not approve of Communist ideas or objectives, and that it shall be a criminal offence for people to hold or to express views in favour of communism or to have dealings with other people who favour communism. Just imagine the extraordinary difficulties and injustices which might occur.[15]

In the same debate, Chifley emphasised the strength of ALP opposition to the principles of Communism, while acknowledging that the Labor Party too had radicals and militants among its members. He also tried to deflect criticism by saying that 'all members of the public service, even though they may not have been engaged in security work, have been subject to close scrutiny'. As far as was known, declared Chifley, no person associated with the CPA in such a way as to raise legitimate doubts about reliability 'is engaged in vital security work'. Alternative work in the public service could usually be provided for employees deemed suspect.[16]

This moderate concession to witch-hunters did not satisfy the Opposition parties, which returned to the attack when Australian press reports claimed that the United States refused to pass on atomic secrets to Britain for fear that they would be leaked to the Soviet Union through Australia's supposedly faulty security. This time the attack focused on the Council for Scientific and Industrial Research (CSIR). Dedman, the Minister responsible, postulated that it would not be surprising if there were a few reputed Communists among the CSIR's 5000 employees, and added:

I have seen in the office of the Commonwealth Investigation Service the files dealing with these persons, and none of them is connected with any matter relating to defence, or defence scientific research.[17]

Many years later, it became public knowledge that in July 1948 the United States notified the Australian government that no more classified (secret) material would be supplied to it. This embargo greatly disturbed Australian Security and Defence advisers, although (as usual in such circumstances) no searching questions appear to have been asked as to whether the classified material provided up to that point had been of significant value. Certainly, no vital atomic secrets had been, or were likely to be, passed on to Australia. The same embargo applied, shortly after, to classified material received by Australia from Britain, in so far as the United States was the original source of that information.[18]

Chifley, alarmed by the American embargo, determined to strengthen security arrangements. Sir Percy Sillitoe, head of the British MI5 organisation, visited Australia to give advice on the subject; and in December 1948, Chifley issued a directive that the Commonwealth Investigation Service (CIS) should carry out security checks on public servants and officers who had access to 'top secret' or 'secret' classified information. Then, in March 1949, Chifley established the Australian Security Intelligence Organisation (ASIO), which took over most of the responsibilities and records of the CIS.[19]

The extent to which Evatt was involved in these developments is not known. As Attorney-General, he had responsibility for the CIS and there is evidence that he was interested in some of its activities, which were by no means confirmed to investigation of subversion or sabotage. For example, Longfield Lloyd, Director of the CIS, reported on the circulation in 1945–47 of certain leaflets among ironworkers and coalminers in New South Wales and South Australia. Headed 'Letter from Lefty' or 'Lefty Writes Again', these leaflets were 'anti-Communist propaganda in the guise of a Communist circular to party members'. In other words, the leaflets were spurious, designed to turn readers away from the CPA by the use of such provocative statements as: 'Always remember that the ultimate purpose of all our tactics is Russian victory in the coming world war, which it will be necessary for the Soviet to make upon Britain and America'.[20]

Evidently, Communists had competitors in the field of dirty tricks directed towards workers engaged in industrial disputes or fights for control of unions. According to Lloyd, Catholic Action was responsible for publication of 'Letter from Lefty'. As indicated by a notation, Evatt read this report; and he appears to have had a high regard for the author. Longfield Lloyd, on the occasion of his retirement, wrote to Evatt, thanking him for 'your very gracious message...[expressing] every appreciation of the service rendered in the security field over all these years, often under difficult circumstances'.[21]

However, in view of Evatt's full work schedule and his responsibilities overseas, it is unlikely that he was able to keep himself adequately informed of any but the most important or urgent security matters. Chifley was more fully informed, though his Defence Department advisers had their own axes to grind. Certainly, it was on Chifley's initiative that ASIO was established, and he appointed a

South Australian judge, G. S. Reed, as its Director-General. Reed had headed a closed court inquiry into national security in 1944 and this presumably brought him to Chifley's attention. Apart from this, the Prime Minister was pleased to appoint someone with the prestige and air of impartiality of a judge. Evatt probably took the same view. Yet it soon became clear that Reed, as Hall puts it, was 'very much under the influence of the Defence Department'.[22]

Australian Communism was also of keen concern to US government officials. They were catholic in their taste for informants, so long as they were anti-Communist. For example, on 23 June 1947 the American Embassy in Canberra sent to the State Department in Washington a long 'Memorandum on Communist Activities in Australia', supplied in confidence by Dr Ryan, a Sydney priest well known as a spokesman for Catholic Action. Ryan's memorandum specified with some accuracy certain trade unions and other institutions in which Communists were said to be dominant or influential. Over a broader social field, Ryan's views—to a modern reader—appear absurdly naive: 'It is noticeable that all these Communist controlled women's organisations agitate for easy divorce, absolute equality of sexes, the introduction of women into heavy industry, wages for housewives, creches, kindergartens and other means of breaking up family life'. Other references in Ryan's memorandum were damning in their false or misleading character. Professor Julius Stone, a Zionist, was described as 'Chief Communist radio propagandist'. Evatt was said to have ordered CIB investigators to concentrate on Fascists rather than Communists, while his personal secretary, Dalziel, was alleged to be 'a well known Communist sympathiser'.[23]

Given such prejudiced reporting, it is not surprising that the US embargo on transmission of classified material to Australia remained in full force throughout 1949. American officials did not trust Evatt. Moreover the Chargé d'Affaires in Canberra reported to Washington that he had been told privately 'by several Australians on the ground' that 'Reed probably lacks the ruthlessness required in the operation of a security service'. The perspective changed in 1950, when Menzies was Prime Minister and Evatt had gone from office: a military intelligence man, Colonel Spry, was appointed to replace Reed as head of ASIO, and the US embargo was substantially withdrawn. Evatt had cause to regret his acquiescence in the establishment of ASIO, an autonomous body operating virtually outside political control. He may have been mollified in 1949 by the retention of formal administrative control of ASIO within the Attorney-General's Department, but in practice this did not mean that ASIO was accountable for its activities.[24]

NOTES

1. J.J. Dedman, interviewed by David Stephens, 28 August 1972, MS 4625 (b), NLA.
2. Quoted by Brian Galligan, *Politics of the High Court*, p. 171. See also H.C. Coombs, *Trial Balance*, pp. 114–16.
3. *CPD*, vol. 193, p. 803.
4. Patrick Weller (ed.), *Caucus Minutes*, MUP, Melbourne, 1975, vol. 3, 1932–49, p. 436.
5. Casey to J. Mitchell, 12 December 1947, Burns Philip General Manager's Correspondence, ANU Archives of Business and Labour. Casey's phraseology was mild by comparison with some of the political and business effusions of the time.
6. Latham to Evatt, 17 May 1948, Latham Papers, MS 1009, Box 1 General Correspondence 1/6413, NLA. Evatt's scheme came to full fruition in the Colombo Plan in 1950.
7. McTiernan suspected that Rich and Williams decided against the government at an early stage of the case. See K. Buckley, 'Edward McTiernan and the High Court' (unpublished MS held by Law Foundation of NSW).
8. *CPD*, vol. 202, p. 702, 8 June 1949. Holt also noted that Evatt, during his absences overseas, was represented in parliament by an acting Attorney-General (McKenna) who was a senator, not a member of the House of Representatives available for questioning there.
9. Evatt Collection, Flinders University. File: Banking Case—Notes of Evatt. See also David Marr, *Barwick*, Allen & Unwin Sydney, pp. 70–4.
10. Brian Galligan, *Politics of the High Court*, pp. 179–80.
11. Evatt to Clarrie (Clarence) Martin, 14 November 1949, Evatt Collection, Flinders University. File: Banking case.
12. *ALJR* (1988), p. 303.
13. 79 *CLR* (1949), pp. 205–6.
14. 79 *CLR*, p. 278 (Dixon), pp. 283–4 (McTiernan).
15. *CPD*, vol. 196, 7 April 1948, p. 619. Menzies was not yet committed to support Fadden on the banning of the CPA.
16. Ibid., pp. 611–12.
17. *CPD*, vol. 198, 30 September 1948, p. 1035.
18. Peter Morton, *Fire Across the Desert: Woomera and the Anglo-Australian Joint Project 1946–1980*, AGPS, Canberra, 1989, p. 104.
19. *Royal Commission on Intelligence and Security, Second Report*, AGPS, Canberra, 1977, p. 17. Under the Menzies government, the 'vetting' procedure was extended to public servants who handled less important ('confidential') material.
20. Longfield Lloyd to Secretary, Attorney-General's Department, 7 March 1947, Evatt Collection, Flinders University, File on ALP Industrial Groups and The Movement.
21. Lloyd to Evatt, 30 September 1949, Evatt Collection, Flinders University, File: Correspondence. See also Andrew Moore, *The Secret Army and the Premier*, p. 243.

22 Richard Hall, *The Secret State: Australia's Spy Industry*, Cassell Australia, 1978, p. 43. Senator McKenna had a hand in the drafting of ASIO's charter, *CPD* vol. 207, p. 3315.
23 US National Archives, RG59 Box 6166. The Commonwealth Investigation Service in 1947 also supplied the US Embassy with a report on Communist Activities in Australia, AA: A467, SF42, Bundle 89, Item 36.
24 Peter Morton, *Fire Across the Desert*, p. 106. Spry was the Australian Director of Military Intelligence between 1946 and 1950.

CHAPTER 25

DEMOCRACY, THE COAL STRIKE AND THE DEFEAT OF LABOR

It is 'most desirable that as far as possible new recruits to the coal industry...be secured from persons who have not formerly worked in coal mines and whose families do not possess coalmining backgrounds'.
JOINT COAL BOARD, 1949

Besides its problems in the High Court, the Chifley government in 1949 was under pressure on several fronts. In federal parliament, the Opposition—including Lang—persistently claimed that the government was 'soft on Communism'; and it may have been partly in order to counter these accusations that the Attorney-General's Department in March prosecuted L. Sharkey, secretary of the CPA, for uttering seditious words. He had told a journalist that if Soviet forces 'in pursuit of aggression entered Australia, Australian workers would welcome them'. In October, under the federal Crimes Act, Sharkey was sentenced to three years gaol (later reduced to eighteen months). Subsequently, Brian Fitzpatrick wrote to Evatt:

We are of course aware that the Crimes Act sedition prosecutions were launched during your Attorney-Generalship. Knowing your long-maintained view of the 'political' and 'industrial' sections of that Act, I believe that you must have consented with reluctance to their revival.[1]

Earlier in 1949, another leading Communist, J. McPhillips, who was an official of the Federated Ironworkers' Association (FIA), was gaoled for one month. He had publicly expressed distrust of the judges of the Commonwealth Arbitration Court, which was considering a basic wage claim at the time. Affronted by this reflection upon their impartiality, the judges—using a power newly acquired under the Arbitration Act of 1947—sentenced McPhillips for contempt of court. Although the court action was taken independently of the government, there is no doubt that Chifley and his colleagues were seriously concerned about the strength of Communists in important trade unions and the way in which Communists were criticising the ALP for its reliance upon the slow processes of arbitration.

At the same time, Industrial Groups in unions were fighting back against Communist advances and tactics. In particular, there were claims that Communists were rigging ballots in certain union elections so as to secure control for themselves. Actually, there was a long history of ballot-rigging in unions and the ALP, but undoubtedly there was substance in allegations about Communist involvement in the practice at this time. This became clear in 1951, when Laurie Short (supported by Industrial Groups) became secretary of the FIA after a court action in which his Communist opponent, Thornton, was found to have rigged a ballot for the position.

There was another amendment of the Arbitration Act in 1949, apparently designed to ensure that elections for union positions were fairly conducted. Prior to this—indeed, since 1928—judges of the federal Arbitration Court had power to conduct a secret ballot of members of a registered union engaged in an industrial dispute. To this, the amendment of 1949 added power for the Court to investigate and rectify irregularities in union elections; and the Court could do so at the request of any member of the union in question.

Evatt, in moving the second reading of this Arbitration (Amendment) Bill in the House of Representatives on 30 June 1949, asserted that 'the proper conduct of ballots for the election of union officials is a matter of vital public concern'. The government's standpoint had been outlined in more detail when McKenna introduced the Bill in the Senate a week earlier. In fact, McKenna was largely responsible for preparing the Bill, which had a long gestation period. Although he did not say so, there was more involved than the question of clean ballots. Democracy in unions was also related to internal union rules and the way in which they operated. The AWU in particular was notorious for the ruthlessness with which its officials dealt with opponents in the union.[2]

Evatt had long been aware of the arbitrary manner in which the bureaucrats of the AWU maintained control over members of their union. This is evident from an entry in Henry Boote's diary at a time when Evatt was still a High Court judge. Boote wrote that Evatt had phoned 'to express his disgust' that AWU officials had gone to see Attorney-General Hughes

to ask him to have the Arbitration Act amended so that the AWU Executive could debar 'Communists or Communist sympathisers' from standing for office in the Union. A most reactionary move, in Evatt's strongly-worded opinion. I agreed.[3]

The episode illustrates the concern of AWU officials in Queensland over the activities of a militant group of pastoral and sugar workers, who had broken away to form the Pastoral Workers and Industrial Union in the 1930s. The union appears to have been dissolved after a while, but its supporters remained a thorn in the side of conservative AWU leaders, who frowned upon strike action. The problem recurred in 1945 when there was an unofficial strike, in defiance of the State executive of the AWU, by workers in the grazing industry of Queensland.

C. G. Fallon, Queensland secretary of the AWU, approached the federal Attorney-General's Department and the matter was dealt with by Senator McKenna in the absence of Evatt overseas. Fallon sought federal legislation making it an offence for any person to cause, or take part in, a strike without the authority of the registered union; and the collection of strike funds by persons not authorised by the union to do so should be prohibited.

McKenna was sympathetic, accepting Fallon's argument that unless some drastic action was taken, Communist influence would result in 'a serious extension of these practices, disruptive of Trades Unionism and of the process of Arbitration'. However, McKenna envisaged problems. In particular, any legislative proposal to prohibit strikes or lock-outs conducted without the authority of the controlling body of the union concerned would encounter opposition from many unions. As McKenna put it to Chifley:

The Trades Union Movement has for many years opposed the enactment of such provisions on the ground that such measures are of a domestic nature to be determined by the Unions themselves.[4]

Consequently, the government took no action, and the matter rested there for two or three years before being revived again in response to pressure from ALP Industrial Groups for legislation on 'clean ballots'. For instance, Short led a deputation of ironworkers to see Chifley on the subject in May 1949. At the same time, the Federal Labor Advisory Council, which included representatives of the Australian Council of Trade Unions, recommended legislation to deal with irregularities in union elections. Thus McKenna, introducing the

Arbitration Bill a month later, was able to say that its 'broad principles' had the support of the ACTU. Evatt, while acknowledging that unions traditionally claimed the right to conduct their own elections without outside interference, brushed aside such objections as being less important than the test of public interest.[5]

In brief, there was more to the Arbitration Bill of 1949 than appeared on the surface. The Industrial Groups, intent upon securing control, had their own conservative agenda, which was no more concerned with the democratic functioning of unions than was the programme of Communist opponents. Court intervention in union affairs was regarded as likely to favour anti-Communists. The antecedents of the Arbitration Bill have been presented here in some detail in order to show the internal party pressures on Labor leaders, including Evatt, at the time. A further factor was the 'cold war' campaigning of conservative parties. Evatt gave his support to the Bill, but he appears to have had little to do with it. Indeed, he was fully engrossed in making a second-reading speech on the more important National Emergency (Coal Strike) Bill on 29 June, one day before he spoke briefly on the Arbitration Bill. Evatt remained conscious of the lack of democracy in the AWU. Later, in the 1950s, he quietly gave Clyde Cameron legal advice on how to challenge the validity of arbitrary AWU rules aimed at disciplining internal critics. Cameron, a long-term opponent of federal AWU officials, put this advice to good use.[6]

Because the passage of the Arbitration Bill overlapped that of the Coal Strike Bill in 1949, it is easy to assume that the two events were integrally connected. This is the more so when account is taken of the antecedents of the Arbitration Bill in attempts to limit the right to strike—which was definitely the aim of the punitive Coal Strike Bill. Yet the arbitration legislation did not arise out of the coal crisis. One conceivable connection is that the determination of the government to restrict Communist power via the Arbitration Bill may have steeled Chifley's resolve to break the coalminers' strike, thereby undermining Communist influence in the labour movement. Certainly, that object was gained, and it made sense for the government to suppose that the strike resulted from strong Communist influence in the Miners' Federation. The irony of the situation was that the miners, in their isolated lodges on each coalfield, were probably more democratically organised than any other union members in Australia. When they responded to Communist urgings for direct action, it was because the miners themselves felt aggressive. In fact, they were often ahead of Communists in this respect. During the war years, Communists frequently failed in attempts to restrain miners, in the interest of the war effort, from going on strike. The coalminers had grim memories of the pre-war depression years and were determined to make gains in the circumstances of full employment which followed the war.

Certain features of the Australian coalmining industry were universally acknowledged: it was vital to the economy; technically backward; and relations between mine owners and those who produced the coal were exceptionally bad. In 1946–47, the governments of the Commonwealth and New South Wales (both Labor) set up a Joint Coal Board, with regulatory powers to rationalise the industry and expand production, as well as to promote the welfare of workers engaged in it in New South Wales, the source State of about eighty per cent of total coal output. A Coal Industry Tribunal, consisting of one man (F. H. Gallagher), was also established as an arbitration authority.

In the next few years, the Joint Coal Board worked to improve production, for example by encouraging mechanisation of mines. Considerable amounts of public capital were allocated for these purposes, and some money was spent on improving amenities for miners, such as washing facilities at pit-tops. These moves were acceptable to the private mine owners, who continued to draw profits from the industry. However, the miners were dissatisfied. Mining remained a hard, dirty and dangerous occupation. The Miners' Federation traditionally regarded the employers as greedy and callous; and the union's panacea for problems was for the nationalisation of coal mines. This was also part of official ALP policy, yet in the postwar years there was no government move to implement it. Instead, miners were urged to produce more, and outbreaks of industrial disputes at a local level gave rise to increasing irritation in the community outside mining areas. A significant indication of the alienation of government officials from miners is conveyed by a confidential Joint Coal Board document in May 1949, stating that the Board considered it

most desirable that as far as possible new recruits to the coal industry... be secured from persons who have not formerly worked in coal mines and whose families do not possess coalmining backgrounds.[7]

If this viewpoint had been made public, there would have been an explosive reaction from the close-knit, clannish mining communities. As it was, the miners felt that too little was being done to improve their working lives, and they wanted action. Early in 1949, the miners' union lodged a claim with the Coal Industry Tribunal for a thirty-five-hour week, substantial wage increases and more generous provision for long-service leave. It was a formidable log of claims, but not outrageously so—miners at Broken Hill and in the New Zealand coalmining industry already had a thirty-five-hour week. From the federal government's point of view, the big problem was that a quick concession of major gains to miners would encourage claims by other unions for comparable concessions, which would then upset the government's anti-inflation policy of dampening down wage claims. Consequently, Chifley insisted that the miners' claims be dealt with through arbitration. He stated in a radio broadcast that 'the miners cannot hope to enforce their claims by the law of the jungle'. It was a trite phrase, which did not impress miners who had memories of the situation in 1929–30, when colliery proprietors successfully defied the law in locking out their workers for fifteen months.

Rather than the dilatory process of arbitration, the miners sought direct collective bargaining, to be followed by strike action if that failed to achieve results. Acting as the Coal Industry Tribunal, Gallagher offered arbitration on the dispute, but only if the threat of a strike were withdrawn. Indeed, Gallagher angered the miners by prohibiting the holding of stop-work meetings to decide whether the miners should go on strike. The Miners' Federation ignored the prohibition order, regarding it as interference with the members' traditional right to strike if they wished; and the aggregate meetings voted heavily in favour of a general coal strike, to begin on 27 June 1949. The decision was strongly supported by Communists, both within the Federation and outside it: they saw the matter as a decisive test of Labor government policy and authority.

The Miners' Federation gave eleven days notice of the approaching strike. This proved a tactical mistake, due partly to the union's democratic procedure in implementing aggregate meeting decisions. Additionally, miners were confident of winning: reserve stocks of coal were low and there was some expectation that the government, to avert a fuel crisis, would agree to a compromise settlement at the last minute. When that expectation evaporated, there were apparently some Communist leaders, experienced in trade union negotiations, who favoured a tactical retreat by the miners from their hard-line position. However, Communist influence in the Federation was not as strong as was supposed and the CPA maintained its firm pro-strike policy in public, believing that the miners would win their struggle. It should be added that Communists, although they had an exaggerated opinion of their own strength, at no time envisaged a coup. This was not a revolutionary situation. [8]

Governments made good use of the advance notice given by the Miners' Federation. Before the strike began, well over 100 000 industrial workers were stood down in New South Wales in anticipation of shortages of coal, and cuts in cooking, lighting and transport facilities were imposed. These moves, intensified once the strike was under way, had the effect of rousing strong feelings of resentment against the miners in the general community, including many workers. Chifley made other arrangements by setting up a sub-committee on the strike. It comprised himself, Evatt, W. P. Ashley (Minister for Shipping and Fuel), Dedman (Defence) and C. Chambers (Army). Evatt threw himself into the work of this body. In particular, he prepared the National Emergency (Coal Strike) Bill, which he introduced in parliament two days after the strike began. The Bill was rushed through all stages in one day, the only dissentient voice being Doris Blackburn's.[9]

This Act was a shocking departure from Labor traditions and policy. It made it an offence for any person to give financial aid to the miners on strike. This applied to those unions which supported the miners as well as the Miners' Federation itself, which was prohibited from providing the usual strike pay to its members. The miners and their families were to be starved into submission. The Act had retrospective effect, so that the federal Arbitration Court, if satisfied that at any time since 16 June money had been paid for strike purposes, could order its repayment by whoever was in possession of it. To clinch matters, the Act placed the onus of proof in legal proceedings on supporters of the miners: unless proved to the contrary, a payment was deemed to be made for strike purposes. As a partial justification of this draconian measure, Evatt said that 'for many years the employees of the [coalmining] industry have worked under unsatisfactory and often degrading conditions. Those times have gone'. Arthur Calwell tied himself in knots in the parliamentary discussion:

For my part, I believe that the strike weapon should not be used...but let me say clearly that no supporter of the labor party will ever deny to the worker the right to strike. [10]

In mitigation of the harshness of the Act, it may be said that it was designed to have effect only until the end of the coal strike, and it was then repealed. Nevertheless, in the interim the Act was used ruthlessly. Immediately before the National Emergency (Coal Strike) Bill became effective law, the Miners' Federation and several sympathetic unions, anticipating the 'freezing' of union funds, withdrew sums totalling £50 000 or more from their bank accounts. In terms of the Act, the Arbitration Court ordered that this money be paid into the court to prevent its use in the strike. Then, when some union officials refused to disclose the whereabouts of the money, the court sentenced seven union officials (five from the Miners' Federation and two from the Waterside Workers' Federation) to twelve months gaol each. This was despite the fact that some, perhaps most, of these men did not know where the missing money was secreted. Della Elliott, who worked in the Waterside Workers' Sydney office at the time, revealed decades later that although the union's leaders, Healy and Roach, did not know the whereabouts of the union's cache of £6000, she knew. With the assistance of her Greek father, she had hidden it in large jars of rice which stood in a storeroom under her parents' home. When questioned in court in 1949, she was not directly asked if she knew where the money was.[11]

The Arbitration Court judge who imposed these swingeing gaol sentences upon union leaders was A. Foster, known earlier as a Labor lawyer. There is an unsubstantiated, though plausible, story to the effect that Evatt influenced Foster's decision through a private telephone conversation. Whatever the truth in that tale, Foster needed little or no urging. His anti-Communist bias is shown plainly in the transcript of court evidence; and it was he who chose gaol sentences of twelve months on the subjective ground of contempt of court rather than under the Coal Strike Act where the maximum sentence would have been six months. It may be added that when the validity of the Coal Strike Act was challenged by unions in the High Court, the application was dismissed with extraordinary celerity on 6 July by a bench consisting of Rich, McTiernan and Williams.[12]

The gaoled union leaders included the president and secretary of the Miners' Federation, and their removal from the scene was welcomed by the government. Nevertheless, the miners remained as determined to win the strike as Chifley, on the other side, was adamant about breaking it. As stocks of coal dwindled, the government's options—short of contemplating economic disaster—were limited. One option was to use the conservative AWU to produce more coal. Before the strike, members of this union were already employed to some extent in open-cut coalmining. There was thus rivalry between the AWU and the Miners' Federation; and after the commencement of the strike, AWU leaders such as Fallon in Queensland and the federal secretary, Dougherty, made it clear that they would be happy to see their members used more extensively in working open cuts on a permanent basis.

The idea was also favoured by R. Williams, Deputy Director of the Commonwealth Investigation Service. When the strike collapsed, he secretly reported his own apprehension that the Miners' Federation would remain strong in future:

The only effective way the Federation could have been weakened would have been to place members of the Australian Workers' Union in charge of the open-cut mines...once continuity of supplies for essential demands can be maintained in future strikes through A.W.U. labour the strength of the Federation would be at an end.[13]

The Chifley government, after consideration, decided against such strong anti-union action, on the ground that it would lead to constant disruptions of coal supplies through demarcation disputes once the strike ended. This objection did not apply to another option: short-term employment of troops to produce, handle and transport coal during the dispute. Virtually from the start of the strike, Evatt (at Chifley's request) was directly concerned with the legal ramifications of this possibility. He examined the terms of the Defence Act and a relevant Army Order, and decided that there was nothing to prevent the government from using the Permanent Forces in an industrial dispute, so long as proper procedures were followed. So Evatt drafted a Minute to be signed by Ministers of the Forces, authorising the use of soldiers in open-cut mining and coal transport in New South Wales, as well as the use of naval personnel to unload imported coal from a ship in Melbourne.[14]

A joint meeting of the federal and New South Wales Cabinets on 27 July 1949 approved the use of troops in the coal dispute, and soldiers (who were all paid a bonus) began work four days later. Incidentally, these men included Army Engineers and Air Force constructional personnel from the long-range weapons site at Woomera. The use of troops was a very clear affirmation of Chifley's 'boots and all' determination to break the strike, and Crisp quotes the Prime Minister's privately expressed appreciation of the 'very great value' of Evatt's legal knowledge in this connection. Yet Evatt was aware that despite Chifley's great prestige in the ALP and trade unions, there was much disquiet among Labor supporters, particularly over the breach of union principle involved in the introduction of troops. Dr Eric Dark, an old friend of Evatt's from university days, wrote to him expressing dismay, and his wife, novelist Eleanor Dark, concurred. Evatt replied at length, noting that Curtin had used military personnel to move vital cargoes during wharf disputes. However, in doing this, Curtin had relied upon a National Security Regulation promulgated for wartime use.[15]

Unlike Chifley, Evatt did not have a closed mind about the coal strike. This is indicated by a curious episode in July 1949, before troops were brought into the dispute. E. Thornton, a prominent Communist and union leader, in an informal approach to John Burton, said that he would like to meet his 'boss', Evatt. When this message was passed on to Evatt, he agreed to meet Thornton, so long as it was a secret meeting at Burton's farm on the outskirts of Canberra. This was arranged but according to Burton, when the meeting was held, each man was tough and unyielding in discussing the coal strike—each was trying to find out what was in the other's mind. Another meeting, again at Thornton's suggestion, was held a week or so later, this time in a different atmosphere. There was a stalemate in the strike situation, and Evatt felt that Thornton was aiming to get the strikers and their supporters 'off the hook'. Consequently, there was exploration of ways of reaching a settlement.[16]

Eddie Maher, a Communist party organiser in the trade union field, was not at this meeting, but he was present when Thornton reported back to other Communist leaders. According to Maher, Thornton said that Evatt's attitude was that the government would adhere to its policy on arbitration, but that if the CPA would recommend a return to work by the miners, the government would look sympathetically at the miners' claims, with one exception. The exception concerned the thirty-five-hour week. Evatt was reported as saying that a shorter working week could not be conceded: if it were, 'Menzies would crucify Labor about a shortage of coal'. Evatt's proposition was that the Miners' Federation should go back to the Coal Industry Tribunal, on the understanding that the government would support some, if not all, of the miners' other claims. Maher's reaction was favourable:

A wink was as good as a nod...in all my experience, you never get things while on strike, you've got to listen and go back, sometimes a deal is being done, sometimes not. You've got to make up your mind. I would say that if that proposition had been put [to miners' leaders] they would have accepted.[17]

However, other Communists reckoned differently, especially as some of their comrades were in gaol, and that was the end of the prospect of negotiations. On the other side, there was a similar rejection of compromise. Evatt, after his meetings with Thornton, told Chifley about them, but the Prime Minister wanted nothing to do with Thornton or other Communists whom he held responsible for the strike.

That concluded the episode, and the coal strike collapsed in August. There is some doubt as to whether the soldiers dug much coal, as distinct from transporting stockpiled coal, but undoubtedly the miners were despondent over the actions of federal and State Labor governments. Miners were also disillusioned by public hostility towards them and the failure of other unions (a great number of whose members had been rendered unemployed) to support them. Communists suffered a resounding defeat, and many people reckoned that the government's stand boosted Labor's electoral prospects. Thus Judge Foster sent his 'best regards' to 'My Dear Bert':

The strike is over and today the men have purged their contempt...The Government has won great praise for its handling of a very difficult task—*I hope the [Arbitration] Court has also come out of the ordeal without loss of prestige...Election prospects over here are excellent.*[18]

As an assessor of public opinion, Foster did not rate highly. Chifley was shrewder in expecting the political benefit for the government to be short-lived; and in fact the ALP was defeated in a general election in December 1949. Considerable sections of the labour movement were disgruntled by the government's fierce reaction to the coal strike.

Neither Chifley nor Evatt made much reference to the coal strike in the election campaign, although they were at pains to rebut Opposition claims that the ALP, as in the recent struggle over bank nationalisation, was wedded to socialism and should be regarded as unreliable in relation to Communism. It was largely to forestall such allegations concerning foreign policy that Evatt and Chifley in October 1949 decided (contrary to public expectations) that Australia should not give formal recognition to the Communist government of China. Until then, Evatt—on the advice of Australian diplomats in Nanking—favoured recognition on the pragmatic ground that the Communist regime was in actual control of China, and Australia would benefit from a trade relationship. Furthermore, the British government, with interests of its own in Hong Kong, was urging Evatt to recognise the People's Republic of China. Evatt decided not to do so—partly, no doubt, because the US government was opposed to recognition, but mainly because of the electoral implications in Australia. Burton's recollection of the matter is that he arranged a meeting of senior External Affairs officials to discuss the question. Evatt came in at the end of the meeting and enquired of Keith Officer as to the consensus of opinion. Officer told him that they were unanimously in favour of recognition, whereupon Evatt said dismissively, 'Keith, you're a Red', and walked out. Chifley then persuaded Cabinet that it would be wrong to commit Australia immediately to recognition of Communist China: the decision should be left to whichever party won the approaching general election.[19]

Besides the factors already noted, there were a number of other reasons for Labor's electoral defeat in 1949. There was widespread public irritation over the maintenance of many restrictions so long after the war, and the government's decision to reintroduce petrol rationing focussed attention upon this point. In contrast, the Liberal–Country Parties promised not only relaxation of restrictions but an extension of child endowment payments to the first child in every family, not merely the second and subsequent children. Menzies appealed specifically to female voters. Evatt's friend, W. S. Robinson, noted these circumstances when he wrote to the American financier, Bernard Baruch, after the election. Robinson added two other points to explain Labor's defeat: 'the antagonism of the Catholic Church to the socialisation of the individual'; and 'the revolt of the outlying or periphery states [Queensland, Western Australia, Tasmania] against the rule of Canberra based on the representatives of New South Wales and Victoria'.[20]

Underlying the Chifley government's defeat were strong currents of hostile opinion in important sections of the population. Among professional people, this was most obvious in the medical profession, whose practitioners viewed the attempt to introduce free medicine as a precursor of plans to transform doctors into government employees. Labor also lost support among businessmen and white-collar workers over the proposal to nationalise banks. According to J. Dedman, in his Geelong constituency 'there were bank officers going round telling people that if the Labor Party got back to power all their savings bank deposits would be taken over by the government'. Throughout Australia, the press was heavily anti-Labor.

With such forces arrayed against the ALP, and given the fact that Chifley's policy of standing on the government's record in office was uninspiring, what is surprising is not that the Party lost the 1949 election but that the margin of loss was not much greater. For the House of Representatives, Labor's vote fell by about four percentage points, to forty-five or -six per cent of the total. True, this translated into a decisive loss of seats: Labor secured only 47, compared with 74 won by its opponents. Nevertheless, the margin in a number of seats was quite slim, so that Labor appeared to have reasonable prospects of recovery in the future.

Evatt held his own seat of Barton, but of course lost his ministerial portfolios. Robinson wrote a letter of commiseration, adding that there were compensations for Bert and Mary Alice Evatt:

At last you can rest, at last you can have some private life—I hope you will take full advantage of them...I suppose however it will not be long before that restless spirit of yours will be stirred to the point of turbulence and we'll hear of you tackling some gigantic literary job or dipping deeply into international affairs for which no-one is better suited than you.[21]

NOTES

1 Fitzpatrick to Evatt, 21 February 1950, Fitzpatrick Papers, MS 4965, 1/4406, NLA. McKenna had been acting Attorney-General when it was decided to prosecute Sharkey.
2 *CPD*, vol. 203, pp. 1812–13.
3 Boote Diary, 27 April 1941, MS2070, NLA.
4 McKenna to Chifley, 9 January 1946, Evatt Collection, Flinders University.

5 Susanna Short, *Laurie Short: A Political Life*, Sydney, Allen & Unwin, 1992, p. 100; *CPD*, vol. 203, pp. 1399–400. The ACTU Congress in September 1949 narrowly endorsed the Arbitration Act amendment.
6 Interview with Clyde Cameron, 3 May 1988.
7 Quoted by Tom Sheridan, 'Planners and the Australian Labor Market 1945–1949', *Labour History*, no. 53, November 1987, p. 112.
8 Kylie Tennant, *Evatt: Politics and Justice*, pp. 251–2; Ralph Gibson, *The Fight Goes On*, Red Rooster, Melbourne, 1987, p. 78.
9 The most comprehensive account of the coal strike is in Tom Sheridan, *Division of Labour*, chs 11 and 12. See also Robin Gollan, *The Coalminers of New South Wales*, MUP, Melbourne, 1963, ch.11.
10 *CPD*, vol. 203, pp. 1677 (Evatt), 1690 (Calwell). In the Labor caucus, some MPs opposed the Bill.
11 Audrey Johnson, 'Recollection of an Old Leftie', *The Hummer* (Sydney), no. 34, 1992, pp. 18–19. Della was married to E.V. Elliott, secretary of the Seamens' Union.
12 Brian Fitzpatrick, in *The Australian Commonwealth*, Cheshire, Melbourne, 1956, p. 84, observed that 'a dozen of Foster's' had long been the colloquial order for twelve bottles of a Melbourne lager beer, but the term acquired another meaning after Foster's sentences in 1949.
13 R. Williams to Director, CIS, 12 August 1949, Evatt Collection, Flinders University.
14 However, members of Citizen Military Forces could not be used in connection with an industrial dispute. This information is derived from a summary in Army Department Minute, 19 October 1950, Australian Archives, A4931, Menzies Ministry Cabinet Decisions, vol. 1, March 1951. We are indebted to Dr Les Louis for this reference.
15 L.F. Crisp, *Ben Chifley: A Political Biography*, Angus & Robertson, Sydney, 1977, p. 363; Evatt to Dark, 28 July 1949, Evatt Collection, Flinders University, File: Miscellaneous Corespondence, 1948–49. Dark reminded Evatt that he had once called Dark his 'political conscience'.
16 Interview with John Burton, Canberra, December 1988.
17 Interview with Eddie Maher, Sydney, October 1987. See also Tom Sheridan, *Division of Labour*, p. 310.
18 A. Foster, Commonwealth Arbitration Court, Melbourne, to Evatt, 25 August 1949, Evatt Collection, Flinders University, File: Attorney General's Department—Miscellaneous Correspondence. On 24 August, Judges Kelly and Kirby in the Arbitration Court decided to release the gaoled union officials.
19 J.J. Dedman, interviewed by D. Stephens, Canberra, 28 August 1972, MS 4625 (b), NLA.
20 Robinson to Baruch, 11 January 1950, W.S. Robinson Collection , Box 5, File 61, Melbourne University Archives. In an earlier letter to Baruch, on 24 March 1948, Robinson described Evatt's address to the High Court in the bank nationalisation case as 'a wonderful job for what I tell him is a questionable cause!'
21 W.S. Robinson to Evatt, 19 December 1949, Evatt Collection, Flinders University.

PART VI

LEADER OF THE OPPOSITION

CHAPTER 26

THE 1951 REFERENDUM: EVATT'S FINEST HOUR

It is fascist in spirit and a definite step towards the police state.
H.V. EVATT

After the defeat of the Chifley government, Evatt talked privately of quitting politics. For a man of his ability and experience, a return to the High Court bench might have seemed fitting, and openings were appearing there. Starke and Rich, content to see Labor out of office, both retired from the Court early in 1950. Sir George Rich, avid for formal preferment, was disappointed by Labor, as he indicated a year earlier in a letter to Evatt, who was then in London. Rich wrote:

I propose to take leave at the end of this year. As senior justice I should have priority in case any juniors have the same idea. From 1913 to 1949 is a bit of a record and added to that are the two years on the N.S.W. [Supreme Court] Bench 1911–1913. In each case I was appointed by the A.G. of a Labour Ministry—Holman in N.S.W. and Hughes Commonwealth. I suppose in England one gets some recognition of services rendered, not so in Australia.[1]

Yet although the retirement of Rich and Starke left two High Court positions to be filled there was no chance of Evatt being appointed to either of them. The appointments were made by the government of the day, and Menzies would certainly not have considered Evatt for such a position. Nor would Evatt have entertained any hope of appointment in the circumstances. Further, it is unlikely that he would have been attracted by possible appointment to a judgeship (not Chief Justice) in the New South Wales Supreme Court. There appears to be no reliable evidence for a story that Evatt angled for this position, and it would have entailed a big loss of face for someone who had been a High Court judge. Rumours abounded. For example, the London *Daily Telegraph* on 20 December 1949 stated that Evatt was a 'probable' candidate to replace Trygve Lie as United Nations Secretary-General.[2]

Certainly, there was no lessening of Evatt's interest in politics and international affairs. When the federal ALP caucus met in February 1950, Chifley was re-elected as leader of the Party, while Evatt defeated Ward for the deputy leadership. A month later, Evatt made a parliamentary speech on foreign policy, in which he noted critically that the new Minister, Spender, had said that at present there was to be no recognition by Australia of the Communist Chinese government. Evatt, in a move to modify his own recent attitude on the subject, said that 'some degree of recognition of Communist China cannot be deferred indefinitely'. He also noted that the governments of the United Kingdom and India had granted such recognition.[3]

Evatt's moderation in speaking about this matter may have been due to more than acknowledgement of his recent opportunism. W. S. Robinson detected a relaxation of manner:

Bert is a 'New Man' now that he has been temporarily relieved of the strains of office. Gracious, tolerant, eloquent and strongly desirous of lending a helping hand to everything proposed for the World's peace and Australia's safety.[4]

Any such relaxation of tension was unlikely to survive the introduction of the Menzies government's Communist Party Dissolution Bill in April 1950. This legislation was designed to outlaw the CPA and to confiscate its property. Other organisations, which in the view of the government were substantially Communist, could also be declared unlawful; and persons who continued to be members of an unlawful association would be liable to imprisonment. Where the government was satisfied that a named person was a Communist, he could be 'declared' as such, and 'declared' persons would be ineligible for employment in government service or as officials of trade unions in key industries.

Basically, the Bill aimed at punishing people, not for their actions but for their thoughts and opinions—to the extent that those supposedly Communist thoughts were abhorrent to the regime in office. Menzies' justification of this move in peacetime was the Cold War. In introducing the Bill, he said: 'We are not at peace today, except in a technical sense'. Evatt responded by saying that the government already had power under the Crimes Act to take court action to obtain a declaration of unlawfulness against an organisation which advocated the overthrow of the constitution by violence, but the government had not used this section of the Act because it wished to avoid court processes. The Communist Party and other organisations were now to be made unlawful directly by Act of Parliament. Evatt added that the Crimes Act had been denounced by Labor leaders for many years, 'not because it did not provide for legal proceedings to be taken, but because it casts the onus of proof, in certain respects, upon those who have to answer cases brought under the Act'.[5]

The question of onus of proof was critical. A person 'declared' by the government was put in the position of having to demonstrate that he or she was not a Communist—a negative which was difficult to prove. Failing this, they would lose their livelihood if employed in the public service or by certain trade unions. The flaws in this procedure became apparent immediately. Menzies, in his introductory speech on the Bill, named fifty-three people as Communists. Most of them, like Thornton and Healy, held important trade union offices. The information was supplied by ASIO, yet shortly afterwards the Prime Minister had to acknowledge that five of these people were either not Communist or did not occupy the trade union position stated. To make matters worse, Menzies claimed that one Labor Senator could easily be 'declared', while one member of the House of Representatives 'might escape only by the skin of his teeth'. The threat was manifest and nobody doubted that Menzies had in mind Senator Morrow and Eddie Ward.

Chifley and Evatt were well aware that Menzies' strategy was directed against Labor as well as the CPA. The ALP was in a quandary. It could oppose the Bill wholeheartedly, to the point of defeating it in the Senate. However, this would enable the government to call for a double dissolution of parliament, and in the ensuing election it was likely that Labor would be defeated on the issue, losing its majority in the Senate. Opinion polls indicated that there was a strong public majority in favour of the Communist Party Dissolution Bill. Furthermore, the government claimed a mandate for the Bill, having advocated the policy in the recent general election.

The alternative strategy for Labor was to shuffle, ignoring the fact that in 1948 a federal conference of the ALP, while denouncing Communism, had agreed that to ban the CPA would be 'a negation of democratic principles'. A further important factor in favour of equivocation was that the election of 1949 had resulted in the strengthening of the bloc of federal Labor MPs, particularly from Victoria, who were supporters of the Movement. Their fervent anti-

Communist Catholic feelings overrode loyalty to traditional Labor principles and objectives. These men were a small minority among Labor parliamentarians, but they represented a potent threat to split the Party if they did not get their way. Chifley, for one, was worried by the religious fanatics in the Party.

The outcome was that the federal caucus in May 1950 decided by a narrow majority not to oppose the Bill in principle but to move certain amendments to it. This was in line with the views of the federal executive of the ALP, and this course was followed in parliamentary debate on the Bill. Chifley felt bound to accept the decision, although he made his own position clear in public, saying: 'I do not want anybody to think I see any virtue in this legislation'. This may be contrasted with the tenor of McKenna's statement in the Senate. He said that the ALP was 'in complete accord' with the broad purposes of the Bill, 'to destroy communism in Australia, and, secondly, to remove Communists from key positions in trade unions and in the Public Service'. Where the ALP disagreed with the government, said McKenna, was on the methods chosen to achieve these ends and the government's disregard for the rule of law.[6]

Evatt worked doggedly in the parliamentary debate on the Bill, moving and speaking to a series of amendments on such questions as the onus of proof. In the process, Evatt and his Party were subjected to much criticism from the government, which pointed to earlier measures on which Labor had compromised its reputation concerning civil liberties, particularly the Approved Defence Projects Protection Act and the National Emergency (Coal Strike) Act. Evatt was also taunted about his supposed involvement in the Australia First Movement internments. On the other hand, there were some encouraging signs of opposition to the Bill outside parliament. Fifty students, members of the Sydney University History Club, signed a letter of support addressed to Evatt. The signatories included Eric Fry and J. Hagan, both to become well known later as labour historians. A number of trade unions strongly opposed the Bill, although the Industrial Groups took a different line.

Menzies conceded some minor points in debate on the Bill, but this made no real change in the situation. Matters were different in the Senate, where Labor used its numbers to make substantial amendments to the Bill. However, when the amended Bill was returned to the House of Representatives, the government majority there refused to accept the amendments. The stage then seemed set for a dissolution of both houses of parliament to resolve the impasse—a solution which would have suited the government in the context of intense anti-Communist feeling associated with the outbreak of war in Korea. In facing this situation, most members of the federal ALP caucus followed the advice of Chifley and Evatt to persist with the amendments and to go to a general election if need be.

As the last moment, this principled stand was overridden by the federal Executive of the ALP. In October, this body, strongly influenced by the party's Victorian and Western Australian branches, went to water. The Executive instructed the federal parliamentary Labor Party to withdraw its opposition to the government's Communist Party Dissolution Bill. As a meaningless face-saver, the parliamentary Party was directed to insert Labor's amendments in the legislation once it regained office in government. The immediate reality was that the prospect of a double dissolution of parliament was averted. The Labor representatives acted as instructed, and probably most of them were secretly relieved to do so. The Bill was signed into law later that month.

L. F. Crisp notes that in the detailed parliamentary debate up till then, 'Evatt handled the lion's share and fought tirelessly a tremendous duel with Menzies'. Kylie Tennant, while agreeing on this, says that initially, in May 1950, Evatt advised the ALP Executive to let the Bill go through parliament as quickly as possible, on the grounds that Labor could not then be accused of supporting Communism; and the Act, when challenged in the High Court, would be judged unconstitutional. Tennant has been followed on this point by later commentators, yet there is no satisfactory evidence to indicate that Evatt gave any such advice to the Party. Crisp, who was in a good position to know, makes no reference to the matter, nor does Leicester Webb. There is actually a simple explanation for Evatt's apparent agreement with the early decision by caucus not to vote against the Bill as a whole but to move amendments to it: Party solidarity and discipline required his adherence to that decision, whatever his personal opinion might have been.[7]

As for the suggestion that from the outset Evatt was confident that in due course a challenge to the legislation in the High Court would be successful, this is inherently unlikely in view of the strong rebuffs which Evatt had recently experienced in the Court. True, he was personally involved in such a challenge after the struggle in parliament ended, but until then he would have preferred to seek a total rejection of the Bill. His subsequent actions made plain his abhorrence of the Communist Party Dissolution Act and the threat to civil liberties which it represented.

As soon as the Act came into force, its constitutional validity was tested in the High Court by a number of unions, including the Waterside Workers' Federation (WWF). Evatt's decision, as a barrister, to accept a brief to represent the WWF in court was taken without consultation with his political colleagues and it created a sensation in the press. It was in accord with the ethics of the Bar, as Menzies conceded, yet it gave supporters of the Communist Party Dissolution Act a good opportunity to insinuate that Evatt was a friend of Communists such as Healy, the secretary of the WWF. Evatt's decision was expected to damage the ALP in public opinion, as the party would be associated with the parallel CPA resolve to test the validity of the Act through its own legal representatives.

As it happened, the dry legal argument in the High Court was beyond the comprehension of most people. The essential issue was freedom of speech, and particularly whether a government could outlaw a political party and 'declare' as punishable other organisations and individuals associated with that party, simply in terms of an Act of Parliament which gave arbitrary power of decision-making to the Attorney-General. The intellectual frailty of the government's reasoning is indicated by its failure to find any instance of the CPA publicly advocating the overthrow by violence of the existing social and economic order since the wartime ban on the party was lifted in 1942. Yet this was the party now regarded under the Act as guilty of subversion, as distinct from the utterance of seditious words by one or two of its leaders.

Chief Justice Latham favoured the government's argument. Indeed, there is reason to believe that on various occasions he gave advice to Menzies and other conservative leaders on political matters, improper though that would be for a person in such high judicial office. Latham, from his time as an Australian Naval Intelligence officer in World War I, hated Bolsheviks and their associates. It was an obsession reflected in his efforts to suppress them while he was Attorney-General in the 1930s; and he remained consistent in upholding the Menzies government's Communist Party Dissolution Act in 1951.[8]

The other High Court judges disagreed with Latham on the matter. McTiernan was most strongly opposed to the Act, but it was not till towards the end of the case that he was 'most relieved' to learn that he would not be alone in opposition. The case was decided not so much as a clear-cut issue of civil liberties as on the respective powers of government and the courts. As Evatt put it in addressing the High Court:

For the Act to give discretion to the executive government to condemn property and take away the civil rights of citizens not upon established facts but on the mere say-so of the executive is to introduce legally an extravagant, fantastic and tyrannical notion into the Constitution.[9]

Evatt's argument relied heavily upon the judgment in 1925 in the *Walsh–Johnson* deportation case (in which he had himself been an advocate) to the effect that it was for the courts, not parliament, to determine the facts—certainly at a time when Australia was not in a state of war. The Commonwealth might legislate to prohibit subversion, but it must be left to the courts to decide, after criminal trials, whether or not associations or individuals were guilty. The point might be expressed with a different emphasis: if fundamental restrictions on liberty were to be imposed, they should be authorised by the High Court, not the government. Moreover, it was remarked that there appeared to be nothing to stop the States from enacting identical legislation. This, in the absence of a constitutional Bill of Rights, meant a rather shaky foundation for civil liberties, but it was ground enough for the High Court judges. In March 1951, they decided by a majority of six to one (Latham being the dissentient) that the Communist Party Dissolution Act was invalid. In a succinct summation, Justice Michael Kirby wrote recently: 'Evatt, the lawyer, was vindicated'. Kirby also notes that South Africa, through its Suppression of Communism Act 1950, provided a model of the kind of repressive society Australia could have become had its own legislation been upheld in the High Court or endorsed by the people in a subsequent referendum.[10]

Ten days after the announcement of the High Court decision, Menzies secured a double dissolution of parliament on the ground that the Senate had 'failed to pass' a relatively unimportant Commonwealth Bank Bill. The point was a technical one, unconnected with the Communist issue—on which the Labor senators had already sold the pass—but it was enough for the government's purposes. In the ensuing general election campaign, Communism was a much more prominent matter than bank legislation. This was particularly so in Evatt's electorate, Barton, where his opponent, Nancy Wake (acclaimed as a war heroine), attacked him for being 'a defender of communism'. Evatt was re-elected with a majority of only 243 votes, although the closeness of the vote may have been related to another factor, which deserves closer analysis than it is usually given.

Evatt is generally considered to have neglected his constituency between elections, and there were numerous complaints about this. Yet this criticism overlooks the fact that federal MPs at that time enjoyed few facilities—no more than an electorate office and a secretary. They did not even have Gestetner duplicators. Attention to a constituency meant not only hard work in dealing with individual problems but attendance at many boring social functions. To someone like Evatt, whose time was more profitably occupied with broader problems and intellectual pursuits, such intense cultivation of a constituency was an unwarranted diversion. Moreover, he had many voluntary supporters to help with local matters. In this sense, Evatt's alleged 'neglect' of Barton was a necessity for him.

The general result of the election of 1951 was defeat for Labor. The Party regained a few seats in the House of Representatives but lost its majority in the Senate. The way was then open for Menzies to push through legislation as the necessary preliminary for a referendum which he expected to have the effect of negating the High Court decision.

Chifley died suddenly in June 1951 and Evatt was elected by caucus to take his place as leader of the parliamentary Labor Party. Thus it fell to Evatt, the following month, to set the tone for Labor's response to Menzies' introduction of the Constitution Alteration (Powers to deal with Communists and Communism) Bill. In terms of the legislation, the people were to be asked to vote 'Yes' or 'No' to a proposal to give parliament constitutional power to deal with Communists and Communism and, specifically, to pass a law corresponding to the Communist Party Dissolution Act which had been nullified by the High Court.

Evatt's response in parliament was trenchant. He described the Bill as totalitarian. 'It is fascist in spirit and a definite step towards the police state'. A week before this, the federal Executive of the ALP ruled that members of the party must oppose Menzies' Bill, although the decision was not unanimous, as delegates from Victoria and Western Australia voted against it. The division illustrates Evatt's difficulties in his own party as he advocated a 'No' vote in the referendum. He realised that the result might depend upon the extent to which Catholics were guided to vote as a bloc.[11]

Clyde Cameron recalls that Evatt said to McKenna:

Now you've got a good position with the Catholic Church, you're a practising Catholic, go and tell the archbishop and the hierarchy generally that it is the intention of Menzies to graft the whole Bill onto the constitution so that it can never be altered without another referendum. It means that...any organisation which supports any of the principles enunciated by Marx and Lenin shall be liable to be declared to be a communist organisation and have the whole of its property and assets confiscated.[12]

Evatt added that McKenna should give the Catholic hierarchy a copy of the *Communist Manifesto*, pointing to the support expressed in it for 'free education'—which might be used by government against any Catholic bishop who advocated free education. Whether persuaded by such arguments or for other reasons, Archbishop Mannix in Melbourne opposed banning the Communist Party and Cardinal Gilroy in Sydney regarded the referendum vote as a matter for individual decision, not ecclesiastical command. On the other hand, Archbishop Duhig in Brisbane favoured a 'Yes' vote; and prominent Catholic Labor politicians reckoned that they themselves were adequate judges of divine wish on the subject. In Melbourne, such federal Labor MPs as Keon and Mullens paid lip-service to Party policy while actually favouring a 'Yes' vote. Evatt is reported to have once remarked on Keon's religious fanaticism: 'When I hear Keon talking I can hear the faggots burning.'[13]

As leader of the federal parliamentary Labor Party, Evatt was committed to opposing the government in the referendum campaign initiated by Menzies. However, the manner in which Evatt opposed was a matter of choice. Labor's position seemed hopeless: in July 1951, a Gallup opinion poll indicated that eighty per cent of voters intended to vote 'Yes', and in August the figure was still as high as seventy-three per cent, with only seventeen per cent favouring a 'No' vote. In these circumstances, a prudent, conventional Labor politician would probably have aimed at maintaining party unity while conducting a low-key campaign. Indeed, the Victorian ALP, in the name of its State secretary, D. Lovegrove, issued a four-page leaflet, only one page of which was concerned with issues in the referendum. The rest of the leaflet was devoted to attacking both the Liberal Party (mainly over inflation) and the CPA (as 'a section of the Russian Communist Conspiracy').

This was not Evatt's way, although he was certainly not defending Communism. Rather, he argued that the methods advocated by Menzies, notably the outlawing of a political party, were unacceptable in a peaceful democratic society and should be rejected out of hand. A perceptive judge remarked later:

Perhaps it took the blinkers of a lawyer or of an international humanitarian, imbued with the words of the common law and the Universal Declaration of Human Rights, to press on against all odds. The choice for Evatt on this issue was between darkness and the light. The clarity of the right side gave Evatt an increasing fervour and conviction.[14]

Perhaps, too, Evatt was influenced by knowledge that, through the exigencies of holding public office and being repeatedly away from Australia, he had drifted away from many old friends. Thus he wrote to J. V. Barry:

Dear Jack,

I have not written to you, but no one appreciates or values more than I your continuous thoughtfulness and generosity—in season and out of season.[15]

Evatt was also aware that some of his long-term supporters were disappointed by some aspects of his recent record as Attorney-General, particularly in relation to civil liberties. Strong advocacy of a 'No' vote in the referendum was an opportunity for him to redeem himself in the eyes of such people. Certainly, he gave them, and others, leadership and hope. In a punishing itinerary, he travelled around Australia for a month, speaking on the referendum wherever a crowd could be assembled. Of course, Evatt was not alone in rousing opposition to the referendum proposal. Left-wing trade union bodies campaigned strongly, and the CPA naturally threw its organising abilities into the distribution of leaflets and the like, spending approximately £40 000 on propaganda. This was a considerable sum for the time, yet a much smaller body, the Summer Hill Citizens' 'Vote No' Committee in Sydney, did proportionately better by raising £12 700 for the purpose.[16]

Most significant was the support for a 'No' vote evinced by intellectuals, not usually noted for active participation in politics. The *Argus* newspaper, on 14 September 1951, gave a report on a meeting of about 1000 people at Melbourne University, at which several professors—including Zelman Cowen and R. D. Wright—spoke in favour of the 'No' case. Similarly at The University of Sydney, Professor J. Anderson (a noted anti-Communist) was among the 'No' advocates. More broadly in the field of the arts, particularly literature, outspoken 'No' supporters included Dame Mary Gilmour, Bernard Smith, Eleanor Dark, Katharine Susannah Prichard, Eric Lambert, J. L. Waten, and C. B. Christesen. Bishop Burgmann, in a diocesan letter, also opposed the 'Yes' case.[17]

Some of these people were friends of Evatt's. There were others, not usually counted on the left, who were equally dissatisfied with Menzies' attitude towards civil liberties. One was Alan Missen, vice-president of the Young Liberal and Country Party movement in Victoria. After he expressed public opposition to official policy on the referendum, he was suspended from office by the Party's State executive, but there were other respected Liberals who agreed with him. On the other hand, nearly all newspapers advocated a 'Yes' vote. Thus on the morning of the referendum poll, a leader in the *Sydney Morning Herald* stated 'We are under attack as a free nation...there is a clear call to every patriotic Australian to rally behind his government at a time of national emergency'.[18]

For those who advocated a 'No' vote, Evatt was a lodestar. He was a focal point in a whirlwind campaign which carried conviction: to him, the principles of liberty and the rule of law were more important than winning a general election. Evatt fought mightily against what he described as 'one of the most dangerous measures that has ever been submitted to the legislature of an English-speaking people'. He won the point but only just. Actually, in the referendum poll, there was a majority of 104 000 in favour of 'No' in Evatt's home State, New South Wales, but over Australia as a whole the majority was only 52 082, and three States (Queensland, Tasmania, and Western Australia) had majority votes for 'Yes'. The closeness of the vote, coupled with the fact that nobody at the outset of the campaign had forecast any result other than a solid 'Yes' majority, testified to the importance of Evatt's role. Geoffrey Sawer wrote to congratulate him, saying 'This is probably the first time in federal politics that a political campaign has altered the opinion of a large majority of the electorate, and it's entirely due to your leadership'. Geoffrey Serle gave a historian's perspective by writing: 'It is perhaps not an exaggeration to suggest that future historians may use this as an instance of the "hero in history" reversing the apparently pre-determined flow of events'.[19]

'Doc' Evatt received very many other congratulatory messages from individuals, Party branches and trade unions. They were heartfelt in expression, while indicating a remarkable variety of interests. Thus the Neutral Bay (Sydney) branch of the ALP added to its congratulations a request 'that full support, both financial and moral, be given to the ALP Industrial Groups in their efforts to give the Labor Party prominence in the Trade Union movement and defeat communism by democratic methods'. H. West, editor of the *Bathurst National Advocate*, pointed in a different direction in a telegram to Evatt on 24 September 1951:

Our late friend Ben [Chifley] couldn't have done better. I do trust that you will be able to deal with the few Quislings within your ranks and put an end to them for ever.

In later years, Evatt may have rued his failure to act upon West's advice at a time when he was at the height of popularity in the ALP, due to his referendum success. The federal Executive of the Party, in November 1951, paid tribute to Evatt's leadership and resolved to place the Melbourne *News-Weekly* in the same anti-Labor category as the Communist *Tribune* and Lang's *Century*. In other words, it was not to be distributed by any member of the ALP. The Executive's decision was due to the fact that *News-Weekly* (organ of the Movement and of Santamaria) had attacked Evatt and other Labor leaders in the 'Vote No' campaign. However, the decision was rescinded six months later in favour of a simple declaration that *News-Weekly* was 'an anti-Labor Party organ'.

Evatt himself evidently decided to try to work in harmony with the Industrial Groups and their associates—a decision which cost him some enthusiastic support on the left. George Petersen, who was then a disillusioned militant worker, looking for an alternative to the CPA in Queensland, puts the point as he saw it:

> *But what was the alternative? Join the corrupt Queensland ALP, then infiltrated by the clerical fascists of Santamaria's movement, and led by such repulsive extreme right wing characters as Hanlon and Gair and the standover men of the Australian Workers' Union? In fact, I did want to join the ALP after the Labor leader Doctor Evatt led the fight to defeat the Communist Party Dissolution Bill in 1951, but one look at the Queensland ALP made me change my mind.*[20]

If the Menzies government had won the referendum, Communists would have gone underground and they were prepared for it. Many trade union militants would have suffered severe restrictions on their activities. Evatt's victory in the referendum put paid to that prospect. However, there were other weapons available for use by a repressive regime. For example, when the WWF, in May 1951, supported a waterside workers' strike in New Zealand by refusing to handle cargo from ports in that country, Jim Healy, the WWF secretary, was charged under the Crimes Act with obstructing trade and commerce. He was gaoled as a result, and other union leaders were also prosecuted. These incidents were part of a concerted Menzies government plan to crack down on militant trade unions. The plan was devised at the end of 1950, when it was reasonable to suppose that the Communist Party Dissolution Act would come into force and that as a consequence there would be widespread industrial upheavals.

A military-style operation code-named 'Alien' was concocted secretly by a small group of senior officers responsible to the Prime Minister. The aim was to ensure the maintenance of essential services and industries in the event of major strike action, and the use of troops as strike-breakers was clearly envisaged. It was also decided to use as a model the procedures adopted by Evatt to bring troops into the coal strike in 1949. This was ironic, and if Evatt had known about the decision he would have been indignant, feeling that the circumstances were quite different from those of 1949. Actually, Evatt never knew about operation 'Alien'. The Labor Opposition in parliament was kept in ignorance of the planning that went on—although it may be taken for granted that ASIO freely supplied a foreign country, the United States, with information on this and other anti-Communist operations.[21]

As it happened, the 'No' victory in the referendum meant that there were no massive industrial battles in the next few years, so that the 'Alien' plan was put into effect in only a few relatively small disputes. Against a conservative government, the ACTU objected strongly to the use of troops and the plan was quietly dropped. Yet there was one other aspect of the affair which would have attracted Evatt's attention if he had known about it. One of the senior officers who elaborated the plan for 'Alien' was the Director of Civil Defence, Brigadier A. W. Wardell—a name which would have brought an unpleasant memory back to Evatt. As noted in an earlier chapter, Evatt, in the course of a visit to London in 1942, unearthed for himself the text of the crucial 'Beat Hitler First' agreement between Britain and the United States. Wardell was Australian Military Liaison Officer in London at that time, and Evatt suspected that Wardell had learned about the agreement earlier but had deliberately refrained from informing the Australian government because of the confidentiality of his official contacts. To an Australian nationalist like Evatt, such divided loyalty was unacceptable. S. M. Bruce, in his own words, 'defended what Wardell had done', but in the upshot Wardell was recalled to Australia. Perhaps he should have been pensioned off then.[22]

NOTES

1 Rich to Evatt, 24 May 1949, Evatt Collection, Flinders University, Miscellaneous Correspondence. Rich was never regarded as sympathetic towards Labor.
2 Kylie Tennant, in *Evatt: Politics and Justice*, p. 258, claims that C.E. Martin, the NSW Attorney-General, refused to recommend Evatt for the appointment in 1950, but there is no mention of the matter in Paul White's comprehensive M.Ec. thesis, 'C.E. Martin: A Political Biography 1900–1953' (Government Department, The University of Sydney, 1986). Allan Dalziel, in *Evatt: The Enigma*, pp. 62–3, appears to have been the originator of the story.
3 *CPD*, vol. 206, p. 918, 16 March 1950.
4 Robinson to Baruch, 21 March 1950, W.S. Robinson Collection, Box 5, File 61, Melbourne University Archives.
5 *CPD*, vol. 207, pp. 1995 (Menzies), 2287 (Evatt).
6 Leicester Webb, *Communism and Democracy in Australia: a survey of the 1951 referendum*, Cheshire, Melbourne, 1954, pp. 25–7; *CPD*, vol. 207, pp. 3312–15.
7 L.F. Crisp, *Ben Chifley*, pp. 388-9; Kylie Tennant, *Evatt: Politics and Justice*, pp. 260–1. Calwell, *Be Just and Fear Not*, p. 75, says that Evatt favoured 'straight-out confrontation'.

8 C.J. Lloyd, 'Not Peace but a Sword! The High Court Under J.G. Latham', *Adelaide Law Review*, vol. 1, 1987, pp. 175–202.
9 Evatt, quoted in David Marr, *Barwick*, p. 86.
10 Michael Kirby, 'H.V. Evatt: Libertarian Warrior', in *Seeing Red*, Evatt Foundation, Sydney, 1992, p. 12. Also in *Seeing Red*, George Winterton's article, 'The Communist Party Case and its Significance', for the best account of the episode.
11 *CPD*, vol. 213, p. 1218 (10 July 1951); Patrick Weller and Beverly Lloyd (eds), *Federal Executive Minutes 1915–1955*, MUP, Melbourne, 1978, pp. 467–8.
12 Interview with Clyde Cameron, 3 May 1988.
13 Concerning Keon, see Janet McCalman, *Struggletown*, MUP, Melbourne, 1985, p. 226. McKenna proved a loyal supporter of Evatt in the referendum campaign.
14 Michael Kirby, 'H.V. Evatt', *Seeing Red*, p. 15.
15 Evatt to Barry, 28 June 1951, Barry Papers, MS2505/1/1657, NLA.
16 A letter of 8 October 1951 from this committee to Evatt stated that it consisted of former ALP members, expelled from the Party during the 1949 coal strike, Evatt Collection, File: 1951 referendum campaign. It is possible that the Committee was a front for the CPA.
17 *Argus*, 19 September 1951.
18 Leicester Webb, *Communism and Democracy*, pp. 80–1; Elizabeth Evatt, 'Referendum 1951: A View from the Media', *Seeing Red*, pp. 38–63. Missen, a Liberal Party Senator later, was a consistent advocate of civil liberties.
19 *CPD*, 10 July 1951, p. 1213; Evatt Collection, Flinders University. Serle's letter, dated 23 September 1951, was written in his capacity as chairman of the Victorian Fabian Society.
20 G. Petersen, 'How Labor Governs in New South Wales' (unpublished manuscript). Much later, Petersen became an outspoken Labor Member of the NSW Parliament.
21 Les Louis '"Operation Alien" and the Cold War in Australia', *Labour History*, 62, May 1992, pp. 1–18.
22 Note by Bruce on conversation with Evatt, 28 March 1942, *DAFP*, vol. v, Document 508; David Day, *Reluctant Nation*, OUP, Oxford, 1992, p. 104.

CHAPTER 27

PETROV, POLITICS AND SECURITY

If any election were held today, Bob Menzies would be swept out of office and Bert Evatt would be PM in his place.
W. S. ROBINSON, IN 1952

The quarter-century following World War II was marked in Australia by rapid growth and economic diversification, coupled with full employment. There was a steady rise in living standards, manifest in ownership (or hire-purchase) of commodities such as refrigerators, television sets, cars and homes. Conservative governments got the credit for such material improvements, though in truth they contributed little: the long boom was a phenomenon common to Western countries. Particularly in the 1950s, the ethos of self-advancement was not favourable to the Labor Party and other collectivist organisations. Indeed, it was a somnolent and culturally sterile decade for most Australians interested in politics or the arts.

There were some important exceptions to these generalisations, including striking episodes of conflict. Fear and hatred of Communism was a theme constantly played upon by conservatives, who linked it with assertions that the ALP itself was suspect. In 1950, Menzies claimed that Australia had only three years in which to prepare for another world war. Richard Casey, as Minister for External Affairs, followed this up in May 1952 by declaring that there was a 'nest of traitors...somewhere or other in the Public Service'. Casey refrained from naming anybody at the time, but other government MPs smeared John Burton by association. Meanwhile, ASIO was investigating. Not to be outdone, Keon, on the Labor side, claimed a little later that the Australian National University had become 'a nest of Communists organising to subvert the educational institutions of Australia'.[1]

Yet the Menzies government, despite its efforts to direct public attention to the issue of Communism, lost some popular support in the early 1950s—and another general election was due in 1954. There were various reasons for decline in the government's public standing, one important factor being a rapid growth in inflation. To counter this, the government resorted to sharp credit restrictions in 1951–52, with serious consequences for many small businessmen facing bankruptcy. There was a recession in the economy which, though short-lived, gave the ALP a good opening to criticise the government. Evatt, as leader of the Opposition, headed the attack. Like Menzies and Fadden, he was unfamiliar with economic concepts, but when it came to preparing a speech on the Budget, the 'Doc' received good advice from an academic economist at the ANU.

Evatt also performed well as Labor spokesman on other policy matters, particularly foreign policy and support for the United Nations. His earlier interest in nuclear energy was renewed by the discovery of the raw material, uranium, at Rum Jungle in the Northern Territory. The considerable extent of this deposit was proved in 1951–52. Later in the 1950s the ALP, led by Evatt, advocated international disarmament and the banning of the atomic bomb. Before this, however, Evatt failed to exploit fully Menzies' approval of British tests of atomic weapons on the Monte Bello Islands off Western Australia and subsequently at Maralinga in South Australia. The nationalist instincts of W. S. Robinson on this question were sharper than Evatt's. Robinson wrote:

Is it not time that you assured the people of Australia that you would not permit the explosion of any bomb at Monte Bello, Woomera or elsewhere in Australia which created the slightest risk to their health and wellbeing? If HM [British] Government desire to test their bombs then they must go east of Australia—the prevailing westerly winds necessitate this'.[2]

Evatt's political progress continued to absorb Robinson's attention. In 1952 he had written to Baruch: 'If an election were held today, Bob Menzies would be swept out of office and Bert Evatt would be PM in his place'. In State politics, Labor gained office in Victoria that year, and in Western Australia in 1953. However, by 1954, with a federal election approaching, Robinson reckoned that Labor's prospects had deteriorated and that the election would be a 'close go' between Evatt and Menzies. In April, Robinson gave Evatt considerable advice on points of policy. The advice was mainly economic in nature, though it included some more general nuggets of wisdom. Thus Robinson commented: 'The [armed] services are clamouring for more money for equipment...[but] everyone appears to admit that another war is further off than for a very long time past.' To quote another example: 'Do not let anyone suggest using the Savings or other Banks Deposits. Don't forget what happened to Lang.'[3]

Leaving aside for a moment other reasons for Labor's defeat in the 1954 election, it may be noted that Robinson attributed it partly to unfavourable developments in New South Wales—he apparently alluded to the Groupers' move to take control of the Party there—and partly to a flaw in Evatt's character:

I'm sorry for Bert, for his intentions are excellent, and his intelligence, except for one failing, of the highest order. His one failing is his apparent inability to secure the trust and confidence of others—he can only expect to do that when he gives others his full trust and confidence.[4]

This was a perceptive remark, which may also apply to Evatt's reputation for rudeness. Yet there was another side to the story, in so far as Evatt's dealings with bureaucrats in the ALP and the New South Wales Labor Council are concerned. George Petersen recalls an occasion, about twenty years after the referendum of 1951, when Bill Coulter MLC (a former union official in New South Wales) gave a long dissertation on Evatt as 'an arrogant rude man who would change meeting plans at the drop of a hat, cancel other meetings, and demand that meetings be organised without notice'. Petersen's comment is pithy: 'Obviously the right wing were running dead in the campaign and they were angry when Evatt demanded that they get off their bums and transform their nominal opposition to the referendum proposal into real activity'. Resentment of Evatt's pushful methods was still evident in 1954 and later.

A general election was set down for 29 May 1954, and the federal parliament rose in preparation for it on 14 April. The previous evening, the Prime Minister made an unscheduled yet sensational announcement. He told parliament that V. Petrov, the third secretary at the Soviet Embassy in Canberra, had sought political asylum, bringing with him important documents concerning Soviet espionage in Australia, and the government proposed to set up a Royal Commission to investigate the matter. This announcement caught Evatt off guard. Indeed, he was not in parliament at the time, having left for Sydney that afternoon to attend a social function at his old school, Fort Street. The government was aware of Evatt's intended movements, yet refrained from giving him notice of Menzies' impending announcement. Actually, Petrov had defected a week earlier, and an ASIO agent, Bialoguski, had been in contact with him over the previous two years. The final phase of the defection process was organised by G. R. Richards, deputy head of ASIO. Richards was the man who earlier had operated against Communists in Western Australia and was suspected of being involved in a frame-up of Australia First Movement sympathisers there in 1942.[5]

In February 1954, the head of ASIO, Colonel Spry, told the Solicitor-General, Bailey, about the prospective defection of Petrov, and Bailey suggested that as a consequence 'a Royal Commission would be a possibility and a fruitful means of *propaganda*'. Spry passed this suggestion on to the Prime Minister when he gave the latter a 'preliminary briefing' on the Petrov affair on 10 February.[6]

Much later, Menzies wrote blandly that he did not recall the name of Petrov being mentioned on that occasion. However, after the election of 1954, Menzies acknowledged that several days before his announcement in April, he:

knew the names of all the people who had been, or were, associated with the Leader of the Opposition, and whose names were mentioned in the Petrov papers, but I remained silent...to the end of the General Election campaign.[7]

In other words, Menzies knew how damaging the Petrov papers might be to Evatt, yet the Prime Minister gave every appearance of behaving with due propriety: he did not overtly make political capital out of the Petrov affair during the election. He did not need to—some of his colleagues, including Fadden, were happy to do so. They dropped hints and warned darkly that the ALP could not be trusted, if elected, to deal with the allegations of espionage. Further, public speculation was greatly increased by spectacular media coverage of official protection being afforded to Mrs Petrov at Darwin airport as two Russian strong-arm men tried to hustle her out of Australia. In these circumstances, it was not surprising that Evatt and his supporters suspected a conspiracy by Menzies, timed to secure a Liberal–Country Party victory in the election. This view held sway among Labor people for many years, and still does among the more hard-bitten or cynical of them.

People on the right in politics, including some gullible academics, had considerable success in discrediting the conspiracy theory after 1984, when many ASIO and Royal Commission papers (including *in camera* proceedings) were made available for the first time to researchers. In particular, Robert Manne made a thorough examination of these papers and wrote a book which was very heavily based upon them. Certain aspects are now clearer than they were in the

1950s. There is no evidence that Menzies deliberately planned or brought about the defection of Petrov in order to influence the outcome of the general election. This does not necessarily absolve ASIO from suspicion of indulging its own ingrained anti-Labor bias in order to help conservative political groups at a critical moment— or to embarrass Evatt if the ALP proved successful in gaining office in government.

Whatever the truth about the timing, there is no doubt that the Petrov affair was very opportune for the Menzies government. Menzies was an astute politician with a flair for drama. The proceedings of the Royal Commission on Espionage were opened a week or so before the election, and the appetite of the public was whetted with a preview of Soviet spying to be investigated, although the names of people involved were not revealed at this stage. Nor was there any mention of the fact that ASIO had paid Petrov £5000 to encourage him to defect with worthwhile information. The Commission then adjourned until after the election. The matter was handled with circumspection, yet it undoubtedly harmed Labor's prospects. The appointment of the Commission came on top of years of anti-Communist hysteria, in which many Australians had come to expect the worst of the left.

Furthermore, if Menzies had been genuinely concerned not to take political advantage of the Petrov affair, he could have deferred his public announcement and the appointment of the Commission until after the election. Of course, the effect of these events on the election result cannot be determined precisely: there were other issues, notably concerning social welfare benefits, to be taken into account. Yet to suggest, as Manne does, that the Petrov affair had a negligible effect on the election strains the limits of credulity. It also exposes Manne's own predilections.[8]

Actually, the ALP made a net gain in number of seats, and it won fractionally more than fifty per cent of the total votes cast in the election. Its opponents remained in office because of the uneven distribution of voters. In the light of the marginal difference between winners and losers, it is reasonable to suppose that the emotions roused by the Petrov affair were decisive in the overall result. Furthermore, the Petrov affair had much more profound effects than influencing the outcome of a particular election. In order to consider this point, it is necessary to look closely at the sources of information available first to the Royal Commission and later to historians. The bulk of the material came from dubious or tainted sources (notably the Petrovs, who were anxious to satisfy their new paymasters). The material was sifted selectively by ASIO, which interpreted it for the benefit of the Commission. Manne, in writing *The Petrov Affair*, did not question the accuracy or honesty of these sources. Moreover, he was 'deeply indebted' to Sir Charles Spry for several conversations— 'among the most enjoyable' in Manne's life. Evidently, he believed what Spry told him, although there is very little indication of just what this was; and the book contains virtually no direct quotations from Spry, so that it is not possible for a critical reader to challenge this source decisively.[9]

Manne and others who followed him never posed one obvious question: why should ASIO and its agents be believed, unless there is independent corroboration of what they say? After all, these people operate in a world of deception. Lying is part of their trade and it is pointless to think of them as honourable individuals. In their own eyes, ASIO staff—like the members of all intelligence agencies—are patriots who, because they have access to secret information, are best qualified to decide where the security interests of the nation lie. The end justifies the means in this view, and the means include dirty tricks. ASIO was not responsible to parliament or any other democratic institution.

Against this, it may be argued that there is a safeguard: all is revealed by public archives thirty years after the creation of a particular body of records. However, there are two important qualifications to this. In the first place, it is standard practice for ASIO to refuse access to those files or pages of its records which it deems too sensitive. Secondly, ASIO may have destroyed or secreted certain files. A strong indication of this came to light recently when R. Holdich, Inspector-General of Intelligence and Security, investigated a complaint by a journalist who had been informed by ASIO that there were no security files on certain Labor politicians. The journalist, D. McKnight, found this difficult to believe, especially as one of the politicians, Jim McClelland, had been a Trotskyist in his youth, before becoming a highly respected member of the Whitlam government.

In a report on this complaint, Holdich stated that he was unable to find any ASIO files on the people in question. He added that ASIO had advised him that:

> *on the basis of the recollections of a number of long-serving ASIO officers...an instruction was issued in 1972 prior to the Federal election that the personal files of leading members of the possible incoming ALP Government should be sent to Central Office where it was believed they were to be destroyed. As the Archives Act was not in force there was no legal requirement to have a disposal authority to destroy such files.*[10]

So much for the principle of preservation of important public records, as well as the naivety of some historians and judges concerning the operations of security agencies! In relation to the Petrov Royal Commission in 1954–55, ASIO had its own game to play. Its prime function was to counter subversion, and undoubtedly there were Soviet agents engaged in secret intelligence work in Australia, as in other countries. There was nothing remarkable or unexpected about this—the same could be said of American, British and Australian agents abroad. In Australia, the problem of dealing with Soviet intelligence operations assumed large proportions in the public mind mainly because of the extreme suspicion engendered by anti-Communist feeling at the time. To judge by results, ASIO had no success: as a consequence of the Petrov Commission, no Soviet agent was prosecuted or convicted for espionage. There was no evidence to warrant any such prosecution. Certainly, there were many Australians—and not only Communists—who were sympathetic towards the Soviet Union, but that was no crime. After all, the two countries had been allies in a terrible war only a few years earlier.

Nevertheless, the Petrov business was a coup for ASIO, seemingly justifying its existence. The failure to provide evidence of espionage was thoroughly obscured by the process of presenting many fascinating (and ultimately inconclusive) leads to the Royal Commission. ASIO focussed particularly upon the activities of people supposedly forming part of what Casey had described as a nest of traitors linked to an alleged leak of information from the Department of External Affairs in 1948. The evidence concerning this, mostly from Petrov, was very superficial and—as Burton told the Royal Commission in secret session—had been known in substance to Security and other government authorities for some years previously and had been investigated. Later in 1955, Burton gave a warning about intelligence organisations:

It is axiomatic that Intelligence Officers who seek to determine long-term Defence and Foreign Policy, would also use their best endeavours...to ensure that any government elected will be the government which pursues policies they favour. Furthermore, they will ensure the smearing...of any person...who might effectively influence public opinion in ways contrary to the policies these services favour. It is for this reason that there has been a singling out during the Commission hearings of External Affairs Department and particularly the Leader of the Opposition and persons associated with him...Petrov and his documents gave an excuse to rehash and to add to, in a way valuable from a political point of view, material already on the files of Security.[11]

Once the general election of 1954 was over, the Royal Commission on Espionage began taking evidence from witnesses, beginning with Petrov. Three members of the Commission were justices of the

Supreme Courts in their respective States. The chairman of the Commission, William Owen of New South Wales, owed his appointment to a process in which Menzies by-passed the State Attorney-General (the standard conduit) and made a direct approach to the Premier, J. J. Cahill—who, according to Dalziel, had an anti-Evatt bias despite being a Labor leader. Menzies also personally selected R. F. Philp of Queensland. All three Commissioners had impeccably conservative credentials: Owen was a member of the Melbourne Club; George Ligertwood was in the Adelaide Club; and Philp was a member of the Queensland Club. In the course of proceedings, it became clear that the Commission was prepared to accept Petrov's evidence as truth, although it was often hearsay in nature or consisted of words put into Petrov's mouth by leading questions from counsel or Commissioners.[12]

The Royal Commission had considerable discretion in procedure. It alone had the power to decide what witnesses to call before it, and those witnesses were subject to penalties if they refused to answer questions. Witnesses were permitted legal representation, but such lawyers could be barred from dealing with the broad questions under investigation. In any case, legal representation was generally of little avail to those witnesses who had left-wing backgrounds or associations. Although no criminal charges were laid, readers of newspapers tended to assume that most of the people called before the Commission to account for themselves had something to hide.

From the outset, there were two men who realised that they were likely to be called before the Commission in due course. This was because Victor Windeyer, counsel assisting the Commission, referred at the pre-election opening proceedings to two particular documents in the Petrov papers, which appeared to emanate from Australians. One of these papers, Document 'H', was described as a three-page commentary on the political leanings and social habits of a number of Australian journalists. In itself, this document was of no particular importance. It did not relate to defence or security matters. Document 'H' acquired significance in the eyes of ASIO and the Commission only because it had been made available to a Soviet press representative by a certain Australian journalist who had compiled it.

From newspaper reports referring to Document 'H', Fergan O'Sullivan, 'Doc' Evatt's press secretary, recognised himself as the author. It was a statement which he had prepared and passed on in 1951, when he was a journalist working for the *Sydney Morning Herald*. O'Sullivan did not become Evatt's press secretary until 1953, but the connection between O'Sullivan and Document 'H' was bound to damage Evatt when it became known. Before this point was reached, O'Sullivan, in June 1954, confessed the facts to Evatt, who was shocked. He dismissed him on the spot as being untrustworthy. When O'Sullivan appeared before the Royal Commission in July, he was legally represented by James Meagher, who later wrote privately:

When I saw document 'H' I realised that, though it was grossly foolish to let such a document get into the hands of a Soviet Press attache, it might be equally useful to an American Press attache, but if found in his possession would scarcely cause any fuss.

Meagher added that the Commission ordered the contents of document 'H' to be kept secret on the ground that it was libellous, but this was 'an unfortunate excuse as it prevented the public from realising that it was in fact so far outside the terms of the Royal Commission as to be truly "a damp squib"'.[13]

Also in July 1954, the Commission considered document 'J', said to have been composed inside the Soviet Embassy by a Communist journalist, Rupert Lockwood, in 1953. Manne describes this document as 'perhaps the least significant part of the haul Petrov brought with him'. Nevertheless, document 'J' contained a list of sources of information and although the document was not published by the Commission, the Chairman (Owen) remarked in court that three of the sources named were members of the secretariat of the leader of the Opposition—O'Sullivan, Dalziel and Grundeman. Evatt made an angry public protest about this disclosure, which was likely to harm him and his Party. It reinforced Evatt's views about a conspiracy, and he came to the defence of Dalziel and Grundeman, being certain that neither of them was involved in espionage.[14]

Bert's brother, Clive Evatt, QC, was ready to represent Dalziel and Grundeman before the Commission, but 'the Doc' insisted on taking the brief himself—partly out of loyalty to his staff, but also because he aimed to expose what lay behind Petrov's defection. It would have been wiser to allow Clive to do a speedy job of clearing Dalziel and Grundeman, but Bert felt that his own future was at stake. So H. V. Evatt confronted the Royal Commission for a considerable period of time in August. In particular, he queried the authenticity of document 'J'. Undoubtedly, the prime author of the material in the thirty-seven-page typescript was Lockwood, but he claimed that some of the material was not his or had been 'recast' by someone unknown.

Evatt's own scrutiny of the document led him to believe that in effect it was a forgery, produced with the connivance of ASIO. In this, he disagreed with the evidence of a police inspector who was an expert on typewriting and handwriting (document 'J' included some handwritten marginal notations). The inspector testified to the Commission that in his opinion the document was solely the work of Lockwood. To counter this, Evatt applied to call another handwriting expert as a witness. The Commission, exasperated by what has been described as Evatt's 'barn-storming' style, refused permission. Shortly after, the Commission refused to allow Evatt to appear before it any longer, stating that his role as an advocate representing Dalziel and Grundeman was incompatible with his political role as leader of the Opposition. What this really meant was that Evatt was getting close to turning an enquiry into Soviet espionage into what Menzies privately termed 'a political dog-fight'. The Prime Minister was worried that Evatt was 'having a considerable measure of success in the public mind' in this respect. In Menzies' view, it should be made plain that Evatt was not fulfilling the role of a disinterested advocate before the Commission, which should dispose of document 'J' in an interim report.[15]

Menzies' thoughts on the subject closely approximated the Commission's decision, some days later, to withdraw Evatt's leave to appear. Then the Commission produced an interim report, strongly identifying Lockwood as the author of document 'J'. There is no evidence of Menzies' suggestions being passed on to the Commissioners, although this could have occurred through unrecorded meetings or telephone calls. Evatt was certainly at a serious disadvantage in terms of Royal Commission powers and procedures. Technically he was not defending two men charged in a criminal court, and it was open to the Commission to object that he was taking up matters not relevant to his clients. Nevertheless, it is extraordinary that the 'prosecution' was allowed to testify to the authenticity of document 'J', whereas the 'defence' was not allowed to do so or to subject this and other Petrov documents to proper forensic analysis. This was a travesty of justice. A further point is that Philip Evatt—who appeared as junior counsel to his uncle at the Royal Commission—believed that the main reason for 'the Doc's' exclusion from Commission proceedings was concern that he might use further examination of G. R. Richards to expose the latter's earlier role in relation to the Australia First Movement.

Brendan Bracken—who, as a Minister in Churchill's government, had met Evatt during his overseas trip to Britain in 1942—offered an insight into one consideration in a letter to W. S. Robinson:

Was our friend Bert wise to appear as Counsel for his Secretaries in this Petrov case? I doubt it. Bert's nerves aren't strong enough for this kind of foray. Moreover, he is appearing before judges who look upon him as a [judicial] renegade.[16]

Evatt's intervention in Commission proceedings and his frequent displays of irascibility in court were partly due to frustration at having no other forum in which to express his views adequately. He was unable to speak freely in parliament, where the subject was ruled *sub judice*. Evatt's prime opportunity did not arrive till October 1955, when the Royal Commission's final report came up for debate in parliament. The circumstances appeared favourable for Evatt. As Fitzpatrick commented, the Commissioners 'couldn't give a basis for a single prosecution'. Some of Evatt's friends had been disconcerted by some aspects of his appearance before the Commission—for example, he wrongly assumed that O'Sullivan had been 'planted' on him by enemies—yet he retained their support. Early in 1955 Justice Barry of the Victorian Supreme Court confided to friends his opinion that the Commission was 'entirely discredited'.[17]

The night before Evatt's parliamentary speech in October, Russel Ward and a few others helped him to 'revise and polish' the text. Evatt said nothing to them about one item which appeared in the speech as actually delivered—perhaps he had not already decided to include it. Yet as Evatt's many friends listened to the speech on the radio they were stunned to hear him, after a promising start, say that he had written to the Soviet Foreign Minister, Molotov, enquiring about the genuineness of the Russian-language documents said by Petrov to have come to the Embassy in Australia from Moscow; and the Soviet reply to Evatt was that these documents had been fabricated 'on the instructions of persons interested in the deterioration' of Soviet–Australian relations. Indeed, diplomatic relations had been broken off by the Russians following Petrov's defection.

Evatt did not claim that the Soviet response to his Molotov letter was proof of fabrication of the Petrov documents. Rather, he said that the Soviet denial of authenticity of the documents was cause for the establishment—by agreement with the USSR—of some form of international commission to settle the dispute. Thus there was an element of rationality, as well as obvious naivety, in Evatt's remarks, but this was lost sight of as government MPs laughed and jeered at the very idea of asking Soviet representatives whether they had agents engaged in espionage in Australia. Evatt had made a fatal blunder, as his own supporters recognised immediately. When Evatt joined them for supper that night, Russel Ward asked why he had been 'so mad as to write to Molotov, and so much madder as to announce the fact'. Evatt replied, as Ward recalls, in an easy tone:

'Oh, that's established judicial practice. In opening a case one must always ask counsel for the accused for his version of the events'.

'But couldn't you see that correct legal protocol was suicidal political insanity?' He couldn't and I'm not sure that he ever did.[18]

The tragedy of the situation was that in the main body of the speech Evatt made a number of valid points. He referred, for example, to the fact that ASIO had recently asked an academic at The University of Sydney to inform on the political views and activities of his fellow-lecturers and students. Evatt said that the same sort of thing was occurring in relation to trade unions, broadcasting stations and the press. He concluded:

We must prevent any attempt to set up an espionage system for spying on our own people...The security service was never intended to be a secret police organisation.[19]

When Menzies replied to Evatt in parliament a week later, he made no attempt to deal with most of Evatt's contentions. Instead, the Prime Minister concentrated on ridiculing and distorting Evatt's statement concerning Molotov. Evatt, said Menzies, preferred the word of Molotov to that of three distinguished Australian judges and the Director-General of ASIO—all of whom had honourable military records from both world wars. Menzies also claimed that 'scores and scores of Soviet intelligence operatives working in democratic countries' had been identified as a result of the disclosures of the Petrovs. In addition the Petrovs were said to have supplied 'invaluable information regarding Soviet intelligence methods and techniques of espionage'. These claims remained unsubstantiated, on the plausible ground that to give details would provide information useful to a potential enemy. It was a self-serving claim which ASIO was happy to build upon in subsequent years, sustaining an ill-deserved reputation for competence which also served to attract large government funding for its operations.[20]

On 26 October 1955, Menzies announced that there would be a general election in December, more than a year earlier than expected. His justification for the decision, in terms of realigning the elections for the House of Representatives and Senate, fooled nobody: the real reason for an early election was that with Labor split and in disarray, Menzies anticipated a decisive victory for anti-Labor forces. He was not disappointed.

Notes

1 Robin Gollan, *Revolutionaries and Reformists*, pp. 273–7.
2 *CPD*, vol. 1 (new series), 30 September 1953, p. 833; Robinson to Evatt, 24 March 1954, W.S. Robinson Collection, Box 6, File 70, Melbourne University Archives.
3 Robinson to Baruch, 11 June 1952, 4 May 1954, W.S. Robinson Collection, Box 5, File 61; Robinson to Evatt, 5 April 1954, W.S. Robinson Collection, Box 6, File 70.
4 Robinson to Baruch, 17 December 1954, W.S. Robinson Collection, Box 5, File 61.

5 Stuart Macintyre, *Militant: The Life and Times of Paddy Troy*, pp. 60–1.
6 Quoted in Robert Manne, *The Petrov Affair*, Pergamon, Sydney, 1987, pp. 46–7. Emphasis added.
7 *CPD*, vol. 4, 12 August 1954, p. 287. Furthermore, it is now known that as early as August 1953, Spry informed Menzies about a prospective Soviet defection.
8 W.C. Wentworth, Liberal MP, in an ABC interview in 1974, had no doubt that there was an effect on the election—rightly so, in his opinion.
9 Manne, *The Petrov Affair*, p. xiii.
10 Report by R. Holdich on Complaints against ASIO, 4 September 1992, p. 23.
11 Statement by John Burton, 15 September 1955, Evatt Collection, File: Petrov Affair.
12 Kylie Tennant, *Evatt: Politics and Justice*, p. 296; M.G. Dunn, 'The Royal Commission on Espionage, 1954-55', Ph.D thesis, University of Adelaide, 1979, p. 84.
13 Quoted in Tennant, *Evatt: Politics and Justice*, pp. 299–300.
14 Manne, *The Petrov Affair*, p. 68. In fact, Dalziel and Grundeman were exonerated later.
15 Ibid., pp. 147–8. See also David Marr's illuminating account in *Barwick*, pp. 111–23. Barwick was persuaded by Menzies to represent ASIO at the Commission after Evatt's first appearance before it.
16 Bracken to Robinson, 26 August 1954, W.S. Robinson Collection, Box 24, File 231.
17 Fitzpatrick to Evatt, 10 October 1955, Fitzpatrick Papers, MS 4965, 1/5657, NLA; M.G.Dunn, 'Royal Commission on Espionage', p. 299.
18 Russel Ward, *A Radical Life*, Macmillan, Melbourne, 1988, p. 224. Incidentally, Ward's publisher, fearful of libel action, made him delete from this book any mention of the name of Colonel Spry!
19 *CPD*, vol. 8, 19 October 1955, pp. 1717–18. When the outraged Sydney academic told his Staff Association about the underhand approach to him, the Association protested to the University Senate. The Senate raised with the Prime Minister the potential threat to academic freedom, but Menzies took no action. Evatt probably heard about the incident through his membership of the Senate of the University of Sydney.
20 *CPD*, vol. 8, 25 October 1955, p. 1874.

CHAPTER 28

THE ALP SPLIT

The (Catholic) Movement should be able to 'completely transform the leadership of the Labor Movement, and to introduce into federal and state spheres large numbers of members...to implement a Christian social program'.
B. SANTAMARIA, 1952

The Petrov affair was a catalyst for a major split in the ALP, although the fissure was a reflection of the very nature of the Party as it had developed historically. It was a political haven for a wide variety of interest groups and factions, ranging from socialist to capitalist in ideology and from liberal democratic to conservative authoritarian in social outlook. Particularly important, especially in ALP leadership, was a large body of Catholic members. These were mainly Irish in origin although other ethnic groups, principally Italian, were appearing by the 1950s. Also by that decade, the solid working-class homogeneity of the Irish in Australia was in process of dilution by upward social mobility: with growth in affluence, more Catholics were attracted to the Liberal Party, especially when Menzies later came out in favour of State aid for private schools.

Naturally, the diversity of interests in the Labor Party led to repeated disagreements and manoeuvring. Yet for a long time the potential for major breakaway movements was contained by a degree of tolerance—recognition that no one faction could expect to have things entirely its own way—and by mutual hostility towards the main enemy, seen as big business personified by the Liberal Party. Over the years, two forces appeared as major threats to the broad encompassing fabric of the ALP. First, there were Communists who, not content with having their own political party, sought to have it accepted as part of the ALP in much the same way as the Fabian Society. Communists aimed to infiltrate and to mould the ALP in their own image, but they were repulsed time and again.

The other big threat to Labor Party unity and independence came from the Industrial Groups and their alter ego, the Movement. The Industrial Groups, established in the late 1940s with ALP connections, were primarily designed to work against Communists in trade unions. The Groupers were right-wing in general orientation. For example, an amendment to the Arbitration Act by the Menzies government in 1951, which strengthened court control by permitting small groups of unionists (non-Communist in practice) to apply to the Arbitration Court for secret union ballots, was welcomed by Groupers—whereas in parliament, the ALP, in line with the views of the ACTU, voted against this legislation. However, apart from this and a parallel tendency to support anti-Communist foreign policy moves, the moderate wing of the Groupers had no distinctive aims. Many trade union leaders among them were content simply to see the defeat of Communist rivals.

The Movement—whose public face was the Catholic Social Studies Movement, directed by Bartholomew Santamaria—was different in important respects. Its membership was restricted to Catholics, it operated secretly, was more dedicated in anti-Communist fervour and embraced elements of a distinctive social policy. Thus Santamaria, noting an influx of Catholic immigrants, advocated extensive immigration and a 'back to the land' policy in the form of providing small subsistence farms, mainly for Italians with a peasant background. In 1953, a Victorian Land Settlement Bill, brought in by a Labor government, included authorisation of the allocation of Crown land to unspecified organisations; and Santamaria's National Catholic Rural Movement was expected to be one of the beneficiaries. However, the Victorian Lands Minister resigned in protest at what he regarded as intimidatory tactics by Santamaria, and the episode strengthened sectarian feelings in Victoria.

Nevertheless, the Movement was remarkably successful in infiltrating the Industrial Groups and, through them, the ALP. Members or supporters of the Movement were appointed to a succession of important positions in the Party and trade unions. Communists in the early 1950s suffered a series of defeats in elections to trade union posts, to the extent that the Communist threat of domination became much less apparent than previously. The corollary of this was that the Industrial Groups lost some impetus: in many cases, the prime justification for their existence disappeared. Yet it was not in the interest of members of the Movement to lose the public cover for their own activities. Consequently, tension developed between those Groupers who were members of the Movement (perhaps thirty per cent) and those who were not—especially as the Movement in a number of cases used its influence against non-Communist union leaders whom it regarded as weak or objectionable.

At the same time, Santamaria became increasingly confident that the Movement would soon be able not only to influence the ALP but to take it over. He expressed this viewpoint confidentially in a personal letter to Archbishop Mannix in December 1952, saying that within a few years the Movement should be able to:

completely transform the leadership of the Labor Movement, and to introduce into federal and state spheres large numbers of members who should be able to implement a Christian social program...This is the first time that such a work has been possible in Australia and, as far as I can see, in the Anglo-Saxon world since the advent of Protestantism.[1]

In short, the Movement was moving beyond its original aims. Santamaria envisaged it as transforming the ALP into a Christian Centre party linked with the Catholic Church in much the same way as in Italy. As part of the change, it was anticipated that the ALP would pursue a firm international anti-Communist policy aligned with that of the United States. These were not wild dreams, and Santamaria might well have achieved his aims but for a last minute intervention by Evatt.

Stephen Murray-Smith, referring to Evatt's work in defeating the anti-Communist party proposal in the referendum of 1951, recollected that 'Doc Evatt got Dinny Lovegrove, Victorian ALP numbers man, to point out to me in precise terms that the vast majority of Labor politicians, state and federal, in fact voted YES'. Even allowing for some hyperbole in that statement, it is safe to assume that most Catholics went along with their co-religionists among Labor politicians in voting 'Yes' in the referendum. Nevertheless, some Catholics in the ALP (A. Calwell and J. Ormonde, for example) were opposed to the Movement even when it appeared to have the support of the Church hierarchy. Indeed, there was some support for Evatt among the Catholic clergy. Cardinal Gilroy had written to Evatt in 1949, expressing his 'gratitude for your courageous advocacy of justice [at the United Nations] for the Cardinal Primate of Hungary and of the internationalisation of the Holy Places [in Jerusalem]'.[2]

Evatt, between 1952 and 1954, had some reason to hope that he could secure the support of Industrial Groups and Catholics. With an eye to the approaching federal election in 1954, he made speeches attacking Communists and supporting Groupers—notably Laurie Short of the Ironworkers' Association. Further, in 1954 Evatt made arrangements to meet Santamaria in Melbourne on several occasions. It is unlikely that Evatt at that time had any real conception of the operations of the Movement or of Santamaria's guiding role in that clandestine organisation. Evatt knew simply that Santamaria was active in lay Catholic circles and could be expected to have some influence over Catholic voters.

Santamaria's later account of these meetings was that Evatt expressed support for Industrial Groups and tried to flatter him, asking what sort of measures he would like a Labor government to introduce if it came to power. Santamaria was 'disgusted' by the manner of Evatt's approach and declined an invitation to assist in drafting the ALP leader's policy speech for the 1954 election. Evatt's version of these meetings was different: his attempt to ascertain Santamaria's view was part of a regular process of consultation with prominent people preparatory to drafting the ALP policy speech. Undoubtedly, Santamaria continued to distrust Evatt. According to G. Henderson (who was a colleague of Santamaria at the time), Santamaria did not want Labor to win in 1954. Rather, says Henderson, Santamaria was looking ahead to 1957. 'In 1957, his own people [the Movement] would be that much stronger in the ALP and in a position to take over'.[3]

Evatt certainly felt that the ALP defeat in 1954 was due, at least partly, to a 'disloyal' group in the Victorian ALP. He probably derived some consolation from an indication of a dissident strain of Catholic thought. This was expressed in a letter of 26 May 1954 (a few days before the poll) from Dermot Mahon at Temora in New South Wales. He told Evatt:

As an Irishman and a Catholic priest who hates communism, may I pay you the tribute of saying that for me you had no need to declare your hatred of communism. Your deeds have spoken long ago.[4]

Shortly after this, the Petrov Royal Commission began taking evidence. When Evatt appeared before the Commission in August and made clear his belief that the Petrov affair was a conspiracy against him and the ALP, Santamaria and his supporters were outraged. Their opinion that Evatt was unreliable—an opinion stemming from his role in relation to the Communist Party Dissolution Bill of 1950 and the following referendum—was strengthened. In the federal ALP caucus some members criticised Evatt, and there was some basis for this in the fact that Evatt had not consulted caucus before deciding to intervene in the Royal Commission proceedings. Thus he was open to criticism that he was neglecting his responsibilities as leader of the Party, especially as he was obviously completely absorbed in the conduct of his case in court.

Very few people knew that Evatt received advice on Intelligence matters from a well-placed private source in the latter part of 1954 and into 1955. This advice came in the form of a series of notes, some handwritten, some typed. In many cases, the notes were unsigned. In other cases, there was a mysterious signature: 'Phil's Friend'. Presumably, 'Phil' was Philip Evatt who, as a young barrister, worked with 'the Doc' (his uncle) in Royal Commission matters. The identity of 'Phil's Friend' is uncertain. Robert Manne was convinced that it was R. F. B. Wake, which seems to be a reasonable supposition. Bob Wake, who had been a Commander in Naval Intelligence during the war, was living in Mosman in 1954–55 and was a friend of Philip Evatt. It seems that the alias of 'Phil's Friend' was adopted because it was assumed that H. V. Evatt's phone was being tapped by ASIO.

Wake's name cropped up in public records as early as 1940, when he was inspector-in-charge of the Brisbane Office of the Commonwealth Investigation Branch. Judging by the incident recorded then, he was unsympathetic to the activities of Fitzpatrick's ACCL: Wake, like other CIB staff at the time, was anti-Communist. He was also anti-Fascist. He believed that politics should be kept out of ASIO and its forerunners.[5] In 1949, Wake was appointed deputy to Judge Reed, the new Director-General of ASIO. Wake told Chifley that he did not expect the appointment to be a very comfortable one, as he had learned from MI5 men who were then in Australia that the Director of Military Intelligence (Colonel Spry) 'whom I [Wake] had not met had an intense dislike of me, and was friendly with Liberal right-wing politicians'.[6]

Evidently, Wake disliked the imposition of military control over Security, and it is not surprising that he was transferred to another public service post (in the Department of Works) soon after Spry became head of ASIO. Wake's story was that he resigned from his Security position. According to Manne, Wake was dismissed by Spry on the ground of erratic behaviour—but it seems likely that Spry was Manne's source of information on this point. Whatever the truth of the matter, Wake was undoubtedly disgruntled and willing to supply Evatt with inside information when the Petrov affair surfaced. Wake probably still had access to some ASIO sources after he left the organisation.[7]

Manne writes off the material supplied by Wake to Evatt as embodying 'a sinister and nightmarish vision'. Certainly, Wake's impression of an international conspiratorial movement with a United States–Vatican axis and various Australian bodies such as ASIO fitting into the picture, was far-fetched. Yet Wake's world-view was not as fantastic as Manne supposed. The Vatican seems to have had very little direct involvement in Australian politics at this time, but it was heavily engaged, alongside US agencies, in Italian politics. As for the US government, not only did it have an intimate relationship with ASIO, but it subsidised the Movement by supplying free of charge anti-Communist propaganda material for distribution in Australia.[8]

Wake, in writing to Evatt about the connection of certain Australian organisations with the Petrov affair, included some interesting factual material. The pattern of analysis of connections, however, was typical of the ASIO methodology of 'guilt by association'. That is to say, if person A was associated with person B, particularly in an organisation, and person B was believed to hold suspect views, it could be assumed that person A shared those views. Despite such fallacious reasoning, some of Wake's intelligence analyses were well worth considering for their background significance. Thus he supplied Evatt with proof that in 1946 a Queensland division of the Australian Intelligence Association was formed in Brisbane, while similar branches were planned for other States. The initiative came from the Director of Military Intelligence (Spry).

The constitutional objects of this Association were unexceptionable, and outsiders might well assume that the purpose of the organisation was to arrange social reunions and provide a network to help former comrades to obtain jobs. However, one of the objects was to keep members in touch with developments in Intelligence in the post-war period; and membership of the Association was open not only to anyone who had been engaged in Intelligence duties in the Australian Military Forces at any time since 1939, but also to personnel currently engaged in such duties.

Perhaps this Association was a precursor of a larger body, known as The Association and headed by General Blamey. In effect, this was a private right-wing force led by former officers, prepared to go into action to put down any 'communist rising', in much the same way as the New Guard of the 1930s had planned. The Association appears to have been disbanded in 1952, after the advent of the Menzies government.[9]

Wake was also suspicious about the provenance of a 'Call to the Nation', an appeal for national unity (excluding Communists) issued in November 1951 by five church leaders and six judges from State Supreme Courts. Behind 'The Call', in Wake's opinion, were certain personalities prominent in ASIO, The Association and the Movement. Ironically, Evatt in 1951 expressed support for 'The Call', perhaps because the appeal was couched in such general moral terms as to be acceptable to almost anyone. Indeed, for this reason 'The Call' was quickly forgotten, although an attempt was made to revive it a year later through the appointment of some ex-officers to provide an organisational drive.

Although Evatt read and filed Wake's numerous scribblings, there is no indication of whether he adopted the viewpoints expressed; but he certainly acquired some knowledge of the activities of various bodies, including the Movement. Evatt's own suspicious nature was inflamed in August 1954 when he learned from a supporter that fifteen months earlier the *News-Weekly* had stated: 'Startling repercussions are expected to follow disclosures soon to be made on the activities of certain members of the Russian diplomatic staff in Australia. As a sample of what will be revealed in the anticipated disclosures, take the case of the third Secretary attached to the Russian legation in Canberra'. This was an unmistakable reference to Petrov, yet *News-Weekly*'s announcement attracted very little media attention, perhaps because nothing happened for a considerable time.

Even so, the *News-Weekly* disclosure on 28 January 1953 was very well founded. At that time, Bialoguski was working to effect Petrov's defection, although it did not actually came about until 1954. Subsequently, on 28 April 1954, *News-Weekly* boasted that it had long ago tipped off its readers about the coming Petrov defection! When these *News-Weekly* items belatedly came to Evatt's attention, he immediately referred them to the Petrov Royal Commission. To Evatt, this was proof of conspiracy: Petrov's defection had been saved up for the 1954 election. Then, probably at the instigation of ASIO, *News-Weekly* denied that in 1953 it had any knowledge of Petrov's impending defection. In a lame fashion, the magazine's editor said that the name of Petrov had been picked up from the addressograph of a trade union in 1953. The more likely explanation was that the Movement's organ had received a highly confidential leak, if not from ASIO directly, then from one of its senior officers. Given the identity of purpose between ASIO and the Movement in relation to Communism, this was not very surprising, but ASIO denied it and the Royal Commission was not prepared to entertain the possibility. Much later, Santamaria, while saying nothing about the 1950s, acknowledged that he had close official links with ASIO in the 1960s. (*Sydney Morning Herald*, 17 March 1990).

When Evatt launched a strong attack upon the Movement and the Industrial Groups in October 1954, most Australians were taken completely by surprise. Over a period of years, the media had reported very little about the Movement and its activities. After all, it was a secret organisation. Yet there were numerous trade union and ALP leaders who had experienced and resented Grouper/Movement efforts to dominate the labour movement. There was already an incipient revolt in Labor ranks, especially among 'trade union "barons" and political machine "bosses" who feared for their independence and their positions of power'.[10] Most important was Tom Dougherty, federal secretary of the AWU, the largest union. The AWU had worked in alliance with the Groupers until mid-1954, when Dougherty came to the conclusion that there was an intention to set up Industrial Groups in the AWU with the aim of undermining his control. Men like Dougherty were happy to make common cause with Evatt, whose onslaught on the Groupers provided the leadership and national focus they had lacked. There were also many ALP members on the left who were delighted by Evatt's reversal of his earlier dalliance with Groupers. Some of his supporters defy classification. For example, the author Frank Clune wrote:

I dooks me lid! Bravo! Viva! That's the Spirit of Eureka; having the courage to hop in and defend your mates. Bash into them, with fists and boots and tongue...until they grovel on their gonads [11].

Although Evatt's decision to expose the Grouper/Movement was unexpected, it was not simply a reaction to criticism of him in caucus by MPs who had close connections with *News-Weekly*. Evatt was angry about such attacks, but fundamentally he was concerned about the integrity of the ALP, which was threatened by a subversive group aiming 'to deflect the Labour Movement from the pursuit of established Labor objectives and ideals', as he put it in a sensational statement on 5 October 1954. He did not then name any member of the disloyal 'small minority group', located particularly in Victoria, but he did refer to the Melbourne *News-Weekly* as their organ.[12]

The secretary of the Victorian ALP responded immediately with a press statement deploring Evatt's attack and linking it to his 'difficulties' before the Royal Commission on Espionage. Laurie Short also issued a statement strongly criticising Evatt. Santamaria was pleased with this, as it indicated that the Industrial Groups were unlikely to sever their connection with the Movement. On the other hand, it opened the way for a broadening of the attack by Evatt and his supporters upon the Movement so as to embrace the Industrial Groups. Dougherty played a major role in this when he published in *The Worker* on 20 October substantial extracts from a speech delivered by Santamaria earlier that year to the annual convention of the Movement in Albury, New South Wales. The speech was entitled 'The Movement of Ideas in Australia', and evidently Santamaria felt that he could speak frankly, without fear of being reported outside the Movement. Actually the speech was tape-recorded and a transcript was leaked months later to opponents of the Movement, including Evatt and Dougherty. Evatt's copy apparently came from J. Ormonde.

The most revealing part of Santamaria's speech, as reproduced in *The Worker*, was a passage in which he criticised what he regarded as a soft and anti-American line on foreign policy favoured by many ALP leaders. They used the memory of Chifley to reinforce their arguments, which led Santamaria to conclude: 'Within the Labor movement we must fight to destroy the Chifley legend'. Santamaria urged the Movement to overthrow the 'Chifley legend' and replace it with a pro-American 'Curtin legend'. Regardless of the historical validity of such legends, the exposure of Santamaria as someone aiming to belittle Chifley's reputation among a great number of Australians who remembered him with affection was highly damaging to Santamaria's supporters. Santamaria's leaked speech was widely publicised within the labour movement.[13]

Evatt rightly saw the ALP Federal Executive as his main hope in the internal struggle against the Groupers and the Movement. The federal body was composed of equal numbers of representatives from each State, and Groupers were relatively weak in Western Australia, Tasmania and South Australia. Consequently, there was a fair prospect of securing an anti-Grouper majority on the federal executive, which had power to discipline State branches of the party. In November 1954, the Federal Executive met to consider statements by both Evatt and a large number of trade unions in Victoria concerning the activities of the Groups there. As a result, the Federal Executive took a majority decision to investigate the affairs of the Victorian ALP and to convene a special conference of the Victorian branch to elect a new State Executive. The rules for election of delegates to the special conference were modified in ways which apparently disadvantaged Groupers. However, opponents of Groupers regarded these changes as simply redressing the balance which Groupers had previously manipulated in their own favour. Besides this, the federal executive ordered withdrawal of official ALP support for Industrial Groups in Victoria.

These decisions favoured Evatt and his supporters. On the other hand, the Movement, influenced by Santamaria, reckoned—perhaps mistakenly—that under the new rules the Groupers were unlikely to secure a majority of delegates to the special conference. The old Victorian executive split along sectarian lines on this issue, with the majority deciding to boycott the conference. Thus, when the conference met in Melbourne in February 1955, there was little opposition to the election of a new anti-Grouper State executive, together with six delegates to a federal ALP conference to be held in Hobart the following month. There followed a dramatic showdown as the credentials of the anti-Grouper Victorian delegation in Hobart were approved, while a rival delegation, representing the old Victorian executive, was excluded from the conference after considerable scuffling.

This gave victory to the pro-Evatt forces. It was narrowly won, and the outcome of the Hobart conference would have been very different but for the credentialling of the delegation from the new Victorian executive and its participation in subsequent voting. Nevertheless, in the tradition of ALP conferences, a narrow majority was as good as a win by a large majority. The defeat of the Groupers was decisive as the Hobart conference went on to decide to withdraw official ALP recognition of Industrial Groups in all States, on the ground that such recognition had materially assisted Groups in 'entering fields other than those intended by their founders'. Evatt himself spoke at length along these lines at the Hobart conference. He also successfully urged the conference to commit the Party to recognition of Communist China—a policy which was anathema to the Movement. Incidentally, Evatt spoke by invitation, as he was not a delegate—which serves as a reminder of the importance of trade unions (in New South Wales as well as Victoria) which allied themselves with the left in the ALP to support Evatt against the Groupers and the Movement.[14]

There were bitter reprisals on both sides in Victoria after the Hobart conference. Without going into detail, it can be said that most Groupers in that State hived off from the ALP to set up a Labor Party (Anti-Communist) in 1955, which was re-named the Democratic Labor Party (DLP) a year later. Similar breakaway movements occurred in other States, though with much less success. Thus in New South Wales, most of the Groupers, after a period of confusion, decided to give nominal allegiance to the Hobart conference decisions and to remain in the ALP. To a large extent they were motivated by desire to maintain the existence of a State Labor government with considerable links to Groupers. Furthermore, the Catholic Church hierarchy in New South Wales differed appreciably from its counterpart in Victoria in attitudes towards the Movement. In particular, Cardinal Gilroy in Sydney did not support the establishment of the DLP there in September 1956. This did not prevent the new party from being promoted by the more bigoted of the anti-Communists. Its first secretary, Jack Kane, had become general secretary of the Groups in New South Wales in 1950, a member of the State executive of the ALP in 1952 and assistant general secretary of the Party from

1953 till the formation of the DLP. Kane was a good organiser but the refusal of many of his former colleagues to join the DLP meant that the new party could do little more than block the federal ALP in elections.

———❖———

Evatt, early in 1955, was involved in an odd situation which well illustrates the atmosphere of bitterness and vicious recrimination within the ALP. At the time, Evatt's attention was fully taken up, not only by the inner-Party struggle but also by the proceedings of the Petrov Royal Commission. It is not surprising that he had no personal time to spare for routine matters such as renewing his annual membership of the ALP. Evatt had been a member of the Party's Canberra branch for many years, as his primary residence was there, in a rented house. A newly-appointed member of his staff was given the job of seeing that the Doc's membership was renewed for 1955, but the staff member failed to do this. In January 1955, a membership ticket was issued to Evatt by a branch in his Barton electorate, but this was of limited validity: he did not reside there, as was required by ALP rules for the issue of a primary membership ticket conferring continuity of Party membership (a pre-requisite for endorsement of a parliamentary representative).

Membership tickets had to be renewed by 31 March of each year, and it was very close to that date before Evatt was alerted to his dangerous position. On 30 March 1955, Evatt himself asked Canberra branch officials to renew his ticket but was told that this could not be done within the required time. In desperation, Evatt the following day sent a telegram to George Godfrey, president of the ALP branch in Mosman (where Evatt lived, in a house which he owned, between parliamentary sittings), applying for membership of the branch. Godfrey replied that he would recommend the branch to approve the application and to date Evatt's ticket as from 31 March, when the application was received. This could not be formally effected until the next branch meeting, in April, but Godfrey was confident. The Mosman branch generally supported Evatt's policies, and Evatt's association with the branch went back to the 1920s.

Groupers in News South Wales were acutely conscious of Evatt's predicament. On 1 April 1955, the Sydney *Sun* published a statement issued by three leading officials of the ALP State executive (Colbourne, Kane and Bowen), which said that Evatt 'is not now a member of the ALP and cannot hold any position in the party'. Godfrey responded publicly, referring to Evatt's application to the Mosman branch. The matter was then considered by the Party's federal Executive on 5 April. By a close vote of seven against five, the executive resolved that Evatt should be permitted to take out a membership ticket and be regarded as having continuity of membership. Two of the five minority votes came from New South Wales.[15]

Then came a special meeting of the Mosman branch on 13 April. Evatt was present and so was Bowen, vice-president of the Party in New South Wales. They clashed dramatically, although this probably had little effect upon the Mosman branch's decision to admit Evatt as a member with effect from 31 March 1955. Then, in a last-ditch stalling movement, the secretary of the branch (a Grouper) told the meeting that he had not brought the ticket-issuing book with him. Indeed it was locked in the vaults of the local branch of a private trading bank, where he was employed. E. L. Wheelwright, who was a member of the branch at the time, recalls that the branch induced the secretary to conform with the branch decision by suggesting that his job might be affected if his employer were to be informed that he was active in the ALP. As Wheelwright says, although the threat was not implemented, it was a dirty trick to play. On the other hand, it pales into insignificance when compared with the breathtaking pettiness of the Grouper attempt to get rid of the party leader on a technicality.

Groupers retaliated against Evatt's Mosman supporters in 1956 by swamping the branch with new applicants for membership. These applicants were:

mostly recruited through local Catholic Churches. None of the new recruits ever uttered a word at Branch meetings, leaving the talking to, and following the voting lead of, three spokesmen. The Groupers' leader, Jack Kane, visited one night with eleven recruits. Then suddenly all of them vanished as if an official boycott of the Branch had been imposed. This gave the opportunity to myself [Godfrey] and the Evatt loyalists to carry a resolution asking the ALP State Executive to withdraw the Mosman branch charter and reform the Branch excluding all Groupers ...The branch was reformed on Jan. 15, 1957.[16]

Evatt was fortunate in gaining Godfrey's support, which actually ante-dated the struggle against the Groupers. For example, on 20 June 1951, Godfrey wrote to congratulate Evatt upon his election to leadership of the ALP, saying that he (Godfrey) had 'always ranked you, with John Curtin and Ben Chifley, as the Big Three of Australian Labor in this generation'. Evatt returned the compliment, proposing Godfrey for an important Party position in 1956. This appears in an informal letter from Evatt to 'Joe' Chamberlain, federal president of the ALP. Evatt attacked the current New South Wales Executive of the Party, saying that it had 'done everything possible to undermine and destroy the Hobart decisions especially in relation to ALP Industrial Groups and the foreign policy declaration'.[17]

Evatt went on in this letter to suggest that the federal Executive should act to install a new New South Wales executive willing to carry out the federal policy of the ALP. As requested earlier by Chamberlain, Evatt put forward several names, including those of Ormonde, Dougherty and Godfrey, for inclusion in a new State executive. Shortly after this, the federal Executive disbanded the New South Wales executive and established a new body on which pro-Evatt forces had a narrow majority. However, there was no clean sweep of Groupers as in Victoria: the new State executive in New South Wales included a number of people previously known as Groupers.

NOTES

1 Quoted in G. Sharp, 'The Movement', *Arena*, Melbourne, December 1992–January 1993, p. 17. Gerard Henderson is given as the principal source of this information. See also Edmund Campion, *Rockchoppers*, Penguin, Australia, 1982, pp. 112–13.
2 S. Murray-Smith, in *Australians from 1939*, ed. Ann Curthoys and others, Fairfax Syme, Sydney, 1987, p. 427; Gilroy to Evatt, 13 December 1949, Evatt Collection, Flinders University. File: Correspondence, Miscellaneous, 1948–49. See also James Murtagh, *Australia: The Catholic Chapter*, Angus & Robertson, Sydney, 1959, p. 208.
3 Quoted by Susanna Short, *Laurie Short: A Political Life*, Allen & Unwin, Sydney, 1992, p. 210.
4 Evatt Collection, Flinders University.
5 Australian Archives, A432, 40/115.
6 Wake's summary of conversation between himself and J.B. Chifley, about August 1949. This document, along with others on Security and the Petrov affair, is located in various files (e.g. 'Phil's Friend') in the Evatt Collection at Flinders University.
7 R. Manne, *The Petrov Affair*, pp. 242–3.
8 John Warhurst, 'United States' Government Assistance to the Catholic Social Studies Movement, 1953-4', *Labour History*, no. 30, May 1976.
9 David McKnight, 'A Very Australian Coup', *Sydney Morning Herald*, 11 November 1989, p. 82.
10 Tom Truman, *Catholic Action and Politics*, Georgian House, Melbourne, rev. edn, 1960, p. 157.
11 Clune to Evatt, 27 August 1954, Evatt Collection, Flinders University, File: ALP Industrial Groups (d). 'Them' in this quotation referred to 'squealers' such as Daly and Keon in caucus.
12 Robert Murray, *The Split*, Cheshire, Melbourne, 1970, pp. 179–85. Murray presents an anti-Evatt view. He argues that Evatt was 'deeply disturbed', indeed paranoid, at the time, although he acknowledges that Evatt 'did not give the impression of unbalance to the men he was cultivating and using to promote the split'. In fact, Evatt's actions were quite rational in the light of what he had learned about the Movement.

13 Short, *Laurie Short*, p. 188.
14 Weller and Lloyd, *Federal Executive Minutes, 1915–1955*, p. 612.
15 George Godfrey Papers, Sydney. According to Godfrey, the person who failed to submit Evatt's membership renewal application in Canberra was a Grouper.
16 George Godfrey, transcript of oral autobiography, Tape 2, Side 1, pp. 40–2, 15 November 1975, ANL.
17 Evatt to Joe (Chamberlain), 30 April 1956, Evatt Collection, Flinders University. By this time, the NSW Executive had formally acknowledged the binding nature of the Hobart conference decisions, but Evatt regarded this recognition as mere lip-service.

CHAPTER 29

THE LAST FIGHT

If mere anti-Communism is to be the primary policy of Labor, all the great principles we support will become of minor importance.
H. V. EVATT, 1954

For many years after the split in the ALP in 1954–55, the DLP functioned as a spoiler in Australian politics. Essentially, its role was negative: if the former Groupers and Movement supporters were to be denied domination of the ALP from within, they would work through the DLP to keep Labor out of office by directing the second preferences of DLP voters to the Liberal–Country parties in elections. To many clerks, artisans and others, the DLP served as a bridge (and a salve for conscience) in their inevitable transition from Labor to Liberal in these relatively prosperous times. Yet many other former Labor voters also switched allegiance to the DLP. The overall strategy was very successful. Although few DLP candidates were elected to parliament, the national DLP vote ranged from 9 per cent of the total in 1958 to 6 per cent in 1969 (the figures were higher than this in Victoria), and the Liberal–Country Party government in Canberra benefited greatly. The ALP did not win a federal election until 1972.

In the light of this long-term trend, questions arise as to Evatt's role in the 1950s. Was the split inevitable? Could it have been avoided or moderated by a more conciliatory approach than Evatt's? The answers are uncertain, of course. It seems clear that an explosion and diversion of some kind was inevitable before long. The Movement was close to achieving its aim of control of the ALP, and in the process it made many enemies. Very broadly, as a Catholic priest put it later: 'The Movement men and women who were extruded from the Labor Party at that time were expelled because, like the communists, they belonged to a political apparatus which was attempting to impose its ideology by stealth'.[1]

If Evatt had not precipitated the split by his forceful attack upon Santamaria and his supporters, a breakaway might have been delayed and been very different in form—it could have been a protest from the left against the diversion of the ALP from its traditional aims. Whether such a protest would have had much success if the ALP had been firmly controlled by the Grouper/Movement faction is doubtful. The history of dissident parties on the left in Australian history is not encouraging. Actually, the question was pre-empted by Evatt's decisive attack upon his opponents while their control was still not firmly established. Timing was crucial. On the one side, by October 1954, 'the Movement was convinced that both Evatt and ALP policies were gravely inadequate to meet the menace of communism'.[2] On the other side was Evatt's view, expressed in a statement to the ALP federal Executive on 27 October that year:

If mere anti-Communism is to be the primary policy of Labor, all the great principles we support will become of minor importance. It will be sufficient to condemn any proposal to show that Communists or Communist papers have supported it...The theory has been used against myself in **News-Weekly** *and in the Caucus. 'He is critical of the Petrovs. So are the Communists. Therefore he is a Communist supporter'...Labor cannot survive on the basis of a party within the party.*[3]

It was generally reckoned by Evatt's enemies—and, indeed, many of his supporters—that opportunism was primarily responsible for his actions at this time. As J. D. Pringle, editor of the *Sydney Morning Herald*, wrote: 'In order to strengthen his own position in the party, gravely weakened by his failure in the [1954] Federal elections and by his attitude to the Petrov Commission, Dr Evatt has decided to launch an attack on Catholic Action.' Undoubtedly, Evatt was very concerned about his personal position in the Party. Yet there is not necessarily a conflict between this interpretation and the reasoned argument quoted above. The target was the same in both cases.[4]

Ross McMullin, in his recent history of the ALP, concludes that 'Evatt's leadership aggravated the split.' McMullin also refers to Evatt's 'increasingly erratic behaviour during 1954'.[5] Equally, it can be argued that there was no realistic prospect of compromise between Evatt and Santamaria and that a decisive severance from the Movement and the Groupers was essential for the health of the ALP in the long run. This goes to the heart of the issue. Patching over the areas of fundamental disagreement may have averted a split, but to what end? Professional politicians in the party generally regarded the winning of office as the main aim, without any overriding concern for the policies to be pursued in government. Power and careers were at stake. On the other hand, many less well-placed members and supporters of the ALP were more concerned with principles and policies. What was the point of winning elections if the ALP was barely distinguishable from its main political opponents?

It was not simply a question of ideology. The ALP had some members who were socialist and were strongly critical of the Cahill Labor government in New South Wales in the 1950s, because it was clearly not interested in any radical reforms despite its legislation to improve the conditions of workers. There were also some prominent ALP members—F. E. Chamberlain, for example—who proclaimed themselves socialist and adhered to principles but in practice did little to further socialist aims. Yet there were other Labor supporters who, while not on the left in the political spectrum, held firmly to democratic principles even if the result was to keep the ALP out of office. Two examples of this may be given. One is George Godfrey who, besides being President of the Mosman ALP, was a leading official of the Australian Journalists' Association and was generally reckoned to be conservative in politics. In addition, he was a Freemason. In 1950, he wrote to Chifley, urging uncompromising opposition to the Communist Party Dissolution Bill:

I believe that there are many members of the Labor Party who would rather see the party go down fighting a good cause (even though the recipients of the exercise of freedom are unworthy) than shabbily sacrifice their principles for, probably, the false hope of electoral advantage.[6]

A second example is a feminist trade unionist, N. V. Williams of Darlinghurst (Sydney), who wrote to congratulate Evatt on his stand 'in the matter of the Royal Commission and on the behaviour of certain elements in the Labor Party':

I don't know whether what is happening now is going to win or lose the next election for Labor. I do know, however, that I would rather see an honestly reactionary 'Liberal' government in power than a Labor government which was white-anted by people who are prepared to go to any lengths in order to defeat and exterminate what is after all a rather small section—the Communists—and who would in that process kill the last remnants of the freedoms we are so fond of boasting about on public occasions.[7]

Although Evatt would never have conceded that a Liberal government might be better than a Labor one, he was in full agreement with the two people quoted above in respect to Labor principles and civil liberties. His attitude towards socialist doctrine was not so clear-cut. He generally favoured economic intervention by the state, but this did not necessarily imply a policy of nationalisation of industries. At the time of the coal strike in 1949 he wrote privately:

my opinion is that certain industries should be controlled and operated by the people through the government, that certain trades can never be so controlled and operated, e.g. retail trades generally, and that there is a third group which should, under certain conditions, be operated by government.

The essential element is that the profit motive should be curbed in the interests of the community as a whole.[8]

In a broader context, Clyde Cameron, who was closely associated with Evatt in parliament in the 1950s, cannot recall hearing him talk about socialism. However, there were occasions when Evatt referred to 'democratic socialism', which he said was:

precisely the same as European social democracy...the views of the social democrat movement of Europe—the British Labor party is an essential part of it—the Australian Labor party, and the New Zealand Labor party are exactly the same.[9]

❖

In parliament, from 1955 to 1956, Evatt's position as federal ALP leader was relatively secure. He was subjected to constant verbal abuse by Keon and other former members of the party but the damage they could inflict was limited—they were no longer members of caucus. Once the Petrov affair was over, Evatt settled down to the standard role of a Labor Opposition leader. Thus he attacked the growth of business combines and monopolies, though seldom in the context of a call for a radically different kind of society. He also supported the Commonwealth Trading Bank against the private banks and alleged that the Prime Minister relied heavily on the views of S. Ricketson, head of the stockbroking firm of Were. Evatt declared: 'What Mr. Ricketson says today, Mr. Menzies says not long after'.[10]

Evatt was deeply concerned by two important issues which arose in federal parliament in 1956. One was over industrial disputes. There had been a number of cases in which action was taken in the Arbitration Court to obtain injunctions restraining unions from continuing work bans; and unions were subsequently fined for contempt of court when such injunctions were not obeyed. In this connection, the High Court in 1956 ruled in the *Boilermakers'* case that the Arbitration

Court, as a non-judicial body, had no power to impose fines or penalties: arbitral powers must be kept separate from judicial powers. The Menzies government responded with legislation to establish a new federal Industrial Court with judges empowered to impose penalties, alongside a separate Conciliation and Arbitration Commission to determine wages and working conditions in the customary manner. This conflicted with Evatt's long-held opinion that administrative bodies with social welfare functions should not be 'hampered too much by judicial restrictions'. More immediately, he pointed out that the new Industrial Court was to be composed of some of the judges who previously exercised its jurisdiction in the old Arbitration Court.[11]

Evatt moved to have the Bill reconsidered, arguing particularly that it contained 'some of the worst features of the existing legislation, e.g. penalties enforceable by process of contempt of court...In practice they have been enforced only against trades unions, their officers and their members'. Menzies in reply said that Evatt, through his Arbitration (Amendment) Act of 1947, had 'put the judges into a position where injunctions could be issued by them as a superior court of record'. This was true, though it should be added that the Menzies government itself, regarding the Act as unsatisfactory, had brought in further changes in 1952. The amendment which Evatt moved in 1956 was defeated by the government, but he had the satisfaction of voicing the growing concern of the ACTU over the infliction of court penalties in industrial disputes. Evatt was no longer inhibited by Groupers from making forthright statements on such matters.[12]

Shortly after this an international crisis over control of the Suez Canal erupted. The British and French governments vehemently objected (though without justification in international law) to nationalisation of the Canal Company by the Egyptian government. In September 1956, an international consortium sent a delegation, headed by Menzies, to Cairo for talks with the Egyptian leader, Nasser. The mission 'led nowhere'; Nasser was not susceptible to intimidation, and Menzies, for all his vain posturing on the international stage, had been given no power to negotiate. On his return to Australia, Menzies made a parliamentary statement in which he canvassed the possible use of force or economic sanctions against Egypt in order to restore international control of the Suez Canal.[13]

Evatt responded vigorously, saying that it was 'appalling' for Menzies to make such a speech on the eve of discussions by the United Nations Security Council. Evatt asserted that there 'never was international control of the canal in the sense used by the Prime Minister': it was in reality control by the shareholders of the Suez

Canal Company, who made high profits. As for Menzies' postulation of the possible use of force, it would, said Evatt, be

completely contrary to the rule of law which has emerged as a result of the Charter of the United Nations...No authorisation of force is provided under the Charter except self-defence against armed force.[14]

On 30 October, Israeli forces, by secret agreement with Britain and France, attacked across the Egyptian border towards the Suez Canal; and this was followed by Anglo-French military action against Egypt. Menzies in effect welcomed the British action. He was not particularly worried by adverse UN reaction, although he was very embarrassed by President Eisenhower's strong opposition to the invasion of Egypt. The Americans were concerned about the effect upon Arab opinion—and upon cheap oil supplies from the Middle East. Menzies, in informing the Australian parliament of developments in the situation, was also on the defensive because Australia (and other British Dominion countries) had not been consulted before Britain acted. Menzies' excuse was that unilateral action by Britain was warranted by the situation of 'great emergency'. This was not at all acceptable to Evatt, who characterised Menzies' attitude as being in line with

the rule of the nineteenth century—the policy of the gunboat diplomat. You go in and try to get what you want. If the people concerned are not acquiescent and do not recognise your superiority, you use armed force. I tell him [Menzies]...that doctrine ought to be dead. I tell him, too, that on the legal conception of the United Nations Charter that doctrine cannot be justified.[15]

Evatt concluded his speech by saying that the action initiated by Britain and France

in effect amounts to an act of aggression. It was condemned by seven out of eleven members of the United Nations Security Council, and I believe that it is opposed to the feeling and conscience of the great majority of the people of Australia.

This was Evatt's last great speech on foreign policy and its impact was forceful. It was highly appropriate for him to emphasise the central importance of the United Nations. As it happened this was the forum in which the Suez crisis was effectively handled, with Britain and France being forced to withdraw their forces under pressure applied mainly by the United States. In short, Evatt was vindicated. Menzies defended himself but was clearly wounded. He said:

Some casual but biased observers have suggested that we have merely 'toed the line'. This is, of course, nonsense. We have not...lacked the capacity for expressing our own views, though we have at all times expressed them as British people.[16]

The interests of the 'British people' (as interpreted by the British government) constituted Menzies' basic reference point, rather than the interests of the people of Australia as expressed by Evatt. Some of Menzies' own Cabinet colleagues, including Casey, were privately not happy about his Suez policy or its effect upon Australian public opinion that year. W. C. Wentworth, in an undated letter (written approximately June 1956) to Percy Spender in Washington, said:

Labor appears to have wrecked itself again on the Evatt—Comm. issue. Believe me, nothing else keeps us in office. The Government's stocks are very low, and not likely, I think, to improve. But Labour stinks so badly it can't win as things are at present.

To judge from Commonwealth Parliamentary Debates in 1958, Evatt was subdued in parliament. Perhaps his health was giving way, without his realising it. However, he was galvanised into action towards the end of the year, when there was a federal election. Evatt himself did not seek re-election for his old seat of Barton, which had become marginal in polling terms over the years. He obtained preselection for a safe Labor seat, Hunter, on the northern coalfields of New South Wales. The incumbent MP, James, decided not to contest the seat again, due to illness. Evatt's loyal supporters in Barton evidently did not feel betrayed by his switch: as national leader of the party he could not be expected to spend a lot of time winning a seat for himself.

Apparently, Evatt decided that the ALP could not win the general election without some dramatic move to neutralise the DLP vote. Accordingly, in the midst of the campaign, he announced at a public meeting that he would resign from the leadership of the ALP after the election—and would not seek re-election—if the DLP would direct its voters to give their second preferences to the ALP. Evatt seems to have been genuine in this offer, described by his secretary as 'an act of political self-abnegation'. Yet most of his colleagues, such as Calwell, had not been consulted beforehand and were aghast at his recklessness, although they refrained from saying so in public in the election campaign. They feared that voters would be bewildered by the prospect of voting for a Labor Party whose leadership would be uncertain till after the election. On the other hand, Evatt's move had the effect of putting DLP leaders on the defensive: after directing so much venom at Evatt, they now had an opportunity to get rid of him.

The adverse aspect of this, from the ALP point of view, was that media attention was deflected from policy issues to the DLP.[17]

The outcome was that the DLP rejected Evatt's offer because it did not indicate that the ALP was prepared to abandon the policy decisions made at its Hobart conference in 1955. With the departure of hard-line Groupers, the Party had moved to the left. In a final effort to influence the Catholic vote, Evatt—apparently with the concurrence of Calwell and McKenna—decided to place newspaper advertisements which gave the impression that Cardinal Gilroy was at least neutral in the contest for votes between the ALP and the DLP. This was a tactical error as it provided an occasion for Archbishop Mannix to issue a statement the day before the election, criticising the use of Gilroy's name. Mannix declared: 'Every Communist and every Communist sympathiser in Australia wants a victory for the Evatt party. This...should be a significant warning for every Catholic and every decent Australian'.[18]

With the benefit of DLP preferences, the Liberal–Country parties won the 1958 election comfortably. Evatt was then re-elected as leader of the Opposition, although the position was contested by Ward, who secured thirty-two votes against forty-six for Evatt. Ward was angered by Evatt's offer to the DLP during the election campaign. Fundamentally, however, Evatt's moderate success in the caucus ballot denoted no more than a recognition that prospective alternative leaders of the party were not outstanding. In the next year, there was a hardening of feeling in caucus that the party could not win a federal election with Evatt as leader and that he must go. Yet many Labor MPs had a genuine respect for him and wished his departure to be a dignified one.

An opening appeared with the impending retirement of the Chief Justice of New South Wales. Evatt, weary of the strains of politics, became interested in appointment to the prestigious but less stressful judicial position. His federal parliamentary colleagues encouraged him in this, and some of them (notably Calwell, who was prospective successor to Evatt as federal Party leader) lobbied the New South Wales Labor government in his favour. Evatt had qualifications for the position, and Bob Heffron, the new Premier of New South Wales, was an old political ally of Evatt. Another old friend, Abe Landa, who was Minister for Housing in the government, strongly upheld Evatt's claim for appointment. However, there were other members of Cabinet who were opposed—notably, R. Downing, the Attorney-General. When Cabinet first voted on the issue in January 1960, it was evenly divided.

Downing's views were a compound of his political position on the right in the ALP and a belief that Evatt was unsuited for the appointment. There were rumours about Evatt's health, along with suggestions that he was mentally unstable. These rumours appear to have circulated among lawyers and senior ALP politicians, especially in Canberra. Of those in the latter group who gave credence to such stories, it must be said that their eagerness to get rid of Evatt through appointment to the position of Chief Justice of New South Wales bespoke only their concern for the party and their own preferment, regardless of potential damage to public welfare. Their attitude was disgraceful, for the function of Chief Justice was important. It was not a sinecure. Evatt himself knew this, but he was unable to take cognisance of his declining ability to cope.

There was at least one other candidate for the position: John Kerr, a one-time protege of Evatt. Kerr had important connections with a number of right-wing trade unions, having long advised and acted for them in legal matters. However, Evatt asked Short of the Ironworkers' Association to persuade a certain New South Wales Minister—who was opposed to Evatt—to change his mind over the appointment. Short agreed to speak to this Minister, who subsequently switched his vote at a Cabinet meeting. Evatt was appointed Chief Justice, whereupon he resigned from leadership of the ALP. It seems that Short's prime motive was his belief that 'removing Evatt from the leadership was the first step to removing alleged Communist influence from the ALP.'[19]

Evatt's term of office on the Supreme Court bench was a lamentable final phase in a brilliant working life. His memory, which had been phenomenally good, failed him; he sometimes dozed on the bench (although he was not unique among judges in that respect); and his mental deterioration was obvious. Michael Kirby recalls that in his own youth as an articled clerk he 'was surrounded by well-groomed young lawyers who mocked this mental giant in his closing months. He was like Lear, disconsolate'.[20]

Fortunately, it seems that no major miscarriages of justice resulted. Evatt's brother-justices covered up for him, sometimes assisting in writing his judgments, although they despaired about his failure to perform such relatively simple tasks as allocating judges to take particular cases. It is a remarkable coincidence that when Sir Owen Dixon (another lawyer who worked extremely hard) retired from his position as Chief Justice of the High Court in 1964, he too was suffering from a nervous breakdown. In his case, the problem occurred suddenly and was never referred to publicly—evidently, he was persuaded to go quickly. In contrast, Evatt stayed on, although his condition was obvious to lawyers who appeared before him in court.[21]

At the Bar, it was bruited that he suffered from cerebral arteriosclerosis—a hardening of arteries which prevented sufficient oxygen from reaching the brain. Some politicians were less precise or careful. Fred Daly, for example, reckoned wrongly that Evatt had Alzheimer's disease. In 1962, the Chief Justice was given leave of absence from the court to go to a conference in Britain, but his health broke down completely while the ship was still on the West Australian coast. He was taken home and he resigned from his position on the New South Wales Supreme Court later that year. He never returned to public life.

When it became public knowledge that Evatt was mentally ill, there was speculation as to when the condition first asserted itself and affected his behaviour. With the benefit of hindsight, many people reckoned that the early stages of the illness could be traced back to indications of paranoia in Evatt's conduct during the Petrov Royal Commission. Other people directed attention to the stresses associated with the great Labor split. Perhaps so, but these conjectures were guess-work, uninformed by medical knowledge. Actually, problems with Evatt's health had cropped up much earlier. He had respiratory complaints and often took to his bed for days at a time, particularly when there was abnormal stress, as during an election campaign. Little public attention was paid to these episodes, which were usually reported as bouts of bronchitis or influenza. It is possible that they were manifestations of a deep-seated malady: epilepsy.

There are six sub-types of epilepsy. The most serious is evidenced by symptoms of convulsion and loss of consciousness, but there is no indication that Evatt was ever afflicted by this form. In any case, most sufferers from epilepsy can lead normal lives with few restrictions: modern drugs can suppress seizures. Nevertheless, people who suffer from epilepsy are generally subject to a degree of social stigma—based on fear and ignorance—and the stigma was greater in the past than it is today. Understandably, therefore, epileptics avoided public disclosure of their condition, if at all possible. Thus the fact that Manning Clark, the historian, was epileptic was revealed only recently, in his autobiography, *Puzzles of Childhood*.

In Evatt's case, there was never any public suspicion or suggestion of epilepsy, nor any direct evidence of it, although there are a few significant indicators. In 1943, while Evatt was in Washington on an official mission, he sent the following cable to Hodgson, head of the External Affairs Department in Canberra:

Please convey the following message to Dr. Gilbert Phillips, 143 Macquarie Street:

'Agree to your diagnosis. Might try combination of Luminal and Dilantin. Letter following'.[22]

No elucidation of this cryptic message has come to light. However, it is a fact that Phillips was a specialist neurosurgeon in Sydney, and luminal and dilantin were drugs used in the treatment of epilepsy, with particular reference to partial seizures. Dilantin was a new drug in 1943, available in Australia to only a few people, notably those of high status. According to medical sources, some side effects of the use of dilantin as an epileptic drug were manifest in swings of mood. This might help to explain some odd aspects of Evatt's behaviour over the years, such as erratic conduct, sudden changes in the way he treated people, and explosive outbursts. It may also be significant that Evatt always seems to have used a chauffeur when travelling by car: an epileptic was not permitted to have a driving licence.

A final piece of evidence concerning Evatt's medical condition relates to his last years, when Sir Douglas Miller, an eminent neurosurgeon, went to see him at his home on one occasion. Sir Douglas did so at the request of Evatt's personal physician, and knowing nothing about Evatt having a history of epilepsy. Sir Douglas recalls the visit as being very distressing. Evatt (in 1963–64) was physically uncontrollable and was completely out of touch with reality. He was demented and Sir Douglas could do nothing to help him. [23]

One other piece of information may have some relevance. In 1959, the Commonwealth parliament considered a Matrimonial Causes Bill, which became law after MPs voted upon it as a non-party matter of individual responsibility. In debate in the Senate, a clause in the Bill which provided for voiding a marriage where one spouse was subject to recurrent attacks of insanity or epilepsy was amended by deletion. Senator Hannan, in speaking to this amendment, said: 'By the use of modern drugs phenobarbital with dilantin...epilepsy is now capable in most instances of being contained.' In support of this argument, Hannan quoted an opinion expressed by Sir Charles Symonds, an authority on nervous diseases at Guy's Hospital in London. Symonds said that sufferers from epilepsy

will need some encouragement and may fairly be told that there are many cases in which the lability is so slight that it is entirely controlled by medicines and the attacks cease...and, further, that there are many more cases in which, though the attacks continue, they are so infrequent as to interfere very little with the patient's life, and their occurrence is known only to his intimates.[24]

When the Bill was returned to the House of Representatives, Evatt spoke in support of the Senate amendment, declaring that he was 'impressed' by Symonds' opinion as quoted. Evatt said nothing to suggest a personal interest in epilepsy and he was not in any way involved in the raising of the matter in the Senate amendment. Even if it be surmised that Evatt suffered from epilepsy, the occasion for a debate on the malady in his last year in parliament was simply coincidental.[25]

According to surviving members of the Evatt family, there was never any suggestion or indication that 'the Doc' was epileptic. Philip Evatt says that there was no sign of mental deterioration in 'the Doc' at the time of the Petrov affair, when on the contrary he was functioning 'at full strength', as usual.

What should be obvious must be emphasised: Evatt's medical problems, whatever their precise nature, do not detract from his great achievements. Hartley Grattan, writing after his death, said:

Evatt was probably neurotic most or even all of his life. Most of us are neurotic to some degree...certainly in his maturity and later life, when I knew him, he was neurotic. But nothing much can be made of this beyond noting and assessing its significance which is, in my view, not definitive in explaining Evatt's public speech and conduct. He certainly was observably eccentric...But I see no evidence that he was psychotic at any stage of his life.[26]

The last few years of Evatt's life were dark and sad, not only for him but also for his devoted family, particularly his wife, Mary Alice, and his daughter Rosalind. He was cared for at home, Mary Alice being concerned to shield him from public exposure and possible ridicule. In addition to emotional pain, heavy costs were incurred in the employment of day and night nurses. The government offered no assistance for the man who had served his country well, and although the family had always lived in comfortable circumstances—Mary Alice had a substantial inheritance from the estate of her parents—it became necessary to sell assets to meet expenses. The valuable Modigliani painting, acquired by the Evatts in the 1930s, was sold in the process.

Herbert Vere Evatt died in November 1965 in Canberra and was buried there. Among those who eulogised him in parliament, perhaps the most sincere was Bert James, rough-hewn representative of the mining constituency of the Hunter, a seat vacated by his father to make way for Evatt in 1958. James ended his speech about Evatt by saying:

Leave him to history. It will be kinder than his present day critics.[27]

Notes

1 Edmund Campion, *Rockchoppers*, p. 114.
2 Patrick O'Farrell, *The Catholic Church and Community: An Australian History*, University of New South Wales, Sydney, 1985, p. 395.
3 Evatt Collection, Flinders University.
4 Gavin Souter, *Company of Heralds*, MUP, Melbourne, 1981, p. 634, footnote 336.
5 Ross McMullin, *The Light on the Hill*, p. 276.
6 Godfrey to Chifley, 1 May 1950, George Godfrey Papers.
7 Williams to Evatt, 13 October 1954, Evatt Collection, File: ALP Industrial Groups.
8 Evatt to Eric Dark, 28 July 1949, Evatt Collection, File: Miscellaneous Correspondence, 1948–49. Evatt was unsure about classifying the coal and steel industries.
9 *CPD*, vol. 18, 27 February 1958, p. 115.
10 Sydney *Sun*, 30 November 1955.
11 Leslie Zines, 'Mr Justice Evatt and the Constitution', *Federal Law Review*, vol. 3 (1969), p. 170.
12 *CPD*, vol. 10, 22 May 1956, pp. 2332–45.
13 Kenneth O. Morgan, *The People's Peace: British History 1945–1989*, OUP, Oxford, 1990, p. 150. The author of this text dismisses Menzies as 'a somewhat surprising emissary'.
14 *CPD*, vol. 12, 25 September 1956, pp. 826–32.
15 Ibid., vol. 13, 31 October–1 November 1956, pp. 2060–6
16 Ibid., 8 November 1956, p. 2116 .
17 Allan Dalziel, *Evatt the Enigma*, p. 145.
18 Robert Murray, *The Split*, p. 348.
19 Susanna Short, *Laurie Short*, pp. 239–40. Kerr became Chief Justice later, in 1972.
20 Michael Kirby, 'H.V. Evatt: Libertarian Warrior', S*eeing Red*, p. 17.
21 Kylie Tennant, in ch. 25 of *Evatt: Politics and Justice*, refers to some of the cases which came before Evatt in his last years. Dixon's mental state is not mentioned in any law book.
22 Evatt to Hodgson, 23 April 1943, Australian Archives, A 4764/3 E. 25.
23 Information from Sir Douglas Miller, Sydney, 14 January 1993.
24 *CPD*, Senate, vol. S.16, 26 November 1959, p. 1926.
25 *CPD*, H. of R., vol. 25, 3 December 1959, p. 3321. Evatt also co-operated with Barwick, the Attorney-General, in supporting the Bill as a whole.
26 Quoted by Frank Poyas in paper delivered to Bond University conference on Evatt, 1990. For information on epilepsy generally we are indebted to Dr. Anne Schlebaum, a Sydney psychiatrist.
27 *CPD*, vol. 48, 9 November 1965, p. 2464.

CHAPTER 30

ASSESSMENT

Evatt 'would have been the most intellectual Prime Minister of the twentieth century, but he remains the great Premier Australia never had'.
IRISH TIMES, *1979*

Psycho-biography is a fashionable modern approach to biographical writing. Those who practice it lay heavy emphasis upon the early childhood experience of the historical figure under consideration, although there is often little reliable information available. On this basis, speculations as to the effects upon later public life may be constructed. Where the linkage between childhood and adult actions is reasonably established, the process can be interesting and useful. Thus in the case of Evatt, some of his actions, which had considerable political consequences, were undoubtedly the result of his personal characteristics. Yet it should not be assumed that such characteristics were the product of his upbringing and family circumstances. Obviously, there were many other children subject to similar influences, such as a mother imbuing a son with ambitious aims, who nevertheless achieved nothing of note.

In other words, the conjectures of amateur psychologists in the field of biography should be regarded critically. The approach may be exaggerated, placing the subject in a distorted perspective. There have been some unfortunate examples of this in Australian historiography, in biographies of Bob Hawke (A. Anston), Robert Menzies (J. Brett) and, most recently, H. V. Evatt (P. Crockett). A general feature is that the author's concentration upon trivia belittles the significance and achievements of the subject of the biography. This is the case with

Crockett's *Evatt: A Life,* which focuses upon Evatt's personal frailties as a means of 'explaining' his career. Thus history is stood on its head. The hard fact that it is deeds and their effects that count—no matter how 'good' or 'bad' the person—is pushed into the background.

Evatt is an obvious magnet for psycho-biographers. There was no shortage of personal flaws for other people to observe—and often to endure. Many contemporaries referred in detail to his egocentricity, arrogance and suspicious nature. His rudeness and lack of consideration for those who worked under him—he expected them to work as hard as he did—were not calculated to endear him to them, even when they recognised his ability. Yet, astonishingly, nobody found any fault in his private life. Disappointingly from the viewpoint of a psycho-biographer, friends and foes agreed that Bert and Mary Alice Evatt were a loving, mutually supporting couple from the time of their marriage. There were no extra-marital adventures. Hartley Grattan described Mary Alice as Bert's 'Companion in Arms'—in politics as well as affection. As for other members of the family, Rosalind describes him simply as 'a great father', who gave her all the affection and attention she could wish for. He was tender and warm-hearted in private life.

In public, Evatt was correctly regarded as extremely ambitious, although few people realised that virtually no great historical figures are ever modest. He was also criticised for constantly seeking publicity—again, something which no politician can afford to despise. In appearance, he was something of 'a character'. He spoke with a broad Australian accent and he may have exaggerated this as a means of identifying himself with ordinary people. At the same time, he was genuinely careless of dress. His clothes often looked as though he had slept in them, his tie was askew and his socks were frequently oddly matched. He never owned a dinner suit. He assumed that he would be judged for important attributes such as his intelligence. He was, indeed, a very serious person. In private conversation, he did not retail dirty jokes—which marked him off from most other politicians. Though confident, Evatt was not really at home in polite society. He preferred the company of writers and painters, with whom he could talk about matters of intellectual life and art.

Evatt is said to have lacked a sense of humour, despite his booming laugh. Actually, he was not humourless and could be quite dry at times. One anecdote concerns an occasion when Evatt was being driven in an official Australian car in London. He drew the chauffeur's attention to the fact that the car was flying a New Zealand flag. Next day, the driver pointed to a newly-installed Australian flag and said, 'Is that all right?'. Evatt replied, 'It would be if it were not upside down'. More typical of a rather juvenile, heavy quality in 'the Doc' is a story relating to Tom Bass's wall-fountain outside the P & O building in Sydney. Evatt had a very high regard for Bass as a sculptor. However, this particular piece of work was popularly believed to resemble a public urinal, with spaces apparently designed for men to stand at in the street. It is said that Evatt, when he walked along that street with a companion in the late 1950s, would indicate the spaces, saying 'That's Owen (of the Petrov Royal Commission) and that's...' The Doc was a good hater.

One other anecdote is worth telling, since it is at variance with most of those told about Evatt. He kept whisky or other alcohol in his parliamentary office to offer to visitors, but he drank very sparingly himself—no more than a glass or two of wine with dinner. Yet towards the end of an international conference in Paris, where Evatt had worked under great pressure, he appears to have been in high spirits and relaxed at a party with journalists and others. According to Charles Buttrose, an Australian press officer who was present, Evatt (balancing a large glass of beer on his head) engaged in a race along a hotel corridor against another person. Evatt also joined in singing a number of Australian songs popular at the time, including one with the refrain, 'We don't want any Chinks in New South Wales'. The story lacks corroboration, but it has a flavour of truth: Evatt shared the prejudices, as well as the better qualities, of his fellow-countrymen. Buttrose adds that next day Evatt felt that he had made a fool of himself, but fortunately for his reputation the incident went unreported in the media.[1]

It is ironic that Evatt, himself a historian of some standing, has not been well treated by historians. True, he was a hero to Kylie Tennant, who wrote with a flair and insight sadly lacking in the experience of professional historians, but she could be written off as a hagiographer who was 'merely' a novelist. Furthermore, when Tennant's biography was published in 1970, the great mass of official material in Australian Archives relating to the period from the 1940s was not open to researchers. Later historians of the period may be classified in two groups: those who specialised in certain aspects, including biography (Fin Crisp for Chifley, and Lloyd Ross for Curtin), while understandably making only passing reference to Evatt; and more general historians who largely reiterated the views about Evatt held by his critics. Some of those critics, such as Hasluck, Watt and Daly, went into print themselves.

Another trendy modern source of information is oral history. It provides useful gleanings, but there are pitfalls. Narrators, speaking privately yet for posterity, are naturally concerned to present themselves in a favourable light, while sometimes taking the opportunity to pay off old scores. These unpublished comments are not freely available for contradiction or qualification by other people. Clyde Cameron, despite his reputation for acerbity, is unusual among contemporary commentators on Evatt in emphasising the good points in his character, along with the weaknesses. Evatt was a compassionate and very generous person—he 'had foibles that were quite ridiculous really', yet there was 'an intrinsic decency in his makeup in relation to other human beings'. Cameron recalls that at the end of a session in which he recorded his views of Evatt for the oral history project of the National Library, he was complimented by his interlocutor for giving a balanced picture, as other people interviewed on the subject had mainly denigrated Evatt.[2]

Some denigrators went public long after Evatt's death. The most splenetic is Peter Ryan, who wrote about Evatt: 'This most disagreeable of Australians lies where he belongs—in the dustbin of history'. More recently Ryan, as a side-blow from his attempt to destroy Manning Clark's reputation, described Evatt as a 'miserably failed Labor leader. One must go back to Iago for so authentic a model of treachery'. To cap it all, Ryan declares Evatt to be a 'monster', comparable to Stalin. Such outrageous statements have no relation to the facts but are worth mentioning as an indication of the depth of feeling which Evatt's name can still evoke.[3]

The other side of the coin is that very many of Evatt's contemporaries held him in high regard. One was Judge Long Innes, who in 1938 wrote from Sydney to a friend in Britain about Evatt's sabbatical trip overseas. Innes thought it likely that his friend (an eminent lawyer) would meet Evatt at cricket Test matches, and he provided a brief sketch of Evatt's career, first in New South Wales politics in the 1920s:

had he stuck to politics he would sooner or later have been Premier of this State, where with his brains and ideals he might have done a lot of good; but I think he thought politics stank a bit, and chucked up an enormous practice to go on the High Court Bench, and will probably some day be Chief Justice of the High Court.[4]

The vicissitudes of war cut across that particular prediction but there was never any question of Evatt's outstanding quality as a lawyer. Geoffrey Sawer believed that Evatt wasted his talents by transferring from law to politics. If a comparison be made on this score between Evatt and Menzies, it seems that the latter was a good advocate and the more accomplished politician—especially in parliament—whereas Evatt was a brilliant lawyer whose work lives on. On the other hand, Katharine Susannah Prichard was more impressed by Evatt's political standpoint and his stature as 'a statesman of international significance'. She also wrote:

Evatt squandered great gifts for Australia and the Australian people. He gave his all: physical energy, emotional intensity, scholarly and juridical attainments. Unlike Deakin, who had his 'secret bread' in an aloofness and inner life of the imagination fed by poetry and religious mysticism, Evatt entered the fray to participate in the welter of the people's struggle for a better life.[5]

George Godfrey, who came to know 'the Doc' well in the 1950s, recorded a remarkable incident. One evening in Evatt's study in his Mosman home, the two men discussed the political turmoil of the day, and Godfrey remarked, 'But you enjoy the heat of battle, Doc, you're a fighter'. Evatt waved an arm at the book-lined study and replied, 'But I'm not, George, I'm a scholar'.[6] As a disclaimer, this is surely unique among the utterances of leading Australian politicians. It reads well alongside a statement in *The Irish Times* in 1979 that Evatt 'would have been the most intellectual Prime Minister of the twentieth century, but he remains the great Premier Australia never had.' This delightfully Irish way of expressing the matter serves incidentally as a reminder that the memory of Evatt lingers on in some other countries.

There was a certain amount of factual underpinning to some of the criticisms levelled against Evatt. As noted in previous chapters, he made some important mistakes during his term of office in government. Without excusing the blunders, it may be remarked that he was an interventionist, impatient for action. In politics, only those who do nothing can claim to have made no errors—a claim which may mean no more than rigid adherence to the status quo. Moveover, in judging Evatt, environmental factors must be taken into account. They influenced the development of his character, while limiting the possibilities open to him. Australian society was relatively egalitarian, so that some very talented people were able to rise to the top in their chosen spheres. On the other hand, Australia was a small country in terms of population and power, and its insular society was narrow and conformist in outlook. Censorship was pervasive and it required a great effort for people with progressive views to break through such restraints. In the 1950s, Evatt had only limited success in efforts to protect Clem Christesen, editor of *Meanjin*, from political discrimination against his journal in the award of grants from the Commonwealth Literary Fund. Christesen had been smeared in the Petrov affair.

Evatt's social background was important. He grew up to be an intellectual and a barrister—nobody ever regarded him as a horny-handed member of the working class. This meant no easy path for him in a political party which proudly espoused the interests of workers. At the same time, he was not an associate of wealthy landowners or (with the exception of W. S. Robinson) members of the capitalist class. In their eyes, he was an outsider. This did not worry Evatt, who was an idealist, cherishing his ideological standpoint. George Parsons, a historian, gives his own uncle as the source for a story about an incident in the 1950s, when Evatt spoke at a very rowdy public meeting—invaded by Liberals—in Sydney. On the way out of the hall, hard-pressed policemen asked Evatt to keep to the right to avoid hostile barrackers. 'Never', the Doc replied stoutly. 'I only walk on the left. Clear a way to the light'.

This was not just braggadocio. Evatt was a rallying point for the left, even if at times he seemed willing to compromise with Santamaria. Sam Atyeo, a loyal supporter of Evatt, wrote to him from Europe shortly before the Doc launched his attack upon the Movement in 1954:

...letters I receive from home have likened your entrance into the Petrov proceedings as a Southerly after a foetid day! Good old Bert—I believe you can again unite the Labor movement which...should be comprehensive enough to take in all the working class and the Socialist intellectuals. The A.L.P. seems to have become the left wing of the Liberals—at times not even the 'left wing'...Let the right wing A.L.P. members join the Liberals. After all the Liberals represent the vested interests—and is there a more influential vested interest than the R.C. church?[7]

Although Evatt did not give the appearance of being class-conscious, he had no liking for members of the ruling class who were imbued with a sense of social superiority. Among Australians, that group included Bruce, Casey and Menzies. Actually, Evatt's opinion of Casey (described by Atyeo as 'the poor man's Anthony Eden') probably mellowed in the 1950s, when Casey as a matter of courtesy gave Evatt advance notice of what he planned to say in a foreign affairs debate in parliament.

In Britain, the task of distinguishing members of the ruling class was much easier, due to the tell-tale private school accent. Evatt's bias against such people in high places was shared by Gordon Childe, who wrote from Britain in 1946, expressing a hope that William McKell, then Labor Premier of New South Wales, would be appointed as Governor-General of the Commonwealth. Childe added a cautionary remark: 'The DO [Dominions Office] is still staffed with Eton and Oxford whoever is the nominal Minister'.[8]

The Australians' suspicion concerning the British ruling class view of 'colonials' was remarkably well founded, as it happened. A year earlier, Lord Addison, the Dominion Affairs Minister, had written privately to his Prime Minister concerning McKell's strong wish to have an Australian appointed as Governor of New South Wales. Addison disliked the idea, although he felt that the British government

should, if possible, avoid any appearance of conflict with any of the [Australian] States at the present when we bear in mind the touchy attitude of Dr. Evatt so far as he represents Australian sentiment.[9]

Addison's Prime Minister by then was C. R. Attlee. The Labour Party was in office in post-war Britain. Evatt had fond hopes of cooperation between the three countries, Australia, Britain and New Zealand, which had Labour governments and might constitute a third, social democratic, force between the USA and the USSR in world affairs. He was disappointed. The British Foreign Office remained under the guidance of conservative gentlemen, and their new Minister, Ernest Bevin, while not being a gentleman, was a tough trade union boss with an anti-Communist background. He was happy to identify himself with the views of his departmental advisers. In the process, he became irritated to find that Evatt frequently took an independent standpoint. On one occasion, Bevin wrote from Moscow to tell Addison that 'there is no satisfying Evatt. He seems to be in an impossible mood, making difficulties for me, wherever he can'.[10]

Although British bureaucrats were offended by Evatt's assertiveness and his refusal to conform to the niceties of international diplomacy, the problem went deeper. It related to important divergencies of national policy and interest between Britain and Australia. British authorities did not comprehend this, nor did they appreciate the extent to which Evatt recognised the benefits of the British Commonwealth connection. Diplomats such as Sir Alexander Cadogan, permanent head of the Foreign Office, occasionally acknowledged Evatt's skills. Thus, in commenting on an Australian argument presented at a Security Council meeting, Cadogan wrote:

Tactics which can command a measure of success when used by a debater at once so well-informed and so quick to seize a chance as Evatt, once again proved useless in the hands of representatives to whom he allowed little or no latitude.[11]

Evatt's great preoccupation in foreign affairs was for the security of Australia, especially in the Pacific region. World War II brought this question to the fore, and Evatt in the post-war years worked hard for an early peace settlement in Asia, giving Australia a leading role and providing harsh treatment for Japan as the aggressor. His basic aim here was frustrated by the development of the Cold War and the US decision to support Japan as a bulwark against the Soviet Union; and Britain's interests were focused on Europe. Evatt had to recognise that there were definite limits to what could be gained by a small country. Nevertheless, he achieved much in pushing against those limits. Evatt's characteristic contribution was his insistence that Australia's voice be heard and considered in international negotiations. He articulated an independent Australian foreign policy. As the American *Life* magazine wrote in celebration of Evatt's work at the San Francisco conference in 1945, 'it isn't easy putting Australia on the map'. Evatt did so in no uncertain terms, in the United Nations forum and elsewhere.

As an Australian nationalist, and as the first English-speaking President of the United Nations General Assembly, Evatt left an indelible mark. His contribution to the creation of Israel was particularly important. So was the 1948 Universal Declaration of Human Rights, which was a precursor of later UN documents such as the International Covenant on Civil and Political Rights. In a sense, Evatt carried over into the UN his long battle against privilege in Australia. He emerged as a champion of small nations, campaigning at San Francisco against the granting of a veto right to the big powers in the UN. Having inevitably failed to carry the day there, Evatt realistically accepted the fact that the UN was flawed by the veto provision. He worked his way around the obstacles where possible, although the Cold War intervened to make this very difficult. At the same time, he never deviated from Australia's defence and security interests.

Of course, Britain, the USA and the USSR all had their own national interests at stake. In the case of Britain, it may be doubted whether her best interests were served in the post-war period by operating as a junior partner of the United States on major issues, but that is too big a question to consider in this book. However, one element in British social structure is relevant here. For all the obvious class differences and tensions in British society, their reflection in political life was blurred. There was a subtle element of traditional deference towards social or intellectual 'superiors', which carried considerable weight until the 1970s, even among rank-and-file activists in the British Labour Party who had a hand in the choice of parliamentary candidates.

Despite Evatt's instinctive distrust of Anglo-Saxons with 'fancy' accents, he appears to have overlooked the significance of ambitious graduates from Oxford and Cambridge in the British parliamentary Labour Party. True, a number of the Oxbridge Labour MPs were on the left in the party, and other progressive intellectuals such as Laski held important party positions, but the education of the Oxbridge contingent had entailed absorption of many of the class assumptions and biases held by their opponents in conservative political groupings. This is not to deny that there were also a number of trade-union MPs who were on the right in politics.

Certainly, the Attlee Cabinet was predominantly right-wing in orientation. In foreign policy, it was virtually indistinguishable from the Tories. Evatt saw the effects of this in nullifying his hopes for a social-democratic British–Australian–New Zealand axis, but he was probably not well informed about opinion and status in the British Labour Party. Things were different in Australia, where the tendency—in the ALP and in society as a whole—was to cut down tall poppies. Evatt ran risks in taking a prominent public stance. Yet he was rightly proud of his efforts to establish Australia as a country of importance in world affairs, and there is significance in the fact that the granite stone on his grave in Canberra refers to him simply as 'President of the United Nations'.

❖

H.V. Evatt was a man of many talents, demonstrated in the fact that he had not one career but several. He was a barrister; a High Court judge; a writer and scholar who was also a significant patron of literature and the arts; an international statesman; and a Labor leader with a very meaningful role, especially in the preservation of freedom in Australia. A common thread linking these careers was Evatt's background as a lawyer: he thought and talked as one, even in international conferences where professional diplomats looked askance at his combative courtroom style. Evatt was a great jurist, whose ideas, writings and legal judgments are still highly relevant.

Three examples of this may be given. First, there is what Robert Menzies later dubbed 'the Evatt doctrine': a broad view of the external affairs power in the Australian constitution, which Evatt made applicable to domestic affairs in certain circumstances. Second, there is Evatt's interpretation of Section 92 of the constitution, which was belatedly vindicated by the High Court in the 1980s—after decades in which big businessmen exploited a contrary interpretation to win wholesale avoidance of tax payments. Third, there is Evatt's penetrating analysis of the reserve powers of the Crown, which is germane to current discussion of constitutional amendment in the light of Australia's possibly becoming a republic.

Regarding Evatt's role in international affairs, let us add that under him as Minister, the Department of External Affairs was transformed. From being a small, somnolent department in the 1930s, it became a much larger one, buzzing with activity. Staff were rapidly recruited and trained and there was a major increase in prestige relative to other Commonwealth government departments. Hasluck and some others resented the authoritarian way in which Evatt treated them, but they relished the enhanced reputation and accelerated promotion which stemmed from the driving force of 'the boss'.

There remains for consideration Evatt's position in Australian politics and the Labor Party. Unquestionably, his finest achievement was in defence of civil liberties against the wave of reaction which followed Labor's election defeat in 1949. Evatt was a tower of strength in the battle for freedom. Without his leadership of the campaign in the 1951 referendum, the Menzies government would have succeeded in outlawing the Communist Party. Had Menzies achieved this aim, the effects would have extended far beyond the Communist fringe, doing incalculable damage to the fabric of Australian democracy.

There has long been debate about Evatt's ability as a politician and over his leadership of the Labor Party. On the latter question, attention has focused upon his central role in the ALP split in the years from 1954. Ideology still enters strongly into this discussion. Conservatives—including those in the ALP—reckon that the split could have been averted but for Evatt's stand, and the party would not have remained so long out of power. That may be true, yet it begs the question concerning the essential nature of the party. Admittedly, the ALP in the past decade or two has changed into an organisation which differs little from its main political opponents in basic policy and outlook. Nevertheless, that evolution was not inevitable, nor was the timing. It might have occurred much earlier and in a different form, had it not been for the struggle against the Movement and the Groupers in the 1950s.

The fact of the present-day dominance of the right in the Labor Party helps to explain a paradox. Today, Curtin and Chifley are acknowledged on all sides as worthy of great respect: they are uncontroversial, and in Labor circles they are above criticism. This is not so in the case of Evatt, partly because of the ALP machine's obsession with power: a leader who fails to become Prime Minister (or Premier) lacks the qualities necessary for myth-making. However, the problem goes deeper. Labor's right wing is wary of what Evatt represented in terms of ideals and enthusiasm. Fortunately, not all has been lost in this respect. The current move by the Keating government towards justice for Aborigines, following the High Court's Mabo judgment, would have been applauded by Evatt—it was he who, in the referendum of 1944, sought unsuccessfully to secure constitutional power for the Commonwealth government (as against the States) to legislate concerning Aborigines.

Whereas the Labor right-wing is perfunctory with respect to Evatt, other conservative forces lose no opportunity to blacken his name. This is illustrated in the writings of such commentators as Peter Ryan and Gerard Henderson. They regard Evatt as a dangerous symbol; and understandably in the light of their own ideology, they resist any recrudescence of what he stood for. Luckily, history is not on their side. Evatt's spirit lives on and in a long-term perspective his contribution will be seen as having universal validity for humanity.

The last words about 'the Doc' may be given over to C. Hartley Grattan, an American historian who had a constant interest in Australia, and Joseph Furphy ('Tom Collins'), the Australian novelist. Grattan's assessment of Evatt was that 'here was a great Australian, a great man, for whom I had through thick and thin an abiding affection'. Furphy's life was not contemporaneous with Evatt's, but Furphy's description of his own classic book, *Such is Life*, could be applied equally well to Bert Evatt's character: 'temper, democratic; bias, offensively Australian'.[12]

Notes

1 ABC Radio tapes on Evatt, broadcast in 1988. Buttrose's contribution was originally recorded twenty years before this.
2 Clyde Cameron, interview with authors, May 1988.
3 Peter Ryan, *Age* Extra, 7 September 1991; *Weekend Australian*, 28–9 August 1993; *Sydney Morning Herald*, 13 November 1993.
4 Long Innes to 'Mick', 7 April 1938, Evatt Collection. File: Overseas Trip, 1938.
5 Quotation from a document in the Evatt Collection, File: K.S. Prichard. It seems to have been written after 1967 and was probably sent to Kylie Tennant. It is also the source of the quotation which serves as a frontispiece to this book.
6 George Godfrey, transcript of oral biography, Tape 2, Side 1, p. 42, ANL.
7 Atyeo to Evatt, 19 September 1954, Evatt Collection. File: Atyeo, Sam. Atyeo, who spoke fluent French, was an intimate companion of Evatt overseas in the 1940s, though he ranked only as a temporary employee of the External Affairs Department. He was dismissed in February 1950, after the fall of the Chifley government. Evatt interceded unsuccessfully on his behalf.
8 V.G. Childe to Mary Alice Evatt, 7 December 1946, Evatt Collection, Flinders University.
9 Addison to P.M., 30 August 1945, PRO, DO 121/10C. McKell was appointed Governor-General of Australia in 1947.
10 Bevin to Addison, 20 March 1947, PRO, FO 371/66580 (W2304/1011/C). US diplomatic counterparts were decidedly more hostile than this in their opinions of Evatt.
11 Cadogan (New York) to Foreign Office, London, 4 April 1946, PRO, DO 35/2000. The Australian representatives referred to were Hodgson and Hasluck.
12 Grattan to Mary Alice, 7 December 1965, Evatt Collection. File: Hartley Grattan; Stephen Murray-Smith (ed.), *The Dictionary of Australian Quotations,* Heinemann, Victoria, 1984, p. 87.

INDEX

Aborigines
  welfare of 219, 220, 418
Advisory War Council 146
  Evatt as member 148, 149, 227
aluminium manufacturing 190–1
Amalgamated Engineers' and
  Boilermakers' Union 40
Amery, L.S. 60, 110
Anderson, Francis 10–12
Antarctica
  Evatt on 269, 271, 277
Anzac Pact see Australia–New
  Zealand Agreement
Arbitration Act see legislation
Arbitration Court, Commonwealth
  see Commonwealth Arbitration
  Court
Argus 21–2, 33
Ateyo, Sam
  friendship with Evatt 120, 308,
    310, 311, 414
Atkinson, Meredith 24
atomic energy, development 290,
  292, 316
  Australian involvement in 286–92,
    336
  Evatt on 287–9, 290, 315, 370
atomic weapons 315–18, 370
  British tests 220, 287
Australia First Movement 173–5,
  176, 177–8, 202–3, 204, 372, 378
Australia–New Zealand Agreement
  226, 234, 238, 239, 246, 248, 250,
  258, 265, 266, 286, 292
Australian Council for Civil Liberties
  (ACCL) 169, 204, 205, 219, 386
  Evatt's support for 170

Australian Council of Trade Unions
  220, 342–3, 367
Australian development
  Evatt on relationship between
    British law and 104–6
Australian Insurance Staffs'
  Federation 98
*Australian Labour Leader: W.A.
  Holman* 16, 26, 81, 119, 129,
  130–1, 144
Australian Labor Party
  ballot-rigging in the 36–7, 38, 72,
    341
  Catholic influence in 172, 204,
    205, 215, 216, 218, 313, 336,
    358, 362–3, 365–6, 382–5,
    391, 397
  caucus 13, 36, 42, 44, 52–3, 58,
    59, 66, 69, 70, 93, 140, 358,
    359, 385
  Communist influence in 72–3,
    329, 335–7, 340, 341, 350,
    357–9, 360, 361, 369, 372–80,
    383–91, 397, 398, 403, 404
  conferences 142–3, 391, 403
  emergence of 129, 131
  expulsions 72, 75, 140, 397
  Evatt on 13, 43, 140, 143, 144,
    371, 384, 389, 391, 393–4,
    396, 414, 418
  federal 36, 84–6, 88, 93, 143, 396
  'Hands off Russia' resolution 143
  Heffron group 140
  Industrial Groupers in 135, 218,
    341, 342–3, 358, 365, 366,
    371, 383, 385, 388–91, 393,
    394, 397, 418

Labor pledge 13, 42, 43
New South Wales 5, 13, 26, 27–8,
    36, 86, 148
  allegations of bribery by
    Nationalists 66
  battle for leadership of 65, 66,
    140
  Cabinet 44, 69, 70
  candidates 43, 72, 73, 75
  conferences 35, 36–7, 66,
    142–3
  executive 66, 140, 143, 393–4
  government 26, 27, 28, 36, 37,
    44, 109, 148
  platform 13, 38, 42, 59, 68
  policies 36, 38, 42, 43
  preselection for 35–6, 38,
    39–40, 42–3, 72
  South Australia 13, 390
  split (1916) 109, 133, 135
  split (1955) 135, 358, 380,
    382–94, 396, 418
  structure and processes of 35–8,
    72, 390
  Victoria 13, 389, 390–1
  Women's Organising Committee
    40
  see also Movement, the; trade
    unions
Australian Law Journal
  on reduction of judges' salaries 101
Australian Railways Union 39, 87–8
Australian Security Intelligence
  Organisation (ASIO) 336–7, 367,
    373, 374–5, 380, 386
Australian Worker 14, 15, 43, 49,
  73, 140
Australian Workers' Union (AWU)
  33, 35–7, 78–9, 80, 340, 347
  disaffiliation with ALP 82, 86
  Evatt on 342, 343, 389
  on wage arbitration 87
aviation industry, civil
  Australian 211, 285, 289
  Evatt on 211, 226, 234–5, 238,
    240–1, 305
  policy 211, 285
  United States and 226, 234–6,
    237–41, 285, 317

Baddeley, J.M. 56
Bailey, J. 36, 37
Bailey, Kenneth H. 196
  on Evatt 202, 207

Balfour Declaration 106, 107, 314
Ball, William Macmahon 118, 251,
  267, 271, 273–4, 304
Balmain Distress Relief Committee
  Evatt contributes to 99
banks, nationalisation of
  Chifley government and 326–30,
    351
  Evatt on 145, 326, 327, 328, 330,
    331–2, 399
  High Court on 327, 330, 331–3
  Menzies on 145
Barry, John V. 112, 195, 204, 364
Barwick, Garfield 331, 332
Bavin government
  on living wage 78, 79
  on railway strikers of 1917 83
  on Workers' Compensation Act
    83
Bavin, T.R.
  Edmunds Royal Commission 31,
    54
  literary association with Evatt
    27–8
  on Forty-Four Hours Week Bill
    53–4
  on Legislative Council 59, 95
Beasley, J. 'Stabber Jack' 140, 142, 148
Beeby, Justice 85
Blackburn, Doris 219, 220, 346
Blackburn, Maurice 169, 170, 175
Bladen, F.M. 125
Bland, William 12, 118
Bligh, Governor
  Evatt on 123–9
Bolton, Geoffrey 245
Book Censorship Abolition League
  118
Boote, Henry E. 14
  friendship with Evatt 73, 130,
    140–15, 142, 146, 342
Bracken, Brendan
  on Evatt 378
Brett, Judith
  on Menzies 192
Bretton Woods Conference 284
Brookfield, P.S. 22–3
Bruce, S.M.
  on Evatt 158–9
  on White Australia policy 62
Bruce–Page government 47, 49
Buckland, G. 142
Burgmann, Bishop E.H. 117, 118,
  120, 140, 364

Burton, J.W. 184, 196, 304, 350, 370, 375
  relationship with Evatt 185, 203, 290, 348
Business Tenants' Association New South Wales 37
Butlin, Brian 120

Cahill, J.J. 398
  on Evatt 376
'Call to the Nation' 387
Calwell, Arthur 204, 209, 213, 215, 326, 346, 384, 403
Cameron, Clyde 37, 314, 343
  on Evatt 147–8, 362, 399, 412
Cantor, M.E.
  appointed to Industrial Commission 78, 79
  Evatt on 81
Cantwell, Ida ('Bill') 63
capital punishment
  Evatt on 54
Casey, Richard G. 63, 142, 369, 375, 414
Catholic Action 336, 337, 397
  see also Australian Labor Party; Movement, the
censorship 168
  literature 102, 117, 118, 170, 173
  press 12, 143, 173
  Evatt on 13, 102, 413
Chifley government 210–13, 217–18, 220, 285, 292, 326, 330, 351
  on coal strike 345, 346, 347, 348, 349, 350
  on nationalisation of banks 326–30, 351
  relationship with Communism 335–7, 340, 341
Chifley, J.B. 49, 176, 265, 336, 359, 390
  on Catholic influence in ALP 358
  death 362
  on development of atomic power 286
  at Edmunds Royal Commission 31, 32
  Prime Minister 210, 325
  relations with Trades Council 216
  relationship with Evatt 326
child endowment
  Evatt on 68–70, 73, 76, 79–80, 81
  federal arbitration awards and 80–1

Childe, Vere Gordon
  friendship with Evatt 8, 14, 23–5, 32, 99
  political views 8–9, 14, 23–5, 99, 414
Chisholm, A.R. 7
Churchill, Sir Winston 153–4
  relationship with Evatt 155, 158, 161, 162–3, 184, 185–6, 237
civil liberties
  and Communist Party Dissolution Act 358, 359, 360–1, 364
  during war years 168–80
  Evatt on 32, 168, 170, 171, 172, 173, 177–8, 196, 197–8, 203–5, 218–19, 364, 399, 416, 418
  Ratliff–Thomas case 170–2, 177
  see also Australian Council for Civil Liberties
Clarke, George 24
Clune, Frank 118
Clyne, T.S. 202–3
coal industry 344–7
  Evatt on 210, 346, 348–9
  see also industrial disputes
Commonwealth
  defence of 288, 292–3, 295, 296, 297
  Evatt on 286, 292–4, 298
  relationship with Australia 285–6, 288, 289, 292, 298
  see also foreign relations, Australian
Commonwealth Arbitration Court 29–30, 47, 80, 81, 84, 85, 86–8, 98, 217, 341, 399–400
Commonwealth–State relations 96–7, 132, 176, 196–7, 200, 206, 210, 214, 217
  Evatt on 76
communism
  Evatt on 41, 42, 72–3, 141, 170, 172, 207, 216, 291, 296, 297–8, 307, 325, 335, 357–66, 385, 397
  see also Australian Labor Party; Chifley government; legislation, Federal; Menzies government; trade unions; World War II
Communist Party of Australia 73, 143, 218, 220, 329, 340, 345, 349
  banned in Australia 170, 172–3, 335, 356–7, 360, 362–3, 364, 418

Evatt on 172, 325, 363
  referendum on 362–7, 371, 384, 385
Conlon, Colonel Alfred
  relationship with Evatt 290–1
conscription 144
  Evatt on 15, 16, 24, 25–6, 133
  referendum 15, 16, 21–2, 24–5
Constitution, Australian
  amendments to 96–7, 179, 196–9, 214, 331–2
  the Crown and the 105–9, 178–9
  Evatt on 13, 96–7, 105–12, 179–80, 334
  High Court on 195, 331–2
  Section 92 331, 332, 333, 417
Contemporary Art Society 120
Coombs, H.C. 184, 189
  on Evatt 190
Coulter, Bill
  on Evatt 371
Country Party 134, 139
Cowan, Sir Zelman 112
Crown, The
  reserve powers of 97–8, 104–12, 178–9
Cullen, Sir William
  Evatt as associate to 10, 24
'Cultural Defence Committee' 118
cultural identity, Australian 104, 119
Currey, C.H. 15
Curtain government 149, 159, 191–2, 193
Curtain, John 143, 144, 153, 154, 390
  character 192
  death 209
  on foreign relations 186
  relationship with Evatt 146–7, 150
  speeches 192, 283, 286

Daily Guardian
  attack on Evatt 43
Daly, Senator J. 88
Dark, Eleanor 348, 364
Dark, Eric 8, 348
Day, David
  on Evatt 162
de Chair, Governor 59, 60, 110
Dedman, J.J. 142, 265, 326, 327, 346, 351
defence, Australian 286, 291–2, 297
  Evatt on 225, 227–41, 245–60, 276–7, 290–1, 295, 296, 305

  see also regional security, Australian; World War II
Democratic Labor Party (DLP) 391, 396, 402–3
deportation
  Evatt on Commonwealth powers 46, 49
  Walsh–Johnson cases 46–9, 53, 71, 73–5, 361
depression (1930s) see Great Depression
Dethridge, G.J.
  on Arbitration Act 86–7
Devanny, Jean 118
development see Australian development
Dixon, Sir Owen 95, 96, 101, 144, 334
Doran, H. 72–3
Dougherty, Tom 389, 390
Downing, Reg 216, 403
Drake–Brockman, E.A. 84
Duffy, Justice 96, 97, 100, 101
Dutton, Geoffrey
  on Evatt 120

economy
  Australian 37, 210–11, 217–18, 284, 294, 305
  international 187–8
Edmunds Royal Commission 30–2, 38, 54
Education
  Evatt on free 39
  high school fees 39, 52
  reforms 40, 42
  see also State aid to church schools
Eggleston, Frederick 118, 192
elections
  federal
    campaigns
      1925 49
      1940 145
      1943 192
      1949 350–1
      1951 361
      1954 370–3, 385
      1955 380
      1958 402–3
    results
      1929 84
      1940 146
      1943 193
      1946 215
      1972 396

INDEX 425

New South Wales
  campaigns
    1920 28
    1922 32
    1925 37, 38, 40–1, 43, 68
    1927 75
    Evatt in 1922 campaign 32
  results
    1917 109
    1925 44
    1927 73
    1930 86
    1932 97
    1941 148
employment
  Evatt on preference to unionists
    13, 42, 54
  post–war policy on 199–200, 217,
    284, 285
  referendum on 217
Evatt, Clive 4, 41, 140, 377
Evatt, Frank 16, 17
Evatt, Sir George Hamilton 16
Evatt, Jane Sophia (Jeanie) 3, 4, 5
Evatt, John Ashmore Hamilton 3, 4
Evatt, Herbert Vere
  admitted to the Bar 17
  art, love of 120–1, 407, 410, 411,
    417
  Associate to the Chief Justice of
    New South Wales 10, 24
  attitude to alcohol 4, 410
  on Australian autonomy 105–6
  battle against unwarranted
    privilege 8, 416
  Beauchamp prize (Liberalism in
    Australia) 9, 12
  born 3
  Chairman of UN Atomic Energy
    Commission 316
  Chairman of UN Commission for
    Conventional Armaments 316
  character 4, 10, 14, 17, 39, 75,
    99, 131, 147–8, 150, 155, 160,
    165, 183, 190, 207, 253,
    325–6, 371, 378, 397, 407,
    409–19
  Chief Justice of New South Wales
    403–4
  childhood 4, 409
  children 83, 99
  death 407
  on dismissal of Lang government
    97–8, 107

'the Doc' 147
education
  academic achievements 6, 7, 9,
    10
  arts degree 7, 9, 10
  bursary 7
  Editor-in-chief *Hermes* 9
  graduation 9, 10
  Law Debating Society 10
  law degree 7, 10, 17
  President of The University
    Sydney Union 9–10
  President of the Undergraduates
    Association 9, 15
  primary 4
  scholarships 7
  secondary 5–7
  thesis 'The Royal Prerogative'
    10, 14, 105, 107
  university 7–10, 14
Engineers case 29–30
essays 9, 12, 13, 14, 24, 43
financial assistance to the poor
  99–100, 102, 114
health 404–7
High Court
  appointed to 88–9, 93–5, 98,
    100
  award wage rates case (1931)
    98
  Kisch case 118
  Garnishee case 96–7
  resignation from 144
  salary on 100, 101, 102
influenced by
  Anderson 10–11, 12
  Childe 8, 14, 24, 25, 33
  Kilgour 6
  mother 4
intellectual life 5, 410
on idealism 21, 25, 32, 33, 37,
  414, 418
King's Counsel 83
lectureship at The University of
  Sydney 33
legal career 21–3, 27–34, 46–9,
  52, 61, 67, 73–4, 76, 82–3, 86,
  87–8, 93–99, 100, 102, 145,
  377–8, 379, 404
marriage 17, 410
membership of Privy Council 158
on natural justice 31, 102
personal finances 100, 102
poetry by 17

political life 4, 10, 33, 35, 140, 142, 283–4, 379–80, 418
  ALP opponents attempt to get rid of him 64, 72, 392–3, 404
  Attorney-General (Commonwealth) 106, 149, 168, 193, 332, 351, 364
  candidate for Balmain 39–44
  candidate for Barton 144, 145–6, 351, 361–2, 402
  deputy leader parliamentary Labor Party 215, 216, 356
  elected to Federal parliament 146
  elected to State parliament 44, 51–2, 75
  expelled from ALP 72, 75, 142
  federal political intentions 40
  joins Australian Labor Party 26, 37–8
  Labor independant for Balmain 72, 73, 75, 83
  leader of parliamentary Labor Party 362, 386, 393, 402, 403, 404
  leaves State parliament 86
  membership of ALP expires 392–3
  Minister for External Affairs 106, 141, 149, 193, 212, 218, 226, 228, 229, 332, 351, 417
  political viewpoints 12, 13–16, 23–9, 37, 42–3, 75–6, 80, 83, 104–5, 123–35, 140–3, 145–9, 207, 218, 302–18, 379–80, 399, 414
  preselection
    for Balmain 38–40, 42–3, 72
    for Hunter 402
  President of Mosman branch 38, 44
  President UN General Assembly 303, 416
  on racial discrimination 18, 313
  religion 4, 5, 8, 10, 40
  social views 8, 10, 12, 26–8, 32, 37, 38, 42, 73, 80, 81, 83, 98, 99, 104–5, 197, 207, 399, 413, 414
  speeches
    on ALP factionalism 36
  campaign
    1925 NSW 33, 41, 42
    1940 Federal 145
    1943 Federal 192
    1945 Federal 385
  parliamentary
    federal 199, 227, 232, 241, 247, 288, 292, 314, 356, 379–80
    state 51–2, 54–5, 56, 59, 76, 83
    overseas 185
  on White Australia policy 61–2, 411
  at San Francisco conference 209, 416
  on Socialism 12, 132
  on sport 4, 5, 8, 10, 34, 38, 129–30
  visits
    England 61–3, 129, 155, 157–61, 164, 176, 183, 185, 189, 211, 288
    Paris 120
    USA 119, 130, 155, 156, 157, 159, 164, 176, 183–5, 189, 209, 211, 229, 284, 302
  works by 13–14, 16, 24, 39, 42, 81, 107–9, 110–12, 114, 119, 123–35, 196, 198, 230, 291
Evatt, Mary Alice 'Mas' 17, 183, 407, 410
  art involvement 120
  assists the poor 83
  influence of Morris 40
  political involvement 40–1, 61, 75, 198
Evatt, Peter 83
Evatt, Philip 378, 386, 407
Evatt, Ray 16
Evatt, Rosalind 99, 328, 407, 410

Fadden, A.W. 149
fascism
  Evatt on 141, 306–8
Fair Rents Act 26–7
Fallon, C. G. 342
  relations with Evatt 147
Far Easten Advisory Commission (FEC)
  Evatt involvement with 268, 269–70, 272, 274, 275, 278
Federated Ironworkers' Association (FIA) 341, 385

Federated Seaman's Union of
  Australasia 47, 48
Fitzpatrick, Brian 118, 119, 120,
    134, 197, 219–20
  member of ACCL 169, 170, 172,
    386
  relationship with Evatt 172, 340
  works by 123, 129
Forde, Frank 174, 175, 177, 178, 215
  Evatt on 209
foreign economic policy
  Evatt on 188, 190, 305
foreign relations, Australian
  Britain 186–7, 228, 230–2, 237,
    238–41, 248, 267, 286, 288,
    289, 292, 295, 296, 298, 414,
    417
  China 350, 356, 391
  Evatt on 62–3, 106, 141, 153,
    157, 158–9, 164, 178–9, 186–7,
    210, 214, 216, 218, 225–41,
    246–60, 264–80, 283–8, 289,
    295, 296, 304, 307, 316, 350,
    356, 370, 400–1, 414, 417
  France 236–7
  Indonesia 246, 250, 251–2, 253,
    254, 256–7, 259–60, 295
  Japan 264–80
  New Zealand 226, 233, 234, 414,
    417
  Soviet Union 375, 379
  United States 186–7, 226, 228–9,
    230–1, 232, 233, 234–5, 237,
    238–41, 248, 268, 278–9, 284,
    285, 292, 295, 298, 387, 390
Forty-Four hour week 37, 53, 55, 70,
  82
Fort Street Boys' High School 5, 7, 99
freedom of speech
  Evatt on 219
Franklin, Miles 118, 119
Fuller, Sir George 41

Gallagher, F.H. 344, 345
Game, Sir Philip
  dismissal of Lang government
    97–8, 107, 108, 110
Garden, J.S. 82
Garnishee case 96–8
Gilroy, Cardinal
  on establishment of DLP 391–2
  relationship with Evatt 384, 403
Godfrey, George 63–4, 398
  support for Evatt 392, 393

Governor-General
  reserve powers of 106, 107–8,
    111
Governors
  reserve power of 59–60, 97–8,
    106–7, 108, 110–11, 112, 124
Grattan, Hartley
  on Australian literature 118–20
  relationship with Evatt 99,104,
    118, 147, 304, 410, 419
Gray, Bridget 3
Gray, Jane Sophia (Jeanie) see Evatt,
  Jane Sophia
Gray, John Thomas 3, 4
Graziers' Association of New South
  Wales 87
Great Depression
  effect on basic wage 80–1
  Financial Agreements Enforcement
    Act 96–7
  history of 81
  Premiers' Plan 100
  and reduction of High Court
    judicial salaries 100–2
Greece
  Evatt on 308–11
Green, T.H. 11

Hall, Bridget see Gray, Bridget
Harvester award 81
Hasluck, Paul 207
Hergenham, Laurie 119
Hermes 9, 15, 16
Heydon, Justice
  Evatt on 81
Higgins, Justice 53
  Evatt on 81
High Court 29–30, 48–9, 71
  appointments 84–5, 88–9, 93–7,
    99, 212, 213, 355
  cases 87–8, 95–9, 199, 206, 212,
    327, 330, 331, 333–5, 360–2
  Evatt on
    appointments 213
    salary reductions 101
  salaries 100–2, 212
Hirohito, Emperor 267, 268
history, Australian
  economic 129
  Evatt on 123–35
Holman government 109, 131–4
Holman, W. A. 109, 130, 131–4
hours of work 36, 37, 53, 70, 217,
  344–5, 349

housing, rental 331
  observations by Evatt 26–8
How Labour Governs 24, 32
Hughes, W.M. 16, 18, 133, 134,
  143, 148, 158

immigration
  Evatt on 61–2, 73, 76, 102, 226,
    233, 304, 313
Immigration Act 46, 47, 48
Imperial Federation 14, 15
Independance, Australian political
    and legal
  Evatt on 105–12, 178–80
India
  Evatt on 296
Industrial Arbitration Court
  New South Wales 30, 54
Industrial Court, federal 400
industrial disputes
  coal 81, 85, 343–51
  and deportation of persons not
    Australian born 49
  federal government sanctions
    against 81
  federal government intervention
    217–18, 342–3, 346–9,
    366–7
  maritime 47–9, 81, 82, 253
  railway
    ARU case 87–8
    NSW 30–2, 38, 43, 51, 54, 71,
      83, 132
  right to strike 47, 102, 132, 219,
    342–3, 345, 346
  shearing 87
  work bans 399
industrial relations
  Evatt on 214, 216–18, 220–1
Injustices within the Law 114
International Federation of Trade
    Unions 61
Ireland
  Evatt on relations with
    Commonwealth 293–4
Isaacs, Sir Isaac 86, 88

Japanese
  policy
    Evatt on 264–5, 266, 269, 271,
      273, 274, 275, 276, 277–9,
      286, 295, 306, 313, 415
    United States on 264, 265–6,
      268–9, 272, 273, 276, 277–
      9, 280, 284, 286, 292, 298

threat to Australia 117, 227–32,
    264–5, 268, 269, 271, 276,
    277–80, 295, 297
  see also Pacific peace settlement;
    World War II
Japanese population in California
  observations by Evatt 18
Jewish refugees
  Evatt on discrimination against
    102, 204
Johnson, J.
  deportation case 46–9, 53, 71,
    73–5, 361
Jose, Arthur 124

Keith, Professor A. Berriedale 108, 109
Kerr, John 99–100, 112, 404
Kilgour, Alexander
  influence on Evatt 6
  on equality of education 7
Kirby, Justice Michael 361, 404
Kirby, Sir Richard 221
  on Evatt 29, 33, 144
Kisch, Egon 118
Kitson, W.H. 61
Knox, Chief Justice 48

Labor Daily 38, 39, 57
  on bribery by the Nationalist Party
    66
  defence of Evatt 43
  on shearers' strike 87
Labor Leagues 35
Labour movement, Australian 5, 12,
    42, 131, 343, 384, 389, 390
  corrupt practices in the 33, 35,
    36–7
  on deportation of unionists 47
  Evatt on 41, 42, 97, 104
  socialist doctrine in 132, 217–18
  support for Evatt from 73
  support for railway workers 38–9,
    43
Labour Socialist International 61
Landa, Abe 174
  friendship with Evatt 75, 100, 403
Lang government 44, 51, 52
  on child endowment 68–70
  conflict with Legislative Council
    58–61, 95–6
  dismissal of by Governor Game
    97–8, 107, 108, 110–11
  establishment of State Insurance
    Office 57–8
  reforms by 58

Lang, John Dunmore 12, 13, 85, 148
  on abolition of Legislative Council
    59–61
  on appointment of Evatt to High
    Court 94
  on Bligh 125
  appears before parliamentary
    Select Committee 66
  battles for leadership of NSW
    Labor Party 65, 66, 70, 140,
    142
  Evatt criticism of 65–6, 68, 70–3,
    83
  forms breakaway Australian Labor
    Party 142
  on rates of premium for GIO 58
  see also Loughlin
Laski, Harold 118
Latham, Chief Justice
  on Communist Party Dissolution
    Act 360
law
  Australian 105–6
  and society 105
  reform 55
le Gay Brereton, J. 7
Legal Service Bureau
  Evatt on 139
legislation
  federal
    Approved Defence Projects
      Protection Act 218–19, 220,
      291, 358
    Australia Act 105
    Australian Navigation Act 179
    Australian National Airlines
      Act 211, 212
    Banking Act 326, 327
    Coal Strike Act 343, 346, 347,
      358
    Colonial Laws Validity Act
      107, 179
    Commonwealth Bank Act 326
    Communist Party Dissolution
      Act 356–7, 358–60, 362–7,
      385, 389
    Conciliation and Arbitration
      Act 86–8, 220, 341, 343,
      383, 400
    Crimes Act 49, 219–20, 357
    Financial Agreements
      Enforcement Act 96–7
    Matrimonial Causes Bill 406
    National Security Act 144,
      169, 175

    Pharmaceutical Benefits Act
      210, 212, 214, 333, 334
    Stevedoring Industry Bill 221
    Statute of Westminster 106,
      107, 178–9
  New South Wales
    Abolition of Capital
      Punishment Bill (1925) 54,
      58
    Arbitration Act 68–9, 70, 78
    Family Endowment Act (1927)
      68, 69, 70, 79
    Finance (Newspapers Taxation)
      Act 66
    Forty-Four Hour Week Act 37,
      53, 55, 70
    Industrial Arbitration
      (Amendment) Bill (1925)
      54
    Liquor (Amendment) Bill 67–8
    Workers' Compensation Act
      55–8, 83
  Victorian
    Land Settlement Bill 383
Legislative Assembly of New South
  Wales
  sitting hours 52–3, 76
Legislative Council of New South
  Wales
  appointments to 133
    of Labor nominees 58–9, 110,
    132
  attempt to abolish 58–61, 95–6
  eligibility of women to join 51
  Evatt on 59, 60–1
Lend-Lease Aid 187, 188, 189, 190,
  238, 285
Liberal Party
  influence of business on 215
Liberalism, Australian
  Evatt on 12, 13, 24, 26
  see also New Liberalism
Liberalism in Australia 13, 24, 39,
  42, 124
literature, Australian
  Evatt's involvement with 118–19,
    123
Locarno Pact
  Evatt on 62
Lockwood, Rupert 377, 378
Loughlin, P.F. 58
  challenges Lang for Party
    leadership 65
Lyons government 96, 118
Lyons 102

McAlpine, A.S. 142
MacArthur, General Douglas 266, 268–9, 270
  relationship with Evatt 272–3, 277
MacDonald, Malcolm 42
Mackaness, George 124
McKay, Claude 140
McKell, William J. 82, 140, 142, 414
McKenna, Senator 341, 358, 362
McNamara, Mr 61
McPhillips, J. 341
Macrossan, H.D. 22, 23
McTiernan, E.A. 27, 28, 29, 44, 72
  appointed to High Court 88–9, 93–7, 98, 100
  Attorney-General 52, 54, 59, 60, 65, 70, 110
  on Communist Party Dissolution Act 360
  federal member ALP 84, 88
  on Garnishee case 96–7
  on High Court cases 102, 334
  on High Court salary reductions 101
  relationship with Evatt 98, 164
  reserve powers of the Crown 112
Malaya
  Communist threat to 297
Mannix, Archbishop 204, 384, 403
  relationship with Evatt 215
manufacturing industry
  Evatt on development of 191
Manus Island 234, 239, 240–1, 285, 297
Marxism 13
Meldrum, Max 118
Menzies government 143, 146, 149, 159, 220
  on Arbitration Act 383, 400
  on Communism 356, 357, 361, 362, 364, 366, 370
  support for State aid for private schools 382
  on trade unions 366
Menzies, Robert Gordon 29–30, 95, 98, 106, 139, 141, 192, 289, 350
  on atomic energy 288
  conflict with Evatt 145, 164, 214–15, 359, 380, 400–1, 417
  legal career 145
  on nationalisation of banks 145
  Petrov affair 371, 372, 373, 376, 378, 380
  resigns as Prime Minister 149
  on Statute of Westminster 178
  on Suez Canal 400–2
  support from Evatt 149
migration
  Evatt attends world Congress on 61–3
Miles, W.J. 15
Milson's Point 4
Miners' Federation 39, 343, 344, 345, 346, 347, 349
Moral, E.D. 25–6
Morris, William 40
Movement, the
  Evatt on 384, 385, 388–91, 397, 414
  influence on the ALP 382, 383–5, 387, 388–91, 396–7, 418
Mungana affair 95
Murdoch, Professor Walter 118
Mutch, Tom 51–2, 73
Mutual Aid Agreement 187

Nairn, Bede 66
National Belgian Relief Fund 15
national service see conscription
nationalism, Australian 104, 117, 367, 370
  Evatt on 14, 399
Nationalist government
  New South Wales 27, 37, 47, 54, 109, 133–4
Nationalist Party
  candidates 73
  structure of 38, 41, 109, 134
Necessary Commodities Commission 27
Netherlands East Indies (NEI)
  Evatt on 246, 247, 248–54
New Liberalism 11, 12
  Evatt on 12, 14
New South Wales Labor Council 42, 47, 49, 73, 82, 371
Newby-Fraser, Revd W. 4
News-Weekly 365–6, 388, 389

Officer, Keith 350
Oliphant, Mark 287, 288, 289, 291
Orange Lodge 39
O'Sullivan, Fergan 376–7, 379
O'Sullivan, T.J.
  criticism of Evatt 42–3

Pacific peace settlement
  Evatt on 264–80, 286, 295, 313, 415

MacArthur on 273, 277
Pacific War Council 157, 184, 229, 233, 235, 265
Page, Earl 154
Palestine
   Evatt on 311–15
Palmer, Nettie 107, 118, 120
   on Grattan 118–19
Palmer, Vance 118, 120, 130, 140
Parliament, Commonwealth
   powers of 13
Peace Conference 105, 303
Pearl, Cyril 173
Peden, Professor John B. 9, 54, 69–70
Petersen, George 366, 371
Petrov Royal Commission
   Evatt and 377–80, 385, 386, 387, 388, 398, 405, 407
Petrov, Vladimir 371–80, 388
Piddington, A.B.
   Kisch case 118
   on living wage 68–9, 70, 78–9, 80
politics, Australian 13, 16, 109, 129, 173, 200, 295
   see also women and politics
post-war reconstruction 210–12, 284
   Evatt on 195–7
   referendum on 197, 198, 200
Potsdam Declaration 265, 267, 268
price-fixing
   Evatt on 27–8
prices, control of 27, 331
Prichard, Katharine Susannah 118, 143, 364, 412
Profiteering Prevention Act 28

Quirk, J. 39, 43

Ratliff, H.
   internment of 170–2, 177
regional security, Australian
   Evatt on 226, 227, 231–4, 238, 239, 240–1, 245–60, 265, 268, 271, 276–8, 277–80, 295, 296–7, 298, 305–6, 318
religious sectarianism 40
Rich, Sir George 96, 98, 101, 212–13, 327, 355
Richards, G.R. 'Black Snake' 203, 372, 378
Riley, E.C. 42
Rivett, Revd Albert 118
Robinson, W.S. 155–6, 157, 158, 161–2, 183, 190–1, 350, 370
   on Evatt 351, 356

Roosevelt, President F.D.
   relations with Evatt 152, 155, 156–7, 184
Rosevear, J.S. 42
Ross, Lloyd 120
   on Evatt 150
Rowse, Tim 11
Rum Rebellion 119, 123
Ryan, Peter
   on Evatt 412, 418
Ryan, T.J. 21

Santamaria, B.A. 218, 365, 366, 382, 383, 384, 385, 388, 389, 390, 397, 414
Sawer, Geoffrey 46, 49, 93, 94, 112, 365
Scott, Ernest 118
   Evatt on 25
Scullin government 84–5, 93, 140
   Garnishee case 96–7
Scullin, J.H. 84, 89
   on High Court judical salaries 100–1
Seaman's Union 47
Select Committee, parliamentary
   on bribery of Labor caucus members by Nationalists 66–7
Serle, Geoffrey 119, 365
Sharkey, L. 340
Shaw, Patrick 278
Shedden, Sir Frederick 153, 163
Sheffer, Mary Alice see Evatt, Mary Alice
Sheridan, Tom 217
Short, Laurie 341
   Evatt on 385, 389, 404
Smith, Bernard 120, 364
Smith, Sir Joynton 33
Smith's Weekly 33, 61, 85
social services 214, 333–4
socialism 12, 25, 132, 206, 217, 329, 350, 398
Socialist League 40
society, Australian
   discrimination in 8, 10
   law in 105
   lower middle 192
   middle-class 5
   originating circumstances 123
   structure 120
   working-class 5, 14, 38, 39, 47, 414
St Andrew's College 7, 23
St Andrew's College Magazine 8

St Mark's Memorial Library 5
Starke, Judge 96, 98, 99, 101, 212–13, 327, 330, 355
State aid to church schools
    ALP policy on 42
    Catholic Church on 362–3
    Evatt on 42
    Menzies on 382
State Insurance Office, New South Wales 57–8
Stephensen, P.R. 118, 173, 174, 175, 177, 202, 203
Storey government 27, 28, 31
Street, Jessie 146
Street, K.W.
    appointed to Industrial Commission 78, 79
    Evatt on 81
Strickland, Sir Gerald 109
strikes see industrial disputes
Strong, Revd Charles 11
Suez Canal crisis 400–2
Sunday Sun 99
Sydney Morning Herald 83, 94

tariffs 186, 188, 189, 190, 284
taxation
    Evatt on 176
    rates of during war years 176
The King and his Dominion Governors 107, 108, 110–11, 112, 124
The University of Sydney 7
    Labour Society 42
    Men's Christian Union 10
    Undergraduates Association 9, 15
    Union 9, 10
The Worker 389, 390
Theodore, E.G. 41, 84, 95
Thomas, M.
    internment of 170–2, 177
Thornton, E.
    discusses coal strike with Evatt 348–9
Timor
    Evatt on control of 246, 247–8, 249, 252, 259, 268, 295, 297
Tolpuddle Martyrs
    Evatt on 114–17
trade
    Australia
        and Britain 284–5, 294
        and United States 187–90, 284
    Evatt on 284, 285, 294–5

    United States policy 187–90, 284, 285, 295
    world 187–8, 285, 294
Trade Union Defence Fund 49
trade unions
    ballot-rigging in 341
    Communist influence 341, 342, 343, 345, 348–9, 357, 358, 359–60, 364, 365, 383–4
    deregistration of 30–1, 47, 220
    Evatt on elections in 341–2, 343
    in England 114–7
    formed during 1917 railway strike 54
    on High Court appointments 88–9
    High Court cases and 98
    influence on ALP 35–7, 82, 215–16, 218, 365, 391
    and the poor 114
    represented by Evatt 82–3, 87, 359–60
    at living wage inquiry 79, 80
    secret ballots 383
    use of lawyers 29, 82–3
    and wage protection 86
Trans-Australian Airlines (TAA) 211
Truth 70
Truth and the War 26

unemployment 37, 81
Union of Democratic Control 265
United Australia Party 139
United Nations
    Evatt involvement with 248, 252, 253, 255, 257, 258, 268, 276, 298, 302–18, 400–1, 416
University of Sydney see The University of Sydney

Wade, G.G. 95
wages 29–30, 36, 84, 217
    female living 80, 220
    living (basic) 220
        Evatt on 68–70, 73–4, 76, 78–80, 81
        Industrial Commission on 78–80
        reduction of 80–2, 86–7, 98
Wake, R.F.B.
    relationship with Evatt 386–8
Walsh, Adela 173
Walsh, Tom
    deportation case 46–9, 53, 71, 73–5, 361
Wardell, Brigadier A.W. 367

Waterside Workers' Federation (WWF) 359–60, 366
Watt, Alan 157, 165
Watt, A.R.J. (Andy) 22, 30, 33
   challenge to deportation law 46, 47–8, 49
Webb, Sir William 213, 268
Wentworth, W.C. 12, 13, 124
West New Guinea (Dutch)
   Evatt on 245–6, 247, 249, 253, 254, 258–9, 295, 297
Whaling
   Evatt on Japanese 269, 270, 271
White Australia policy 14
   Bruce on 62
   Evatt on 61–2, 232–3, 257, 313
Whitlam government
   dismissal of 112
widows' pensions 200
women
   living wages for 80, 220
   and politics 40–1, 51, 61
women's rights in law 73–4
Wood, George Arnold 13, 14, 15
Woodward, E.A. 16
Woomera rocket range 218–20, 287, 290, 291, 292
workers compensation
   Evatt on 55–8, 66, 71, 83, 98
   High Court cases on 98
   historical background to 55–7
Workers' Educational Unit 24
workers in industry
   Evatt on 51, 53
working conditions 29–30, 53, 84, 217–18, 219
   reform of 37
   see also hours; wages
World War I
   Evatt on Australian involvement 15–16, 25–6, 105
World War II 139
   Australian defence during 152–65, 182–6, 225–6, 227, 228–9, 246–8, 264, 265
   'Beat Hitler First' policy 159, 160, 161, 163, 182, 226, 228, 230, 264, 265
   civil liberties during 168–80
   Communists support for 141, 172, 343
   concept of a National Government during 146, 149
   crimes 268
   Darwin air attack 163
   declaration of war against Japan 106, 174
   Evatt on
      Australian involvement 141, 145, 148–9, 152, 155–65, 227, 229, 252, 265, 266
      Japanese involvement 149, 152–5, 158, 159, 163–4, 205, 227–8, 230, 246–7, 250, 260, 264, 266
      occupation of Japan 265, 266–8, 271, 272
      post-war reconstruction 195–6, 318
      supply of British aircraft 185–6
      supply of United States aircraft 183, 184–5
   internment during 169, 171–2, 174–5, 176–8, 202–5
   Japanese surrender 265, 266, 267
   restrictions in Australia during 143
   WW1 agreement 159, 161, 162, 163
   see also post-war reconstruction
Wran, Neville 134–5
Wren, John
   relationship with Evatt 215, 216
Zines, Leslie 106